Praise for *The Gun*

"... magisterial ..."

—*The Atlantic*

"He writes both with technical precision and the humanity that comes with understanding the invariably unhappy and all too often horrific consequences of the weapon's effects. All this makes for a delicate and at times fascinating balancing act, as Mr. Chivers the enthusiast and expert shares the page with Mr. Chivers the historian and journalist—the expert dealing well with the detailed mechanics of his subject, the journalist at other times brilliantly illuminating the book with highly effective vignettes of human courage, ingenuity and, mostly, suffering. . . . Mr. Chivers's account of the general development of automatic weapons and the men who pioneered them is impressive."

—*The New York Times*

"In *The Gun*, Pulitzer Prize–winning journalist, former Marine officer and Persian Gulf War veteran C. J. Chivers sets out to 'lift the Kalashnikov out of the simplistic and manipulated distillations of its history.' He succeeds admirably by putting the gun into its social, historical and technological context in an evocative narrative."

—*The Washington Post*

"... in his fascinating book, *The Gun*, Chivers offers a compelling perspective on 20th-century warfare as he traces the rise of the Kalashnikov. At the same time, he offers some intriguing clues about what kind of weapon might turn out to be the Kalashnikov's successor in the 21st century."

—Slate.com

"Chivers draws links between machines and their cultures very convincingly. The breadth and depth of his strategy is as compelling as it is educational. His book treats guns not just as tactical devices, technological marvels and instruments of death and terror, but as psychological snapshots of the nations that produced them—and monuments to a bloodthirsty, ingenious race that has spent centuries fighting over land, money and God, and won't stop any time soon."

—Salon.com

"... for disciplined and devoted scholars of the history of modern war, politics, and ideology, and how the automatic weapon has forced the transformation of the essence of combat . . . a colossal effort . . . appears to have created a history-laced masterpiece."

—*Marine Corps Gazette*

"The story of this particular weapon [the AK-47] becomes in an important sense the story of the violence and threat at the heart of the more than sixty years since the gun was first introduced . . . If there is no longer much, if any, pacifist discourse on ending the production of weapons, the trade in weapons is perhaps one area where the developed world might act with greater energy and will. If *The Gun* achieves what it deserves, this will surely be one of its primary lessons." —*National Interest* (UK)

"Chivers does an excellent job in *The Gun* in giving an in-depth history of the . . . AK-47, the so-called everyman's gun, in exemplary, muscular prose backed up by prodigious research." —*VVA Veteran Magazine*

"This superior history . . . [is] written incisively and researched exhaustively." —*Booklist*

". . . eye-opening . . . it's hard to resist a narrative that ends with a world awash with a weapon that has killed more soldiers and civilians than all the high-tech planes, missiles, bombs, WMDs and America's sophisticated rifles combined. An entertaining work that combines technical details, biographies, political maneuvering and insightful military history." —*Kirkus*

"In *The Gun,* former Marine and *New York Times* correspondent Chivers writes a paean to the planet's most ubiquitous small arm. . . . [he] tells the AK-47's story as a Tolstoyan epic. . . . With Venezuela planning to construct its own AK-47 factory, the Kalashnikov's story is anything but spent." —*Time*

". . . as accessible and compelling to the general reader as it is for the military specialist . . . Chivers's mastery of history and engineering is matched by his mastery of language. For all the detail and technical data, *The Gun* is a riveting read." —*The Guardian*

"Chivers, a *New York Times* senior writer who served in the Marine Corps in the Gulf War, combines a soldier's experience with a historian's skepticism. . . . The greatest strength of *The Gun* lies in the stories told by rank-and-file gunfighters. Chivers devotes space to child soldiers in Uganda, Marines in Southeast Asia and Kurdish bodyguards in northern Iraq. One by one, they describe what it's like to shoot, and be shot by, this killing machine, a device that can unload hundreds of bullets in a minute." —*Bloomberg Business Week*

". . . a fascinating, exhaustive history of the rifle's origins, development and unprecedented influence on the world we live in. Chivers brings experience and impressive research . . . to put the AK-47 into a social, historical and technological context . . . the bonus is that he also produces a compelling narrative." —*The Times of India*

"... in the investigative tradition of Seymour Hersh, combined with the precision of John McPhee ... *The Gun* is nothing less than a history of modern warfare."
—*BookForum*

"C. J. Chivers makes a convincing case ... [with] experience and impressive firsthand scholarly research."
—*Los Angeles Times*

"... outstanding history of an exceptional instrument of war."
—*Publishers Weekly*

"In his fascinating book, Pulitzer Prize–winning journalist C. J. Chivers shows how the world was forever altered by the pursuit of automatic weapons."
—*New York Post*

"In originality, in depth of research, in vividness of writing, in insight ... Chivers's book stands alone."
—*Field & Stream*

"[Chivers displays] impressive research—of a kind not possible on the AK-47 and Mikhail Kalashnikov—and deft descriptions of individuals and their experiences. ... Mr. Chivers focuses our attention on an ordinary item that has been vastly more destructive and done more to define the character of warfare today than any other weapon."
—*The Wall Street Journal*

"*The Gun* demolishes the Soviet propaganda."
—*Winnipeg Free Press*

"... a formidable feat of research and writing. The story of the Kalashnikov is a fascinating one, which encompasses both the darkest days of the Cold War and the asymmetric warfare of the early 21st century. In telling it, Chivers adds a number of illuminating asides on technological developments and wider strategic concerns. In marshalling these myriad sources, he has produced surely the final word on one of the most iconic weapons of our times."
—*The Independent*

"What makes *The Gun* readable is its humanity. ... Chivers wants to show a richer context, and he succeeds thoroughly."
—*Military Times*

"... this exhaustively researched account ... explodes several myths ... Chivers has done outstanding work."
—*Star Tribune* (Minneapolis)

"Pulitzer-winning war reporter C. J. Chivers takes readers on a fascinating ride from the introduction of the Gatling gun during the Civil War to the birth of the AK-47 after World War II to today's front lines. It's not just the story of the AK-47 but also unparalleled military history."
—*Garden & Gun*

"... an objective, fast-moving biography and analysis of this infamous utensil of death."   —*The Dallas Morning News*

"... justly lauded as one of the finest war correspondents of his generation ... he has a former infantryman's eye and ear for the staccato cadences of small-unit combat ... this book is testament to his erudite understanding of military history."   —*The Wilson Quarterly*

"... [a] rich, engrossing, and comprehensive narrative. ... This is a fascinating book. The research is extraordinary and Chivers's background as an officer in the Marine Corps provides the credibility to fully explain why and how this rifle with its stubby black barrel, dull brown stock, and distinctive banana clip has become one of the most frightening outputs of the Cold War. Vivid reportage by a journalist at the top of his game places this weapon in its historical context."   —TucsonCitizen.com

"Pulitzer Prize–winning *New York Times* reporter Chivers's book is an engrossing history of the evolution of machine guns since the mid-19th century, which makes it a history of modern warfare. ... The result is gripping and original interpretive history, highly recommended."
                                        —*Library Journal* (starred review)

"... a rich, engrossing, and comprehensive narrative history of this groundbreaking weapon. ... Chivers gives us a gripping, exhaustively researched, and far-reaching assessment of the most important weapon of our time. ... And with its probing historical analysis, vivid reportage, and provocative moral dimension, it will be equally compelling to those concerned with the origins, dynamics, and resolution of global conflict."   —Ammoland.com

"As others have written books about cod, salt and cotton, Chivers has crafted the singular general history of modern man's most plentiful and efficient killing machine."   —*Boston Book Bums*

"Chivers had several hundred opportunities to get it wrong in the 496 highly technical but eminently readable pages of *The Gun,* but he doesn't. Instead, he paints a context-rich picture of how a Soviet assault rifle has become the most widespread implement of war in the world."   —*The Oregonian* (Portland)

"The best book so far about what is probably the most influential weapons system of our times."   —*The New York Review of Books*

THE GUN

C. J. CHIVERS

SIMON & SCHUSTER PAPERBACKS

NEW YORK   LONDON   TORONTO   SYDNEY   NEW DELHI

Simon & Schuster Paperbacks
A Division of Simon & Schuster, Inc.
1230 Avenue of the Americas
New York, NY 10020

First Simon & Schuster trade paperback edition September 2011

SIMON & SCHUSTER PAPERBACKS and colophon are registered trademarks
of Simon & Schuster, Inc.

For information about special discounts for bulk purchases,
please contact Simon & Schuster Special Sales at
1-866-506-1949 or business@simonandschuster.com.

The Simon & Schuster Speakers Bureau can bring authors
to your live event. For more information or to book an event,
contact the Simon & Schuster Speakers Bureau at
1-866-248-3049 or visit our website at www.simonspeakers.com.

Designed by Kyoko Watanabe

Manufactured in the United States of America

10   9   8   7   6

The Library of Congress has cataloged the hardcover edition as follows:

Chivers, C. J.
   The gun / C. J. Chivers—
1st Simon & Schuster hardcover ed.
      p.   cm.
   Includes bibliographical references.
   1. AK-47 rifle—History.   2. War—History.   3. Machine guns—
Technological innovations—History.   4. Firearms—Technological
innovations—History.   I. Title.
   UD395.A16C47   2010
   623.4'424—dc22   2010020459

ISBN 978-0-7432-7076-2
ISBN 978-0-7432-7173-8 (pbk)
ISBN 978-1-4391-9653-3 (ebook)

For Natalya K. Estemirova

Bezstrashnaya Natasha

Fearless Natasha

The Investigator

Murdered for her work in Chechnya

An Example for All

February 28, 1958–July 15, 2009

"Inventors seldom benefit themselves. They benefit the people."

—*Richard J. Gatling, inventor of the Gatling gun*

CONTENTS

Stalin's Tools of War

*Outside an Institute Known by a Codeword, Nadezhda,
on the Steppe in the Kazakh Soviet Socialist Republic*

The atomic bomb rested on a tower one hundred feet above the ground. Known as RDS-1, it was shaped like a huge metal teardrop with rivets and bolts along its sides. Everything had been prepared. Inside its shell was a uranium and plutonium charge equal to about twenty kilotons of TNT, making it a rough equivalent to the weapon the United States had used to destroy Nagasaki four years before. In the hours after midnight the scientists had departed, and now, shortly before dawn on August 29, 1949, they gathered at their instruments in a control bunker more than six miles away, where they were watched by Lavrenty Beria, chief of Stalin's secret police. Detonation was set for 6:00 A.M. The Soviet Union was moments from entering the atomic age—ending the American monopoly in atomic arms, securing the Kremlin's status atop a global superpower, and giving the Cold War its sense of doomsday menace. This was a decade after the purges, two decades after the brutalities of collectivization, and in a postwar period in which German prisoners of war were used as forced labor and captured Soviet soldiers returned from German camps had been interrogated, incarcerated, and, sometimes, put to death. Beria's methods of pursuing Stalin's will were well-known. The lead physicist, Igor V. Kurchatov, and his team were anxious. If the bomb did not work, some of these scientists expected to be shot.

The test range, on an arid basin northwest of Semipalatinsk, a frontier city where Russians had been sent to exile since czarist times, was a methodically assembled period piece. Soviet soldiers and laborers had built it at a pace a dictator could muster. The anticipated detonation site had been divided into sectors. Within each, work cadres had erected structures and placed objects in common military and civilian use: a railway bridge, buildings of various dimensions and design, automobiles, concrete bunkers, aircraft, artillery pieces, armored vehicles, tanks. Live animals had been tethered throughout, some unprotected and others within buildings or vehicles, to determine how an atomic explosion's shock wave, heat, and radiation might affect live tissue at various distances and in various states of exposure and protection. Pigs had been selected because their hides were thought to resemble human skin; rabbits because their eyes were thought to be like those of a man. Horses were used because they could be fitted with gas masks. Looming over the scene were reinforced concrete towers, each nearly forty feet high and anchored on foundations sunk deep into the ground. The towers, containing instruments and cameras, had been lined with lead plates and connected with subterranean cables. Never before had Soviet physicists had such an opportunity. They did not intend to waste it. It was not enough that RDS-1 explode. The Soviet scientists planned to measure its effects on the buildings, equipment, and animals ringed round.[1] All of this work had been cloaked in the strictest secrecy that Beria could organize. Kurchatov's research center, roughly an hour's bouncing drive away over a dirt road, was on no maps. It had its own postal code, which often changed. One code name was *Nadezhda,* the Russian word for hope.

And now it was time.

There was an enormous white flash, then an extended bright glow. A sky-splitting roar and blast rushed outward, blowing asunder buildings, twisting the bridge, buckling bunkers as it blew through. In the first instant the soil near the tower had been liquefied, becoming a molten syrup that shot through the air, coating flat surfaces and the ground in a searing, radioactive caramel. As the wave whooshed through the nearest sectors, tank barrels and artillery pieces bent like reeds. Farther out, animals were roasted; then farther, they were singed. Farther still, they were bombarded with radiation that would erupt into burns that would kill them later, as the scientists documented their declines. The blast wave took a half minute to sweep over the steppe to the command bunker, which shuddered. When the rumbling subsided, Beria, Kurchatov, and his team stepped outside and looked at a steep-sided mushroom cloud, sucking up smoke, soil, and debris as it rose.[2] Timber and dust spun high overhead. Success.

Inside Factory No. 74 of the Izhevsk Machine, Engineering, and Motor Plant Complex, in the Russian Soviet Federated Socialist Republic

As diplomatic cables about the atomic explosion moved from embassies in Moscow to Western capitals, about eleven hundred miles to the west of the test site, in a Russian industrial city in the Ural range, another of Stalin's secret military projects was gaining momentum. Within the dark brick walls of a set of immense factories, a product was being prepared for mass production. Teams of engineers, armorers, and factory supervisors were fine-tuning its design. Communist Party leaders insisted that these factories were engaged in the manufacture of automobiles. But this product was neither a vehicle nor any of its parts. It was a weapon: a strange-looking rifle, deviating from the classic forms.

At a glance, the new rifle was in many ways peculiar, an oddity, a reason to furrow brows and shake heads. Its components were simple, inelegant, and by Western standards, of seemingly workmanlike craftsmanship. The impression it created was the puzzling embodiment of a firearm compromise, a blend of design choices no existing Western army was willing yet to make. It was midsized in important measures—shorter than the infantry rifles it would displace but longer than the submachine guns that had been in service for thirty years. It fired a medium-powered cartridge, not powerful enough for long-range sniping duty, but with adequate energy to strike lethally and cause terrible wounds within the ranges at which almost all combat occurs. The weapon was not merely a middleweight. It was a breakthrough arm. It could be fired automatically, and at a rate like those of the machine guns that already had changed the way wars were fought. It could be fired on single fire, like a rifle of yore. None of the Soviet Union's Cold War opponents had managed to conceive of, much less produce, a firearm of such firepower at such compact size. And this new weapon had other useful traits. It had little recoil compared to most rifles of its time. It was so reliable, even when soaked in bog water and coated with sand, that its Soviet testers had trouble making it jam. And its design was a testament to simplicity, so much so that its basic operation might be grasped within minutes, and Soviet teachers would soon learn that it could be disassembled and reassembled by Slavic schoolboys in less than thirty seconds flat. Together these traits meant that once this weapon was distributed, the small-statured, the mechanically disinclined, the dimwitted, and the untrained might be able to wield, with little difficulty or instruction, a lightweight automatic rifle that could push out blistering fire for the lengths of two or three football fields. For the purpose for which it was designed—as a device that allowed ordinary men to kill other men without extensive training or undue complications—this was an eminently well-conceived tool.

The Army of the Soviet Union had given its new firearm a name: the AK-47. While Soviet physicists had been teasing out the secrets of the atom, the army's Main Artillery Department had selected the AK-47 in a secret competition soon after the end of the Great Patriotic War, as the Soviet Union called their war against Hitler's Germany. The acronym abbreviated two Russian words, *Avtomat Kalashnikova*, the automatic by Kalashnikov, a nod to Senior Sergeant Mikhail Timofeyevich Kalashnikov, a twenty-nine-year-old former tank commander to whom the army and the Communist Party formally attributed the weapon's design. The number was shorthand for 1947, the year a technical bureau in Kovrov, a city east of Moscow with its own hidden arms plants, had finished the prototypes. In the time since, factories in Izhevsk had been tooled up to produce it. Within twenty-five years it would be the most abundant firearm the world had known.

During this time, the American intelligence community would fixate, understandably and properly, on the Soviet Union's nuclear programs. The activities in Izhevsk would be missed. As the mushroom cloud towered over the Kazakh steppe, no one noticed the arrival of Stalin's new firearm. No one would pay much mind as these rifle plants, and others across the Eastern bloc and in nations aligned with the Soviet Union or the socialist ideal, would ship off their automatic rifles by the untold millions during the years ahead. And no one would have predicted, as the world worried over nuclear war, that these rifles, with their cartridges of reduced size, would become the most lethal instrument of the Cold War. Unlike the nuclear arsenals and the infrastructure that would rise around them—the warheads, the mobile launchers, the strategic bombers and submarines—an automatic rifle was a weapon that could actually be used. And none of the Cold War's seemingly infinite and fantastic array of killing tools could more readily slip from state control. In this way, 1949 became the year of a mismatched but fated pair, RDS-1 and the AK-47, whose descendants were to work in consonance and shape the conflicts ahead. The nuclear umbrella froze borders in place and discouraged all-out war between the conventional armies stacked in Europe, helping to create conditions in which the Kalashnikov percolated from continent to continent, nation to nation, group to group, man to man, maturing as its numbers grew and its reputation spread into the age's dominant tool for violence in conflict zones. At first the distribution was piecemeal and incremental; gradually, it became almost unchecked. By the early 1960s, after the Cuban Missile Crisis had startled its participants and as the war in Vietnam was expanding and quickening, the Kremlin and the White House comprehended that their mutual nuclear arsenals had made total war unwinnable. Small wars and proxies would be the means through which the Cold War would be fought.

The Kalashnikov Era had arrived.

We are living in it still.

This book focuses on the most important series of infantry small arms of our time, and as most commonly encountered in the field: the original AK-47 and its derivates, knockoffs, and companion firearms that have flooded armories and arms bazaars around the world and become a primary weapon of guerrillas, terrorists, and many armed criminal gangs. It examines their origins, design, production, distribution, stockpiling, export, and use as one of the predominant tools of war of the past half-century—a status they are likely to retain for at least a half-century more. But this is not an account solely of a weapon's ubiquity on the battlefield. Nor is it a treatment of the AK-47 only for the sake of examining the AK-47. That is not to say that the Kalashnikov line by itself is not an expansive and interesting subject; it is. But a richer context is essential. These weapons occupy a place in history beyond the questions of when, where, and how they have been manufactured and used. The significance of the automatic Kalashnikov lies deeper than its origins in Stalin's Soviet Union, its technical utility as a killing tool, its famed reliability and ease of use, the awesome size of its number or the multiplicity of its meanings—though these themes are all essential.

The richer context is this: The automatic Kalashnikov offers a lens for examining the miniaturization and simplification of rapid-fire firearms, a set of processes that when uncoupled from free markets and linked to mass production in the planned economies of opaque or brittle nations, enabled automatic firepower to reach uncountable hands. It also provides a lens for examining national arming decisions, in the East and the West, and the many practices of arms transfers to other states and groups, often to disastrous effect. The results have shaped war and influenced security and development in large sections of the world. This is the story, then, of how fully automatic rifles, lightweight and often concealable tools that perform their intended tasks with reliability and efficiency, came into existence and widespread use.

In the narrowest sense, these weapons were born of a set of ugly and overpowering political forces of the early to mid-twentieth century. Nazism, Stalinism, and the exigencies of the Cold War combined to give assault rifles their early shape. But their roots reach much further back in time; they are the result of evolutionary processes in firearms and ammunition development and changes in military and economic thinking that accompanied an industrializing and polarizing world. The factors and actors that finally conjured compact automatic rifles into existence were able to do so because of this much longer and richer history. The journey through this history is populated by geniuses and fools, ruthless villains and naïve idealists, self-promoting salesmen and incorrigible profiteers, a pantheon of killers of all stripes and, now and then, people who wanted the killing to stop. Along the way the journey offers a tour of the ignorance and folly of many governments and their colonels and generals, as well as a passage across the grim political landscape of the Soviet Union and many of the most dreadful battlefields of modern times, upon which soldiers found themselves using the wrong tactics or carrying the wrong gear. It is also the story of how the United States, whose industrial revolution in the nineteenth century became the incubator for rapid-fire arms, and which as it became a superpower would stand against the Soviet Union and dictate small-arms choices to fellow NATO member states, repeatedly misread the path of automatic arms development. Ultimately, in the 1960s, American soldiers and Marines found themselves outgunned.

Automatic arms had evolved in the Eastern bloc to the Kalashnikov line. The United States was far behind. Such mistakes began in the mid-nineteenth century and continued, at key moments, for more than one hundred years. Last, in the latter half of the Cold War, the chronicle shifts again, to an account of how Kalashnikov-pattern rifles migrated from military possession to guerrillas, thugs, bandits, child soldiers, and a host of other users at odds with the stated, or perhaps supposed, reasons of their design. These weapons began as a means to equip standing armies. But the nations that made them lost custody of them, and then control, and now in much of the world they are everyman's gun.

In examining the AK-47 in this way, this book attempts to lift the Kalashnikov out of the simplistic and manipulated distillations of its history that have come to define it, inadequately. The carefully packaged history of Soviet times, a cheerful parable for the proletariat, was that the weapon sprang from the mind of a gifted if unlettered sergeant who wanted to present his nation an instrument for its defense. This was a message made in the Communist Party's propaganda mills. It required redaction and lies. In publishing this account, the Soviet Union resorted to enough invention, some of it cartoonish, that even Mikhail Kalashnikov eventually publicly criticized it, albeit lightly. As a historical account, the official narrative was not only embellished and redacted, but poorly framed. It emphasized the heroic spontaneity of a single mind and intentions for the weapon at odds with the weapon's most characteristic uses. The AK-47 did not result from an epiphany at the workbench of an intent Russian sergeant. Heroism, in the classic sense, was nonexistent here. Spontaneity, according to a close reading of the available records, played almost no role. The automatic Kalashnikov was the result of state process and collective work, the output not of a man but of committees. And its wide distribution and martial popularity did not occur because the rifle is, as General Kalashnikov often says, "simple, reliable, and easy to use."[3] Ultimately, it was its production by the tens of millions by governments that gave them away or lost control of them that made the Kalashnikov the world's primary firearm. One way to understand the nature of its familiarity is this: Had the AK-47 been created in Luxembourg, few people would likely have ever heard of it. But Luxembourg could not have created this weapon, because it lacked the Soviet bureaucracy and the particular historical pressures that ordered the Kalashnikov to its form within the USSR. This assessment is meant as no insult to Mikhail Kalashnikov; rather, it is meant to show the fuller and more interesting processes that pulled assault rifles into existence and global use, and to draw out the inner workings of the Soviet Union during a time it saw itself as in great peril. The Soviet state is the inventor here—both of the weapon and its fables. Far too many people regard the study of weapons as an illiberal art. The chronicle of automatic firepower, viewed through the AK-47 and its infiltration across the world, suggests otherwise. But first fable must be cast away.

Such an inquiry could begin at many points over a roughly one-hundred-year span. Here, it will start with Dr. Richard J. Gatling, whose invention in 1862 of the Gatling gun provided armies with their first reasonably effective rapid-fire arm—a massive, misunderstood, and often unwanted weapon that became the precursor to the rest. The early Gatling system weighed, more or less, a ton. It had no more mobility than an artillery piece, and required a crew of men to fire and a train of mules or horses to move about the battlefield. In its early forms it was temperamental, prone to jamming, and often despised by traditionalists who did not understand what it pointed to. And yet it was, in the history of conflict, of singular importance: Distinct shapes of modern war and instability can be traced through the miniaturization and proliferation that followed Gatling's designs. In 1949, the Soviet selection of the AK-47 as its standard military arm marked a decisive moment in this evolution. A superpower had managed the effective miniaturization of a rapid-fire arm that could be wielded by a single man in almost all the typical situations in which a firearm might be useful. Gatling's ton became, in a fully loaded Kalashnikov, about ten pounds—a weapon compact enough to be worn beneath a coat. To compete with this new weapon, combatants faced a choice. Either use the Kalashnikov, or come up with a rifle that could match it in a fight. War reorganized around Stalin's gun.

Why does this remain a subject, more than half a century on? One weapon alone has been a consistently lethal presence in modern war: the infantry rifle. Tanks can rout conventional armies. GPS-guided ordnance can scatter combatants. Land mines, suicide bombers, and improvised explosives have attracted more attention in recent years. Yet the rifle remains preeminent. Whenever an idea organizes for battle it gathers around its guns. Few weapons are as accessible or can be as readily learned. No other weapon appears in as many conflict areas year after year. None is as sure to appear in each future war, if only because no other weapon is as well suited for as many missions and tasks. And of all the rifles available for war today, the Kalashnikov line stands apart as the most abundant and widely used rifle ever made. Virtually everyone has seen a Kalashnikov. With its stubby black barrel with a parallel gas tube above, its steep front sight post, and the distinctive banana clip, its unmistakable profile has become a constant presence in the news. It is the world's most widely recognized weapon, one of the world's most recognizable objects.

More than six decades after its design and initial distribution, more than fifty national armies carry the automatic Kalashnikov, as do an array of police, intelligence, and security agencies. But its fuller terrain lies outside the sphere of conventional force. The Kalashnikov marks the guerrilla, the terrorist, the child soldier, the dictator, and the thug—all of whom have found it to be a ready equalizer against morally or materially superior foes. A roster of its handlers holds a history of modern strife. Celebrated by Soviet propagandists as a tool for self-defense and liberation, its first lethal uses were for repression—crushing uprisings in East Germany in 1953 and in Hungary in 1956, and for shooting fleeing civilians trying to cross the Iron Curtain's borders. Once it grew beyond border and crackdown duty in Eastern Europe, and became an automatic weapon for global combat service, it was instantly a groundbreaking firearm, a weapon that rearranged the rules. In the 1960s, when American Marines encountered AK-47s in urban warfare, at Hue City in Vietnam, they discovered that a single guerrilla with a Kalashnikov could slow a company's advance; they used cannon to rubble buildings in which AK-toting Viet Cong marksmen hid.[4] Its power, today a battlefield norm, was at first of an almost unseen sort, at least among the weapons that could be wielded by one man. Interest in it was immediate. Engineers in Finland and Josip Broz Tito's Yugoslavia secured early versions of the weapon and developed unlicensed knockoffs straightaway. After leading the revolution that put him atop Cuba, Fidel Castro amassed stores of Soviet assault rifles and distributed engraved Kalashnikovs as gifts. Idi Amin armed his Ugandan forces with Kalashnikovs and appointed himself president for life. Yasir Arafat procured them for the PLO and the many terrorist groups that spread from Fatah. Since it first entered the martial consciousness, no matter the year or theater, the Kalashnikov has appeared. Its followers cross all lines. The Egyptian army outfitted itself with Kalashnikovs. Islamic Jihad used a Kalashnikov to assassinate the Egyptian president, Anwar Sadat. Its durability and availability have made it more popular with the passing of time; the great numbers of its manufacture and the multiple sellers offering it ultimately ensured that it would be turned against the army that created it, as was the case in the Soviet-Afghan War and then again in Chechnya.

By the 1980s, with several sources simultaneously arming both sides of the Afghan conflict, the country filled with AK-47s and their derivatives. A durable assault rifle can have many lives over the decades of its existence, and in Afghanistan the weapons were recycled repeatedly, passed from fighter to fighter by many means. In the Panjshir Valley, a chasm in the mountains north of Kabul, the rifle sometimes became a family heirloom. The valley had been the scene of some of the most intense fighting in the early years of the war; its canyons became backdrops for mujahideen legend. Several times the Soviet army thrust armored columns up the valley, sometimes enveloping the guerrillas by using helicopters to land troops on mountain passes to cut off withdrawing mujahideen. Each time the Soviet forces controlled territory briefly before being subjected to persistent attacks. The valley was never conquered, and its villages were never co-opted or tamed. First among the Soviet army's foes was Ahmad Shah Massoud, the ethnic Tajik commander whose charisma and tactical adroitness became part of Afghan lore. Massoud's fighters were fit and skilled. But they too suffered. After one Soviet incursion, Massoud attended the funeral of a dead guerrilla. He lifted the man's Kalashnikov and carried it to the deceased man's younger brother, Ashrat Khan. The commander's mastery of quiet ceremony, like his sense for tactics, had reached a high state of polish.

"Do you want to be a mujahid?" Massoud asked.

Ashrat Khan extended his hands. He accepted the rifle.

"Yes, I am going to take my brother's weapon," he said. "I am going to be with you."[5]

At moments such as these, the Kalashnikov's infiltration of the martial world was nearing completion. Afghans were using it for the same purpose that Mikhail Kalashnikov insisted had motivated him—to defend their native land. Ashrat Khan became a fighter. He eventually lost his brother's Kalashnikov in combat, but he obtained another and survived the war.

The rifle assumed uses that were at once soldierly and ceremonial, and over the decades it reached far beyond conflicts in which the Kremlin played a primary role. When Sheik Ahmed Yassin, the founder of Hamas, was mourned in 2004 by his followers in Gaza, his casket was guarded by masked men at the ready with folding-stock AKs. The scene was a throwback. Six years earlier along the Cambodian-Thai border the body of Pol Pot was attended by teenage gunmen carrying an Asian version of the same gun.

Mastering a Kalashnikov is one of the surest ways to become an underground fighter in our time. In Belfast both sides of the Irish question used them in clashes and political art. In Afghanistan and Pakistan student notebooks from al Qaeda camps showed that the opening class in jihad curricula was a lesson on Kalashnikov's *avtomat*. Along with the rocket-propelled grenade, the portable mortar tube, and the makeshift bomb, the automatic Kalashnikov completes the quartet of weapons for the resistance in Afghanistan and Iraq, where insurgents rely on the local version, the Tabuk, which was churned out in the 1970s and 1980s in a state-owned Iraqi factory with Yugoslav technical help, then cached throughout the country before American tanks rolled in from Kuwait. No pariah seems far from his personal inventory of this dated Russian design. In his first taped message after the attacks of September 11, 2001, Osama bin Laden held a microphone near his beard and told the world that "the winds of faith and change have blown." It was his movie, he could put in it anything he wanted. Beside him was a Kalashnikov leaning against a rock.

Bin Laden understood the symbolic potency of his choice. Others keep their Kalashnikovs near for more practical tasks. By the time Saddam Hussein was pulled from a hole in Ad Dawr, in late 2003, the fugitive president had distilled his possessions to a modern outlaw's basic needs: two AK-47s and a crate of American cash. (He also had a pistol, a 9-millimeter Glock.) Kalashnikovs are not just tools for the battlefield. They guard South American coca plantations and cocaine-processing labs. In Los Angeles they have served bank robbers and urban gangs; in the northwestern United States survivalists squirrel them away in antici-

pation of the worst. African poachers use them to thin wildlife populations and defend their illegal trade against antipoaching patrols, which
carry Kalashnikovs, too. In the western Pacific, the aboriginal Chukti
people fire Kalashnikovs at migrating gray whales, the post-Soviet manifestation of an ancient hunt the Chukti call traditional, even as they slap
magazines into place and click their infantry arms off safe. Given that
the automatic Kalashnikov was conceived with the intention of shooting
160-pound capitalists, its use against 30-ton marine mammals would
seem ill-advised. But the rifle at hand is the rifle that gets used. Kalashnikovs are regularly at hand.

No one can say for certain how many Kalashnikovs exist today. Their
production in secrecy, often in some of the planet's harshest dictatorships,
has made precise accounting impossible. One point is beyond dispute.
They are the most abundant firearms on earth. Since the Soviet army chose
the AK-47 for distribution to Soviet ranks, automatic Kalashnikovs have
been made in Albania, Armenia, Bulgaria, China, East Germany, Egypt,
Hungary, Iran, Iraq, North Korea, Poland, Romania, Russia, Yugoslavia
(now Serbia), and the United States. Knock-off versions, incorporating
the main elements of Kalashnikov's operating system, were developed in
Croatia, Finland, India, Pakistan, South Africa, and Israel. (The Israel
Defense Forces were so impressed, and concerned, by the performance
of Egyptian Kalashnikovs in the Six Day War in 1967 that Yisrael Galili
and Yaacov Lior borrowed the AK-47's main features to create a series of
weapons at Ramat HaSharon.) More Kalashnikovs are made every year
(though at a lesser pace than in decades past). Venezuela plans to build a
new plant, which could be used to arm groups throughout the region in
a new round of opaque handouts. A single comparison provides a sense
of the automatic Kalashnikov's spread. The second-most-abundant family
of rifles is the American M-16 family; fewer than 10 million have been
made.[6]* Serious estimates put the number of Kalashnikovs and its derivatives as high as 100 million. There could be one Kalashnikov for every
seventy people alive.

Where did all these rifles go? Huge numbers filled state arsenals, issued

---

*Other older and more traditional rifles would displace the M-16 from second place if they
were still in widespread service, but they fell from common use with the spread of assault rifles.
The British Lee-Enfield line, for example, was manufactured in greater numbers than the M-16
during its many decades in use across the old British Empire.

to Eurasian communist armies and stockpiled around the Cold War's anticipated fronts. Untold millions were sold, others simply given to those thought to need them by the KGB and the Soviet army or their cousins in other communist states. During decades of influence jockeying, the Cold War saw the shipment of enormous quantities of Kalashnikovs to proxy forces, from the Viet Cong to militias in Beirut. Lists resemble tour guides to troubled lands: Russian, Chinese, and North Korean Kalashnikovs were carried by the North Vietnamese Army; Polish Kalashnikovs were shipped to the Contras; East German Kalashnikovs went to Yemen; Romanian AKs armed the Kurds; Russian and Bulgarian AK-47s supplied Rwanda; the United States directed Chinese and Egyptian Kalashnikovs to Afghanistan's anti-Soviet mujahideen. Chinese Kalashnikovs are abundant in Uganda and Sudan. By the time the Iron Curtain fell, it had become difficult to travel outside Western democracies without seeing Kalashnikovs in some form. There are more Kalashnikovs circulating now than then; when state socialism collapsed, arsenals were looted and weapons locked within were trucked away for sale. For people who study the universe of disorder, automatic Kalashnikovs serve as reasonably reliable units of measure. Arms-control specialists and students of conflict look to the price of Kalashnikov assault rifles in a nation's open-market arms bazaars to determine both the degree to which destabilized lands are awash in small arms and the state of risk. When prices rise, public anxiety is considered high. When they sink, the decline can indicate a conflict is ebbing. Because there is no surer sign that a country has gone sour than the appearance of Kalashnikovs in the public's grip, they can also function as an informal social indicator, providing another sort of graduated scale. Anywhere large numbers of young men in civilian clothes or mismatched uniforms are carrying Kalashnikovs is a very good place not to go; when Kalashnikovs turn up in the hands of mobs, it is time to leave.

In the aftermath of the Cold War the overabundance of automatic Kalashnikovs has remained a persistent factor in terrorism, crime, ethnic cleansing, and local and regional destabilization. Their widespread presence empowers unflagged and undisciplined forces to commit human rights abuses on a grander scale, raises the costs and exacerbates the dangers of peacekeeping missions, emboldens criminals of many sorts, stalls economic development, and increases the social burdens of caring for the wounded, the orphaned, and the displaced. Having been shipped to regions rife with the tensions of poverty, poor governance, and high ethnic, religious, or nationalist sentiment, the *avtomat* has helped to instigate and expand conflicts. And the prevalence of the Kalashnikov has helped the modern underground fighter to transform himself into today's protean, shadowy enemy, giving shape to the Pentagon's term for the conflicts in which the American military is almost irretrievably enmeshed—asymmetric war.

Studies of military small arms have documented their role in a stubborn toll of instability, injury, and death. The United Nations convened a conference in 2001 by noting that small arms were principal weapons in forty-six of the forty-nine major conflicts in the 1990s, in which 4 million people died. In 2004 Human Rights Watch identified eighteen nations where child soldiers are still used. For most of these wars and most of these young conscripts, Kalashnikovs are the primary arm. The available American casualty data from Iraq show that bullets fired from the Eastern bloc's family of firearms remain, injury by injury, the most lethal wounding agent on the battlefield. (In Afghanistan and Iraq, bombs have killed more soldiers. But of all the ways a soldier could be wounded there, bullets have been more likely to kill than any other. Put another way, soldiers wounded in bomb blasts have a statistically greater likelihood of survival than those who have been shot.) Moreover, Kalashnikovs outlive strife; bandits find them as useful as soldiers ever did. Even a single Kalashnikov can set a nation in motion. In 1989, after the drifter Patrick Purdy opened fire with a Kalashnikov on a schoolyard in Stockton, California, striking thirty-four children and a teacher, Congress began work on the assault weapon ban. Purdy did not use a true automatic Kalashnikov. His rifle was not an automatic. It had been modified to shoot a single bullet with each trigger pull, making it no more dangerous (and arguably less, considering the medium-powered cartridges it fired) than the rifles in many a deer camp. The facts hardly mattered. The mere appearance of a Kalashnikov in a schoolyard crowded with children, *its look,* was enough to put Congress in a lawmaking mood.

Look is important to Kalashnikovs. In their march from secrecy to ubiquity Kalashnikovs have become more than weapons. They have become symbols—first of the industrial success of Stalin's Soviet Union and the socialist way, later of popular insurrection, armed liberation, and gangland stature, more recently of jihad. A Kalashnikov can be appropriated for most any cause. An AK-47 with bayonet attached appears on the flag of Mozambique; it shares that flag with a hoe and a book, as if it were one of a young nation's foundational tools. Another Kalashnikov-like rifle, held aloft by a defiant fist, adorns the emblem of Hezbollah. Here its meaning is different. The flag is not about victory, not yet. It's about the fight. In Hollywood the Kalashnikov suggests the bad guy, the lunatic, the connoisseur tough. "AK-47—the very best there is," the actor Samuel L. Jackson said in one of his well-known roles. "When you absolutely, positively got to kill every motherfucker in the room."

These mixed meanings make a potent brew. The Kalashnikov stirs feelings, for and against, and the savvy have learned to tap its many meanings for their own purposes. In Missouri in mid-2009, when Mark Muller, the owner of a car dealership, wanted to generate interest and lift flagging sales, he offered a voucher for an AK-47 with the purchase of every pickup truck. The offer was a gimmick. True AK-47s cannot be legally owned by most people in the United States, and the dealership offered a coupon worth only half the price of the semiautomatic version sold in American gun shops. Once again, as is often the case in conversations related to the Kalashnikov, facts did not matter. Nonsense prevailed. Muller's sales promotion generated international attention: A broadcast team from Al Jazeera turned up, as did another from Russian state television news. The coverage triggered old arguments. What does this weapon mean? Is it the sinister product of sinister forms of government, set loose on the world via dark processes that were, and often remain, all but unchecked? Or does its reliability and simplicity make it a symbol of the virtue of our best tools, a companion to the utility of a well-performing pickup truck? Muller was pleased. He appeared before the cameras brandishing a Kalashnikov in its semiautomatic form, enjoying free publicity while spurring business and tweaking the anti-gun crowd at the same time. Like many a man who has used a Kalashnikov, he held up his rifle for the cameras and grinned—the rascal's pose. The Kalashnikov was put to yet another use.

Several declarations are necessary.

First, a matter of classification: For the purposes of this book, the Kalashnikov series includes the original forms and common descendants of the AK-47, including the AKM, the AKS, the Chinese Type 56 and

North Korean Type 58, the Type 68, the East German MPiK, the Hungarian AMD, the Polish PMKM, the Egyptian Misr and Iraqi Tabuk, the Yugoslav M70, the AK-74, and a host of other derivatives and copycats. These rifles are commonly—although incorrectly—lumped together and referred to as the AK-47 by many commentators. To be precise, the actual AK-47 was an early model in the line and is not nearly as widespread as the varieties that followed. But the name has become, in public discourse, a shorthand for an entire family of arms. This work also examines, to a much lesser degree, the original and follow-on forms of the RPK (a light machine gun that closely resembles the AK and is often mistaken for it), the PK (a general-purpose machine gun also designed by a team working under Mikhail Kalashnikov's name), and the SVD (a semiautomatic sniper rifle designed by Evgeny Fedorovich Dragunov and approved by the Soviet Army in 1963; Dragunov worked in the same factory as Kalashnikov and his SVD incorporated several design features of the Kalashnikov system). Why cover these arms together? Because this group forms a system of arms created from the mid-1940s to the mid-1970s to equip the Eastern bloc. They are an interrelated bunch, often made in the same factories by the same people, and designed to be distributed and used together. They share essential characteristics—ruggedness, reliability, simplicity, and profligate mass production. And because they use only three basic cartridges, made in factories that have been tooled globally to feed these now widely distributed weapons, as a group they provide a means to examine the methods and consequences of military small-arms proliferation around the world.

Second, this book, though covering a wide expanse of time and geography, attempts a comprehensive account, not a complete account, of these weapons and their place in a larger history. There are two reasons. The first is obvious. The Kalashnikov series is a sprawling subject. No single treatment can address all of its uses. An effort of such scale would require volumes and cover much of the history of more than a half-century of ground war. To cover every weapon and step in the evolution would require more time and space than one book allows. But there were milestones along the way, and consequences that fit categories. Many of these central processes and moments can be readily described. The second reason is less obvious but an even more limiting factor. On the subject of the assault rifles made by the former and current socialist worlds, impregnable obstacles block full illumination. Important matters will remain unknown until archives are open and independent researchers are allowed to assemble honest accounts of arms plants and arming decisions in Russia, North Korea, China, and many other nations. The weapon was principally a product of secretive governments, and unpleasant facts surrounding its distribution have left governments and exporters with little incentive to share their roles openly. Further, Russia, where the *Avtomat Kalashnikova* originated in Soviet times, has expressed itself on the subject mostly through propaganda, which over time and through repetition has hardened into national fable. The fuller versions remain officially suppressed, lost to the combined and corrosive effects of the censors and the near chanting of half-truths and lies. Myths have risen around the weapon, as have honest understandings. Separating the two is a challenge for any researcher, particularly in a period when important state archives remain sealed and when many institutions and groups, ranging from Kalashnikov's family to the manufacturers of the weapons that bear his name, are invested in self-serving versions that cannot be fully verified and do not appear sturdy enough to withstand scrutiny. The story of the Kalashnikov is further complicated by accounts of soldiers, activists, and journalists, Eastern and Western, pro-gun and anti-gun, whose statements often flow from legend, fancy, or, in the case of the ideologues, ulterior motives. Such distillations have been repeated so often that they can appear to the casual observer to be fact. Last, elements of the weapon's story are difficult to assemble because of the weapon's frequent involvement in crimes. The criminals who have used them left no archives. Many have had a marked unwillingness to discuss their work. And yet for all of these obstacles, the weapons exist in such huge quantities and in so many visible fashions that a rich history can be assembled with rigor. And the questions whose answers are unknown or unresolved, the blank spots—like those of a redacted Soviet text—can be pointed out and encircled with analysis and the available facts.

Third, this book does not attempt to address the core arguments over the Second Amendment of the Constitution of the United States. There are several reasons for this. The book is principally concerned with events and activities outside the United States, and with roles that automatic weapons play in conflict zones and regions of instability. Their effects upon stable, developed, Western democracies are of an entirely different order, and so of limited interest in this treatment. Where this book does examine events within the United States, these events are mostly matters of nineteenth-century conflict, arms development and sales, military policy, and the evolution of tactical choices in officers' circles. The Second Amendment, and the many questions of individual rights and public policy that surround it, is another subject. This is especially so because throughout the period of their existence, the Kalashnikovs discussed here, which in the United States are classified under federal law as weapons covered by the 1934 National Firearms Act—essentially, as machine guns—have not been available to most American citizens. As such, they are largely removed from the main disputes over how to define and legislate the right to bear arms in the present day. Moreover, the Kalashnikov rifles that are in circulation in the United States are almost all semiautomatic arms, and fire a single shot for each trigger pull. For this reason—the fact that they are not fully automatic weapons—they are not Kalashnikovs as the rest of the world understands them.

Fourth, on the subject of sources: To explore the more challenging periods or characters, especially within the Soviet Union and the nations of the Warsaw Pact, the middle portion of this book brings together conflicting sources and positions them against each other. Many sources are sound. Some are not verifiable, but have enough merit to be included with attribution and explanation. Some are suspicious or outright false and are declared to be so in the text. The value of the dubious sources is that they demonstrate both a portion of the lies that have been circulated and the reasons why. The Soviet Union deployed falsehoods for practical purposes, and its propaganda—pernicious and sustained for decades— has indelibly informed the public understanding of the Kalashnikov line. It is worthwhile, then, for a reader, when examining Soviet military history from official and contemporaneous Soviet sources, to remember the words of General Aleksei Yepishev, chief political commissar of the Soviet armed forces. In a helpfully apt summary of much of what was published in Soviet times, Yepishev dismissed the complaints of Georgy K. Zhukov, marshal of the Soviet Union, whose memoirs were being "edited" by a Communist Party rewrite team in ways that removed criticism of Stalin, made them more celebratory and platitudinous, and included cameo appearances by senior communist officials who demanded that they appear in the text, no matter their relevance to the story. (Leonid Brezhnev, who never saw Zhukov in the war years, was among those who insisted on being named.) To Zhukov's objections, Yepishev said: "Who needs your truth if it stands in our way?"[7] This is part of the nature of official Soviet history, and it frames one of the challenges to objective researchers of the period. And for exactly this reason, Soviet sources are useful, even necessary, when clearly shown for what they are. They go to the very character and motivations of actors involved, and provide readers with a basis for a healthy skepticism of official stories in the national stock.

The nature of available sources drove choices in structure. The book is arranged to present three periods of a history: the origins of rapid-fire arms, the development and mass distribution of Eastern bloc assault rifles, and the effects these weapons have had on security and war. The middle section in places offers differing accounts and allows for triangulation. This approach has utility in presenting contradictory statements by Soviet propagandists and by Mikhail Kalashnikov about the invention and development of this weapon, and about the designer's personal history. Again, it provides a foundation for skepticism. The clarity with which Soviet and Russian falsehoods are visible should not be taken as an indication that Western sources on Western arms told the truth. Sometimes they did; other times they did not. Arms designers and military officers in the West, and one now-defunct firm with a prominent place in this book—Colt's Firearms Division of Colt Industries—engaged in untrustworthy behaviors. But there is a difference between Western sources and sources with a Soviet influence. In the West, the availability of materials in archives, and laws that allow at least a modicum of public access to once-classified reports, allow the Western portion of this history to emerge in a crispness of detail that is not yet possible in much of the old Soviet space, where legends, though challenged and under strain from post-Soviet disclosures, manage to live on.

Fifth, a note to the collector, enthusiast, industrial historian, or forensic investigator: This book does not attempt to provide a full field guide to Kalashnikov-style weapons, the ammunition they fire, and the factories that produced them. Such a reference would be, without question, a valuable resource, including as a tool for helping soldiers and law enforcement officers to trace collected weapons to their sources. It would also be a different book. But the field-guide notion is worth addressing here. A small number of firearms references have attempted this, at least in part, and the United States military has quietly built an arms database, known as CHUCKWAGON, that provides this service to its users. The Pentagon's database includes data not just on weapon types by style and serial numbers and their sources of production but also on intermediate handlers, including governments and units that have possessed distinctly identifiable weapons at certain times. But for private citizens, none of the publicly available tools are complete, and all of them have errors. Most of them also repeat legends and common mistakes.[8] An effort to provide that service here would no doubt include errors as well, partly owing to the secrecy and deception of many Kalashnikov producers, and partly because the official database, which might be used to refine such a record for the public, is closed to unofficial users.

Sixth, for those interested or invested in the continuing disputes about what cartridge and rifle combination would be best for conventional military duty in 2010 and beyond, this book does not recommend one cartridge or weapon over others. It deals bluntly with problems that surrounded the American military's introduction in the 1960s of the M-16 rifle and the 5.56-millimeter cartridges it fired—a reaction to Kalashnikov proliferation that, in its early years, resulted in a weapon not ready for war. But the most pressing problems of that era were addressed well more than a generation ago, and much of the historical discussion is not relevant to comparisons between rifles offered for government service today. Moreover, the highly charged rifle-selection disputes that persist—between advocates of the SCAR, the M-4, the XM8, and many others, including new variants of the Kalashnikov line—are not treated here. That could be another book. The experiences of soldiers and Marines described in this book do have bearing on that conversation. They suggest that those who choose new rifles for military organizations should be wary of hype, and of salesmen pushing new products. The best tests of an automatic rifle occur in the body of experience accumulated during its service in combat over time. Many of the choices offered today have not been widely used by many hands, or have been used by secretive forces whose operations are not transparent and whose experiences are not sufficiently known and available for considered reflection and review. It is not the ambition of this book to champion one rifle over others. Based on what is publicly known, the limits of any endorsement are too great.

Similarly, this book avoids a celebration of the Kalashnikov's technical merits. The AK-47 was, in hindsight, a predictable assimilation of converging ideas of military small-arms design. It came into existence via smart borrowing of others' work and emerged as a compromise between established classes of firearms. Like all compromises, it was imperfect. Its descendants do have remarkable traits. Mostly they have been well made. But they are not engineering miracles or monuments to perfection, as often portrayed. Limitations and weaknesses inhabit the Kalashnikov design. These emerge starkly, for example, when the distances between a shooter and potential targets stretch out. For this reason, the Kalashnikov line has showed itself in Afghanistan and Iraq to be more than adequate for insurgents seeking to undermine weak governments or to prey on the unarmed, but less useful against a well-trained conventional foe possessing rifles and machine guns with longer effective ranges. Eastern bloc assault rifles were exceptionally well matched to fighting in Vietnam, where humid conditions and short ranges were common and these rifles gained early fame. For conventional desert fighting, the Kalashnikov is not ideal.

Last, this book also avoids making sweeping public-policy proposals. It is descriptive rather than prescriptive. It documents a portion of a history and delineates a set of problems. It does propose, unequivocally and without qualification, that like the atomic bomb and the weapons of mass destruction that followed it, the Kalashnikov is a Cold War weapon with a legacy as yet unresolved, a legacy that continues to threaten people and security across much of the world. It further proposes that because governments have focused elsewhere, these weapons and the people who have put them to ill use have killed and maimed more people, and dragged many regions deeper into disarray, than they might have otherwise. Still further, it proposes that the Kalashnikov, while a special case, is representative of a larger group of weapons. This book does review certain means of ameliorating the effects of widespread assault-rifle proliferation, but it deliberately leaves questions of the best means of relief and abatement—methods that might bring a degree of peace and stability to many troubled lands—to other hands. This is in part because as an effort at assessing the Kalashnikov's history, and it effects, this book is not aligned with any interest group or side.

C.J. CHIVERS

KANDAHAR, AFGHANISTAN

JULY 2010

I

ORIGINS

CHAPTER 1

The Birth of Machine Guns

An Invention of No Ordinary Character

Rᴄʜᴀʀᴅ ᴊ. ɢᴀᴛʟɪɴɢ ᴡᴀs sᴇᴇᴋɪɴɢ ʙᴜsɪɴᴇss. ɪɴ ᴛʜᴇ ᴍᴇᴛɪᴄᴜʟᴏᴜs penmanship of a man born to a land-owning Southern family, he began a letter to President Abraham Lincoln.

It was February 18, 1864, late in the American Civil War and an extraordinary period in the evolution of firearms: dawn in the age of the machine gun and yet a time when officers still roamed battlefields with swords. At forty-five, Gatling was a medical-school graduate who had never practiced medicine, opting instead to turn his stern father's sideline as an inventor into a career. For twenty years he had mainly designed agricultural devices. Dr. Gatling, as he liked to be called, came from a North Carolina family that owned as many as twenty slaves.[1] But he had moved north to Indiana for business and marriage, and when the war began in 1861 he did not align himself with the secessionists who formed the Confederacy. He knew men on both sides. Far from his place of birth and away from the battlefields, he had taken to viewing the contents of the caskets returning to the railroad depot in Indianapolis. Inside were the remains of Union soldiers, many felled by trauma but most by infection or disease. Seeing these gruesome sights, Gatling shifted attention from farm devices to firearms,[2] and to the ambition of designing a rapid-fire weapon, a pursuit that since the fourteenth century had attracted and eluded gunsmiths around the world. "I witnessed almost daily the departure of troops to the front and the return of the wounded, sick and dead," he wrote. "It occurred to me that if I could invent a machine— a gun—that would by its rapidity of fire enable one man to do as much

battle duty as a hundred, that it would to a great extent, supersede the
necessity of large armies, and consequently exposure to battle and disease
would be greatly diminished."³

Gatling did not fit any caricature of an arms profiteer. By the available
accounts, he carried himself as a neat and finely dressed gentleman. He
was kindhearted to his family and associates, soft-spoken at home, and
self-conscious enough that he wore a beard to hide the smallpox scars that
peppered his face.⁴ He made for a curious figure: an earnest and competitive showboat when promoting his weapon, but restrained and modest
on the subject of himself. He was, his son-in-law said, "an exception to
the rule that no man is great to his valet."⁵ One interviewer noted that he
professed to feel "that if he could invent a gun which would do the work
of 100 men, the other ninety and nine could remain at home and be saved
to the country."⁶ He repeated this point throughout his life, explaining a
sentiment that he insisted rose from seeing firsthand the ruined remains
of young men lost in a fratricidal war. His records make clear that he was
driven by profits. He never ceased claiming that compassion urged him
on at the start.

Gatling was neither a military nor a social visionary. But he was a
gifted tinkerer and an unrelenting salesman, and he found good help.
His plans proceeded swiftly. Though there is no record of his having prior
experience with weapon design, by late 1862, after viewing rival guns,
drawing on his knowledge of agricultural machinery, and enlisting the
mechanical assistance of Otis Frink,⁷ a local machinist, he had received a
patent for a prototype he called the "battery gun." "The object of this invention," he told the U.S. Patent Office, "is to obtain a simple, compact,
durable, and efficient firearm for war purposes, to be used either in attack
or defence, one that is light when compared with ordinary field artillery,
that is easily transported, that may be rapidly fired, and that can be operated by few men."⁸

Gatling's battery gun, while imperfect in its early forms, was a breakthrough in a field that had frustrated everyone who had tried before. Since
medieval times, the pursuit of a single weapon that could mass musket
fire had confounded generations of military-minded gunsmiths and engineers. Gunsmiths had long ago learned to place barrels side by side
on frames to create firearms capable of discharging projectiles in rapid
succession. These unwieldy devices, known as volley guns, were capable

in theory of blasting a hole in a line of advancing soldiers. They had limitations in practice, among them slow reload times and difficulties in adjusting fire toward moving targets and their flanks. Ammunition was a problem, too, as was the poor state of metallurgy, although this did not discourage everyone, and the lethal possibilities of a machine that could concentrate gunfire attracted would-be inventors of many stripes. One of the few highly detailed accounts of the early models suggests an inauspicious start. In 1835, Giuseppe Fieschi, a Corsican, rented an apartment on Boulevard du Temple in Paris. In a room overlooking the street he secretly constructed a frame of thick oak posts and attached twenty-five rifle barrels, all in a space of roughly a meter square.[9] Each barrel was packed with multiple musket balls and a heavy charge of powder, then aligned to aim together at a point on the street below. Fieschi waited. On July 28, his intended victim appeared: King Louis-Philippe. Fieschi fired his makeshift device, and a volley flew from the apartment window and slammed into the king's entourage. In the technical sense, the "infernal machine," as his device came to be known in Europe, was both a success and a failure. It had a terrible effect. A piece of lead grazed Louis-Philippe's skull, just above his face, and others cut down his company, killing eighteen people. But an examination of the gun later suggested that while it worked well enough as a tool for assassination or terror, it was hardly ready for the battlefield. Four barrels had failed to fire. Four others had ruptured. Two of these had exploded, scattering lead inside the assassin's rented room and gravely injuring Fieschi, who was captured and saved from his injuries by the French authorities, to be executed later by guillotine.

Several hundred years of near stagnation in rapid-fire design, coupled with such mishaps, did not make machine guns an attractive idea to investors or customers alike. There was reason as well for potential purchasers to suspect nonsense in the claims of the movement's dreamers, whose folly preceded Fieschi. In 1718, James Puckle, of London, had received an English patent for a rapid-fire flintlock that he proposed to manufacture in two forms: one for firing round balls at Christians, and another for firing square blocks at Muslims. The weapon, he wrote, was for "defending King George, Your country and Lawes, to defending yourselves and Protestant cause."[10] Puckle was nearly two centuries ahead of the machine-gun age. His proposal to subject Muslims to what he expected to be the crueler effects of square projectiles in some ways foreshadowed the punishing ways that rapid-fire weapons would be used to suppress indigenous tribes late in the nineteenth century, including columns of Mahdist fighters in British campaigns along the Nile. It also suggested that he knew next to nothing of ballistics. Investors steered wide. The gun never went into production.

By the Civil War, the new manufacturing capacity in the United States was moving the craft of gunsmithing into the realm of mass production, putting it firmly on the terrain of the speculator and engineer. Puckle's fancy fell to more practical men. Since the 1850s, with improvements in metallurgy, toolmaking, and precision labor, there had been a flurry of fresh design efforts, and war in the 1860s had proven to be a stimulant to arms makers and their salesmen. A six-barrel rapid-fire weapon known as the Ripley had been conceived of in Troy, New York, although it had not made it out of the prototype phase. General Origen Vandenburgh, of the New York State Militia, had been conducting tests of his own line of volley guns, and envisioned what he called "their life-destroying efficiency at every point." An arms race had begun, although initially it was driven more by private designers and profit-seekers than by armies or governments. "We involuntarily look for the most deadly weapon by which men can destroy each other in the open field, and not without ample cause, for decisive struggles, on which national results will depend, will be decided there," General Vandenburgh told an assembly of British officers in 1862.[11] The general's loyalty to the nation seems to have been less well developed than his desire for sales receipts. After the United States military refused to adopt his weapon, saying, among other things, that it took nine hours to clean after firing, the general took it to England, found a manufacturer, and offered his weapon's "life-destroying efficiency" to the Confederacy, which bought at least one. He was not the only Northern businessman supplying the enemy. A firm in Rochester, New York, offered a new volley gun, the Requa, with twenty-five .58-caliber barrels arranged in a single row. The Confederate Army had incorporated a few of these weapons into its forces as well; a quick and well-supplied crew could fire seven volleys through a Requa in a minute, 175 bullets in all.[12] Another gun, the Union Repeating Gun, fired repeatedly through a single barrel by the means of a hand crank. Then came Gatling.

The sketch that accompanied Gatling's patent application showed that he had given the concept of rapid fire an ingeniously effective form. He had placed six heavy rifled barrels in circular fashion around a central axis, a design somewhat like a revolver in reverse, with the barrels spinning, rather than a cylinder behind them. A hand crank on the right side rotated each barrel through its turns firing, as ammunition was fed from a canister above. The weapon was a sight. It rested between two carriage wheels, like a small cannon. One writer gave it a name: "the little death angel."[13] It was an angel with curious parentage. Gatling appeared to have borrowed heavily from previous gun designers—the crank and hopper from the Repeating Gun, the six barrels of the Ripley. He also drew from himself. His first battery gun shared design elements with a cotton planter and rotary cultivator, except that it directed evenly spaced bullets, not seeds, where the handlers intended them to go. The result was still not a true automatic weapon. Gatling's gun was manually operated. It required external assistance from the soldier at the handle to produce continuous fire, and it bore little resemblance to the automatic infantry arms in service today. But Gatling had created a weapon that fired with great rapidity and considerable accuracy, and was a technically sound step closer to the firearm manufacturer's ideal of automatic fire. The term *machine gun* had not yet entered military jargon or the public imagination, but here was the forerunner: the 1862 Gatling, the first reasonably reliable weapon that could provide continuous rifle fire. It needed only to be debugged, and for the ammunition industry to catch up.

Modifications to the battery gun followed, as did public demonstrations. Witness accounts and ordnance test reports show that nothing quite like the effect of a Gatling gun had ever been seen. With this bulky invention, two men could produce controlled and withering streams of bullets beyond the ranges at which infantrymen of the time typically fought. Newspaper editors in Indiana cheered the arrival of a mechanical killing tool. "The newly invented gun of Richard J. Gatling, of this city, was put through an experimental trial yesterday, with blank cartridges, at the State House square, in the presence of the Governor and a large crowd of citizens. It operates very successfully and will certainly prove to be a weapon of war both novel and deadly."[14] Indiana's governor, Oliver P. Morton, had been impressed enough that he ordered state tests. The initial examination was promising. "The discharge can be made with all desirable accuracy as rapidly as 150 times per minute, and may be continued for hours without danger, as we think, from overheating," the three reviewers wrote. The weapon's endurance while firing was an essential improvement over the Repeating Gun, which, with a single barrel and the characteristics of metals of the time, was vulnerable to malfunction caused by extreme heat. (One test in England would find that the Repeating Gun's "barrel grew first red and then nearly white hot, large drops of fused metal poured from the muzzle, and the firing had to be discontinued from fear of worse consequences.")[15] The Gatling gun's evaluators were impressed. "The very low price at which the gun can be made, its superiority in every respect, induce us to hope that your Excellency will order enough to be immediately constructed for a fair experiment in the field."[16] Early praise did not spur sales on a significant scale, but Gatling's prototypes had made him a leader in a pack of arms designers—many of them genuine, some charlatans—racing for business.

These designers sought customers, and Gatling hoped to manufacture his line for the Union Army, the institution most likely to make him a very rich man. He also had little choice. During the war, the United States had imposed an embargo on arms exports. Sales contact with the Confederacy would be treason, and aside from the War Department there were few potential customers. The great size of the Gatling gun, and its relative complexity, made it a tool for institutions, not individuals. Gatling had spent the war years trying to entice the army into a deal, and had been helped by Governor Morton, who urged Peter H. Watson, an assistant secretary of war, to consider the Gatling gun for Union Army service. Good connections did not matter. Always Gatling had failed. The army showed no interest in his bullet-spitting contraption. A limited trial in 1863 by the navy indicated that the design had merit. The battery gun, wrote Lieutenant J. S. Skerrett, who supervised the tests, "has proved itself to be a very effective arm at short range; is well constructed, and calculated to stand usage to which it would necessarily be subjected."[17] The navy ordered a small number of Gatlings. But the army did not budge.

The Union Army was engaged in some of the most ferocious fighting ever seen, the fate of the American experiment was at stake, and many other young technologies were being applied to wide-scale use in war: rail transport, the telegraph, the repeating rifle, and more. All that Gatling had managed was a side arrangement in 1863 with Major General Benjamin F. Butler, a politician turned general in command of the Massachusetts Volunteers. General Butler often acted according to his own whim, and at the request of Gatling's agent in the East, a demonstration was performed for him in Baltimore as he made his way south toward the war. He bought twelve guns on the spot for one thousand dollars apiece, along with twelve thousand cartridges. It should have been a promising start, but much went wrong. Gatling claimed to have paid $769 per gun to the machine shop he had contracted to manufacture them. Had his company received one thousand dollars for each of the dozen guns, there would have been at best a small profit after his agent's commission. But Butler's cash did not find its way to the inventor. "I never got any of that money," he complained. "My agent went to Chicago with it, where he failed in business before he had made a settlement. So you see I was, so far, badly out of pocket."[18] Moreover, if the weapons had ended up in the hands of a different and more experienced general, they might have been put to imaginative work, and Gatling's full loss could have been offset by a rush of orders. But Butler is remembered more for his foul reputation among Southerners than as a tactician.[19] He retains the distinction of being the first army officer ever to bring modern rapid-fire arms to war. Yet he used them little. Butler's Gatlings were apparently employed in the defense near Richmond,[20] where they were effective in repelling a Confederate attack, and again at a fight along the James and Appomattox rivers. But little else is known of them, and they did not leave a strong impression in the Union Army, or influence the direction of the war.

As Gatling pondered his business in February 1864, nearly three years into the Civil War and with no significant sales on his books, the only other known use of his battery guns had been in mid-July 1863 at the *New York Times,* a Republican paper and stalwart backer of President Lincoln. The city had been shaken that summer by protests against draft laws that allowed citizens to buy their way out of Union conscription with a payment of three hundred dollars. The large fee meant that only the rich could afford a waiver. Class rage flowed, mixed with racist anger against blacks, who many white citizens thought would be competing with them for jobs. After an attempt to hold a new conscription lottery in July, rioters clashed with the police and roamed the city, burning buildings and beating freed slaves. At least several hundred people were killed. The *Times* had supported the draft laws and editorialized against the rioters. It backed its words with a bizarre reserve at its offices on Park Row: Gatling guns ready to turn back any mob. Accounts of the newspaper's armory have varied. By one, Henry Jarvis Raymond, the *Times'* editor, was said to have personally manned a Gatling from behind a north-facing window that commanded a view of the street, and to have urged one the *Times'* principal stockholders to join him if necessary. "Give them the grape, and plenty of it," he said,[21] although the guns were never fired. On the night of July 13, mobs had ransacked the offices of another pro-Lincoln paper, Horace Greeley's *New York Tribune,* before being driven off in a club-swinging melee with the police. The next night, fresh mobs appeared, but seeing Gatling guns pointing from the *Times'* front entrances, the rioters chose to converge once more on Greeley's office, which the managing editor had arranged to have lined with wet newspaper to keep down the risk of fire. The crowd seethed with menace but withdrew when its members saw Greeley's staff had taken arms, too, and rifles bristled from the windows.[22] Where the *Times'* Gatlings came from has been lost to history, but the newspaper's offices weathered the riots without suffering so much as a broken window.

The deployment at the *Times* and the brief trial by Butler's troops were anomalies. Whatever the merits of the battery gun—and as yet it was not perfected and the ammunition it fired was problematic—the bureaucratic obstacles against it were substantial. Throughout the war Gatling's ambitions had been undermined by Brigadier General James W. Ripley, the army's prickly and by-the-book chief of ordnance, who was nearing seventy years of age and was not inclined to entertain new ideas. Ripley had devoted himself to trying to standardize the Union Army's mismatched collection of weapons, and was annoyed by the parade of salesmen with their gimmicks and untried wares, who were seeking to add ever more arms to an already sprawling assortment.[23] (If war is an incubator for industry and weapons development, it is also a phenomenon that attracts profiteers and quacks. Ripley faced problems that will always accompany a government that has the power to make an arms salesman instantly rich. Several decades later, the British minister of munitions would describe the phenomenon perfectly; "I was, naturally being deluged at the Ministry of Munitions with letters and calls from people who had some new invention or improvement to propose. The great majority of these ideas were, of course, useless, and many of them came from cranks and lunatics.")[24] In Ripley's case, the forces working against standardization were extraordinary. Both sides had been unprepared for war when war arrived. The Union Army had grown from 16,000 officers and men to a force of 486,000 in a matter of months,[25] and Ripley was tasked with finding them arms and ammunition. The arming risked becoming frantic and slipshod; as the war progressed, between the Union and the Confederacy there were no fewer than 370 different types of small arms on the battlefields, in at least sixty-five calibers. This count did not include the personal arms that many soldiers carried to the fighting.[26]

Gatling also faced darker problems. He had been born in North Carolina, to slave-holding parents, and had settled in the North. Rumors circulated that he was a Confederate sympathizer masquerading as a businessman, and had built his weapon in Cincinnati, near Southern lines, so that rebel troops might seize his arms stores in a raid.[27] It was a peculiar form of war hysteria, and like most forms of hysteria, it was illogical. In the eyes of the federal government, the gun was not good enough for United States service, and yet the government feared that the other side might secure and use it against the Union's troops. By February 1864, having invested heavily in a weapon that yielded little return, Gatling had had enough. He sought the ear of President Lincoln, to whom he composed a sales pitch, right down to the enclosed brochure. "Pardon me for the liberty I have taken," the inventor began. "I enclose herewith a circular giving a description of the 'Gatling Gun,' of which I am inventor and patentee.

"The arm in question," he added, "is an invention of no ordinary character."[28]

As Gatling posted his letter, war had reached its bloodiest form yet. The Industrial Revolution, and the American zest for capitalism, were proving to be incubators for weapons development, and the soldiers of the time faced firearms and artillery that were becoming more powerful and more precise. Ordered into battle at close ranges, in solid-colored uniforms and in dense formations, they were easy marks at short distances, and suffered miserably from bullet and shrapnel injuries, as well as from diseases stalking both armies' filthy camps. In the 1850s, the United States Army had switched from using round musket balls and chosen to issue Minié balls, which were faster and more accurate. The Confederacy, whose senior ordnance officers came from American service, chose Minié balls as well. This meant that both Union and Confederate units, going into battle in close-order drill, were blasting away at each other with rifles of terrible power.[29] Enormous amounts of lead were in the air. War records suggest that the Union Army alone procured more than one billion rounds from foreign and domestic suppliers. At two hundred yards, the Minié balls fired from most service weapons could penetrate from nine to eleven inches into white pine; at six hundred yards, they penetrated more than five inches. Experiments with cartridges of the time found that even stray rounds traveling far from the barrel, slowed to the speed of 362 feet per second, would pass effortlessly through an inch-thick pine board, or shatter the leg bone of an ox.[30]

Accounts of the carnage were accumulating. More than 50,000 casualties at Gettysburg, nearly 35,000 at Chickamauga, another 30,000 at Chancellorsville. And as arms and ordnance plants churned out new developments, the medical arts had not kept pace. Even the lightly wounded faced agony. Anesthesia was only beginning to enter widespread use, which, as one chronicler noted, often meant that "nine-tenths of surgical skill was speed."[31] Amputations were performed in tents and commandeered buildings at battle's edge, at times by surgeons who sawed off shattered limbs from one partially sedated soldier while his wounded comrades queued up and watched, waiting their turns.[32] This was also before the causes of infection were known. Working in ignorance of bacteria, the surgeons who accompanied the soldiers into battle often did not wash their hands or change instruments between patients, many of whom either expired from putrefying infections after their wounds were sutured or arrived at convalescent hospitals away from the front feverish, weakened, and at risk. "Our house is one of constant death now," the chief nurse at the Union Hospital in Washington had written to her mother in New England, as Gatling was seeking his patent in 1862. "Every day some one drops off the corruption of a torn and wounded body."[33] Two days after Gatling's patent was awarded, she lamented of laboring to save the wrecked and infected men in the hospital's dim halls and cold rooms, an environment beset by "universal depression." "When the day dawns one of my men has gone, and before the hour of supper time comes we close the eyes of two more, one the only son of his mother!"[34]

The names of these lost sons filled lists in the newspapers around the land, North and South. By the time Gatling wrote Lincoln, about half a million Union and Confederate soldiers were dead, by far the largest toll that the nation had ever suffered in war, and ever would. Hundreds of thousands more men had been wounded. These were staggering numbers for a nation with a population of 31 million. (The proportionate equivalent would be roughly 5 million dead Americans in the first three years of the most recent war in Iraq.) They were even more staggering considering that neither the Union nor the Confederate tallies included civilian tolls. Gatling offered to help end the bloodletting through a counterintuitive means: more efficient slaughter. He hoped that President Lincoln would see that his weapon—"very simple in its construction, strong and durable and can be used effectively by men of ordinary intelligence"—was "providential, to be used as a means in crushing the rebellion."

The decision to seek the president's attention was not unwise, but it was poorly timed. In June 1861, at the outset of the war, Lincoln had expressed enough of a personal interest in the Union Army's weapons that he had agreed to meet with the salesmen of the Union Repeating Gun, designed, depending on which patent application one believes, by either Wilson Ager, Edward Nugent, or William Palmer.[35] Its vendors were no strangers to overstatement. They called their offering "an Army in six-feet square." It was a single-barreled weapon with a revolving cylinder set just behind the stationary barrel, which made it more like a huge revolver than Gatling's eventual development. The cylinder was turned via the working of a hand-crank. And as each of the .58-caliber projectiles flew from the thirty-five-inch barrel, at a rate of 120 rounds a minute, new paper cartridges rolled into place from a metal box mounted above.[36]

Lincoln believed in technology, and he thought that the right weapons, made with the Union's industrial advantages, might hurry the fighting along toward victory. When the Repeating Gun's salesmen arrived from New York and checked into the Willard Hotel in Washington, the president ventured down Pennsylvania Avenue from the White House to participate in a demonstration in the loft of a carriage house. Empty cartridges were used, but Lincoln, manning the crank himself, was able to see the cartridges cycle from the box above, through the cylinders, and drop out below. It was the first time a head of state had such a personal encounter with a rapid-fire firearm—a sales phenomenon that within a few years would become common practice in Europe. Lincoln was impressed. He called the weapon the "Coffee Mill," a homespun nickname coined at the sight of cartridges falling from the hopper and out onto the ground through the movement of a handle, which made the contraption vaguely reminiscent of a grinder.[37]

A few days later the president attended a firing trial with live ammunition at the Washington Arsenal. By the year's end he had instructed the army to order sixty of the guns. The first fifty were bought for $612.50 apiece, plus 20 percent, the following July.[38] With that order, J. D. Mills, the salesman, became the first arms dealer to sell a machine gun,[39] a career path many would follow. Gatling hoped to be next.

The mood for revolutionary weapons in Washington, however, was different in early 1864 than it had been in 1861. More than two years of intense fighting had passed since Mills's sales coup, and no fewer than twenty-five different "machine-gun devices," as one American military officer called them, had been submitted to ordnance officials.[40] Lincoln had pushed for another early machine gun, known as the Raphael Repeater, but General Ripley had stymied that weapon, too. And the Coffee Mills that Lincoln had managed to urge into service, and Butler's Gatlings, had been of little consequence, for many reasons. Some were the weapon's fault, others not. Paper cartridges were prone to failure. Coffee Mills had seen combat under Colonel John W. Geary in Middleburg, Virginia, in 1862, when they pushed back a Confederate cavalry squadron.[41] But the colonel later returned the guns to Washington and complained they were inefficient and unsafe. The single barrel, firing heavy bullets and exposed to the bullets' friction and the great heat of the powder that propelled them, was prone to overheating. The loads of ammunition required to supply the weapons were a heavy burden for the men and draft horses needed to move the weapon into position for a fight. There were also reports that the weapons' parts broke, causing the entire system to fail. The rebels' Requas had also not redeemed themselves. The Confederate volley gun weighed nearly fourteen hundred pounds and tended not to work when its ammunition was exposed to moisture. Rapid-fire weapons were too new, and the army's officers too unfamiliar with them, for machine gunnery to find a place in the war.

Worries about logistics and performance were not the only factors that had dampened enthusiasm. An absence of imagination played a part.

The federal and Confederate officers had been unable to conceive of an essential tactical role for these new weapons. Officers were simply not sure what to do with them. They regarded them as offshoots of artillery, not as infantry arms. Rapid-fire arms stood garrison duty. They watched over bridges. Butler dragged them along as his unit walked across the South. They were not pushed to the center of battlefield duty, and, as near as the surviving records and accounts of the fighting tell, were never used in the offense. No one quite knew how, and no one was advocating for them from within.

Gatling sensed what he was up against. His claim to Lincoln—that the gun he offered was of no ordinary character—was certainly true. Unlike the guns his competitors sold, his weapon was showing signs in field trials that it did not overheat and was a step closer to making the elusive goal of rapid fire real. He wanted Lincoln to know that what he offered was not another curio, and far surpassed the lackluster machine that had intrigued the president almost three years before. He included a postscript in his letter: "I have seen an inferior arm known as the 'Coffee Mill Gun' which I am informed has not given satisfaction in practical tests on the battlefield. I assure you my invention is no 'Coffee Mill Gun'—but is entirely a different arm and is entirely free from the accidents and objections raised against that arm."

Performance did not matter. The Confederacy by 1864 had both bloodied the Union's formations and become so weakened by the materially superior federal troops that the promise of a swift victory brought on by a new and terribly efficient weapon was neither as inviting, nor as believable, as it might have been before. Gatling waited for an answer from a president whose attention had drifted. Lincoln did not intervene on Gatling's behalf. There is no record that he troubled to reply.

The time was not spent idly. Work on the Gatling gun line continued. Gatling had initially had his weapons manufactured in Cincinnati. In 1864, upon making another model with many refinements, he commissioned the Cooper Fire Arms Manufacturing Company, of Pennsylvania, to build an improved prototype. The new model was much more reliable and efficient. Gatling's sales agent, General John Love, a well-connected retired army veteran and graduate of West Point, offered the weapon for trials to the Army Ordnance Department in January 1865. General Ripley, who had thwarted Gatling from the beginning, had retired. His eventual replacement, Brigadier General Alexander B. Dyer, was twenty years younger than his former boss and more amenable to examining new submissions. The latest Gatling's performance was of a much higher order, and new developments in ammunition meant the weapon now fired metal cartridges, rather than the paper cartridges used in the earlier guns. Trials were ordered. The army's ordnance corps began to see its potential. "Dr. Gatling's gun seems to possess all the good qualities claimed for it," a test supervisor wrote. "It is therefore merely a question of whether such a piece would be of use in actual service."[42]

The Gatling gun had largely missed the war that spurred its creation, but it had found official support at last. Machine guns were no longer the fancies of men like Puckle. They were nearing commercial success, and were soon to be put to use.

CHAPTER 2

Machine Guns in Action

Merely a Life-Exterminating Weapon[1]

On August 24, 1866, the American army entered a contract to purchase one hundred Gatling guns, signed under the hand of General Dyer, who had assumed command of the Ordnance Department two years before.[2] Much had changed in the short time since General Dryer ordered the improved Gatling guns to be put through performance trials. General Robert E. Lee had surrendered the Army of Northern Virginia at Appomattox. President Lincoln had been assassinated at Ford's Theater. The Gatling Gun Company had entered an agreement with the Colt Patent Firearms Company, in Hartford, Connecticut, which gave Gatling the manufacturing capacity to handle large orders. And the army had turned much of its attention westward, to the resumption of subjugating Native American populations and tightening the government's hold on the vast wilderness territory that it claimed.

The latest army tests had led to enthusiastic reports. The weapon now had inside backing. "The moral effect of the Gatling gun would be very great in repelling an assault, as there is not a second of time for the assailants to advance between the discharges," a report noted in 1866. The chief tester found as well that the weapon was suited for the demands of the field. "The machinery of this gun is simple and strong, and I do not think likely to get out of order. I had the oil rubbed off this gun, drenched it with water, and then exposed it for two nights and a day to the rain and the weather, but though it was quite rusty, it was fired 97 times in a minute and a half, one man turning at the crank. In my opinion this arm could be used to advantage in the military service."[3] Positive reviews accumulated in the navy, too. "From the examination made of the gun, and the report the tests hereto appended, the board is of opinion that, as an auxiliary arm for special service . . . it has no known superior."[4]

Parallel developments had made Gatling's weapon more reliable. The improvements to the weapon proper in 1865 had been matched by advances in ammunition manufacturing, which made cartridges with solid metal casings available. The new gun, with the new casings, was an altogether more effective system. Gatling in time admitted that perhaps his earlier sales efforts had been rushed. When he had written Lincoln, it seemed, he had been peddling an unreliable weapon. "The machine gun was not of much practical use until the metal cartridge had been perfected," he said, "and that was not till after the war was ended."[5]

The end of the war also brought an end to an American embargo on exporting arms. The American army was small, and with a large recent order, Gatling knew that there were natural limits to domestic sales. He also knew that the more nations that fielded Gatling guns, the more appealing they might become to others. With the export ban lifted, he searched for business overseas. He enlisted the help of international sales representatives, offering salaries and commissions. Company officers, including Gatling, went abroad. At their urging, trials were held in Holland, Berlin, Versailles, Vienna, and Denmark. Sales started slowly. But the efforts hinted at the new markets' prospects. In 1867, the company sold the rights to Russia to make guns for its own use, and sold one gun to the Argentine Republic and another to the Royal Bavarian Arsenal. The Dutch bought two more, and the following year, in 1868, the royal Danish government ordered three. Word was spreading of the weapon's potential, reaching those controlling the purse strings of several governments.

Then came a break. Czar Alexander II of Russia was trying to exert his empire's influence over distant lands and indigenous populations. He sought arms, the best available, and in 1865 the czarist bureaucracy in Saint Petersburg assigned Colonel Alexander Pavlovich Gorloff to be the empire's military attaché in England and the United States. Colonel Gorloff, an arms-design expert from the Russian artillery, was directed to canvass arms and ordnance circles in the West and see what might be procured. Russia has long produced able military agents, and Colonel Gorloff, given wide latitude by his country, was one for his time. He had refined manners, spoke exquisite English, and had experience as the former secretary of the nation's Artillery Commission, where he had helped design Russian cannon. Upon arriving in the United States, he found himself drawn in particular to two systems: Smith & Wesson revolvers and Gatling guns. He introduced himself to American companies and comprehended the potential of repeating weapons with remarkable speed. By 1867 he convinced the czarist government to enter an agreement with the Gatling Gun Company to allow the Russian government to manufacture Gatlings.[6] In May 1869, Colonel Gorloff submitted an order to have seventy guns made in the United States; within months he ordered thirty more. Russia was moving quickly. While the prevailing attitude among officers of almost all professional armies was to dismiss machine guns as nearly useless, the czarist military distributed them without an agonizing or time-consuming debate. Within a year, every Russian artillery brigade would field a battery of eight Gatlings made for Russian-caliber cartridges.[7]

Russia's officers seemed much more determined to use Gatling guns than the inventor's own countrymen. Even after General Dyer and other ordnance officers recorded the Gatling's curious new powers and placed orders, the United States Army could not figure out what to do with them, aside from the obvious use in guarding forts and other fixed points. Some officers shunned them. "Against my wishes I was detailed to command them," wrote Edward S. Godfrey, a recent graduate of West Point assigned to the Seventh Cavalry in Kansas in 1867 and ordered to oversee "four Gatlings hauled by two mules each." He knew next to nothing about them, and had trouble finding soldiers to man them; this detail, like many others, apparently had been neglected since the guns had been delivered to Seventh Cavalry's post. "The only Gatlings I had ever seen were in the ordnance museum at West Point," Godfrey groused.[8]

The Russian purchases were made before Gatling himself knew just how powerful and well made his weapon had become. A test in Vienna, on July 9, 1869, showed the new weapon's ferocious capabilities. At a distance of eight hundred paces, a Gatling crew took three trial shots and then opened fire with a Gatling gun of half-inch caliber. The target, fifty-four feet wide by nine feet high, simulated the sort of large enemy presence—a formation of soldiers, perhaps, or a boat or an artillery piece—that gunners would fire upon by traversing their weapon slightly and distributing fire for maximum effect. The crew took 216 shots. Two hundred and thirteen bullets struck home. At twelve hundred paces, a larger Gatling gun fired 191 shots for 152 hits.[9] The results should have led to a self-evident conclusion: This was a weapon that could cut down the massed formations—the columns, lines, and squares of tightly grouped infantrymen—common in that day.

The following month, another test, at Karlsruhe, Prussia, pitted one hundred well-drilled infantry soldiers equipped with the *zundnadel-gewehr,* a breech-loading rifle known as the "needle gun," against a single half-inch-caliber Gatling. This time the target was seventy-two feet across but only six feet high. The competitors were given a minute each to fire as accurately and often as they could manage from a position eight hundred paces away. The one hundred Prussian riflemen produced a rolling barrage displaying the effects of what until that time had been seen as rapid firing: 721 shots, roughly one aimed shot per man every nine seconds. An examination of the target showed that much of the shooting had, in effect, been little more than noise. Only 196 projectiles struck the target, a success rate of 27 percent. The Gatling gun fired 246 shots and recorded 216 hits, or nearly 88 percent.[10] Gatling's gun had almost achieved its creator's vision: Two men, not one, had done the work of one hundred men and with only about one-third the ammunition. The first part of Gatling's theory about efficiency was proving correct. Technology was rendering the conventional infantry tactics of the era obsolete, although the conventional infantry did not yet know it.

More orders arrived. In 1870, a sales agent traveling the Middle East reported that he had in hand an order from Egypt for twenty-four guns. The company's hired agency in Europe had paid off, too. In the late spring, the agent, L. W. Broadwell, traveled to Constantinople and arranged demonstrations for Halil Pasha, the grand master of artillery for the Ottoman Empire. With a new drum feed, he wrote, the .42-caliber Gatling "has never before worked so well—no more hitches of any kind." He negotiated a contract to sell two hundred Gatling guns, to be manufactured under contract in Vienna, to the Turkish forces,[11] whose artillery experts had moved more quickly than even Colonel Gorloff.

With several hundred Gatlings working their way into service in armies at Europe's edges, the Europeans were busy with their own experiments with rapid rifle fire. Though they still favored the volley-gun design, they were developing guns that reduced the time between volleys and fired at rates comparing favorably with Gatling's claims. The most successful result had been credited to a Belgian army captain in 1851, and was modified by Joseph Montigny, a Belgian engineer, who designed a cylinder holding thirty-seven fixed barrels, which were fired in an almost simultaneous sequence by a single clockwise turn of a crank. Montigny's offering was a completely different concept from Gatling's, and owed more to the volley guns, like the failed Vandenburgh, than to guns in American service. The French called the gun the *mitrailleuse,* or grapeshooter, a name that suggested its officers conceived of it as a new kind of artillery more than as an infantry arm. Reloading was achieved by removing a rear plate that had holes arranged to match the barrels. A soldier would insert a preloaded replacement plate into the grooves and close the breech. The mitrailleuse was ready for its next blast. Volley firing was thereby straightforward. A gunner would give the crank one swift turn, and bullets would fly. A fresh platter of bullets would be rushed into place, and the crank would be spun anew. Montigny claimed a trained crew, well supplied with ammunition, could repeat the cycle as often as twelve times in a minute, for 444 shots in all, discharged in volleys spaced only a few seconds apart.[12] His tests, like those of the Gatling gun in Vienna and Karlsruhe, pointed to the lethal consequences for any massed infantry formation caught in the path of rifle bullets concentrated by a machine. At eight hundred yards, a cluster of thirty-seven bullets fired from a Montigny remained in a grouping roughly ten feet high by twelve feet wide. On paper, these were fearsome statistics. In the late 1860s, while Gatling was busily trying to sell France his improved weapons and personally attending field tests of his weapon in Versailles,[13] Montigny convinced Napoleon III, the French emperor, to order that the mitrailleuse be distributed to French troops.

Manufacturing began in supposed secrecy at a French arsenal in Meudon, outside Paris. The secret could not be kept. French newspapers crowed about a devastating weapon soon to be unveiled, one that would fell the Prussians in rows. Inside European martial circles, officers' clubs awaited the result, even as they shared the details of the emperor's hushed work. "The secret is so jealously guarded by our friends and allies, that it would be an ill return for much official kindness and hospitality shown me, to publish that which after all I have unofficially and indeed almost accidentally learned," declared one British major to an assembly of

officers in London. The speaker, G. V. Fosbery of Her Majesty's Bengal
Staff Corps, was an early proponent of rapid-fire arms. On the subject
of the *mitrailleuse,* he opted for both disclosure and titillation. The guns,
he said, actually seemed to fire about 300 shots a minute (not the 444
proposed), and the French had applied themselves to learning how to
fight with them. "The weapon is a most formidable one, it is admirably
constructed, and equipped for service, and will, I doubt not, produce, if
brought into action, effects almost as astonishing as those of the breech-
loader, and cause a general impatience to be possessed of the new arm."
The officers did not have to wait long for the gun to be revealed. Napoleon III declared war on Prussia in 1870. The huge guns—each weighed
nearly three thousand pounds—were towed toward the opening battles
hidden under tarps, along with a few Gatlings. In this war, France expected its rapid-fire weapons to be decisive.

When Prussian and French soldiers met in the countryside, the out-
comes were inconsistent. There were moments when rapid-fire arms were
extremely effective, including a one-sided engagement captured in an account by a correspondent for the London *Journal.* The writer described
the effect on a distant infantry formation that was caught in the open, and
suffered almost exactly the effect predicted in the 1868 tests in Vienna:

> A column of troops appeared in the valley below us, coming from
> the right—a mere dark streak upon the white snow; but no one in
> the battery could tell whether they were friends or foes, and the com-
> mander hesitated about opening fire. But now an aide-de-camp came
> dashing down the hill, with orders for us to pound at them at once—
> a French journalist having, it seems, discovered them to be enemies
> when the general and all his staff were as puzzled as ourselves. *Rr-rr-a*
> go our Gatlings, the deadly hail of bullets crashes into the thick of
> them, and slowly back into the woods the dark mass retires, leaving
> however, a track of black dots upon the white snow behind it.[14]

This was a minor episode in a war with more than two hundred thousand conventional combatants, and might not be expected to have been
either widely witnessed or grist for extrapolation among the tacticians
of the time. Another event, however, built on it. At the battle of Mars-
la-Tour, in August 1870, about thirty thousand Germans encountered a

retreating French force roughly four times their size. The battle would be a rout, with the outnumbered Germans forcing the already disoriented French deeper into indecision and withdrawal, and contributing to the capture of the French emperor and the Prussians' march on Paris. Lost in the scale of fighting and the political significance of the outcome was the riddling of the Thirty-eighth Prussian Infantry Brigade, which, backed by artillery, attacked a French division and its mitrailleurs. The official report presaged some of the accounts that would later circulate in World War I. It stated:

> . . . that these troops encountered a murderous infantry and machine-gun fire, and were obliged to fall back, their losses *"amounting almost to annihilation;"* that cavalry attempted to protect the shattered remnant of the brigade, "but that on account of the violent mitrailleuse fire, the leader was unable to deliver home his attack." The 38th Brigade (5 battalions) went into action with 95 officers, 4,546 men and sustained the loss of 72 officers and 2,542 men killed, wounded and prisoners. The proportion of killed to wounded being as 3 to 4.[15]

These accounts, for all that they suggested, did not receive wide circulation in the war's immediate aftermath, in part because two problems emerged in the Franco-Prussian War that the promoters of the mitrailleuse had not anticipated. First, no matter Major Fosbery's insistence to the contrary, the weapons were so new that the French had not yet matched the technology with tactics covering how to use them. They were usually badly employed. The second problem was that the Prussians arrived on the battlefield equipped with an innovative weapon of their own: Krupp's breech-loading artillery, which was made not of iron, as most artillery to that point had been, but of steel. The strength of steel made Krupp field pieces more powerful and accurate than any artillery yet seen, and their breech-loading quality meant they could be fired more rapidly and with gun crews at less risk as they reloaded. The French mitrailleurs, often setting up in the open and with scant idea how best to use their newly issued weapons, were easy marks for the Prussian artillerists, who dropped shells on them from beyond the Frenchmen's range, silencing one team after another. The abandoned weapons littered fields and roads, war trophies that the Prussians and their allies from across the German empire did not want. "The Germans took something like 600 of the French mitrailleurs," noted one British officer in attendance with the German command, "and never attempted to make the slightest use of them."[16]

Victories received more coverage than defeats. Set against the rout of the French army, the Germans' indifference to the veritable stockpile of rapid-fire guns was the sort of assessment shared among correspondents and military attachés, who focused on instances in which the French weapons failed to work rather than on those in which they did. The Franco-Prussian War, which the French had hoped would usher in the era of battery arms, had the opposite effect. Skepticism, even hostility, to the idea of machine guns soared among the traditionalists, who, in their own view, had been right to resist the weapons from the beginning. Informed of the French military's fate after putting its faith in rapid-fire arms, a British military committee in 1871 saw that the Gatling could be useful for fort or coastal defense. But it sniffed at the Gatling's utility in continental warfare: "The committee are decidedly averse to the employment of mitrailleurs for advancing with infantry, or indeed attacking in any form, except when the enemy is provided with an inferior artillery or no artillery at all."[17]

By now, however, enough weapons had been shown to enough military officers, and distributed to enough armies and navies, that given time even the most stupid of military men would eventually grasp just how well rapid-fire arms could kill. Notwithstanding the French debacle, a few officers in the British service continued advocating their use. The British government had ordered a Gatling gun for tests in 1869,[18] beginning the process that would see British expeditions depart with Gatlings on their vessels and assign them to troops on colonial duty. Gatling and his sales agents kept lobbying, and test guns were subjected to performance trials in Shoeburyness, England. At a range of six hundred yards, in two minutes' time, a Gatling gun's bullets all but ventilated its target, peppering it with 522 hits. This was more than the shrapnel holes produced by two British artillery pieces (283 and 142 each) or the impacts in a target fired upon by a Montigny mitrailleuse (127). In three contests between weapons firing from unknown ranges at 134 man-sized dummies spread about a field, the results were similar. Each time, no weapon was able to hit the dummies with the speed or frequency of the Gatling gun.[19] William H. Talbott, the company president, declared that the trials were "no ordinary triumph,"[20] and was hopeful that the right people had been converted to the company's cause. "The Gatling gun behaved elegantly," he wrote. "The Duke of Cambridge said in my presence 'It was a most powerful and wonderful gun.'"[21]

And then the Gatling made its British field debut. Troubles broke out on the Gold Coast of West Africa in the 1870s, when the Ashanti, a tribe with ambitions of restoring control of a seaport to keep open trade routes, besieged a British garrison at Elmina, a slave port established by the Portuguese in what is now Ghana. The British had only recently purchased the territory from the Dutch. The fort at Elmina held. But the region remained restive and the English forces present were too thin to do more than defend what they held. Major General Garnet J. Wolseley was appointed commander of the King's West African Army, and tasked with putting the new protectorate into order and quelling the Ashanti threat. He arrived with his forces in January 1873 and quickly moved columns inland, skirmishing as he went and establishing a forward outpost at the River Prah. The incursion alarmed the Ashanti king, who wanted to know the invaders' intentions. He sent a messenger to find out. The British built on the example of the editor of the *New York Times,* and decided to show their hardware. After all, a Gatling gun was intimidating. Especially when fired.

> Two days after the arrival of Sir Garnet, an ambassador came down from the king with a letter, inquiring indignantly why the English had attacked the Ashanti troops, and why they had advanced to the Prah. An opportunity was taken to impress him with the nature of English arms. A Gatling gun was placed on the river bank, and its fire directed upon the surface, and the fountain of water which rose as the steady stream of bullets struck its surface astonished, and evidently filled with awe, the Ashanti ambassador.[22]

The shooting into the River Prah marked the first recorded use of a machine gun in colonial service. It was a simple demonstration of power, a performance not much different from what Gatling and his salesmen had been putting on since his early efforts on Indiana's statehouse square. Initially it did nothing to change the Ashanti ambassador's mind. But an artillery captain present with General Wolseley recorded another result. The emissary and the detachment of Ashanti scouts that accompanied him were given quarters in the camp. Not long after the exhibition, the sound of a gunshot woke the encampment at 1:00 A.M. Rushing to the source of the noise, the British soldiers found that one of the Ashanti scouts had placed the muzzle of his own weapon against his throat, pushed his toe against the trigger, and fired the weapon into his head. The Gatling, the captain wrote, had made an impression after all.

> It was a strange and ghastly sight, the dead man lying on the guard bed with his brains scattered on the side wall, shown by the lantern light. At first the other messengers expressed ignorance as to the cause of the act, but a court of inquiry was held on the 5th and witnesses were examined. One of the Ashantis then said that the dead man, Quamina Owoosoo by name, had expressed his opinion that all the scouts were going to be killed, and only the messenger allowed to return, and had consequently blown out his brains. Sein Quaku, the messenger, spoke to the same effect, and it appeared that they had all been more or less surprised and astonished at the firing of the Gatling; and that this man, being of rather a cowardly nature, had determined to destroy himself.[23]

The demonstration firing into the River Prah was only a foretaste of what the weapons could do to a technologically unsophisticated foe. It fell a few months later to Russia, which had pushed the guns ordered by Colonel Gorloff out into soldiers' hands, to show what could happen when machine guns were fired at men.

In 1873, Czar Alexander II was expanding his empire's authority over the khanates of Central Asia, trying to bring the defiant hinterlands and overland trade routes under Russian control. His soldiers faced a holdout at the city of Khiva on the banks of the Amu Darya, where the ruling khan, Muhammed Rahim, refused to recognize Russian rule. The khan held a small collection of Russian slaves, which provided the court in Saint Petersburg with all the public-relations material it needed to portray its campaign as a civilizing mission. Columns of imperial troops advanced across the desert toward the city, battling snowstorms in the spring and later parching heat. The khan was defended in part by the

Yomud tribe, a group of Turkmen warriors whose horsemen had earned a fierce reputation by defeating Persian troops in battle. Viewed by the Russians as Islamic fanatics, they were the local manifestation of steppe warriors that had preceded Genghis Khan: able riders, brave and bearded, and at home on terrain that taxed the Russians foot soldiers' enthusiasm for warfighting on the enemy's land. They were not modernized in any military sense.

One afternoon in mid-1873, a Yomud detachment found a Russian supply train trudging through the steppe near the ruins of Zmukshir, near Turkmenistan's present border with Uzbekistan. The Russians formed a large square of wagons and braced for attack. A nervous night passed. At about 3:00 A.M. the Yomuds came at last. It was an eerie horse charge in the darkness, punctuated by the horsemen's shrieks. Inside their square, the Russians had with them two of Colonel Gorloff's Gatling guns, which had been shipped over the Caspian Sea and dragged across the Karakum desert by pack train. The guns were under the command of an officer, Captain Litvinoff. From the account he left behind, there can be no doubt that the captain had spent considerable time thinking about their use. The Yomuds' shrieks, meant to be unnerving, only helped him to perfect his detachment's response. If any one moment marked the battlefield arrival of machine guns, this might have been it.

> At the first howls of the enemy, I hastened to form a cover for my guns. I put on the right wing 10 privates, on the left 15 sharpshooters and 12 men of my battery command, with whom I could dispense for the present. These men were also armed with rifles. Leaving thus with the battery guns only the most indispensable men to assist in the firing, I took myself the crank-handle of the first gun, and invited Captain Cachourin to take the handle of the other gun, and enjoined on all my group not to commence the fire before the word of command was given. The guns formed an obtuse angle with each other, as it was necessary to direct them to the precise spot where the shoutings of the enemy were heard, and whence they were approaching us. We had not long to wait. The cries of the Turcomans who had succeeded in breaking through the lines of our detachment and turning their flanks suddenly rose from all sides, and became deafening. Though it was dark we perceived in front of us the

galloping masses of the enemy, with uplifted glittering swords. When they approached within about twenty paces, I shouted the command "Fire." This was followed by a salvo of all the men forming the cover, and a continuous rattle of the two battery guns. In this roar the cries of the enemy at once became weak and then ceased altogether, vanishing as rapidly as they rose. The firing at once stopped, and, as no enemy was visible, I ventured to get a look at the surrounding ground, availing myself of the first light of dawn. At some distance to the right of our square stood the 8th Battalion of the line. Between it and us, at every step, lay prostrated the dead bodies of the Yonoods [Yomuds].[24]

The newest Gatling guns, meanwhile, were being put to military tests that showed they were capable of feats beyond anything Gatling had conceived for them. On the morning of October 23, 1873, at Fort Madison, Maryland, ten drums of 400 cartridges were fired through a Gatling gun in twelve minutes and twenty-eight seconds. In the afternoon of the same day, another 28,000 rounds were fired at a similar rate. Cartridges were expensive, and Gatling, who worried over costs, had never subjected his guns to such extreme use. So many rounds were fired without rest that the barrels emanated a heat "sufficient to scorch dry white pine."[25] The gun performed nearly flawlessly. The following morning, after the gun had been cleaned, 63,600 more cartridges were fired in less than four hours without so much as cleaning the barrels. Gatling was on hand, and was astounded. On the night of October 26, complaining of a severe headache from the racket of firing, he penned an excited letter to General Love. His meticulous handwriting had abandoned him; he smeared ink repeatedly on the page. The trials, he wrote, "have been a great success." The 100,000 cartridges had been fired almost without a problem, and only a few—one out of every four of five thousand, he said—had missed fire. "I never expected the gun to be able to produce such results," he wrote. The officers who had come to watch had departed pleased. It was a triumph. "I can say of a truth," he wrote. "No trials ever made with the gun before, or will, be equal in value to us."[26]

The events in the field and on test ranges in 1873 secured the place of machine guns on the battlefield. The fall of that year marked a peculiar moment in the history of the distribution of rapid-fire arms. Gatling guns had earned their supporters and found their way into armies. But the company that made them continued to struggle, and the records that remain of the company's internal unease offer insights into unflattering facts behind the Gatling legend. Even as Gatling sought the trust of the Colt Patent Fire Arms Company, his company and its officers were laboring to keep knowledge of their poor finances from reaching their partners' ears. The company had amassed thirty-one thousand dollars in debt in Indianapolis; Gatling and his colleagues wanted to suppress knowledge of it. They sent letters to one another discussing how to keep the debt in Indiana. It was essential, they agreed, to prevent details of the company's position from being known in Connecticut, Gatling's new home and the center of his business. "It would have a bad effect [in Hartford] on the credit and standing of the co.," Gatling warned.[27] The company secretary, Edgar Welles, agreed. These were men with high reputations in Indiana and Connecticut, who had connections in Washington. They were not above deceit. The company would suffer a "black eye," Welles said, if it were known that it had "a debt of that size and no cash in the treasury."[28] By late 1873, the company had managed to pay down at least four thousand dollars of the debt. But it had done so by juggling its books, receiving financing from outside Indianapolis at a better rate, while trying to collect further on its accounts receivable to cover the balance. Gatling was nervous. But he saw reason for hope. If the collections could be made, he wrote, "and we can sell the guns (or only a part of them) on hand we will be all right financially. Money matters are still tight, and I hope ere long we may have money plenty."[29]

There were other pressures as well. Selling machine guns had become a business with a bright future, but the company faced competition as orders arrived. Gatling had been an innovator, and he had devoted himself to the field. Now new rapid-fire guns—not only the mitrailleuse but the Hotchkiss and the Gardner—were in development or coming to market. Moreover, Alfred Nobel, the Swedish inventor and arms manufacturer, had taken an interest in the Gatling guns in Russia and begun to work on them. He told L. W. Broadwell, Gatling's main agent in Europe, who handled the Russian account, that he had improved the weapon so much that the Nobel version was a new weapon altogether. Pressured by worries over money and reputation, Gatling's nerves overcame his customary politeness. "I am often amused at men claiming my invention," he complained to General Love, "as their own."[30] He added that he was willing to pay "liberally for any valuable change or modification which adds to the effectiveness of the invention; but, such men have no right to take my original invention—the gun itself [and] make some changes into it and call it their gun or their system.*"[31]

At last good news came with the difficulties. At the end of 1873, the navy, after the results of the hundred-thousand-cartridge endurance test, placed an order for fifty guns. The Gatling Gun Company, it seemed, might survive. More promise followed. William W. Belknap, President Ulysses S. Grant's secretary of war, sought appropriations of $292,600 from the Forty-third Congress to purchase 209 Gatling guns, principally to be used for defense of forts.[32] It stood to be the company's largest order yet, and Gatling passed many months worrying over the fate of the appropriations. As the matter stalled on Capitol Hill, his correspondence grew in irritation. Gatling was not a military man, and his mechanical skills did not extend to tactical matters. He had never served in uniform, much less in war, and knew little of how war was actually fought. He was deeply impatient, and issued instructions to General Love to lobby with all his power not to let the appropriations fail.

It is now a well established fact that the Gatling is the best military arm for certain kinds of service (fort defense etc.) in the world and the nation should have them so the men can in time of peace learn all about how to work them to the best advantage. It is a shame that a nation like Russia should have four times as many Gatling guns as the Un. States—Even poor Turkey has more than this country. Forts are of little use without arms—our forts are weak [and] need being strengthened [and] no way can they be more cheaply [and] better strengthened than by being supplied with Gatlings. It is a criminal neglect of duty for members of Congress to refuse to vote money for the nations [sic] defense [and] when such appropriations are asked for by the Chief of Ordnance and the Secretary of War.[33]

---

*The underlined words retain the underlines in Gatling's handwriting. The [and] replaces an addition sign.

A desire for profit eclipsed Gatling's judgment and good form. He suggested pandering to the congressmen of North Carolina, where he had been born. "When they learn the gun is the invention of a native of their own state, they will not fail, I think, to vote for the appropriation." He proposed planting stories in the press. "If you and Mr. Welles could get some articles published in the Washington or N. York papers, stating the necessity of strengthening the National defence (without making reference to the Gatling gun) it would do much good."[34] As the vote drew near, he grew even more anxious and prepared to have General Love hold a firing demonstration in Washington for members of Congress. The shooting, as he envisioned it, could be held on the public roads. "I got permission from the Mayor of Washington on former occasion to fire the gun against an embankment (formed by the grade of the street) near the Capitol," he wrote, "so members of Congress would not have far to go to see the firing."[35]

The appropriation was denied. Gatling's bouts of nervousness, however, had not been necessary. Even without a large congressional appropriation, the company's sales were strong, and its debt had been paid down. Between August 1, 1873, and October 8, 1874, the company recorded sales of 245 guns, and 174 of them were paid for, including 52 for the American army, 26 for the navy, 51 for China, 10 for Brazil, 4 for the Spanish Cuban government and an assortment for New York, Indiana, Pennsylvania, Connecticut, and Iowa.[36]

Step by step, machine guns were creeping into use. The Gatling Gun Company was solvent. Other companies had formed in the United States and Europe and were readying their own guns—the Gardner, the Nordenfelt, and the Hotchkiss—for trials. The guns were in use in colonial and wilderness service and were being fitted to naval vessels. But there remained resistance to issuing them to continental armies. No powerful interest group backed them, and many opponents saw little use for them, in part because of the results seen in the Franco-Prussian War. Commentators were skeptical, or outright against. "The deluded French soldier has ere this found out that the new engine of warfare is not all that he had been taught to believe," wrote the editorialists of the *Saturday Review.* The machine gun, they informed London, had seen its value inflated "by diligent Imperial puffing" and could expect little productive martial use. "The instrument will not bring about a revolution in tactics. It will accomplish no real change in the art of war. It is not, in the broad sense of the word, a new arm or a new power."[37] The magazine *Nature* was more open-minded, but assumed a politely hedged stance. "It does not follow, because it is not good for all purposes, that it may not be useful in some. There are obviously many positions in which it might inflict great damage on an enemy."[38]

By 1873, the Gatling Gun Company had sold fewer than one thousand guns, but it had sold enough of them, and there was enough curiosity arising from the accounts of the use of machine guns in battle, that a few officers were taking interest. Some of the officers who made a study of the French and Prussian battlefield reports concluded that the weapons had performed well enough when the French used them wisely, and that machines guns were a weapon with a certain future. A small contingent of officers advocated their use, sometimes to ridicule. One of these officers, Captain Ebenezer Rogers, of London, wrote a letter to Gatling late in the summer of 1873 to say that he had lobbied inside the British military to have the Gatling, which the British military had not yet adopted for widespread use, sent to Africa for the Ashanti War. He enclosed a picture of himself. Gatling liked what he read. Captain Rogers, he said, judging from the enclosed photograph, was "a very fine appearing gentleman." There was a whiff of opportunity here. "The truth is," Gatling continued, "Capt. E is doing us a good service in England [and] his efforts should be encouraged."[39]

Captain Rogers sent another letter to Gatling, urging the company to push the British services to send six or eight of his guns to the Gold Coast. Gatling balked at this, thinking that a telegraph to the British secretary of war might offend the G. W. Armstrong Company, which had entered a licensing agreement with the Gatling Gun Company in 1869 that allowed the British firm to make Gatling guns for sales in Great Britain for five years. But Gatling was even more taken by the captain. "You will see from the letter," he told General Love, "that he's still quite warm to the cause."[40]

Rogers was not alone. More proponents were awakening. Lieutenant William Folger, a former officer in the American navy who worked with Gatling, foresaw machine guns becoming so popular and widespread, and a product that would create such an intensive competition between manufacturers, that he urged the Gatling Gun Company to set aside its disputes with Alfred Nobel and its resentment of the other guns and buy them out. He envisioned a super-company, which would manufacture entire systems of automatic arms and dominate global markets. "The world of inventions should be watched, [and] the Nobels' and Hotchkiss' should be taken in or bought. This fabrique would at the same time manufacture infantry arms—the best magazine for the next machine gun etc etc [*sic*] and in a short time become a sort of controlling feature among the arms companies. The Gatling cannot last forever, and the company should already look for something to replace it."[41]

The vanguard had preceded Captain Rogers and Lieutenant Folger by only a few years. General Vandenburgh, of the New York militia, had traveled to London and made a presentation to the Royal United Services Institution in 1862, in which he reasoned that a machine that could mass rifle fire would be devastating once brought into use. Major Fosbery, who helped tweak the design of the Montigny mitrailleuse, had presented his own strong opinions in favor of rapid-fire arms to the same organization in 1870. Major Fosbery's lecture remains important, even if his premature endorsement of French tactics eroded his credibility in officers' circles. He was peering into the future, more perceptively than his critics. He had misread the French army and not foreseen the effects of Prussian artillery. But his solid mechanical understanding of machine guns—he had handled every gun of the time under consideration for service—was giving him glimpses of World War I.

The major had collected data on the effects that various weapons had on targets at various ranges, including data that showed how much shrapnel actually whistled through the air around a bursting artillery shell.[42] He did the math and found that six twelve-pound artillery guns of the time could subject an exposed group of soldiers to about three hundred bits of shrapnel per minute. Six French mitrailleuses, which were proven to be less effective than Gatling guns, would be able to fire 2,664 well-aimed bullets into the same place during the same time. It was a chilling set of numbers. He let his listeners consider it. "What would be the result of the concentrated fire of several batteries of mitrailleurs on an exposed formation I leave it to your judgment to determine from the data I have placed before you," he told the officers gathered in the room.

Major Fosbery's logistical math similarly favored the mitrailleuse. It weighed less than half as much as a field artillery piece, needed one-third as many horses to tow along on campaign, and was fired with one-half the number of crew. Major Fosbery's data had little influence in the British military. He understood why. "The invention in its present state is a comparatively new one," he said, "and like all new things will find many opponents simply because it is so, whilst the status quo will never want an advocate."[43]

With this groundwork laid, Captain Rogers continued the cause.

In his own presentation to the officers' institution in 1875, after Gatlings had been deployed to Central Asia and to the Gold Coast, he declared that it was "no longer possible to ignore the existence of mitrailleurs with the armies of all countries, every state in Europe having adopted some type of machine gun." He offered lists: Turkey, Egypt, China, Japan, and Tunis all had Gatlings, and Russia already owned "a formidable array," with 400 Gatlings organized in units with eight guns apiece. British intelligence, he said, had determined that 328 of the guns were in European Russia, 48 were in the Caucasus, and 24 had been deployed to the empire's distant reaches in eastern Siberia and Turkestan. The distribution had been swift.[44]

Captain Rogers predicted the bloody utility of machine guns on colonial duty, where small contingents of European soldiers, sometimes racked by fever, might encounter vast formations of African warriors, unschooled in the tools of modern warfare and not backed by the industrial economies that could produce them. He urged the British officer corps to see the obvious. Machine guns were more than an equalizer. They would allow Britain to strengthen her rule. "Gatlings are peculiarly adapted to colonial defensive operations, as well as for retaliating demonstrations against troublesome neighbours, in countries where our enemies are numerous but ill-armed, where the roads are few and unsuited to wheel traffic, and where the surprise caused by the overwhelming discharge of a battery could carry with it an irresistible moral effect."[45] With a few machine guns, he said, Europeans might use lopsided violence to put down rebellions around the world.

What was not publicly known, as Captain Rogers gave his undiluted endorsement of the future of machine gunnery, was that Richard Gatling and the Gatling Gun Company had been sending him money to encourage his enthusiasm for their arms. Late in 1873, as more correspondence kept coming from Captain Rogers, Gatling and Love had committed to incorporate Captain Rogers into their sales push. "I enclose a letter just rcvd from Capt Rogers," Gatling told Love. "You must keep in correspondence with him—He is a man that can do us much good."[46] The two men developed a plan to arrange for Captain Rogers's payment, hoping it might induce him to work even harder on the company's behalf. General Love, an old army hand who himself had gone on sales trips to Europe with letters of endorsement from President Grant, appears to have suggested it. Gatling approved. "I fully agree with you that we should pay Capt. Rogers for his services rendered," he wrote. "Mr. Welles will write Capt Rogers today and tell him to draw on Colt's agency." The first payment was twenty British pounds. Gatling also told General Love that he would sweeten it with a personal letter containing five more British pounds, which, he said, "will make him feel kindly towards us and inspire him to continue to write in favor of the gun."[47] How much, and how often, Gatling paid Captain Rogers is not known; their full correspondence does not exist. But the captain was a willing recipient and became a veritable promotional service in uniform. "My dear Gatling," he wrote late in January 1875, as he was preparing the lecture for his fellow officers. "Your letter of the 8th January has just reached me with its unexpected enclosure which however I regard as a substantial recognition of my devotion to the subject at hand and your just estimate of the opportunity afforded by my lecturing at the Royal U.S. Institution."

Captain Rogers might have made a similar presentation without the money; his attraction to the gun predated the payments. And the British military might have settled on the Gatling as a service arm without his efforts—Gatling guns had outperformed any competitor in several tests. But Dr. Gatling and General Love had invested in quite a performance. The British captain reprised the Gatling gun's history with relish and read aloud the American translation of Captain Litvinoff's repulsion of the Yomud charge two years before near Khiva (he even repeated the American mistake, calling the attacking horsemen "Yonoods"). He described Captain Litvinoff walking through the scattered collection of the dead horsemen at dawn, and then he reached a conclusion almost fantastic. "Mark, too, the immediate moral effect produced by this automatic man-slayer," he said. "Its very snarl hushed the war cries of the savage foe. It caused the Yonoods to reel in the saddle and wheel their fiery steeds back once more in the desert; all, that is, who did not bite the dust. I cannot fancy that they returned for wounded men. I cannot fancy that there were any to take away."[48]

The officers were skeptical. In the period for comments and questions after Captain Rogers finished, several officers weighed in against him. "It seems to me that Captain Rogers has somewhat exaggerated the importance of this weapon," said Captain J. F. Owen, of the British army. "The question for us seems to be, are the advantages of the Gatling such as to counterbalance the disadvantages of taking extra impediments into the field?"[49]

The following summer, the outcome of another distant battle hinted at a possible answer. In 1875, a group of Native American tribes left the reservations the government had designated for them in the western territories along the Rocky Mountains, and tensions between the American government and the region's native populations soared. President Grant issued an ultimatum: Return to the reservations by the New Year, he said, or be considered an enemy force. Several tribes formed a coalition under a spiritual leader, Sitting Bull, and defied the president's demand. In spring 1876, a large American contingent set out to subdue the refusing tribes. The United States Seventh Cavalry Regiment, under the command of Lieutenant Colonel George A. Custer, was among the units assigned.

On June 25, after several weeks in the field, Colonel Custer's column came upon an Indian encampment on the Little Bighorn River in territory now part of the state of Montana. Thinking the encampment was small and vulnerable, the colonel decided to attack from two sides. He ordered Major Marcus A. Reno, his senior subordinate, to advance on the camp with three cavalry companies from the south. Colonel Custer planned to swing round to the north with five more companies and trap the Indians between his forces. Two other elements, including his logistics train, were given supporting roles. Major Reno began his advance but quickly discovered the native camp was not as small as he had believed, and occupied by a large number of Sioux and Cheyenne warriors. The divided American cavalry was no match. Major Reno withdrew under fire and fell back into the protection of cottonwoods and undergrowth, where the cavalrymen dismounted and fought from the ground. Colonel Custer's assessment of the size and readiness of the native force had been wrong. He had come upon the camp of Sitting Bull and much of the defiant native coalition, which had many more warriors than the United States Army's scouts in the field had detected in the weeks before the campaign. Major Reno's command soon found its position among the cottonwoods untenable; the troops retreated farther, scrambling across the river and leaving behind their dead and more than a dozen of their unwounded fellow soldiers. They dashed pell-mell to the comparative safety of a hilltop. There, to their great fortune, they were met by one of the other detachments of American soldiers. These combined American forces began to dig in, anticipating a large Indian attack. The Indians' attention, however, had been diverted from the major's weakened command. It had turned to Colonel Custer.

The regimental commander's detachment, with slightly more than two hundred cavalrymen, had continued unknowingly toward the river camp. It was quickly enveloped. From their hilltop, Major Reno's men heard some of the resulting ferocity, including the booms of volley fire during the brief time Colonel Custer's group managed to fight as a unit and resist. Caught by the Indians in unfamiliar terrain and out of the reach of reinforcements, the soldiers were pinned down, then overrun. It was a highly unusual event. The Indians had been elusive. Combat with them was usually swift and fleeting. In this case, however, a small American contingent had collided with the indigenous warriors during a brief period when they were massed. The battle was over in an hour or less. Every man in the colonel's command was killed. The victorious Cheyenne and Sioux stripped many of the dead soldiers of their clothes and mutilated and scalped corpses. Precisely what happened between the moment when Major Reno's detachment galloped away and the time when the last man in Colonel Custer's contingent fell has never been fully known; no cavalrymen survived to tell. But the disposition of the dead soldiers, discovered when another American unit came upon them the next day, and the available Indian accounts, indicated that Colonel Custer's group made a wall with the carcasses of dead horses, to little effect, and tried to fight off an Indian charge by the old tactic of volleyed rifle fire. Rifles were not enough. The charge broke the lines. Pandemonium followed, with panicked soldiers dropping weapons and scattering on foot, only to be hacked down by pursuing horsemen.

Colonel Custer, young and intense, had been a public personality. His defeat ignited controversy and an investigation. The investigation found many grounds for criticism of the colonel's decisions, among them that he had been offered Gatling guns, but had left them behind as he rode off to campaign. Thinking they would slow his movement, he opted to plunge into the Indian territory with cavalry armed with single-shot Model 1873 Springfield rifles, and not any rapid-fire arms. The army had recently issued the Springfields; their slower rate of fire was seen as a means to reduce ammunition consumption in distant territories, where resupply was slow and difficult. Colonel Custer fit the old model of officer who rejected the value of machine-gun fire. His position had merit: The Indians' superior speed and mobility made it difficult for American units to bring firepower to bear on them, and his Gatlings would have been pulled along on carriages, no doubt slowing his advance as he reconnoitered territory. But at his command, the American government's plans to bring its material superiority against its enemies were turned upside down. Instead of being able to concentrate fire against a concentrated Indian force, densely packed and in the open, Colonel Custer's soldiers were armed with rifles designed to help preserve their bullets. Red Horse, a surviving Indian chief, was surprised by the Americans' weakness. The Sioux, he said, drove Colonel Custer's isolated cavalrymen:

> . . . into confusion; these soldiers became foolish, many throwing away their guns and raising their hands "Sioux, pity us; take us prisoners." The Sioux did not take a single soldier prisoner, but killed all of them; none were alive for even a few minutes. Those different soldiers discharged their guns but little. I took a gun and two belts off two dead soldiers; out of one belt, two cartridges were gone; out of the other five.[50]

No one can say with certitude how the battle might have gone if Colonel Custer had arrived for the fight with rapid-fire weapons. Historians argue both sides, some taking his position.[51] If Colonel Custer had brought his Gatlings, he might not have reached Sitting Bull's encampment that day. But Colonel Henry J. Hunt, the former chief of artillery for the Army of the Potomac, excoriated Custer posthumously for failing to bring the weapons that he had been issued. The Gatlings, he said, would have kept the Sioux and the Cheyenne attackers at bay.

> At the Custer massacre Reno reached the neighboring "bluffs" and saved his command . . . Custer, when attacked by overwhelming numbers, tried to do so, failed, and *his* command was exterminated. A battery or half-battery of Gatlings would have been a moving "bluff," with power to fight and specially fit for keeping "swarms" of Indians in check. The guns would not have "staggered about" from weariness after a forced long march, as Sitting Bull describes our soldiers to have done. Nor would they have lacked the rapidity of fire which that chief claimed. Under their protection our men could have moved about in comparative safety, or at least to cover. The presence of such a battery would have probably saved the command.

Colonel Hunt did not mention the Russian experience three years earlier, moving from oasis to oasis across the Central Asian steppe, where, like the men under Colonel Custer's command, the Russian and Cossack detachments risked encountering a mobilized indigenous foe on unfamiliar terrain. Outside Khiva, the Russian Gatling guns had stopped a charge cold, as surely as if it had hit a wall. Colonel Custer never had the chance to try. Colonel Hunt fumed at the thought of an officer leaving a Gatling gun battery behind in war. He suggested it was an oversight so galling it could be considered illegal, a dereliction of an officer's oath to follow the orders of the government that gave him authority and paid his wage.

> I know of no good reason why one should have not been on the ground, if they had been kept mounted in accordance with the expressed will of Congress.[52]

Not all of the American army's officers failed to use the guns. Brigadier General Oliver O. Howard used a pair of Gatlings in 1877 in the campaign that ultimately forced Chief Joseph and the Nez Perce onto a reservation. The guns were carried in packs on mules, and General Howard's troops were well enough drilled that they were able to rush them forward when the general caught a band of retreating Indians crossing the Clear-water River near Kamiah, in what is now Idaho. "The whole force was put to a brisk run to the river crossing," wrote Thomas A. Sutherland, a newspaper correspondent covering the campaign. "General Howard with Captain Jackson was the first to reach the destination, as the road taken by Whipple was more circuitous. The Gatling gun was hurried into position and under command of Captain Wilkinson did good work in driving the Indian sharpshooters from their different breastworks on the mountains opposite."[53]

That encounter was not on the order of what Colonel Custer had faced. It fell to British soldiers to show what an outnumbered force, equipped with modern weapons, might do when faced with a native charge. In spite of high-ranking objections, British curiosity about Gatling's weapons had been significant enough that machine guns were being sent out with expeditions and units on colonial duty. Their arrival coincided with fresh troubles in the crown's empire. When the British invaded Zululand in 1879 with a large force, they brought with them several Gatlings, including the British army's first Gatling battery, which was under command of J. F. Owen, the officer who had criticized Captain Rogers's enthusiasm for machine guns four years before in London. Owen had been promoted to major, and his guns were used in skirmishes and several battles. Two were present for the war's final large battle, at Ulundi.

In early July, the British moved toward Ulundi, the Zulu capital, and set up camp nearby. The British commander, Frederic Thesiger, Lord Chelmsford, sent a message demanding that the Zulu king surrender the artillery pieces and roughly one thousand rifles that his fighters had captured after a stinging defeat of the British earlier in the year at Isandlwana. The king did not reply, and British watering parties came under fire. On the morning of July 4, Lord Chelmsford ordered his roughly five thousand troops to battle. His units marched across the Mahlabathini plain, passing the chopped-up corpses of their comrades who had been killed in skirmishes the previous day. As they drew near the huts of the seat of government, which were ahead behind high grass, they were entering what in any other circumstance but this—a technological mismatch of drilled European troops with modern weapons facing indigenous Africans with shields and spears—would have been an inescapable trap, much like what

Colonel Custer had faced three years before. The British walked into an encirclement, outnumbered several times.

> As the mounted men scrambled out of the donga, the inGobama-khosi regiment rose from the midst of the grass and, as if on signal, other regiments appeared at wide intervals on either side. The silent black masses parted the waving grass, displayed their shields and began to move forward, joining the regiments coming down from the heights as they reached them, until the center of the basin was ringed with dark groupings.[54]

The British formed a square and watched, tightening ranks and readying weapons. The Zulu defenders, estimated to be twenty thousand men, merged and stamped their feet, harassed lightly by the Seventeenth Lancers, a unit of British cavalrymen, who opened fire and peppered the walls of Zulu warriors as their horses cantered in the shrinking open space. The Lancers were outnumbered by thousands. The enclosing circle grew smaller. The British cavalry taunted the Zulus, but they knew, like Colonel Custer's men, that they would have small chance in a head-to-head fight. They withdrew within the square as the larger clash became imminent. The Zulus advanced slowly until the British artillery opened fire. Then the Zulus broke forward at a run.

For all of his professions of humanitarianism and assurances that machine guns could serve as such a powerful deterrent that they would make wars safe, Richard Gatling had never addressed this.

> The battalion opened fire with rifle fire and the rattling bursts from the Gatling guns stitched the crashing volleys together. Regiment after regiment surged forward, and the lines began to melt away in the hail of bullets scything the slopes. Succeeding waves charged over the contorted bodies that littered the grass, and shining faces of the warriors, with gleaming eyes and set teeth, bobbed up and down over the rims of their shields. Raw courage had brought them that far, but bravery alone could not force a way through the crescendo of fire, and the warriors sank to their knees to crash full length in the dust or tumble head over heels in mid-stride. Not a Zulu reached within thirty yards of the British lines.[55]

The Gatling guns had jammed several times, but were still effective. A charge by the Zulu reserve was broken, and then Lord Chelmsford ordered the cavalry back out, to pursue. The Seventeenth Lancers cheered as they bore down on their retreating victims, and cut them with lances and swords. The Zulu charges had been broken in thirty minutes. Most of the mopping up was completed within the hour. Several of the British soldiers had brought champagne on the march, and now, with clusters of African bodies glistening on the field, and the British killing the wounded in vengeance for past defeats, some men shared warm toasts. Lord Chelmsford ordered Ulundi to be set afire. His command had left its camp before 7:00 A.M. It faced the Zulu charge at 9:00 A.M. "Ulundi was burning at noon," he telegraphed home.[56] The British, with their superior firepower, had completed the destruction of the Zulu nation in a morning, though they were on enemy terrain and outnumbered roughly four to one. One British officer and ten enlisted men were killed.[57] The rout had reached proportions almost absurd, but was also demonstrative of what rapid-fire weapons could do when applied to people who did not have them, or who were ordered in the open by commanders who did not appreciate how machine gunnery worked. Colonel Custer had left his guns behind. The killing at Ulundi had shown their utility in what one officer called "wars with people who wear not trousers."[58] They would not be left behind anymore.

Still the dispute over the utility of rapid fire raged back at home. At the Royal United Services Institution in London not long after Lord Chelmsford returned to England, another American arms designer, William Gardner, spoke on the merits of machine guns in conventional battle. Gardner had served as a captain in the Union Army during the Civil War, and knew his way around a battlefield. In 1874, he had developed hand-cranked weapons, available in time with two to five barrels arranged in a row, like organ pipes. His guns competed with Gatling's better-known models. Unlike Gatling, Gardner had drawn from his military experience and understanding of tactics to canvass the literature and develop practical theories for machine-gun use. In his lecture in London, he laid out proposals for machine gunnery that would in time become standard practice for infantrymen in the field, including using the guns from a distance against an enemy to fix him in place while other soldiers advanced. And he was realistic, avoiding Captain Rogers's breathless hyperbole and conceding that the problem of unwanted stoppages was critical. Jamming had been attributed in the main to poorly manufactured European cartridges, which were not sturdy enough to withstand the forces of extraction from a gun firing at a high rate of speed, and often were bent or broken in place, stopping firing altogether. But Gardner's observation was also a veiled attack on his product's main rival, the Gatling gun, and lingering British concerns about its reliability. "I prefer a pair of walking boots to a balking horse," he said, "and a club to a machine gun very liable to jam."[59]

After his lecture, Gardner faced the doubters. Lieutenant General Charles Pyndar Beauchamp Walker, who had traveled with the crown prince of Prussia during the Franco-Prussian War and assimilated the Prussian assessment of rapid-fire arms, did not contain his contempt. "The introduction of this engine into the French armament was, as I have already expressed myself, a gigantic swindle," he said. "The results have been in no way commensurate with the expectation formed, and although the weapon is probably capable of improvement and certainly very formidable under certain conditions, I do not think it will ever take the place which its upholders expect."

The general listed objections, including that the French guns often fell out of use because they malfunctioned. He cannily echoed Gardner's own statement about a club, to suggest, indirectly but pointedly, that perhaps the infantry would be better armed with blackthorn mallets. "I am reminded of the old Irish saying which I heard a great many years ago, when first in that country, that the 'shillalah never missed fire,'" he said. "The Irishman prefers a stick to any other weapon; there is no jamming there."[60]

Lord Chelmsford, who had led the forces in the Zulu War, and knew something about a machine gun's value, intervened politely. But as an officer with colonial experience and not a presumed expert in continental warfare like General Walker, he treaded carefully. "I think myself that machine-guns have been rather harshly judged," he offered. "I cannot help but thinking there is a future for these machine-guns, and I think there is a future for them not as employed with artillery, but as employed with infantry. I can safely say, at all events in such wars as we have to carry on in South Africa, that machine-guns attached to infantry, if they are of simple and reliable nature, carrying the same ammunition as the infantry arm, would be of inestimable value."[61]

Gardner, like Gatling, was able to handle rejection. He showed no sign of offense. By this time he had designed multiple models of his machine guns and was breaking into markets. His guns had performed admirably at recent British tests, and one version from his line had been accepted for service in the British navy. An exhibition of them was available in the building. Soon his guns were to go ashore in landing parties in Africa, and meet indigenous charges, too. He opened his reply with polite confidence. "I have only some crude ideas to express, and I express them in a crude way," he said. "But I believe in what I say."

Gatling knew about Gardner. In what resembled turf encroachment, Gardner was having his weapons manufactured at a Pratt & Whitney factory in Hartford, not far from the Colt factory where Gatlings were made. And Gardner's line of guns was enjoying warm press coverage and satisfying reviews in competitive military trials. Gatling had market share to preserve. He wanted to put Gardner and the others in their place. The field was getting ever more crowded. Dr. James H. McLean, a fraud who had passed himself off as an inventor in Saint Louis, was even echoing Gatling's own theories of world peace through awesome firepower and offering an entire range of quick-firing weapons, with catchy names designed to attract sales: the General Sherman, the Vixen, the Annihilator, and, with a wink, the Lady McLean.[62] The Gatling gun risked losing ground. The aging inventor took out newspaper advertisements, calling his would-be rival out.

> Many articles have recently appeared in the press, claiming the superior advantages of the Gardner and other machine guns over the Gatling gun.
>
> In order to decide which is the best gun, the undersigned offers to fire his gun (the Gatling) against any other gun, on the following wagers, viz:
>
> First, $500 that the Gatling can fire more shots in a given time, say one minute.

Second, $500 that the Gatling can give more hits on a target, firing, say, one minute—at a range of 800 or 1000 yards.

The winner will contribute the money won to some charitable object.

The time and place to be mutually agreed upon.

R. J. Gatling
Of Hartford, Conn.[63]

The advertisement appeared in 1881. In a similar advertisement published a few weeks later in England, Gatling added a line suggesting the depth of his annoyance. "The trials of the above character," it read, "will do more to determine the efficiency of the guns than newspaper articles so cleverly written."[64]

Twenty years after designing the first Gatling gun, Gatling was white-haired and wealthy, an elder statesman in the machine-gun trade whose name was known round the land. He wanted his life's most successful work to be above all challengers. It was a sentiment that was unnecessary in the short term, and pointless in the long.

In the short term, the British were still taking his weapon on colonial campaigns, mounting them on seagoing vessels, boats, outposts, and armored trains. The problems with ammunition used by European forces had been largely solved, and there would be little more talk of jams. The naysayers in officers' circles could block their armies from purchasing Gatling guns for continental service. But there were other markets—for navies, for police forces, for yachts, for mines, and for penitentiaries—all of which his company would try to tap. And yet his dream of assigning the Gatling to the world's ground forces was soon to end. Gatling had spent two decades designing and marketing rapid-fire arms. Through official indifference and hostility, and the perplexity of friends, he had set the stage for machine guns. And Hiram Maxim was about to take it.

CHAPTER 3

Hiram Maxim Changes War

That Patent Music Box for Perforating Men[1]

HIRAM MAXIM WORKED A CARTRIDGE INTO THE ACTION OF HIS prototype gun. It was an unusual-looking device: a narrow and dull metal box with a single protruding rifled barrel. For a trigger it had a small metal bar at the back end of the gun, and on its right side was a lever, resembling a switch, that could be used to adjust the rate of fire. Maxim had obtained the necessary Royal Laboratory machine-gun cartridges, the sort fired by a Gardner gun, and he intended to use them in his creation's first firing test.

Powerfully built and dark-eyed at forty-four, Maxim had started his career in industry in rural New England. He was a picture of supreme confidence. As a young man he had earned his living as a maker of bedposts, wheelbarrows, wagons, and rakes, and as a decorative carriage painter. But his mind outpaced both the lifestyle and products the local mills offered, and he had become a prolific inventor and successful businessman in the electric and gas industries in New York. A few years earlier he claimed to have beaten Thomas Edison in the race to invent the light bulb, only to have Edison submit the necessary patent papers first. Had Maxim won that race, everything might have been different. He might have remained in the United States and enjoyed a life of fame and wealth, as Edison did. Instead he had moved to Europe, and in a professional lull in London had begun to work on machine guns that would not need a man to do more than depress a trigger to produce continuous fire. His weapon had no hand crank to turn. It did not need one.

He had the six cartridges in place,[2] and he gave it a try. In roughly half a second, all of the cartridges were gone. The bullets had been fired in a little more than a blink. This was a new kind of gunfire, *automatic fire,* the manifestation of the vision Gatling had had almost a quarter-century before. Everything was about to change.

Hiram Maxim was a designer with a story, and an ego, like almost no other. He was born in 1840 on a small farm in central Maine, an isolated and impoverished region. By his own long and often unverifiable account of his life, his excellence had begun with birth. "For many years there has been a tradition that there was always one very strong member in the Maxim family," he said. "And I think I am entitled to be recognized as the strong member of the generation in which I was born." His attraction to labor started early, as did his sense of mischief. At the age of eight, he said, he felled a gigantic fir tree with a butcher's knife, chipping at a groove around its base all day for a week. The tree toppled and fell. The little Maxim watched with awe. A farmer soon complained to him that he had robbed his cows of their pasture's only shade. Maxim was unmoved. "This was the proudest moment of my long and eventful life," he wrote shortly before he died. "Nothing since has equaled it." After he became famous in Europe he was remembered back in Maine as "the worst boy for miles around."[3]

His confidence, which veered into arrogance, was beyond measure. By the time he was a teenager, Maxim considered himself an "expert in geography" and "a natural all-round mechanic." He claimed to be so handy that he could do all the work of the experienced craftsmen in the workshops of Maine, and in less time. And he was growing into the strongest man in town. Accounts of his strength were Bunyanesque. As a young man, he singlehandedly moved a row of enormous pork barrels from a sled, lifting barrel after barrel. Each barrel, he said, weighed six hundred pounds. His strength became such a curiosity that townsmen urged him to fight, examining him the way a buyer examines a horse. "All agreed that I had the make-up of a successful boxer," he wrote. "I had already thought of taking up the art, feeling convinced that I could very soon become a champion."[4] The local men arranged a match on Independence Day between Maxim and the town's best boxer. Within minutes, he had beaten the reigning champion senseless and was fighting the next-most-feared man. Maxim claimed he punched his second opponent into unconsciousness, too.

Maxim and his son's memoirs are busy with accounts of fights. Between descriptions of his inventions and his travels, they are an inventory
of brawls and beatings worthy of a Victorian-era comic hero, invincible
but reluctant, who always defeats those who provoked his peaceful genius
to feats of strength. In one episode Maxim laughed into the face of a man
who menaced him with a pistol. In another he hoisted a robber who
tried to waylay him. Maxim casually tossed the criminal over a fence. He
insisted fighting was a distraction that was beneath him, yet he reveled
in telling of it smugly, and saw himself as the best man at it he ever met.

Maxim never attended university. But he educated himself by reading
scientific literature and books, from which he taught himself chemistry,
physics, and mathematics—complements to the tool-handling and design
skills he was learning in his father's shop. His mind was undistracted by
most vices: at the end of his life, he claimed never once to have smoked
tobacco, tasted alcohol, or consumed caffeine. (Women were another matter. He was hounded with allegations of deceiving and abandoning women
as he moved in search of work. As he neared the age of sixty, three different
women claimed to have been married to him—at the same time. In the
end, he left three separate families.)[5] He held himself above the common
man and ordinary pursuits. While he was at the mill in Maine, the Civil
War began. The young men organized into a company, which marched on
the streets. Maxim briefly joined them, but he loathed the marching and
found the military mentality of his peers grating (he later compared them
to the Boy Scouts). Contemptuous of soldiering, he returned to the mill.
A local doctor told him he had made the right decision. Military service,
by Maxim's account, was beneath a man of Maxim's gifts.

> He thought that I was altogether the most promising young man in
> Dexter; that I was a very hard worker, without any bad habits; that
> it might be all right for those less gifted than myself to go to the war,
> but it was my duty to stay at home and work; also that I would find
> soldiering a very hard job indeed. So I made up my mind to give it
> up and refused to go on.[6]

Early in the war, Maxim left the United States for Huntingdon, Quebec, and he found jobs as a mill worker, sign painter, and briefly as bar-
tender at a small hotel, where he delighted in serving diluted whiskey to

customers and in watching the patrons fight.[7] Next he moved to Fitch-burg, Massachusetts, and took a position in an uncle's metal works, learning the machinist's trade. Later he became a draftsman in Boston, making precision drawings of gas machines. He was collecting modern skills, and an insider's knowledge and appreciation of business and of leading industries of the day. "I left no stone unturned," he said, "to become expert at everything I had to do."[8]

When he was not engaged by his bosses, he was inventing products and widgets of every sort. He had begun tinkering as a boy. As a teenager, he designed a mousetrap that reset itself automatically. From then on, he said, he was "a chronic inventor." And so it went: first mousetraps, then tricycle wheels and silicate blackboard for a schoolhouse, later pumps and guns and curling irons and an early model airplane. He moved to Brooklyn for a machinist's job at the Novelty Iron Works, and made his home near Carroll Park.[9] He opened a side business as a gas fitter and then invented a gas-distributing machine. Its promise enabled him to form a company with an office on Broadway, across from City Hall, that manufactured and installed his gas-distributing machines in buildings, bringing them a new means of having light and heat. His inventing continued, to his success and dismay. After Maxim claimed to have beaten Edison in the race to design the electric light, Edison's fame and wealth filled him with jealousy and pique. When he displayed his own lamp, and people asked him if it was Edison's, he grew angry enough that he told a business partner that "the next time anyone said, 'Is it Edison's?' I would kill him on the spot." He nearly had the chance. One day, while Maxim was traveling, a New Jersey farmer saw him carrying a lamp.

> He sat down on the opposite side of the ferry-boat and stared at me. Finally, he came over and said, "Excuse me sir, but what is that 'ere machine—what is it for?" I looked at the fellow and made up my mind that he had a wife and family at home, so I replied, "It is only a sausage stuffer," and thus saved the poor fellow's life.[10]

Practical jokes and Maxim went together. Some of his antics were little more than mischief. In Brooklyn, he enlisted the help of his young son, Hiram Percy, to harry a police officer who was paying Sunday visits to a housemaid who worked for a family across the street. The officer and the maid met behind an entryway gate. Maxim was suspicious. He told his son that the two of them were "sparking" over there, and that this would have to stop. "If they spark on Sundays, how do we know that they will not spark on other days," he said. "We cannot have this policeman spending his time sparking when he should be watching for bad people." He unfolded his plans before the boy. When the policeman returned the following Sunday, hidden in the umbrella basket of the Maxims' home was a long brass tube, similar to a blowgun, which Maxim had made. Maxim took a position behind the curtain of an open window, loaded a dried white bean into the pipe, aimed, and expelled the little missile high into the air, banking it off the upper facade of a three-story building directly above the suspected dalliance. After a half-dozen shots, the policeman stepped from behind the gate and looked up at the windows of the three-story building. He thought someone was dropping beans from above. Seeing no one, the officer returned to the pleasures behind the gate. The bean blower opened fire anew. The officer reappeared and walked about the sidewalk purposefully, staring at the windows with his back to Maxim's window. The police officer saw nothing and went back to his business with the maid. Maxim fired a third time. As the officer ran out the gate, Maxim was "rolling around in gales of merriment."[11]

Maxim's foxing of the police officer and the maid was tricky, and it had risks. But it was not cruel. His household staff suffered worse. Maxim churned through employees and was frequently annoyed "by the stupidity of the average cook or housemaid." He gave them nicknames, including a series of people he assigned the name Stupid. "I remember Stupid the Fifth very distinctly," his son recalled. "I thought this was her real name." Maxim had read an item claiming that the skin perceives contact with very cold objects and very hot objects in the same way. One weekend at their home, he decided to test the theory on one of the Stupids, an Irish woman in his employ. He heated a metal poker above an oven grate until it glowed red and placed a duplicate poker in a container of alcohol and snow, chilling it to a temperature below freezing. As his intended victim worked nearby, he paced about the kitchen with the glowing poker, testing it on firewood, which produced smoke. In a voice the maid could not miss, he told his son that such irons were used to burn brands into the necks of cattle, and how painful that would be. He put the poker back on the burner, left the room, and returned, having hidden the chilled poker in his coat. Everything had been prepared for the maid's confusion. Maxim lifted the heated poker from the stove again, and suddenly acted as if it were too hot to hold. He waved it about and stepped toward the maid, bringing it close enough for her to see its glow and feel its heat. He backed up. When the maid looked away from her employer's odd spectacle, he withdrew the cold poker from under his jacket, slapped it against her neck, and gave a shout—"Look out!" Then he hissed, as if she had been seared. The cook screamed, bunched her apron where the poker had touched, and collapsed. Maxim's wife rushed into the room. The cook shrieked. She thought he had branded her. She shrieked again. Maxim, with his two pokers, was laughing.

> After a great amount of effort my mother succeeded in getting the woman's hand down from her neck, and the surprising fact was disclosed that there was not even a mark visible, which threw my mother into complete confusion. She was very excitable and for some time she and my father and the cook shouted at cross purposes at one another, nobody listening to anybody else and nobody being able to make head or tail of what the others were talking about. My father saw that he must have gone too far, and did his best to explain that it was an experiment he had been conducting, that nobody had been hurt, and that it was all very funny if only the others would see it in that light; and besides, things had come to a pretty pass if a man could not experiment in his own house.[12]

The cook quit on the spot.

This is the man who would give the world automatic weapons, those most efficient killing tools. Not surprisingly, disputes followed Maxim wherever he went. One of his brothers loathed him so much that there was talk in London of arranging a duel. His son, or rather, the one son he acknowledged in public, labeled him a bad father. Maxim weathered court cases that accused him of misdeeds ranging from patent infringement to trigamy. He was accused of having evaded Civil War service, an embarrassing charge for an arms designer and salesman. (The history is unclear here and the dispute remains unsettled. Maxim claimed that because two of his brothers served, he, as the last remaining son, was exempt. But available census records in Maine show that Maxim had more than two brothers, and one, Leander, who was four years old in 1850, would have been too young to serve as the war began and Maxim decamped for Quebec. This does not prove that Hiram evaded military service, but it suggests that his explanations for not serving, aside from seeing military service as beneath him, do not square with facts.)[13] Later, after his automatic weapons were in mass production, he quarreled with Alfred Nobel, just as Richard Gatling had. Maxim and Nobel both claimed to have been the first to patent smokeless gunpowder, which, as it allowed gunners to remain concealed when they fired upon an enemy from a distance, became an essential military product after it was introduced. (British courts ruled that Maxim had settled upon the chemical formula first.)

For all of the arguments and struggles that surrounded him, no credible counterclaim about the invention of the automatic weapon ever emerged. The claim was Hiram Maxim's alone, and he cherished it.

This is not to say that Hiram Maxim necessarily told the truth.

Maxim gave different accounts about the origins of his interest in automatic weapons. In the more commonly cited account, machine-gun design became his personal project while he was on assignment in Europe. His employer, the United States Electric Lighting Company, had transferred him to an affiliate in London but asked him first to visit Paris and Brussels. There he was to undertake the tedious task of reviewing copies of European patents related to electricity. The work required many months. At an industry exposition in Vienna, Maxim met an American who offered bizarre advice. The electric business was getting crowded; the man recommended that the inventor open another line of work. "Maxim, hang your electrical machines!" he said. "If you wish to make your everlasting fortune and pile up gold by the ton, invent a killing machine, something that will enable these Europeans to cut each other's throats with greater facility—that is what they want." In another account, he identified the American who made the suggestion as a "Jew" he knew previously from the United States.[14]

Whether the account is true remains anyone's guess. Maxim was comfortable with embellishment, and in published accounts of the exchange he did not share the other man's name. He did say that the man was not serious. That did not matter. Maxim was serious enough.

At the time, all of the weapons sold in the machine-gun class were manually operated. The Gardner, the Gatling, the Nordenfelt—with each of these weapons, continuous fire was realized by continuous turning of a hand crank or movement of a mechanical arm. The effect was like that of a manual pump. As long as the gunner's arm kept cranking, and cartridges were in the feed system, bullets would be fired. If the gunner's arm stopped working, so did everything else. By 1884, these technologies were mature, well machined, and impressive for what they were. Maxim had a different approach. He had fired a rifle before, and felt its kick. The recoil was enough to bruise a shoulder. It was also evidence of wasted energy: Only a portion of the powder's energy was used to force a bullet down the barrel and out the muzzle. Could not some of this unused energy be harnessed, cartridge by cartridge, blast by blast, to do the tasks performed by the crank?

Returning to Paris, Maxim sketched out the concept of the automatic rifle, modeling an early draft on an existing pattern: the Winchester rifle.[15] He was too busy to pursue it. His assignment to review patents on the Continent was ending, and he had commitments awaiting him in England. Maxim had been told that the electrical office there would pay half his salary, with the balance underwritten by the American firm. He arrived in London and found the lighting concern's director unwilling to disburse the wages. Maxim asked the director how much he would be willing to pay. The director replied, "One guinea a year." Hiram Maxim and electricity were all but done. He remembered his Paris drawings and the idea of harnessing recoil to make an automatic gun. "It occurred to me," he said, "that this would be a very good opportunity for me to commence experiments."[16]

Over the years Maxim offered a range of stories about when he first undertook such work. He told one interviewer that he made his first designs in 1873, but did not have time to test them for a decade.[17] In a third version, he said his interest reached to 1854 when his father conceived of a hand-cranked, single-barrel machine gun. He hoped it would fire one hundred rounds a minute. Maxim would have been fourteen years old then; he claimed he made drawings and models of his father's ideas over the next two years at the family wood shop in Maine. His uncle, who owned a metal works in Massachusetts, examined the plans and announced they would cost one hundred dollars to manufacture but not be worth one hundred cents.[18] The three accounts are not mutually exclusive, though the third description, if true, would have placed Maxim's involvement in hand-powered machine guns neatly ahead of Richard Gatling's. Maxim liked to be first.

Whether Maxim was a reliable correspondent on matters related to the development of the Maxim gun is another question. Ian V. Hogg, one of the most objective researchers of firearms and their origins, suggested that Maxim did not act nearly as independently as he made it seem. Citing records of the 1880s from the British military's director of artillery, Hogg wrote that the first time the British military heard of the Maxim gun, word of the weapon came from Albert Vickers of Vickers, Sons & Company, a metallurgical concern. In September 1884, it seemed, Mr. Vickers told the British military that he had "several machine guns ready for inspection" and identified himself as "one of the part owners of the patents." Within a week, the British military had decided to provide cartridges for demonstration trials, and by early October the superintendent of the Royal Small Arms Factory had visited Maxim's workshop. A demonstration shooting was held in late January 1885 for several British military officials, who were impressed. From the records, Hogg deduced that Maxim had entered an early partnership with Vickers, and perhaps had his financial backing.[19] The available records also show that by early November 1884, the Maxim Gun Company had incorporated, and that Albert Vickers and Robert R. Symon each had 417 shares with an initial value of twenty pounds each. Maxim was a minority shareholder, with 416 shares.[20]

Whatever the precise nature of his earliest backing, two things are clear. First, Maxim had more support—financial, technical, and social, the third being important to penetrate the business world in a foreign country—than he publicly acknowledged. Second, as Maxim turned his attention to firearms full-time in London, he was well placed to open a new business. He was in his early forties and had experience in manufacturing, engineering, design, sales, and patents. He had made ample money in the early utility industries, and he possessed a rich mix of theoretical and practical skills. He opened an experimental workshop in Hatton Garden, hired assistants, and worked out his drawings. He focused on the guts of an automatic weapon, wasting no time on elements already well-known. The barrels came from the London office of the Henry Rifled

Barrel Company, where the company's superintendent tried to dissuade the American inventor. "Many engineers and clever men imagine that they can make a gun, but they never succeed," he said. "They are all failures. So you better drop it, and not spend a single penny on it. You don't stand a ghost of a chance."[21]

He ignored the warning. Maxim knew his problems were not in the marketplace—he would be offering something different from all machine guns then available. His problems were in the industrial climate of his new home. The Industrial Revolution had not blossomed as fully in England as it had in the United States. Maxim found London technologically backward. The workers were unfamiliar with modern tools then in common use in American mills. And as he procured those tools, he discovered that many were unwilling to work with them. Others followed schemes to slow work and deceive their bosses, extending the time taken to complete a task, so as to maximize wages.

Maxim claimed he often worked alone, pursuing a design for which there were no models. "When tools were required for the various machines I forged them out and tempered them myself," he said.[22] One apparatus allowed him to measure the force and other characteristics of recoil, and with this data he built the interrelated components for model guns that he hoped would perform the chores of all firearms—loading, firing, removing the empty case, and reloading. He made several prototypes. Finally, he settled on a concept whereby when a gunner fired the first shot, the force of the recoil would slide the barrel backward about three-fourths of an inch. After the bullet left the muzzle, this backward motion would unlock the chamber where the spent shell casing was seated and begin the empty casing's extraction. Simultaneously the force of the barrel's rearward travel would knock a heavy metal rod toward the rear of the weapon, where it would meet a thick and powerful spring that would throw it forward again. As the bolt was rushed forward by the spring, it would catch a new cartridge and lock it in the chamber, where the firing pin would strike the cartridge's primer and fire the gun again. The blast that propelled the second bullet down the barrel knocked the bolt backward again, beginning the cycle once more, and so on, a cycle at a time, each lasting as little as one-tenth of a second, until the trigger was released or all the ammunition gone.[23]

By early 1884, after testing several designs, Maxim had a working model based on these principles, which fired at adjustable rates as fast as six hundred rounds per minute. The invention was reported in London newspapers. Maxim was almost immediately visited by England's upper crust. The Duke of Cambridge, who at the time was the head of the British army, was an early visitor. Maxim became so busy with guests, he said, that he could work productively only at night and on weekends. "It was a veritable nine-day wonder," he said.

As the new weapon was receiving its inaugural praise in Maxim's shop, England was consumed by a long-running difficulty in eastern Africa. The Egyptian province of Sudan had been swept by Islamic rebellion in 1881, and in 1883 Britain had decided to evacuate its citizens and the Egyptian military presence from the capital, Khartoum. A popular officer and former administrator of the province, Major General Charles Gordon, was dispatched to organize the city's defense and coordinate the exit. He arrived to discover the situation desperate. By midspring 1884 the Islamic forces controlled the approaches to the city, trapping the Egyptian contingent and General Gordon in a siege.

Britain, pressured by public demands for a rescue, ordered General Wolseley, who had brought the first Gatling gun to Africa during the Ashanti War, to go to Gordon's assistance. Khartoum rests at the juncture of the White and Blue Nile rivers, and General Wolseley initially chose to ascend the river with all of his forces. But as his relief expedition bogged down, he ordered Colonel Herbert Stewart and more than eleven hundred men to break off and attempt an overland route. The foot column set out with a camel train toward the beleaguered capital. Colonel Stewart's detachment became known as the Desert Column. They were the forerunners of the special forces; many had been selected from top English families and for their fitness for the difficulties ahead. Theirs was a colonial misadventure of the first order. On January 16, 1885, while moving between wells on arid terrain, the column encountered near Abu Klea a large Arab force blocking the route to the next watering point. The Arabs, carrying shimmering green banners, outnumbered the British column by as much as ten to one. Night fell before the two sides clashed in force.

At dawn the Arabs began a war dance, and an exchange of distant fire ensued. The Arab shooting was intermittent and not especially accurate, but bullets occasionally slammed into Colonel Stewart's men. The wounded soldiers were loaded onto camels. The colonel understood that the math did not work; the column could not withstand a prolonged contest of attrition. He ordered a square formed and marched toward the green banners at about 10:00 A.M., hoping to provoke the Arabs into a fight in the open, where the Europeans' superior weapons and their battle-drill training might give them an advantage. A naval contingent, led by Lord Charles Beresford, pulled a five-barreled Gardner gun along with the stumbling square. Lord Beresford was peculiar and excitable. He opted to ride a white donkey instead of a camel. But he was devoted to his Gardner and wanted to see what it might do.

The two sides skirmished as the square moved over the broken ground. The Arab units swerved and probed, seeking weakness in the lines. At last they selected the rear of the square, which was having trouble maintaining formation, for their full attack. They closed the distance in phalanxes led by flag-carrying sheiks. "After them came the fighting men, armed with javelins and hatchets, knobkerries and knives," a survivor would later write. "These were not the sharpshooters who had been firing Remingtons, but warriors chosen to exterminate the infidel."[24]

The British riflemen fired into the flanks of the phalanxes as the Arabs moved for the weakest point. The shrieking attackers momentarily wavered, but their numbers were great; they rushed on. Lord Beresford's eagerness to use the Gardner overcame his tactical good sense. The naval contingent broke ranks, rolled the gun and carriage outside the formation, and prepared to meet the charge and cut it down. Lord Beresford, ready at the crank, would test his gun at last.

They were tearing down upon us with a roar like the roar of the sea, an immense surging wave of white-slashed black forms brandishing bright spears and long flashing swords; and all were chanting, as they leaped and ran, the war-song of their faith, *"La ilaha ill' Allah Mohammedu rasul Allah!"*; and the terrible rain of bullets poured into them by the Mounted Infantry and the Guards stayed them not. They wore the loose white robe of the Mahdi's uniform, looped over the left shoulder, and the straw skull-cap. These things we heard and saw in a flash, as the formidable wave swept steadily nearer.

I laid the Gardner gun myself to make sure. As I fired, I saw the enemy mown down in rows, dropping like nine-pins; but as the men killed were killed in rear of the front rank, after firing about forty rounds (eight turns of the lever), I lowered the elevation. I was putting in most effective work on the leading ranks and had fired about thirty rounds when the gun jammed.[25]

The moment that machine guns' critics had long warned about had arrived. Outside the exhausted and bloodied square, Lord Beresford and his little naval detachment stood exposed. They were alone, facing a charge, and with a silent gun.

To clear it the feed-plate had to be unscrewed, and Beresford and a chief boatswain's mate named Rhodes began to do this. Within minutes the enemy were on top of them. Rhodes was speared and killed instantly, and so was the naval armourer beside the gun. Beresford was luckier. He was saved momentarily by the feed-plate dropping on his head and knocking him under the gun, and was then hit by the handle of an axe, the blade of which missed him. He caught a spear blade that was being thrust at him, got to his feet, and was then borne backward by the rush into the front rank of Number 4 Company.[26]

The fighting went to hand to hand on the line, with British soldiers thrusting bayonets while the Arabs hacked with axes and stabbed with spears. The Gardner was briefly in enemy possession, but the British made a rush and reclaimed it, even though it was jammed. By now there were other problems. The attackers had flowed into a gap that had opened in the square. There were so many British camels within—more than one hundred—that the Arabs could not capitalize at the moment they might have broken down the British formation and commenced its slaughter. Their confusion among the animals allowed time for Colonel Stewart to recover. The opposite line of the square, following a drill no infantryman would ever wish to execute, faced about and fired into the square's center, striking some British soldiers on the far ranks but breaking the Arab attack. An Arab retreat began. Nine British officers and sixty-five soldiers were killed, including everyone who had tended to the Gardner gun, except Lord Beresford, the officer who had put it to use in foolish fashion and was spared the fate of the unlucky men he had led. A count of the Arab dead found eleven hundred corpses.[27]

The hand-cranked Gardner gun, for all its potential, had failed. The brief sequence told less about the potential of rapid-fire arms as devices for mass killing than it did about the enduring pitfalls of cumbersome machine guns, low-quality ammunition, and early design. Once Lord Beresford had found the proper range and engaged the lead of the approaching charge, he had managed only six turns of the crank before it seized up.[28] He had made eight more turns before adjusting the elevation. After the battle, he walked among the Arab dead and confirmed the awful power of the big weapon: "I observed that the rows of bullets from the Gardner gun, which was rifle calibre .45 inch, with five barrels, had cut off heads and tops of heads, as though sliced horizontally with a knife."[29] Lord Beresford liked that. But it lasted only fourteen turns—seventy bullets against thousands of attacking men. A machine gun good only for a moment's work was not much good at all.

The Desert Column fought another engagement en route but Colonel Stewart was wounded and he ceded command. His unit arrived at Khartoum one day late. The city had fallen. General Gordon had been beheaded. His killers displayed their grisly prize by wedging it in the branches of a tree. Colonel Stewart later succumbed to his wounds. London was crestfallen.

What was bad for Britain was good for Maxim. Episodes when manual machine guns failed could only aid his cause. And then it happened again. Two years later an Italian column roughly half the size of Colonel Stewart's expedition was caught by an Ethiopian force making an overland movement in what is now Eritrea. In late January 1887, the Italians set out after one of their garrisons, in Sahati, was attacked by Ras Alula, a renegade Ethiopian commander. The reinforcements, 524 men led by a lieutenant colonel, had two Gatling guns. As they walked toward the hills near the town of Dogali, the enemy was alerted of their movement. Ras Alula was a skilled commander and, by contemporary accounts, had ten thousand warriors under his control. He began maneuvering his forces early in the morning to cut Sahati's reinforcements off. The Italians had little wartime experience with their Gatlings. But they had brought them into exactly the sort of tactical situation that the Gatling Gun Company's surreptitiously paid lecturer, Captain Ebenezer Rogers, had proposed at the Royal United Services Institution a dozen years before. A small force on colonial duty, facing a much larger force, the captain had said, would find a Gatling most useful for turning back primitive subjects. Unless the Gatling did not work.

As Ras Alula constricted his hold on the Italians' route, Lieutenant Colonel Tomasso De Cristoforis, the Italian commander, ordered his troops to higher ground. The fighting began. Within a half hour, both Gatling guns were jammed. The Italian soldiers could not revive them. The colonel managed to send out a messenger with a note saying the machine guns were down and help would be welcome. But there was not enough time. This fight would be determined by older rules.

> At one o'clock Ras Alula, having completed two concentric circles around them and closed inwards to within a short distance, gave the order to charge. Then the hand-to-hand fighting began; the Italians having opened fire at the longer ranges had by this time exhausted their ammunition, but each man defended his life with bayonet and sword. To the last man they struggled against an enemy twenty times their number, falling one by one on the position they were hold-ing; 23 officers killed and one wounded; 407 men killed and 81 wounded. Such is the death roll of that sad and glorious day.[30]

When a patrol from the main garrison arrived the next day, it found the Italian wounded hiding under the Italian dead.

Maxim had not made his weapon merely to satisfy his curiosity, or out of patriotism. A sense of concern for soldiers' fates seemed to interest him not at all. He was in the gun business for fame and money. He sought sales. After his gun was unveiled, it was quickly examined for its fitness for military service, and Maxim incorporated suggestions from British officers to transform it from a technical marvel to an instrument more suitable for combat use. Chief among his tasks was simplification, so the gun could be broken down, cleaned, and reassembled with no tools beyond a soldier's hands. Belts of 333 cartridges were made, which could be fed into the gun easily, one after the other, to keep the Maxim firing. The feed system was simplified so that component parts could be removed and replaced in as little as six seconds.[31] Maxim also reduced the weapon's weight. His machine gun would not be like the big Gatlings or Gardners when they entered the market. It would be a fraction of the size, a full system under 150 pounds. The other guns were still large enough to be confused with artillery.

A newly formed concern, the Maxim Gun Company, was ready to market his product, and it quickly became evident that there were advantages to not being first: The sales groundwork laid by Gatling and Gardner had made his path easier. So had the uneven performance of the Gatling gun at Ulundi, and the failures of the Gardner at Abu Klea, and then the massacre at Dogali. In 1885, Maxim's gun was fired for the public at an inventors' exhibition in South Kensington, and next were a series of trials in England and France, and in Italy, where the gun was submerged in the sea for three days and put to tests without cleaning. Upon watching a test in Vienna, Archduke William called it "the most dreadful instrument I have ever seen or imagined." And placed orders with its inventor.

No matter the Maxim's superior performance, it faced clever interference. At one shooting trial between Maxim's guns and those of his competitors, a sales agent for the Nordenfelt gun lingered among the reporters waiting outside the test-range gates. The Maxim beat the hand-cranked Nordenfelt handily, but could not defeat the agent's guile. The competitor's agent addressed the reporters in a hasty news conference. "The Nordenfelt—it has beaten all others," he told them, and so the stories read the next day.[32] Maxim also could not attract attention across the Atlantic; his competitors and potential partners in America barely replied to his mail. "I wrote to all the prominent gun and pistol makers in the States telling them that the automatic system would soon be applied to firearms of all sizes from pocket-pistols up, and advising them to work my system, which had been broadly patented in the States," he said. "I did not receive a single favourable reply."[33]

The American army was similarly unimpressed, in part because it was in a period where it was under orders to buy American-made arms, but also because early tests raised concerns about reliability and durability.[34] Nonetheless, a few officers were scolding the others for not paying developments in machine gunnery adequate mind. "There can be no question that these guns will prove an all-important factor in deciding war, and the nation which best employs them, and fully understands their working and organization, will come off the victor," one artillery colonel wrote in an article in a leading tactical journal. The colonel, Edward B. Williston, pilloried the ignorance permeating the American officer corps. "Generally speaking, not one officer in a hundred has any special knowledge of the subject of machine guns, and very little is known of their construction, capabilities or proper uses," he wrote. "The guns issued to the Army are either used to ornament posts . . . or they are carefully housed and greased to prevent rusting." A terrible tool had appeared, to snickers. "It has been the fashion," he said, "to decry the guns."[35]

In 1887 Maxim submitted guns to the British for naval trials, and the navy bought three. Royal enthusiasm for the gun ran so high that Albert Edward, Prince of Wales, recommended it to his nephew, Kaiser Wilhelm II, the emperor of Germany, who requested a demonstration competition between a Gatling, a Nordenfelt, and a Maxim. The Germans already had tested machine guns, but were not satisfied with them; they had yet to design ammunition casings sturdy enough to bear the strain of rapid fire. The Maxim worked flawlessly, firing 333 rounds in less than thirty seconds. The kaiser approached the gun and placed his finger on it.

"That is the gun," he said, "there is no other."

At that moment, Hiram Maxim had effectively achieved what he would be most remembered for. The companies he was affiliated with would sell more guns to many buyers, and he would continue his inventing, and would try to design an airplane. With uncanny martial prescience, he would predict aerial bombing before airplanes had even been made. But the demonstration for the kaiser was his moment. Once the kaiser had seen the efficiency and ease of use of the automatic machine gun, Maxim had offered his weapons for sale to the powers that would become the central military actors in World War I.

While Europeans placed their initial orders, the most important test results were trickling back—from battle. A Maxim gun was first used in 1887 in the jungles along Africa's western coast, about sixty miles inland from Freetown, against a small, recalcitrant tribe. As colonial episodes went, the uprising was minor. But it proved to anyone watching closely what a Maxim could do. The insurgent tribesmen, whom the British called the Yonnies, occupied a network of crude forts in the jungle, from which they had been raiding neighboring towns and threatening the area's trade. The colonial administration sent to London for help. Sir Francis de Winton was dispatched from England, and arrived to marshal a small force: four hundred men from the First West India Regiment, a hundred local Sierre Leone police officers, and a few dozen sailors from the sloop HMS *Acorn*. The sailors had brought along a small artillery piece and a Maxim, which they carried ashore.

The force marched for Robari, the insurgents' stronghold. When they arrived, they found a tiny fortress, less than eighty yards across, ringed by a deep ditch and a mud wall. Eleven watchtowers looked down over the approaches. The Yonnies were confidently inside. Against enemies with primitive equipment, the Robari defenses might have proved sturdy. But the fort's builders had never seen the type of weapons the British dragged down the trail. The invading force stopped on the opposite bank of a stream, took stock of the defenses, and went to work. From a distance of less than five hundred yards, they leveled the artillery piece and fired into the buildings and walls. The tribesmen scrambled to the roofs to remove the thatch and contain the risk of fire, and unwittingly presented themselves as targets to a weapon they had not known existed. The result was reported by *MacMillan's* magazine.

> The Maxim, which here administered rather than received its baptism of fire, was turned on them, and they dropped off the roofs by dozens. . . . When the leading troops entered the gate on the Mafenbeh side there was not a living Yonnie left in the town, although there was no lack of their dead.

The British saw the rout for what it had been: "a complete, if not particularly glorious, victory." Then they ransacked Robari. Three days later, de Winton began to move on the tribe's smaller forts, where he repeated the slaughter. The destruction of Ronietto made for a particularly ugly account. A Yonnie waved a white flag of surrender, and yet the tribe fought on. The British reply was so overpowering that *MacMillan's* compared it to cleaning out a nest of wasps. This was a new kind of war. Point a machine, and killing men was like killing bugs.

> The gates were flung open, and the defenders came streaming out. The Maxim was planted opposite one gate at a distance of little over two hundred yards, and under the frightful rain of bullets that it

poured upon that narrow entrance not one of the hapless wretches
that came out escaped alive. The slaughter of the war-boys on this
occasion was greater than at any of the other towns. It was necessary
to give them a lesson to respect flags of truce, and in any case one
severe example is with the savages the most merciful in the end.[36]

The growing interest from buyers, combined with the results of field tests
and in West Africa, brought more interest from potential partners. It was
obvious that the Maxim gun outperformed all the manual guns of the
era, and one competitor realized it was better to join efforts with Maxim
than to be pushed out of the field. In 1888 Maxim joined with Thorsten
Nordenfelt, an arms dealer, financier, and steel producer from Sweden, to
form the Maxim Nordenfelt Guns and Ammunition Company Limited.
The firm manufactured his patterns from a factory in Crayford, a short
drive to London's east. Nordenfelt's switch from Maxim rival to Maxim
partner signaled the beginning of the end for sales of manual machine
guns. With the association of his new partner, Maxim also picked up the
sales support of Basil Zaharoff, a corrupt and mercurial arms salesman
with an array of contacts in the war ministries of Europe. It had been
Zaharoff, known in his time as the Merchant of Death, who had tricked
the journalists after the firing trials in Vienna. Now he was on Maxim's
team. His black arts would be used on Maxim's behalf.

As its inventor's business prospects were brightening, the Maxim gun
continued making the rounds in Africa. In 1893, in what became known
as the Matabele War, the British South Africa Corporation moved to put
down a rebellion by Ndebele people, an offshoot of the Zulu nation in the
area that would become Rhodesia, and then Zimbabwe. The corporation
had at its disposal fewer than one thousand police officers, soldiers, and
mercenaries in all. The forces of the opposing king, Lobengula, outnumbered the whites by many times. While they were not as uninformed as
the defenders of Robari and Ronietto—the Ndebele had knowledge of
the power of the colonial columns' other weapons—they began the war
without the benefit of knowing about a Maxim gun.

As one of the British columns moved toward the capital, Bulawayo,
the Ndebele picked at it along the way, trying to ambush or surround it.
Each time the Maxim helped push them back. George Rattray, a British

gunman who had traveled to Matabeleland in his late teens,[37] had joined the expedition, and sent a detailed account of several skirmishes home to his mother in Surrey. By his description, the British with their Maxims were all but invincible. They moved across the countryside toward the capital, razing villages along the way.

> We continued our march straight for Bulawayo capturing cattle as we went, burning every Kraal we came near and destroying the grain, the niggers having left everything behind. I suppose we have burned about some six thousand huts.

About twenty miles short of the capital, the column met resistance from two experienced Ndebele regiments. A skirmish became a larger clash as the regiments pressed near. This time the Maxim did more than hold the attackers off. The Ndebele, Rattray said, were "mown down just as if with a scythe." The events showed how far machine-gun and ammunition technology had advanced since the 1879 Zulu War. Rattray's long letter home described Ulundi in reverse. Rather than depending on the support of the infantry's rifles to assist in battle between jams, the machine guns left little work for the infantry to do.

> Our two foot regiments, the redoubtable foot sloggers, were ordered out with fixed bayonets to clear the bush. This they did in about twenty minutes, the firing on both sides being heavy but strange to say not a man of ours was hit while the Matabele dropped in all directions. The enemy then retired leaving over 1500 dead.[38]

Accounts of this sort accumulated, including the most lopsided tally perhaps ever recorded to that time—a claim that about four dozen policemen with four Maxims withstood repeated charges, killing more than three thousand African men in front of a police station. The round numbers are suspicious. But the larger point is unmistakable. A few hundred men with a few Maxims had subdued a king and his army, and destroyed the enemy's ranks. Hiram Maxim's business was secure.

This was obvious in the market as well, where the Maxim's rise signaled the Gatling's decline. In 1876, after weathering worries over debt and sales, the Gatling Gun Company had been solidly in the black. Its

$31,000 in debt had been paid down,[39] and the company had sales that year of seventy guns, signaling the start of a period of profit. Gross receipts for the fiscal year were $81,290. Profits were $47,495.[40] Then came Maxim. By the end of its 1889 fiscal year, the Gatling Gun Company had grossed $13,006.48 on gun sales, and had only $1,794.55 in hand. It sold thirty-seven guns that year, a small fraction of what it had sold fifteen years before.[41] The American army had tested the Maxim at least twice—in 1888 and 1890.[42] In 1888 it had been intrigued, but the gun was withdrawn by the owners before follow-on tests were held. In 1890, the Maxim was found to be less reliable and more prone to rusting in endurance tests than the Gatling, which by then had been largely perfected. But by 1894, the U.S. Navy testing board had recommended the Maxim for acceptance for the fleet over the Gatling and several other weapons.[43] With the prospect of obsolescence looming, the Gatling Gun Company was developing a means to relieve gunners of the chores and risk related to turning the crank.[44] Its proposed solution was to attach an electric motor to keep the barrels spinning.

By this time, Gatling had refined the basic operations of his gun and embarked on the process of miniaturization. Gatlings of the time weighed 224 pounds, the carriage an additional 202 pounds, and the limber another 200.[45] With a reasonable load of ammunition, the weapon, ready for movement about the battlefield, weighed more than a half ton. To expand markets, the Gatling Gun Company offered a smaller and more portable model, sold under the name Camel gun. The Camel gun was made not for forts or warships, but for overland patrols and expeditions. It fit into a case that could be lashed to the back of a pack animal. A portable tripod completed the kit, and allowed the gun to be set readily on the ground most anywhere required. These were essential developments. In the short term, they allowed Gatling guns, first created to ride on a timber between large wheels, to get off the roads and level ground and out into the infantry's terrain. In the long term they marked the first step toward the shrinkage of rapid-fire arms, which would make them available to a much longer list of users.

By 1892, the Gatling gun was down to 74 pounds.[46] In 1895, the Maxim Nordenfelt Company took miniaturization further, down to 40 pounds—25 pounds for the gun and 15 more for a tripod, the pair fitting together in a pack.[47] These smaller guns were not mainstays in the fighting. But they established, change by change and pound by pound, that rapid-fire arms could be reduced in mass.

The Maxim's success in the field, and the interest of many nations, helped the company's prospects for raising capital or finding partners. Hiram Maxim's actual state of affairs were not rosy. Maxim was a difficult man—cantankerous, arrogant, impulsive, rude—and he was a designer by personality, not a manager. His company's affairs were sloppy, and by this time he was extremely deaf. One of his directors, to communicate with him, had to pull on Maxim's earlobe, lean close, and bellow. The company had factories at Crayford, Erith, Dartford, Birmingham, and Stockholm, but Maxim was regarded as so disruptive that the company barred him from entering the assembly-room floors, and set aside a work-shop for him where he might spend his time without wasting everyone else's. The company itself had been a far-flung and overcapitalized con-cern, and equipment was often idle. A directors' report in 1890 noted that one factory had three to four times the necessary capacity. The company had a product that was gaining reputation and generating enthusiasm. But it leaked money.[48]

Nonetheless, the product was good enough that the firm would survive mismanagement and all of the disruptions Maxim would muster. Vickers purchased the Maxim Nordenfelt Guns and Ammunition Company for 1.35 million British pounds in 1897, becoming Vickers, Son & Maxim, and helping the Vickers family to position itself against their rivals in the armaments trade, Armstrong.* By this time, Maxim's patterns were being turned into guns in England, Germany, France, Spain, and Sweden, and Maxim expected them to be made in the United States. "The automatic system has now been adopted by nearly all nations, great and small," he said proudly at a public lecture. "We are now giving employment to a large number of men. Our works are fully employed."[49]

And this did not mention the manufacture of Maxims abroad, in Germany, where a firm had astutely arranged a licensing agreement that passed the full technical drawings of a Maxim gun to German possession. Step by step, the demonstration before the kaiser was leading to its result:

---

* Maxim's difficult personality would not help him in his relations with Vickers. He would retire in February 1911. On a motion in March by Albert Vickers, one of Maxim's earliest supporters, the firm would quickly strike the word *Maxim* from the company name and its correspondence, becoming Vickers, Ltd.

trenches bristling with machines guns in World War I. The gun works at
Spandau would provide the German armies with thousands of the Maschinengewehr 08, a Teutonic Maxim knock-off, for the start of the war.

Two battles at the close of the nineteenth century showed, once and for
all, what machine guns could do when supplied with well-made ammunition and properly employed.

The first was in July 1898, when the American army landed in Cuba
with intentions to oust the Spanish. Although the Maxim gun was sup-
planting all other machine guns in Europe, the American army had not
purchased any. As war with Spain approached, its main rapid-fire arm remained the Gatling, which it had accepted for service thirty-two years before. The army gathered and provisioned itself in Tampa, where the man
who was to show the army how to use its guns at last, Second Lieutenant
John H. Parker, arrived with the Thirteenth Infantry. Machine guns had
been invented by Americans. They were a quintessentially American product. But aside from limited use against the Native American populations
in the western territories, the American guns had scarcely been put to a
combat test. Lieutenant Parker had been studying machine guns and the
available literature on them, and had spent his brief career working out
theories for their use. He had been born in Missouri in 1866, the same
year the Gatling gun was officially, and belatedly, accepted in the United
States Army. He found it scandalous that decades had passed since the
weapons' introduction, to such little effect. The army's tactical mind, he
concluded, was moribund, beholden to nonsense it had heard from European circles. "The rules of war established by pen soldiers do not form
the basis of actual operations in the field," he wrote. "Deductions based
on the drill-made automatons of European armies are not applicable."[50]

Lieutenant Parker, at thirty-one, was sure-footed beyond his experience and years. Up to this point, his military record had been undistin-
guished. He had ranked forty-ninth of the sixty-two graduates of the
United States Military Academy's Class of 1892,[51] and he had neither
previous combat service nor connections in civilian circles or the army's
senior leadership, which he was given to deriding. Not much about him
suggested he could bend the army to his will. "He was, apparently, a safe
man to ignore or snub if occasion or bad temper made it desirable to

ignore or snub somebody, and, above all, had no political friends who would be offended thereby."[52]

Not much suggested that the army was any more ready for machine guns than it had been when General Ripley was thwarting Richard Gatling's sales efforts during the Civil War. From 1872 through 1890, the American army had issued to its forces 253 Gatling guns in three different calibers, plus 32 other machine guns, including Gardner, Lowell, and Hotchkiss guns. On one level, this was impressive. The army had shrunk to fewer than thirty thousand men;[53] considering its small size and the fact that it had been through decades without fighting a modern conventional foe, it was well equipped with rapid-fire arms. Yet almost no one knew how to use them effectively, and few people were interested in finding out. "Distributed, apparently according to no considered plan, to the various military establishments then existing throughout the continental United States, their maintenance was the duty of the local Ordnance officer," an official historian of the subject found. "The post commander appears to have been without specific instructions as to their employment, and, unless he possessed a native curiosity concerning their characteristics (which was rarely the case), they remained wholly unused from the beginning of his tour of duty to the date of its termination."[54]

Up to this time, the most intensive use of a machine gun on record had been at a territorial prison in the desert near Yuma, now in Arizona, where a Gatling had been mounted by the guards above the penitentiary walls. In 1887, a group of inmates, many incarcerated for stagecoach robberies and other violent frontier crimes, organized a prison break. Two prisoners overpowered the warden as he walked through the yard, breaking his skull and shooting him with one of his own pistols. Simultaneously, another twenty attacked the prison office, which fell under their control. Now equipped with the collection of rifles and pistols taken from the office, the inmates tried to fight their way out. A dozen managed to escape through the gate and into the desert. Their freedom lasted only as long as it took to get the Gatling aimed and cranked; three-quarters of the fleeing men were promptly knocked down.

No Gatling gun was ever worked more rapidly and unerringly than that on the penitentiary walls at that time, and the Winchesters in the hands of another guard on the walls fired a ball every three seconds. Nine of the fleeing convicts dropped wounded in their tracks. Three more threw up their hands as a sign of surrender and walked back to the prison yard.[55]

The United States did not have the problems with machine-gun cartridges that had plagued Europe; its Gatlings, though bulky, worked well. And by the start of the Spanish-American War, the army had smokeless powder, which made the guns harder for any enemy to spot when they fired. But still they had little support. Colonel Custer's attitude toward the guns—that they were not worth their weight and hassle—remained a common view. A few voices did rise on behalf of the weapons, but they were mostly boosters in the local or scientific press. The *Times* of London had come to the not especially difficult conclusion that with a Gatling gun "a continuous shower of ounce bullets can be poured upon the spot where the enemy is the thickest, swept along the line of troops or scattered over the field like a jet of water from a fire hose."[56] Other newspapers noted similar Gatling gun properties, even if the analysis they derived from what they saw could be a stretch. "So destructive has its efficiency been made that it may almost be termed a peace preserver rather than a demolisher," the *Washington Post* declared. The *Indianapolis Sentinel* went further, invoking deterrence with the certitude of those who would later embrace the security of mutual assured destruction in the nuclear age. "We believe the Gatling gun will change the whole aspect of war in due time," its editors wrote. "When six guns can pour a steady stream of bullets at the rate of 3,000 a minute into the enemy, it is easy enough to see that 100 guns would make it prudent not to advance an inch; but on the contrary, retire as soon as possible. With a few hundred Gatlings on both sides, armies would melt away like dew before the sun, and men would soon learn to settle their disputes by arbitration, or some other means less destructive of life." The *London Broad Arrow* took a position closer to reality, seeing not deterrence, but a full list of practical uses. "The new model Gatling is a terrible instrument, capable of awful doings on occasion, as for instance, when it is desired to sink a torpedo boat, or enter the embrasures of a fort, mow down a column, sweep the streets in a riot, clear a bridge or drive back a skirmisher swarm."[57]

The army still had no experience with the weapons in a major battle. Gatling use had been limited to six skirmishes with Indians, the defense of forts and boats, and, by one account, the possible pot-shooting of a grizzly bear.[58] The misapprehensions of the tactical potential and roles of rapid-fire arms fit neatly into the historical precedents. To produce and field these new weapons, a nation would need industrial capacity and a modern bureaucracy; this was because the costs of production were high, and maintaining a large and reliable supply of ammunition was demanding. But possessing these qualities, and distributing the new weapons to military commanders, did not mean that armies were ready for them. It was not merely that armies were often caretakers of tradition, and therefore fundamentally conservative institutions, or that they were led by the oldest members, whose battlefield experience was often dated and who might be the least likely officers to innovate. They were also fragmented within, prone to rivalries between services and competing ideas of how budgets should be spent.

Lieutenant Parker saw the army's lack of vision as a waste. He was a seemingly fearless and hot-blooded young officer, and clever, too. Six months before the outbreak of war, before he was garrisoned to Tampa, he had written the War Department and proposed with characteristic self-promotion and confidence "the first correct tactical outline of the proper use of machine guns ever filed in any War Office in the world." For good measure he had included drawings and specifications for a new machine-gun carriage, which would move the guns and their ammunition over varied terrain at the pace of the infantry. The War Department, he claimed, "did not even acknowledge receipt."[59]

The war brought fresh chances to revisit the question. As the forces gathered in the damp heat, Parker lobbied to assemble a specialized machine-gun unit, an organization the United States had never previously sent to war. Yet he managed to prevail and was placed in charge of a section of Gatlings with thirty-seven men selected from multiple units. The result was a detachment that had the feel of a theoretical crusade; his was a personal project, conducted "without proper equipment, adequate instruction, or previous training, in the face of discouragements and sneers."[60] The lieutenant brought the guns ashore in Cuba in late June and began moving forward with the infantry and cavalry on the march toward Santiago. The force halted for four days just short of the Spanish trenches, and in the wait for battle Lieutenant Parker drilled his soldiers for several hours a day. They practiced loading and reloading so that they might make continuous fire over a long period of time, and they worked on clearing jams, so that any gun that malfunctioned could be brought quickly back into the fight.

The lieutenant had more ambitious ideas for his Gatling than defending held ground. He wanted to push the guns to the fore and pour bullets onto the enemy positions as the infantry and cavalry advanced. He believed that when the time came for a charge, the guns should be right there, providing covering fire. Machine guns were modern killing tools, and tools that spread fear. Why leave them behind at a decisive time, when heavy fire was needed? Thirty-five years had passed since General Butler bought a dozen Gatling guns in Baltimore and marched them onto Confederate soil. No one had tried what Lieutenant Parker proposed. He insisted his detachment was ready. On July 1, the Americans went into the attack.

The troops moved across the San Juan River in the sweltering summer heat toward the trenches outside Santiago, where the Spanish infantry had dug in. This was not a case of a modern army with modern weapons facing aboriginal rushes or a primitively equipped foe. One conventional force was moving against another on carefully prepared ground. And the lieutenant was pushing his soldiers and their bulky weapons forward as if they were any other infantrymen closing for an attack.

> The bullets were singing by our ears, and some of the men had narrow escapes. One was struck on the ear, and another had a portion of the leather from the toe of his shoe shot away. Some of the men were unable to keep up with the guns, but continued to follow as fast as they could run. One was sunstruck, another ruptured himself badly. A short distance beyond the ford of the San Juan we found an open space from which the works of the enemy were visible at a distance of from 600 to 800 yards. We dashed on to the farther edge of this opening so as to take advantage of some foliage for cover. Mauser bullets were dropping all around us, and as we unlimbered a bullet chipped the pommel of a driver's saddle. Another cut a mule's ear, and again we heard his cheerful song.
>
> It was but the work of an instant to indicate the range and point out the objectives. The guns began grinding instantly, and we could see the dirt fly and the straw hats of the Spaniards duck wherever we

pointed a piece. The effect upon the enemy was for a moment that of paralysis. Then they caught sight of Sergeant Green's gun, which was in the open, and concentrated a hideous fire upon the little battery. This was hard on us, but it relieved the firing line. The light screen of foliage immediately in front was no impediment to our own fire and no protection from that of the enemy. About one minute after we went into action all of Green's men were knocked out except himself and Corporal Doyle. Sine, who was feeding, struck me as he fell, shot through the heart. Greene [sic] jumped off the gunner's seat and ran for ammunition, leaving Doyle alone with the piece. I took the vacant place, and Greene [sic] began to pass all the ammunition for several minutes, until some of the men who had been left behind caught up and began to help.

Suddenly I perceived the Spaniards getting out of their trenches; at the same time I heard a yell from Sergeant Steigerwald at one of the other guns. It was like the ferocious cry of an infuriated lion. Doyle turned his head to look. At that I reached over, hit Doyle a jolt with my fist and pointed at the flying groups. He gave one glance and then the crank seemed to fairly fly.

By this time two men were feeding the gun, and we kept them busy. The other guns were turned up also to the highest rate. We ground out cartridges at the rate of 850, perhaps 950, per gun per minute during that last little spurt. It lasted only about two minutes, but it was here that our guns got in their most deadly work. When we got to those trenches the sights we saw were horrible. Where we had been aiming, there were masses of tangled writhing squirming wounded and dead Spaniards, and it was not until then that we fully realized the awful destructiveness of our work.[61]

A member of the burial detail for the Spanish soldiers later told Parker that forty-seven men appeared to have been killed by machine-gun fire. The figure sounds much more realistic than some of the earlier British accounts from Africa, with their round numbers. But body counts were not the issue. The effect in paralyzing the Spanish infantry and reducing their tactical options midfight—this was the observation that mattered most. It marked a shift in war. Machine guns were hereafter going to be a feature of almost every aspect of infantry battle, although not everyone yet realized it. After the war, Lieutenant Parker told all listeners, including many newspaper editors and correspondents, what had occurred. He wrote a book about the battle, in which he claimed he had proven his theory correct and turned the conventional wisdom upside down: Machine guns were immensely destructive, and thus effective, in offense and defense alike. "The infantry and cavalry had been pounding away for two hours on those positions," he wrote. "In eight and one-half minutes after the Gatlings opened the works were ours." His account was confirmed by Colonel Theodore Roosevelt, the commander of the First United States Volunteer Cavalry, known as the Rough Riders, whose charge had overrun Kettle Hill in the same battle for Santiago's outskirts. In the foreword of Lieutenant Parker's book, the colonel said that Gatling guns had been more effective in the fight than American artillery, and had boosted American morale.

> On the morning of July 1st, the dismounted cavalry, including my regiment, stormed Kettle Hill, driving the Spaniards from their trenches. After taking the crest, I made the men under me turn and begin volley firing at the San Juan Blockhouse and intrenchments [sic] against which Hawkins' and Kent's Infantry were advancing. While thus firing, there suddenly smote on our ears a peculiar drumming sound. One or two of the men cried out, "The Spanish machine guns!" but, after listening a moment, I leaped to my feet and called, "It's the Gatlings, men! It's our Gatlings!" Immediately the men began to cheer lustily, for the sound was most inspiring. Whenever the drumming stopped, it was only to open again a little nearer the front. Our artillery, using black powder, had not been able to stand within range of the Spanish rifles, but it was perfectly evident that the Gatlings were troubled by no such consideration, for they were advancing all the while.[62]

Roosevelt hedged his endorsement of machine gunnery, but barely. He proposed creating permanent machine-gun units for the wars ahead.

> I have had too little experience to make judgment final; but certainly, if I were to command either a regiment or a brigade, whether of cavalry or infantry, I would try to get a Gatling battery—under a good

man—with me. I feel sure that the greatest possible assistance would
be rendered, under almost all circumstances, by such a Gatling battery, if well handled; for I believe that it could be pushed fairly to the
front of the firing line.[63]

Lieutenant Parker had four Gatling guns under his command. Several
months later, in autumn 1898, the British military brought many more
machine guns—of the newer Maxim variety—into battle in Sudan and
put them to their most lethal use yet. The latest campaign along the Nile
reached back to 1895, when the British government decided to reassert
its influence over Sudan, hoping that a conquest of the Islamic forces in
the desert would establish a firmer colonial presence from Cairo to the
Cape of Good Hope. A large expeditionary force, more than eight thousand British soldiers accompanied by nearly eighteen thousand Egyptian
and African troops, was placed under the command of General Herbert
Kitchener. It massed in Egypt and prepared for the arduous trek and river
movement up the Nile to destroy the forces of the Khalifa, the Sudanese leader, and reclaim Khartoum. The campaign would serve a second
purpose: to avenge the beheading of General Gordon in 1885. A feat of
logistics and administration made the final clash possible. Kitchener built
a railroad through the desert to keep his soldiers well supplied. An escort
of gunboats accompanied them as they traveled upriver. The Maxims were
brought overland wrapped in silk, to prevent them from collecting sand
and grit.[64]

By late summer 1898, with the British columns nearing the capital at
last, the Khalifa prepared to annihilate them outside Omdurman, on the
Nile's western bank and to Khartoum's north. War drums beat in the city,
and before dawn on September 2, General Kitchener's soldiers formed
into order near the village of Karari, anchoring one end along the river
and the other at the end of an arc that swept across a plain. Thousands of
Sudanese warriors, called Dervishes by the British troops, had spent the
night in the field, readying to turn back the invaders. Winston Churchill,
then twenty-three years old and a correspondent for the *Morning Post,* was
with the British cavalry as the two sides closed the last distance between
them. The battle unfolded around him in a series of unequal scenes, as
the lightly armed and technologically unsophisticated Sudanese fighter

moved toward an enemy equipped with repeating rifles, artillery, and batteries of Maxim's guns. Some of the Sudanese men carried rifles, but they were a mixed collection of rusting older patterns. The fighters themselves lamented them. Roughly half of the Khalifa's soldiers had no firearms at all.[65]

The indigenous army numbered into the tens of thousands. As many as eight thousand Sudanese men streamed forward for the first frontal attack. The Maxims had a longer range than their limited assortment of rifles. Even before bullets were fired, while the Sudanese formations were far off, the British artillery began dropping shells in the midst of the dense charge, stopping men in clusters. The opening minutes of fighting consumed a column led by Ibrahim al Khalil, and defined the day. Al Khalil went into battle with two horses, Aim and End, and after the artillery barrage, Aim had been killed. The commander pushed on.

> The plain was filled with thousands of corpses. Yet they had had the enemy in sight for only half an hour. Aware of his acute disadvantage in the face of this massive firepower, Ibrahim decided, at a distance of 800 yards from the *zariba,* to veer to the right and enter one of the khurs* where he might pause, take stock, realign his forces and continue the attack. There he would be only 1,200 yards from the *zariba.* He motioned to his men to follow him to the right. Then at this moment, 0705, he was hit in the chest and head. He fell from his horse. End also fell, for he too had been hit. The Maxim machine-guns had opened fire, and one of their first victims was the commander of the Kara army. It was remarkable that he had survived so long, for throughout the long artillery bombardment he had been in the front line. Four horsemen dismounted and bore Ibrahim back amid a shower of bullets. The ferocity of the fire was such that the army's pace was checked, preventing it from turning to the right to shelter in the khur. But even so the scattered survivors continued to advance. Shells exploded on all sides. Many men fell; few rose again. When they had the chance they fired their guns, but it was an unequal contest. Moreover, the twelve machine guns of the three steamers were all now firing at a range of about 1,000 yards. Shaykh

---

*An estuary or creek; the Sudanese commander sought protection for his forces in a ditch.

Babikr Badri, who was a few miles away, described the regular volleys as being fired at intervals and the enemy fired on them with
a sound like runnnn. The command now fell on the shoulders of
Muhammad Ishaq who tried to rally the reduced force. He indicated
the new direction with his hand, but was immediately and fatally
struck by a whole volley of bullets. In the open space there was no
cover for a warrior to concentrate his aim and direct his fire, apart
from a few scattered bushes, and even when these were reached the
machine-gun fire was directed at them, and men and trees were torn
up without discrimination.[66]

By eight o'clock in the morning, the mismatch was obvious. Thousands of Sudanese soldiers had been wounded or killed, and not one
had managed to come close enough to the British lines to throw a spear.
Churchill watched the charges lose momentum, waver, and stop. The remaining Sudanese men tried to get away. There was little chance for that.

As the shells burst accurately above the Dervish skirmishers and
spearmen who were taking refuge in the folds of the plain, they rose
by hundreds and by fifties to fly. Instantly the hungry and attentive
Maxims and the watchful infantry opened on them, sweeping them
all to the ground—some in death, others in terror. Again the shells
followed them to their new concealment. Again they rose, fewer than
before, and ran. Again the Maxims and the rifles spluttered. Again
they fell. And so on until the front of the *zeriba* was clear of unwounded men for at least half a mile.[67]

The British cavalry, the Twenty-first Lancers, organized for a sweep
of the plain and pounded out from the lines and across the ground to
exploit the enemy's helplessness and confusion. Roughly four hundred
horsemen strong, they rode unexpectedly to a large and deep depression, and met a Sudanese force in hiding. The horsemen were too close
to stop, so instead they accelerated and collided with the wall of men in
the trench. For ten seconds, both sides were stunned. They continued to
fight while intermingled, slashing and stabbing and shooting into one
another, sometimes with muzzles pressed almost to one another's flesh.
Then the British broke through, but not before having lost more than a

quarter of their horses and suffering seventy wounded or dead men. Less than two minutes had passed since the two groups collided. The British survivors regrouped and wheeled back to prepare to repeat their charge, as riderless horses or horses carrying sagging, bloodied men wandered uselessly about. The Lancers had just completed the last effective British cavalry charge in history. It had been an anachronism in real time, and an example of older, outmoded ideas of tactics urging men to do what Maxim guns no longer required.

The cavalrymen galloped to the Sudanese flank, dismounted, and the two sides exchanged rifle fire as the Sudanese fighters retreated, allowing the British to recover their dead. General Kitchener in the meanwhile had directed his units to move forward and capture Omdurman, and his forces were attacked en route by a massive concentration of the Khalifa's fighters. The British set their Maxim guns and shattered charge after charge. The battle passed with astonishing quickness. Churchill, a veteran of the seesaw skirmishes against Pashtun tribes on the Afghan and Pakistani frontier, was both astonished and horrified. A huge collection of drilled fighting men had been cut down, almost extinguished, by modern arms. The British force had suffered forty-eight dead, including those lost in the cavalry charge. Contemporaneous estimates of the Sudanese dead exceeded ten thousand, and sometimes were twice that. It was not yet noon. "Within the space of five hours," Churchill wrote, "the strongest and best-armed savage army yet arrayed against a modern European power had been destroyed and dispersed with hardly any difficulty, comparatively small risk, and insignificant loss to the victors."

Three days later Churchill accompanied a British horseback patrol that toured the plain, which was covered with the grisly remains of the local army's dead, and a far smaller number of the wounded, some of whom were trying to crawl with their wrecked frames to the Nile, for a drink. His report of the ride is among the most chilling pieces of battlefield correspondence from the nineteenth century, and the most complete assessment in its time of the power of automatic fire.

A strong, hot wind blew from the west across the great plain and hurried foul and tainted to the river. Keeping to windward of the thickest clusters, we picked our way, and the story of the fight unfolded itself. Here was where the artillery had opened on the swarming masses. Men had fallen in little groups of five or six to each shell. Nearer to the zeriba—about 1,000 yards from it—the musketry had begun to tell, and the dead lay evenly scattered about—one every ten yards. Two hundred yards further the full force of the fire—artillery, Maxims and rifles—had burst on them. In places desperate rushes to get on at all costs had been made by devoted fearless men. In such places the bodies lay so thickly as to hide the ground. Occasionally there were double layers of this hideous covering. Once I saw them lying three deep. In a space not exceeding a hundred yards square more than 400 corpses lay festering.

Churchill was shaken. "I have tried to gild war," he wrote, "and to solace myself for the loss of dear and gallant friends, with the thought that a soldier's death for a cause that he believes in will count for much, whatever may be beyond this world." But he was unable to square the sights before him, acre upon acre of the remains of soldiers on their own land, with his understanding of war waged by a "civilized Power."

> There was nothing dulce et decorum about the Dervish dead; nothing of the dignity of unconquerable manhood; all was filthy corruption. Yet these were as brave men as ever walked the earth. The conviction was born in me that their claim beyond the grave in respect of a valiant death was not less good than that which any of our countrymen could make.

The patrol continued on. Its members traced the outlines of the battle by following the lines and piles of corpses. Churchill had participated in the charge of the Twenty-first Lancers; he knew of its exhilaration and frantic terror, and had been within the rushing wall of four hundred horsemen crashing at high speed against a denser wall of dismounted men. As he roamed away from the location of the Lancers' victory, out onto the plain near the Nile, he came to the spot where another cavalry charge—this one by the Baggara, who were aligned with the Khalifa—had been stopped by Maxims. The result had been utterly different. The area of the Baggara attack was marked by a sun-bloated collection of dead horses and men. Churchill saw immediately the distinction between the charges. It was as if two events from different eras had occurred side by side on the same field. The British cavalry had faced rifles, swords, and spears, and made it up to and through the Sudanese lines, just as their tacticians had imagined, and much like cavalrymen from another time. The collision eroded the will of the defenders, and as the British turned around, reorganized, and attacked again, the Sudanese men fled. The Baggara faced a line thick with machine guns. A few European men, peering down metal sights and pressing metal buttons with their thumbs, had filled them and their horses with bullets, bringing them to a not quite instantaneous stop.

> Every man had galloped at full speed, and when he fell he shot many lengths in front of his horse, rolling over and over—destroyed, not conquered, by machinery. At such sights the triumph of victory faded on the mind, and a mournful feeling of disgust grew stronger.

Battle had changed. Modern weapons were no longer curiosities. The questions about their reliability had been put to rest. Sudan would fall back under British control. War had entered a new phase.

> Now only the heaps of corruption on the plain, and the fugitives dispersed and scattered in the wilderness, remained. The terrible machinery of scientific war had done its work.

For this victory, General Kitchener would be named Kitchener of Khartoum and propelled to celebrity and ahead of other British officers in his career. And other movements were afoot. Adolf von Tiedemann, a German military attaché, had toured the right flank during the battle and taken notes of the work of the Maxim guns. He estimated that more than half of the Sudanese deaths were caused by them, and saw the ruinous effect of reliable and massed automatic fire used against soldiers who moved into it in traditional military style.[68] While London celebrated, the attaché was sending back his reports. Germany would soon increase its production of Maxim guns.

Reaction to the sudden dominance of machine gunnery on the battlefield was mixed. By 1893, after British expeditions had gunned down the

Yonnies and the Ndebele, the British Parliament was debating the merits and morality of machine gunnery. Several politicians found the startlingly lopsided killing unfair and suggested it was counterproductive. "Treaties with savage Chiefs were not of much value," the parliamentarian A. C. Morton told his fellow members in 1893. "They were very often brought about by the aid of Maxim guns, aided not infrequently by the whisky bottle." Hilaire Belloc, the deeply Catholic French writer who had taken residence in England, was also made uneasy by the ready application of machine gunnery in colonial governance and the callous attitudes that accompanied it. In 1898 he published *The Modern Traveler*, a narrative poem about a trio of Englishmen who traveled to Africa for profit and tried to exert their will. One of the characters, a feckless stockbroker named William Blood, relied on machine guns even to settle a wage dispute.

> Blood thought he knew the native mind;
> He said you must be firm, but kind.
> A mutiny resulted.
> I shall never forget the way
> That Blood stood upon this awful day
> Preserved us all from death.
> He stood upon a little mound
> Cast his lethargic eyes around,
> And said beneath his breath:
> "Whatever happens, we have got
> The Maxim Gun, and they have not."
>
> He marked them in their rude advance,
> He hushed their rebel cheers;
> With one extremely vulgar glance
> He broke the Mutineers.
> (I have a picture in my book
> Of how he broke them with a look.)
> We shot and hanged a few, and then
> The rest became devoted men.

As General Kitchener was marching across the desert in 1897, Rudyard Kipling had already commandeered the word *Maxim*. He made it a

verb, describing a British sergeant, a man "with a charm for making riflemen from mud," training his colonial charges in the arts of military rule.

> Said England unto Pharaoh, "I must make a man of you,
> That will stand upon his feet and play the game;
> That will Maxim his oppressor as a Christian ought to do."[69]

In early 1899, Kipling followed with another poem, "The White Man's
Burden," encouraging the United States to invade the Philippines. By
now machine gunnery was a symbol with many meanings. Opponents
of colonialism mocked Kipling's poem for its racist undertone. Henry
Labouchère, a parliamentarian who had used his office to condemn the
activities of the British military and trading companies abroad, wrote a
jeering retort, "The Brown Man's Burden." It was an anticolonial and
anti–machine gun screed, summarized in verse.

> Pile on the brown man's burden:
> And, if ye rouse his hate,
> Meet his old-fashioned reasons
> With Maxims up to date.
> With shells and dumdum bullets
> A hundred times made plain
> The brown man's loss must ever
> Imply the white man's gain.
>
> Pile on the brown man's burden,
> compel him to be free;
> Let all your manifestoes
> Reek with philanthropy.
> And if with heathen folly
> He dares your will dispute,
> Then, in the name of freedom,
> Don't hesitate to shoot.

What did Maxim think? He seemed never to express misgiving at the
uneven killing taking place under his name. There were signs he ap-

proved of and encouraged it. As his fame rose, Maxim became friends with Lord Wolseley, who by then had led two campaigns during which hand-cranked weapons had jammed at crucial times. The general took an early and sustained interest in Maxim's invention and saw it as a superior arm. Maxim in turn enjoyed Lord Wolseley's company, even seeing him as an equal, which, given Maxim's personality and sense of self, was a rare thing. "I sympathized with him deeply because he seemed to be afflicted with a very active imagination," he wrote, adding that it was "a trouble that I had suffered from for many years." When the two men discussed machine-gun use, Lord Wolseley asked Maxim to consider making a machine gun that would fire a larger cartridge, something that might pierce the side of ammunition carts from great distances. Maxim saw the request as a distraction from his gun's main purpose: killing men, especially of the uncivilized sort. "I told him that such a gun would not be so effective as the smaller gun in stopping the mad rush of savages, because it would not fire so many rounds in a minute, and that there was no necessity to have anything larger than the service cartridge to kill a man."[70]

The bloodletting that accompanied British colonialism, represented by the Maxim gun, disturbed liberal members of Parliament. After the initial reports of flattening native formations and shredding native defenses were circulated in London, some of the members decried machine gunnery, worrying even that Maxim guns undermined the cause of Christianity by having Christians associated with such a fearsome thing. Maxim showed little interest; his mind was insulated by a sturdy disgust for all talk of the Christian faith, which he saw as a retreat for the mentally weak and a corrosive on modern life. "The Biblical story of the world and man is, even on broad lines, as far as possible removed from the truth," he wrote. The central narrative of the testaments, he said, "is indefensible." He relished insulting it. "Our civilization," he concluded, "has been retarded more than a thousand years by the introduction of Christianity."[71]

His views on race were equally severe. "A black man," he declared, "has no rights that a white man is bound to respect." Late in life, he described belittling blacks in the United States in the service of his early business interests. Before taking a trip to Atlanta in the early 1870s to oversee the installation of one of his automatic gas machines at the grand Kimball House hotel, he bought a photograph of "a New Guinea nigger; it was the niggerest-looking nigger I had ever seen." Maxim thought the picture might charm his Southern hosts. At the time, Pinckney Pinchback, the son of a slave and the slave's master, was serving as governor of Louisiana, to many a white Southerner's dismay. Maxim wrote the words "Governor Pinchback" on the photograph and carried it in his pocket. At moments he deemed convenient, he produced his photograph for his white clients. It was a Maxim calling card. "Whenever we were discussing niggers and politics I used to take out this photograph and hand it to them," he said. *What are we coming to,* some of the men would exclaim. *Next we will have a gorilla.* Maxim maintained his sense of racial superiority, and his disdain for blacks, throughout his life.[72]

There were signs that some of Maxim's contemporaries understood the role Maxim and his guns had assumed, and were not positively impressed at the ease with which he accepted it. In 1900, Lord Salisbury, Britain's prime minister, attended a banquet of the British Empire League, where Maxim was being feted. The inventor was sixty now, white-haired and with a thick, jutting goatee. He had amassed wealth as his guns had been taken into service by armies across Europe. When Lord Salisbury's turn came to compliment him, the prime minister was ready with his toast.

"Well, gentlemen, do you know, I consider Mr. Maxim to be one of the greatest benefactors the world has ever known?" he said.

Maxim was curious. "And how?" he asked.

"Well," said Salisbury. "I should say that you have prevented more men from dying of old age than any other man that ever lived."[73]

If Maxim had a response, it was not reported by the newspaper correspondent in attendance. The premier's subtly caustic remark did not reflect the official stance. Maxim guns had brought victory to England. Maxim's place was secure. In victory was glory, and official gratitude. He was knighted the following year.

CHAPTER 4

Slaughter Made Industrial: The Great War

Must buck up as I am not dead yet.[1]

RICHARD GATLING'S VISION HAD BEEN WRONG. GIVING ONE SOL-
dier the tool to do the killing of one hundred did not supersede large
armies, and exposure to battle had not been diminished so that men might
be saved for their countries. By the early twentieth century, industrialization had brought forward all manner of martial developments. Some were
natural evolutions in well-established arms: more reliable ammunition
that propelled bullets at extraordinary velocities, more powerful explosives, better steels that allowed for artillery to fire more lethal shells with
greater precision and over longer range. Others were breakthroughs that
made long-awaited technologies ready for war: submarines, war planes,
hand grenades, poison gas. All of these would become characteristic men-
aces of World War I. None of them worked the way Gatling had proposed. Weapons designed to cause more casualties tended to cause more
casualties, not fewer. Machine guns fit into this intricate mix of killing
tools, and more people were dying before them, many more people than
Gatling's vision had allowed. The remaining questions were behavioral.
When would the professional military class realize that machine guns had
become a permanent presence in battle? What would they do about it?
Machine guns, and the possibilities they created for using massed fire for
killing massed soldiers on a large scale, presented new puzzles for officers
to ponder and solve. The killing fields of Omdurman and Lieutenant
Parker's innovations in offensive tactics outside Santiago had been widely

publicized, providing an impetus to explore the questions at hand. But battlefield results did not bring focus to the necessary minds. Machine gunnery remained misunderstood by senior officers in armies around the world.

The marketplace, though, was enthused. Even before machine guns shaped the outcome of closely watched battles, Maxim guns had been finding customers near and far. Demand meant opportunity. Other designers wanted market share, too. New weapons emerged. In 1889, John Moses Browning, a second-generation American gunsmith whose father had operated a small gun works in Utah, began trying to harness another form of energy from a bullet's discharge: the muzzle blast. Like almost anyone who had fired a rifle, Browning had noticed that the report of a rifle was accompanied by the rush of gas that followed the bullet out of the muzzle. He had seen how the blast knocked aside bulrushes in marshes in Utah. This represented unused energy. Browning wanted to put that energy to work. But how to capture gas rushing through a barrel, especially with a bullet in the way, moving at more than two thousand feet per second? Browning held a series of firing experiments,[2] and ultimately made a prototype weapon with a vent inside the barrel, near the muzzle, to provide an alternative route for a portion of the expanding gases; essentially, a tap. In this system, in the tiny fraction of a second after the bullet passed the vent but before it left the barrel, gas whooshed at high pressure through the vent and forced a rod backward, down the length of the gun, toward the trigger. The excess gas was animating a lever. Now it was only a matter of mechanics for that pulse of energy to be converted to the work once done by hand: extracting the spent casing, loading and locking a new cartridge into the chamber, and, as long as the trigger remained depressed and ammunition available, firing the next round to start the cycle anew. By late November 1890, the Browning Brothers Armory, in Salt Lake City, had offered this new design to Colt's Patent Fire Arms Company in Hartford. Five years later, a gas-operated automatic* sold under the name Colt Model 1895 entered the market.[3]

All the while, as Maxim's guns were heading out on colonial expeditions, other weapons were being assembled in gun works around Europe.

---

* Almost sixty years later, this would be the concept used to make the AK-47 an automatic rifle and usher in the assault rifle era.

In Austria, a grand duke and a colonel had created the Skoda machine gun, which a factory in Pilsen produced in many calibers. An Austrian captain had designed another gas-operated machine gun by 1893, and the Hotchkiss firm in France purchased the patent. Nordenfelt introduced a true automatic in 1897, and by 1902 the Madsen automatic machine gun was being touted by the Danes; soon it was tested by the British and the Americans.[4] The German gun works at Spandau, prodded by the kaiser, was busily producing its own Maxim knock-offs. Arms firms saw machine guns as weapons of the future. The era of the hand-cranked gun—the Gatling and its brethren—was all but over, even if a few Gatlings and Gardners remained in military armories. Richard Gatling died in 1903 at the age of eighty-four, at his son-in-law's home in Manhattan's Upper West Side, after returning from a meeting at the editorial offices of *Scientific American*. His business had gone bust. His capital was gone. He had kept his entrepreneurial spirit to the end. Recently he had accepted five hundred dollars from one of his sons to help underwrite a new venture in agricultural plows.[5] But the armaments industry had moved on. Rapid-fire arms had entered the automatic age.

Military officers, especially senior officers, took longer to catch up. The gap between what the arms industry could see and what professional military circles could not created one of the most baffling chapters in the intertwined histories of military technology and tactics. As the services pondered machine guns, traditionalism permeated most Western officer corps. Old prejudices endured. Old arguments continued, though not quite as fiercely as in decades past; the sheer volume of killing at Omdurman had shown that machine guns had a place in battle. It was not because of hostility so much as because of conservatism, along with administrative disarray and sluggishness, that tactics did not adequately shift. The ignorance was not as total as sometimes portrayed.[6] Many armies exchanged their bright uniforms of the nineteenth century for dull-colored field uniforms in khaki or gray. In such attire, soldiers became more difficult for enemy soldiers to spot in rifle and machine-gun sights. And soldiers were instructed to spread out in battle, five paces between each man, to avoid being struck in large numbers by single artillery rounds or bursts of fire. But these changes should have been obvious enough. The blindness that afflicted the senior officer class was extraordinary. In addressing the more difficult questions of developing tactics and doctrine for fighting with and against modern automatic arms, institutional inertia trumped individual intellect. For a range of reasons related to how armies often work, the brighter officers, the gadflies, and the converted who advocated for a material and intellectual investment in machine gunnery were not heard. Some of these officers recognized the potential of concentrated firepower. Others saw the obsolescence of nineteenth-century battlefield tactics and the cherished traditions that adhered to them (one well-known officer observed that "the only advantage in cavalry is the smarter uniform").[7] Some were simply curious, enlivened by tangible shifts in technology or assessments of battles past. Evidence had shown that modern weapons had become sufficiently lethal that opposing soldiers rarely were able to maneuver close enough to one another for a hand-to-hand fight; combatants were getting shot or torn by shrapnel before they could engage in those old-fashioned scrums. One French officer noticed from a review of war records that of sixty-five thousand German casualties listed in the Franco-Prussian War, swords had killed six men.[8] But many advocates of machine gunnery either were of junior grade or had achieved their experience in colonial campaigns in Africa, the Middle East, and Asia. Having used machine guns on practice ranges or to turn back aboriginal rushes, not professional armies, they were regarded as insufficiently schooled in the ways of war between European states.

In the United States, John H. Parker, now an army captain, had published two books on machine gunnery and proposed tactics for the offense and defense. By the early 1900s, he was busy testing a cart that could carry the guns, equipment, and ammunition swiftly about battlefields.[9] He had also proposed an organization for a separate machine-gun service, with units dedicated solely to automatic guns. This followed a kernel first put forth in 1880 by William W. Kimball, an American navy officer, who had recommended selecting American sailors for duty with machine guns for shore defense, for firing from ship to ship, and for pummeling the types of close-in targets that the navy anticipated facing, such as a hostile landing party or torpedo boat. Lieutenant Kimball and Captain Parker were radicals. They sketched out the notion of a professional machine gunner, a specialist who would work within a team. In their visions, these men were to be selected for their stamina, daring, and smarts. "In order that the gun may work up to its full effectiveness, the machine gunners must have a very considerable degree of intelligence, and the utmost steadiness; compared with infantrymen armed with single loading shoulder pieces, they must be as clever mechanics are to common laborers—they must be capable of working with a killing machine instead of a killing tool."[10] These officers' precise organizational proposals would never be accepted, but their underlying idea was sound. Professional machine gunners, with separate training and distinct duties, would in time become common. But not yet.

In the early twentieth century, the idea did not take hold. The military bureaucracy moved bureaucratically. Ordnance officials in the United States continued to test machine guns, and while there was a sense that machine guns had a place in battle, no one was quite sure where. One army major, commanding a battalion at Fort Leavenworth, requested a pair of machine guns for his battalion and the army provided them;[11] this hardly signaled that the army as an institution was fully invested in trying to find the weapons' ideal use. Enthusiasm was further dampened by lingering worries about reliability. The American army had purchased Colt's Model 1895 guns and used them in the war in the Philippines, but they were air-cooled and tended to overheat; officers in the field found them fussy. This enduring reputation for unreliability undercut the advocates' cause. Worries about ammunition consumption were also an obstacle. How was an army supposed to supply units with guns that fired 500, 600, 700, or 800 rounds a minute? The answer, which eluded the quartermasters and generals, was that technical rates of fire were theoretical. In practice, machine gunners fired in short bursts. When facing machine-gun fire, targets were either knocked down or scattered. No target presented itself for very long. Ammunition consumption did pose new logistical challenges. That was irrefutably true. But these challenges were not the impossible demand that detractors imagined them to be.

Richard Gatling, an inventor of killing technologies who cast himself as an idealist, had been a crusader for rapid-fire arms as instruments for peace. Hiram Maxim, the self-taught engineer and mischief-maker from backwoods Maine, became a premier vendor of machine guns in nearly perfected form and converted Gatling's dream into wealth. Under their hands, machine guns had sprouted from the industrial conditions of nineteenth-century America to become global products that allowed armies to arm themselves for killing on a prodigious scale. But machine gunnery in the United States military remained a haphazard field. The

American military entered the twentieth century with inventories of weapons of different calibers and designs, without a machine-gun doctrine, and with neither a standard arm nor a clear training plan. In 1903, the army held new tests and selected a Maxim water-cooled gun as its new standard machine gun.[12] This decision would not long hold. There was similar confusion in Britain, even though the British army had adopted the Maxim ten years earlier. Russia had already become a minor machine-gun power. It had embraced rapid-fire arms since the Gatling gun first became available after the Civil War, and had since procured Maxims and distributed them in the field. Otherwise, only Germany kept pressing ahead, manufacturing guns and designing a doctrine to use them in special machine-gun units, which colonels and generals could control, moving them about the battlefield as necessary so firepower could be massed at critical moments and places, roughly as Captain Parker had suggested.[13] Germany had certain psychological advantages over the other Western powers as it pursued its arming spree. It had not been interested in machine guns until Kaiser Wilhelm II saw Maxim's gun in 1887; this meant that it began its association with machine gunnery with a weapon that worked well, and it did not have to overcome an internal institutional bias stemming from having invested in Gatlings or Gardners that jammed in the era when ammunition was unreliable.

Elsewhere, as machine-gun salesmen worked European officer clubs and test ranges, armies hewed to their traditions, assuming that when they fought again they would fight much as they had before, perhaps with victory to be carried by a decisive charge. Courage was praised, the philosophies of disciplined unit formations preached. War was seen as an activity to be carried by determined men, whose foes were broken by fright during a stoic advance to the bayonet fight. The attitude was well established in successful military units: Moral force was superior to material might, and men were supreme. In its way, the attitude marked one of the older and more enduring vulnerabilities of military units steeped in their past success and lore. Unleavened by an understanding of the changing tools available for battle, the attitude led men who should have known better to believe that machine guns were mere devices. Years after officers had personally observed the effects of machine guns in war, the brass clung almost mystically to the romance of close-quarter battle and championed tactics that Maxim guns had made obsolete. In their bias some officers even scoffed at the rifle. "It must be accepted as a principle that the rifle, effective as it is, cannot replace the effect produced by the speed of the horse, the magnetism of the charge, and the terror of cold steel,"[14] one turn-of-the-century British training manual said.

Such were the daydreams. They could not be extinguished, even by clear accounts from distant wars. Military bureaucracies, as they considered incorporating machine guns into their armies, dawdled indecisively in every Western country but Germany. The thinking was fully blinkered. Senior officers recognized the effects of withering bursts of fire upon massed combatants, having heard reports of the felling of heaps of Arabs and Africans who advanced in formation toward machine guns. They were somehow unable to accept what might happen when such fire was directed against their own ranks. And then they were given another chance.

In 1904, after years of competition between the Russian and Japanese empires in the northwestern Pacific, the contest erupted into the Russo-Japanese War. Here machine guns and poor tactics were to combine for the bloodiest results yet. The origins of the war were simple. During the Boxer Uprising, from 1898 through 1901, Czar Nicholas II had dispatched Russian troops to Manchuria. He had not withdrawn them when the uprising ended. Instead, the Russian garrison grew, angering Japan, which saw Russia encroaching on its sphere of influence. Negotiations for a Russian withdrawal led nowhere, and in 1904 Japan struck, attacking the Russian navy at the Yellow Sea harbor of Port Arthur and sending infantry across the Yalu River to push overland for the port. En route, the Japanese divisions met Russian units, which were equipped with Maxim guns, organized into a company per division. Each company had sections of eight Maxims equipped with sixty-six hundred cartridges per gun.[15] The czar's infantry was not highly regarded. "The Russian soldier, when sober and not brutalized by slaughter, is a great, strong, kind, superstitious child; as good a fellow as ever stepped, but always a child," wrote the correspondent present for the *London Times,* who was a former colonel himself. "Given an educated and highly trained corps of officers of a good class, capable of instructing, caring for, and leading him with judgment and skill, the Russian soldier would go far. But there is no such corps of officers in Russia."[16] No matter the poor reputation, machine guns turned the Russians into lethal defenders of held ground. After a battle along the approaches to the port, a Japanese lieutenant, Tadayoshi Sakurai, examined captured Russian Maxims. The Japanese army had its own collection of Hotchkiss machine guns, and its officers were beginning to use them in effective ways, especially in firing in support of Japanese attacks. But Lieutenant Sakurai had seen machine gunnery from the other perspective. He knew what happened to Japanese units when they faced Maxim guns. He looked upon the captured Russian Maxims as almost otherworldly tools. His description marked one of the earliest first-person accounts of the experience of coming under modern automatic fire. "This was the firearm most dreaded by us," he wrote:

> A large iron plate serves the purpose of a shield, through which aim is taken, and the trigger can be pulled while the gun is moving upward, downward, to the left, or to the right. More than six hundred bullets are pushed out automatically in one minute, as if a long continuous rod of balls was being thrown out of the gun. It can also be made to sprinkle its shot as roads are watered with a hose. It can cover a larger or smaller space, or fire to a greater or less distance as the gun wills. Therefore, if one becomes a target of this terrible engine of destruction, three or four shots may go through the same space in rapid succession, making the wound very large. . . . And the sound it makes! Heard close by, it is a rapid succession of tap, tap, tap; but from a distance it sounds like a power loom heard late at night when everything else is hushed. It is a sickening, horrible sound! The Russians regard this machine as their best friend, and certainly it did very much as a means of defense. They were wonderfully clever in the use of this machine. They would wait till our men came very near them, four or five *ken** only, and just at the moment when we proposed to shout a triumphant Banzai, this dreadful machine would begin to sweep over us with the besom of destruction, the results being hills and mounds of dead.[17]

---

* A Japanese unit of measure, approximately six feet. By Lieutenant Sakurai's estimates, then, the Russians were opening fire at a distance of about thirty feet.

Japanese ground forces besieged Port Arthur late in summer 1904. They found that the Russians had prepared. The port was on a peninsula, and the soldiers had spent months fortifying the hills overlooking it. They had also dug extensive trenches and filled the lanes though which the Japanese soldiers might attack with barbed wire. Lights were rigged to cover the approaches in darkness. Maxim guns watched over it all; by one count, thirty-eight Maxims in all.[18] Circumstances were ripe for disaster. The Japanese infantry was fired with a culture in which to die in a battle was a supreme honor, and its officers faced a tactical problem for which their training offered no obvious or doctrinal solution. This was not entirely their fault. Until that time, there were no widely understood tactics for overcoming the types of modern defenses before them; the book on machine gunnery and tactics had not yet been written. The result was a horror. Eager for battle, the Japanese officers ordered human wave attacks across the open ground. One of the attacks, the Ninth Division's assault on East Panlung, showed war's new shape.

Sappers were sent first, at night, and managed to breach the Russian wire in several places, cutting open lanes through which the infantry of the Seventh Regiment might follow. The Japanese regimental commander ordered the First Battalion through the wire in the darkness before 5:00 A.M. The soldiers went up the hill without cover and were stopped in place by sweeping machine-gun fire; not a man advanced through the breaches. The regimental commander led the remaining battalion in a second attack over the same ground. He was quickly killed. The Second Battalion suffered the same fate as the first. In the predawn gloom, the division commander tried to watch from afar. He knew nothing of what was happening, beyond that the volume of Russian fire was deafening and the absence of a Banzai call was discouraging. The scene which revealed itself at daybreak was worse than any sense of foreboding had anticipated: "The hillside was thickly strewn with dead and dying, and in front and around the gaps in the wire entanglements the dead bodies were piled three or four high. No progress had been made anywhere, and the small surviving force of the gallant 7th was cut off from retreat by the murderous fire."[19] The division attacked again by daylight, sending another regiment of men over the same ground, bayonets high. These men, too, were cut down. A night attack ended in the same fashion.

This was but one episode among many. For weeks the Japanese

attacked. The Russian garrisons were too isolated to resist indefinitely. In the end, the Japanese soldiers captured the port. But by the time Port Arthur changed hands in early 1905, the Japanese commanders had lost more than forty thousand[20] of their army's soldiers in the war, and they had repeated their tactical mistakes throughout, sending exposed troops forward again and again. Lieutenant Sakurai, whose infantry company was annihilated, summed up the mentality of soldiers sent on a mission understood to be suicidal. "We were all ready for death when leaving Japan," he wrote. "Men going to battle of course cannot expect to come back alive. But in this particular battle, to be ready for death was not enough; what was required of us was a determination not to fail to die."[21]

In the lieutenant's last action, he almost got his wish. The soldiers set out on foot with twenty-inch bayonets affixed to their Type 30 carbines, picking their way through stacks of corpses from the waves before. The company commander, a captain, brandished a sword in the charge. He was killed. This was Lieutenant Sakurai's moment. "From henceforth I command Twelfth Company!" he shouted. His command would be brief. He ordered a renewed charge, but soon the fire was thick and the men around him were few. What had been a company was a handful of survivors, including the lieutenant, who had been shot through the right hand. The Russians counterattacked. The remnants of Twelfth Company fell back, consolidated, and were trapped as the Russians brought up machine guns to finish the fight. The lieutenant was wounded and suffered the indignity of survival. It meant that he was able to tell what happened at the end. "Men on both sides fell like grass," he said.[22]

This was not a distant colonial fight. It was a head-to-head conventional war between rival empires and soldiers bearing modern arms, fought in the presence of Western military attachés. The attachés observing the battles did a mixed job of assessing and reporting the discernable facts. Some noted that the Russian guns were effective. Lieutenant Colonel A. Haldane, a British attaché, wrote that Japanese attacks were "checked by machine gun and rifle fire, and there is no doubt that a strong feeling exists in the infantry that the presence of machine guns with the Russian army confers upon it a distinct advantage."[23] American reports were uneven. One officer reported that the Japanese had used their own machine guns quite effectively, and that Japanese officers had learned during the war that machine guns could be used offensively as well as in defense of held ground—an echo of what Captain Parker had proposed for ten years, and had proved outside Santiago. But another American officer wrote that "the machine gun [had] played a useful but not great part in the war."[24] As a body, those who could carry the word out—military observers and war correspondents alike—were distracted from the obvious: that in the age of machine guns assault tactics urgently needed to be rethought. Colonel Louis A. La Garde, of the United States Army Medical Corps, later reviewed casualty data from the war and noticed something that should have been readily observable by any attaché on hand: the military futility of a bayonet charge. Of 170,600 Russian soldiers documented as wounded or killed, bayonet wounds accounted for 0.4 percent.[25] More wounds, Colonel La Garde found, were caused by stones. And yet some Westerners present at the war still succumbed to a fascination for the spirit of the Japanese soldiers, missing the technical and tactical points while filing dispatches describing what they regarded as fanaticism, whether bizarre or sublime. What did Westerners have to learn from the Japanese experience, after all, when everyone knew that no Western army would resort to attacks by human wave? One correspondent's dispatch was typical:

It is said that when men have made up their mind to die they act and speak like gods. That day, when the fight was at its fiercest and the bullets were falling like rain, Lieutenant Sakamoto, who had been sent out towards the right flank on scouting duty, found himself pressed by a greatly superior force of the enemy and unable either to advance or to retreat. He sent an orderly to ask the commanding officer for final instructions. The reply was, "Go back and say to the Lieutenant, 'Die.'" The orderly, saluting, rode off. What a grand order—"die." The one word, "die"![26]

Germany drew a different lesson. Kaiser Wilhelm II had continued his support for machine guns, and by 1899 the German military had four-gun machine-gun batteries. In 1908, each regiment had batteries of six guns, and the German army underwrote extensive inquiry and experimentation into how best to use them. All the while, the gun works at Spandau were producing more of its Maxim clones. The other Western militaries breezed through the early twentieth century without clarity on

how they might use machine guns in the next war. Brigadier General
J. Franklin Bell, the American army's chief of staff, noted that his service
did not have a doctrine, or even a plan, for the guns on order.

> The War Department is now confronted with this situation: We have
> adopted a type of gun, mount and pack outfit, and contracted for a
> considerable number [120 for field service and 75 for coastal fortifi-
> cations], and actual deliveries [80 guns] are being made pursuant to
> this contract; but no plan for the distribution and use of these guns
> has been formulated.[27]

Everything was set for disaster when World War I broke out.

In summer 1914, as one nation after another declared war, Germany invaded Belgium and made a thrust into France. Under prewar agreements,
Great Britain was committed to provide France with military aid. Much
of the British army was spread about the globe on imperial duty, but the
British Expeditionary Force, or BEF—a contingent of six regular British
infantry divisions and another division of cavalry—quickly crossed the
Channel and took its place between the beleaguered Belgian and French
militaries. Though the expeditionary force was small (Kaiser Wilhelm II
called it a "contemptible little army"), it was experienced, highly trained,
and professional, and it made a determined fight. But it was outnumbered
and outgunned. Within weeks its ranks were thinned. Soon the BEF was
joined by the British version of reserves, known as the Territorials. These
units, too, suffered heavy losses.

The near destruction of the core of the British regular army meant
that Britain resorted to a massive recruiting drive to build what Lord
Kitchener, now the minister of war, would call the New Army. "We have
been asked who will volunteer for Foreign service and I have said I will,"
wrote Alfred Chater, one of the men mobilizing for war, in a note to his
girlfriend as he made his choice that summer. "It was put to us in such
a way that unless one is married it is almost impossible to say anything
else." A letter soon after was rueful: "It would be a splendid experience for
those who come back."[28] The early months in Europe saw a war of movement, with armies racing across the countryside trying to outflank each

other and check each other's advance. But gradually the lines extended, and extended more, and settled by the fall into the Western Front. The opposing sides faced each other across a maze of trenches, pillboxes, and barbed wire. A modern form of siege warfare set in, as the Allies waited for replacement units to reinforce the lines and allow for an offensive to dislodge the entrenched German troops.

The imbalance of firepower was devastating. The German army went to war with more machine guns, and distributed them more widely, than any of their opponents. It began the war having issued sixteen machine guns to every infantry battalion, while the British army had issued two—thus part of the mismatch faced by the British Expeditionary Force in the war's opening months.[29] In 1892 the German gun works at Spandau had entered into an agreement with Ludwig Loewe and Co. (later the Deutsche Waffen and Munitions Fabrik) that gave the German firm the right to manufacture Maxim-pattern machine guns for sales to Germany and its united governments. Though many German officers initially resisted machine guns, the events at Omdurman and the Russo-Japanese War had made their impression, and by the early twentieth century, manufacturing had begun in earnest of the German modification Maschinengewehr 08, or MG08. The German military had at least forty-nine hundred of these Maxims by the start of the war. Manufacturing accelerated after hostilities began.[30] Even Germany's colonial troops were equipped with machine guns, which led to one of the failed British actions outside of Europe and demonstrated yet again that the British military mind did not yet grasp matters at hand.

In November 1914, a British naval and infantry force moved against East Africa, hoping to push aside the thin contingent of German soldiers along the coast and assert British control over the continent. The crown's plan included an attack on Tanga, a seaport located in what is now Tanzania. An amphibious British force, accompanied by Indian units, landed outside the city and passed through most of the tropical forest around the port. The enemy's pickets were waiting. As the invasion force drew within six hundred yards of Tanga's outskirts, the Germans and their colonial units opened fire. "Bullets came thick, men falling in all directions," wrote Captain Richard Meinertzhagen, a British intelligence officer who went ashore in the landing party's little boats. "Half of the 13th Rajputs turned at once, broke into a rabble and bolted, carrying most of the 61st Pioneers with them." In the afternoon, the invasion force managed to round up enough of its scattered soldiers to push forward and into the city. "I had collected some 70 Rajputs and two private soldiers of the North Lancs and got them back to the firing line," the captain wrote. As these small contingents pressed on, they were met by machine guns in the hands of native African soldiers under German command. This was both a reversal and precursor. For decades the British had used machine guns to bloody effect in Africa. Now Africans were pointing machine guns back.

> Machine guns were deadly and swept every approach, every house spitting fire. The Kashmir Infantry and two companies of Rajputs were doing well. I particularly admired the pluck of young Hammick of the Rajputs, quite a lad and appearing to revel in bullets. I joined on to some Kashmiri Dogras and we were doing well, taking house after house near the Customs House, when we came to a broad street which was an inferno of machine-gun and rifle fire. This brought us up short. My party was twenty-five men, and nine fell at the first attempt to cross.

Facing heavy fire, the British and Indian soldiers lost their hold on the city. Soon the troops had "dwindled away or were shot and I found myself with two men in the Customs House," Captain Meinertzhagen wrote. The British attack was broken. Soldiers were scattered along the route of their advance, many shaking with fear. Bullets had struck beehives in the trees, and the insects swarmed upon the miserable force, stinging soldiers cowering on the ground. A British ship, in the harbor, was shelling the shore randomly. Some of the incoming rounds exploded among the British troops. The breakdown was complete. "Most of the men had gone, we were all parched with thirst, ammunition was short and the last remnants of the British firing line were a few British officers, each fighting their own battle," the captain wrote. Tanga would remain in German hands. British plans were checked by machine-gun fire. Africa was not ever to be the same, though the salient point about machine gunnery was largely lost on the defeated soldiers, who commiserated not about the difficulties, even the pointlessness, of using old tactics against these modern weapons, but about being defeated by Africans.

"The Lancs are very dejected at having lost so many friends, for their best have gone," Meinertzhagen wrote. "They also feel the disgrace of losing a fight against black troops. They are not a first-class battalion."[31] The captain offered a similarly dismissive reaction to the Rajputs' fear when they first came under fire. The Indians, he wrote, "were all jabbering like terrified monkeys." Both comments were instructive. Racism still informed colonial operations. And Captain Meinertzhagen, who published his diaries years later and with the benefit of seeing the outcome on the Western Front, could not, even with the passing of time, understand the technical picture for what it was: Intensive machine-gun fire could hardly be beaten back by men with rifles using tactics of yore.

By this time, the Western Front was taking on an air of permanence, and the war in Europe was settling into the shape for which it would be remembered. The trench systems were a complicated and carefully considered network. A set of forward trenches served as the front line, supporting trenches were dug farther back, and the reserve trenches farther still—all part of a defense in depth that could absorb an enemy thrust. Along the lines, trenches rarely ran in straight lines for any distance; soldiers dug them according to the contours of the countryside—the sides of hills, across knolls, in positions overlooking concealed routes of approach—in ways that gave the occupants a commanding view of the ground out front. This maximized their defensive potential by providing clear fields of fire into likely infiltration routes. On level ground trenches were typically cut into the earth in zigs and zags, a precaution so that if an artillery or mortar shell landed squarely inside, or an enemy infantryman lobbed in a grenade, the blast would be contained and casualties would be limited to the few unlucky souls in one small bit of ditch. But the defense was not simply linear, weaving, and wide. It was buttressed by strong points, concentrations of soldiers and weapons in woodlots or higher ground where they could fight from even more sturdy positions. These strong points were often near enough to one another to be mutually supporting by interlocking fire. In front of all this were listening posts, from which sentries could give early warning of an attack or approaching patrol. And throughout the front proper, snipers scanned the terrain from concealed positions, ready to shoot any man who dared to expose himself by day. When the sun was up, the warrens of earthworks could seem eerily deserted, save for noise and the smoke rising from cooking fires. Soldiers learned not to lift their heads above their parapets until after dark. This lesson was reinforced by the fate of the incautious, who often were shot by high-powered rifle bullets in the head.

Between the opposing trenches was No-Man's-Land, a ribbon of unoccupied territory that resembled the ground where Japanese soldiers had perished by the thousands at Port Arthur. No-Man's-Land was narrow in many areas, and soldiers listened to their enemies' voices. "In my part of the line the trenches are only 50 or 60 yards apart in some places, and we can hear the Germans talking," Captain Chater wrote his girlfriend after arriving in France. "They often shout to us in English and we respond with cries of 'waiter!'"[32] In other places, one thousand yards separated the soldiers. This open ground was watched over by machine guns and by artillery observers, who were ready to call down fire onto troops in the open by day, or at night, to send flares aloft that might illuminate enemy patrols. The machine guns of the time only faintly resembled their predecessors of fifty years before. No longer were they wheeled about on heavy timber frames between carriage wheels, to be mistaken for cannon. They had shrunk, some of them to under one hundred pounds, including their tripod mounts and other gear, and could be rigged low to the ground. The tripod served as a stable firing platform, making the guns far more accurate than handheld rifles, and allowing gunners to traverse the barrels in sweeps. Smokeless powder in the cartridges of the time meant that gunners crouching behind a machine gun, firing through a slot in the earth, were difficult to spot.

Given the intricacy of the defenses, and the difficulties they posed, large battles were rare. The soldiers on both sides of the trenches followed routines: a full alert, known as "stand-to," at dawn and dusk. Nightfall brought patrols or manual labor repairing earthworks, filling sandbags, and the like. The soldiers slept in snatches by day. Helmets, the most valuable piece of personal defensive equipment in the entire war, were rarely issued to British soldiers during the first two years of fighting, and heads were unnecessarily exposed to shrapnel and ricochets. Front-line officers carried pistols and swords, weapons that were useless except at exceptionally short range. The British Lee-Enfield rifles were not often fired. Riflemen almost never saw a clear target. The large British bayonet was almost

universally issued, though as one historian dryly observed, it was principally "useful for chopping wood and other domestic work."[33]

New battalions arrived at the Western Front with roughly one thousand men. Without major battles, they could expect to lose thirty soldiers
a month to injury or death, and another thirty to disease.[34] Those not
struck by German ordnance or weakened by illness endured a singular
ordeal: a maze of rats, rot, tinned food, infection, and trash. They were
soaked and muddy much of the year and bitterly cold in winter. Random
violence—a sniper shot or an incoming artillery or mortar round—was a
constant threat. To fortify the young soldiers, many officers issued swigs
of rum before missions, hoping to lift spirits in the face of the fear and
ugliness ahead.

In fall 1914, as the British units fought in these woeful conditions, new
volunteers were being rushed through preparations to take their place.
Swarms of men were being kitted out and drilled. Equipment remained
scarce. "Rifles and bayonets are also at a premium," wrote Private Arthur Anderson, a teenager who joined the Second Battalion, Ninth Royal
Scots. "Only a matter of dozen ancient patterns of each being available
per company, with the result being that our progress in rifle drill is somewhat slow."[35] Private Anderson was a meticulous penman and easy writer,
and his diary documented the state of British training as he was converted from a Scottish boy to an infantryman in kilt, deemed ready for
war. By late November, he had been issued a rifle. In December his unit
was practicing maneuvers in city parks, and later in a system of training
trenches dug into a golf course at Riccarton. There was much prewar mo-
notony and dreariness: inspections, inoculations, church parades, bland
food, and crowded quarters. The practice trenches offered a hint of real-
ism and could have been used to drill a wide range of tactics for attacking
German lines defended by machine guns, except that thoughtful tactics
for that sort of battle did not yet exist. Brigadier General Ivor Maxse,
a senior British officer regarded as a premier tactician, dispensed wisdom
that looked not much different from what the Japanese army had tried at
Port Arthur. "A single line will fail; two will usually fail, three lines will
sometimes fail, but four will usually succeed," General Maxse said—an
official endorsement of attack by human wave.[36] Private Anderson waited

to be old enough to ship to France. In the interim, he stood picket duty against amphibious landing and collared drunken soldiers home on leave. His record of the training he received reads like the chronicle of an alert and intelligent young man sent nonchalantly to die. "The rest of the time is taken up with the usual routine of drills and exercises," he wrote, "and putting in a good deal of firing practice and bayonet fighting."

British fascination with the bayonet persisted in the face of all evidence that it was a weapon long outmoded. In theory, the mettle of disciplined men moving forward into fire to slash and stab their foes was enough to unnerve almost any enemy force. In practice, moving forward with a big knife into machine-gun fire, across open ground and in extended lines, was not much different from Zulu warriors attacking British Gatlings with spears at Ulundi in 1879, or Sudanese men rushing with swords toward General Kitchener's Maxim guns along the Nile in 1898. Casualty reports from World War I were not fully reliable, especially in real time. Lists were incomplete or repetitious, and there was no standardized method among the Allies for collecting and distributing information crucial to assessing the wounding agents in war. But the available statistics, for all of their flaws, virtually roared on one point: Bayonets were unquestionably ineffective in what war had become. One military critic wrote in February 1916 that data collected from a French army corps that had been in heavy action found that bayonets caused 0.5 percent of casualties, while shells, grenades, trench explosions, shrapnel, and bullets accounted for a combined 92.5 percent (7 percent of the injuries were of undetermined cause).[37] That even one-half of one percent of the casualties were caused by bayonets was a testimony less to their martial utility than to the fact that both sides insisted on fighting with them. Such data might have suggested to the war's planners, and to the designers of infantry-school curricula, that perhaps it was time to explore an alternative set of weapons and means of fighting. And yet as fresh troops were being drilled to enter the war, prowess with the bayonet remained near the center of infantry training. Thus the British manual on the subject, a terrifying period piece:

> The bayonet is essentially an offensive weapon. In a bayonet assault all ranks go forward to kill or be killed, and only those who have developed skill and strength by constant training will be able to kill. The spirit of the bayonet must be inculcated into all ranks, so that

they go forward with the aggressive determination and confidence of superiority born of continued practice, without which a bayonet charge will not be effective.[38]

There happened to be other factors that made bayonet charges ineffective; Hiram Maxim and the European gun works that received licenses to manufacture his patterns had seen to that. But the romance with cold steel endured. Traditions—and bad ideas—die more slowly than men.

As Private Anderson waited for his turn in France, news from the front was grim. The Royal Scots' First Battalion suffered heavy casualties soon after it landed, and two of his friends were killed. By this time, early in 1915 and after a winter of misery, British troops had shed illusions of war. The early cheer had vanished. One noncommissioned officer, A. J. Rixon of the London Irish Rifles, also left a diary of his experiences. It was a laconic account of daily life and tactical choices that filled him with anguish and disgust. "Trenches are like a maze only a trifle more dangerous," he wrote, describing the difficulty of moving any distance on even the friendly side of the line. "An awful time. 1½ miles doubled up like a pocket knife. Reached the corner but then had to go along a road about a mile under fire all the time. One man hit in the leg, almost wish it had been me, if this is a usual thing."[39] As his unit prepared for an attack, his diary entries assumed an air of helplessness and dread. "Once more I wish I was single, no game for a man with responsibilities cant do as would like.* Life not my own."[40] When he watched another unit return, his emotions almost overwhelmed him. "Not many came out unwounded, those who did all have souvenirs, helmets etc. Some wounds sickening but boys bearing up wonderfully no grumbling. Enemy throwing petrol bombs on wounded, and many burned to death ammunition exploding in meantime. Snipers refuse to let S.Bs† go near wounded between lines many shot if attempt to move. God help enemy if boys ever get at them." Sergeant Rixon was not a young man. He was thirty years old and responsible for keeping his company's soldiers ready and leading them in battle. But he was spent. Worn

---

* The spelling and grammatical errors of Rixon's shorthand are retained here.

† Stretcher-bearers.

down and confused, he was near despair. "The language in this trench is awful," he wrote. "Fed up with everything. Its not war but murder."

The resolve he finally found within was rooted in resignation. "Must buck up," he wrote, "as I am not dead yet."

Still the tactics had not evolved. The London Irish Rifles went into battle with its soldiers marching in extended lines across No-Man's-Land. Sergeant Rixon saw the madness of this even while urging his men along, enforcing the absurdity by shouting orders to keep the formation intact. He described himself as:

> . . . personally being more or less guilty of inanely and with parrot like frequency exhorting the boys to keep their 5 paces, although after the first 300 yards I couldn't see more than 50 yards each side of me, owing to the smoke, and vision obscured by smoke helmet. I realised after a time that my efforts were being wasted the smoke helmet smothering my voice so shut up, confining myself to watching if any of the boys went down so as to replace them by carrying men whom we had with us for that purpose. I don't wish to give the impression by the above that I was absolutely coolness itself; I wasn't by any means, but in a horrible state of funk, as men were falling all around me.[41]

As the army gained experience of the sort that was unraveling Sergeant Rixon, the replacement soldiers were drilled to fight in the same ways. Back in Scotland, Private Anderson's battalion's "bayonet fighting team" was preparing for a military tourney and exhibition for local dignitaries. "When the great day arrives the weather is broken, and by the time it is our turn to go on the rain is coming down in torrents and the ground is practically deserted, with the exception of the judges and a few notables, all of whom are comfortably settled in a covered stand," he wrote. "Clad only in shorts and singlets we bravely carry through our performance." The British army had at last realized that it needed machine guns in far greater numbers than it had them. A royal warrant in fall 1915 had ordered the creation of a Machine Gun Corps.[42] And in addition to the redoubtable Vickers, the British army was also issuing Lewis guns, light machine guns of American design that had been rejected in the United States but that were being quickly produced at a gun works in Birmingham, England. The gun weighed less than thirty pounds and could be moved about the battlefield much more quickly than the heavier guns of the day. But in all of Private Anderson's diary, there is no mention of machine-gun training for the war. He was busy mastering his rifle's potential as a twentieth-century spear.

All the while, the battalion was shrinking. Its members were being sent to France as replacements for the ravaged battalions on the front. In April 1916, Private Anderson's turn to ship out came, and he departed for the French countryside, where he soon encountered garish sights. Almost two full years into the war, some soldiers were not yet in dull-colored clothes. "French soldiers, in their red and blue uniforms, are also much in evidence now, and much amusement is caused by the sight of French Cavalry, complete with brass helmets and breast-plates," he wrote. "In some cases the helmets are covered with sacking and breast-plates daubed with some dull substances, but there is no doubt that such a get-up could hardly be considered appropriate to modern war conditions."

Private Anderson was assigned to the infamous Labyrinth, a warren of trenches below the Germans in Vimy Ridge. A French unit had held the position in the winter, before the Scots arrived, and had buried its dead soldiers in the parapets; as the soil eroded in the warm spring rains, decomposing bits of corpses slipped out, filling the trenches with nauseating smells and occupying the attention of rats. Private Anderson had his first encounter with the German machine guns, Maxim's offspring from Spandau, when he was part of a night patrol sent into No-Man's-Land. A stray round passed through another soldier's knee. The young Scots huddled near the wounded man, hoping he would not cry out and reveal their location. It was no use.

> The Germans heard all right, but their fusillade of bullets passed wide of us. We completed our job and, helping our wounded man along, returned cautiously in what we trusted was the right direction. No sounds could be heard from the trench before us, and we were compelled to lie flat in the mud, hoping to get some sign to let us know we were at our own lines. After a bit, getting fed-up lying in the dirt our sergeant decided to risk giving a shout. Fortunately for us it was answered by one of our own sentries, and we scrambled back to the shelter of the trench, but not before my dear old friend

Miller, hit by a bullet, dropped dead over the parapet. This is a hot spot for machine-guns.

Private Anderson's indoctrination continued its ghastly escalation. In mid-May 1916, the Germans began a heavy bombardment along the lines. Within two days shells were landing and exploding on Private Anderson's sector through the night. His unit was put on alert ahead of an anticipated ground attack. The battalion began to lose men in the barrage, including a captain, who was carried past dead. The side of his head was gone. That evening the German artillery fell silent. The attack came.

They are moving across the open being pretty well bunched up in places, and affording an excellent target. Our front-line is unable to stop their advance however, and we in the support line get orders to open fire, and pour a steady rifle and machine-gun fire into them. By now, also, our field guns have started shelling and the attackers are being badly cut up but they reach our front line, which has now been vacated, and our own troops are doubling back over the open to our support trenches.

British guns pounded their own front-line trenches, hoping to dislodge the German soldiers. Private Anderson knew what this meant. He waited for the order to counterattack. When it came, he experienced his first taste of running into concentrated machine-gun fire.

It is still twilight when the signal is given and we go over the top, advancing across the open ground with difficulty, as two lines of trenches have to be "jumped" by means of narrow bridges, which causes much congestion. Everyone is in the charge; stretcher-bearers, signalers and the Lewis gunners, and we make our way blindly forward through a chaos of bursting shells and machine-gun bullets. It is only possible to see one's nearest neighbors in the smoke, the sense of direction is entirely lost, and there is an awful feeling of being very much alone. The noise, which at first was deafening, is hardly noticed after a few minutes, shell splinters and bullets are practically ignored, and dead and wounded lying in the way are only looked upon with a sort of mild interest. The sole idea seems to be to keep on until something happens. It appears as though it would be impossible to get through such an inferno, but at last we reach the trench. The Germans have put up a stout resistance but we managed to get about sixty prisoners before they break away for their own lines.

The fighting stalled. Anderson's company had retaken its trench. Thirty-five of its soldiers were killed. Nearly one hundred others were wounded. The trench routine returned.

Equipment can drive tactics. In a nimble military organization it often does. The British misapprehension of machine guns was related in part to the fact that British units had few machine guns of their own, which meant few officers and soldiers had experience with automatic fire before facing it from the opposite side. Those who did gain a sound technical and tactical understanding were often incapacitated or killed, which resulted in a regular winnowing of hard-won knowledge. Where were the British machine guns? This was a question being asked at the top. During 1915, David Lloyd George, then serving as the nation's minister of munitions, tried to determine why the British were underequipped with a weapon that the enemy had stockpiled. He found that from August 1914 to June 1915, the British military requested only 1,792 machine guns from the Vickers plant. "This would work out to two machine guns per battalion with none left for training at home," he wrote, with palpable anger, and "no margin for losses or breakages." The munitions minister, soon to become the British premier, excoriated the senior officer class. "It took our generals many months of terrible loss to realise the worth of the machine gun. They were converted by representations from officers who had witnessed its deadly effect in action. The farther they were from the fighting line the less impressed were military commanders with the power and peril of the machine gun," he wrote. He added a caustic aside: "It is an incredible story for anyone who had no actual experience of the fanatical hostility displayed by the Higher Commands to any new ideas."

In summer 1915, the munitions ministry confronted Lord Kitchener about the military's pitiable requests for automatic arms and demanded estimates for future manufacture. Kitchener, having commanded the British and Egyptian forces at Omdurman, might have been expected to know something about the machine gun's value in combat. But in a meeting with Sir Eric Geddes, one of Lloyd George's deputies, he was indifferent. He had no idea how many guns the forces would need. Nor was he able to offer guidelines for purchases through early 1916.

"Do you think I am God Almighty that I can tell you what is wanted nine months ahead?" Kitchener said.

Geddes insisted. At last Kitchener answered that "the proportion was to be two machine guns per battalion as a minimum, four as a maximum and anything above four was a luxury." Geddes was disgusted. ("This was the opinion of the Secretary of War, who was looked upon generally as our greatest soldier," he wrote.) He asked Kitchener to sign a memorandum to that effect.

Geddes, satisfied that he had a document that would enable him to deliver more machine guns to the front, presented the memorandum to Lloyd George. Lloyd George was aghast. He had quietly taken to talking on his own with soldiers returning from the horrors of France, and had been told repeatedly that the troops needed more machine guns. As minister of munitions, he had no authority to exceed the secretary of war's request. He seemed not to care. He almost tore up Kitchener's memo, but Geddes managed to save it for posterity. Lloyd George then broke policy.

"Take Kitchener's maximum [four per battalion]," he said. "Square it, multiply that result by two; and when you are in sight of that, double it again for good luck."

In this way, over the objections of its most senior officer, the British military began to get its guns. By 1918 it would have 138,349 more machine guns on order. It planned for nearly 200,000 more in 1919. The stock on hand in June 1915, roughly at the time of the spat between Geddes and Kitchener, was 1,330 machine guns in all. Lloyd George was unapologetic to the end. "Nor do I think that the Army ever had cause to regret that the supply proposed by Lord Kitchener in July, 1915, was increased sixteenfold. Photographs taken of dead Highlanders lying in swaths in front of a single German machine gun on the battlefield of Loos, which I saw some weeks later, taken by Colonel Arthur Lee and brought to me, finally disposed of any qualms I may have had at having taken upon myself the responsibility for overriding military opinion."

Military opinion was overridden. The material side of machine gunnery was now being addressed, at least for the British. The tactical side remained far behind.

Two years into the war, in summer 1916, Kitchener's New Army was deemed sufficiently ready to attack. The Allies chose to open a French and British offensive in the countryside near the River Somme, a rural area of northwestern France, striking along a wide belt of front. The battle was meant in part to take pressure off the French at Verdun, where Germany had launched an offensive of its own. For the early part of the war, the front near the Somme had been entirely a French sector. By late 1915, as the Royal Scots arrived at the Labyrinth, British troops had been assuming command on the lines. The ground was hardly ideal for an attack. No-Man's-Land here was wide-open, usually treeless, and covered with a fine, chalky soil. Cover was all but nonexistent.

By this time, the Machine Gun Corps had come into existence, and gunners attended an eight-week course. Lloyd George's requisitions were having an effect in the field. A division now had 204 machine guns at its disposal; at the start of the war, a division had 24.[43] But while the British had become materially more formidable, their tactics for storming enemy positions remained undeveloped. A veteran French captain from the 153rd Infantry, André Laffargue, had begun working out new methods. His ideas held promise. Laffargue had survived traditional attacks across open ground, into the teeth of German defenses. He grasped that machine guns were not only defensive weapons. Like Captain Parker in the United States, he proposed that the weapons be rushed forward and used to suppress enemy positions as the infantry moved close. "The machine gun should be pushed as far as possible in front of the halted line of fire," he wrote. "It will enable the infantry line to advance for some time under the cover of its fire; it is the tooth of the attack."[44] Through bloody experience, Captain Laffargue had also learned that enemy machine guns needed to be knocked out for an attack to have a realistic chance of success. He proposed that light artillery move behind the attack, like a gigantic rifle, to blast German machine guns by direct fire whenever German guns appeared. He also proposed a detailed reconnaissance of any trench to be attacked, with the intention of locating the enemy's machine guns so that they might be silenced before they reaped their toll. "The weapon that inflicts the heaviest losses on infantry is the machine gun, which uncovers itself suddenly and in a few seconds lays out the assailants by ranks. It is therefore absolutely necessary to destroy them before the attack or have the means of putting them out of action as soon as they disclose themselves."[45] Captain Laffargue's proposals were not flawless; he still believed in the value of rigid open-order formations. But he also urged riflemen to fire their weapons as they advanced, and to suppress German fighters as they fired back. Taken together, his proposals were well enough regarded in French military circles that Joseph Joffre, chief of the French General Staff, circulated an article Laffargue wrote throughout the French army. It was translated into English by the *Infantry Journal,* an American publication, and given wide circulation among officers in 1916.

None of the proposals appeared to influence British planning for the offensive ahead.

The orders were given: The attack on the Somme would begin with a nearly weeklong artillery and mortar barrage in late June, and on July 1, eighty-four British battalions, more than sixty thousand men, would attack on foot across a sector eighteen miles wide. No operation of this size could be kept secret. Spies worked the lines, and the pilots of German aircraft and spotter balloons watched the buildup. For weeks rumors of the impending offensive filled conversations in the trenches on both sides. "Apparently the Germans know as much about the coming offensive as we do," Private Anderson wrote in his diary, before the battles began.[46]

The preparatory barrage appeared terrible, but the Germans had dug sleeping shelters within their trench systems, and they took cover within them with their weapons, ammunition, and even beer.[47] They watched from relative safety, keeping watch on No-Man's-Land and the British lines with mirrors and trench periscopes.

The troops gathered before dawn on July 1. The barrages lifted. At 7:20 A.M., the British engineers detonated explosives in shafts they had cut deep under the German lines. The blasts heaved dirt high into the sky and left craters of smoldering earth. A brief calm ensued. The British soldiers had been told by their officers that the artillery would destroy the German defenses and kill so many German soldiers that survivors would be unable to resist. Confidence was distributed like rum. Bunkers would be crushed, the officers said, and the barbed wire defending them would be severed. The British infantry would quickly carry the other side. At 7:30 A.M., Zero Hour, the time came to find out if any of this would be so.

The first battalions, their soldiers laden with backpacks and loads of at least seventy pounds, carrying Lee-Enfield rifles with bayonets affixed, climbed out of their trenches. As the soldiers stepped over the top, some of them, observing a tradition that marked their boyishness, kicked footballs gamely out into the stillness. The leather balls bounced into No-Man's-Land, a zone almost without cover. In front of the British soldiers, and in most places uphill, were the German front lines. The British began to walk, in formation, lines of men moving forward parallel to the frontage ahead. This was not the full madness of nineteenth-century close-order drill, but it was close. German machine gunners opened fire. Some of the British soldiers were knocked back into the trenches by bullets before they had taken a step forward. The companies formed up and pushed on in waves, deeper into the trap their officers had designed for them. Survivors recounted the scene.

> From their trenches came the "tac-tac-tac" of the guns as they traversed to and fro along the endless lines of advancing men. Whole waves were swept over by the fire. The dead lay in long rows where they had fallen, the wounded lay with them, pretending to be dead, or took cover wherever they could—in a fold in the ground, in one of the rare shell holes. Many huddled behind the body of a dead comrade. If a wave or part of it was missed in the first sweep, back would come the traverse of fire seeking out the survivors. The long line of men came forward, rifles at the port as ordered. Now Gerry started. His machine guns let fly. Down they all went. I could see them dropping one after another as the gun swept along them. The officer went down at exactly the same time as the man behind him. Another minute or so and another wave came forward. Gerry was ready this time and this lot did not get so far as the others.[48]

Watching from behind their machine guns, German soldiers were amazed. They had weathered fear and frustration through the shelling, waiting for the immense attack they knew was coming. As they peered over their parapets in the sudden quiet, the sights astonished them: thousands upon thousands of men, strolling exposed in neat lines. The British

carried their rifles across their chests, in the drill-field posture known as
port arms. "The English came walking, as though they were going to the
theatre or as though they were on a parade ground," one German soldier
said. "We felt they were mad." Another saw waves in which the men were
so densely packed they "were like trees in a wood."[49] Some of the Germans
whooped. They were professional soldiers, the product of a German military system in which conscription was nearly universal in early manhood,
and civilian men maintained and updated their skills through mandatory
reserve duty into early middle age. They had never seen such targets before. The time for killing was at hand. One German machine-gun team
alone would fire at least twenty-five thousand rounds.[50]

In this withering fire, a Yorkshire battalion, Company A of the Seventh Green Howards, lost 108 of 140 men in minutes. An even more galling destruction fell upon the Tyneside Irish, a brigade of three thousand
men, which had to cross almost a mile of open ground behind its own
front-line trenches just to reach the British edge of No-Man's-Land. It
took twenty minutes under fire to complete this march. Bullets slammed
into the soldiers the entire way. The surviving Irish were ordered on, to
press the attack across five hundred yards of open space and breach the
German lines. They plunged forward, through the bloodied remains of
the battalions that had gone before. Somehow they managed to cross
the ground and get a toehold in the German lines. Of the three thousand men who had stepped off, fifty fighting men remained.[51] The New
Amy, Lord Kitchener's grand two-year project to replace the battered
British Expeditionary Force with volunteers from all walks of British
life—the mines, the factories, the clerks, the schoolhouses—was being
cut down in an hour. The Dervishes had fought this foolishly. So had
Japanese soldiers, who saw duty in death. Now the British army was doing
it, too.

A darker hour for England would be hard to measure. By one estimate, 30,000 British soldiers were killed or wounded in the first sixty
minutes. The midday tally reached 50,000. By the end of the day, 21,000
British soldiers were dead, 35,000 wounded, and 600 more had been
taken prisoner. The survivors were emotionally devastated. One lance
corporal, a signaler who had not been assigned to advance, watched his
friends try to cross, only, he said, to be "mown down like meadow grass."
He stayed back, weeping.

Private Anderson's battalion was not ordered to attack the first day. Several days later, as the battle continued, his unit raided German trenches. Before returning to the British side, his platoon lost several men, and a bullet struck and splintered his rifle stock. After several months of war, his platoon had been wrecked. "Of the old crowd only Wightman, Davidson, Tommy Graham, Harvey, and the hefty Irishman Connell and myself remain, as well as Reid and Crossley," he wrote. Two sentences later he added: "A German sniper also got 2nd Lieut. Stewart through the head when he was having a look over the top."[52] Tens of thousands of men had been lost. Front-line life remained the same.

As news of the slaughter on the Somme trickled out, Hiram Maxim, now seventy-six, was retired comfortably in London. If he was troubled by the killing being done with his namesake invention, he revealed no sign of it. If anything, he seemed proud. After the war had begun, he had published an essay in the *New York Times* boasting of inventing both the automatic machine gun and the smokeless powder that made it a more effective killing machine. His principal concern appeared to be to make sure that he received credit ushering these developments to form. In 1915, in his memoir, *My Life,* he crowed more. "I was the first man in the world to make an automatic gun," he wrote. "The gun was very light, small, and effective, and the automatic system, which was thoroughly worked out by myself, went into universal use throughout the whole civilized world. It is astonishing to note how quickly this invention put me on the very pinnacle of fame."[53] He maintained his detachment and dark humor to the book's end, where he lamented that an inhaler he had designed to relieve congestion brought him no fame at all. "It is a very creditable thing to make a killing machine," he wrote, "and nothing less than a disgrace to invent an apparatus to prevent human suffering."[54] Maxim died in November 1916, a few weeks after the end of the Battle of the Somme, which caused more than a million casualties to the armies involved without changing the fundamental contours of the Western Front. To the end he never showed a public hint of regret. Given his history and the record of his public statements, this is neither surprising nor especially significant. The time of sales pitches, claims of inventive genius, and disputes over patents had passed. Machine guns were now firmly in the domain of the common foot soldier, and soldiers both understood their uses and gave the weapons their meaning

War was not for the likes of Gatling and Maxim; neither ever experienced it firsthand. That experience fell to others. It was these young men, who suffered what modern battle had become, who would best explain the experience of automatic fire, as Wilfred Owen did. In 1918, just before he died, Owen wrote "Spring Offensive," which described a British unit resting behind a hill before trying to cross a valley. The front had been broken by then. The Allies were chasing the retreating German forces. The British unit emerged on open ground and discovered that the Germans were ready with a delaying action. Owen described what Maxim could not. In his poem, the soldiers were a hardened and exhausted bunch. To them the war was old and horribly familiar, and experience had scoured away any expectation of glory, or even of nation or heroism. The soldiers were simply tired. Some felt a sense of foreboding before they tried to cross the valley. It was as if, Owen wrote, they knew "their feet had come to the end of the world." Then they moved out, to be memorialized in Owen's elegy for the common soldier, written a month before he himself was killed in action.

> Soon, they topped the hill, and raced together
> Over an open stretch of herb and heather
> Exposed. And instantly the whole sky burned
> With fury against them; earth set sudden cups
> In thousands for their blood; and the green slope
> Chasmed and deepened sheer to infinite space
> Of them who running on that last high place
> Breasted the surf of bullets, or went up
> On the hot blast and fury of hell's upsurge.
> Or plunged and fell away past this world's verge,
> Some say God caught them even before they fell.[55]

More than fifty years after Richard Gatling gave the world the first reliable rapid-fire arms, the basic questions about machine gunnery had been answered. All doubts about their utility had been erased. All serious military powers armed their ranks with them in large quantities and provided the soldiers assigned to them with generous amounts of ammunition. By late in World War I, spurred at last by an understanding of the futility of attacking well-defended trenches and machine-gun bunkers with masses of knife-wielding infantrymen, ideas about firepower and tactics were shifting, swiftly and finally. Machine guns were being put into use in all forms of warfighting that could be waged within the distance that a bullet could fly. Light machine guns were mounted on aircraft to strafe ground targets and to shoot other aircraft down. Heavy machine guns were mounted on turrets and used to pound boats, aircraft, trucks, and cars. Tanks were created in part so that men could move against machine guns, and to defend themselves, tanks had machine guns mounted on them, too. The British Machine Gun Corps, which began with only a few machine guns and a royal warrant, would grow to have more than 170,000 soldiers and officers, and would suffer more than 62,000 casualties, making it an important part of the history of the war.[56] Infantry tactics changed, moving away from inflexible formations and frontal attacks to approaching the enemy via infiltration and with precision supporting fires. The human wave—or extended line, or whatever euphemism the officers endowed it with—was falling from use in professional Western military units, though it would be seen again in a variety of forms in more centralized or less-developed militaries or guerrilla groups. Drab clothing and camouflage became the necessary standard to improve the odds of a soldier's survival in the era of automatic arms, especially as tracer rounds, which allowed machine gunners to see precisely where their cone of bullets was flying, came into widespread use. By late 1916, as the Battle of the Somme ended and the understanding of its carnage was settling into military and political minds, and as the imperious and unshaken Sir Hiram Maxim was carried off to his grave, the skepticism about machine guns was gone. By the time of the Armistice, in 1918, another question had moved to the fore: How to make automatic weapons smaller, so that their firepower could be carried by a single man?

The question was not entirely new. Hiram Maxim had sketched out an automatic rifle in his earliest efforts to make machine guns, and he dabbled briefly with a possible design. Since the 1890s, other arms designers had been trying, with great frustration and limited success, to make the first reliable and manageable automatic rifle. The idea had proved to be as frustrating as the Civil War–era efforts to make hand-cranked battery guns. One of the first reasonably successful entries was the Madsen, a short-lived Danish creation that was not issued to its army. But there had been many other efforts at a semiautomatic and automatic rifle: by Ferdinand Ritter von Mannlicher, by John Browning, by Peter Paul Mauser, and by other arms engineers and gunsmiths.[57] A Russian armorer, Vladimir Grigorevich Fedorov, began work on an automatic rifle in 1906, and by World War I had produced a working model, though it suffered from problems and was never perfected or moved to mass production. In World War I, a number of machine guns appeared on battlefields at sizes considerably smaller than the big Maxim and Vickers and Colt guns, and had been successful enough in the trenches. These smaller guns, the Lewis among them, hinted at the possibilities of miniaturization. But they remained far too large to be considered rifles, and because they fired rifle-caliber ammunition at a great rate, they were not weapons to be used for any length of time by a single man. The rifle ammunition of the time was large and powerful, capable of propelling bullets out of muzzles at velocities approaching three thousand feet per second. The effect downrange was exactly what ballisticians thought they wanted: a long, flat trajectory for bullets that could strike a man with tremendous force and potential for lethality more than a kilometer away. But one unhelpful and inseparable result was that the heat and recoil associated with firing these cartridges strained lighter-weight weapons and soldiers alike, and made designing small but sturdy automatic rifles, which would blaze though this high-powered ammunition in rapid-fire mode, exceptionally difficult, as Fedorov was finding as he experimented in Russia. And therein was the problem: the ammunition. As long as designers sought to make an automatic rifle that would fire contemporary high-power ammunition, the field of automatic-rifle design remained frustrated by technical problems, and largely undeveloped.

By 1915, after World War I had settled into a siege on the Western Front, Germany took another path toward a portable weapon that could be rushed forward to clear trenches. The underlying concept was the same. Germany sought a weapon that would concentrate fire, but would be small enough to be wielded by a single man, who would carry all of its ammunition, too. With such a weapon, firepower would be as mobile as the infantry, able to go anywhere a man could walk, without much slowing him down. In the narrow confines of trenches, and in the maze of barbed wire in No-Man's-Land, large rifles were often a hassle rather than a help. German arms designers understood that rifle ammunition was too powerful for small automatics, at least if a solution was to be worked out quickly enough to influence the war. It chose to seek an automatic weapon that would fire the comparatively low-powered and lightweight 9-millimeter pistol round, a class of ammunition that was already in the German inventory and could quickly be produced in quantities necessary for war. The concept had promise for the trenches, and it suggested a style of warfare that had not yet been seen. It would also reduce the weight of a soldier's ammunition load. The requirements for such a weapon were established by the Rifle Testing Commission in late 1915.[58] Working from the Theodor Bergmann weapons factory in Suhl, a German designer, Hugo Schmeisser, gave the concept its shape: the Bergmann Maschinenpistole 18, or MP-18, which had a wooden rifle stock for shoulder fire, but a squat, fat barrel that gave it a blocky appearance. It weighed just over nine pounds, could be fitted with magazines that held twenty or thirty-two rounds, and fired its bullets at more than twelve hundred feet per second. In all it was just over thirty-two inches long, a foot shorter than many standard infantry rifles in the war. This was the submachine gun. It became an ideal complement to the evolving German infiltration tactics being worked out by General Oskar von Hutier and the elite *Stosstruppen,* or shock troops, who before the war's end would master the tactics of pinpoint attacks and breaches of front lines.

The MP-18 was the first submachine gun to see combat, but similar ideas were being pursued elsewhere. By 1915, the Italian army had already fielded small quantities of the Villar Perosa, a two-barrel automatic weapon that fired 9-millimeter pistol ammunition, though the gun was fired off a bipod and was used as a lightweight machine gun for fighting in the mountains, and not as a submachine gun.[59] A new company in the United States, the Auto-Ordnance Corporation, was at work on its own weapon for trench warfare. Led by General John T. Thompson, a retired army ordnance officer, the company's engineers were quietly developing a submachine gun chambered to fire .45-caliber pistol ammunition. The war ended before the result, the Thompson gun, was put to a test.

The era of automatic fire was almost fully developed. Two ends of the automatic-fire spectrum had changed the way that people experienced organized violence. The Maxim gun and its offspring had altered how armies

were organized and how war was waged, and had killed men in quantities beyond counting. And the MP-18 had been considered a worrisome
enough development after its brief debut that the German military was
specifically prohibited from possessing them by the Treaty of Versailles.
The next question was obvious. Might not there be something between
the great weight and power of a true machine gun and the lightweight
and ferocious MP-18? Was it not possible to design an automatic rifle that
combined the traits of both? Such a weapon would allow foot soldiers to
be as mobile as ever, but more lethal than before. If small-arms design was
an evolutionary process, and so far it had been just that, then this class of
weapon was inevitable. Only details remained. What country would first
design and field such a weapon? And when?

II

INVENTION AND DISTRIBUTION

Every day Svetlana Vladimirovna works a long shift at the machining factory beside the smelter at the edge of her city in central Russia. The factory makes the best beds in the Soviet Union, all of them of exceptionally fine steel. But no one in Svetlana's city, including Svetlana, has a bed. This is an unfortunate but perfectly understandable matter of policy. The comrades who run the factory, and who have designed such magnificent and marvelous beds, better than any beds in America, have decided in the spirit of the revolution and correct socialist principles that they must give beds first to all of the hospitals, and to the army, and to the universities, and to the collective farms, and to many other important institutions necessary for the people and the government in the world's most rapidly and inevitably advancing socialist society. To do this, the factory must work round the clock. Three shifts a day.

And only rarely stopping on holidays. It is understood that the workers need beds. But it is not yet the workers' turn. Only recently did the cosmonauts receive beds!

And so everyone who works at the bed factory returns home after each shift and sleeps on the floor.

One summer Svetlana's sister, Natasha, who long ago married a man in Leningrad and moved away, returned for a visit. She was appalled that after ten years Svetlana still had no bed. After all, Svetlana was strong of hand and skilled with tools and one of the best machinists at the bed factory. "My dear sister," Natasha said. "You have not been thinking correctly. It is very easy to have a bed. Each day you must steal one piece of bed from the parts bins at the factory and smuggle it home. And after a week or two you must assemble the parts. Then you will have a bed. And you will never again sleep on the floor."

Svetlana listened closely. "My dear sister," she sighed. "It is you who are not thinking correctly. We have tried this many times. We have stolen the bed parts and carried them home. We have assembled them in the room. And every time, after we finish, we discover that instead of a bed we have an automatic Kalashnikov."

—SOVIET-ERA JOKE

CHAPTER 5

Stalin's Contest:
The Invention of the AK-47

So young, and he's already pulling a fast one! He's a good actor, make
no mistake!

—A peasant carpenter in the Altai krai, circa 1925, commenting on
young Mikhail T. Kalashnikov, as told by Kalashnikov to a writer
who collaborated with him on an autobiography

SENIOR SERGEANT MIKHAIL T. KALASHNIKOV STARED OUT FROM
the window of his office, his back turned to the door. He was tense with
suspense. It was early 1946, the first winter in Russia since the defeat
of Nazi Germany, and there was activity on this day at the Research
Proving Grounds for Firearms and Mortars, or NIPSMVO, a Soviet
weapons-testing center near the village of Schurovo, about sixty miles
southeast of Moscow. The proving ground, or polygon, as the Russians
called it, was a secluded military garrison, bustling with officials and frequently shaken by the sounds of small-arms fire and explosions. Officially
the polygon was encased in a hush. NIPSMVO was a garrison that did
not exist, a secret post with a mix of arms design and technical intelligence
responsibilities that the USSR wanted to keep hidden from the West.
Nestled into the thick forests that ringed the capital, it had been built
early in the 1900s, in czarist times, to be a self-contained military town
for testing and evaluating Russian and foreign arms. Over the years, as

the nation had militarized under Leon Trotsky's and then Stalin's commands, arms development had become a pressing matter of state security. The proving ground had grown. By the 1940s, it had barracks, offices, communal apartments for families, a canteen, a store selling basic goods, a modern metal shop for refining and repairing prototype arms, a ballistics laboratory, and environmental chambers to submit weapons to grueling simulations of Russian and Asian field conditions. The design offices provided workspace for staff for teasing out new ideas, and a hotel hosted visiting officers and specialists, who were ever rotating through.[1] Around the main buildings were several small-arms firing ranges, each a kilometer long, that had been cut through stands of trees. An old bus shuttled designers and testers between the ranges and the main post. Sergeant Kalashnikov, a wounded veteran of the war, had worked here intermittently since 1942, after, by dint of what seemed an innate mechanical sense, he had been transferred while on convalescent leave from the Soviet tank forces to an environment where his talents and drive might be harnessed. Already he had been at work on new weapons and had made prototypes of a submachine gun and a self-loading carbine. Both designs had been rejected. Since fall 1945 he had become excited again. He had been consumed by the most significant project he had participated in yet: a submission to a secret Soviet contest to design an automatic rifle.

The war against Nazi Germany had ended in May, but a new arms race had been joined. The workers at NIPSMVO had learned in August that the United States had dropped atomic bombs on Hiroshima and Nagasaki. Sergeant Kalashnikov and his colleagues listened over the polygon's public address system to the announcement that the Pentagon had developed and used the most terrible weapon yet. Two cities had been left smoldering. In the war against German fascism, the citizens of the Soviet Union had suffered invasion and partial occupation. The Communist Party had feared its own destruction. Now it faced something worse: the prospect of atomic war. The mind-set that had gripped the arms specialists during the war—a mood that combined anger, fear, resolve, and a sense of duty—was invoked once more. The staff at the polygon was driven to conceive of weapons that would ensure the safety of the *rodina,* the great Russian homeland, and equip fraternal socialist forces in the expanding Kremlin sphere. "Again designers were urged to hurry and implement their projects," Kalashnikov wrote. "The quality requirements were noticeably tightened."[2]

The world had yet to develop a reliable and lightweight automatic rifle, a firearm that could fire at the rate of a Maxim gun out to typical combat ranges and yet be managed by a single man. Throughout fall 1945, Sergeant Kalashnikov and a larger design collective had worked on a submission for the contest's first phase, which required competitors to submit a packet of technical specifications. The Main Artillery Department wanted a weapon that fired like a submachine gun but out to greater range. It issued the guidelines. The weapon must be compact, lightweight, highly reliable, simple to manufacture, easily operated, and composed of a small number of independent parts. And it must fire a new cartridge, only recently designed by Soviet ammunition experts. Sergeant Kalashnikov's team made hundreds of sketches, detailing each of the proposed weapon's main parts, trying to put a practical form to the commission's request.[3]

Kalashnikov was not an engineer, armorer, or metallurgist; he had little formal design or technical-drawing training, and had not attended school beyond his midteens. But a group of specialists was assigned to work with him, giving his ideas shape on the drafting table. The sergeant had a reputation for working almost ceaselessly, taking only a few hours for sleep. Often his collective remained at the shop until midnight. Gradually the paperwork began to show the proposed design. A lieutenant colonel, Boris L. Kanel, conducted the barrel-strength analyses. A draftswoman, Yekaterina Viktorovna Moiseyeva, rendered the drawings. Her papers showed a weapon that hinted at what would in time become the AK-47: an automatic rifle in which the excess gas of each shot was vented via a port into a tube above the barrel, and this energy was captured by a piston and then used to eject the spent shell casing and begin the next cycle of fire. The idea of a gas-operated weapon, conceived by Hiram Maxim seventy years before and given shape in the late nineteenth century by John M. Browning and the Colt Model 1895, was being put into a miniaturized form inside the Soviet Union, at least on paper.

Kalashnikov was not the first. Many had tried a similar design elsewhere. And other Soviet designers had been working on similar systems during the late war and postwar period. But this particular Soviet push for a gas-operated automatic rifle was different. The Red Army's designers were cogs in a much larger machine, working within a government that was hungry for a new weapon, and willing to expend deep human and material resources on finding a satisfactory result. The only hurdle, once a design was worked out, would be the judges' review.

Sergeant Kalashnikov's packet had been submitted to the Main Artillery Department by a deadline in late 1945, along with fifteen other entrants from around the Soviet arms-design community.[4] The test commission planned to review the competing proposals and select several entrants to proceed to the next phase—constructing their guns for firing trials. The sergeant wanted what all designers wanted: to see his ideas take shape in metal. The Russian winter gripped the test range. He waited.

The sergeant, a small and intent man with pale blue eyes and a face pitted by the faint scars of childhood disease, was worried. Over the course of a week, he had heard that other collectives had been notified that their designs had met approval, and they could proceed to the next stage. For his case, there was only silence. Perhaps he had failed again. He knew well that his path to arms design, and his entry into the inner workings of the Soviet military complex, had been unlikely. He had been born in near penury and raised from peasant stock on the steppe of central Russia, just north of the current border with Kazakhstan. Though he did not talk openly about his past with his army peers, his and his family's lives had been a tour through many of the characteristic miseries of the early Soviet period. The sergeant worked in secrecy. He kept secrets of his own. He dared not speak of his family's suffering at the hands of Stalin's state, including that his father, Timofey A. Kalashnikov, had been declared a *kulak,* and exiled as an enemy of the people, when the sergeant was an eleven-year-old boy. He spent the rest of his childhood and early teenage years in Siberia, a run of bitter and difficult years. But the Great Patriotic War had reshaped him, just as it reordered much of Stalin's Russia. He had made his peace with the Communist Party, the institution that had nearly destroyed his family.

Kalashnikov had been conscripted into the Red Army's tank forces in 1938. In 1941, soon after Hitler betrayed his nonaggression pact with Stalin and launched the invasion of Russia, he had been wounded in battle. Kalashnikov's wartime experiences, and his newfound access to educated and accomplished people inside the Red Army, had given him the handholds he needed for a social and professional climb. The sergeant had many talents, not the least of which was a twinkling charm. His politics took shape: He became an ardent nationalist and patriot, committed to the Soviet Union and to its survival. In addition to his mechanical abilities, Sergeant Kalashnikov possessed a mind informed by an unerring survival instinct. He repeatedly endeared himself to the officers and party officials who determined his fate. The war against Germany drew him into the system that had brutalized his family, and he had come to align his interests with the interests of the national cause. He knew what was at stake, and how to articulate his place in it. "Nazi enslavement or victory!" he would later write. "The potential for a man worrying about the fate of his homeland in years of trouble is really unlimited!"

Now he was at a critical moment. He had found a place in the army's armaments-design branch, and had found security as well, as much security as was possible for a young man in Stalin's Soviet Union. His salary was fifteen hundred rubles a month, several times more than many Soviet workers received, and at least twice the national average.[5] Still, he was nervous. The contest was a chance to excel even more and to earn greater security yet. Under the Soviet system, successful *konstruktors,* as the state arms designers were called, were given status, prizes, awards, and perks. But Sergeant Kalashnikov was only twenty-six years old. He lacked the reputation and sense of protocol of other designers. Moreover, the submission papers had to be completed with bureaucratic Soviet precision, and he was competing against some of the most established names in Soviet arms circles. He expected rejection.

Yekaterina Moiseyeva, the draftswoman, appeared at his door. Kalashnikov knew her as Katya. In their months working together, the pair had fallen in love. Other members of the collective had played endless practical jokes on them, sending them each on contrived errands or with contrived questions so that the two might meet. "May I come in?"[6] she asked.

She brought news. "Our bureau has authorized me to congratulate you on your victory in the contest," she said, and held out her hand.

The sergeant turned his back. He thought it was another of his colleagues' jokes. She seemed confused, too, and walked away, leaving him to stare at the winter outside. He had failed again.

More members of the team rushed to his door. "Come on, hurry over to the headquarters and then to the shop!" one said. This was Russia; they suggested toasts. Inside the polygon's headquarters, he was told officially. His proposal for an automatic rifle had been selected for the next phase.

* * *

From this moment forward, by his own telling, Mikhail Kalashnikov was on the path of designing the weapon that would be designated by the Soviet military as its new standard infantry arm. The result would become an object familiar to the world's eyes: a stubby black rifle, with a banana-shaped magazine, a steep front sight post, and a dark wooden stock. After many modifications over many years, from Sergeant Kalashnikov's initial design would flow the family of assault rifles now universally known as the AK-47—an acronym for *Avtomat Kalashnikova-47,* the automatic by Kalashnikov designed in 1947. The significance of this secret contest was unknown in the West and not immediately evident even within the circle of officers who made the equipment decisions for Soviet land forces. But of all the many programs pursued in the Soviet arms complex in the years ahead—the ballistic submarines and transport and attack helicopters, the intercontinental missiles and strategic bombers, the armored vehicles and titanium-hulled tanks, and even the atomic bomb itself, which at the same time was the focus of a team of physicists in a project supervised by Lavrenty Beria, the feared leader of the secret police—none would claim as many lives as this seemingly mundane and uncomplicated invention. The man credited with its design would benefit, too. Sergeant Kalashnikov, a low-ranking *konstruktor* in a sprawling bureaucracy, was destined to receive promotions that in time would elevate him to the honorary rank of lieutenant general. His surname would become an informal global brand. He would receive state prizes, ruble bonuses of enormous value in the parsimonious Soviet Union, an apartment, and eventually a dacha, or summer cottage, on the shores of a wooded lake. His second wife—Katya of NIPSMVO—would wear fur.[7] And he would be appointed by the authorities as a deputy in the Supreme Soviet, the rubber-stamp national legislature that seated itself before Stalin and his successors in grand sessions within the Kremlin's tall red walls. For a peasant once in exile, he was now in a breathtaking climb.

How exactly would all of this come to pass? Rough accounts of the contest, and of the early development of the Kalashnikov series, are known from official and personal versions. The basic outline is familiar. Sergeant Kalashnikov, the story goes, was a gifted young soldier, unde-veloped but eager to serve his nation. His intuitive design skills, coupled with a desire to confront the marauding Germans and drive them from Russian soil, was given an outlet and direction by the Red Army and the Communist Party, enabling him to rise from obscurity and invent for his imperiled nation a rifle that was more reliable and effective than any previous design. By this account, everyone is put in a good light. Kalashnikov is the quintessential proletarian hero, a simple and seemingly unassuming man, a commoner, whose natural gifts and loyal dedication helped the Soviet Union arm itself and its friends against the encroaching West. And the Red Army, through the wisdom of its commanders and the timely and prescient intervention of Communist Party officials, channeled his raw talent for the workers' good. The durable frame of this story has been passed down through government accounts and repeated often enough over the decades to have entered twentieth-century martial lore. But what were the precise circumstances and events that led to the creation of this weapon, now a centerpiece of modern war, and led to this previously unheralded man receiving credit for it?

The story becomes trickier at a finer grain of detail. The broad history of the evolution of military arms, deduced through ordnance reports, ballistic and technical studies, sales brochures, transcripts of officer and designer seminars, soldiers' accounts, medical records, and a host of materials in institutional archives, is crowded with legends, quacks, apocryphal tales, and deliberately deceptive characters. Military secrecy has obscured many chapters; trade secrecy has prevented a full understanding of others. With the history of many weapons, the task is further complicated by the fact that essential sources have often not been fully trustworthy. Richard Gatling hewed in public to a profoundly naïve dream and presented himself as a proper Southern gentleman who pitched up ready for America's industrial age. In private he plotted with no small amount of cunning—hiding and shifting his company's debt, paying a uniformed British army officer under the table to promote the weapon at officers' clubs, and concocting cagey plans to boost government support and sales, even if it meant planting stories in the Washington press. Ultimately, late in life, he admitted that he had offered his weapon for sale before it was ready. Hiram Maxim, an accomplished cad, suspected draft dodger, and accused trigamist, presented multiple and conflicting accounts of the origins of the Maxim gun. His ego was so immeasurably large that much of what he left behind in writing and in the transcripts of his public remarks was a celebration of himself. He was mischievous to boot, a prankster, which lent his memoirs and many of his statements the feel of an inside joke. This has made tracing a complete set of independent and verifiable details of his weapon's development, at least through what might seem its most important source—Hiram Maxim—a frustrating if not impossible task. The result is that it is often easier to evaluate any given weapon's impact and significance than it is to determine the exact circumstances of its invention.

But little in any independent inquiry into the evolution of automatic arms can compare in degree of difficulty to an examination of the origins of Kalashnikov's AK-47. The reasons are manifold. First and foremost, the weapon came into existence inside one of the most secretive and paranoid military systems the world has known. Within this system, the state-directed process was long, fundamentally bureaucratic, scattered across multiple cities and testing sites, and conducted in a cone of near silence by scores, if not hundreds, of participants. The rules muzzled contemporaneous accounts beyond the limited statements made by the authorities, and Soviet authorities were given to lies. Later, when Mikhail Kalashnikov and his namesake weapon entered proletarian lore, the Soviet mythmaking mill produced simplified distillations and outright false official accounts. Inventions, handy fables, and propaganda wormed away at the story for decades, institutionalizing falsehoods and calcifying legends, many of which then became part of the narrative in the West, where further repetition hardened and certified official Soviet accounts. As for Mikhail Kalashnikov himself, he sometimes complained of the false accounts and at other times participated in them, including in his first encounter with a researcher who eventually became a curator at the Smithsonian's National Museum of American History. At their first contact, by letter in the early 1970s, Kalashnikov recommended a clumsily and transparently falsified official account of his personal biography and the weapon's history.[8] The subterfuge was understandable in its context, part of both a bureaucratic and a diplomatic dance. Kalashnikov consulted with a senior KGB official in the region where he worked before replying to the letter, and his response was passed through the acting Soviet military attaché in Washington. Such conditions left little room for candor. The caution was characteristic of its time. Perhaps it was justified. Though Kalashnikov did not know it, the civilian researcher was quietly collaborating with, and seeking advice from, a senior American technical intelligence official, the very man whose primary responsibility for the United States government was to examine and evaluate Eastern bloc small arms. Whether the researcher's role was intentional or not, from a Soviet perspective he was acting as an agent.[9] Kalashnikov's deception was expected, to the point of being reflexive. The reflex fit the time.

Years later, toward the end of the Soviet period, Kalashnikov presented, in both his writings and his scores of public interviews, a somewhat more expansive account of the weapon's development and design. This brought more detail to the discussion. But as Kalashnikov circulated more accounts, he sometimes contradicted himself and thereby made the history even more debatable. Memoirs might be expected to help, as they would presumably be rendered with more deliberation and care than extemporaneous remarks in interviews, and Kalashnikov would be able to consult his own records to check facts and shape revisions. And yet for a man with a reputation for mechanical precision, his memoirs are a sloppy affair. He has written several, or, put another way, several have appeared under his name (two were cowritten with other authors, and at least one of his critics suspects there has been a ghostwriter, too).[10] They beg for an editor, and not just because his accounts veer between sentimental, doctrinaire, folksy, and at times scalding. Stylistic shifts are a mere nuisance. Deeper problems lie in the shifting facts. Accounts of key events differ from text to text. Simple errors intrude in some places; in others, he has reclaimed chunks of the official history or other writers' work and recast it.[11] Throughout the memoirs, his recollections and the dates, even the years, for important events change. The dialogue changes as well, often in ways that alter the meaning of events as he recalls them. Even what might seem the most basic details come unmoored. (Was the AK-47 accepted as the winner of the design contest in late 1947 or in early 1948? Kalashnikov's memoirs have said both. The answer, from other sources, is clear: January 1948. How exactly was Kalashnikov wounded? Again, there are many answers, depending on the memoir.) An independent researcher is left to wonder: Is Kalashnikov simply imprecise? Or is he a serial embellisher and cunning censor? The record indicates that he was, variously and sometimes simultaneously, all three.

Sorting through these varied accounts and small details might be possible with extended and detailed interviews with Kalashnikov, or with unfettered access to primary documents. But Kalashnikov, while he makes himself accessible, is nearing senescence. He spent his life in a system that discouraged openness, encouraged deception, and punished disobedience, and he arrived at old age adept at evasion; in his memoirs, he openly admits to misleading Soviet officials and the public about his past, and in interviews he mixes a proletarian and peasant persona with gentle refusals to answer almost all questions he labels "political." He often answers questions with stock lines he has repeated for years, or decades. When pushed, he grows dismissive. The Soviet legacy endures in other telling ways, too. In the matter of archives, important collections that would be expected to contain information on the weapon's development, and the roles of participants, remain closed. Primary documents have not been shared, even with the museum that bears the designer's name and celebrates his work. And many documents are presumed to have vanished. "Here if something is once classified it will in most cases be classified until destroyed," said one prominent Russian firearms researcher.[12]

Since the collapse of the Soviet Union, which created possibilities for more openness, other factors added to the uncertainty. Freed from silence by the disintegration of the Soviet Union and the fall from power of the Communist Party, two participants in the competition in the 1940s, including a Red Army major who helped evaluate the prototype assault rifles, staked partial claims on the weapon's parentage. Moreover, further research suggested that the renowned German arms designer Hugo Schmeisser, who was captured by the Red Army after Nazi Germany's defeat, worked at the same arms-manufacturing complex where the AK-47 was first mass-produced and modified—raising the possibility that the weapon's production, if not its design, was directly influenced by an expert and innovator who was effectively held as a prisoner. Kalashnikov was also accused in a Moscow newspaper of lifting important components of a competitor's design and applying them to his final submission, the prototype that became the basis for the AK-47. Two post-Soviet Russian-language accounts using official sources—one by a participant in the contest's evaluation, and another by an arms museum curator—lend support to counterclaims, though they do not dismiss the central narrative outright.

Mikhail Kalashnikov is a proud, energetic, and sometimes intense man, and as a lingering proletarian hero, whose narrative has served both his interests and the interests of the state, he always rebutted such claims emphatically, often with thinly masked fury. But strong and angry denials serve only as denials; absent full access to the primary documents, sorting through the exact lines of parentage remains impossible, at least without taking leaps of faith, which many of the people who embrace the stock story have been willing to do. These leaps fit patterns. First they were expected as part of the Communist Party's recasting of history; history, during the bulk of Kalashnikov's work life, was as the party defined it, and the public was to accept the fabricated and debased versions as presented. Later, accepting the updated but still self-serving versions that emerged in post-Soviet years was a requisite part of access to Kalashnikov, which many writers cherished and did not jeopardize with inconvenient questions. Fighting this tide was not easy. In Russia, the simple story is a minor industry. Its upkeep has been a determined project.

As a result of these processes, the precise circumstances are, at best, historically unsettled. But a middle view is possible within a wider context. It is this: Any distillation that treats the AK-47 as a spontaneous invention, the epiphany of an unassuming but gifted sergeant at his workbench, misses the very nature of its origins as an idiosyncratic Soviet product. The weapon was designed collectively, the culmination of work by many people over many years, and the result of a process in which Senior Sergeant Kalashnikov was near the center in the mid and late 1940s. This process was driven not by entrepreneurship or by quirky Russian innovation and pluck, but by the internal desires and bureaucracy of the socialist state. The motivations that fueled it were particular to a moment in history. The Soviet Union, once a technologically backward society that had been brutalized and organized by Stalin's police state, had been militarizing throughout its existence, and it had recently been fully transformed into a military-industrial economy by war and its fear and hatred of Hitler. As Hitler exited the stage, this economy's potential for arms-making was harnessed again, this time to a mix of almost religious revolutionary ideology—socialism was, according to the party's core teaching, to sweep the world in an irresistible advance—and to a rational suspicion of the United States, with which it was compelled to compete.

Out of these forces, the competition for an automatic rifle was ordered. Unlike the Maxim and Gatling guns, the Soviet result, as near as a close reading of the available accounts can allow, flowed from official directives and widespread collaboration and not from a flash of inspiration. The AK-47 was a product of Stalin's state, not of a single man; it was the work of a government and the result of the vast resources the government applied to creating it. Kalashnikov himself has hinted at this himself. "When I grew older, I understood that my invention was not only the culmination of the fervent desire of all of our soldiers to have a worthy weapon to defend our Homeland but also what is often described in seemingly trite words—the 'creative energy of the people,'" he said. "I am sure that the AK-47 has become the embodiment of this energy. And let it be a common monument to us all—people whose names are known and the nameless. Let it be a symbol of the people's unity in a time of trial for the homeland."[13] Later, in a public presentation in Russia commemorating the sixtieth anniversary of the weapon's design, he expressed the fuller view more clearly. "Today we are celebrating the work of a big collective," he said. "I was not by myself sitting at a desk. It was a thousand-strong collective working at different factories."[14]

Such declarations are, of course, narrow. What makes the origins of the AK-47 interesting are not these easy platitudes, but the larger insights its story provides. The Soviet Union of the late 1940s was at a high point in its history. When it focused on technical tasks, it could excel. And when it focused on creating an automatic weapon that could be carried and managed by almost any man, it was able to quickly make one of the world's superproducts, and one of the truest symbols of itself. The weapon, which Kalashnikov emphasizes as a defensive tool and a shared monument to the population's creative energy, was rather a marker of the planned economy under totalitarian rule, a nation that could make weapons aplenty but would not design a good toilet, elevator, or camera, or produce large crops of wheat and potatoes, or provide its citizens with decent toothpaste and bars of soap. This is not to say that the planned economy was completely inefficient, though broadly it was. In the planned economy, when the plan worked, the nation got what its planners ordered. Main battle tanks became sturdy, reliable, and fearsome. Refrigerators barely worked. The AK-47 and its descendants in many ways form an apt emblem of the Soviet legacy, a wood-and-metal symbol of what the socialist experiment came to be about.

* * *

Certain aspects of the history are unchallenged.

The project that would change military rifles as combatants under-stood them began in strict secrecy in the Soviet Union just after the end of the Great Patriotic War. The Workers-Peasants Red Army was seeking a replacement for the infantry rifles, some of them dating to the turn of the century, that had served for decades as a standard arm for Russian and Soviet land forces. The Soviet Union had tried fielding automatic rifles for years, with disappointing results in battle. In the fight against the much more fully equipped German troops many Red Army soldiers found themselves carrying a Mosin-Nagant rifle largely unchanged since 1891.[15] A hurried effort during the late war years by a prominent Soviet designer, Sergei G. Simonov, had produced a serviceable but not quite satisfactory carbine that was matched to a new, smaller cartridge than previous Soviet rifles had fired. Simonov's result, the SKS, *Samozaryadny Karabin Sistemy Simonova,* the self-loading carbine system by Simonov, was a semiautomatic. It was light, simple, and inches shorter than most infantry rifles of the time, which made it easier to handle in thickets, in urban combat, in armored vehicles, or on parachute duty. But it fired only one round for every pull of the trigger, and was fitted with a fixed ten-round magazine. The Red Army's Main Artillery Department was in-terested in an individual soldier's weapon with more firepower. For more firepower, something else was needed.

The project's early luck had not been good. Another *konstruktor,* Aleksei I. Sudayev, had been working on a true automatic rifle for the new cartridge, and soon after the war his project had undergone two cycles of prototypes and tests. Sudayev was a young man, but already a celebrated figure among Soviet designers. Working in Leningrad during its encirclement and long siege, he had designed a submachine gun and helped oversee its production within the city, all in conditions approach-ing starvation. The weapon was issued to the Red Army soldiers who finally pushed the Germans back.[16] His energy seemed boundless, his talents immense. His second prototype for an assault rifle, the AS-44, was submitted in 1945. The evaluators found it promising, but heavy. They directed Sudayev to develop a third prototype of lesser weight. Sudayev fell severely ill in 1945 and died the next summer at the age of thirty-three, stalling the rifle's development. By then the Main Artillery Department had decided to commit the country's military infrastructure more fully to the cause. It had issued a new set of instructions. A competition among design collectives throughout the arms complex would be held, and each would offer proposals for an automatic rifle—for the army's review.

The contest's timing all but predicted its result: A weapon would be created and it would be mass-produced. The Great Patriotic War had radically altered the Soviet Union. Since the October Revolution, the population of the former Russian empire had suffered civil war, collectivization, purges, and labor camps. The revolutionary promises of socialism had given way to the centralization of a police state and single-party rule. The People's Commissariat for Internal Affairs, the NKVD, had grown in size and role, and its secret police had become a principal arm of a government that ruled by violence and fear. By the time of Operation Barbarossa, Hitler's plan to invade the Soviet Union in 1941, show trials had thinned the ranks of the Bolshevik revolutionaries and party luminaries. Much of the senior military leadership had been liquidated. Within schools, factories, and families, people were forced to denounce those near them, producing fresh crops of counter-revolutionary suspects to be arrested, tortured into confession, and sentenced to execution or forced labor in the network of GULAG camps. Stalin's personality cult had overtaken the land, and the national conversation was smothered by official propaganda and state lies. The nation was being consumed by the general secretary's whim, and the whims of those who acted under his hand.

The German invasion changed the national mood. The Third Reich's thrusts onto Russian soil had rallied a terrified people with a sense of shared peril and common purpose, and provided an impetus for militarization and industrialization on a scale not imagined immediately after the Bolshevik coup. Hitler's armies drove almost effortlessly through the Soviet Union's outer defenses, upending the Russian belief, central to the party's propaganda, that the Red Army would stop all enemies at the edge of Soviet soil. "We will never concede an inch of ground" was one popular slogan.[17] The reality was different. Many divisions along the border were not dug in. Many units had no maps. Many officers were on leave. As the Germans attacked, Stalin issued an order that deepened the confusion. Awakened in the predawn hours and told of the attack by Marshal Georgy Zhukov, the general secretary was in disbelief. "That is provocation," he said into the phone. "Do not open fire."[18] Russian units were routed.

Ukraine and much of western Russia, the location of a large portion of the Soviet Union's population and the nation's industrial base, fell under Nazi occupation, abandoned by the battered Red Army as it retreated. A drive for modernization had preceded the war. Stalin's Five-Year Plans, coupled to prison labor made available through repression, had rushed the Soviet Union through centralization and development apace, and the military sector had benefited. A huge pool of talent had been directed toward arms production and design. Laboratories, design bureaus, and research centers were dedicated to help.[19] As the German Blitzkrieg bore down on Moscow, creating cascades of refugees, the nation was energized more. The Soviet Union tottered. Its defense establishment swelled.

By 1944, three years later, the ordeal and the turnabout had both been spectacular. The Soviet Union had lost as many as 20 million of its citizens, including nearly 8 million soldiers—losses that dwarfed those of all other participating nations. But the tide had shifted. Germany's army, pressed from east and west, was nearing collapse. As the war approached its end in 1945, the Red Army, its ranks swelled by mass conscription, pursued the retreating German forces. The Kremlin gained control or primary influence over an expansive swath of territory extending from the Baltic states through Central and Western Europe and looping back to the banks of the Black Sea and almost into Yugoslavia, where Tito's resistance had evicted the Germans and a socialist state had taken hold. Stalin's prewar visions of socialist expansion had come to pass. This belt of nations would fall under Soviet influence and become the front line of the Eastern bloc, the buffer zone.

Stalin knew that large military forces would be necessary to occupy and administer this new socialist frontier, and to face down the West. These forces would need weapons. The timing was ideal for arming them. The Soviet Union had gone through an industrial transformation and remained on a war footing. It now had a labor force skilled in making weapons. Its arms and munitions factories, which had grown in size and number and worked around the clock in the war years, were producing weapons at an extraordinary rate. By one official estimate, in slightly less than four years of war, the Soviet Union managed to manufacture 12 million rifles, more than 6 million submachine guns, and almost a million machine guns—more than 13,000 weapons a day.[20] But this was an average over a four-year period during which production in the first years was small. By the end of the war, at least one enterprise, the sprawling gun works at Izhevsk, claimed at peak production to be making 12,000 weapons each day by itself, consuming fifty tons of steel every twenty-four hours.[21] This was the state of Stalin's defense complex as it considered its needs for a new infantry arm, a small automatic rifle that could be issued to every man.

Stalin liked contests. The dictator believed they motivated designers of military equipment, winnowed ideas and accelerated development's pace. Contests were central to the Red Army's research efforts across a spectrum of design pursuits, including not just infantry arms but aircraft, too.[22] He rewarded winning designers and at times summoned them before him— a terrifying prospect, considering that some designers, including the air-craft engineer Andrei N. Tupolev, worked from a *sharaga*, a secret NKVD research camp, where he was a prisoner living under fear of even worse.

The extremes were Sovietesque. When the Hero of Socialist Labor prize was introduced in 1939, Stalin arranged that the first of the med-als be given to him—and only him. The second prize, issued in 1940 by the Presidium of the Supreme Soviet, was awarded to Vasily Degtyarev, the weapons designer. In 1941, the Soviet Union awarded nine more, all to designers of military equipment and arms. (The prize was meant to recognize achievements in culture, the economy, and the arts; that ten of the first eleven prizes went to arms designers says something about na-tional priorities.) One of the recipients in the third batch was Aleksandr Yakovlev, another aircraft designer, for whom Stalin had a special fond-ness. After asking Yakovlev directly about the due date for an expected fighter plane, the general secretary said that if the deadline was met, "the drink would be on me."[23] Yakovlev was wary of this offer. The system had its perks, but the men who led it were mercurial, fickle, and exception-ally dangerous. Things often were not as they seemed. Another successful designer, Yakov G. Taubin, whose work gave the Red Army a reliable automatic grenade launcher, and who had also been awarded high state honors, was arrested early in the war and accused of being a supporter of Mikhail N. Tukhachevsky, a senior Red Army commander who had been arrested, tried in secret, and executed in 1937. Tukhachevsky's liquidation had been part of the purge's effort to remove the dictator's potential rivals, including figures popular in the public eye. Taubin's design successes did not save him once he was in the clutches of the state. Nor did the fact that the charges against Tukhachevksy had been contrived, and his supposed network of plotters did not exist. Taubin received no trial. His service to the Soviet Union ended in October 1941. He was summarily shot. The system often wasted men, no matter their potential and their willingness to be of service to the same system that by turns rewarded and persecuted them. Arms designers had better prospects for survival than most Soviet citizens. But even they were not fully spared. No one was immune.

Against this backdrop, the rifle project also fit within a larger pattern by which the Soviet army exploited what it could from Germany as design efforts were intensified. The Soviet Union's war with the Nazis, its postwar occupation of German arms plants, and its interrogation of German designers and engineers had exposed the army both to its own weaknesses and to the most modern and carefully considered developments in German military designs. Throughout the 1940s, the Soviet Union had upgraded its suite of military equipment, often incorporating concepts from preexisting German systems. By the late 1940s, all of the defense sectors were at work on new weapons. The T-34 tank was being replaced with the T-54 and T-55 main battle tanks (which in time would be replaced by the T-62, the T-72, and the T-80, all of which would themselves be continually upgraded). Soviet submarines were being updated, influenced in part by German design. Aviation bureaus were experimenting with helicopter prototypes, and Stalin had browbeaten the Soviet Union's fixed-wing aircraft designers and instructed them to hurry jet aircraft into production. The Soviet Army was also in midproduction of its first rocket-propelled grenade, the RPG-2, an antiarmor weapon based on a Nazi-era German pattern. (Further development would lead, in the 1960s, to the RPG-7—a system that, like the Kalashnikov, has lasted for decades.)

At NIPSMVO, one of many centers in the Red Army's constellation of research institutes, the contest for a new class of automatic arm was to proceed in phases. In the first phase, the design bureaus were ordered to submit technical descriptions of their proposals by a deadline late in 1945. The most promising candidates would then proceed to a second step: making working prototypes for tests. The competition was not only a state secret. It was veiled in anonymity, at least at the start.

Each design collective was to work separately from others, and to submit documents under a pseudonym, so the review commission's members would not know which submission came from which bureau. There was reason for precaution. Among the participating designers were established names, and past experience had shown that favoritism was a risk. Stalin had been rumored to have liked Fedor V. Tokarev, another famous Soviet armorer, and in a previous contest, in the 1930s, the desire by officers on the commission to please the general secretary was said to have led to the selection of a Tokarev rifle design over other submissions, including a better weapon proposed by Simonov.[24] Tokarev's weapon had not been a success, though that was not entirely Tokarev's fault—all the arms designers, in the Soviet Union and the West alike, who had tried making automatic rifles that fired the heavy rifle ammunition of the time had encountered difficulties. But the new contest drew from the lessons of the old. The use of pseudonyms was meant to prevent the taint of political interference from influencing the commission's decisions, and to give all participants, even unknowns like Sergeant Kalashnikov, a fair chance, at least at the first cut. Kalashnikov's team convinced him to submit his packet under the name "Mikhtim," a shorthand for his first name and patronymic. "I was young then and felt a little awkward about it," he said. "But my friends told me not to be shy."[25]

As the collective worked, the Soviet project differed sharply from the earlier age of rapid-fire arms design, when General Origen Vandenburgh or Richard Gatling or Hiram Maxim labored with small teams in private workshops, puzzling over plans they hoped would find financial backing and a manufacturer to convert them into products for sale. The Soviet contest was wholly different. It was a state-directed pursuit, a process born of Leninist ideology and Stalin's will, freed from the restraints of Western patents and combined with Red Army administration. It was a secret matter of state security, pursued on a large scale and according to a full set of rules, not the individual entrepreneurship and inventiveness of a Gatling or a Maxim. Moreover, the Soviet state was not merely issuing demands and timelines and serving as the evaluator. It was the primary influence in determining the nature of the weapon to be created. This influence extended beyond the contest's guidelines. It involved a cardinal decision, without which the AK-47 would be impossible: the selection of the cartridge the rifle would fire. It was a new cartridge, the M1943, unknown in the West, but destined to be the most common rifle cartridge on earth.

The origins of the M1943 preceded the Red Army's experiences in the war. In the 1930s the German army developed a prototype cartridge of intermediate size, the 7.92 Kurz. Until that time, the ammunition used by the riflemen of major powers was almost universally of high power, both by today's general-issue rifle standards and for the tasks that they could reasonably be expected to perform. Armies had been bewitched by the ballistic possibilities of high velocity, which could lead to long range, flat trajectory, and, with a heavy bullet, devastating wounds to victims struck. To fire heavy bullets at the great velocities then desired, bullets were seated in long cartridge cases that carried large charges of propellant. The globally used British .303 round, a mainstay from the turn of the century through the 1940s, was 78 millimeters long in all, as was the French MAS round used in World War II. The American round stretched to about 85 millimeters, and the Russian was just more than 77 millimeters long. Shifting away from these big rounds in favor of something smaller had proven difficult in Hitler's Germany, and impossible elsewhere. Armies remained invested in them, materially and psychologically. Who, after all, would propose undertaking the substantial costs of overhauling ammunition factories to produce a cartridge that, on paper at least, was *less* lethal?

After World War I, however, groups of ordnance officials and infantry officers had been asking whether such cartridges were necessary, and whether fidelity to ideas of maximum velocity and stopping power was a handicap forced on the ranks by tradition rather than sound analysis. What was the point of a rifle bullet that could strike a man two kilometers away now that soldiers wore camouflage and moved by infiltration? There were few targets at ranges beyond a few hundred yards, and when targets did present themselves out farther, not many marksmen could be expected to hit them. Rifles seemed to have been designed for tasks that did not exist, at least not for the typical foot soldier in the situations he was most likely to face. (Snipers, as specialists at long-range marksmanship, were another matter, but not every conscript needed a rifle capable of fulfilling sniper duty.) To those willing to question the status quo, the drawbacks of traditional rifle cartridges were obvious. To fire effectively out to this excess range, rifles had to be made heavier, which consumed more resources, drove up their costs, and made many models unwieldy. Their ammunition was heavy, too, meaning that it was expensive and soldiers carried fewer rifle cartridges than they otherwise might.

Between the wars, Germany was the first nation to pursue fully the concept of a smaller round, though German officers quarreled, too, about the merits of reducing a cartridge's power. The Treaty of Versailles officially had idled most of Germany's arms industry, but officers and their friends in industry actively circumvented the treaty and surreptitiously continued research and manufacturing. As early as 1934 the Wehrmacht's Army Weapons Office had secretly issued a contract for a smaller round to the GECO firm, which developed the M35, a cartridge that was 55 millimeters in total length. In 1935, once the M35 rounds became available, Heinrich Vollmer, a designer from Biberach, worked out a rifle to fire them. Vollmer's rifle was almost thirty-eight inches long and weighed a little more than nine-and-a-quarter pounds, making it shorter than a standard rifle but within the typical weight range of rifles of the time. And it had a feature that had eluded everyone who had tried to design a rifle of this size: It could fire automatically, like a machine gun. The smaller cartridge had allowed Vollmer to solve the decades-old problem of miniaturization. In a short time, he had made a rifle that hammered out rounds at a rate as high as one thousand rounds a minute but did not weigh more than its single-shot cousins. Twenty-five of Vollmer's prototypes were made by hand for testing. The Army Weapons Office liked the weapon. The army itself did not. It was not approved, which may have been due to a pair of concerns regarding production: The M35 round would have required extensive retooling at ordnance plants to be brought into mass production, and the rifle was complex in design and tedious to manufacture, making it less than ideal for soldiers and a military economy alike.[26]

In 1938, the Weapons Office started again from scratch, issuing a contract to a second ammunition firm, Polte, which began its own tests for an intermediate round. This led to the 7.92 Kurz. *Kurz* means short. The word summarizes what Polte produced. In making the new cartridge, the firm had taken the 8-millimeter Mauser, the army's standard high-powered rifle cartridge for its rifles and machine guns, with an overall length of 82 millimeters, and trimmed it, creating a version with a shorter case and shorter bullet length. The result was a similar but lighter bullet but within a cartridge that was 49 millimeters long from end to end. The Kurz offered an industrial advantage over the M35. Because it was based on the 8-millimeter Mauser, producing it would not require as many changes to factory lines to bring it into large-scale use. The result had other favorable qualities. In the most basic sense, a shorter cartridge case meant less propellant would be put into the cartridge to drive the bullet down the barrel and out the muzzle. This reduced the power of the round to roughly midway between pistol and rifle ammunition, though the 7.92 Kurz round leaned more toward a traditional cartridge's power. It was also lighter in weight, which meant supply chains and individual soldiers could carry a larger number of rounds of ammunition into combat without increasing their load. Manufacturing it required fewer resources and cost less money. And because the cartridge had less energy, it had less excess energy, which meant it would produce less recoil. Any rifle that would fire it, if designed well, would be easier to handle than conventional rifles of the time, and might allow recruits to be trained in marksmanship more swiftly.

On April 18, 1938, even before the Kurz round took final form, Hugo Schmeisser, who had designed the Maschinenpistole 18 on a hurried schedule during World War I, was tasked with working out plans for a new class of rifle at his shop in Suhl. The rifle was to have an effective range of eight hundred meters and be capable of automatic or semiautomatic fire. It was also to be designed for ready mass production. The initial name would be Maschinenkarabiner—or machine carbine—a small rifle that would fill the gap between submachine guns and machine guns, and create new possibilities for infantrymen to mass firepower. Though the Germans were in a hurry, it took Schmeisser two years to make a prototype, during which time Hitler launched World War II. His first effort was machined from solid steel. The Weapons Office wanted a weapon with components fashioned from stamped sheet metal, which would be cheaper and trim manufacturing time. Schmeisser had limited experience in sheet-metal processes, and as the German army was busy fighting in Europe, another firm, Merz in Frankfurt, was assigned to rework his prototype in stamped metal. At last, in summer 1942, the Merz gun works, working with Schmeisser, delivered fifty prototypes of the Maschinenkarabiner 42. By then Hitler had invaded the Soviet Union, too.

Schmeisser's automatic rifle was the world's first intermediate-power automatic rifle to be approved for mass production and general issue to the infantry—a medium-range weapon firing at rates that rivaled machine guns and could be managed by a single soldier. The rifle was compact and had modest recoil and limited muzzle rise. And it was versatile. It could be fired one shot at a time or on automatic, as each soldier and situation required. A concept with scintillating military promise had been given shape. Schmeisser had won a race; another firm, Carl Walther, also tried to offer a prototype, but it did not produce as many by the deadline. Schmeisser's model went into action. Most of the prototypes were sent to the Russian Front for combat trials, and several were used against the Red Army in early 1943 by a battle group under the command of Major General Theodor Scherer. The group survived a months-long encirclement after Russian ski troops severed its supply lines in Cholm. One account credited the new weapon's firepower with helping the Germans to keep the Russians back. "It was this circumstance that made it possible for them to hold out," the account read, "until they were relieved."[27] Germany tooled up for production, though critics in the military complained about integrating a new class of ammunition and the risk of complicating supply. The next version of the gun mixed subterfuge with refinement. Hitler had discovered that the army was experimenting with an intermediate weapon and was firmly opposed to it. As a veteran of World War I, including the Battle of the Somme, he retained a commitment to powerful cartridges. To avoid the Führer's scrutiny, the weapon's proponents relabeled the modified arm as a Maschinenpistole, and dubbed it the MP-43. This version merged elements of the Schmeisser and Walther prototypes, and slowly went into production under its misleading label. By early 1944 production had reached 5,000 pieces a month, and 9,000 of the rifles were made in April. The Wehrmacht was clearly satisfied. Production was projected to reach 80,000 rifles a month by 1945—a pace nearing a million a year—signaling that the Wehrmacht planned to distribute its invention widely.[28] By then Hitler had swung round and become a strong supporter. He renamed Schmeisser's automatic yet again: the *sturmgewehr,* or storm rifle, which in translation became assault rifle, the designation that stuck. A new class of firearm had been named.

Schmeisser's weapon was short-lived in battle; Germany's defeat ensured that. But in the long competition among nations for perfected infantry arms, it marked a critical moment: the arrival of the reduced-power automatic rifle. The *sturmgewehr* was only an inch beyond three feet. Like a submachine gun, it cycled out blistering automatic fire, not with short-range pistol ammunition, but with bullets that traveled at more than twenty-two hundred feet per second and had the power to incapacitate a man beyond the ranges ordinary to modern combat. It was not a full machine gun; it had no large-capacity feeding device, no tripod or sled or traversing equipment that would enable it to be firmly emplaced and used for fixed fire—the sort of accurate, long-range menace that allowed the Maxim gun and its descendants to rule the open ground of Omdurman and the Somme. But it was an exceptionally versatile firearm, well suited for all single-shot shooting at a rifleman's typical combat ranges, and its automatic fire made it ferocious for close combat and effective for suppression fire to cover an infantry unit's movement. As German units fell back late in the war, the *sturmgewehr* was picked up by Soviet troops. The Red Army grasped the significance of the weapon falling from its enemies' hands. A shift in rifle capabilities had occurred. The Red Army set out to replicate it, but with a more fully considered gun.

The first Soviet step was not to make an assault rifle. It was to make a cartridge comparable to the Kurz. Exactly when the Red Army began to work on its own intermediate bullet remains an open historical question,[29] though its interest predated the *sturmgewehr*. In czarist times, an armorer and inventor, Vladimir G. Fedorov, understood that overcoming the design problems inherent in automatic rifles would require developing a smaller cartridge. His experiments demonstrated the difficulties of using high-powered cartridges in smaller weapons. Little came of his ideas. His work stalled. In Soviet times, when denouncing imperial figures was welcome and safe, he blamed the lack of enthusiasm for his work on Czar Nicholas II. The czar, Fedorov said, had spoken openly against an automatic rifle at a lecture at an artillery school in 1912, and worried aloud about the amount of ammunition it would consume. The czar's opinion, Fedorov said, was influential, and became "widespread at the time amongst the high-ranking military commanders. That was why armourers, myself included, could not obtain noteworthy assistance in work on the automatic rifle."[30] The truth was more complicated. Soviet authorities did not offer much initial support either. In the 1920s, the Red Army discontinued production of Fedorov's rifle and stopped purchases of the slightly smaller Japanese cartridges it fired. For two more decades the Soviet military committed itself to its own traditional rifle cartridge, the 7.62x54R—the same high-powered round that had been in service since the early 1890s.*

But at roughly the same time that the *sturmgewehr* was appearing in battle, opinions were shifting, and the Red Army was developing an intermediate cartridge of its own. Soviet officials claimed that Russian designers had begun working in earnest on this cartridge in 1939, and the project had been suspended after Germany invaded Poland that year, which was followed by the Soviet invasion of Finland and the start of the Winter War. The demands of wartime production, by this account, pushed the pursuit of an intermediate cartridge aside.[31] Interest intensified on July 15, 1943, when at a conference of Beria's intelligence service, the NKVD, analysts presented two smaller cartridges used by other armies in the war—the German 7.92 Kurz and the American .30 Carbine, which was fired by a small, semiautomatic rifle issued to support troops.[32] That year, two Soviet cartridge experts, Nikolai Elizarov and Boris Semin, were at work refining the idea, and soon the pair had made a cartridge satisfactory to the Main Artillery Department: the M1943, a .30-caliber round with an overall length of 56 millimeters. The cartridge looked like little else in mainstream circulation. It was more than a full inch shorter than the standard .30-06 Springfield cartridge used in American rifles. But it was not entirely new—it closely resembled the M35 round developed by the GECO firm in Nazi Germany and used in Vollmer's rifle. The similarities between the M35 and M1943 raise the possibility that Soviet spies obtained them even before the *sturmgewehr* was fielded, or that German technicians had shared details of the round or samples during trade agreements between Germany and the Soviet Union from 1939 to 1941, when, with Hitler's permission, Soviet military delegations extensively toured German munitions plants.[33] Whatever its genesis, the M1943 fulfilled for the Red Army the niche that the 7.92 Kurz had filled for the Wehrmacht. Like the Kurz, the M1943 round flew from the muzzle at velocities closer to two thousand feet per second than the nearly three thousand feet per second traveled by the American round. In the eyes of ballisticians who favored high-velocity cartridges,

---

* The 7.62x54R cartridge remains in use today. PK machine guns and SVD sniper rifles, and their many derivatives, are chambered for this round.

such numbers marked the M1943 as a bantamweight, a round with limited range and knockdown power. To Soviet arms designers, these numbers were academic. Results were more important. Tests had shown that at six hundred meters, the new cartridge penetrated three pine boards each 2.25 centimeters thick, nearly three inches of wood in all.[34] Soviet ballisticians thought this was more than enough power and penetration to wound or kill a man at that considerable distance, which was beyond the range at which most fire from rifles found a mark. Experience had also shown that the *sturmgewehr* was not a weapon infantrymen wanted to face, at least not when armed with bolt-action arms with which to fire back. The M1943 had economic advantages, too. The army's engineers noted that for every million rounds manufactured, the M1943 saved four tons of the alloys used for cartridge cases, a ton and a half of propellant, and more than a ton of lead. By March 1944, the M1943 was in production.[35] Now weapons would have to be made to fire it.

Soviet willingness to experiment with an intermediate cartridge, and the urge to field a new class of weapons around it, marked another instance of Russian ordnance officials recognizing the value of nascent military technology before many competing nations. Both imperial Russia and the Soviet system that replaced it had proven adept at this sort of intelligent mimicry. The Kremlin's armies had not been early leaders in machine-gun design, but they had been smart borrowers of technologies and ideas from elsewhere. The results had been impressive. In the nineteenth century, czarist military officers had been among the first to see the value of Gatling and Maxim guns, and had integrated them into Russian formations and put them to effective combat use ahead of almost all the world's other armies. Soon after the turn of the century, Russia started the work that in time put it at the vanguard of the shift to automatic rifles. Vladimir Fedorov had understood the utility of machine guns in the Russo-Japanese War, and had been intrigued with the idea of a small automatic rifle. From 1909 through 1913 he led a research program to design a suitable weapon. Working with the slightly smaller Japanese cartridges, he made a nine-and-a-half-pound automatic rifle that saw limited service in World War I. His rifle never saw mass production. Thirty-two hundred were made over roughly ten years,[36] and production was cancelled after the October Revolution. But Fedorov's program bridged the Bolshevik coup. He survived the revolution and offered his services to the new socialist state. In 1918 he was sent to Kovrov, a center of arms production to Moscow's east, to help open new gun works there. He supervised much of the factory's early development, recruiting designers and workers and helping to make the plant a principal producer of machine guns and submachine guns used in the Great Patriotic War.[37] During his decades as a prominent armorer, he published widely on military and ordnance topics and became a giant in the insular clique of Soviet firearms designers. Through his outsized influence, an appreciation for automatic arms became entrenched among the Red Army design teams, and informed Soviet arms development.

This institutional affinity for automatic arms took another shape in the Great Patriotic War, when the Red Army embraced submachine guns. The Soviet Union had few submachine guns at the war's outset. As German armor and artillery neared Moscow, Stalin discovered that the Red Army had almost none of the weapons to issue to troops tasked with the city's defense. "The enemy was threatening the capital, and we had to look for two hundred submachine guns needed for those going behind the enemy's lines," he said later. "We did not let anyone sleep then."[38] The shortage was in no small part his own fault—the dictator's purges of the Red Army's senior officer corps had sent many experts and proponents of automatic arms to their deaths.[39] But the Soviet Union found that its submachine guns were easy to manufacture. State arms factories and small "victory workshops," many of them under siege in Moscow or Leningrad, produced huge quantities of the PPSh, a stubby eight-pound weapon with a distinctive circular magazine and a vented cooling shroud. The PPSh, which fired pistol ammunition, had completed its design and trial phase only in 1940. It was compact, simple to operate, and inexpensive to manufacture, and gave Soviet infantrymen firepower at close range. Its ease of manufacture was related to its design, which envisioned its being produced in part with electric welding and cold stamping, techniques considered beneath firearms by many Western manufacturers. The Soviet choice made sense. "The technology of manufacture of the PPSh ensured a considerable saving of metal, reduced the production cycle, and did not require complicated specialized tools and equipment," one Soviet officer noted.[40] This also meant that highly skilled workers were not needed for its production, and were available for other work.

As weapons go, the PPSh was neither handsome nor refined. It was a triumph of pragmatism, expediency, and unpretentious Soviet ideals. One reviewer said it fit a pattern: "The Russians excel in calculated crudity. In these burp guns, the plumbers have all but eliminated the gunsmiths."[41] Aesthetics matter to many gunsmiths. They mattered not at all to a nation that risked falling under Nazi control. Known among Soviet conscripts as the *pe-pe-sha,* the dumpy submachine gun was popular with Red Army troops and was regarded well enough that when German soldiers captured them, as they often did, they carried them, too. This is the highest vote of confidence an infantry arm can achieve, and this submachine gun, rushed into production to save the nation, became a familiar prop in Soviet symbols of the Great Patriotic War, appearing endlessly in murals and statuary. But the effect of the PPSh, and of other Soviet submachine guns that appeared later in the war, was deeper than its tactical or symbolic power. It helped cement in the Red Army an appreciation for automatic arms that could be wielded by a single man.

For all of these reasons, in 1945, the Soviet military was well positioned, intellectually and industrially, to pursue a concept that had little traction in the West: a rifle of reduced power. By the time of the Nazis' collapse, the Red Army had experienced decades of satisfactory service from the Mosin-Nagant rifle line, with roots in czarist times, which had followed the traditions of the era and fired a powerful round down a long barrel and achieved velocities in excess of twenty-eight hundred feet per second. And the Red Army had been similarly satisfied with its line of submachine guns. The idea of a weapon roughly midway between the two was not radical. It was evolutionary, and a matter of common sense.

The Red Army knew this, and as the Cold War began it leaped ahead of the Pentagon. The United States, the heavyweight among Western military powers, whose arming decisions would eventually determine which weapons NATO militaries would carry, retained its commitment to powerful cartridges. Inside Stalin's Soviet Union, the approach to arms design was more flexible, more informed, more interested in what other nations had tried. The intensity of the police state also played a role. The internal risks and frantic subcurrents, along with the preeminence of the intelligence service as an instrument of bureaucratic power, kept the system and its participants alert. Pride in the intellectual pilferage of the enemy's weapon designs made Soviet design processes less convention-bound. By early 1946, the Red Army had chosen its candidates to give a new class of weapon a Soviet form. Senior Sergeant Kalashnikov had made the first cut. He was an unlikely contender, given his history and credentials. But he was in the race.

Mikhail Kalashnikov was born in the remote village of Kurya, in the Altai region of south central Russia, in 1919, two years after Vladimir Lenin and the Bolsheviks he led had toppled imperial Russia and begun to force upon the Russian peasantry their vision of the proletarian state. Kurya rests just north of the Kazakh steppe and west of the Russian and Mongolian highlands. It is a flat, dry, windswept place bisected by the winding and turgid Loktevka River, a lonely agricultural zone far from the capital that claimed it. Kalashnikov's illiterate mother and semiliterate father were religious Cossacks, and had moved from the Kuban region of the North Caucasus and settled on the steppe after Czar Nicholas II had granted land to peasants willing to relocate.[42] Mikhail was the eighth of his mother's eighteen children, and suffered the privations of his time. Frontier hardships were shared. The family lived in a dank log cottage lit by kerosene lamps; the structure shook and groaned in storms. Some of the rooms had dirt floors. Only eight of the family's children would survive childhood. His mother, Alexandra Frolovna, buried so many of her children that she recycled names, giving two of her deceased sons' first names—Ivan and Nikolai—to boys she delivered later.[43]

Kalashnikov was weak himself, small and prone to illness. He contracted smallpox at age five and carried the disease's scars for life. He was sick enough at age six that his parents had a casket assembled for him, though he recovered to outlive everyone who watched over him. The coffin maker spat with anger. "Such a snotty little one," he said, and added, "pretended he was dead."[44] (In another account, Kalashnikov said the carpenter offered a different insult: "So young, and he's already pulling a fast one! He's a good actor, make no mistake!")[45] As he grew, Kalashnikov saw himself as a weakling, and was eager to be a *muzhik*, a real Russian man. Work served as an early outlet and a means to develop a sense of self. From age seven to nine he guided a horse and plow in the fields around the village and took pride in the labor, using his stature as a plowman to tease the boys not assigned to the fields. "I know the price of bread," he would think. "And you are small fry."[46] Kalashnikov enjoyed working with his hands and using tools. He attended school, learned to read and write, and took a liking to poetry, including writing simple verses. He understood that he was being raised in a traditional, elemental way: a Russian from hearty Russian bloodlines, eager for work, capable, steeped in vital folk values.

In 1928, after Lenin had succumbed to dementia and strokes, and Joseph Stalin had succeeded him as general secretary, Stalin and the party turned their attention to private agriculture. Stalin was dissatisfied. The agricultural sector, much of it in the hands of small landowners, was a nettlesome anticommunist symbol. As the nation industrialized, and more food was needed in the cities, he was angered by grain prices and production levels. The party tried requisition. Threats of expropriation of food drove production further down. Stalin decided to bring the peasants to heel, and to reverse the czar's redistribution of land by bringing food production under state control. By 1929 the solution was selected. Peasants' land would be seized, and peasants forced to work on collective farms. Agriculture was to be a state enterprise.

In the pogroms to subdue farmers and to pursue the party's plans, Kalashnikov's village was not spared. Government commissioners appeared and surveyed homes, livestock, and food stores; meetings with the villagers were held, sometimes overnight. The commissioners confiscated property and grain. Their plans assumed shape. Agriculture was to be centralized to stamp out a Soviet invention—the parasitic and counter-revolutionary *kulaks*—and to increase food production for the nation. The farmers were to be forced together to work on *kolkhozy,* the collective farms. Those deemed unsuited for communal work were to be exiled, so as not to disrupt the party's plans.

The effects were immediately evident. Tensions simmered in Kurya, pitting families against one another and dividing households. Even classrooms were not immune; children were listed as rich or poor. Those fortunate enough to be classified as poor enjoyed newfound social leverage, which some officially poor children used as license to taunt classmates labeled rich. True wealth was scarce. In 1930 the commissioners returned. The Kalashnikov family was blacklisted, too. As part of collectivization, the state had taken to seizing the grain and slaughtering the livestock of suspect farmers. Kurya suffered a social frenzy. The small jealousies of the less-well-off families were given an outlet in the denunciation and public hounding of more successful families. The means of identifying *kulaks* were crude. Large families often kept more livestock to feed the larger number of mouths in the home. And a family that possessed more livestock than its neighbors could attract the commissioners' attention. The Kalashnikov family was large. Mikhail Kalashnikov was confused. "It was not that easy to understand who was who," he said.[47] In 1929, at the age of ten, Kalashnikov experienced his first heartbreak in a manner peculiar to the police state. His childhood crush, Zina, a dark-eyed girl he knew from school, stopped attending class. Zina's parents had been denounced and blacklisted, and her entire family was deported in the night. Kalashnikov heard of her fate the morning after she had been shipped away. "I passed her house several times a day, hoping for a miracle," he said. "What if I saw her tender face again, what if she smiled at me again? But that was not destined to happen."[48]

A group of men drove farm animals seized from several *kulak* families into their yard and hacked the animals to death with axes. The yard filled with terrified, bellowing animals, and then with carcasses as the blood flowed. The family was gripped with fear. It was divided as well. Mikhail had two older sisters. One, Nyura, had married a poor peasant. Her household was spared attention. The other, Gasha, had married Kurya's most ardent party man. She severed ties with her parents and siblings ahead of their deportation; her siblings pretended not to know her. A few days after the slaughter in the yard, government sleighs arrived. The Kalashnikovs were taken away in the cold, except for Viktor, one of Mikhail's brothers, who hid in a neighbor's home. He was turned in by another villager and arrested. He served several years of forced labor, including time spent digging the White Sea Canal. (Kalashnikov has given different accounts of his brother's sentence. By one, Viktor was sentenced to seven years of labor, but when his sentence ended two more years were added because he dared ask the camp chief why he had been convicted. In another, Viktor was sentenced three years, but had three years added because he tried to escape three times. In this version, he asked why he was sentenced and received an immediate sentence of another year. Kalashnikov's memoirs are crowded with such jarringly inconsistent recollections.)[49]

After travel northward by sled and railway livestock car, the Kalashnikov family was relocated to western Siberia and assigned by a party superintendent to a run-down hut in Nizhnaya Mokhovaya, a village in the marshy taiga near Tomsk. They were classified as "special deportees" and forbidden to use the word *tovarisch,* or comrade, which was above them. They were told they were mere citizens, nothing more. The family was not under guard. The Kalashnikovs had not committed grave political crimes, and the area was too remote and inhospitable for it to be necessary to post guards over deported farmers. The authorities required Timofey Kalashnikov to report periodically to the local administration. The administration did not need to worry. A family had nowhere to run. Restarting an agricultural life in an unfamiliar climate, without seeds or the usual tools, the family found life worse than what it had known. In the spring Timofey Kalashnikov and his five remaining children—all sons—worked to clear an area for cultivating food, fighting off swarms of insects as they dug and tilled. Within a year Mikhail's exhausted father fell sick. He succumbed in the winter, and the family was not able to bury him during a Siberian blizzard. Kalashnikov recalled watching over his father's body, expecting the man to rise and speak.

> A snow storm was raging while Dad lay dying, and after he died it got even worse. One could not leave the house in such weather. So Dad's body was kept in a cold room in our house for a week. We had been so happy in such weather when we lived in Kurya. The wood in the stove would be burning, Mom would be combing yarn, my sisters knitting, my brothers making something, one of us would be reading verses from a book, and then Dad would begin to sing all of a sudden . . . Shivering from the cold I went up to the door of the cold room in which Dad's body was lying and listened for a long time. It seemed to me that I was just about to hear him say something softly in his confident deep voice. . . . But no, he did not sing of the "sacred Baikal," the tramp was not running down a narrow path and the Cossack was not galloping across a valley, across the faraway "Caucasian land." There was only the vicious snowstorm raging around our hut.[50]

The next year, Mikhail attended a school in which the teachers were deportees, too. The school, which was to prepare exiled children for adulthood and the modernity the Soviet Union craved, had no paper. Kalashnikov's mother remarried to a Ukrainian exile with three children of his own, and their combined household endured. They subsisted in poverty, but wood outside could be used for heat, and with it they built a new log home. Mikhail Kalashnikov resisted settling into an exile's life. As a young teenager, he was homesick and decided to return to Kurya. There he found the ashes where his family home had stood. It had been razed. He returned to Nizhnaya Mokhovaya, but soon, hoping to begin again in a place where he was not known as an exile, he fled with a friend to the small outpost of Matai, in the Kazakh Soviet Socialist Republic, near the border with China. The pair moved in with his friend's relatives, and Kalashnikov began working as a clerk at a rail yard of the Turkestan-Siberian Railway. Within a few months, he was recruited into the Komsomol, the Young Communist League. He had taken steps that would change his life. Kalashnikov remained in Matai for two years. During this time, a period of surreptitious rehabilitation, he became a *tovarisch* again, though he lived with the worry of discovery. "I was haunted by the fear that someone might learn about my past as a deportee," he said.[51]

In late 1938, Kalashnikov was drafted into the Workers' and Peasants' Red Army and assigned to duty in western Ukraine, near Poland. As a small-statured man, he was well suited for the tight confines of tank service, and was sent to a school for tank mechanics and drivers. His small size also meant that he was bullied in indoctrination camp, and he struggled to develop military bearing. But the Red Army was a social leveler, and in time Kalashnikov found a place in its ranks, though he was not impressed with all aspects of his service, particularly in matters of readying for war. Hitler's attack was to catch the Red Army in a Stalin-enforced slumber. This was the army—out of touch with its responsibilities—that had conscripted Kalashnikov. It did little to ready him for the tasks ahead. "We weren't at all prepared," he said. "The soldiers hadn't been given the necessary training. We'd hardly learned how to shoot."[52]

Tanks require continual maintenance and frequent repair, and Kalashnikov's assignment to a tank unit put modern tools in his hands. The workshops became his new outlet, as the horse and plow had been years before. He soon designed a device that measured the hours on a tank's engine and submitted it to a competition sponsored by the Red Army in 1939. The army was struggling to determine the actual number of engine hours on its fleets of tanks, due to the behavior of Soviet tank crews.

Why? Because when you work in a tank you get dirty very quickly. They would put all their clothes into petrol and then hang them out to dry. They would then write down all the petrol they used and fake the petrol receipts. That is why the fuel was used in such huge amounts. After a certain number of hours a tank is supposed to be repaired. Since they did not start the tank but instead wrote down the hours of work, the equipment was repaired but without needing it. Therefore we needed a device that would count the real numbers of hours that the tank was used.[53]

The tank was a central instrument of the Soviet army. Kalashnikov said his interest in such a machine and its well-being earned him both a commendation and a meeting with Georgy K. Zhukov, the general commanding the military district that covered Ukraine. The general transferred Kalashnikov to a tank plant in Leningrad in 1941, to work on the device.* Kalashnikov's conversion was nearly complete. With war threatening, the Red Army was a repository of national pride and a sense of communal commitment. Kalashnikov had limited contact with his scattered family. The party and the army were becoming surrogates, anchoring him in the complex and formerly hostile Soviet world. Young Kalashnikov, a son of an enemy of the people, whose brother had just finished a long term of hard labor, was being drawn into the system that had set upon his family. He was finding purpose, community, respect—and perks.

Then came the war, in June 1941, which would turn Kalashnikov finally and completely into a right-thinking Soviet man. The Wehrmacht's opening actions surprised Stalin and his generals. While German planes and artillery attacked their targets, the Blitzkrieg rolled over the borders and smashed an army that had not armed itself adequately and was not on alert. The Germans pushed on. As they overpowered Soviet defenses, front-line Soviet commanders either were in disbelief or dismissed the sounds of battle as noise from maneuvers.[54] The Kremlin seemed paralyzed; Stalin did not make a public statement for almost two weeks. Propaganda filled the air. The German columns advanced across Russian soil.

---

*Zhukov's memoirs are silent on this meeting. Though they were heavily edited by the party officials who watched over the Soviet armed forces, they make no mention of Kalashnikov whatsoever. See *The Memoirs of Marshal Zhukov* (London: Jonathan Cape, 1971).

The Red Army and the party leadership sank into confusion and recrimination. In Leningrad, Kalashnikov was ordered from the tank factory back to his regiment, promoted to the rank of senior sergeant, and sent to fight as the commander of a newly issued T-34 tank.[55] The T-34 was one of the more successful pieces of military equipment in Soviet history, a durable, quick machine, and a technical match for the German Panzers. It was a welcome replacement for the aging T-26s that Kalashnikov's regiment had driven before. But the Red Army units remained inadequately trained and poorly led, and the soldiers were mismatched against the German Blitzkrieg.

Not too many years later, after Kalashnikov became an approved symbol of the proletariat, a biography was necessary for him. This manufactured biography required whitewashing entire chapters of his life and inventing approved substitutes to bring him to this moment: the transformative experience of combat against the Germans. Such were the demands of saccharine Soviet mythmaking, part of the propagandists' norm for framing the population's understanding of their nation and figures the party chose to make historic. (Marshal Zhukov's memoirs were to become a classic case).[56] In one moment in the tale built around Kalashnikov, he was at a bunker on the front lines reading a letter from his mother, who had written, "How are you whipping the enemy there?" She then described the secure condition of the Kalashnikov home in the Altai steppe, in lovely Kurya, where the family had recently repaired the roof. Sergeant Kalashnikov closed his eyes and dreamed of the home he had left behind. Everything was about progress.

> How many beautiful hours he had spent as a child there! There was a tower from which it seemed one could see a whole miraculous world which lay beyond the Altai steppe; filled with shavings from the shop in which they were born, everything like now, tractors or machinery thundering so that in tens of courtyards chickens flew up into the sheds from fright.[57]

The story was Soviet invention, a fabricated homespun yarn. It was also striking in the audacity of its deception, which Kalashnikov tolerated and participated in for years. Sergeant Kalashnikov's mother tended to no home in the Altai. The home had been seized during collectivization when she and her family had been exiled. And there was not much need for fixing a roof on a home that party arsonists had burned to the ground. As for fond memories of the family's life at the edge of "the miraculous world," Kalashnikov later said he returned to the ruins of his childhood house once. The collective farmers complained of his visit. "Misha was looking for something on the site of your house," one of them said to his sister. "Must have been after gold."[58] There was no such letter from Kalashnikov's mother. And the Germans were not being whipped. Rather, by October, German Panzers were overrunning Bryansk, a city in western Russia along the route between Kiev and Moscow. Kalashnikov's regiment, newly equipped and reorganized, was fighting them in the rolling countryside to the city's south. And his experience of the war was much different from the predetermined struggle described in the party's propaganda organs.

What really happened in Kalashnikov's tank company has been lost in the multiple retellings. But he and the legends alike say he was wounded, apparently by an exploding shell during a skirmish. In one account, Kalashnikov said a group of Soviet tanks had become separated from the main unit, and he opened his turret hatch to look around. At that instant, he said, a shell exploded nearby, blasting shrapnel through his chest and back.[59] In another account, a shell slammed into his tank. "A big boom echoed in my ears and an amazingly bright light blinded my eyes for an instant," he said. He was knocked out. In the explosion a piece of the tank's armor struck him. "I do not know for how long I remained unconscious. Perhaps, I was out for a considerable time. . . . Somebody was trying to undo my overalls. I felt as if my left shoulder and arm were someone else's. . . . A fragment of the tank armor had passed through my left shoulder after a direct hit."[60] The official Soviet account, formerly embraced by Kalashnikov, was the most dramatic of all. In this version, Kalashnikov's platoon commander, his head bandaged and bloodied, fought off a German assault on his regiment's right flank. The officer managed to maneuver his platoon of T-34 tanks behind a group of Panzers, scattering the German infantry with machine-gun fire. The commander's tank was immolated in an explosion, and Senior Sergeant Kalashnikov—shouting, "The dirty swine, they set fire to our commander!"—rushed his own T-34 forward to help. Kalashnikov's tank was struck. A bright light flashed. He passed out. The account continues: "How long this went on, Kalashnikov didn't know. When he opened his eyes, he saw Kuchum. 'Mish, Mish, are you alive?'" In this version, Kalashnikov was wounded only in the shoulder; there is no mention of chest or back wounds.[61]

The account followed the mores of the Soviet hero tale. Soon Kalashnikov regained consciousness and was able to walk. Soaked in blood, he rode outside his damaged tank, exposed on the vehicle's armor, to help his company pick a withdrawal route. He then refused medical treatment and left his unit only when his company commander ordered him to a hospital. In later accounts, Kalashnikov has said that in fact when he regained consciousness he found his tank company had vanished. By one of these later accounts, his wounds were serious enough that he could not fight, and after hiding for two days in a bunker he was ordered by a doctor to travel to a hospital on a truck. In another account, he said his battalion commander ordered him to the hospital. The various versions Kalashnikov has circulated all converged briefly at the same point, a moment in which Kalashnikov was transported by truck with a group of wounded fellow soldiers.

Setting aside the diverging particulars of Kalashnikov's final battle and his medical case, the larger situation was certain: The Red Army was being routed as the wounded sergeant was driven off in search of a hospital. From the strategic confusion sowing fear in the Kremlin down to the tactical disarray of the units scattered around Bryansk, disaster was near. The German units were about to capture the city, which they would occupy until 1943. Panzer columns and light motorized patrols roamed the countryside. The truck with the wounded Red Army soldiers stopped at a village that seemed deserted, and Kalashnikov, the driver, and a lieutenant with burned hands reconnoitered the town. They were spotted by a German patrol, came under fire, and escaped. But as they returned to their friends, they discovered that the Germans had found the truck. Next came an incident that appears in all his memoirs: The Germans, Kalashnikov said, executed the wounded Soviet soldiers with close-range automatic fire. After the Germans drove away, the three surviving Soviet soldiers emerged from hiding and gathered at the truck to look in horror upon the dead and dying men, whom they had left only a few minutes before. "Our lieutenant was already vomiting and suddenly I doubled over, too, and threw up," Kalashnikov wrote.[62]

The official Soviet account is again much more dramatic. In it, as the truck moved through the countryside, Kalashnikov and the other wounded soldiers talked at length and in detail about the need for a new automatic weapon in the Red Army. When they reached the deserted village, Kalashnikov volunteered in spite of his injury to reconnoiter the town and set off with another soldier. They were fired upon by a German patrol but escaped and returned to a place near the truck and saw that the Germans had surrounded it. As they watched, the doctor protested about a Nazi soldier touching a wounded Russian, and a German hit him with a rifle butt. One of the Red Army soldiers on the truck—Kuchum, who in this version had tended to Kalashnikov after he was wounded—wrestled a gun from the Germans and killed a German officer, but was shot dead in the struggle. The Germans then leveled their submachine guns and opened fire. "Barbarians!" the Red Army doctor shouted as he died. Kalashnikov opened fire with a pistol, but it was no use. He was chased away by the Germans' superior firepower. Like much in the Soviet version, it is an engaging, powerful, and fully unverifiable tale.

By Kalashnikov's later telling, the three survivors wandered the countryside and were taken in and hidden and fed by a peasant, who happened to be a doctor. The man cleaned the soldiers' wounds and dressed them with new bandages. The soldiers hid in a pile of hay for two or three days, and at last, after more days of walking, reached Red Army lines near the village of Trubchevsk. "We gave ourselves up as prisoners of our own army, since we'd crossed German lines and weren't carrying any papers," Kalashnikov wrote. "Every Russian soldier's worst nightmare was to fall into German hands: We'd avoided the worst, and were safe. After a short interrogation, the lieutenant and I were sent to hospital, while Kolya reassumed his job as an army driver."

Sergeant Kalashnikov's first sustained treatment for his injuries was at Evacuation Hospital 1133 in Yelets, a city about four hundred miles south of Moscow.[63] There he stayed into early 1942, among wounded soldiers in a crowded ward. In Yelets, he said, his interest in arms design took serious shape. "My roommates included tankers, infantrymen, artillerymen and sappers. We often argued about the advantages and shortcomings of various kinds of weapons. I did not take active part in those debates, yet they made an impression on me. I listened with particular interest to those who had themselves attacked the enemy with a submachine gun or checked enemy attacks on their trenches. Their description of how the automatic weapon worked in close combat was most convincing."[64] In Yelets, Kalashnikov said, he was racked with nightmares of the execution of the wounded soldiers in the truck, and of being underequipped against German troops. "I woke up, my heart beating fast, only to hear the moans of my neighbors. They were having nightmares, too, and woke up one by one: a wonderful silence fell on the room, but not because everybody was asleep—on the contrary. I, too, lay in the dark with my eyes open and thought: How come? We had been told before the war that we would not incur heavy casualties and that we would fight with up-to-date weapons. But now, whoever I asked said that he had to share a rifle with another soldier when fighting. . . . Where were our automatic arms?"[65]

Kalashnikov said he began reading *Encyclopedia of Arms,* by General Fedorov, the czarist and Soviet armorer, which he found in the hospital library. As his understanding of arms grew he started to sketch possible designs. "That helped me forget those nightmares," he said. "And the constant pain would seemingly go away for a while." A wounded lieutenant from a paratrooper regiment befriended him, he said, and encouraged him to work. (In the official Soviet account, Kalashnikov was urged on by a Moscow storekeeper who had become an army scout.)[66] The collection of wounded soldiers, by Kalashnikov's telling, together knew the history of most Soviet and German weapons on the battlefield. Kalashnikov absorbed their words, he said, kept at his sketches, and imagined ways to equip the beleaguered Soviet troops.

In early 1942 he was granted a convalescent leave and boarded a train intending to return to Kurya. His two sisters still lived there. En route, however, Kalashnikov said he changed his mind, choosing to head to Matai, where the railway depot might provide a workshop. He wanted to try to convert his sketches to a submachine gun. According to Kalashnikov's memoirs, the chief of the locomotive department granted his request and assigned several people to assist him, including a welder, a fitter, and a machinist. A group of women at the depot's technical bureau helped with the drawings. After three months, he said, his ad hoc design team had its prototype—a "black lacquered submachine gun number one," he called it, which fired 7.62x25 Tokarev pistol cartridges.[67] (How long Kalashnikov worked on the first prototype is a subject of confusion. His memoirs say three months. In an interview, he said he worked "about half a year.")[68] Once the crude prototype was ready, the team held firing tests, first to ensure that it functioned and then to examine its accuracy. The official Soviet version is again more colorful. According to Kalashnikov's party chronicler, the depot chief was not interested in helping the sergeant, but a Communist Party organizer saw the error in this, intervened, and convinced him to allow Kalashnikov to work on the depot's grounds. Often in the official version, party officials appear to provide well-timed pushes.[69]

Sergeant Kalashnikov settled into Matai, taking up residence in a single-story wooden home and fathering a son, Viktor Mikhailovich, who was born late in 1942.[70] By then Kalashnikov had moved again, away from the child and the child's mother.[71] Once the weapon was finished, a local official decided to send the weapon and the sergeant to the military registration and enlistment headquarters in Alma-Ata, the capital of the Kazakh Soviet Socialist Republic. Kalashnikov made the train trip, drinking vodka along the way with fellow travelers. He arrived in the capital, presented himself to a lieutenant serving as the commissar's adjutant, and announced that he, a tank sergeant on convalescent leave, had made a new weapon. He said he would like to show it to the commissar. He was arrested. "This was war time and everybody was very much on guard," Kalashnikov said. "The question was, where did this staff sergeant get the means to develop a machine pistol?"[72]

Relieved of his weapon and of his belt, Sergeant Kalashnikov spent four days locked in a guardhouse, asking each of his cell mates, as they were released, to contact people on his behalf. On the fourth day the adjutant appeared and arranged his release. (Unsurprisingly, the official version makes no mention of an arrest.) A car waited outside, to bring the sergeant to the republic's Central Committee. Kalashnikov, it seemed, had enlisted the help of local party contacts he had made in Matai during the late 1930s as a member of the Komsomol. The official who met him affected the mannerisms and dress of Stalin, as many officials did at the time. He had no expertise in small arms, but, by Kalashnikov's telling, he was impressed that the weapon had been created in a railroad workshop by a sergeant with no special training. He arranged for Kalashnikov to continue his work at an institute in the city under the mentorship of a specialist in aircraft weapons. Hundreds of Soviet design institutes and manufacturing enterprises had relocated to the east, out of reach of German columns and aircraft. Working from a small adobe building, Kalashnikov refined his weapon at the Moscow Aviation Institute, which had moved to Alma-Ata.

Later, he was sent to the Dzerzhinsky Artillery Academy, which had relocated from western Russia to Samarkand, in the Uzbek Soviet Socialist Republic. There, early in the summer of 1942,* Kalashnikov met Major General Anatoly A. Blagonravov, a Soviet academician who worked during the war on automatic arms. The general examined Kalashnikov's prototype. It had technical problems and was not better than submachine guns already in Soviet use, including the PPSh. Kalashnikov has offered different versions of this meeting. In 1968 he said General Blagonravov reassigned him to the academy. "What did you do then?" an interviewer asked him. He answered: "What I was advised to do. I had to remain at the Academy and study."[73] In later accounts, and in the official tale, Kalashnikov said the general intervened quickly on his behalf, having understood that whatever was wrong with Kalashnikov's submachine gun, the fact of its creation demonstrated the sergeant's commitment and talent. He recommended that Kalashnikov be transferred to a setting where he could pursue his design ideas full-time. In one memoir, Kalashnikov quoted from the recommendation he said the general made.

> Despite a negative judgment on the submachine gun as a whole, I note the large and laborious work done by Comrade Kalashnikov with great love and persistence under extremely unfavorable local conditions. In this work Comrade Kalashnikov displayed indisputable talent in designing the submachine gun, especially if one takes into consideration his insufficient technical education and a total lack of experience in gunsmithery. I consider it advisable to send Comrade Kalashnikov to study at a technical school, at least to short-term courses for military technicians in accordance with his wish, as the first step possible for him in wartime.[74]

---

*In one memoir, Kalashnikov dates the meeting as July 2. In another, he gives the date as July 8. In an interview in 2003 Kalashnikov suggested that the meeting was in June (from the typewritten notes of an interview provided to the author by Nick Paton Walsh, correspondent for the *Guardian,* who interviewed Kalashnikov in Izhevsk).

In Tashkent, the Uzbek capital, General Blagonravov's letter was presented to Lieutenant General Pavel S. Kurbatkin, an officer who had helped defeat the *basmachi* Islamic uprising in the region twenty years before, and who commanded the Central Asian Military District. The general ordered Kalashnikov to Moscow, to the Main Artillery Department. His journey to Schurovo began. On the train, he rode with Sergei G. Simonov, an established designer. The two discussed the sergeant's prospects. General Blagonravov had told Kalashnikov to read widely and to study all existing firearms. "Without knowing the old you will not make the new well," he had said.[75] Simonov offered similar advice.

Suddenly Simonov squinted and smiled;
"Now tell me: Do you like to dismantle things?"
"You bet!" I exclaimed. "And I put something back together and then take it apart again to see every projection, every groove, every depression, every washer and every screw in order to understand exactly how everything works."
"Well, then, when we get to the testing range, the first thing you should do is dismantle and assemble every gun. Feel the metal structures with your hands and eyes—and you will understand everything better, and it will be easier for you to perfect your gun."
"I'll do that, Sergei Gavrilovich," I assured Simonov.
I thought I saw him glance at my tanker's insignia.
"We all must do our jobs! Otherwise one could end up firing a pistol from a tank."[76]

Upon arriving at Schurovo, Kalashnikov frequented the polygon's museum, which had an extensive collection of Russian and foreign weapons. "The specimens of arms displayed gave a graphic picture of the evolution of arms," he said. "I took rifles, carbines, pistols, submachine guns and machine guns in my hands and thought about how unique various designing solutions were, how unpredictable the flight of creative thought could be, and how similar Russian and foreign arms sometimes were." He added: "Sometimes I noticed that originality did not always go well with expediency."[77] Kalashnikov was also drawn to another collection: prototypes of Russian and Soviet firearms that had not been se-

lected for production. All of these weapons had flaws, but many had
an unusual component or represented a novel approach. Kalashnikov
tried to determine what about each weapon had made it a failure and
inspected weapons from this scrap heap to see if any had a valuable feature, unrelated to its disqualification, that might be applied in a future
design.

For much of the next two years, Kalashnikov shuttled between Schurovo and institutes in Tashkent and Alma-Ata. He tried to perfect his
submachine gun, but the Red Army's evaluators rejected it, saying that
it still did not improve on existing models and was too complicated. (By
the account of one of his supervisors at Schurovo, Kalashnikov's work
was of little promise: "Those samples were not even tested, since they
were very primitive. . . . I can state with responsibility that during his
work in Kazakhstan he did not create anything useable.")[78] In late 1943,
he participated in a contest for a light machine gun and was selected
as a finalist. Again his submission did not win approval. "The failure
wounded my pride," he said, and claimed that after these disappoint-
ments, he considered leaving the armorer profession and returning to
the front. Instead, he said, he was encouraged to remain at his job by
the chief of the polygon's Inventions Department. In October 1944 he
tried to work out a semiautomatic carbine matched to the new M1943
intermediate cartridge. His project was discontinued when Simonov's
entrant became the front runner. Every gun he had tried to design had
failed. "I suffered probably a hundred times more failures," he said, "than
other designers."[79]

Early in 1946, three and a half years after leaving Central Asia for his new
career, Sergeant Kalashnikov had his break: selection to continue in the
trials to design an *avtomat* for the M1943 cartridge.

After being chosen for the second phase, he was transferred from
Schurovo to Kovrov, an industrial center. Roughly two hundred miles east
and north of Moscow, Kovrov was officially a city whose workers manufactured excavators. In accordance with the Soviet cover assigned to it,
the plant where Kalashnikov was assigned was engaged in the manufacture
of motorcycles. In fact it was dedicated to the production of automatic
arms, including many of the machine guns and submachine guns that

had driven the Nazis off, among them the PPSh. When Sergeant Kalashnikov arrived, the plant had recently been awarded the Order of Lenin, the Soviet Union's highest award, for its successes arming the Red Army. During the war, the Communist Youth, working with factory workers who logged eleven-hour days on the assembly lines, constructed a new shop and production center for the Goryunov machine gun.[80] Nationalist fervor in Kovrov ran strong, at least among the officials. "A special exultant atmosphere reigned there," Kalashnikov wrote.[81]

The assignment came at a difficult time for Kalashnikov. Repression and war had scattered the Kalashnikov family, and now that the war was over, news of his family's grief was reaching him. Two of his older brothers—Ivan and Andrei—had been killed. The husband of his sister Gasha, who had been the dedicated party man in Kurya, had been lost in the war, too. The direct family tally meant that of the seven male members in Timofey Kalashnikov's peasant household in 1930, only two survived the next fifteen years unharmed—Timofey died in exile, Viktor had been sentenced to a labor gang, Ivan and Andrei were killed in action, Mikhail had been wounded. This sort of suffering distilled the sorrow of the Stalin years. The war losses also gave meaning to the nation's pride in its role and sacrifices in defeating Hitler's Germany—the Soviet Union's greatest accomplishment and a subject used to distract attention from the system's cruelty and failures. Kalashnikov was too busy to return home and comfort his bereaved relatives. The *avtomat* project demanded his attention. His life was also changing. Though he had a young son and wife in Matai, on the Kazakh steppe, he had fallen in love with Katya, the draftswoman at the NIPSMVO design bureau. He was filled with longing as he left for Kovrov. Katya had to remain behind.

For a young arms designer on an important project, Kovrov held professional promise. Revered names in Russian armaments circles had worked at the plant, including Fedorov and Vasily A. Degtyarev, a Fedorov protégé and Stalin favorite who had been promoted to general-grade rank and given a black ZIS, the imitation Packard limousine manufactured by hand for the party's elite. When the arms plant received the Order of Lenin, General Degtyarev had been granted the Order of Suvorov, a decoration typically given to leaders who excelled in combat. Such was the general's stature. He had achieved the rarefied place of rewards and fame that Stalin's machine doled out to its favored sons. Kovrov was a place for arms-design greatness. And with the push for an *avtomat,* there was fresh urgency and opportunity. A cadre of draftsmen, engineers, machinists, and other specialists were pressed into service. Kalashnikov was soon paired with his new bureau.

Over the course of a year,[82] the collective made a batch of prototype rifles. The outline of what would become the AK-47 was only faintly evident:[83] the weapon's overall length, the steeply raised front sight post, the distinctly curved magazine, and the characteristic gas tube above the barrel. But many Soviet efforts at automatics looked like this; these were not unusual traits. The resemblance to the eventual design was superficial. Internal components were still to be reworked. Kalashnikov and his collective nonetheless were proud. They had a gun. "At last the time came," he said, "when we could actually touch the whole thing, glistening with lacquer and lubricant."[84]

Sergeant Kalashnikov worked alongside Aleksandr Zaitsev, an engineer who had recently left the army. One design feature was essential. They chose to make their prototypes' parts loose-fitting, rather than snug, thinking that this might make the weapons less likely to jam when dirty, inadequately lubricated, or clogged with carbon from heavy firing. This was a counterintuitive choice to many Western designers, who had experience with the precision tools that allowed assembly lines to work within tight tolerances and mill parts to an exacting fit. Some Russian designers favored that approach, too. "Tokarev had adopted one principle which determined the overall shape of his weapons: all the elements were stuck to one another so that not even dust could get in," Kalashnikov wrote. "My approach is different: all the elements are spaced out, as if they were hanging in air."[85] The approach was not original. It had been used by Simonov for the SKS and by Sudayev in the AS-44—the weapon that had been the front runner until Sudayev fell sick.[86] It appeared to reach to the stamped-metal Soviet submachine guns, which were made with a looser fit to accommodate the anticipated shrinking and stretching associated with stamping and pressing metal sheets. It was becoming a trait in general-issue Soviet small arms and would distinguish them from their Western counterparts. To those who did not recognize the reasons behind the choice, the AK-47 could seem crude. Anyone who removed the return spring from a Kalashnikov, for example, would find that many parts, when not held by its tension, would slide and rattle. This was not crudity. This was exactly as the AK-47 was designed, and contributed to the weapon's ability to withstand field use.

In 1947 the teams gathered with their prototypes back at Schurovo for the field trials, to be held from June 30 to August 12.[87] The new weapons would compete against one another, while three others—the AS-44 prototype made by Sudayev, a captured German *sturmgewehr,* and a PPSh—would be used as controls. Kalashnikov was of two minds. In Schurovo he was reunited with Katya, and the pair was married at the garrison. "The testing range became our registry office," he said.[88] His personal life had taken a shape that would last for decades. His professional confidence was strained. He was anxious about the tests and wished that if he was to be eliminated, the elimination would be quick. His weapon, listed as the AK-46, was heavy, weighing more than nine and a half pounds.[89] He doubted its design. "My situation was not enviable as I was becoming increasingly critical of my imperfect creation," he said.[90] He worried and fretted, listening to the rifles being fired, and was able to distinguish the sound of his from the others. Once, as the AK-46 was being put through a course that included ten shots, the shooting ceased after a few rounds. The silence tormented him. Had his weapon jammed? The tester who answered the phone laughed. "A moose crossed the firing line so we had to stop shooting,"[91] he told him.

Ultimately none of the submissions were accepted outright in the second phase; all had defects. Several weapons were eliminated, and three[92]—those submitted by Aleksei A. Bulkin, Aleksandr A. Dementyev, and Kalashnikov—were ordered to be reworked and brought back for a second round. Their *konstruktors* were issued detailed instructions for improving their arms and sent to their workshops.

The AK-46 test rifles that Kalashnikov brought to the firing trials were much different from the rifles he would return with a short while later. An overhaul was to occur, which would give generations of assault rifles their distinctive qualities. At this point, the available record, already obscured by propaganda and conflicting statements, becomes cloudy once more. Many years later, Kalashnikov, by then a lieutenant general and a Soviet hero in the mold of General Degtyarev, would describe his thinking as he prepared. "In order to achieve the best results in this 'run-off' contest, I had to make a breakthrough in the design, not just improve it,"[93] he said. By this account, at Kalashnikov's insistence, he and Aleksandr Zaitsev made a series of changes that fundamentally altered the prototype and assured its selection.

The pair had already borrowed features from Allied and Axis weapons and others from his own previous work. In a hurried fashion in late 1947 at the design bureau in Kovrov, a new weapon emerged. Kalashnikov and Zaitsev shortened the AK-46's barrel by 80 millimeters. They altered its main operating system, combining the bolt carrier and the gas piston into one component, a modification that closely resembled the previous prototype by Bulkin. The alteration proved invaluable. By reducing the number of parts, it made the rifle easier to disassemble and clean. A second result was more important. The combined bolt carrier and gas piston were now massive, and by giving these parts heft, the designers provided the AK-47's operating system an abundance of excess energy every time a shot was fired. Each time the piston and bolt were pushed backward by the gas vented from the barrel into the expansion chamber, this energy was available to push through any dirt or accumulated carbon inside the weapon. The massive operating system, combined with the looser fit from the earlier prototype, would later give the rifle much of its legendary reputation.

The team was at work on other components, too. The trigger mechanism was also overhauled—a project that seems to have been led by Vladimir S. Deikin, a Soviet army* major and test official assigned to work with Kalashnikov.[94] The bureau also changed the safety catch, removing the AK-46's small selector lever and replacing it with a large sheet-metal switch. As a result of this revision, when the weapon was on safe this lever served as a protective cover over the bolt and the area around the chamber and blocked sand, dust, and dirt.[95] They also designed a large, one-piece receiver cover. The modifications completed much of what would become the AK-47 and made the already simple prototype more simple still. Time was tight. The field tests had ended in August. Revised prototypes were due back at NIPSMVO in mid-December. Zaitsev said that by working

---

* The Red Army was renamed the Army of Soviet Union in 1946, during the time that the design team in Kovrov was working with Kalashnikov; the term Red Army no longer applied.

day and night, the group managed to finish the documents for the new design in a month, and a month and a half later had made the first of the new models in wood and steel. By November they had made three models. "We felt that we were on an uphill path," he said.[96]

Exactly who was responsible for all of these final modifications is unclear. General Kalashnikov would describe a near epiphany, a eureka moment. "I came up with several new ideas that turned my life upside down. I completely altered the general structure. As the rules of the competition didn't allow me to change its overall design, I had to pretend I was working on a mere improvement. Sasha Zaitsev, my faithful right-hand man from the start of the competition, was at this time the only person aware of my real plan."[97] He added, "Our design represented a real leap forward in the history of automatic weapons construction. We broke all the stereotypes that had dominated the field."[98] He also claimed the changes were related to an inherent flexibility in his design style.

> Often times designers become affixed to a certain idea and hesitate to discard it. They are so attached to their original concept, you could say, like a spinster to her cats! I am just the opposite. Today this idea seems good, tomorrow I might just toss it. The day after I might do the same until such a point, when I can feel the design is completed. When you work with somebody who is afraid to discard an idea that has outlived its usefulness, you notice that they find it difficult to part with it. They think their accomplishments should last for all times. I am referring here to the need for a certain flexibility (of mind), i.e., the ability to test as many ideas as possible and not get too attached to any one in particular. This enables one to develop models of high reliability. . . . There is no limit to improvement![99]

That was Kalashnikov's version. Zaitsev remembered events differently. He said that in fact he had conceived of the changes. Kalashnikov, he said, opposed them. His recommendations were made at Kovrov after Kalashnikov returned from NIPSMVO with the judges' recommendations. "I suggested the Kalashnikov assault rifle be entirely redesigned," Zaitsev wrote. Kalashnikov resisted, Zaitsev said, because he thought there was not enough time to overhaul the design before the final trials. "I managed to convince him I was right."[100] D. N. Bolotin, a Soviet arms writer who was friendly with many designers, thought enough of Zaitsev's account to include it without challenge in his published work.[101] Aleksandr Malimon, an officer who worked as a test officer at the polygon, also chronicled Zaitsev's contributions as matters of fact.[102] These accounts present a credible challenge to Kalashnikov's accounts, which blended the official Soviet biography with post-perestroika inserts and edits.

Further challenges to the rifle's parentage have also suggested that Kalashnikov had not been forthcoming about the origins of the AK-47. Central to these claims were two allegations that flowed from forces both historical and personal. After the Soviet Union's collapse, many legends were questioned by a population weary of propaganda and state lies; this larger re-examination led to a revisiting of the official story of the AK-47. Kalashnikov appeared to have drawn some of the attention on himself. Several colleagues thought the designer, who had basked in state glory and enjoyed benefits and favored treatment for decades, had assigned in his writing and public remarks too much credit to himself. They came forward with a fuller story.[103] Their counterclaims, largely ignored in the West, have proven long-lasting within arms circles in Russia.

One allegation asserted that Kalashnikov's final prototype included a primary design feature—the integrated bolt carrier and gas piston—lifted from Bulkin's earlier submission. Bulkin led a design bureau from Tula, a city south of Moscow that was another center of Soviet arms production. Unlike Kalashnikov, who was adept at endearing himself to his army and party superiors, Bulkin had a quarrelsome personality. He was not well liked by the judges.

The other allegation asserted that Kalashnikov had inside help from a testing officer at the range, Major Vasily Fyodorovich Lyuty, who provided Kalashnikov many ideas he applied to his prototype. Lyuty, who worked at Schurovo, claimed that he shepherded the early Kalashnikov design through a disappointing first showing and overruled a stern report from U. I. Pchelintsev, a testing engineer, which concluded: "The system is incomplete and cannot be further developed." In all, Lyuty claimed, he recommended eighteen changes to the first prototype, which Kalashnikov accepted. Pchelintsev's rejection letter was then rewritten.

I felt the test frustration deeply with Mikhail, because we were friends. This is why when he asked me, as the chief of the testing unit, to have a look at the gun and Pchelintsev's account to out-line the improvement program, I agreed of course. In fact, I took up all the subsequent business in my hands, thank God I had the knowledge and experience needed for it. Having studied the test report scrupulously I came to the conclusion that the design had to be redone almost anew, since according to my calculations 18 im-provements of different complexity had to be made. I told Mikhail about it and explained what, and most important, how, this can be done to the *avtomat*. With the account of my remarks, I changed Pchelintsev's conclusion and recommended the gun for further improvement.[104]

Major Lyuty added that after the first round of tests, he and Ka-lashnikov worked side by side, along with Colonel Deikin, and the trio made the prototype that became a finalist. Major Lyuty later fell into official disfavor. He was arrested in April 1951 and taken to Lubyanka, the headquarters of the Soviet intelligence service, where he was beaten and accused of preparing a terrorist act against party leaders, of circulating anti-Soviet propaganda, and of participation in a counterrevolutionary group. He feared he would be executed. After torture and with coaching from another inmate, he agreed to confess to involvement in anti-Soviet propaganda. He was sentenced to ten years. Lyuty served four years in a labor camp, cutting wood near Kansk, and then was transferred to a *sharaga* near Moscow, where scientists and designers served their sen-tences. In 1954, after Stalin died, he was rehabilitated and returned to work, but not before Kalashnikov had become a proletarian legend and model of socialist virtue. Kalashnikov's public standing precluded serious challenge to his record in Soviet times.

On one level, claims that the Kalashnikov design bureau, by appro-priating elements of Bulkin's design or accepting help from a test officer, tainted the contest do not account for the nature of the Soviet army's pursuit of new arms. The Soviet Union did not operate by Western rules. Notions of intellectual property were incompletely formed. Of-ficials encouraged designers to copy features of any weapon that could be usefully applied to their prototypes, even weapons in development by competitors.[105] Kalashnikov's final design did not copy Bulkin's test model in full; it incorporated a central idea but changed details, including the location of the cams. Kalashnikov never denied that he was an aggressive borrower. Collecting good ideas from existing firearms was, to him, fundamental to sound design. One of his reflections was resonant on this point. Sometimes originality does not go with expediency, he said. The first *avtomat* that his bureau produced for the M1943 cartridge, the AK-46, borrowed from John C. Garand, the designer of the standard infantry rifle for the United States, and his bureau tinkered with variations on Schmeisser's trigger assembly, obtained by studying captured German arms. More broadly, as tests for an automatic weapon proceeded from Sudayev's AS-44 to Kalashnikov's final prototype, many submissions by different designers came to resemble one another in significant ways. Design convergence seemed to have been a welcome byproduct, even an aim, of holding competitions.

Kalashnikov always rebutted his accusers. He berated a Russian newspaper for publishing a story arguing that he had copied Bulkin's work in an untoward way. "Certain people would like to cast doubt on the paternity of the AK-47," he wrote. "I'm 83 years old, but fortunately I'm still here to reply to those mendacious accusations!" The questions persisted. The changes in his prototypes just before the final phase were so striking, and a central change bore enough physical and conceptual resemblance to Bulkin's earlier design, that they pointed to the broader nature of the AK-47's creation, which had been cocooned in a simplistic narrative for decades. They suggested that the weapon came into existence via expansive collaboration rather than springing from the mind of one man.

Whatever the exact origins of the final changes and whoever deserved the credit—Kalashnikov, Zaitsev, Bulkin, Lyuty, Deikin, and others—the AK-47 had taken its recognizable form. And many of its mechanical merits were evident. Kalashnikov described an encounter with Vasily Degtyarev, the general who had designed some of Russia's most successful arms. The meeting, if the account is to be believed, said much about the redesigned weapon's potential. It occurred as the last prototype neared completion. The general and Kalashnikov met at Kovrov. Someone in the group proposed that they show each other their work. "Cards on the table," he said.

The graying sixty-six-year-old general and the twenty-eight-year-old sergeant presented their weapons. Kalashnikov had disassembled his, so the general could examine each part. These two men were not the sort who would be expected to meet like this. The general had been predestined to be an armorer. Born into a family of czarist gun-smiths in Tula in 1880, he began working in the city's arms factory at age eleven. Like Fedorov, he endeared himself to the Bolsheviks after the October Revolution and began working on automatics. As Leon Trotsky was building a socialist army, he worked at the gun works at Kovrov, which became his home. Fedorov was aging. Degtyarev was heir apparent to be the Soviet Union's *konstruktor* emeritus. His chest was adorned with state prizes and medals; his party contacts were extensive. With his short gray hair, parted to the side, he vaguely resembled Nikita Khrushchev, though he had a restrained and dignified air. He looked at the AK-47, the work of unknowns. As Kalashnikov tells it, he was impressed.

> All of a sudden, General Degtyarev made this staggering declaration: "The way Sergeant Kalashnikov has put the components of his model together is much more ingenious than mine. His model has more of a future—of that I'm certain. I no longer wish to participate in the final phase of the competition."
>
> He'd said all of that loud enough for everyone to hear. I can remember the moment perfectly well. The general was in uniform, decorated with his medal, the star of a Hero of Socialist Labour. I think that it was very brave of him to think in this way. It was an act of great honesty, and indeed nobility—especially in view of the fact that he was one of the "favourites" of the regime.[106]

This story also shifted in its multiple tellings. Kalashnikov told a cura-tor of the Smithsonian Institution, whom he befriended, that General Degtyarev made his declaration during the final testing.[107] In another memoir, he recalled the moment differently. In this version, soon be-fore the final tests, officials from the Main Artillery Department visited Kovrov.

> Degtyarev gave a tired smile, as if under the pressure of an invis-ible weight. His movements seemed sluggish to me and he shuffled noticeably. However, he quickly became animated when he saw our prototype. "Well, let's see what the young are up to now." Degtyarev

started to examine each part, each component of the prototype which
I was taking apart right on his table. "Yes, it's a clever piece of work,"
said Degtyarev as he took the bolt carrier and the receiver cover in
his hands. "Your solution to the fire selector problem is certainly
original." Speaking aloud, Degtyarev did not conceal his opinion. At
the same time, we were inspecting his assault rifle. It seemed rather
heavy to us and more improvements could have been made as regards
component interaction. But Degtyarev, after scrutinizing our prototype again, this time as an assembled unit, suddenly concluded: "I do
not think there is much sense in sending our prototypes to the tests.
The design of the sergeant's prototype is better and more promising.
You can see it with the naked eye. So, comrades," he said addressing
the officials, "perhaps we will have to send our prototypes to a museum." . . . Degtyarev, a man of high morals, was most exacting and
honest in everything.[108]

The varying accounts of a meeting that obviously held high significance to Kalashnikov are important for another reason: They diverge not
only from each other but from the official Soviet version. The jumble
hints yet again at the unreliability of the long-standing narrative of the
AK-47's invention and of many of its sources. In his memoirs, Kalashnikov said he had never met Degtyarev until this moment. In interviews
with the curator,[109] and in the Soviet account, Degtyarev was a presence
earlier. Kalashnikov, in the Smithsonian interview, said he met Degtyarev
in a competition for an automatic rifle for the 7.62x54R cartridge; this
would have been at least two years before. The Soviet biography both
contradicted Kalashnikov's chronology and produced a sentimental vi-
gnette that propagandists spun around the designer for decades. In it,
Degtyarev had a cameo, serving as a wizened Soviet hero offering advice
to an armorer-to-be at a firing range on a summer day. The sound of
grasshoppers rose from the fields. Kalashnikov was nearly overcome with
excitement, but dared to ask a question.

"Comrade general," the senior sergeant said suddenly, "What qualities in your opinion are necessary for a designer-gunsmith?"
    Degtyarev turned toward him. "A gunsmith? Ah then, have you
been chosen as a gunsmith, Kalashnikov?"

Surikov* pricked up his ears. So this was Kalashnikov! And it seemed that Degtyarev remembered his name. He looked first at Degtyarev then at the questioner, trying not to miss a word. The question was interesting.

"Gunsmiths are made of the same clay as everyone else. So let's simply say: what qualities does a gunsmith need. I think that first of all it's a love of work and persistence. I have spoken more than once of creative fiber. I'll say this to you now: this fiber is a love of invention which gives a man no rest. Even in your sleep you see your machine as it would be if it were manufactured real . . ." Degtyarev paused and looked up toward the top of the pine trees. "I don't know if you can develop this creative fiber. I have felt it since my very earliest years. But as to persistence it is possible and necessary to cultivate it. I discipline myself constantly."

He was silent. No one wanted to break the silence.[110]

This was the sort of narrative that informed the West's understanding of the AK-47's origins. To a large extent, it still does.

In many ways, it is easier to describe what the first AK-47 was, than to describe its origins. To understand how this automatic rifle worked, it is necessary first to grasp the operation of a more simple firearm. The process begins with a cartridge, which provides both the bullet that will fly out of the muzzle and the energy that will propel it. The bullet is at one end, crimped watertight to a metallic case. Inside the case is a granular propellant, known, in layman's terms, as gunpowder, though modern smokeless propellants are much different from the true gunpowder of the nineteenth century and before. The propellant stores latent energy. Once a cartridge is seated snugly in a weapon's steel chamber, the rifle is fired when its firing pin strikes a small primer at the bottom of the cartridge case. In a flash, the primer ignites the propellant, which is converted at nearly explosive speeds to gases. The release of energy liberates the bullet

---

* Surikov, a colonel, worked for the Main Artillery Department; in this account he has been assigned to nurture Sergeant Kalashnikov's development, and ventured to a firing range to find him and to convince him to enter the contest for an *avtomat* (author's note).

from the crimp in a manner reminiscent of the way a champagne cork flies from a bottle. The bullet has nowhere to go but down the length of the barrel, so it accelerates through the open path toward the muzzle, pushed by expanding gases. As the bullet moves it picks up spin imparted by grooves in the barrel, known as rifling, that force the bullet to rotate on its central axis. The spin will stabilize the bullet in flight, reducing drift and allowing it to travel truer to the shooter's aim. As the bullet leaves the barrel the excess energy that put it to flight is manifested in several ways—recoil, muzzle flash, noise, and a rush of gas venting into the air.

To make a rifle that will fire automatically using energy from the cartridge, designers must capture some of that excess energy and convert it to the work of clearing the spent shell casing from the chamber, reloading, and firing the next round. In the design chosen by the Kalashnikov team, the rifle bleeds a portion of gas via a diversion. This is done through a small port in the top of the barrel, about 5.5 inches from the muzzle, that slopes backward at a forty-five-degree angle. Each time a bullet passes the port, pushed by the expanding gases, excess gas rushes through the port into a tube seated above the barrel that serves as an expansion chamber. Within the chamber is a piston. The gas forces the piston backward, toward the shoulder of the shooter, in the split second before the bullet leaves the muzzle. The piston is integrated with a bolt carrier, and as this entire assembly moves backward it unlocks and withdraws the bolt from the chamber and extracts the empty cartridge case. As the bolt continues backward and clear of the chamber, the spring-loaded magazine, mounted at the bottom of the weapon, forces the next cartridge up and into place. The piston and bolt's journey is meanwhile arrested by a return spring, which now, fully compressed, pushes the piston forward and seats the fresh cartridge snug in the chamber, where it is struck by the firing pin, restarting the cycle. The system is theoretically simple. In the AK-47, it was mechanically simple, too. To describe it today is to describe a well-known technology, like that of a lightbulb, a water pump, or the carburetor on a 1965 Ford. In late fall 1947, a weapon that could do these things reliably at this size was more than new. It was a product that fit the aspirations and carefully cultivated image of the Communist Party, and the army that served it, and the needs of soldiers in war.

* * *

The Kalashnikov prototype would still undergo fine-tuning, but it was now the clear front runner. It was both imperfect and special at once. What made it special? Later, after extensive testing and considerable refinement, its simplicity and its reliability would become known. But even before those results were understood, both as a mechanical device and as a combat firearm, it marked a profoundly smart compromise. Whenever an army sets out to choose a rifle, it faces choices, and many of the choices inherent in rifle design are difficult. It is easy to draw up specifications, a wish list of what a rifle might do. The ideal rifle for a nation's combat forces would be a weapon with a long range, a high degree of accuracy, and knock-down power against any man the shooter could see. It would be eminently reliable in a variety of climates and field conditions, light in weight, and small in size, with an intuitive, ergonomic design that would make it easy to master and comfortable in the hand. Soldiers would be able to move quickly with it through confined spaces, as when entering and exiting an armored vehicle, running though a doorway, climbing through a window, or rushing through underbrush. It would also be able to be fired semiautomatically (one round at a time) for shooting precisely at distinct targets, or automatically (in bursts) for overpowering close-in targets and for delivering a high volume of bullets to suppress an area or enemy force. When fired, this rifle's recoil (or "kick") would be light. Its muzzle rise would be minimal, so that when fired automatically its bullets could be fired level to one another, and not move gradually upward, first over the target, and with subsequent rounds, even higher, into air. Moreover, the ideal rifle would be easy to take apart, simple to clean, and a cinch to reassemble—so well considered that a user could put it back together intuitively. Not only would it have few moving parts, it would have no small or fragile parts that might be lost or broken when servicing a rifle at night, or in the woods, or in combat. It would resist rust inside and out, and would not tend to seize up or become sluggish when dirty, blackened with carbon, or coated in sand or mud. All of these traits would make it an ideal device for the infantry, or for arming civilians for civil defense. But it would not be enough for a rifle to be perfect in field use. The nation would have preferences, too. The treasurer would want the weapon to be inexpensive and long-lasting, so as not to be replaced for many years.

And the generals would ask that it be easy to manufacture, so that it could be available now and mass-produced quickly in the event of war.

Such a rifle does not exist. It probably never will. There are many reasons for this, but they all come down to compromises. In choosing one feature, designers eliminate other traits. Take muzzle velocity, which is an element of effective range. The instant a bullet departs a rifle's muzzle, gravity and the environment work on it, and it begins to decelerate and to drop. To achieve the high velocities required for long range, barrels must be long enough for a bullet to build up speed. In this manner, they depart the muzzle at such velocity, say twenty-five hundred or more feet per second, that they do not drop significantly over the course of two hundred or three hundred yards. But as barrel length increases, more steel is used, and the rifle becomes heavier, more cumbersome, and more expensive. Want a rifle that has long range and loads itself between shots? Adding such features adds complexity. A manually loaded bolt-action rifle can be as straightforward in construction as in use. Self-loading abilities require new components, and choices of gas tubes, springs, pistons, and rods. Add automatic fire, and the rifle needs some sort of selector switch that lets the shooter choose between settings: safe, semi, and automatic. And adding automatic fire means that the rifle will be subjected to more strain and much more heat. This requires a stronger, heavier design to withstand these burdens and remain reliable and safe. This will drive up weight and costs, too.

Until World War II, when rifles were designed, they were designed to have some, but not all, of these traits. Then came the breakthrough couples—the 7.92 Kurz and the *sturmgewehr,* followed by the M1943 cartridge and the Kalashnikov design bureau's final prototype. As compromises go, these cartridges and rifles represented a pair of design feats. And after the German models fell out of production, their Soviet offspring appeared. Like the 7.92 Kurz, the M1943 claimed the largely uncharted ballistic territory between pistol and rifle rounds. But it cheated a little toward the rifle. And the AK-47 prototype took its place between the submachine gun and the traditional infantry rifle. But it cheated toward the submachine gun in size and weight. The result was a weapon that had the necessary firepower within the ranges at which most combat occurred, and yet was, at last, light enough to be carried by one man, along with a robust load of ammunition. The numbers made it clear. Rifles often were too big for the full range of uses. The Russian semiautomatic rifles in the Great Patriotic War, designed by Tokarev, exceeded four feet in length and weighed nearly nine pounds unloaded. The M1 Garand, the standard American infantry arm in World War II, exceeded forty-three inches and weighed almost ten pounds. Submachine guns were of a welcome size, but lacked range. The PPSh was thirty-three inches long and weighed eight pounds. The early American Thompson gun was almost a yard long and weighed nearly eleven pounds; a later form shed almost two inches but still came in heavy, at ten pounds and nine ounces. The Kovrov design bureau's final prototype was just over thirty-four inches long and weighed slightly more than eight pounds—it was, at a glance, a weapon the size of a submachine gun that had much of a rifle's power.

More than four years after the introduction of the M1943 cartridge, at last came time for the final field trials for an automatic weapon that would fire it. Tests began in NIPSMVO in mid-December 1947. Evaluating a proposed infantry rifle is an intensive process, typically involving engineering examinations, a series of firing tests for durability, accuracy, and reliability, and troop trials examining ergonomics and ease of use. The ballistics of the rifle and cartridge combination are also studied, including the so-called terminal ballistics—the effects the rounds have on objects they strike, from a wooden board to a car windshield to various parts of the human body, which can be determined, to a degree, by shooting large live mammals (adult pigs are a favorite; goats have often been used) or human cadavers.[111] Rifles are subjected to extreme cold and heat, and subjected to firing courses at various ranges and rates of fire. Some weapons face lengthy firing drills while slicked with excessive lubricant, others with no lubricant at all.[112] Testers try to break prototypes, and submit others to such extended firing, without rest or time to cool, that barrels can melt and wooden stocks can smolder, even burst into flames.[113] Kalashnikov has provided few details over the years of the engineering testing of the weapon, and scant other details have been made public, though Western technical intelligence officials would conduct engineering tests on Kalashnikov rifles in the 1950s and early 1960s after defecting Soviet soldiers were dispossessed of their arms as they slipped through the Iron Curtain.[114] Parts of the environmental testing have been shared.

At NIPSMVO, the loaded rifles were submerged for long periods in swamp water, then expected to fire. Then came the "sand bath," with each rifle dragged through ash, broken bricks, and fine sand—first by the barrel, then by the stock—until the rifles were filthy and every opening in the weapon was clogged. "After that, without any sort of cleaning . . . they were fired," Kalashnikov said.[115] Again uncertainties stalked the designer. "Despite myself, I began to doubt that further shooting would proceed without failures," he wrote. Zaitsev consoled him. The prototype fired almost flawlessly. "Look, look," Zaitsev said, during one course of fire. "The sand is flying in all directions, like a dog shaking off water—look."[116] This was the result of two design choices: loose fit and massive operating parts.

The weapons were subjected to extreme cold in a special chamber. Kalashnikov said the weapons were also exposed to salt water to determine how they would withstand its corrosive effects. The AK-47 proved more reliable than the others, though accuracy remained a Soviet army concern. "The advantages of my modification were blindingly obvious," he said. "I was jubilant."[117] Next the weapon was dropped from heights onto a concrete floor so it would land on its barrel, then its stock. The weapon survived and functioned normally afterward. For assessing terminal ballistics, Kalashnikov said, the rifles were fired at dead animals. The soldiers requested vodka for this duty, Kalashnikov added; this was considered an unpleasant task.

Tests continued until January 11, 1948.[118] The results were presented to a thirteen-member technical and scientific commission, which decided Kalashnikov's *avtomat* most closely fulfilled the requirements of the 1945 order. Mikhail Kalashnikov's submission had won. It was not without flaws, and needed much follow-on work, which would be assigned to other engineers. But it was an acceptable descendant of the *sturmgewehr*. As the news was released, an assistant rushed to Kalashnikov. "Today you must dance, Mikhail Timofeyovich," he said. "The *Avtomat Kalashnikova* has been accepted as the standard weapon."[119] The AK-47, a rifle that had existed only for weeks, was heading for production.

CHAPTER 6

The Breakout: The Mass Production, Distribution, and Early Use of the AK-47

K. Marx and F. Engels taught that in order to win victory over the class enemies the proletariat had to be armed, organized and disciplined. A resolute rebuff had to be given to any attempt on the part of the bourgeoisie to disarm it.

—Andrei A. Grechko, Soviet minister of defense[1]

THE AK-47 ARRIVED TO A TIME AND GEOPOLITICAL SITUATION like no other. Through technical intelligence and the dedication of enormous resources, Stalin's military had developed a firearm with promise to be the standard weapon for legions of socialist workers and peasants. A working prototype of a compact automatic rifle had been made that was well suited for most uses in modern war and could be readily mastered by conventional conscripts and violent revolutionaries alike. Yet the assault rifle's practical merits do not explain the proliferation that followed. The AK-47 was not to break out globally because it was well conceived and well made, or because it pushed Soviet small-arms development ahead of the West.[2] Technical qualities did not drive socialist arms production. It was the other way around. Soviet military policies mixed with Kremlin foreign-policy decisions to propel the output that made the AK-47 and its knock-offs available almost anywhere. Were it not for this more complicated set of circumstances, the AK-47 would have been a less significant weapon, an example of an evolutionary leap in automatic arms that became one nation's principal infantry rifle. Mikhail Kalashnikov would have remained an obscure figure, a man with a surname—like that of Schmeisser or Garand—recognized by specialists, not as an informal global brand.

In the long history of automatic arms and their roles in war, there were periods when everything changed. In the 1860s, Richard Gatling began selling the first rapid-fire arms that worked well enough for battle. His guns offered small or isolated military detachments a one-sided advantage in colonial actions. In the 1880s, Hiram Maxim contributed an awesomely lethal efficiency when he invented the first truly automatic gun and peddled it in Europe's officer courts. From 1916 through 1918 machine guns became common to all modern ground forces, at terrible cost to men led by officers whose tactics had not kept pace with the instruments of war. Then came the Soviet Union and the design stimuli resulting from World War II. From 1943 to the early 1960s, and centered on the 1950s, automatic arms reached an evolutionary end state. Everything changed once more. In the 1950s, socialist assault rifles gained international acceptance, and the sprawling infrastructure for their mass production in multiple countries was created and set in motion. The developments were often subtle and seemingly unrelated—a technical decision here by one entity, a political decision there by another. The result, as decisions accumulated, was an improved AK-47 and assembly lines opening in one nation, then another, while these weapons began to show up in battle, first as rarities, then curiosities, and then almost everywhere.

What fueled proliferation? Two larger phenomena drove the AK-47's spread from the secrecy of Schurovo to near ubiquity in conflict zones. They can be distilled into categories: the Kremlin under Stalin, and the Kremlin under Khrushchev. Viewed through the prism of the Soviet Union's industrial psychology, Stalin was the AK-47's creator, the impatient dictator whose engineers conjured to existence weapons of all kinds, and whose arms plants perfected and assembled them at a hurried pace. This phenomenon predated the development of the gun. The same forces that led to the *avtomat*'s creation predicted a certain degree of its abundance, even—perhaps especially—during a time when Kalashnikov-producing nations lagged in producing consumer goods. The assault rifle was a priority product in the planned economy of Stalin's police state, which saw itself under threat and was preparing for inevitable war. The emphasis on fielding assault rifles fit neatly into the larger pattern. As the Soviet Union expanded its nuclear arms programs, it overhauled its conventional equipment and engaged in arms races with the West across an array of items: attack aircraft, submarines, radar systems, tanks. Cold War urgency pressed Soviet engineers to improve the AK-47 and its follow-on arms and rush them to mass production. Production was linked to the strength, even the survival, of the state. All the while, as the force of Stalin's personality and the particulars of his fears gave rise to the Soviet assault-rifle industry, the world was being divided into camps. The AK-47 emerged in time to become the principal firearm of one of them. These historical pressures forged the AK-47 into something more than a mere defense product; it was a national, then an international, requirement. But even Stalin could not last forever. Someone else would send the rifles around the world. Nikita S. Khrushchev, who would replace him, became the Kremlin's arms dealer, the man whose government passed the weapons out and whose decisions would serve to expand assault-rifle production to outsized levels.

In the mid-1950s, while the Soviet Union staggered out of Stalin's reign, the Kremlin was in a unique position. It was both the world's standard bearer for socialism and a nation with the military power to help fraternal nations with their armament desires. Soviet arms became a form of Soviet political currency. Nations queued up, seeking their share, as did revolutionary groups, and, later, terrorist organizations. As the AK-47 gained acceptance and approval in the Soviet army, the Kremlin used it as a readily deliverable tool in the game of East-West influence jockeying, both as a diplomatic chip to secure new friendships and as an item to be distributed to those willing to harass or otherwise occupy the attention of the West. The trends gave energy to each other. As AK-47 production gathered momentum, the Kremlin also began pursuing a more activist foreign policy, and this policy shift encouraged the distribution of more military technology, for reasons practical and political. On the practical side, convincing allies and potential allies to select Soviet equipment expanded standardization. By circulating Soviet patterns across the contested world, Kremlin arms deals made interoperability with Soviet troops easier in the event of future wars and as notions of socialist revolution spread. This was an especially useful pursuit for cartridges and firearms, those most basic tools of war. Standardization also made client states accept that in the event of their own local wars, they would need to be resupplied via the Kremlin. The result was a logistical and psychological arrangement that created dependencies serving Kremlin interests. On the political side, sharing military technology cemented allies and made new friends for the Kremlin, all the while helping to frustrate the West. Clients and customers brought an intangible benefit, too. Foreign acceptance of Russian firearms created the impression that Soviet equipment was preferable to Western military products. For a nation that struggled to manufacture decent elevators and shoes, in a system in which wool shirts were not necessarily wool, approval of a Soviet weapon served as a refreshing endorsement of an industrial base often making shoddy goods.[3]

For all of these reasons, the period centered on the 1950s marked the most important years for the Kalashnikov line. The weapon had been developed. Now it would be debugged, and the man credited for its invention would be given public stature and material rewards and would be regarded as a proletarian hero—the role he would live for decades. The infrastructure would be built to manufacture the assault rifle across the socialist world, and the Russian assault rifle would see its first combat use—both by conventional forces and by insurgents. The United States military, all the while, would misjudge the meaning and significance of the AK-47's arrival. Beyond dismissing the value of the socialists' main firearm with parochial superiority, it would develop weapons for its own forces that would fail when it mattered most, losing one of the most important but least-chronicled arms races of the Cold War.

For the initial step in these processes, the Soviet army had to organize a base of domestic production, first to improve the AK-47's design and then to equip its combat divisions. The *avtomat* was a standout compromise firearm, but like all compromises it was not perfect—not at all. The prototypes had flaws, and initial production proved problematic without extensive fine-tuning and a few major changes. In 1948 the army ordered rifles for field trials to be assembled in Izhevsk, one of the country's rifle-manufacturing centers.[4] The accounts of when this occurred vary. By one, Mikhail Kalashnikov said that in January 1948, the day after the announcement of the AK-47's victory at Schurovo, he and a small team were transferred to the Izhevsk Motor Plant No. 524, which was officially manufacturing motorcycles.[5] Izhevsk was an isolated industrial city almost six hundred miles east of Moscow, a community closed to most outsiders, hemmed off by dense forests and Russian suspicions. It had been a center of rifle production since czarist times. During the revolution, the gun works had gone over to Lenin and his party and helped arm Trotsky's new forces. If socialism promised a grand new order of workers' rule and higher living standards, it did not happen here. Izhevsk was a dingy factory town, with block upon block of bland apartment buildings surrounding factories belching dark smoke. The Orthodox church at the city's center had been converted into a movie house. The brick-walled gun works, near the shore of a cold polluted lake, was sealed off by foreboding iron fences. A nearby steel plant kept it fed. Far from Moscow and Leningrad, this drab milieu was to be Kalashnikov's new home.[6]

The initial manufacturing efforts posed problems. The AK-47 remained an unfinished idea, a set of integrated firearm design concepts that together made an automatic rifle. It needed substantial refinement. Lingering concerns about the weapon's accuracy prompted the army to hold more tests, and, at one point, to try reducing the power of the M1943 cartridge.[7] Durability was a concern, too, as some parts, including the return spring, were insufficiently sturdy.[8] A batch of rifles was assembled and in May 1948 a second plant—Factory No. 74, the Izhevsk Machine Engineering Plant, or Izhmash—was ordered to produce the AK-47 as well.[9] Once the first batch was finished, the rifles were sealed in special containers and sent to the army. Two months later, Kalashnikov was summoned to the Main Artillery Department in Moscow, and then rode by train with Nikolai N. Voronov, chief marshal of Soviet artillery, to the location where the field tests were held. Kalashnikov claimed to have already been a favorite of Voronov. The marshal, he said, had helped free up funding for the AK-47 prototypes after a lower-ranking general had refused it.[10]

Field trials are a normal stage in preparing a rifle for military service. What was revealing about this trial had little to do with the tests themselves, but with Kalashnikov's behavior around senior officers. On the train back to Moscow, Marshal Voronov called Kalashnikov to a meeting, where Voronov questioned him in front of a group. As Kalashnikov described it, the session was less an interrogation than an ice-breaker, an effort to learn more of a young noncommissioned officer the Soviet Union was to catapult to fame. Voronov's questions covered Kalashnikov's family and background—those years before Kalashnikov became a *konstruktor*. This was a potentially treacherous patch for a *kulak's* son. The sergeant, mindful of the dangers, resorted to deception. "I obviously couldn't relate my real life story to them," he said. "If I had done so, I would surely not have been allowed to carry on with my career as a designer. God knows what might have happened to me." Life in Stalin's Soviet Union had conditioned him. He was familiar with the methods of editing autobiography. "I'd prepared a long time in advance for it," he added. "I 'omitted' certain details."[11] During this meeting, Voronov asked Kalashnikov if he wanted to remain a soldier or would prefer to be demobilized to reserve status and become a civilian designer. Kalashnikov chose civilian life. The process began for his discharge. (The promotions Kalashnikov would receive in future years—lifting him to lieutenant general—were ceremonial, given for political reasons, not because of military service.)

Work continued on the rifle. Some changes in 1948 were significant. The ejector was redesigned, to be similar to that of the SG-43, a medium machine gun. The return spring was thickened, to increase its reliability and longevity. Some changes were nettlesome and demanded time. One engineer eventually worked for four years to improve the structural integrity of the hammer.[12] A small change was ergonomic—the operating handle was recast to a crescent shape, like that of the American Garand, which made it easier to manipulate. There were others. No matter the changes, the AK-47's accuracy could not be significantly improved; when it came to precise shooting, it was a stubbornly mediocre arm.* The army faced a choice: proceed with a less accurate assault rifle, or delay distribution of a weapon with tremendous firepower to every Soviet soldier. The

---

* Just how mediocre? Two decades later, the U.S. Army would hold long-range firing tests with Kalashnikov variants, including three Soviet, two Chinese, and a Romanian model. At 300 meters, expert shooters at prone or bench rest positions had difficulty putting ten consecutive rounds on target. The testers then had the weapons fired from a cradle by a machine, which removed human error. At 300 meters, the ten-rounds group fired in this manner had a minimum dispersion of 17.5 inches, compared to the 12.6 inches with an M-16, the American assault rifle fielded in Vietnam as a reaction to the Kalashnikov's spread. From Long-Range Dispersion Firing Test of the AK-47 Assault Rifle, U.S. Army Foreign Science and Technology Center, August 1969.

army decided to proceed, opting for less precision to keep production moving forward.[13] As a result, the primary socialist battle rifle would never be as accurate as many others, and this relative inaccuracy—a tradeoff for reliability—would be grounds for sustained criticism in future decades.[14]

After all of these efforts, the AK-47 had other flaws as well. After the final round was fired from a magazine, the bolt of a Kalashnikov rode forward and remained closed, as if another round had been chambered and the rifle were ready to fire again. This made it impossible to tell whether a weapon that had been fired repeatedly was loaded or empty; here was a shortcoming in design. It meant that a combatant, midfight, might not realize his weapon had no cartridges. (The bolts of many other automatic rifles lock in an open position when a magazine is empty. This signals immediately that it is time to reload, and leaves one step fewer in the loading cycle—because the bolt is already open, it need not be pulled back, which might save a second when seconds count.) Another flaw was potentially less serious, but still a sign of poor conception. The rifle's selector lever, of which Mikhail Kalashnikov was proud, was stiff and noisy when it was manipulated between safe, automatic, and semiautomatic settings. For a soldier trying to be silent—as in the moment before an ambush—this pitfall posed a problem.

As more people contributed, the Soviet assault rifle, already a composite creation designed by multiple contributors, became still more of a people's gun—a weapon whose shape, functions, and features were determined by the desires of a committee and the efforts of collective work. Dmitri Shirayev, a Soviet and later Russian armorer who said that many of the AK-47's designers were denied public credit for their contributions, assigned the weapon a telling nickname: The ASS-47, an acronym for *Avtomat Sovetskogo Soyuza*—the automatic made by the Soviet Union.[15] (Shirayev coined this title, the ASS-47, in a Russian magazine article after the Soviet Union collapsed. He worked at a government arms-research center at the time. The day after the article appeared, he was fired.)

The improvements to the AK-47's mass-production models may have been clouded further still, given what is known about the whereabouts of the German designer Hugo Schmeisser, who had been captured by the Red Army and relocated to Izhevsk after the war. Schmeisser was intimately familiar with an assault rifle's difficult path from drafting table to assembly line and had been through many redesigns with his *sturmgewehr*.

He would have seemed the ideal engineer to assist with overcoming the problems faced in converting the AK-47 from contest winner to factory product. Schmeisser lived in Izhevsk during pivotal years of the rifle's refinement. Neither the Soviet Union nor Russia has been forthcoming with details of his work. His contributions, if any, remain a historical question mark.[16] A pair of rival views predominates. One says that there could be no explanation for Schmeisser's presence in Izhevsk, of all places in the Soviet space, except to capitalize on his knowledge of assault rifles and the nuances of their mass production. It could not be a coincidence, in other words, that the preeminent German assault-rifle designer happened to be in the city where the Soviet Union sought to replicate his work. The other view holds that Schmeisser, as a foreigner, was not allowed near the early AK-47, the technical details of which in the late 1940s and early 1950s were still classified. His presence in Izhevsk, in this view, was to work on well-established weapons. Shirayev took this position. "The only thing Schmeisser did in Izhevsk was learn to drink vodka," he said.[17]

Whoever was behind each design change, the improvements satisfied the army. In summer 1949, the army formally designated the AK-47 the standard rifle for Soviet forces. Then a problem demanded the engineers' attention. The original weapons had been made with a stamped-metal receiver. The receiver is the part of the rifle that contains the trigger group, holds the magazine, and in which the bolt moves back and forth—the housing containing the rifle's guts. The original AK-47 design did not lend itself to the available Soviet manufacturing processes, and workers were unable to manufacture the rifles in large quantities without many rejected receivers. This threatened production. A new engineering team, led by Valery Kharkov,[18] was assigned to find a fix. Kharkov's team arrived at a solution—a solid piece of forged steel was machined into shape, grind by grind, to fashion a replacement part. From the perspective of quality, the solution was admirable. The solid-steel receiver was singularly strong.[19] From the perspective of the Soviet economy, and of an army eager for its new rifle, the fix had drawbacks. Machining a receiver from a block of steel meant wasting much of that steel. More than four pounds was milled away for every receiver, a considerable loss, considering that a receiver weighed less than a pound and a half. It also consumed time—requiring more than 120 operations by laborers for one part alone. The lost steel and hours increased costs. The available sources differ on when production of the rifles began. One account from Izhevsk said that by late 1949 both AK-47s—the original version and the variant with a solid steel receiver—were put into side-by-side production.[20] Another, more thorough account said the engineers did not work out an acceptable version of a milled receiver until late 1950, when the modified weapon was approved by a commission.[21] What is uncontested is that Kalashnikov's original design was phased out. The variant with a solid-steel receiver, its production made possible by a modification designed by others, was to be the predominant form of AK-47 for the next decade. The rifle was distributed in two forms—a wooden-stock model and an otherwise identical model with a collapsible metal stock, which, when folded, reduced the length to less than twenty-six inches overall. The folding-stock rifle was designed for paratroopers and soldiers who needed a shorter firearm, such as tank crews and armored troops. Automatic rifles had assumed a tiny form. At less than two feet two inches long, the collapsible Kalashnikov was now shorter than a regulation tennis racket. It had roughly the weight of an axe. Dr. Gatling's vision had come to this.

With his namesake rifle undergoing refinement, Mikhail Kalashnikov experienced his first tastes of material comfort and fame. In 1949 the Soviet Union awarded him the State Stalin Prize, one of the highest honors the government gave to its citizens. The prize, in recognition of the AK-47's selection for general service, included a bonus of 150,000 rubles— a breathtaking sum for a laborer in the years after the Great Patriotic War. The bonus equaled almost thirteen years' worth of salary for the more fortunate workers in Izhevsk.[22] Kalashnikov had lived across a spectrum of Soviet economic circumstances. Life on the Altai steppe had been grinding. In exile he had fared better than only the hungry and thinly clothed prisoners of the GULAG. The Red Army had provided him an economically stable lifestyle, though conditions for enlisted men were decidedly spartan. Once Kalashnikov became an arms designer he enjoyed comforts unavailable to many Soviet citizens, particularly during the war. His salary of fifteen hundred rubles in 1945 was several times that of a typical laborer. For seven years, during the war and in the lean period after, he had been adequately provided for. The Stalin Prize was life-changing. It vaulted Kalashnikov to a rarefied place in the Soviet social and economic hierarchy. Instantly, he could afford things most of his fellow citizens could not. His family, by one account, was the first in Izhevsk to own a refrigerator, a vacuum cleaner, and an automobile.[23] "At the time in Moscow shops there appeared Pobeda cars manufactured at the Volga car factory," he said. "The price tag was 16,000 rubles. Myself, a senior sergeant at that time, I bought a car."[24] *Pobeda* is Russian for victory. The automobile bearing this name was a popular postwar sedan, but very hard to obtain. Ownership of a Pobeda often marked a man with connections. Only 235,000 were made in nearly thirteen years, a tiny figure in a nation of roughly 200 million people. Kalashnikov was among the fortunate few to acquire one. Photographs from the time show Katya, his wife, in a glistening knee-length fur coat. He was twenty-nine years old in a parsimonious nation suffering shortages. He had managed a vertical social climb, to considerable reward.*

The news that a Stalin Prize had been awarded to a sergeant was published in Soviet newspapers, pushing Kalashnikov into mainstream Soviet conversation. He was a person of note now, a model citizen. The story of the unlettered enlisted man from a tank regiment, wounded in battle, who conceived of new tools to defend the Motherland, was the type of proletarian parable the Soviet Union wished to project. Stalin had killed off many of the party's leading figures. The purges had thinned the ranks of promising citizens across society. New heroes were necessary, especially those who would be unquestionably subordinate to Stalin, and thus pose no threat. Kalashnikov was one of them. It was a role for which he would prove eager and well tempered, though it required lying. As his story circulated, it again was an edited biography. His time as an exile, his father's death, his flight to the Kazakh rail yard—these things were not told. Kalashnikov had relocated to Izhevsk, where the assault rifle was soon to be manufactured by the millions. He was married to Katya, who had borne him a daughter. His life had assumed its shape: soldier-

---

*Nelly Kalashnikova, Mikhail Kalasnikov's stepdaughter, strongly objected to portrayals of her family as poor, and of Kalashnikov as a pauper or victim of a threadbare system. On Mikhail Kalashnikov's eighty-fifth birthday in 2004, she was quoted in *Tribuna,* a Russian newspaper: "Do not tell everybody that my father was very poor. Compared to other people we were well off. . . . Our mother was an extremely beautiful woman and used to buy the best hats and expensive fur coats. Father loved to buy coats for her and he could afford it."

konstruktor, heroic genius, representative proletarian man. The years of wandering and wondering were over. Kalashnikov had obliterated his past and found the Soviet version of the good life. Neither he nor the party would endanger this by raising unwanted facts. "Could I have brought to light this part of my life in those straightforward times?" he said. "Of course it would have told upon my relations with the authorities. They would have found many things in my revelations which, from their highly ideological point of view, would not have let me become what I am now. Who would have allowed me to work in such a secret domain as weapons?"*[25]

In 1950, the Communist Party extended Kalashnikov's favored status further. That year, at age thirty, he was chosen to be a deputy in the Supreme Soviet—Stalin's compliant legislature. Kalashnikov described his reaction, when told of his candidacy, as "flabbergasted." Soviet elections were ostensibly free but entirely rigged. He knew his election was a matter of form. He also understood that he had at best a passing familiarity with Udmurtia, the region he was to represent. He had relocated there two years before. "Apart from my factory colleagues, I knew nobody and nobody knew me," he said.[26] Ignorance of local affairs was not an obstacle to holding office. The job was ornamental, and seats were filled by archetypical socialist citizens. The legislators' grand gatherings in the Kremlin brought together a selectively assembled body of cosmonauts, musicians, gold medalists from international athletic competitions, decorated labor-

---

* Kalashnikov's comments about secrecy, a staple in his writing and remarks in later years, do not square with either the story of the AK-47 or the trajectory of his own considerable public life. In one memoir, he wrote, "I, Kalashnikov, was surrounded with an impenetrable veil of secrecy." The veil has been a canard, a post-Soviet line that Kalashnikov and his handlers have repeatedly used, perhaps to increase his Cold War cachet. The record does not support this characterization. Kalashnikov and his work were not only acknowledged by Soviet authorities; they were celebrated and publicized. The attention fit an established tradition for prominent Soviet small-arms designers, who were the opposite of secrets. *Konstruktors* were often pushed into view and praised as model patriots, men whose labors secured the homeland. This reflected the pragmatic side of propaganda. What was the point of trying to keep a secret that could not be kept? A rifle was unlike ballistic missiles or the submarines that carried them, items that were used by small numbers of people and did not change hands. Once a rifle entered mass production and went into general issue, no matter the amount of secrecy that had enveloped its development, it was a secret no more. It was a basic tool, carried by millions of pairs of hands. With the AK-47, publicity was more than an option for the Communist Party. It was an opportunity, and Soviet propagandists acted immediately. In late 1949, after the *avtomat* was selected as the army's standard rifle, Kalashnikov was featured on the cover of *Sovetsky Voin,* a magazine in general circulation within the military. A range of publications continued to cover him from then forward.

ers, and the like. They were not expected to deliberate or to provide checks and balances to Stalin's power. They were expected to vote as they were told. Kalashnikov was assigned to the budget commission, though he had no training in economics or financial matters. The job had its material rewards, however, including regular travel to Moscow to stay in the Soviet Union's finest hotels. As a deputy, Kalashnikov also exercised his connections to Dmitri Ustinov, who had been Stalin's commissar of armaments during the war, to secure a four-wheel-drive car—a well-chosen entitlement for life in Udmurtia, with its heavy snowfalls and unpaved roads. In spite of the privileges, the first session Kalashnikov attended, in 1950, was grounds for dread. When he arrived at Spassky Gate, the Kremlin's entrance, he worried he would be discovered as a former exile. He didn't need to shudder. His past was not known. No guard would stop him. Once inside, he looked upon Stalin for the first time. The general secretary inspired fear like no other, the dictator atop his personality cult and the leader whose policies had cast Kalashnikov's family into the wilderness. Kalashnikov had become his devotee. He was enthralled.

> I was filled with awe. I remember with perfect clarity the way he came into the great hall in which we had gathered. Stalin was wearing his eternal semi-military suit. He sat in his place, the same one as ever, in the midst of a total silence. And then there was [a] thunderous outbreak of applause that lasted an eternity, since nobody wanted to be the first to stop! After several minutes, Stalin gestured with his hand, asking for quiet in the assembly. All at once, you could have heard a pin drop.[27]

And then the dictator died. The reign of terror closed with a whimper. After a dinner with party officials and Lavrenty Beria, Stalin was found on the floor of one of his residences on March 1, 1953, incapacitated by what seemed a stroke.* He died on March 5. Kalashnikov was devastated. He had separated Stalin's predation on the Soviet Union's people from the despot himself. When party newspapers had written of enemies of the

---

*How Stalin died is a matter of historical dispute. Beria, according to Vyacheslav Molotov, a member of the inner circle, boasted of dispatching the dictator with rat poison.

state, of saboteurs and lurking assassins, Kalashnikov accepted the propaganda. He wanted the traitors—many of whose plots were fabricated by the dictator himself—put to death. Stalin's infiltration into Kalashnikov's mind had eclipsed the most basic human relationships. "He was almost closer to us than our own parents," he wrote. "When Stalin was buried, the whole population wept. We felt that life couldn't go on without him. Fear of the future gripped our hearts."[28] Kalashnikov was not naïve. He knew the terror. But he accepted the sinister side of the system that had chosen him for rewards. He had joined the Communist Party. He had become a party man.

The shifts were tectonic. Beria became a deputy prime minister and set out upon what seemed a program of domestic reforms, officially banning torture, a jarring idea given the violent excesses of the *chekists* he had led. Beria was not to last. A plot to remove him was organized by Nikita Khrushchev and other party figures. He was arrested on June 26. His reversal of fortune was total. He had been untouchable, the man who sat beside Stalin and supervised the incarceration and killing of uncountable Soviet citizens, the architect of a great sorrow. Now he was exposed and alone. Shorn of his wire-rimmed spectacles, he groveled in a letter from his cell, offering to work as a laborer anywhere.

> Dear comrades, you should understand that I am a faithful soldier of our Motherland, a loyal son of the party of Lenin and Stalin and your loyal friend and comrade. Send me wherever you wish, to any kind of work, [even] a most insignificant one. See me out, I will be able to work ten more years and I will work with all my soul and with complete energy. I am saying this from the bottom of my heart, it is not true that since I have held a big post I would not be able to perform in a small position. This can easily be proven in any region or area, in a Soviet farm, in a collective farm, on a construction site of our glorious Motherland. And you will see that in 2 to 3 years I will improve my behavior strongly and will be still of some use for you. I am to my last breath faithful to our beloved party and our Soviet government.

Beria's last breath was not far off. He was tried in the fashion he would recognize: in secret, on largely fabricated charges, before a court that offered no appeal. After the verdict on December 23 he was blindfolded, gagged, and shot.[29]

The events of 1953 allowed the Kremlin to reconsider its role at the international socialist vanguard. The changes—first in personnel, then policies—were integral to the assault rifle's spread. Khrushchev became general secretary in the autumn, inheriting both the foreign-policy port-folio and the military-industrial complex. He grasped ways the two could be linked.

One early challenge was in institutionalizing security arrangements in the European buffer zone. In World War II, the Soviet military had moved onto foreign territory previously under German occupation and become the region's premier military power. During the war the Red Army equipped and trained fighting units in Eastern Europe that became foun-dations for new national armies, all subordinate to Soviet command. For the Cold War's opening years, such relationships were sufficient for the Kremlin. But in 1949, Western powers had formed NATO and sponsored the creation of the Federal Republic of Germany. The Kremlin replied by founding the German Democratic Republic on the portion of Germany under Soviet occupation. Moves and countermoves continued. In 1955, West Germany joined NATO. The Kremlin's parallel step would stoke assault-rifle proliferation in ways that persist: It bound its satellites to-gether into a mutual-defense agreement of its own, the Warsaw Pact. The treaty was signed by eight nations—the Soviet Union, Albania, Bulgaria, Czechoslovakia, East Germany, Hungary, Poland, and Romania—in May 1955. Its initial significance was retaliatory and symbolic, a tit-for-tat escalation. In the event of armed attack on any one member, the others agreed to come to the attacked nation's aid. The parties also declared, in a bit of doublespeak boilerplate, that they would strive for "effective measures for universal reduction of armaments." The armaments buildup was actually just about to begin, spurred by the treaty's fifth article, in which the members accepted a unified command.[30] In fall 1955, when the details of the command were circulated via a top-secret memorandum from Moscow, the commander's deputies were instructed that they would be responsible for supplying "military items, in accordance with accepted systems of armaments."[31] The language referred to Soviet-pattern weap-ons, including the most common weapons of all—cartridges and fire-arms. The instructions formalized the idea of standardizing equipment in the Eastern bloc, a concept that became a Warsaw Pact cornerstone. The goal became:

> . . . constant modernization of weapons and combat equipment and the development of new and more sophisticated prototypes of weaponry. The Soviet Union plays a leading role here. Possessing a powerful military-economic potential and scientific-technological base, it gives the necessary assistance to fraternal countries in strengthening their defensive might. Not only direct deliveries of new types of weapons and combat equipment are made, but also licenses and technical documentation are transferred for their production. Joint scientific research and test-design work is conducted, and scientific-technological consultations are widely employed.
>
> The Soviet state plays a large role in the creation and development of the defense industry in the fraternal countries. One of the important ways for coordinating military-technical policy is to standardize weapons and combat equipment of the allied armies, which simplifies their material-technical support in case of military operations.[32]

In this way, most Eastern bloc soldiers would carry the same weapons,[33] which fired the same ammunition, thereby streamlining production and training while reducing the expenditure of research-and-design energy for weapons that had already met the state's standards. This made military sense, albeit for a war that never came. Looked upon years later, a different result is obvious: The political and industrial groundwork for overcapacity in assault-rifle production had been laid. Plants producing AK-47s, their derivatives, and the ammunition they fired were sponsored and subsidized in Bulgaria, East Germany, Hungary, Poland, and Romania. These countries not only would arm their military and security services with them, but would become assault-rifle exporters. Dangerous rules applied. The assault rifle was a socialist military product. Its production, sale, and distribution were not controlled by market forces. They were connected to centralized decisions and national goals. The fine print of the Warsaw Pact had put the Kalashnikov assault rifle at the center of a socialist arms franchise, an example of the law of unintended consequences viewed through the prism of the Cold War. Production would surge under the the unified command's directives. And the bloc's members would provide arms for conflicts long after their alliance was no more, extending the treaty's influence beyond the region in indelible ways.

Under Khrushchev, the Kremlin also distributed arms and arms technology beyond its European vassals. There were two principal types of arrangements: first, direct transfers of finished goods, and later the transfer of licenses and technical specifications to produce them. In September 1955, within months of the Warsaw Pact's signing ceremony, Khrushchev had discovered the political practicality of the arms industry and the new alliance, too. Using Czechoslovakia as a cover, the Kremlin organized a huge arms sale to Gamal Abdel Nasser of Egypt.[34] The deal included tanks, airplanes, artillery, and Czech small arms, and equipped Egyptian forces for war with the young Israeli state. It also thrust the Kremlin into Middle Eastern brinksmanship, putting it into competition with the West and presaging arms deals with Egypt, Syria, Iran, Iraq, and elsewhere.

As Khrushchev's agents closed his deal with Nasser, the Soviet army was arranging for the first arms plant outside Russia to manufacture AK-47s. The plant, an urgent project for China, had origins reaching to a secret collaboration between Stalin and Mao. In late May 1951, Xu Xiangqian, chief of staff of the People's Liberation Army, had led a delegation to Moscow. Mao's victory over the Kuomintang, the party of Chiang Kai-shek, and the founding of the People's Republic of China had reinforced Stalin's almost religious conviction of the allure of socialism and global revolution. The Chinese wanted to update their arms industry. The Soviet Union was the natural source. There was precedent. Soviet arms technicians had surreptitiously helped Mao's arms production since at least 1949, even while the Kremlin maintained diplomatic ties with the Kuomintang. In the summer of 1949, a senior Chinese revolutionary, Liu Shaoqi, who later became China's head of state, secretly traveled to Russia, where he met Stalin and appealed for help in arming the People's Liberation Army. The Soviet Union sent two hundred technicians to assist the effort, including eighty who rode back to Manchuria on the same train with the Chinese delegation. This was part of a slyly hedged Kremlin bet to put the Soviet Union in the winner's camp. In November 1950, as the Korean War was accelerating, Mao asked Stalin for a long list of weapons for the war, including more than 140,000 rifles, 9,000 machine guns, and 1,000 pistols for pilots. Within two days, Stalin personally approved a list. In August 1951, Mao sought more aid, enough to arm as many as sixty divisions. The Soviet army agreed to provide specifications for eight weapons, including Mosin-Nagant rifles, 82-millimeter mortars, machine guns, pistols, and an antiaircraft gun. Documents were transferred and a Russian delegation traveled to China for at least four months, to outfit plants and train workers. By 1953, production had begun, and cooperation expanded to include artillery and tanks. The AK-47 was still in its earliest production runs; the Soviet army did not initially share the specifications.

Four years later, under Khrushchev, the impetus for Chinese production of Kalashnikov-pattern rifles began, by one account, with a minor diplomatic jolt. In June 1955 a Chinese delegation toured the arms plant in Tula, where China's second machinery minister, General Zhao Erlu, saw Slavic laborers producing the SKS. The minister was furious. The only data for rifles provided in 1951, by this account, had been for the M-44 Mosin-Nagant rifle, a weapon based on designs that were decades old. China wanted newer guns. Negotiations resumed. The Soviet army promptly agreed to share the technology behind the M1943 cartridge and both rifles that fired it—the SKS and the AK-47.[35] (Another Chinese account described a less dramatic transfer of SKS and AK-47 technology. In this version, as part of Khrushchev's courting of China early in his tenure as general secretary, the Soviet military offered the technical specifications for the two rifles, beginning with an exchange of letters in early 1955. The AK-47, by this account, was offered as a replacement to the PPSh, which the Chinese had been manufacturing with Soviet approval for several years.) This much is clear: Production of the Type 56, the first Chinese version of the AK-47, began in a blandly named arms plant, Factory 626, in Beian.

Khrushchev had moved quickly. At the time of Stalin's funeral, the AK-47 had been made only in Izhevsk. Three years later, with the beginning of Chinese production, the world's two largest military forces had parallel assembly lines. By 1958, the Kremlin would share AK-47 technology with North Korea. The Soviet Union's escalating military aid to Egypt would then expand to tool a Kalashnikov plant there. Between these deals and the rolling openings of assault-rifle assembly lines in the Warsaw Pact* the Kremlin had ensured production of the Kalashnikov at

---

*All the Warsaw Pact nations except Czechoslovakia would adopt the Kalashnikov system as

a scale no other firearm had ever seen. The next questions were not industrial or political. They were tactical. How would the assault rifle be used?

The armored column growled through the streets of Budapest and came
to a stop in Boráros Square, idling near the eastern embankment of the
Danube River. Leading the formation were six Soviet tanks, including
three T-54s, the most powerful tank the Soviet Union had yet made.
Behind them were armored personnel carriers, bitterly known as "open
coffins," in which Hungarian soldiers had been crowded against the better
judgment of their commanders, who worried for their lives. These vehicles were followed by more tanks still.[36] This was an assault group staging
to attack. Their objective would not be easy. Several blocks away, behind
dense rows of buildings and warrens of narrow streets, stood the Corvin
Theater, an insurgent stronghold. It was the morning of October 28,
1956. The armed popular uprising in Hungary was entering its sixth day.
    The Hungarian fighters waiting to meet the column's advance hid
in four- and five-story buildings, watching from windows to the streets
below, waiting for whatever came next.[37] Circumstances had transformed
them into impromptu urban fighters. They had seen enough of Hungarian state terror and Soviet occupation to turn out spontaneously, an
unanticipated force that had leaped onto the world's stage. Some were
not yet old enough to shave. Others were veterans who had been Soviet
prisoners of war. The adults came largely from the workers' ranks.[38] Together they formed a hard-nosed group: clean-cut, lean, rugged, intent.
The weather was chilly by day in Budapest in midfall; the nights cold.
Rebels wandered their turf in trench coats, lending them a sartorially
proper air. One worker fought with a bowler on his head. He had found it
in the rubble. After he brushed off the brick dust, it became a whimsically
unforgettable highlight to his rebel dress.[39] Though many insurgents were
spread throughout Budapest, the Corvinists, as they were called, were
among the most daring and determined of the lot. Their stubbornness
made them a priority. Soviet generals and Hungarian hard-liners wanted

---

their standard rifles, and often as police weapons, too; and would subsidize plants producing
large numbers of Kalashnikov knockoffs. Albania, however, would not receive its technical aid
for production from the Soviet Union. China would provide that assistance.

to crush them as a lesson for the rest. But how? The area was an urban trap. Most of the neighborhood's buildings were constructed of thick stone and highly defendable. Within them the Hungarians had selected shooting positions from which they could pour out interlocking cones of fire. The Kilián Barracks—a fortress—stood nearby, and rebels took positions here as well, expanding their zone of control. Details had been tended to. To give warning of approaching threats, the rebels had posted spotters on rooftops. They had organized medical care and a field kitchen. They had made a jail for captured troops. They had assembled obstacles and barricades on the streets, so that fighting vehicles would have to slow down and pick their way through tight passages, exposing them to attack.[40] They placed cooking pans on the pavement to resemble mines, a trick to frustrate the tanks more. At the theater's doorway, the Corvinists had an artillery piece.[41]

For the fight against the massing troops, the Corvinists had gathered arms. Some carried a Mosin-Nagant rifle or a PPSh submachine gun taken from government stocks. Others brandished pistols. This was not an especially impressive suite of small arms for an army in 1956. For a guerrilla force in existence for less than a week, it was a feat. And the insurgents were blessed by convenience: A gas station was located near the theater, providing fuel for Molotov cocktails*—bottles filled with gasoline and adorned with a wick to be lit before being thrown. When the glass shattered, the wick ignited the gasoline in a whooshing blaze. In the Corvinists' kill zones, charred vehicles littered the streets. Dozens of soldiers had died. Now they waited for the next thrust. Soviet generals had ordered an advance in two prongs, ending with tanks blasting at the theater as the infantry stormed forward, finishing the insurrection at last.

In the story of the assault rifle, the mid-1950s brought milestones: the AK-47's combat debuts. The first known use of the AK-47 outside of tests and exercises was in East Germany in 1953, when Soviet divisions put down a smaller and less-organized uprising in Berlin. But in 1953 the assault rifle had yet to be issued to Soviet forces in large quantities.

---

* Named for Vyacheslav Molotov, one of Stalin's top party men, who had been the Soviet foreign minister until his ouster a few months before.

It was not abundant. Three years on, as insurgents in Budapest gathered their bottled gas and looted guns, thousands of the Soviet Union's front-line soldiers carried AK-47s into Hungarian neighborhoods. The newsreel footage of soldiers flowing into the capital, new rifles in hand, framed events to be repeated by centralized regimes for decades. They were a myth-buster. One point at the center of Soviet and Russian statements about the assault rifle and the immense industrial capacity behind it, and fundamental to Mikhail Kalashnikov's descriptions of his life's purpose and work, was that the AK-47 was made for national defense and dis-tributed later as a liberation tool. These are the oft-repeated lines. Against this fable, the weapons' premieres in Berlin and Budapest served as more than chronological markers. They informed a fuller understanding of the AK-47 and the political system that circulated it. The AK-47 was chris-tened with blood not as a tool for liberation or to defend the Soviet Union from invaders. It made its debut smashing freedom movements. It was repression's chosen gun, the rifle of the occupier and the police state.

The beginning established a pattern. The Kalashnikov was rarely a Soviet weapon of defense. It was to be the weapon of East German border guards who shot unarmed civilians fleeing for the West, and the firearm used in the state-directed violence against demonstrations and uprisings before the Soviet Union finally tottered and fell. It would be used in Prague, in Alma-Ata, in Baku, in Riga, and in Moscow. It would see crackdown service repeatedly in other strong-arm states—at Tiananmen Square in China, in Andijon in Uzbekistan, and Bishkek in Kyrgyzstan—almost any place where a government resorted to shooting citizens to try to keep citizens in check. It would be used by Baathists to execute Kurds in the holes that served as their mass graves. It would shoot the Bosnian men and boys who were herded to execution in Srebrenica in 1995. But this was all so obvious that it barely deserves elaboration, save as a cor-rective to the authorities' distortions. The fight for Hungary had another value. The Kremlin's image tenders could influence the conversation about their nation's actions and the supposed purposes of its arms. They could not control the ways that war and violence actually worked. There would be too many Kalashnikovs for their uses to be determined, much less fully obscured, by the centralized states that made them. Once Soviet soldiers drove into Budapest the omen appeared, the hint of what was in store. No sooner had the AK-47 been carried into combat than it became the rebels' arm, too.

Like the way power and personalities had changed in Moscow, the violence in Budapest in 1956 said much about the Soviet system. The Kremlin had a clear-eyed view of the hardships in Hungary. Since 1953, the leadership of the Communist Party had discussed in detail the ways its policies had failed the Hungarians, and how the national government it backed had alienated the nation. The Kremlin chose to crush the popular uprising nonetheless, worrying less about Hungary than about the prospect of losing a nation in the socialist camp, or appearing weak.

Hungary had been under Soviet occupation since the end of World War II. The country was ruled through much of the period by a dictator, Mátyás Rákosi, who was propped up by the Kremlin and applied the tools of state terror wholesale. Repression, Rákosi-style, took pages from Stalin's book: a sadistic secret police force, labor camps, *kulak* lists, show trials, executions. Religion was suppressed. Single-party rule was established. The dictator was unchallenged. Stalin and Rákosi forced Hungary through a program of industrialization, collectivization, and militarization. Sovietization deepened popular resentment and shifted part of the hatred for Rákosi toward Moscow. Three months after Stalin's death, the party summoned Rákosi to the Kremlin and spelled out Hungary's wretchedness with exactitude. Beria denounced Rákosi to his face while referring to him in a chilling third person. "It is not right that Comrade Rákosi gives directions regarding who must be arrested; he says who should be beaten," he said. (Beria himself was to be arrested within two weeks, on orders of the comrades in the room.)[42] Vyacheslav Molotov, the foreign minister, extended the line, describing a nation paralyzed. He questioned, if only rhetorically, whether socialism in this form was better than what it had replaced.

> They initiated a persecution against 1,500,000 people in a population with 4.5 million adults in three and a half years. There were 1,500,000 violations in this time. They punish for everything, and punish insignificant acts arbitrarily . . . they resort to all kinds of manipulations to ensure a forced industrial development. For instance

there was [only] 57% wool in a particular fabric. They left the name and price of the material, but they took the wool out of it. They significantly worsened the quality of milk. This resembles fraud. They have lost contact with the population, they do not express the interest of the population in many questions. Is this why we chased the bourgeoisie away, so that afterward the situation would be like this?[43]

Khrushchev stepped in. "Comrade Rákosi is primarily responsible for the mistakes," he said.[44] Rákosi was a thick-necked, confident man; a bull. He had bragged in the past of killing rivals, saying their liquidation was "like cutting off slices of salami."[45] But he was cornered. He did not resist. "Regarding hubris, that's an illness that one cannot detect, just like one cannot smell one's own odor," he said. "If the comrades say this is the case, I accept it."[46] He was promptly deposed. Imre Nagy, a reformer, was appointed prime minister. Nagy eased the repression at home and began a program he called the New Course. There was only so much he could do. The economy was moribund. Consumer products were in limited supply. Agricultural production was low. Years of terror had exhausted the population. And while Khrushchev spoke of a fresh direction, Hungary's arrangements with Moscow still broke in Moscow's favor. No end seemed in sight. Rákosi returned to power in 1955 and Nagy was sidelined. The political turbulence sent mixed signals. Rákosi was removed from office once more in summer 1956. It was too late. Tensions erupted in a public demonstration on October 23, when tens of thousands of people turned out to protest the national government and Soviet interference. Stalin's statue was pulled down, nationalist flags appeared, a crowd massed outside Parliament. Students marched to the radio station, intending to broadcast sixteen demands. The list included the withdrawal of Soviet troops, an election of party officers by secret ballot, the dissolution of the government, public inquiry into the crimes of Rákosi, a reassessment of Soviet-Hungarian relations, and an examination of the merits and practices of the planned economy. The confrontation with the authorities was at hand.

The radio station was under guard of the Hungarian State Security Police, or ÁVH, the loathed secret police. The students never made it into the broadcast booth. The crowd milled outside. The ÁVH fired warning shots. The students held their place. Then someone—who it was remains in dispute, though blame typically falls on the ÁVH—shot into the crowd, killing several demonstrators. Rioting began. Groups of fighters formed in many of Budapest's districts, overwhelming the police. The crowds emptied jails and looted arsenals. Fighting broke out in one neighborhood, then another, later in rural areas and towns. Some police units sympathized with the insurrection and gave weapons to the people. Others did nothing to stop their activities.

The Soviet Union and its proxies had previously weathered challenges from Europe's captive populations. In June 1953 in Berlin and in June 1956 in Poznań, Poland, the authorities had shot into crowds. An official understanding had taken hold: State violence was an acceptable tool to push the people into line. For order, blood was a fair price. But the Kremlin had never faced a general national uprising, or the prospect that a satellite's government would join the opposition as it grew. Notes from the Presidium meeting that day in Moscow show that the Kremlin considered intervening militarily from the first moments. Khrushchev raised the idea, though he seemed not quite ready.[47] An interim solution was found: Soviet troops stationed in the republic would assist Hungarian forces. Before dawn on October 24, an army corps garrisoned outside Budapest moved for the capital, hoping a display of force might bring calm.[48] In some places, the Soviet troops were met by unarmed crowds. In others they met resistance. In areas like the Corvin Passage, the resistance was organized and intense, and Soviet soldiers were cut down. This was not a riot. Many civilians had resolved to fight.

One corps was not enough. Its units entered Budapest tentatively, without a full reconnaissance, unsure of their mission and what to expect. They could depend on the loyalty of neither the Hungarian army nor the regular police. Their armor lacked adequate infantry support, which rendered many patrols blind and vulnerable to ambush. Often Soviet soldiers located insurgents only by drawing their fire—the 1956 version of a perilous form of combat patrol, known among soldiers as the move-ment-to-contact. The circumstances gave the rebels unusual advantages for a force of their experience, and limited the Soviet soldiers' ability to apply their superior equipment and firepower. In such conditions, the newly issued AK-47s could make little difference. But they did make an impression. In one of the few available Soviet accounts of the fighting, emissaries from the Kremlin sent an encrypted cable back to Moscow describing lopsided shooting. The emissaries, Anastas Mikoyan and Mikhail Suslov, told of skirmishes "between single provocateurs or small groups of provocateurs on the one side and our own machine gunners and automatic riflemen. Our own troops were firing more, responding with volleys to single shots." Another translation of the cable, unearthed after the Cold War, summarized how Soviet firepower allowed a new generation of soldiers to fight. "Our men did more of the shooting. To solitary shots we replied with salvos."[49]

On October 24, the government fell. Nagy returned to office. He tried to balance conflicting pulls, working with the Kremlin while feeling the revolution's ineluctable draw. The Kremlin escalated. On October 25, Soviet divisions from outside Hungary crossed the border. Hungary, a member of the Warsaw Pact, was being invaded by its fraternal mentor, which had pledged to protect it from invasion. The Soviet military had decided that it must destroy the Corvinists. A conventional idea was settled upon: A Hungarian army unit, working with Soviet armor, would storm the theater. Hungarian commanders protested, sensing there would be too much bloodshed for the troops navigating the narrow streets, and too much danger for civilians who lived in apartments lining the route. During the final briefing by a Soviet division commander, as the armor idled on Boráros Square, it emerged that the tanks were not equipped with compatible two-way radios. There would be no ready way for government forces to communicate. Hungarian officers refused to participate. The Soviet officers were stuck.

The bungling grew. The column's lead tanks—three Soviet T-34s, the same class that Kalashnikov commanded during the war—departed alone for a reconnaissance.[50] Because they had no radios, no one could call them back, and no one knew what they faced once they clanked out of sight. Ninety minutes passed. Three T-54s—the Kremlin's newest tanks—were sent to look for the wayward soldiers. An hour later, two T-54s returned. One was damaged. All the other tanks had been destroyed. The operation was a failure in every sense. The remainder of the column waited at the square into evening and the troops were told they would attack the next day. But by then the two sides had agreed to a cease-fire. The curfew was lifted that night. By October 30 the fighting died down. Elation swept the Corvinists. Soviet units were withdrawing. Nagy announced the end of one-party rule, and the new government pledged free elections. The rebels, by all signs, had prevailed.

In the quiet of a city exhaling, a quintessential sight of the past half-century appeared for the first time. Outside the shattered facades of the buildings, rebels roamed the streets, posing for news photographers. A few of them carried AK-47s. Which Hungarian rebel first captured an AK-47 and turned it against the army that created it cannot be said. Thousands of men fought in Budapest, and Soviet soldiers were repelled and forced to abandon equipment in many places, just as they left behind some of their dead. But the streets around the Corvin Theater were where the rebels' images were made. The names of most of these men were not recorded. At least one had his back to the camera; his identity is anybody's guess. But one man's name was remembered: József Tibor Fejes, twenty-two years old, fresh-faced, sharp-eyed, purposeful, and seemingly unafraid.

On at least one day, Fejes dressed in a dark suit. On others, he was less formal. One picture showed him wearing trousers with their left knee torn. One item in his wardrobe was consistent: he wore a bowler, tilted to one side. Fejes was the worker who had been seen during the fighting wearing his hat. *Keménykalapos,* his colleagues called him; the man in the bowler hat.[51] Fejes's roguish confidence made him a darling of the photographers, including Michael Rougier of *Life,* who snapped a crisply focused frame of the rebel facing the lens. In it, Fejes stood with other insurgents, an AK-47 slung beside his left arm. The AK-47 was destined to become a symbol of resistance fighters almost everywhere, a weapon with innumerable spokesmen. Fejes had nonchalantly assumed the requisite pose and begun to flesh out this historical role. He did so before Fidel Castro, before Yasir Arafat, before Idi Amin. He was years ahead of the flag of Zimbabwe, which would expropriate the AK-47 as a symbol. He was ahead of Shamil Basayev and Osama bin Laden, who would convert the product of an atheist state into a sign of unsparing jihad. József Tibor Fejes was the first of the world's Kalashnikov-toting characters, a member of a pantheon's inaugural class. He presents a complicated profile. On one level, his activities offered a fine example of the assault rifle's almost instantaneous insinuation into modern ground war. On another, he provided an instructive case of how an untrained man with a fearsome weapon can blur right into wrong.

Who was he? Fejes came from a broken working-class family and had known hardship in many forms. He had been born in 1934 in Budapest, and his parents divorced when he was a toddler. He was raised in an orphanage before moving in during 1942 with a farmer's family for seven years in Romania. He attended school through the fifth grade. Farming life did not suit him. He fled the countryside and was put into a juvenile correctional facility in 1949. Later, he became a metalworker and locksmith, landed a job as an apprentice, and grew into a fit young man, a survivor of Hungary's leanest years. In 1956, Fejes returned to Budapest and found his mother. He lived with her only three days and then moved in with his father. He worked briefly at a shipyard, then at another business. He had survived abandonment, war, and incarceration and brought himself through to adulthood with scant help. He had a job. He might have had a chance, until the revolution changed his path.

Fejes turned out with the demonstrators as the protests began. He was present, by some accounts, for the toppling of the Stalin statue. By others he left work at noon on October 24 and attended demonstrations at the Yugoslav and American embassies, and chanted anti-Soviet slogans, including "Russkies Go Home!"[52] Rumors moved through the crowds. Fejes heard one: that students had been arrested and taken to a police precinct. He joined a group to free them. At one precinct, they found no students. They changed plans. They demanded weapons at another police building, on Vig Street, where they "broke into the building and occupied it, seized all arms and weapons found there."[53] Soon Fejes and the group rode a truck of guns to the Corvin Theater, where they joined the insurgency in its earliest hours. He and several other men entered a food store and retrieved, depending on who is to be believed, cheese, coffee, meat, biscuits, and three boxes of sugar, or roughly a half pound of meat and a bottle of beer, which he drank. Fejes was present throughout the fighting, often in a theater window but later beside the artillery piece at one of the theater's doors. On the night of October 26, he said, he obtained his AK-47 when another fighter presented it to him in the alley. "My fellows explained to me how it worked," he added.[54] The next day, during the fighting, he stole a Russian Pobeda wristwatch from the corpse of a civilian.[55]

After the cease-fire, Fejes stayed active. He directed traffic. He guarded a Red Cross warehouse. At one point he argued with the police, who wanted to confiscate his weapon. He refused to give it up, saying he had captured it in the fighting. It was too much of a war prize, and in the context of the times, had been legitimately earned. The rules were loose. Lines of authority were unclear. Fejes obviously saw himself as legitimate. After the cease-fire agreement was reached, he and his father filed a request for a permit to own the weapon legally. He volunteered for the National Guard, as the Nagy government's quickly deputized formation of paramilitary fighters was called. These actions suggested Fejes wanted to work within the law. But he was young and untutored in the rules and ways of war, and either his personality or his revolutionary certitude carried him too far. Judgment and caution deserted him.

On October 30, armed rebels were searching people on Rákóczi Square. They were emotional and intent, looking for members of the secret police. Several of them stopped a lean young man with flowing hair, a fine mustache, and a good chin. Their detainee was smartly dressed, with a sweater over his shirt and a neatly knotted tie. He had just stepped from his flat, which he shared with his wife. A search turned up a weapon and an identification card showing him to be an officer of the ÁVH. The rebels encircled him, cutting off escape. He was Lieutenant János Balassa, and he was trapped. What happened in the next seconds would be disputed. But at least two men pointed their weapons and opened fire. Witnesses said one was Fejes, who leveled his AK-47 and shot into the defenseless officer's guts.[56] This was not combat. It was a curbside execution. In an instant, Lieutenant Balassa was dead, the AK-47 had been implicated in what would become a characteristic use, and the fate of József Tibor Fejes was sealed.

The murder at Rákóczi Square, largely forgotten, was a signature moment in the evolution of automatic arms.

In the first decades of production of rapid-fire arms, several obstacles restricted who could own and use them. Armies, navies, state militias, territorial prisons, and the like could acquire them, but not the common man. More than the behavior of salesmen kept machine-gun circulation within the authorities' hands. There were factors rooted in the weapons' characteristics. Machine guns were expensive. They were technically complex. They were cumbersome. Many men had to be trained and pressed into service to operate and maintain them. Over time the guns would shrink. But machine guns, their associated equipment, and their ammunition were still heavy, and their operation was not intuitive. They remained almost exclusively instruments of the state.

The Soviet Union was changing all this. It had created the circumstances for the crossover arm, the weapon that would let automatic-rifle fire jump from institutional control. The AK-47 was small. No mule was required here. While not a precision rifle, it was accurate enough for most shots a man might be expected to take. Its ammunition was lightweight. Almost anyone of teenage years or beyond could carry a few hundred rounds. Its variant with a wooden stock could be hidden beneath a blanket. The variant with a folding stock could be slung inside a coat. It provided flexibility, allowing whoever carried it to fire a single shot with each trigger squeeze or to hold the trigger back and blast out bursts. The evolution of automatic arms had reached its most successful form. Gatling's dream—firepower "for *men* of ordinary intelligence"—was now available for a *man* of ordinary intelligence, for the individual, whether he was in uniform or not, trained or not, legal or not, supervised or not. It could be handled by a child. And this highly functional distillation of firearms technology had become the output of planned economies, which could manufacture them in numbers beyond what anyone, outside the minds that organized socialist police states, would need or want. Industrial and political currents in the Soviet Union had lined up in ways that were converting the AK-47 into the world's gun, the automatic rifle for everyman, a tool designed for military use that would elevate the danger to people not directly engaged in war.

There had been, in an instructive way, a precedent: the Thompson submachine gun, whose arrival to markets also predicted what was to come. Something about submachine guns caused alarm. They emerged in World War I and provided an excellent solution for many types of close combat, though they had all the expected limits related to short-range pistol ammunition. Worries over their use had been great enough that in 1919 the Treaty of Versailles banned the MP-18, Germany's first submachine gun, from its postwar army.[57] History would have it that it was not armies with MP-18s that would give submachine guns their reputation. That role fell to civilians once they wrapped their hands around the Thompson gun.

The Thompson gun was less than thirty-four inches long, weighed ten and a half pounds, and fired fat .45-caliber pistol rounds. It was the brain-child of retired brigadier general John T. Thompson, a former Army ord-nance officer and longtime advocate of automatic arms. In the 1890s, as a captain, Thompson had helped Second Lieutenant John H. Parker obtain Gatling guns for the Spanish-American War; his place in machine-gun history was secure before he founded a gun firm. Thompson was more like Richard Gatling than Mikhail Kalashnikov. Upon retiring from the army, he pursued his weapon's development as a business, with a private design team, wealthy backing, and an eye on profits. No state committee was involved, though one root of his design tapped his prior government work. Thompson chambered the Tommy Gun, as it was nicknamed, for the pistol round that he had championed, based on his military-funded studies, as ideal for killing men.

How Thompson came to this decision was a bizarre journey through the world of small-arms development and military science. In October 1903, the secretary of war asked Thompson and an army surgeon to test the available pistol cartridges and determine which possessed "the stop-ping power and shock effect at short ranges necessary for a pistol for the military service."[58] This was subjective work, and the officers were allowed to choose the methodology they thought best. Thompson's partner on the project, Major Louis A. La Garde, had served as a surgeon in the Spanish-American War and been fascinated with questions of ballistics throughout his long career. Experiments suited him. La Garde had tested cartridges tipped with biological agents and established that the flash of high tem-peratures and pressure involved in blasting a bullet out of a barrel did not kill bacteria, as some men assumed. "We fired bullets from different kinds of hand weapons which were previously contaminated with anthrax germs into susceptible animals at varying distances up to 500 yards and the animals died of anthrax in the majority of cases," he wrote in one of his many studies.[59]

Some of La Garde's work spoke of an eccentric's whim; other projects had practical value. By firing into cadavers in the 1890s, he traced the ways that wounds from bullets changed as bullet technology changed. In that study, the ambition had been to examine the effects of rifle fire on what the army called "the human frame." La Garde conducted his tests in 1893 at the Frankford Arsenal in Philadelphia. His methods were clini-cal to the point of being mechanical. He used tackle to position cadavers so bullets could strike the targeted areas of the body squarely. He set up barrels of sawdust to catch the bullets after they passed through, allowing their recovery and examination. The arsenal did not have the ranges required for shooting at long distance, and long-range shots would naturally introduce imprecision. So to reproduce the impact of bullets fired from far away, La Garde shot cadavers with cartridges with less powder from a distance of twenty-eight feet. Lighter charges propelled bullets at reduced speed, thereby simulating bullet strikes from farther out. La Garde was driven by curiosity. He wanted to divine the effects of bullets on various body parts. Shot by shot, he methodically shattered the cadavers in his care. He fired into one upper arm, then the other, one femur, then the other. He shot ankles, hips, and knees, and then shoulders and elbows. He shot skulls, sending bullets through heads at various angles and orientations. He shot feet. He shot a pelvis. He collected the bullets after each shot. Upon examining them and assessing their degree and type of deformation, La Garde tried to determine how they had caused the damage they had caused. Gunshot injuries were common, in peace and in war. Much about them was misunderstood. He was trying to peer forensically into the split-second mechanisms of wounding deep inside the human body. Throughout it all he kept notes and compared them with observations of the torn tissue and broken bones. Based on this work, La Garde concluded that the newer, faster-moving and smaller-caliber bullets caused less tissue destruction, and were therefore more humane, than the heavier lead bullets used in most war to that time. He predicted that wounds from the newer rounds would be such that surgeons would be required to amputate limbs less often than in wars past.[60] La Garde worked in the presecrecy era, before much of the military's work and deliberations were routinely classified and withheld from public review. He was a different breed. He published accounts of his work openly, and when it attracted controversy he defended his methods with vigor. After a few years, when the gunshot injuries of the Spanish-American War had been treated and examined, conclusions from this study were proven right.

The pistol tests were another matter. It was one thing to document how different bullets smash different bones. It was altogether another to measure concepts as ill-defined as "stopping power" and "shock effect." But this was the order, and Thompson and La Garde tried. The officers agreed to an imaginative set of trials. The field of firearms ballistics, like many applied sciences, is populated by scrupulous practitioners and passionate quacks. At times it can be difficult to tell the types apart. This was to be the case here. La Garde's rigor departed him entirely.

First the pair decided they needed cadavers and made the necessary arrangements at the Philadelphia Polyclinic Hospital and New York University's medical school. On the grounds of these institutions, they suspended cadavers by their heads so that their feet hung clear of the floor. Barrels of sawdust provided a backstop. Thompson and La Garde produced their tools: a collection of common pistols of the time* and assorted cartridges, some with full-metal jackets, others with lead points, and one with a cupped front end that its salesmen dubbed "the Manstopper." The shooting began. Eventually the officers would examine each wound, recording effects on flesh, organs, and bones. First they did something novel. In the instant each bullet smacked each cadaver, they estimated the degree of oscillation—in a word, the *swing*—of the struck limbs. "The force of impact was noticed to throw the limb back in the direction of the flight of the bullet, and in regaining its normally suspended position, the member was apt to sway back forth several times,"[61] the officers wrote to the War Department. Their observations led to a numerical rating that no serious scientist would regard as valid—a number between 1 and 100, assigned by assessing the movement with the naked eye. (The .45 round was rated an 80 or an 85, depending on the type of bullet fired.)

It was not enough to plumb how bullets tore through the dead or made hanging corpses sway. To gauge shock effect, the captain and major decided that they also needed to observe the varied ways and rates at which living creatures might die after suffering different types of pistol fire. So, after satisfying themselves that they had learned what could be learned from the cadaver shoots, the officers proceeded to the Union Stock Yards in Chicago, where they obtained livestock for the next stage. The first stockyard test posed a simple question: How does a pistol bullet affect a steer or cow when fired at close range? Animals were tied by turns to posts. The officers lifted their pistols, stepped near, took aim from roughly thirty-six inches away, and fired into each animal's rib cage. Then

---

*A Colt .38-caliber revolver, a Luger 9-millimeter, a Colt .45-caliber revolver, and more.

they backed up to watch. Observations recorded of the first animal, a bull weighing about thirteen hundred pounds, were typical.

> Two shots through both lungs from left to right; second shot four inches in front of the first. Animal dropped at the end of four minutes. Was apparently not much disturbed by the first shot, only throwing head slightly, but he was shocked by the second shot. Blood flowing from nostrils immediately after the first shot, showing that the lung was probably perforated. He was in a death struggle at the end of four and a half minutes; dead at the end of five.

The experiment on the fourth animal, a bull of the same size, might have suggested that cattle were not the best surrogates for studying the effects of bullets on men.

> First shot: Bullet entered from left to right; animal was shocked by the report. The bullet was intended to traverse the intestinal area as much as possible. At the end of the forty-five seconds the animal was breathing somewhat rapidly.
>
> Second shot: Two minutes from first shot. Bullet struck to the right and below where the first entered. Animal was again shocked by the report of the revolver and, of course, by the force of the blow.
>
> Third shot: Three minutes and ten seconds from first shot. Animal very much shocked by the loudness of the report; his breathing became faster, but he soon quieted down.
>
> As it became evident that the animal would not die immediately from the wounds already inflicted, he was shot in the head at the end of six minutes and thirty seconds from the time of the first shot, with no apparent effect.
>
> Sixth shot: At the end of seven minutes and fifteen seconds, the animal, still standing, was shot in the ear, with no apparent effect.*
>
> Seventh shot: At the end of eight minutes and fifteen seconds, the animal still standing, was shot behind the ear. The animal continued to stand, the shots having failed to reach a vital spot, it was determined to kill him in accordance with the method practiced at

---

* The report makes no mention of a fifth shot.

the slaughter house. At the fourth blow on the head with a hammer he fell to the ground and expired.

Captain Thompson and Major La Garde shot eight cows and steers before shifting to what they called "quick-firing" tests, the object being "to fire a sufficient number of shots in rapid succession to cause the animal to fall to the floor." The first cow withstood six bullets and sagged to the ground. The second cow absorbed ten, though "owing to a hitch in the working of the pistol, there was an interval of one minute between the third and fourth shots." The third animal was still standing after twelve bullets. The officers decided to dispatch it with a hammer. And so on.[62]

The work was of dubious value. The data sample was small, the method of observation crude. By today's standards it would be considered unethical and inhumane. It was influential nonetheless.[63] The officers concluded that the caliber of a pistol bullet was the most important factor in lethality. Bullets with larger diameters, they deduced, caused wounds with larger diameters, which brought about incapacitation and death more quickly than narrower, faster rounds. A wealth of other studies in wound ballistics would later show wounding to be more complicated than this. But based in part on these conclusions, the United States adopted the .45 as its standard pistol round. Thompson's affinity for the .45 round outlasted his military service. The lessons he thought he learned from watching swinging corpses and death throes in the stockyard led him to design the Thompson gun as a .45-caliber weapon. The thinking was linear. When fired rapidly through a pistol, the .45 round had brought a standing cow to the floor more quickly than any other pistol round: Six shots and a 950-pound brute was on her side. If it could do that job, imagine what it might do if fired at a rate of more than six hundred rounds a minute into a 160-pound man? This, on paper at least, was what the Thompson gun offered to all buyers.

Thompson's intentions were patriotic as well as commercial. He conceived of his submachine gun during World War I—a "trench broom," he called it, for cleaning German soldiers from fighting holes. But he did not get his prototype developed before the war's end. When he had it ready for sale, the timing was terrible. The American military budget was in a postwar contraction. Procurements were hard to find. Thompson hawked his gun with zeal from his Auto-Ordnance Corporation

offices on Broadway in Manhattan. Calling it a trench broom hardly
served his interests. Germany had surrendered. The prospects for another trench war were uncertain. Government markets were picky and
fickle; armies did not know what to prepare for next. The American
military acknowledged the mechanical soundness of Thompson's gun,
but still favored traditional rifles. Thompson presented the weapon to
police departments. Police officials had misgivings, too. A submachine
gun had a place in certain types of battle. But proposing automatic
arms for use against criminals seemed to many police chiefs to be a risky
inclination toward overkill, considering the danger to bystanders. Yet
all was not lost. Unlike Gatling's massive weapon, Thompson's gun had
characteristics that commended it to customers outside government.
And its legal path was clear. Until this point, automatic arms had been
military arms. No one had conceived of a law to regulate their sale to
private parties, because private citizens had not seemed to be a potential
market for the weapons that had appeared before. The Auto-Ordnance
Corporation turned its sales attention to civilians. The United States
had a love affair with firearms. Why not offer a firearm with extra pop?
The corporation appealed to both the nation's folklore and its cinematic
sense of self. One Thompson gun advertisement showed a cowboy firing from his right hip at armed horsemen charging his porch. In the
ad copy, four of the marauders' horses have been relieved of riders by
the bullets of the Tommy Gun. One rider is falling backward from
his saddle, rifle high, having just been shot. Two more horsemen, one
of whom is galloping away, appear to have had second thoughts. This
was Madison Avenue merged with righteous carnage, step right up and
buy your own. "The Thompson Submachine Gun. The Most Effective
Portable Fire Arms in Existence," the advertisement read. "The ideal
weapon for the protection of large estates, ranches, plantations, etc."
Thompson's most thorough historian summed up the Auto-Ordnance
pitch, and the predicament that accompanied it.

> A company that could fancy a cowboy mowing down bandits, or
> envision a householder pouring machine gun fire into his darkened
> dining room in defense of the family silver, might well have mis-
> judged its markets. But the submachine gun was legally available to
> anyone, and lack of police and military interest made it, by default, a

civilian weapon. And so it came to pass that the Thompson—manu-factured in peacetime, sold on the commercial market—was, in a sense, a machine gun for the home.[64]

A natural problem flowed from this sales ambition. The portion of the civilian population interested in purchasing submachine guns could have been expected to include more than the trespassed-upon homeown-ers suggested by the pitch. Unfortunately for the brigadier, this was the case. The Tommy Gun became a weapon of choice for mobsters, bank robbers, rum runners, and other members of the villainous classes of the 1920s and 1930s, all of whom gave submachine guns a bad name fast. The military's objection to the Thompson—that submachine guns were not effective across the distances at which the infantry often fights—was irrelevant in the underworld. Criminals did not worry about fighting off the massed rifles of well-drilled line platoons. They worried about each other, and they worried about the police. When their disputes turned violent, they settled them by pistol and shotgun fire, across distances at which people could hear each other curse. For these purposes and at these ranges, the Tommy Gun, with bullets that earned their respectability by knocking over cows, was a most useful tool.

Once civilians started filling orders, scandal was not far behind. In 1921, a shipment of Thompsons bound for the Irish Republican Army was discovered on a vessel soon to depart Hoboken for Dublin, which nearly caused a major diplomatic row between Washington and Lon-don.[65] The company's officers dodged indictment, though suspicions lingered that some of them knew more about the Irish deal than they let on. In 1923 the *Saturday Evening Post* questioned the merits of the gun's existence, and worried aloud over the uses to which it might be put.

> Except as an arm for trench warfare or semimilitary police forces having to deal with armed risings, it is difficult to see what honest need they can meet; yet we are faced with the fact that they exist and are on the open market for anyone who wants to buy them. Here, one would say, is an arm that is useless for sport, cumbrous for self-defense and could not serve any honest purpose, but which in the hands of political fanatics might provoke disaster.[66]

The Thompson was not particularly cumbersome for self-defense, and arguments still rage about the best definitions for legal sport and honest purposes in nations fortunate enough to have the stability and the forums to quarrel over such things. But the *Post* summarized well enough some of the risks that followed when small automatic arms designed for the most intimately violent of military tasks were made available to anyone. A few years later, the prediction proved at least partly right. In the mid-1920s, the weapon began to turn up in the hands of Chicago gangsters as they descended into a bootlegging turf war. Thompson's solution for overcoming the tactical horrors of the Western Front reached firearms notoriety by 1929, when hit men in police uniforms ordered seven men against a garage wall in Chicago's North Side and killed them all with Tommy Guns. Thompson was distressed. His public-relations troubles did not improve in the Depression. Pretty Boy Floyd, Machine Gun Kelly, Bonnie and Clyde, Ma Barker, and John Dillinger led a list of headline-generating outlaws who came to be associated with the Thompson and the menace of illicit firepower—good for bandits convincing bank tellers to open vaults and for shooting out of encirclement when trapped by the police. Not so good for everyone else.

The Thompson had a spectacular run, but its long-term effects as a public danger were less than what might appear. The Auto-Ordnance Corporation was one small company. Its production was not especially large. The gun entered outlaw lore aided by a rambunctious press. It managed to point to the future perils of assault-rifle proliferation. Yet it was an isolated case. This was because its breakout period occurred in a stable Western nation with functioning police, courts, and legislatures and a durable public compact. There was also the important matter of scale. Perhaps a few hundred Thompsons reached criminal hands in the United States. They caused minor havoc and national uproar, but the United States took steps for the public's safety before popular ownership of submachine guns became widespread. It began to make law. In 1934, Congress passed the National Firearms Act, part of a series of state and federal laws that restrict the sale, ownership, or use of automatic arms in the United States. Ultimately, after a brief and noisy heyday, Thompson's trench broom served to illustrate how stable nations with responsive governments can adjust to shifts in weapons technology. These were not the sort of nations where the AK-47 would leave its longest-lasting marks.

The AK-47 existed on a different order of magnitude, and was controlled by a different political culture. It was being assembled in enormous quantities by governments that, while they lasted, would show small concern for where the weapons went, or to whom. And after these governments fell, many of their automatic arms cascaded out of their possession. The arms flow began with a trickle. It began with József Tibor Fejes.

Fejes had carried his captured AK-47 with straight-backed rebel confidence. His cause seemed to have prevailed.

Soon after the cease-fire, the Kremlin adopted a conciliatory tone. It published in *Pravda* a declaration of respect, equality, and noninterference in the domestic affairs of its European satellites. By all appearances, the insurgents had won. They had forced Khrushchev to accept a new point of view about Soviet relations in the buffer zone. The revolution shifted from violent to political, at least on the surface. On November 1, 1955, Prime Minister Nagy delivered a radio address declaring Hungary's departure from the Warsaw Pact, and proclaiming its new unaligned status. Hungary was leaving the Soviet orbit. For Hungarians the proclamation was a moment of national self-determination. For the Kremlin, the radio address challenged Soviet authority over the nations in its grip and threatened to unravel a carefully choreographed alliance. For Nagy, the address was a reactive step; he had received reports of new Soviet military activities. The conciliatory declaration in *Pravda* had been a trick. On October 31, Khrushchev had decided to invade Hungary again, and with a much larger force. For a few days, as it massed troops, the Kremlin maintained the ruse. The Soviet leadership negotiated with Nagy's government over details for withdrawing Soviet forces. Almost everyone took the bait. On November 1 in Washington, Allen Dulles, the director of the Central Intelligence Agency, addressed the National Security Council after digesting the news. He marveled at the insurgents' success:

> In a sense, what had occurred there was a miracle. Events had belied all our past views that a popular revolt in the face of modern weapons was an utter impossibility. Nevertheless, the impossible had happened, and because of the power of public opinion, armed force could not effectively be used.[67]

Public opinion was not so powerful after all. That night, Soviet troops started a reconnaissance of the capital. On November 3, the Soviet and Hungarian delegations met for negotiations. The meeting ended when General Ivan Serov, director of the KGB and Dulles's Soviet counterpart, placed the Hungarian delegation under arrest. The remaining plans were already in motion. The commander in chief of Soviet armed forces had given his orders, reminding the soldiers that Hungary had sided with the Nazis in the Great Patriotic War. The Soviet invasion, he said, was justified under the Warsaw Pact, which bound the troops to the task of "carrying out their allied obligations."[68] Shortly after 4:00 A.M. on November 4, the nature of Soviet allied obligations was made known. The full attack began.[69]

The Soviet army called the crackdown Operation Whirlwind and launched it with the codeword *grom,* Russian for thunder. Armored divisions rolled into Budapest from multiple directions, this time with an ample complement of infantry. Nagy managed a radio broadcast to say the Hungarian government was at its post and Hungarian troops were fighting. Then he fled to the Yugoslav embassy. János Kádár, a rival politician who had secretly betrayed Nagy and received Kremlin backing, announced that a new government had been formed. The attack was overpowering. Soviet units quickly encircled the Hungarian Ministry of Defense and army buildings and barracks, neutralizing any chance of an organized conventional defense. In Moscow, Georgy Zhukov, the Soviet minister of defense, told the Central Committee that Soviet troops had seized communication centers, military depots, Parliament, the central committee of the Hungarian Workers' Party, and three bridges. The rebel government was in hiding, Zhukov said, and searches had begun. Then came the problem of Fejes and his colleagues at the rebels' stronghold. "One large hotbed of resistance of the insurgents remains in Budapest around the Corvin Theater," Zhukov said. "The insurgents defending this stubborn point were presented with an ultimatum to capitulate. In connection with the refusal of the resisters to surrender, the troops began an assault."[70]

The attack surprised the Corvinists. As many as two thousand fighters were near the theater, part of the new National Guard. But they were not as alert as before, and this time the Soviet military did not probe piecemeal or hesitate. It drove in heavy and hard. A tank regiment and a mechanized guard regiment rolled forward after artillery had prepared their path. Many rebels fought, but there was small hope of stopping such a force, and gradually most slipped away, yielding ground. The Soviet soldiers used flamethrowers and explosives against the holdouts. "By sunset," said Yevgeny I. Malashenko, acting chief of staff for the Soviet corps that resided in Hungary, "we had broken the resistance in the whole area."[71] The revolution was crushed, although at tremendous cost. The Soviet military suffered as many as 722 dead and 1,500 wounded. The bulk of their casualties came in the first week of fighting, before the cease-fire. Another 67 soldiers disappeared outright, likely to a mix of battle and defection to the West. The Hungarians suffered up to 20,000 people wounded. Depending on the source, 2,000 to 3,000 Hungarians were said to have been killed.[72]

József Tibor Fejes survived. What he did during the final Soviet invasion was not evident from the fading court records left behind; sources vary on whether he participated in the battle for the theater. But he had returned to his father's flat by November 5. By then the rebels' situation was desperate. Many tried to escape, some fleeing on foot toward Austria. Fejes opted to try to resume his former life. He reported back to work, where, in a sign of the depth of popular support for the revolution but also that Fejes's employer knew something of his armed activities, his salary was doubled. He settled back into the routines of labor and collecting wages, his AK-47 slung from his shoulder no more. The choice was fraught with risk. With the uprising extinguished, the Soviet Union and the ÁVH set out to destroy its participants and symbols. The immediate problem was Nagy, who had been granted sanctuary at the Yugoslav embassy. The Kremlin resorted once more to lies. The new Moscow-backed prime minister, János Kádár, signed a document for the Yugoslavs guaranteeing the former premier's safety. Assured of their security, Nagy, his circle, and their families left the embassy on November 22, expecting to be escorted home. Like the Soviet declaration in *Pravda*, and the faked negotiations to withdraw from Hungarian soil, the promise was a trap. Soviet intelligence officers stopped the bus and placed Nagy and his entourage under arrest. (After a secret trial, Nagy would be hanged.)

Next came reprisals against the revolution's rank and file. Between the end of the revolution and mid-1961, 341 people were executed and 22,000 sentenced to other punishments, mostly prison terms. Tens of thousands of others lost homes or jobs. More than 100,000 people were punished. Familiar Soviet slurs were recycled; the accused found themselves labeled *kulaks* or fascists. The reprisals took time to gain momentum. The case-load was large. At first Fejes faded back into his laborer's life. He hid in plain sight. His luck could not hold. He had been visible on the streets with his AK-47 throughout the cease-fire, and his employer appeared to know of his insurgent past. Beyond participating in the fighting, he and his AK-47 had been present at the killing of Lieutenant Balassa. This was the last sort of crime the government was not likely to overlook, the more so because Balassa was a legacy—his mother worked in the ÁVH. She could push for his case from within. All this, and Michael Rougier's photograph of Fejes had been published in *Life*. He was the revolution-ary poster boy, the young fighter with a captured assault rifle, wearing an eye-catching hat. Such high-profile evidence could bring a man maintain-ing a low profile no good. A clipping with the photograph went into the government's file. The authorities zeroed in. Fejes was arrested on April 30, 1957.[73] In a closed trial in early 1959, prosecutors described his sup-posed actions after Lieutenant Balassa, broken by bullets, fell to the street. Balassa had been struck in the neck, chest, lung, and elsewhere. Witnesses said Fejes stood over the body, removed Balassa's documents, and waved them for all to see. "He was an officer of the secret police," his accusers said Fejes shouted. "I killed this officer!" After the killing, prosecutors said, Fejes accused another man of being a member of the ÁVH, too. He released him after examining the man's palms and deciding that their rough condition indicated hard physical work; this, the prosecutor said, showed that Fejes was the leader of an operative revolutionary unit tasked with killing members of the police.

Fejes said this was all a lie. He said he had been posted to guard a cor-ner with another young man, nicknamed the Mute. But Fejes said he had argued with the other guards and was told to go away. As he walked off, leaving the Mute behind, he said, he heard gunshots, and turned around, frightened, to see Lieutenant Balassa falling. He joined the crowd only after Balassa was dead.

> I saw that person who shot the alleged ÁVH member. That person was short, bulky and was wearing a brown short coat, army trousers, boots and a winter hat. He had a Soviet type submachine gun, with

which he shot his victim dead. The murderer afterwards left the site
for the direction of Baross Street, but he returned shortly afterwards
to get the victims ÁVH I.D., then he left again. I was afterward assigned by the armed persons the task to guard the tank at the corner
of Rákóczi Square, which I guarded for over one hour and a half.
During that time came civilians and diplomats to take photos. They
took pictures of me, too, because I was standing next to the tank.
That is how I got into the pictures.[74]

The crowd around Balassa was dispersed, he said, when a Hungarian
soldier shot his weapon in the air. In all, Fejes said, he was at the scene of
the murder, looking at Lieutenant Balassa's corpse, for ten or eleven minutes. Then he took his position guarding the tank. The trial was before a
stern and famously progovernment judge. As the judge questioned him,
Fejes tried to stay alive.

"I never tried my automatic gun," he said. "I did not even shoot any
shots with it, but it must have been very good, I guess." He added later, "I
had nothing on my mind, no particular reason when I joined the freedom
fighters, I was not even familiar with the situation here."

The prosecutors' case was not ironclad. Elements of the evidence were
suspect. The case relied in part on a written statement from an anonymous witness—a police-state tactic that could allow evidentiary invention
to convict innocent men. The prosecutors presented a coroner's report of
Balassa's exhumed remains that claimed he had been shot in the skull. In
the photograph of Balassa dead on the curb, his head was intact. Fejes's
defense attorney pointed to inconsistencies in the testimony, and to a witness who said that Fejes did not fire his AK-47 during the shooting. But
Fejes's AK-47 did not help him. Rougier's photograph imbued the young
man in the courtroom with the air of a tough and accomplished fighter;
certainly a man could not have acquired such a weapon by easy means. A
prosecutor called him "Defendant Fejes, the bowler hat hero, an iconic
figure of the counter-revolution," who "carried out homicide, robbery
and looting." Fejes had the right to speak last. He adopted the language
and essential points of view of his accusers and begged for his life.

I plea for a merciful verdict. I did not participate in the counter-
revolution intentionally, it was curiosity that drove me into it. I am

not at fault in the Balassa incident. I was sent away from Rákóczi Square for I was conducting the checks in an improper way and only when I began to walk away did I turn around because I thought they were shooting at me, but that was when they in fact shot at Balassa. I plea to receive a light verdict because I am a common child of a worker, when Balassa got shot I even felt disgust towards the freedom fighters and I left them.

It was no use. Fejes was convicted of participating in events aimed to overthrow the people's republic, of unlawfully seizing state property, of theft, and of the murder of an officer of the law. The sentence was death. His appeal was rejected. At 7:18 A.M. on April 9, 1959, József Tibor Fejes was hanged. He was suspended on the gallows for thirty minutes, and then pronounced dead, the end of the journey of the first known revolutionary to carry what would become known as the revolutionary's gun.

Within the Soviet Union's design bureaus the family of arms built around the AK-47 was being finished. A new suite of Soviet firearms was emerging, pushing the Soviet army and its allies ahead of the West in efforts to field a basic set of infantry arms for the Cold War. The AK-47 was established and accepted, though problems in its original design had not been resolved. Throughout the mid and late 1950s, a team led by Mikhail Miller, an engineer in Izhevsk, worked to improve the early production models, experimenting on the gas system, the weapon's rate of automatic fire, the wooden stock, and more. The team also sought an acceptable stamped-metal replacement for the solid-steel receiver. Miller's group made multiple test rifles, and in 1959 Izhevsk launched production of an updated Kalashnikov, the AKM, the *Avtomat Kalashnikova Modernizirovanny*, or Modernized. The new Kalashnikov featured a stock made of laminated wood, which was determined to be stronger than solid wooden stocks. It had a new trigger group that included a device to slow the rate of automatic fire. Engineers hoped this would make the weapon easier to control. And the AKM had a sheet-metal receiver, which reduced the rifle's weight from the nearly nine and a half pounds of the previous version to less than seven pounds. With the AKM's arrival, the AK-47 was phased out.[75] The AKM became the basis for the most commonly encountered versions of the Kalashnikov line.

Mikhail Kalashnikov's status as exemplar for the working masses solidified. In 1958, as weapons bearing his name circulated throughout Soviet military, intelligence, and police units, and were passed to the Warsaw Pact, the Politburo designated Kalashnikov a Hero of Socialist Labor. The certificate accompanying his elevation praised his role in "reinforcing the power of the state."[76] This was curious language for an award issued for contributions to economy and culture, and especially so after the manner in which the state's power had been brought to bear in Hungary. It said more about the Soviet view of its assault rifle than most of its other declarations ever would. The award generated more coverage, and in 1959, Kalashnikov received more publicity still, including a profile of his life and work in *Voyenniye Znaniya,* a military magazine. The secret man was hardly a secret at all. He was a well-packaged public entity. Later, he said, "the avalanche of letters began after I had received the first state prize and has continued ever since. As if a floodgate had been opened."[77]

Simultaneously with the completion of the AKM, the Main Artillery Department oversaw the development of complements. The first system, the RPK, or *Ruchnoi Pulemyot Kalashnikova,* the handheld machine gun by Kalashnikov, was the smallest step forward. It was in the simplest sense a heavyweight AK-47, with a longer, heavier barrel and a bipod near the muzzle. These features gave the weapon greater range and accuracy than the assault rifle, and made it more suitable for sustained fire. Many of its parts were interchangeable with the AKM, including the magazines, and it was issued side by side with the AKM, although to fewer soldiers. Mikhail Kalashnikov was pleased. He sensed where the Soviet Union was headed—mass standardization based on the AK-47's basic design. "I cannot get rid of the thought," he said, "that Izhmash was predestined to become the father of domestic and actually world weapons unification."[78]

Next was the PK, or *Pulemyot Kalashnikova,* the machine gun by Kalashnikov. This filled the medium-machine-gun role for infantry companies, with greater range, accuracy, and stopping power than the RPK. It was meant to become the general-purpose machine gun for Soviet forces. In the initial effort to develop such an arm, a machine gun by Grigory I. Nikitin and Yury M. Sokolov was the front-runner. Ultimately, a design team in Izhevsk, with Kalashnikov as its titular head, presented its submission. The army had been satisfied enough with the AK-47, AKM, and RPK that it thought that the machine gun under the same name might enjoy similar popularity and success. It selected the submission from Izhevsk for service in 1961.[79] The PK weighed nearly twenty pounds unloaded and fired the larger 7.62x54R cartridge; it was to be a successful weapon and found in service alongside Kalashnikov rifles almost anywhere they are used. The basics of the Kalashnikov line were now complete. Future arms in the series would all be modifications of these underlying designs.[80] (The remaining element of the Eastern bloc's primary suite of small arms—a semiautomatic sniper rifle known as the SVD, or *Snaiperskaya Vintovka Dragunova*—was also in its research and development phase. It would be fielded in the early 1960s.)[81]

For Kalashnikov, this period should have been a time of professional and personal satisfaction. Instead it brought troubles. Kalashnikov's fame had fueled resentment, and as his stature grew he faced a species of social persecution that inhabited the post-Stalin Soviet Union. In 1956, Khrushchev issued a speech to a party congress, "On the Personality Cult and Its Consequences," in which he denounced Stalin's brutal excesses and the fealty and adoration that surrounded him. The speech, given in secret, was quickly leaked for public consumption. Its transcript was a powerful document. Once the population understood that the party leadership was questioning party symbols and behavior, it had a line of attack to settle scores against those who had benefited during the Stalin years. Kalashnikov's turn came while he was testing the PK in Samarkand. At a meeting of his collective in Izhevsk, a worker denounced Kalashnikov as arrogant and accused him of ignoring the suggestions and ideas of laborers in the plant. The diatribe fit the times. The Soviet Union's decorated designer was being cast as a man whose ego was outsized.[82] Kalashnikov was not present to defend himself. The troubles grew. An article about the meeting appeared in the factory newspaper under the headline "On Overcoming the Personality Cult and Its Consequences," a play on the title of Khrushchev's speech. The text detailed the worker's grievances and provided examples of Kalashnikov's supposed transgressions. Upon returning, Kalashnikov noticed his friends' discomfort around him. He was dejected. "I had always believed that I had been working for the Motherland to strengthen its defenses," he said. "But it appeared that people had misunderstood me."

The Idea of Concentrated Firepower, Miniaturized and Mass-Produced

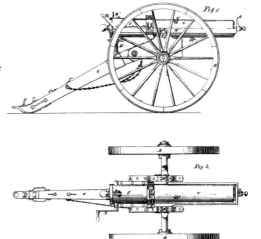

The first reasonably effective rapid-fire arm was the Gatling gun, shown here in patent drawings submitted by its inventor, Dr. Richard J. Gatling, in 1862. Gatling claimed he entered the weapons business to save lives. His weapon was not a true machine gun; firing it required a man to turn a crank. But it was the precursor to the rest.

As the killing powers of rapid-fire arms became understood, and manufacturing technology improved, new types of weapons—machines guns, submachine guns, automatic rifles, and assault rifles—entered markets. With time they were brought down in size and price, and connected to planned economies that produced them whether there were customers or not. The lethality, availability, and small size of assault rifles ultimately made them attractive to most anyone, including terrorists. Here, a Kalashnikov with its stock removed, which had been worn on a makeshift sling under the parka of a man who attacked a police station in Nalchik, Russia, during an insurgent raid in 2005. Its owner was dispossessed of it when he was killed. The keys beside the weapon provide a sense of scale. A fully outfitted Gatling could weigh a ton. A Kalashnikov like this weighs less than 8 pounds. (*Photo by C. J. Chivers*)

Richard Gatling—inventor, salesman, cunning businessman—shown late in life. He made a small fortune from the Gatling gun before it was displaced from markets. He died having borrowed money from his son. (*Photo courtesy of the Library of Congress*)

Hiram Maxim, accused trigamist, suspected draft dodger, and self-taught inventor from backwoods Maine, who decamped for London, where he invented the first true automatic weapon, the Maxim machine gun. His weapon changed war. Maxim guns were first used against men in lopsided fighting in colonial Africa and then helped turn World War I into a grisly hell. Maxim, the man, seemed untroubled by it all. He died proud. (*Photo from* My Life *by Hiram Maxim*)

. . . and Battlefield Success, and Horror

John H. Parker, U.S. Army, one of the first officers in conventional infantry service to grasp the significance of machine gunnery. In the battle for Santiago in 1898, his hastily assembled Gatling detachment pummeled entrenched Spanish positions as the infantry advanced—a new use of rapid-fire arms that earned praise from then-colonel Theodore Roosevelt. Parker was seen as an attention-seeking radical, and mostly was ignored by the army he served. (*Photo from Parker,* History of the Gatling Gun Detachment of the Fifth Army Corps at Santiago)

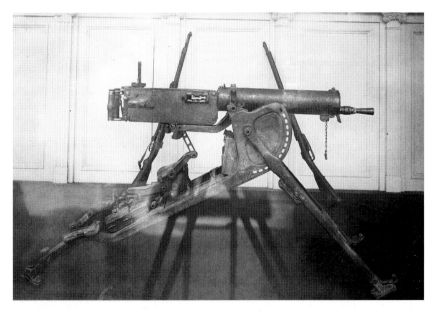

The MG08. The primary German version of Maxim's machine gun. Maxim and his partners sold his weapons and the rights to manufacturer them indiscriminately, including to nations that would become the enemies of his adopted country. The German military grasped what other Western armies did not, and the MG08 shaped the Western experience of World War I, wrecking untold lives. But it was still large—an instrument of the state, not of the individual man. (*Photo courtesy of the Library of Congress*)

The celebrated face of a breakthrough arm. Mikhail T. Kalashnikov, the noncommissioned officer the Soviet Union credited with designing the AK-47, the descendants of which would become the world's most abundant firearm. Shown here roughly two decades later, as a decorated Soviet hero. The rifle's origins are more complex, and more interesting, than the Soviet fables that helped make Kalashnikov's last name an informal global brand. (*Photo courtesy of the Ezell Collection, College of Management and Technology, UK Defence Academy*)

The guts of an AK-47. The weapon is of exceedingly simple design, and its durability is such that this early AK-47, manufactured in 1954 in Izhevsk, was still in use in 2010 in Marja, Afghanistan. Note the few parts and their intuitive relationship to one another; from top: the receiver cover, the recoil mechanism, the bolt carrier with gas piston. Note as well the external pitting, but the relative cleanliness inside. This was a fully functional rifle, made one year after Stalin died and still performing exactly as the Soviet Union intended more than half a century later in a war against the West. (*Photo by C. J. Chivers*)

中阿两国人民永恒的、牢不可破的战斗友谊万岁！

The Soviet Army shared assault rifles and the technical information to manufacture them with like-minded states. By the 1950s, the weapon was being produced in the Warsaw Pact countries, China, and North Korea. It was also shared with Egypt and other states. As its numbers grew, it became a symbol. Here, a Chinese-Albanian propaganda poster drew resolve from the rifle's presence, an accent to the thick-necked, strong-handed optimism of the propaganda-poster genre. The caption reads: "Long live the long-lasting, unbreakable fighting friendship between the Chinese and Albanian people."

Fuller accounts, and honest assessments, were much more complicated than the propaganda would have it. József Tibor Fejes, far right, the first known insurgent to carry an AK-47. Fejes obtained his prize after Soviet soldiers dropped their rifles during their attack on revolutionaries in Budapest in 1956. This photograph, taken after a cease-fire agreement, appeared in *Life* magazine, and drew the attention the ÁVH, the secret police, who tracked Fejes down. The Hungarian Revolution marked the AK-47's true battlefield debut. (*Photo from the Budapest Municipal Archives*)

(*Photo courtesy of
Hermann–ullstein bild /
The Granger Collection*)

(*Photo courtesy of AKG–ullstein bild / The Granger Collection*)

One essential element of the Kalashnikov legend, as told by Mikhail Kalashnikov and the Soviet and Russian governments alike, is that the AK-47 was designed for national defense and then distributed for liberation struggles. The script misses a characteristic use: as the strongman's tool for crackdowns. The case of Peter Fechter (inset), an East German teenager, provides a more complete view.

Fechter tried to scale the Berlin Wall in 1962. Border guards opened fire on him with bursts of Kalashnikov fire. One round struck his hip. His fingers tell the rest of the story—they are coated in clotted blood from his efforts to save himself while the men who shot him watched. The Kalashnikov has been turned by government troops against civilians in Berlin, Budapest, Prague, Tbilisi, Almaty, Moscow, Beijing, Baku, Bishkek, and a long list of other places where regimes have used violence to hold power.

(*Photo courtesy of Bera–ullstein bild / The Granger Collection*)

The weapon continued to spread far from its makers' hands. By 1962, the breakout had accelerated. A Dutch soldier, from Bravo Company. 41st Infantry Battalion, in Western New Guinea. He is holding what may be the first AK-47 captured by conventional Western forces in battle, a rifle picked up after being abandoned by an Indonesian Special Forces team. The Soviet Union had provided the rifles to Indonesia. The new period of Kalashnikov proliferation had begun. (*Photo courtesy of a former officer in the unit who wished to remain anonymous*)

VIETNAM: WHERE BOTH SIDES USED ASSAULT RIFLES AS PRIMARY ARMS FOR THE FIRST TIME

The young men of Second Battalion, Third Marines, were among the first Marines in Vietnam to receive the American answer to the AK-47: the M-16 assault rifle. From left to right are four lieutenants whose troops were issued rifles that failed: Mike Chervenak, Roger Gunning, Chuck Woodard, and Bill Miles. (*Photo courtesy of Chuck Woodard*)

The M-16 and its ammunition had been rushed into production. The early versions were plagued with reliability problems. The problems were largely resolved later, but its bungled and bloody introduction was a searing experience for men asked to put their faith in their commanders and their country, which failed them in war. The nature of war had abruptly changed. For the first time, the soldiers from an industrial nation were outgunned by an agrarian local population, for whom the Kalashnikov assault rifle was a battlefield leveler.

The military identification of Mike Chervenak, who spoke out publicly against the failures of M-16 rifles in combat—and was punished for it. (*Courtesy of Mike Chervenak*)

Staff Sergeant Claude E. Elrod, who led First Platoon, Hotel Company, Second Battalion, Third Marines, on July 21, 1967. The photograph was taken shortly before the fight against the North Vietnamese Army for Ap Sieu Quan, the day that ultimately would force the Marine Corps to admit its rifles were failing—and demand replacements.

After the battle, Hotel Company settled into the deserted village. First Lieutenant Chervenak is standing on the left, in a dark tee shirt. He was enraged, and set out to document the problems.

Marines inside Ap Sieu Quan, with M-14s against a wall. The Marine Corps had issued M-16s to replace M-14s, which were not supposed to be carried. Many Marines, not trusting their M-16s, procured M-14s through underground means and ditched their newer weapons. At Ap Sieu Quan, when at least forty of Hotel Company's M-16s jammed, the M-14s allowed the grunts who had them to protect Marines whose rifles had gone silent. (*Photos courtesy of Claude Elrod*)

The 1986 log book of preconscription training of Soviet students in Pripyat, the worker's town beside the nuclear reactors at Chernobyl. The book was left behind after the power station exploded, bombarding Pripyat with radiation, and remained on the contaminated grounds in 2005.

Results of the students' timed drills with Kalashnikov assault rifles—part of the curriculum in Soviet schools. The log book was a marker of both the rifles's ease of use and the extent to which assault rifles had penetrated Soviet society. The practice persists in post-Soviet Russia. (*Photos by Joseph Sywenkyj*)

The Kalashnikov's durability in the field and its ease of use, along with its slight recoil, have made it a weapon most anyone can use. These traits, coupled with its near ubiquity, have made it a primary arm of child soldiers. A boy soldier in the Tamil Tigers, Sri Lanka, 1992. (*Photo by Suzanne Keating*)

Drawing by a former child soldier from the Lord's Resistance Army, an millennial insurgent group that originated in Uganda in the 1980s. Armed with simple and lightweight assault rifles, the group has survived more than a quarter century in the field. (*Photo by C. J. Chivers*)

帝国主义和一切反动派都是纸老虎

After its introduction, the AK-47 crept into national and insurgent propaganda alike, and can be seen in statuary, symbols, banners, and posters from Central America to North Korea. The caption reads of this poster was typical of its form: "Imperialism and all anti-revolutionists are paper tigers." The weapon has similarly been appropriated as a mark of martial credibility and determination by dictators, criminals, rascals, and jihadists, a malleable icon that can convey whatever those who carry it wish to convey.

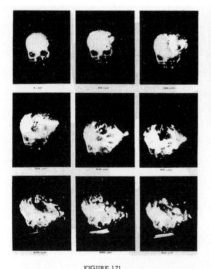

FIGURE 171

ENLARGED HIGH-SPEED MOTION-PICTURE FRAMES OF SKULL 5576, SHOT WITH AR-15 (1/14) RIFLE AT 50 M RANGE (U)

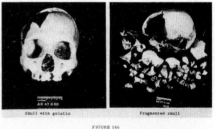

FIGURE 166

SKULL 5633, SHOT WITH AK-47 RIFLE AT 100 M RANGE (U)

In 1962 and 1963, the U.S. Army held classified tests examining the weapon's lethality against that of American rifles. With cadavers procured in secret from India and with live goats, testers at Aberdeen Proving Ground fired into defatted and decapitated human heads that had been filled with gelatinous pseudobrains. The tests—hurried, macabre, free from peer review or public scrutiny, and ultimately useless—were a milestone of strange Cold War "science." An embarrassed army covered them up for nearly fifty years. The effects of a bullet fired by an early American assault rifle passing through a human head were recorded, on a high-speed camera. The so-called terminal effects of an AK-47 round were displayed on another panel, after a tester fired into the skull. (*Photos from* "Wound-Ballistics Assessment of M-14, AR-15 and Soviet AK Rifles," *U.S. Army, 1964*)

Sometimes, choosing not to display a Kalashnikov can have meaning, too. A member of Al Aqsa Martyr's Brigade, the Palestinian terrorist group, brandished an M-4 in an interview with the author in 2002. Carrying a rifle used by Israel signified defiance or fighting skill—to acquire its enemies' rifles, the group depends on corruption or battlefield capture. Displaying the enemies' guns is a common propaganda device, used the world over. (*Photo by Tyler Hicks / The New York Times*)

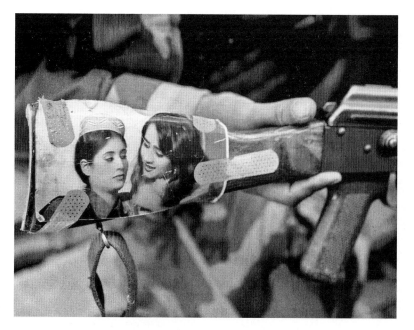

Among those who use them, assault rifles can be intensely personal objects or symbols with many meanings. In 2009, an Afghan National Army soldier in Korengal Valley, Kunar Province, decorated his Kalashnikov with unveiled images of women—a seeming rebuke to the Taliban. (*Photo by Tyler Hicks / The New York Times*)

By the time the Kalashnikov line had entered its second half-century of service, it was firmly entrenched as a primary tool of violence in destabilized lands. The Soviet Union had fallen, the Warsaw Pact had dissolved. The armories and stockpiles were loose, and the weapon was so common in the field that it was scarcely remarked upon. Its effects were easy to find, and chilling. A wounded Taliban fighter, captured by the Northern Alliance in late 2001, on the approach to Kabul. The man was dragged from hiding onto a dirt road, and executed in a frenzy. What the Kalashnikov era has often looked like, in a way rarely documented by camera. The rifle is still used in crackdowns, too. (*Photos by Tyler Hicks / The New York Times*)

Karzan Mahmoud, at far right of bottom row. A bodyguard for a Kurdish prime minister in Northern Iraq, Mahmoud was shot repeatedly by assassins with Kalashnikovs not long after this photograph was taken in 2002. The doctors documented twenty-three bullet wounds in his shattered frame. Mahmoud survived. Later, he wondered whether Mikhail Kalashnikov feared for his soul. (*Photo courtesy of Karzan Mahmoud*)

For a near decade after going to war against the Taliban in Afghanistan in late 2001, the United States has become a busy distributor of the assault rifles of the former Eastern bloc. Here, a swiftly formed unit of the Afghan National Auxiliary Police in Uruzgan Province, Afghanistan, 2007, armed with a fresh batch of Kalashnikovs. These units were later disbanded, often without recovering the weapons, the whereabouts of which are unknown. (*Photo by Tyler Hicks / The New York Times*)

Since their inception, Kalashnikov assault rifles have displayed remarkable durability in harsh conditions. Above, an original Soviet AK-47, manufactured in Izhevsk in 1954. The rifle was still in service in Afghanistan, now in the hands of an Afghan soldier, in 2008. (*Photo by C. J. Chivers*)

The Kalashnikov, centerpiece of the former Eastern bloc's suite of small arms, remains the predominant infantry rifle in use today worldwide. Here, an Afghan patrol in 2007 with arms provided by the United States, approaching a village on a raid with a platoon of paratroopers from the 82nd Airborne Division. There is little reason not to expect the Kalashnikov line, and the consequences of its wide distribuition, to persist for many decades more. (*Photo by Tyler Hicks / The New York Times*)

Kalashnikov described the complaints as petty. Workplace jealousies, it seemed, had found an outlet in the bizarre atmosphere of that time. But workers' newspapers could scarcely be published, particularly in a factory under as close party supervision as an arms plant, without approval of factory bosses and their party liaisons. And published denunciations carried risks. The repression had subsided. Khrushchev's Soviet Union was incomparably less violent than Stalin's, notwithstanding the treatment of Beria. But apparatchiks could have their standing downgraded over accusations related to a personality cult. Kalashnikov's fidelity to Stalin was unbending. His fears were likely considerable. He hinted at this. "I could not defend myself before each employee of our giant plant," he said. The stresses of the period affected him physically, he said, and he developed cardiac arrhythmia. But Mikhail Kalashnikov was ever the survivor of the Soviet Union's ugly undercurrents. He sought help from what he vaguely called "our major client" and continued to work. His instincts and connections served him well. At a collective meeting some months later the secretary of the factory's party committee raised the accusations. This time he defended Kalashnikov. His standing was preserved, even as his role in arms design became less important.[83]

By the early 1960s Mikhail Kalashnikov was no longer especially significant to socialist arms production, beyond his status as a public figure. The weapons carrying his name had been created. They were bound for proliferation independent of what he said or did. Their rates and locales of production, their distribution, their many uses—these were out of his hands. He was a front man now: the story and its face. And across the Eastern European satellites the production of the Kalashnikov line had gathered momentum.

Poland was the first European nation to produce the rifles, beginning work on their arms in 1956. Bulgaria, East Germany, Romania, and Hungary followed. As new assembly lines opened, they would receive state subsidies and be given priority in the delivery of the resources required for production—metals, labor, tools, fuel, and when required, security. The German experience offers a view of the process, albeit with a special set of deceptions required by the Kremlin's public stance that Germany would not be allowed to militarize again. This posed problems. Officially, the German Democratic Republic was a peaceful nation that had forsworn armament production. It was not to be engaged in the gun trade. To hide the work, assault-rifle production was classified and compartmentalized. Rifle parts were made in sites scattered around the countryside, sometimes in small family shops, and brought to a secluded plant. There, the many secret components came together, like pieces in a puzzle, in the form of a gun. Then the rifles were shipped to their destinations, either for East German security forces or foreign customers.

The final assembly point was in Wiesa, a village in the Erz mountains away from main cities and roads. To produce rifles this way, the communists imitated the Wehrmacht, which had experience circumventing restrictions. After World War I, the Treaty of Versailles had mandated a sharp reduction in German armed forces. It also imposed limits on the types and numbers of weapons Germany could garrison. Article 180 allowed for 84,000 rifles and 18,000 carbines (it even mandated the type, down to the style of bayonet), 1,926 machine guns, 252 mortars, and 288 heavy guns. Only one factory, the Simson works in Suhl, was approved to manufacture rifles. Other arms plants were ordered to disassemble their production lines, and, in an early swords-to-plowshares clause, expected to manufacture civilian products, including precision tools. The treaty was impressive on paper. On the ground it did not work. German officers and gun manufacturers used many forms of subterfuge to dodge compliance. In 1922, the former Royal Rifle and Ammunition Factory in Erfurt, which had been shuttered under the treaty, opened a new gun works, ERMA, and surreptitiously resumed production. By 1932, the plant had one thousand employees. Another firm, Rheinmetall-Borsig, spirited away more than two thousand tons of arms-making machinery and hid them in warehouses in Holland under false declarations. Using a front company, it bought stock in a Swiss firm near Bern and began manufacturing machine guns that would have been forbidden at home. In 1926, a group of officers founded the Statistical Corporation, or Stage, which entered the arms-manufacturing business, too. And so on.[84]

The gun works at Wiesa followed this pattern, but added Soviet touches. One step required finding a site for a final assembly line. The army selected a formerly private textile plant that had been nationalized and declared a people's company in 1949. The plant had been owned by the family of Kurt Schreiber, a local businessman. During World War I, its main building served as a POW camp; captured French and Russian officers were held there. After the war, it became a factory again. It was a bucolic setting, a stately building on a hillside with neatly kept fields abutting its fences. After World War II, the party seized the plant. By 1950, several Schreiber family members who had faced charges upon protesting their loss (their descendants call the basis for the seizure "a legal farce") had fled to West Germany. This cleared title for the site's next use. In 1956, East Germany's military received sample AK-47s and technical specifications from the Soviet Union. In February 1957, the commandeered plant reopened as a secret arms factory. That year the government seized adjacent property, taking some of the best farmland on the slope.[85] It extended fences, hired police officers, installed security lighting along the perimeter, and built a guard shack at the gate. Watchdogs appeared. They slept by day in a pen in the compound's interior and roamed the fences at night. Their presence was a sure indication of something important within. Construction changed the place, updating it along bland Soviet lines. Dull concrete buildings and a warehouse sprouted. Rail service was extended to reach within the fences. Beneath one of the main buildings, secured behind heavy iron grates, a firing range was opened for testing the weapons before packaging and shipment.

Across the region, skilled workers were hired and trained, and a bus line was created to carry them back and forth to work. There was no bus service for anyone else. The arms-plant jobs, which paid more than what was generally available elsewhere and came with access to a workers' cafeteria that served hearty meals, were coveted and hard to land. Each applicant had to pass a background check. Those from families with a history of private business ownership or who had relatives in the West were turned away. Those offered positions were required by the Staasi, the secret police, to sign an oath pledging never to reveal what took place in the plant. "You were not allowed to tell your own wife what you did," said one former employee. Such measures were nonsensical, he added. Like most everyone else, "she already knew."[86] The plant was given a cover: It manufactured tools and home appliances. Over time the villagers coined a knowing joke. That strange plant on the hill, they said, makes a wonderful coffee filter.[87]

By 1958, rifle production had begun. A bustling gun works grew. Under police escort on the country roads, truck drivers brought in components that had been forged and machined elsewhere.[88] The barrels came from Suhl, from a plant said to manufacture bicycles.[89] Smaller gun works contributed other parts. A few were machined within the Wiesa compound. The first result was the Maschinen Pistole Kalashnikov, or MPiK, a copy of the original design. Soon more than one thousand people were employed by the works, and the plant became the engine of the local economy in a time when German citizens were still suffering postwar shortages of everything from fresh fruit to building supplies to schnapps. Some townspeople were pleased, and welcomed the good fortune of having a large employer near their homes. Others were afraid. They thought that by choosing Wiesa for a rifle plant, the party had made their village a target. "We always knew, and we were told," one local man said, "that in case of war Wiesa would be one of the first places to disappear from the planet."[90]

Production was slow in the first years. But output rose under harsh quality-control measures, and enough rifles were made to equip the Nationale Volksarmee, the Staasi, and a list of foreign customers, including Iraq, Algiers, Yemen, India, and the Republic of Congo. Rail cars would arrive. They departed filled with green wooden crates containing ten assault rifles each. If the estimates of production levels are accurate, as many as three hundred thousand crates left the grounds. Many were trucked to Dresden. Others went to Rostock, a port on the southern coast of the Baltic Sea, on their way to export. The secrecy of the gun works in Wiesa was short-lived. Virtually everyone in Wiesa knew. Much of East Germany did, too. The covers—the bicycle plant in Suhl, the appliance plant in Wiesa, the idea that East Germany did not manufacture rifles—grew to be absurd. Assault rifles peddled by East German front companies in Berlin turned up in wars in Africa and the Middle East. And yet over the years, day by day, the unstated rules of totalitarianism demanded that the people of Wiesa feign indifference, even ignorance, as the muffled crack of gunfire rose from the basement firing range each night. "I decided that up to the edge of the fence was mine," said one of the plant's neighbors. "After that it was a foreign country, and I couldn't care about it."[91]

Others did care. Little attracts more attention among armies than word that another military force has a new weapon and is investing heavily in its production. Whispers about new weapons can be an emotionally and intellectually powerful variety of intelligence; they inspire curiosity and often worry. Such was the case in many foreign capitals when the AK-47 began to be seen. As the Kremlin hardened its foreign policy, outside interest in the weapon grew. Foreign intelligence services and arms technicians collected specimen rifles. One of the earliest collections was made in 1956 by Erkki Maristo, of the Finnish military's ordnance department, who was at the center of a minor Cold War intelligence caper. In the mid-1950s, the Finnish Defense Forces were exploring available options for a new service rifle and wanted to test existing designs. Intelligence sources had brought news of the M1943 cartridge and the AK-47. In May 1956, Lieutenant General Sakari Simelius, chairman of the Finnish Small Arms Committee, saw the AK-47 on a visit to the Soviet Union. Like the Soviet army, the Finns had experience with submachine guns and had no bias against lighter-powered automatic arms. They had studied the *sturmgewehr* closely and battle experience had taught them that weapons built around traditional European rifle cartridges were not necessarily the best choice for defending their thickly forested nation, where many engagements were fought at close range. The Soviet weapon might fit Finnish needs. How to obtain a sample? Direct sale from Moscow seemed impossible. No defector had carried an AK-47 across the Soviet-Finnish border. The defense forces found another means—a businessman with connections in Poland who agreed to arrange a clandestine purchase. As part of Warsaw Pact standardization efforts, Poland was beginning to manufacture its version of the AK-47. After the businessman's inquiries, an early rifle was offered for sale. In fall 1956, Maristo sailed by ferry across the Baltic Sea as a private citizen and landed in Poland. In Warsaw, he was shown one of Poland's prototype Kalashnikovs. He purchased it for an undisclosed price. The rifle was disassembled and the parts smuggled home on a Polish commercial vessel sailing from Gdansk to the Finnish port of Kotka, where it was picked up by the Ministry of Defense and reassembled for analysis.[92]

The Finns were enthused. They wanted more samples. On March 15, 1957, working through a company called Ankertex OY, the defense forces purchased one hundred more Polish Kalashnikovs, making Poland an early commercial exporter of assault rifles and equipping the Finns with the samples they needed for reverse engineering.[93] In the 1960s the Finns began production of an exceptionally well-made Kalashnikov knock-off, the RK-60, which was updated in 1962 and became the Finnish Defense Forces' standard arm. (The Finns' selection raised questions of which nation had pulled off a masterful bit of small-arms intrigue. Was Maristo's collection trip to Warsaw a Finnish intelligence coup? Or had the Finns been lured into a well-orchestrated KGB double game? The Finns' decision to adopt the 7.62x39 round and a Soviet-pattern could be seen as serving Soviet interests. Finland and Russia shared a long northern border, and as an unaligned state Finland was not a NATO member. There is ample evidence that the Soviet Union gladly aided the Finns' choice. In 1960, it sold 20,000 AK-47s to the Finnish Defense Force, and in 1962 sold another, smaller quantity. The weapons were to expedite assault-rifle training. Once the RK-62 was adopted in Finnish small-arms munitions stores were incompatible with NATO's weapons, but compatible with the Soviet Union's. The Finnish decision gave the Soviet military a logistical edge along its northwestern frontier.)

As the Finns tested their Polish guns, AK-47s kept reaching foreign hands. A confidential 1958 report to the Netherlands General Staff, prepared by intelligence officials and the Dutch inspector of armaments, detailed the exploitation of a folding-stock Kalashnikov that had been manufactured in 1952. The Dutch intelligence service sensed the weapon's production momentum and deduced part of the Soviet army's intentions. It noted that the AK-47s seen in intelligence photographs through 1956 had been assigned to the infantry, whereas more recent images showed them with artillery, signals, and antiaircraft soldiers. The analysts ventured that "it is very likely that this weapon will become the only Soviet shoulder weapon."[94] The report was both prescient and understated; the weapon was moving well beyond Soviet possession.

Arms specialists in Yugoslavia also pursued Kalashnikov technology. Josip Broz Tito, Yugoslavia's prime minister, headed a socialist nation that might have been a candidate for early standardization, had relations with the Kremlin not been strained.[95] When the Soviet army transferred technical specifications elsewhere, Yugoslavia was left out. It obtained neither sample rifles nor the aid needed to manufacture them. Engineers at the Zastava arms plant in Kragujevac, however, had been experimenting with automatic-rifle designs since 1952, working with captured specimens of the *sturmgewehr*. In 1959, they got their break. First, two AK-47s came into their possession, apparently after a pair of Albanian border guards passed them off upon defecting to Yugoslav soil.[96] Engineers at Zastava made metal castings from the rifles but did not glean enough data to copy them. Tito then came through personally. On a foreign visit to a nation that had received Soviet military aid, he retrieved more AK-47s. These were passed to the engineers to finish their work. (During this time, Tito traveled to Egypt, Indonesia, and India, any one of which might have provided him the sample arms; which country did so has remained a state secret.)[97] By the end of 1959, the Zastava plant was developing an AK-47 variant.[98] The work was done by industry. Unlike the Finns, the Yugolav military was not interested in issuing the AK-47, fearing its soldiers would consume too much ammunition.[99] The factory pushed on alone. Its assault rifles would in time become widely exported, and would be present in many wars.[100]

One nation alone had the most puzzling reaction to the AK-47 and its creeping movement across the globe: the United States. Throughout the crucial period of the AK-47's design, development, and mass distribution, American military officers did not foresee or understand the significance of what was happening at its enemy's test ranges and arms plants. The American intelligence and arms-design failures were almost total. On the level of anticipating security threats, the Pentagon did not recognize the risks to its forces or its allies from the AK-47's capabilities and global production. And as for designing infantry firearms, it remained obstinately committed to high-powered cartridges and rifles that fired them. Part of the bedrock belief was tradition. As with the European affection for bayonet and cavalry charges at the turn of the century, America was the victim of romance—with old-fashioned rifles and the sharpshooting riflemen who carried them. These were integral to national frontier legend. An unshakable devotion to these legends, and to technical and tactical choices that adhered to them, showed itself repeatedly. At the late date of 1916, after legions of men had died miserably in Europe, wasted in the trenches before the machine guns and artillery of the industrial age, the United States Army continued to operate a School of Musketry at Fort Sill. Names matter. This name spoke to a mentality that handicapped American ground officers through the twentieth century's first six decades, and left the services unprepared for shifts in technology that were putting lightweight automatic rifles into its enemies' hands.

Time and again, senior officers upheld tradition and missed signs. The

American army watched events in Europe as its involvement in World War I drew near. When it entered the war in 1917, in spite of the nation's industrial might and its role as the incubator of machine guns, the army contributed little to the rapidly expanding tactical field. It had more than fifty years of association with machine guns. But it had not yet developed a sound machine-gun doctrine. The record spoke of indifference and neglect. In 1904, during the Russo-Japanese War, an American military attaché reported observing a Russian machine-gun battery fire 6,000 rounds in a minute and a half, and 26,000 rounds in two days of battle. When the army experimented with machine-gun platoons in 1907, it issued each platoon 1,000 rounds to fire—for an entire year.[101] An allotment of that size provided small chance to develop marksmanship, and smaller chance still to experiment thoughtfully with tactics. It also made everything lucidly clear. No matter Omdurman, never mind the army's own experience outside Santiago and in the Philippines, forget the horrifying effectiveness of machine guns in the battle for Port Arthur. Machine guns and machine gunnery were not a prominent part of army thought. By 1909, the army had 282 Maxims for its entire force. Then it replaced them—after minimal testing—with the Benet-Marcie, a French design that, soldiers discovered after procurement, broke down under heavy use.

Louis La Garde, the army surgeon who had organized the cadaver and livestock firing tests, summarized a persistent ideal, which was common to American infantry thinking before the United States plunged into the war. "With a high muzzle velocity and a flat trajectory, little remains to be desired in the present rifle," he wrote in 1916. The present rifle, in 1916, was the M1903 Springfield—a high-powered, bolt-action rifle almost forty-five inches long. La Garde saw value only in making the round more powerful, so a bullet fired over level ground would fly so flat and so far that as it traveled across more than a half-dozen football fields, it would neither rise above nor fall below the height of a standing man. This was the weirdly disconnected domain of ballistics theory. A round that flies in this fashion would remain a hazard for a man standing upright on perfectly flat ground from any point from the rifle's muzzle out to more than a third of a mile. Such theories appeared sensible on chalkboards, as long as one looked past certain facts. First among them was that in combat such terrain does not exist. The second fact was every bit as important:

People under fire tend not to remain exposed and standing up. La Garde had a busy mind. He liked to think about bullets. He examined gunshot injuries like no other officer of his time. But he was no tactician. The most positive development he could foretell would be fielding a bullet-and-rifle combination such that "the continuous danger space for a height of 68 inches extended from the present range of 730 yards to a range of 1,000 yards."[102]

After the war, the army studied the possibility of a semiautomatic rifle. Tests showed the value of a lower-pressure round—the .276 Pederson—as a replacement for the .30-06 cartridge fired by the M1903. The .276 might have pushed the United States ahead of everyone else in developing semiautomatic and automatic shoulder arms. But the opportunity was lost. General Douglas MacArthur, the army chief of staff, rejected the study after being told that it was still feasible to design a semiautomatic rifle that fired the heavier, faster round. It was in fact feasible. A better question might have been whether it was preferable. The old round remained the standard; the lighter round was shelved. Because no other nation fielded an intermediate round quickly, and the German *sturmgewehr* was not distributed in the quantities necessary to influence the fighting against American soldiers in late World War II, the United States did not suffer directly from MacArthur's decision, at least not immediately. In the short term the opposite occurred. The army developed a semiautomatic rifle, the M1 Garand, which fired its big cartridge. The Garand was powerful and reliable, if somewhat unwieldy in the old-school ways. But American soldiers fought World War II with one of the most successful semiautomatic rifles ever made. Over the longer term MacArthur's decision had an insidious effect. The Garand was a perfect dinosaur—a highly developed and successful weapon of a type that was soon to die. Its success hardened the bias against smaller rounds.

And yet there was still a chance for the United States to move in the direction that rifle technology was headed, and to get there years before the Soviet Union won the race. In 1941, the army recognized that in spite of its commitment to big rifles for its infantry, it needed a lighter and shorter weapon for entire categories of soldiers—those who carried and fired mortars, or were members of machine-gun crews, or drove tanks and trucks, or tended to wounded soldiers, or carried radio gear. There were any number of people on the battlefield for whom a large rifle was a burden and a pistol was too inaccurate to be of much value. For these soldiers, the army fielded a semiautomatic rifle with an intermediate round—the M1 carbine. The M1 carbine weighed slightly more than five pounds and measured less than a yard. It fired a short .30-caliber cartridge that propelled bullets from its muzzle at less than two thousand feet per second. It had a box magazine, and could hold up to thirty rounds. The rifle was popular with many soldiers and Marines. Several million were made. Like many new calibers and new weapons, the M1 carbine-cartridge combination had problems. Many veterans worried that the step down from the .30-06 cartridge had been too steep, and that the carbine's round lacked range and knockdown power. The carbine was known to jam, especially in cold weather. But with this combination, the United States had a format in hand to improve upon in the natural step toward a general-issue lightweight automatic. The chance was lost. After World War II, when the search began for an automatic to replace the Garand, the army remained devoted to traditional cartridges. It selected the Garand format.

Allegiance to tradition informed more than the weapons the Pentagon chose to pursue. It colored how the Pentagon perceived the arrival of the assault-rifle era. When the equipment and lessons of World War II were analyzed, the Soviets recognized the value of the *sturmgewehr*. The Americans did not. Forgetting even the biases informed by convention, the oversight merits consideration. Immense collections of German war records were captured and read by the Allies, allowing deep insight into the Wehrmacht's war machine. Designers involved were interrogated. The *sturmgewehr* represented a groundbreaking change in infantry arms, and the United States Army held the thinking behind it. It possessed captured samples. It occupied many of Germany's arms factories. It held the German plans and the German machine tools. It had access to the workers. But the significance of the Nazis' development was lost on the officers and technicians responsible for American weapons design. The United States understood what Hugo Schmeisser's automatic rifle *did*; it did not understand what it *meant*.

Looked back on, the adherence to old thinking appeared startling, given the information available in the 1950s to the army and its general staff. Shortly after World War II, the army contracted with private researchers, detached from its customs and bureaucracy, who made pointed recommendations for new training and equipment. The group, called the Operations Research Office, combed classified data and literature in offices at Johns Hopkins University and secretly reached conclusions that challenged two preeminent American chestnuts: the value of the long-range rifle and the belief in the shooting skills of marksmen. Available data showed that whatever the abilities of soldiers on rifle ranges, under the stress and visibility conditions of actual war, the preponderance of combat shooting was more pedestrian than legend suggested. Casualty studies showed that most bullet hits in World War II were random, like shrapnel wounds, and most happened at short range.[103] There were good reasons for this. It was not simply that riflemen were bum shots. Tactics had a hand. The United States had been late to machine gunnery, but by the end of World War I, and throughout its military operations thereafter, it usually used machine guns well. And one common element of modern infantry fighting involved a reliance not on the precision aimed fire of the individual, but on the massed area fire of the group. The means and style of conventional ground warfare had changed. Concentrated firepower was often used to pin down an enemy as much as to kill him, while friendly troops moved in close. This suppressive fire, studies showed, was frequently applied without soldiers' putting their weapons' sights to their eyes, unless a distinct target presented itself, which was often not the case. In firefights like this, what was the purpose of such a rifle as La Garde had championed, which could strike a standing man seven hundred yards away? Soldiers often were relying on volume of fire more than on precise plinking at great range, and creating volume of fire required carrying hundreds of bullets, which was not easy to do if those bullets were heavy and large.

These were the kinds of questions and conversations in play overseas, questions that the Red Army had settled to its own satisfaction in 1943.

The data, and the studies, were not enough for the Pentagon of the 1950s. Not even the Americans' closest allies could dissuade the generals from their antiquated point of view. Like their Soviet counterparts, British technicians analyzed the German 7.92 Kurz round and recognized its many qualities. They developed the .280 round as a prospective replacement for the long-standing British .303, a large cartridge that had been used all the way back to the slaughter at Omdurman. The British insights were smart but ill timed. Just as it grasped the direction that military rifle design was headed, Britain was not in a position to head there itself. A young but already stultifying bureaucracy inhibited its choices: NATO. Having experienced the maddeningly complicated logistics of World War II and the problems of multiple allies using multiple cartridges for weapons that performed the same tasks, Western powers wanted standardization. No one ally could select its own cartridge, because all the allies wanted to have the same round. A consensus was needed. A bureaucratic fight ensued, the result being that the Pentagon could not be convinced to switch to a significantly smaller round. NATO had no choice but to follow the United States' lead. In 1953, the 7.62x51-millimeter round— a traditional cartridge closely resembling the cartridge that American weapons had used for decades—became NATO's pick. Like the .276 Pederson twenty years before, the British .280 was dropped. The choice presented familiar problems. The United States Army went to work nonetheless on a heavy automatic rifle to fire its selection. It produced the M-14, which would become, for a few years, the standard battle rifle for GIs. To handle the heat and energy of the heavy cartridge, the M-14 had to be big. And it was big in every sense: Its version that could fire automatically weighed more than twelve pounds and stretched almost four feet long. Certainly it was powerful. Lethality tests would show that it produced an awesomely destructive effect on human skulls and legs.[104] But with this power came costs—not just the weight and length penalty, but punishing recoil and determined muzzle rise. Only the strongest soldiers could expect to control it on automatic, and then only briefly.

The decision had been made that bound the United States to an unwieldy automatic rifle for the next war, and bound NATO members to big rifles, too. The alternative choices made by the Soviet army were disregarded or ignored. Five years after the AK-47 became the Soviet standard infantry arm, American military manuals were silent on the weapons' existence, even though it was a weapon American soldiers would inevitably face. The Ordnance Corps' 1954 manual, *Soviet Rifles and Carbines, Identification and Operation,* made no mention of the rifle whatsoever, while noting that "the information presented herein is based upon the latest and best material available."[105] The declaration verged on the inexplicable, considering that the Soviet Union had publicly acknowledged the AK-47's existence in 1949. By the summer of 1955, the U.S. Ordnance Technical Intelligence Service, working from the Aberdeen Proving Ground, a testing center in Maryland similar to the Soviet center in

Schurovo, began to catch up. It completed translation of the 121-page Soviet technical manual for the AK-47. The manual, published in Moscow in 1952 and stamped SEKRETNO, Russian for secret, had recently come into American possession.[106] The United States acquired at least one new Soviet assault rifle shortly thereafter.[107] In June 1956, the U.S. Army's Technical Intelligence Office issued a classified report detailing the results of exploitation tests of an AK-47, which it labeled, incorrectly, a submachine gun. The army followed up seven months later with another classified report on what it called the SMG (submachine gun) Kalashnikov. The Americans were swift in one respect. They had obtained an AK-47 ahead of the Dutch, the Finns, and the Yugoslavs, and less than a year behind the Chinese. Those responsible for intelligence collection had done well. The analysts and ordnance officers were another story. The American army spent much of the next decade dismissing the AK-47 as a weapon of limited value—a submachine gun that was fine for bungling socialist conscripts, but beneath the far-shooting American infantry. The term *submachine gun,* repeated in military reports and official correspondence for years, was pejorative, as if the AK-47 did not deserve to be discussed in the same conversation with hard-hitting American battle rifles. Snickering was an accepted norm.

Then the army's ordnance branch was shown up. On its September 1956 cover, *GUNS* magazine leaped ahead of official sources with a profile of the M1943 round. The article included a drawing of an AK-47, though the caption mislabeled it as the "Avtomat 54" and the "PPK-1954." Notwithstanding these small errors, the writer, William B. Edwards, a well-known firearms correspondent of his time, understood his facts. He declared the intermediate cartridge "a bold step toward uniform ordnance supply." He recognized the weapon's lineage and noted its resemblance to the *sturmgewehr.* And he had a scoop within his scoop— he had fired the *avtomat.* Little was yet known in civilian circles about this weapon, but Edwards had managed to wrap his hands around one, and a selection of M1943 cartridges, too.[108] He proved a good judge of the AK-47's merits. He liked how the weapon felt and predicted its eventual trajectory, calling it "a remarkable weapon for general issue."[109] Edwards also noted that it was much easier to handle than the automatic rifles that NATO was wrestling with to fire the Pentagon's larger round.

Firing full-auto, the gun handled very well. The straight stock and light charge produced little kick. The former Russian accent on muzzle brakes seems to have been corrected by using the new cartridge and while the gun jumped around, counter-recoil of the bolt and gas piston parts partly resisted the cumulative kick of full-auto weapons. The contrast between the Russian full-auto carbine and the FN* experimental rifle also tested by the U.S. for possible N.A.T.O. adoption was marked. . . . The light-cartridge machine carbines like the Avtomat 54 are more easily controlled.[110]

No matter. In 1956 it was already too late. Insularity reigned. The Pentagon and its ordnance officers had arrived at their decisions, and the United States military and NATO would proceed with bulky firearms based on old ideas. The American army continued to see itself as an outfit that ruled the battlefield with big rifles—big, powerful, flat-shooting rifles—with the knockdown power to flatten enemy soldiers beyond the limits at which enemy soldiers could be seen by the naked eye. It all made perfect sense, at least to anyone impervious to the evolving arts and sciences of tactics and rifle and cartridge design.

Infantrymen tend to know things that senior officers do not, and a clearer view of what soldiers wanted, once they saw their choices, emerged when Western units encountered the AK-47 in the field. By the early 1960s, had the American officers responsible for arming the troops been watching closely as war evolved, they might have noticed the reaction of Dutch soldiers on colonial duty in Asia. In 1961, in preparation for the escalating dispute between Indonesia and the Netherlands over the Dutch holdings in Western New Guinea, Abdul Haris Nasution, Indonesia's defense minister, traveled to Moscow and purchased AK-47s for the army's parachute commandos. Later that year, Indonesia invaded Western New Guinea, beginning a brief jungle war. On April 26, 1962, an Indonesian Special Forces team jumped into Dutch-administered territory, carrying the new rifles. In late July or early August, while in a patrol base near Kampung Wermera, the Indonesian team was discovered by B Company of the Forty-first Infantry, a Dutch unit led by First Lieutenant A. W. van der Steur. Caught off guard, the Indonesian commandos withdrew with

---

* Fabrique-Nationale de Herstal, a Belgian firearms manufacturer.

such haste that some of them left their assault rifles behind. Lieutenant van der Steur's soldiers took them, becoming perhaps the first Western forces to confiscate Kalashnikov rifles on the battlefield. The Dutch soldiers liked their captured arms. Until that day, B Company carried a mix of American M1 carbines, British Sten submachine guns, and Bren light machine guns, along with 9-millimeter pistols. They immediately recognized the Kalashnikov for what it was—a well-adapted hybrid, a weapon that blended the qualities of the weapons they already had and fulfilled many roles very well. They carried their AK-47s for the remainder of the campaign, during which they noticed something else: Even in the jungle, the weapon resisted rust.[111]

These observations were all to be resonant very soon. The United States was returning to Asia for another war. Backed by the world's premier economy and fortified by the belief that its sense of innovation was unrivaled throughout the world, the Pentagon had allowed the Soviet Union better than a fifteen-year head start on designing and organizing the production of a nation's most basic fighting tool. The Pentagon faced a gun gap. Its unlucky soldiers and Marines would soon pay for it in blood.

III

AFTERMATH

THE CONSEQUENCES OF THE AK-47'S GLOBAL SPREAD

CHAPTER 7

The Accidental Rifle

So carry your rifle (they don't give a damn),
just pray you won't need it
while you're in Vietnam.

—From the poem "Rifle, 5.56MM,XM16E1," by First Lieutenant
Larry Rottmann, U.S. Army, a public affairs officer in Vietnam in
1967 and 1968 who said the army forbade all discussion about
malfunctioning American M-16s

THE MARINES OF HOTEL COMPANY'S FIRST PLATOON SPREAD OUT
as they walked through the shin-high grass. They were gripped by unease.
In front of them was their next destination: the village of Ap Sieu Quan,
a narrow cluster of buildings surrounded by paddies and dikes just south
of the demilitarized zone in the Quang Tri province of Vietnam. From out
in the field, the village looked deserted in the rising late-morning heat.
The Marines sensed menace awaiting. At least three North Vietnamese
Army battalions had infiltrated the area, an agricultural belt in the coastal
lowlands where the jungles and mountains drained into the South China
Sea. Many of the NVA units were patrolling. Others were dug in and
concealed. Hotel Company's Second Platoon had been hit by a North
Vietnamese unit in Ap Sieu Quan a short while before. Now the company
was converging. The Marines were exposed as they moved. They saw the
low-slung buildings ahead. The only approach passed over open ground.
We're walking across the savannah, Private First Class Alfred J. Nickelson

thought, cradling his M-16 rifle and scanning as he kept pace. *They can see us for miles.*[1]

Hotel Company was one of the bloodied outfits in Second Battalion, Third Marine Regiment, which in 1967 served as a mobile reaction force for much of Vietnam. It was July 21. Early the previous morning, several CH-46 helicopters had landed a few miles to the northwest, left the company behind, and roared back into the air and banked toward the USS *Tripoli,* their ship, off the coast. The insertion had marked the opening of Operation Bear Chain, a mission to interdict their enemies' food and ammunition caches along the road running from the Communist-controlled north toward Hue City, Da Nang, and Saigon. The navy and Marine Corps had given the battalion a label: Special Landing Force Bravo. In theory, the battalion resided on amphibious ships as a theater reserve. In practice, its units were constantly ashore, shuttled from fight to fight.[2] Upon departing the ships, the Marines would remain in the bush for several days to several weeks, then return for a rest and refit, and quickly be sent to the next fight. This had been the rhythm for months. Mission by mission, firefight by firefight, booby trap by booby trap, mortar blast by mortar blast, the rhythm had exacted its toll. The battalion's ranks had been thinned. The survivors were tired. Even after absorbing the replacements that showed up between operations, the platoons fought at one-half to two-thirds strength, including men who had been wounded but were judged fit enough to send back out.

For the United States military, which had defeated the Japanese army in the early 1940s and repelled communist divisions from South Korea a decade later, the enemy in Vietnam presented a confounding foe. The Viet Cong guerrillas and North Vietnamese regulars were marginally educated, lightly equipped, minimally trained. More than half of the NVA soldiers in late 1966 had six years or less of education, and three-quarters of them had less than eighteen months in their army.[3] They were peasants, agrarian villagers indoctrinated in Marxist-Leninist ideology and fighting according to tactics articulated by Mao. Some of their deficiencies were striking. American intelligence officials marveled that few of them had undergone significant training with live ammunition before being sent on missions against South Vietnamese and American forces. Many captured enemy fighters said they fired their weapons for the first time only in combat.[4] And yet by summer 1967, as Hotel Company rushed toward Ap

Sieu Quan, the Viet Cong and the North Vietnamese Army were killing nearly eight hundred American servicemen each month.

One reason for their success was their weapons. Nikita S. Khrushchev was gone from the Kremlin, forced into retirement in a bloodless coup in 1964. But his practice of using arms transfers as a foreign-policy lever continued, and the People's Republic of China had followed the Soviet example with haste. By late 1964 China had distributed huge quantities of its Kalashnikov assault rifles* in Southeast Asia. A large fraction of the Viet Cong and North Vietnamese Army combatants now carried a new assault rifle. In some units the saturation rate was as high as 75 percent, and many soldiers had been given a basic load of 390 cartridges to go with their new gun.[5] The majority of the combat fatalities among the United States forces were caused by small-arms fire.[†] As the staccato din of the Kalashnikov was heard in battle each day, and American casualties mounted, the Eastern bloc assault rifle at last captured the Pentagon's attention. Carried by proxies, the main rifle of an army whose nation lacked the technical sophistication to have its own modern gun works, it had become a marker of the Kremlin's influence on how war was experienced by combatants of limited means. No young army or guerrilla force had ever gone to war with more rifle firepower, with more ability to fight a technically and materially superior foe in a straight-on infantry encounter. The Viet Cong and North Vietnamese Army were beneficiaries of a new form of martial leveling. Indigenous forces had long faced outsiders backed by industrial economies and the guns they produced. The firepower disadvantages had been extreme. Armed with rapid-fire arms and ammunition stores the local men could not hope to match, conventional soldiers had maintained influence over distant lands with small expeditionary detachments. The AK-47 provided a complication: The locals could now fight like never before. The class of fighter that had stepped

---

*The Type 56 assault rifle, the clone of the AK-47 made in Mao's China since the Soviet army passed the technical specifications to the People's Liberation Army in the mid-1950s.

†The available data, compiled in the database of the Wound Data and Munitions Effectiveness Team, or WDMET, showed that 51 percent of American combat fatalities in Vietnam during the period under study were caused by small arms, 36 percent by fragmentation munitions, and 11 percent by mines and booby traps. From Ronald F. Bellamy and Russ Zajtchuk, *Textbook of Military Medicine. Part I. Warfare, Weaponry and the Casualty. Conventional Warfare: Ballistic, Blast and Burn Injuries,* Chapter 2, Assessing the Effectiveness of Conventional Weapons (Washington, D.C.: Office of the Surgeon General, 1989), p. 65.

from the rubble in Budapest in ones and twos—the Kalashnikov-carrying guerrilla, a common man with portable and easy-to-use automatic arms—was now in the field by the tens of thousands.

On this day, before Second Platoon had moved ahead to sweep Ap Sieu Quan, Hotel Company had been told that the village had been cleared by an American unit the previous night. Until the platoon was ambushed near a church within the little village's confines, the Marines were not expecting a fight. The North Vietnamese soldiers were dug in. The platoon could neither budge them nor get itself out. The company commander, Captain Richard O. Culver, Jr., directed Staff Sergeant Claude E. Elrod, First Platoon's commander, to push off the NVA and retrieve the American casualties, weapons, and radios. The other platoons moved to close off the village.

As the distance shrank, Staff Sergeant Elrod moved near the front of his platoon, between his radio operator and a three-man M-60 machine-gun team. Sweat rolled down his light frame. Ordinarily a lieutenant would lead a rifle platoon, but the battalion was short of officers. Too many officers had been shot. The staff sergeant had joined the special landing force just after the battalion had participated in the fight for Hills 861 and 881, one of the bitterest battles in the war. Upon checking into Hotel Company, he learned that the executive officer, First Lieutenant David S. Hackett, a Princeton graduate, had been shot through the head and killed. The Second Platoon commander, Second Lieutenant Bruce E. Griesmer, had been wounded. A new officer, First Lieutenant Michael P. Chervenak, had arrived to take Lieutenant Hackett's place. Officers were otherwise in short supply. Staff Sergeant Elrod was told he would lead First Platoon. That was two months ago. Already he had been wounded. He had been hit with shrapnel and a rifle bullet a few weeks before. The bullet had passed through his side without striking a vital organ or severing a major blood vessel. The shrapnel injuries had been light. Luck had kept him alive. The corpsmen on the USS *Tripoli* had removed his stitches the day before. Now he was in-country again, leading his platoon, heading toward another village on another operation in the kaleidoscope of action that defined the battalion's tour of some of the worst of Vietnam.

Staff Sergeant Elrod was crossing the last dike before the village when a bullet smacked a bamboo branch near his head. He heard Kalashnikov rifles firing as he dropped. Down the Marines of First Platoon went, shouting, returning fire, dashing into motion in the pandemonium of initial contact. The staff sergeant ordered the machine-gun crew to set up and cover the squads in the field. He had already arranged for a three-man fire team to provide security around the gun, and he watched those men run into place as the M-60 opened fire. *Good,* he thought. The Marines were doing what they do. He shouted to his radio operator and told him to tell Captain Culver that the platoon was engaged.

There are moments in modern firefights when combat can become, in an instant, a lonely and isolating experience. Since late in World War I, after automatic weapons, artillery, and mortars had become prevalent in battle and tactics evolved to account for them, foot soldiers had learned to spread out, scattering the targets they presented and limiting the danger to the group of any one machine-gun burst or exploding shell. This dispersion reduced risks to units. In certain circumstances, it also served to increase the individual's sense of disassociation. At these instants of scattering, each combatant's surroundings could suddenly change. One moment the soldier was part of a group. The next, in the confusion of sudden battle as each man took steps to survive and fight back, he could find himself alone. A man's world compressed to a small, frantic, and companionless space, punctuated by the disorienting roars and blasts of incoming and outgoing fire.

Private First Class Nickelson had entered one of these inner zones. A bullet had passed so close by that it seemed to clap beside his ear. More bullets thumped the soil around him. He pressed himself down, hiding in the grass, trying to make himself small. He felt utterly apart. For a few seconds, he had the selfish thought of a trapped man in what might be his last moment alive. *All these guys out here in the field to shoot,* he thought. *Why are they trying to shoot only me?* Then he collected himself. He knew that each man's fate was tied to the platoon, and that the platoon survived only if it fought. He would fight. He lifted his head and saw a Vietnamese soldier in a tree line. He raised his M-16, lined up the rifle's sights, and eased back on the trigger. He had set his M-16 selector switch on automatic. One round blasted out. Then nothing. His M-16 had jammed. "Oh, fuck," he said.

At the village's edge, Staff Sergeant Elrod estimated that he had met a North Vietnamese platoon. NVA platoons were often small, but their weapons could make them potent. The Marines of the 1940s and 1950s had faced human-wave attacks in Asia. This was something else. Two dozen of this new breed of combatant could stop two hundred. First Platoon's Marines were scattered and flat to the ground. Bullets whipped around them. The staff sergeant needed firepower to match what was coming in. But something was wrong. The Marines assigned to protect the M-60 were not firing. They were crouched and madly working on their M-16s. He ran to one of them. The man's rifle was jammed. The staff sergeant looked at the others. Their weapons were jammed, too. The United States Marine Corps, built around its riflemen, was in battle with rifles that did not work. The platoon was exposed, under fire, and many of its members were busy working on guns gone silent. The machine-gun team nearby was under intensive fire. The gunner, a corporal, was struck in the head. The assistant gunner took his place. He was hit, too. Adrenaline pulsed through the staff sergeant. He was slicked with sweat, furious, confused. He wanted to kill. Why wouldn't his platoon's automatic rifles work? He slipped behind the machine gun and started to fire. First Platoon was stuck.

Of the many enduring effects of the international distribution of the Kalashnikov assault rifle, its influence on the American military was among the least understood and most profound. The AK-47's utility for guerrilla war, terror, and crime could have been readily foreseen. The bad choices it spurred in the United States military were not so predictable. Nor were their effects.

Throughout the 1950s, the United States had missed the significance of the spread of Soviet and Eastern bloc small arms. By the 1960s the institutional ignorance could no longer hold. Jolted alert by the communist assault rifle's large-scale arrival in Vietnam, the Pentagon realized that in the matter of rifles it was outmatched. The American army abruptly selected the M-16 for general service in the war. Had the early M-16 been a reliable automatic rifle, this might have been a straightforward and simple development, a story as old as war. One side gets a new weapon, the other side matches it in kind. In this way, the war in Vietnam became the first large conflict in which both sides carried assault rifles—initially in small numbers but eventually as the predominant firearm. But the American adoption of assault rifles flowed from reaction rather than from foresight or planning, and it was painful and bungled. The early M-16 and its ammunition formed a combination not ready for war. They were a flawed pair emerging from a flawed development history. Prone to malfunction, they were forced into troops' hands through a clash of wills and egos in Defense Secretary Robert S. McNamara's Pentagon. Instead of a thoughtful progression from prototype to general-issue arm, the M-16's journey was marked by salesmanship, sham science, cover-ups, chicanery, incompetence, and no small amount of dishonesty by a gun manufacturer and senior American military officers. Its introduction to war was briefly heralded as a triumph of private industry and perceptive management, but swiftly became a monument to the hazards of hubris and the perils of rushing, and a study in military management gone awry.

The origins of the problems emerge in especially sharp relief when viewed in contrast to the Soviet Union's much more successful rifle program. The AK-47 and AKM had resulted from methodical state-directed pursuits. The M-16 arrived in troops' hands by another route. The American system was neither capitalist nor fully state-driven. It was a disharmonious hybrid. Long-standing arms-development practices had failed; what replaced them was worse. The infantry rifles carried to war by generations of American servicemen had largely been conceived within the army's ordnance service, and then manufactured by private firms commissioned to mass-produce the patterns. The sprawling army ordnance community—known as the ordnance corps—was a network of arsenals, laboratories, and far-flung commands that together had evolved into an empire within the armed services, replete with its own biases and mores. Its powers were substantial, as was its reputation for insularity. Tended to by a mix of experts and bureaucrats, the ordnance corps exercised de facto veto power over arms designed by anyone else. If the community had been objective and fair-minded, this power might have been well used. But the corps' talents had over the decades been undermined by dogmatism. In the years after World War II, those responsible for American small-arms development had shown little interest in the foreign concept of assault rifles, and they had not understood the significance of German and Russian developments in the field. The parochialism was so firmly established that it had earned a label with its own acronym, which described the ordnance corps' attitude toward firearms created by outsiders. The acronym was NIH: *Not Invented Here.*

By the early 1960s, the army's ordnance officials had lost the arms race of their lives. As a result, just when the American armed services grasped that they needed a smaller automatic rifle, there was nothing suitable in the government design pipeline. Instead, the Pentagon reached into private industry for the AR-15, as the precursor to the M-16 was called. This seemed sensible. The mighty industrial economy of the United States had helped carry the country to victory in World War II, and now its universities and factories were producing an ever-varying stream of consumer goods. This economic and intellectual muscle, seemingly tireless and nimble, was a bewitching force. Its slogans were seductive. It had become an article of political faith in Washington that the American businessman was the world's most astute, and the American engineer the most innovative and sound. The evidence was all around. The United States churned out practical and coveted products like few other economies: televisions, phonographs, ovens, blenders, handbags, shoes, fishing reels, vacuum cleaners, and automobiles. If market forces could bring forth the Mustang and the Corvette, certainly they could produce a superior infantry rifle, too.

This might have been a valid conclusion, had American industry been involved in assault-rifle development in any robust sense. But when the Pentagon went seeking an assault rifle that could hold its own against the AK-47, it was working from a position far behind that of its enemies. It had spent twenty years misapprehending the shift in the evolution of automatic arms. Now it was in an inexorably escalating war with almost no choices from the private sector. McNamara's Pentagon was right on one point. The M-14 was not the best all-purpose rifle for what war had become, especially in a tropical delta or jungle. To compete against guerrillas armed with Kalashnikovs, the United States needed more firepower than the M-14 provided, and in a lighter rifle. It needed, in short, more lethality per pound, more ability to lay down suppressive fire, and more ammunition per combat load. It needed a rifle with which its soldiers would be mobile, quick, and deadly. The AR-15 offered all of these features, at least on paper. But none of this necessarily meant that the AR-15 was the best choice as a replacement. The AR-15 was, rather, the most well-known—and hyped—of the very few products available. It rose to the generals' attention through neither a meticulous development cycle nor an expansive market competition. It arrived by default. The supporters of the AR-15, and its salesmen, insisted that it was ready for war. It was not.

It had not yet proven its reliability in objective field tests.[6] Questions of its performance dogged it. As it was handed out, modified and renamed the M-16,* many troops were not trained on it or equipped with the necessary equipment to clean it. Its proponents in the Pentagon first believed the most optimistic forecasts about the M-16's suitability for battle. Then they dismissed reports of problems when its performance did not match the hype. Moreover, the M-16's ammunition was neither fully developed nor subject to strict technical standards. For all these reasons, the M-16 was not a ready equalizer. It was the accidental rifle, pushed into service by a confluence of historical forces that left the United States military in a rush and unwilling to explore a wider set of options or a more careful course. These were conditions for disaster, as the Marines of Second Battalion, Third Marines were finding out.

An account of the M-16's ascension from California curio to the American military's standard firearm could begin in many places, but the conditions that gave the process its velocity began with the inauguration of President John F. Kennedy in 1961. Kennedy brought with him Robert S. McNamara as secretary of defense. McNamara was a graduate of Harvard Business School, a former top executive at Ford, and a believer in an approach to decision-making called "systems analysis," which had been conceived in the 1950s at the Rand Corporation. Systems analysis centered on intensive study of problems and options, with examinations of costs, benefits, and risks of potential decisions. Its introduction to the Pentagon, along with a cadre of McNamara's disciples, who called themselves the whiz kids, was a frontal challenge to the military establishment. McNamara's followers saw themselves as a rarefied pool of talent, and they merged their boss's aggressive management style with a Kennedy mandate to look past contingencies for nuclear war and develop the doctrine, organization, and equipment for flexible responses to conflicts overseas. This meant limited war, which in the context of the Cold War further meant the ability to counter the Eastern bloc in proxy fights. Several of McNamara's officials turned their attention to the question of the rifle.

---

* The new name brought the rifle into line with the military's standard designations. M stood for model; thus the M1903 springfield, the M1 Garand, the M-14, etc.

The rifle conundrum was a significant one. America's military machine had entered the nuclear age with an array of fearsome killing tools. The air force had supersonic jets and intercontinental missiles. The army was fielding a new line of battle tanks to enhance its armored divisions that had settled into Western Europe. The navy had launched a nuclear aircraft carrier that steamed under the power of nuclear reactors sealed within its hull. Yet when it came to the most basic tool of empire and of war—the infantry rifle—the American military had sputtered and stalled. The government had spent more than a decade bringing forward the M-14, only to discover in simulations and in Vietnam that soldiers equipped with M-14s were outmaneuvered and outshot by opponents with AK-47s.

The early 1960s were an unsettled time in American small-arms development. A pair of discordant ideas guided the army's plans. On one hand was the M-14, a rifle firmly rooted in past designs. But the M-14—for that matter, any rifle—was both a nod to the army's sense of what a rifle was supposed to be and regarded as the last of its kind, the end of the line. The army was developing what it called the Special Purpose Individual Weapon, or SPIW. As conceived, SPIW was to be the automatic dart gun for the Cold War, James Bond supplants Rifleman Dodd. It would fire bursts of needlelike flechettes from one barrel and grenades out another. By the early 1960s the project had met delays, and a variety of engineering problems was giving it the feel of unattainable whimsy. Its lightweight darts seemed less than ideal for punching through helmets, windshields, and armor plates. They struggled even to resist deflection in vegetation or heavy rain. The optimists who supported SPIW said a fully functional version might be ready in the mid-1960s and would replace rifles altogether. In the interim, troops would have their new M-14s. In the matter of shoulder-fired arms, the United States Army in the early McNamara era was very strange indeed. It simultaneously upheld old ideas about rifles and hitched its future to a fantastic dream. Somehow it had missed the weapon that was both feasible and the direction in which small-arms evolution had actually headed: the assault rifle.

McNamara sensed at least this much. In October 1962, after his aides had examined the gun gap, he wrote a secret memorandum to Cyrus R. Vance, the secretary of the army. The memorandum was a marker of bureaucratic exasperation. "I have seen certain evidence," he wrote:

. . . which appears to indicate that: 1. With the M-14 rifle in 1962, we are equipping our forces with a weapon definitely inferior in fire-power and combat effectiveness to the assault rifle with which the Soviets have equipped their own and their satellite forces worldwide since 1950.

This was a painful declaration for the United States' most senior military official at the height of the Cold War—a frank admission that the Soviet Union had leaped ahead of the United States in an important way. McNamara left no room for the army to equivocate. He knew that the army had rejected the AR-15 in tests. He also knew that the M-14, an army darling, was vulnerable to criticism. It had been created according to old ideas, after long delays and at steep cost overruns. It was heavy and long. Its ammunition was burdensome. It was difficult to manage on automatic fire, enough so that most M-14s issued to troops were configured to fire one round at a time.* And tactically it felt obsolete. Tests at Fort Ord and at the Hunter Liggett Military Reservation in 1958 and 1959 had discovered that five to seven soldiers armed with AR-15s produced more firepower and were more dangerous than eleven soldiers provided with M-14s.[7] Small automatic rifles with little recoil and lighter ammunition allowed soldiers to move and shoot more quickly and accurately and over a longer period of time.

The defense secretary's disdain for the M-14 could hardly have been more bluntly expressed. As far as he could determine, he wrote, the AR-15 appeared "markedly superior to the M-14 in every respect of importance to military operations." McNamara's displeasure with the M-14 was well placed. But it led to narrow thinking—*the M-14 is not the best rifle, therefore the AR-15 is.* A more systematic view would have recognized that the AR-15 was not necessarily the best option. It was, by any reasonable assessment, only the beginning of an American effort to design an assault rifle. Rifle manufacturers in the United States had not yet invested heavily in developing small-caliber, lightweight assault rifles, judging correctly, at least in the short term, that there was no government

---

*A lock was installed on most M-14s to prevent them from being used on automatic fire. In every ten-man rifle squad in the army in the early 1960s, two men were given the M-14 capable of automatic fire, known as the M-14E2; this version was equipped with a bipod and other features that drove up its weight.

customer for them. The AR-15 was not the product of full competition within its class. It was almost the only rifle of its sort. The industrial base had not been tapped.

But McNamara's pan came with orders that pushed the Pentagon on its course. He asked the army to share with him its views on the "relative effectiveness" of three rifles: the AK-47, the AR-15, and the M-14. And if the M-14 was not the most effective of these three, he wanted to know what action the army recommended taking.[8] The instructions were implicit and strong. Prove that the M-14 was superior to the AK-47 and the AR-15, or plan to make changes.

For those trying to sell the AR-15, McNamara's Pentagon was the break they had gambled on. The new rifle had sprung from ArmaLite, a private concern in Southern California. In business terms, ArmaLite was an infant and an upstart, a company that began as a workshop in the Hollywood garage of George Sullivan, the patent counsel for Lockheed Aircraft Corporation. Sullivan was an aeronautical engineer fascinated with the possibilities of applying new materials to change the way rifles looked and felt,[9] and he had collaborated with an inventor and arms salesman, Jacques Michault, to develop plans for rifles that departed sharply from existing designs in the West. In 1953, Sullivan met Paul S. Cleaveland, secretary of the Fairchild Engine & Airplane Corporation, at an aviation industry luncheon.[10] The pair talked about lightweight firearms and new techniques that might be applied to manufacturing them. Cleaveland mentioned the conversation to Richard S. Boutelle, Fairchild's president, who was an aviation-minded gun buff, too. Boutelle and Sullivan soon agreed to collaborate under Fairchild's sponsorship, and the company was founded in 1954 as a small Fairchild division. From the beginning, ArmaLite had energy, optimism, and curious possibilities for sales. Boutelle was a glad-handing dreamer hooked up to the jet age. A former major in the Army Air Corps and a passionate big-game hunter, he carried himself as an engineering visionary and salesman, and brimmed with ideas for bold modern products that might make Fairchild a global powerhouse. Boutelle spoke of his intention to manufacture "a lightweight train, a gasoline-filled aerial tanker, even a mechanically operated wild-turkey call." His core business was in aircraft. He hoped a Fairchild turboprop passenger plane—the F-27 Friendship—would unseat the DC-3 as the dominant civilian air frame of the time.[11]

Not long after forming, the company hired a former Marine with a background in aviation ordnance, Eugene Stoner, as its senior design engineer. ArmaLite's tastes reflected those of its parent company. Stoner worked not with traditional steels and wooden stocks, but with aircraft-grade aluminum, new alloys, and plastics—materials that made firearm traditionalists cringe. Fortunately for ArmaLite, the Fairchild executives had a sales approach as novel as their weapons. Boutelle's long-standing friendship with General Curtis LeMay of the air force gave ArmaLite unusual access to an alternative market inside the Pentagon. By 1956, the air force had taken an interest in the AR-5, a collapsible rifle that ArmaLite proposed for inclusion in survival kits for air crews. The rifle weighed two and a half pounds and could be disassembled and stored inside its own plastic stock. According to ArmaLite, it even floated. The AR-5 never entered mass production. But it made ArmaLite, a firm that emerged from almost nothing at all, a contender for contracts in a business in which new firms usually met closed doors.

Stoner kept working. By 1956, ArmaLite was showing the AR-10—an automatic rifle that fired the standard NATO cartridge but ditched traditional lines and dress. If the AK-47 was stolid and proletarian, the AR-10 had the sleek look of 1950s modernity itself. Its receiver was forged aluminum alloy. Its stock and hand guards were molded plastics. It had a large handle at the base of its barrel that let it be carried like a briefcase. And it weighed less than automatic rifles under the U.S. Army's review. Like the AK-47, the AR-10 could be fired on automatic or on single-shot semiautomatic fire. Its self-loading features were made possible by putting to work the same excess energy harnessed in the Kalashnikov: It diverted gas from burning propellant through a port in the barrel and back toward the shooter, where its energy was used to keep the rifle moving through its firing cycle. But rather than drive a piston, the expanding gases were routed through a narrow metal tube that blasted gas directly against the housing that held the bolt. This energy was sufficient to drive the bolt carrier and bolt backward and clear the chamber of the freshly emptied cartridge case. A return spring slowed the rearward motion of the bolt, then reversed it and forced the entire assembly forward again.

A prototype AR-10 failed spectacularly when its barrel burst in army tests. The timing of ArmaLite's offering was serendipitous nonetheless. An advanced prototype of the M-14, known as the T44, was on an inside track to become the military's new standard rifle. But within the bureaucracy, an insurgency was afoot. Several senior officers believed that an automatic rifle based on a smaller-caliber cartridge brought more benefits than those offered by the T44. They were examining the possibility of taking the German and Soviet intermediate cartridges a step further, with an even smaller and lighter round that could be propelled at velocities previously unrealized in any standard arm. The concept was known as small-caliber, high-velocity, or SCHV. One of the idea's supporters, General Willard G. Wyman of the Continental Army Command, observed an AR-10 demonstration. ArmaLite, if nothing else, had an innovator's spirit. Wyman arranged a meeting with Stoner, at which he asked him to design a version of his AR-10 to handle a .22-caliber round. Stoner and ArmaLite agreed. This informal compact marked a turning point in American rifle design.

ArmaLite faced a significant technical hurdle. It was one thing to make a smaller rifle, and another to make a smaller rifle that would be accurate and deadly at great range. The United States Infantry Board, an organization responsible for testing new tactics and equipment, had initially accepted the notion that the rifle should be accurate out to three hundred yards. But the army set a more demanding standard: The miniaturized AR-10 was to be able to strike and penetrate a steel helmet at five hundred yards.[12] This was an arbitrary requirement, more suited to presentations in conference rooms than related to the conditions of most warfighting. But ArmaLite had no choice. Stoner redesigned a .222 Remington round, a commercially available cartridge well suited for long-range varmint shooting. For a rifle round that would be fired at men, the .222 Remington was, in a word, tiny—at least by existing military standards in either the East or the West. It was 2.13 inches long and fired a bullet that weighed only fifty-five grains,[13] roughly one-tenth of an ounce, which was less than half the mass of the Soviet bullet. Stoner altered the cartridge so it was slightly longer and could be filled with more powder. The result was a new round: the .223 (and later, the 5.56-millimeter round), the lightweight but high-powered ammunition for ArmaLite's new project. The company dubbed its new weapon the AR-15.

The AR-15 looked like nothing else in military service anywhere. It had all of the nontraditional features of its bigger brother, the AR-10, including an aluminum receiver, hard plastic furniture, and the odd-looking carrying handle. But it was thirty-nine inches long. It weighed, when unloaded, only 6.35 pounds. Its appearance—small, dark, lean, and synthetically futuristic—stirred emotions. A rifle, after all, was supposed to look like a rifle. To its champions, the AR-15 was an embodiment of fresh thinking. Critics saw an ugly little toy. Wherever one stood, no one could deny the ballistics were intriguing. The .223's larger load of propellant and the AR-15's twenty-inch barrel worked together to move the tiny bullet along at ultrafast speeds—in excess of thirty-two hundred feet per second, almost three times the speed of sound. The initial AR-15 and its ammunition were in place. The first steps in an American shift in rifles for killing men had been made.

Now came the matter of selling it. But to whom? Outside of ordnance circles, several officers saw promise in the SCHV concept.[14] But as a rifle that emerged from the private sector, and had such unusual characteristics, the AR-15 met predictable resistance in the army's ordnance corps. The M-14 had been approved as the new standard rifle in 1957. The AR-15 arrived just as the army thought the conversation about rifles had closed. The idea of reconsidering the years of effort and enormous spending behind the M-14, and challenging the prevailing thinking with a high-concept minirifle, amounted to small-arms heresy. The entrenched interests offered ArmaLite little hope. The Fairchild Engine & Airplane Corporation, meanwhile, risked foundering. Its aircraft-marketing plans had not worked out. Nor had Boutelle's other schemes. The company was starved for cash. On January 7, 1959, Fairchild transferred manufacturing rights for the AR-15 to Colt's Firearms Division for $325,000 and a royalty-sharing guarantee with Stoner and Cooper-MacDonald, Inc., the independent arms-dealing firm that arranged the deal.[15] From that point forward, the weapons were to be made in Hartford, Connecticut, by the descendant of the firm that had manufactured Gatling guns, and put the world on the path toward automatic arms.

With Colt's, the sales push entered a new phase. Robert W. MacDonald, a principal at Cooper-MacDonald, was a graying curmudgeon given to hard-nosed deals. He had made a name for himself selling explosives in Asia.[16] His firm had collected a neat $250,000 finder's fee from the

$325,000 ArmaLite-Colt's licensing deal. But he stood to make more money—a lot more money—if Colt's found customers for the AR-15.* First he faced an arms-trade policy hurdle. He could not sell the rifle to America's potential enemies. And under mutual-aid provisions, he could sell it to Washington's allies only if it was compatible with American arms. For the AR-15 to have international sales potential the rifle first had to be introduced, somehow, to American military use. MacDonald put his ample imagination to use, even as Colt's pursued its own plans.

In summer 1960, Colt's took the AR-15 on the road, including to police departments around the United States, where their sales team fired into a variety of objects (automobiles were a favorite) and engaged in almost giddy declarations of their rifle's powers. "The penetrating effects of the .223 round are devastating from a practical standpoint," one company summary read. "We are in a position to state that there is not a commercially manufactured automobile in this country that can withstand the penetrating effects of this weapon and cartridge." The summary described the effects of roughly three hundred rounds fired into a 1951 Pontiac Catalina, which was shot in a demonstration for the Indiana State Police. The range was seventy-five yards.

The .223 cartridge will penetrate:

1. Bumper steel.
2. Frame steel.
3. Motor block (only enters, does not exit).
4. Both sides of car (broadside shot).
5. Trunk lid, back seat, front seat, dashboard, firewall and in some cases on into the radiator when fired from rear to front.
6. Wheel drums, coil springs and shock absorbers.
7. All glass (laminated shatterproof or tempered glass).

---

*Under the license sale arrangement, MacDonald would receive a cut of both Fairchild's and Colt's future receipts. This included a 1 percent commission from Colt's for the selling price of every rifle sold, and 10 percent of Fairchild royalties, some of which were calculated on a sliding scale. For sales to military customers, the combined formula guaranteed him 1.225 percent. These were considerable incentives for MacDonald to try to have the AR-15 adopted by the American military. (For a detailed review of the license deal, see "How a Lone Inventor's Idea Took Fire," *Business Week*, July 6, 1968.)

A few weeks later, Colt's added a suggestive demonstration at a sales pitch to the police of Glastonbury, Connecticut. Its salesman put two large cans of water on the front seat of a 1955 Pontiac Tudor, paced off sixty yards, and opened up. The water cans were surrogates for a driver and passenger. Colt's let everyone know just how poorly those would-be criminals in a getaway car had fared, and how well the bullets fired by the AR-15 had performed: "The bullet will still penetrate both sides of vehicle after passing through two 5 gallon cans of water placed in front seat of the automobile to simulate a body in the car. Both cans were ruptured and torn apart at the seams upon impact." A single bullet fired by an AR-15, by the implicit wink in this kind of statement, was capable of a bad-guy-stopping twofer—it could pass through a door, then one man, and then another man and then out another door. Bonnie and Clyde would have no chance. The summary's conclusions almost gasped. The AR-15, it read, "can be fired full automatic off the finger tips" and "can be fired off the stomach or chin or with one hand holding only the pistol stock. The recoil is so negligible as to be insignificant." It added, "There is not a piece of metal or steel on a commercially manufactured automobile that cannot be penetrated by the .223 cartridge," which will also "penetrate most commercially used building materials."[17]

Such sales copy was straight from the days of the Auto-Ordnance Corporation and the Thompson gun, though it was targeted against law enforcement officers and not yet the general public. As this cocksure sense of the AR-15's formidability was being assembled, the most successful demonstration of all was held. In mid-1960, while automobiles were being pierced, punctured, and shredded by Colt's sales team, MacDonald arranged for General LeMay, then the air force's vice chief of staff, to be invited to Boutelle's sixtieth birthday party at Boutelle's gentleman's farm in Maryland. Much of the farm had been converted into recreational shooting ranges. General LeMay, like Boutelle, was a gun buff. The invitation was crafted to appeal. A sample AR-15, the new miracle gun, would be on hand for the general to fire. The party was held over the Fourth of July. The hosts set up three watermelons at ranges of 50 and 150 yards and invited the general to try his hand at shooting them. What followed was one of the odder moments in American arms-procurement history. Watermelons were bright and fleshy in ways that water cans were not, and when struck by the little rifle's ultrafast bullets, the first two fruits exploded in vivid red splashes. General LeMay was so impressed that he spared the third melon; the party decided to eat it. No doubt this was great fun for the arms salesmen. It was also nonsense. But salesmanship was salesmanship. MacDonald understood that the air force had its own small-arms needs and wanted its own automatic rifle for defending air bases and strategic-missile sites. He also knew that General LeMay was unimpressed with the M-14. Colt's, for the price of three watermelons and Independence Day cocktails, had a high-level convert.

MacDonald had cultivated the right man. The air force began putting the rifle to tests. In 1961, General LeMay became air force chief of staff. In May 1962, the air force entered a contract with Colt's to buy eighty-five hundred rifles. This was a small order. But just like that, the AR-15 formally entered the American military arms system, via a side door. Colt's automatic rifle was now a viable product for foreign and domestic sales.

McNamara did not share with Vance what had convinced him of the M-14's definite inferiority to the AK-47 and AR-15. But the evidence circulating in the Pentagon in late 1962 was both theoretical and empirical. The theoretical side was strong. Charles J. Hitch, a former Rhodes scholar serving as comptroller for the Department of Defense, had recently completed an analysis of the American military's rifle programs. In it, Hitch endorsed the idea of the lighter-weight automatic rifle with smaller ammunition. The study marked a provocative tweak of the old guard. It suggested that systems analysts might, after all, be able to see things the traditional military could not. With it, the Pentagon had at last formally seconded ideas accepted by the Wehrmacht and the Red Army during World War II. The United States military was catching up. The empirical side was weaker. Hitch was more than attuned to the assault-rifle concept. He was smitten by a product: the AR-15. Classified reports from Vietnam, where hundreds of these new rifles had undergone combat trials, were giving the AR-15 high marks and providing a surprise. Reports from the field claimed that when a bullet fired from the AR-15 struck a man, it inflicted devastating injuries.

The causes were apparently twofold. First, the metal jacket of early AR-15 bullets tended to shatter on impact, sending fragmentation slicing through victims.[18] (In the army, this was variously seen as attractive and worrisome. In classified correspondence, some officers were thrilled by the perceived wounding characteristics, which one prominent army doctor described as "explosive effects." Others wondered whether the .223 round might be illegal under international convention.)[19] Second, the bullets often turned sideways inside a victim, a phenomenon known as yaw. In one respect, the effects of yaw somewhat resembled what could be seen on the surface of a lake when a speedboat turned sharply. In this case, the energy delivery manifested itself as a shock wave within a human body, which could create stretching or rupturing injury to tissue not directly in a bullet's path. By turning, the bullet also crushed and cut more tissue as it passed through a victim, creating a larger wound channel.

The supposed effects of these phenomena on men were described in the first known battlefield trials of AR-15s, which had been coaxed to life in Asia via another of MacDonald's sales masterstrokes. In 1961, Mac-Donald had made contact with the army's Advanced Research Projects Agency, which had offices in Saigon and Bangkok. Among the officers eager to work with the new rifle was Lieutenant Colonel Richard R. Hallock, a paratrooper from World War II who was proud to be associated with the whiz-kid culture and was attracted to rifle development, though he had limited experience with ballistics, procurement, testing, or weapon design. He was, however, an able writer of memorandums. His office proposed a study. In December 1961, McNamara approved the purchase of one thousand AR-15s for American military advisers to distribute to Vietnamese government soldiers. The approval worked on two levels. It gave an outlet for McNamara's interest in the new rifle and aligned with President Kennedy's decision a month before to increase military aid flowing from Washington to South Vietnam. The United States was envisioning warfare with new roles for Special Forces and helicopter-borne battalions. Vietnam was becoming a showcase for this thinking. The futuristic AR-15 seemed a tantalizing fit. Enthusiasm for the rifle was running high enough that as the test was approved, President Kennedy's military aide presented him with a sample AR-15 to look over in the Oval Office, and Kennedy was photographed playfully handling this peculiar little rifle, which was secretly being shipped to Vietnam.

Lieutenant Colonel Hallock and the agency dubbed their test Project AGILE—"a comprehensive field evaluation" of the AR-15 under combat conditions. The name in itself might have been a warning that this was not to be real science. Throughout much of 1962, Vietnamese units carried the new American assault rifles into combat. Excited vignettes trickled back. In May, Colonel Cao Van Vien, commander of the Vietnamese Airborne Brigade, reported that his soldiers had shot two Viet Cong guerrillas with their experimental weapons. One guerrilla had been hit in the wrist. The bullet severed the man's hand, which remained behind when he escaped. This was not necessarily revelatory. The typical Vietnamese fighter weighed about ninety pounds. Any number of military cartridges might shatter the lower forearm of a ninety-pound man upon smacking the radius and ulna squarely. And a data sample of one injury was not grounds for extrapolation. But context was absent from the report, which emphasized gruesome wounds with descriptive glee. "An AR-15 bullet pierced the head of a VC from the nape of his neck to his forehead," the report said of the injury to the second guerrilla. "The hole in the nape of the neck was about bullet size. However, it came out his face and took off almost half of it. The face was unidentifiable. Firing range: from 50 to 70 meters."[20] This injury was easier to grasp, if only because it was familiar. Autopsy reports and medical literature had long shown that human heads shatter when penetrated by military rifle bullets. The description, in other words, should have been unremarkable. But the macabre cheerleading leaking from the field evaluation was a mere hint of what lay ahead.

The secret report of Project AGILE, submitted in August 1962, was short on dispassionate observation but long on product boosterism. Like the Vietnamese colonel, Lieutenant Colonel Hallock and his team gushed with satisfaction. "On 13 April, 62, a Special Forces team made a raid on a small village," their report noted. "In the raid, seven VC were killed. Two were killed by AR-15 fire. Range was 50 meters. One man was hit in the head; it looked like it exploded. A second man was hit in the chest; his back was one big hole." A Ranger unit detailed similar effects on five guerrillas ambushed on June 9. Ranges were thirty to one hundred yards. The inventory was chilling:

> Back wound, which caused thoracic cavity to explode. 2. Stomach wound, which caused the abdominal cavity to explode. 3. Buttock wound, which destroyed all of the tissue of both buttocks. 4. Chest wound from right to left, destroyed the thoracic cavity.

5. Heel wound, the projectile entered the bottom of the right foot causing the leg to split from the foot to the hip.

The report claimed that in another firefight a Vietnamese Ranger fired a three-round burst into a guerrilla fifteen meters away and both decapitated the man and severed his right arm. In order to accept these descriptions at face value, one would have to believe that in a small sampling of injuries the AR-15 had caused two traumatic amputations—a type of injury rarely observed from rifle bullets. But such coolheaded skepticism did not work its way into the report. A sales pitch was gathering momentum: The AR-15 was the most lethal rifle the world had known. The Project AGILE report did not stop there. It listed advantages beyond the AR-15's capacity for producing theatrically grotesque wounds. The new rifle was small, light, and easy to handle. The authors claimed it required very little maintenance. Its reliability was unsurpassed. They recorded only one shortcoming: A plastic handgrip along one rifle's barrel had cracked. This they explained away with laconic bemusement, observing that the break occurred while moving a stubborn prisoner, and "the soldier concerned had placed the handguard against a VC head with considerable force." MacDonald's Saigon pitch proved to be another salesmanship triumph. The report, from its title to its conclusions, could not have read better for Colt's had MacDonald dictated it himself. Its claims exceeded even the contents of AR-15 sales brochures.[21]

Cyrus Vance had little to do but follow his boss's orders. He passed McNamara's instructions to General Earle Wheeler, the Army's chief of staff, who ordered tests to determine the "relative effectiveness" of the AK-47, the AR-15, and the M-14. Here began the next strange chapter in the M-16's march out of obscurity. Evaluators have many ways to measure a rifle's utility for war. There are tests for accuracy, reliability, and durability. There are means to assess ergonomics. How the rifle performs tactically— the number of shots, hits, and near misses fired by soldiers as they attack and defend in controlled simulations—can form another set of useful measures. At General Wheeler's instruction, evaluators at American commands around the world were put to work to rank the three rifles along these lines. This was a sensible idea. It was also a flawed plan. General

Wheeler wanted answers by November 30—a deadline almost certainly too tight for findings that would be meaningful, much less conclusive. But President Kennedy and Secretary McNamara wanted answers. The Pentagon was galloping headlong. The army's internal correspondence was frantic. "Initiation of testing will not await submittal or approval of final detailed plans," one of the instructions read. "Representation at tests will be kept to a minimum. . . . Tests should not be influenced or delayed by the requirements for observers."[22]

To see how this kind of haste could lead to poor judgment and shoddy science, one need look no further than the army's attempt to measure the three weapons' lethality. The tests sought to answer a seemingly simple question. What happened when a bullet fired from each rifle actually hit a human being? Implicit in the work was the related question: Which weapon would most surely cause incapacitation, the state in which a wounded enemy combatant would no longer be able to fight? Answering such questions was the realm of a sometimes-scientific field known, in what could seem a double entendre, as "terminal ballistics." The practitioners of this now secretive art were the professional descendants of Louis A. La Garde, the turn-of-the-century surgeon who had fired into cadavers and livestock to explore the means by which bullets tore through skin, bones, and flesh. In the United States, many of them worked at the army's Biophysics Division at the Aberdeen Proving Ground in Maryland, where General Wheeler's project became a major undertaking. More than 90 percent of the division's staff participated, overtime pay was freed up, and to meet the tight deadline many people worked nights, weekends, and on holidays. The division chose four methods to evaluate the rifles.[23] Its staff would measure the velocity of the bullets at the muzzle and at various points downrange. They would fire into blocks of a special gelatin designed to simulate human tissue. They would fire into live castrated male Texas Angora goats, which were the laboratory's preferred animals for experimentation, and in ready supply. And in tests that would later cause their study nearly to disappear from government records, they would fire into amputated human legs and decapitated human heads.

Organizing a supply of legs and heads presented problems. In 1902, then-Major La Garde could make arrangements at a private medical college and shoot dangling corpses on the university grounds. Such options were not available in 1962, at least not on short notice. But the men who

led the study—Arthur J. Dziemian and Alfred G. Olivier, who later would
be expert witnesses before the Warren Commission's investigation into the
assassination of President Kennedy—had tools at their disposal that were
unavailable to La Garde. First, they could shield their work from public
review. The Cold War's atmosphere of secrecy allowed a cone of silence
to be lowered. Dziemian and Olivier needed only to claim that shooting human legs and heads was a matter of national security, and warn
everyone involved that disclosing the strange doings of the Biophysics
Division was punishable under counterespionage law. This ensured that
the work would be classified, and remain classified, and that whatever the
scientists did would barely be known. Second, the United States was now
a global superpower with deep resources and long reach. For a project with
the interest of the president and the secretary of defense, the ballisticians
could make cadaver-procuring arrangements that had been impossible in
La Garde's day. And so it came to pass that in order to satisfy McNamara's
curiosity for a comparison, for the 1962 lethality tests a batch of human
heads were made available via shipment from India. Neither the laboratory's classified report nor the limited correspondence about the tests that
survived disclosed precisely how the army procured them. Nor did the
authors say how they disposed of the human remains after subjecting
them to gunfire. All that survived was a 286-page record of the tests and
the testers' conclusions, along with telltale signs of the army's embarrassment about the entire affair.* But if the record did not illuminate all of

---

* The embarrassment had grounds beyond the origins of the cadavers used. The twenty-seven
severed heads were ultimately subjected to tests of little apparent value. And there are hints in
the report of a lapse of scientific judgment that cast doubts on the value of the entire study.
According to the report, Dziemian and Olivier used AR-15 ammunition different from the ammunition the American military used in Vietnam. Throughout the war, American troops would
use a metal-jacketed round, just as the military had been using in other cartridges throughout the
century. But in the Biophysics Division's test in 1962, the cartridges were described by Dziemian
and Olivier as propelling "bullets with a lead core and no metal jackets." These rounds could be
expected to create wounds of a much different nature from those made by military ammunition,
and their use in the tests risked undermining judgment about the relative lethality of the tested
weapons. But there is a hurdle to knowing with certainty what really occurred: the secrecy and
cover-up of the work. Was the reference a clerical error? The photographs of the ammunition
released to the author by the United States government were low-quality digital scans and provided no help in determining the bullets' composition. Ultimately, it is not possible to tell from
the records released to date. The study's final report did have other clerical errors, so it remains
possible that this, too, was a clerical error. This was one of the pitfalls of secret tests, which were
subject neither to peer review nor to public scrutiny. Both research lapses and editorial lapses
could pass, and did pass, unchallenged.

the details, it did illuminate something else. It showed just how bizarre, and off track, the American reaction to the AK-47 had become.

The tests opened at 9:30 A.M. on October 26 at one of the proving ground's outdoor ranges. It began with live goats. The morning was chilly and overcast. The goats, which weighed between 62 and 145 pounds, had been sheared and secured inside holding racks. They were oriented at right angles to the gunners, each goat so his right side presented itself as a target. The gunners sat at a shooting table, leaned forward, looked through telescopic scopes, and fired. Thirty goats were shot that day. Goat No. 12658, an eighty-pound billy, was first. After each goat was struck, the testers released the wounded animal from the rack for the next research step: "observation of the clinical response of the animal to the trauma." This included measurements of the volume of blood lost (in milliliters); the "time to permanent collapse" (in seconds); the "direction of fall" (vertical, from the rifle, toward the rifle); and survival time, which was determined by counting the elapsed seconds from the impact of a bullet with a goat until the "cessation of heartbeats." (The goats that did not die quickly, and seemed destined to live beyond a few hours, were "sacrificed by electrocution.") To ensure nothing was missed, a 16-millimeter Dynafax motion-picture camera recorded each billy's fate, and the carcasses were examined by necropsy. Goat No. 12658 was hit with a bullet from an AR-15 at a distance of either twenty-five or one hundred meters, depending on which chart in the report is to be believed. He had a quick end. The bullet passed through the animal's liver, at least one lung, and the gastrointestinal tract. Permanent collapse came forty-four seconds later, when the billy fell toward the rifle. His heart ceased beating within five minutes. In the course of the study, 166 goats were shot in all, at ranges of twenty-five to five hundred meters.

The leg tests began on October 29, when gunners fired into human limbs that had been amputated from cadavers, frozen, and then thawed for testing day. The gunners shot from a distance of fifty meters, aiming for thighs, calves, and feet. On November 3, the gunners turned their attention to the processed heads from India. For these tests, the skulls were, according to Dziemian and Olivier, "unbleached and undefatted." To ready them, each was encased in ballistic gelatin, which allowed tissue gaps inside the cranium to fill with fake tissue and form what the authors called a "pseudobrain." The gelatin outside was sculpted close, to create "about the same resistance to penetration by the bullets as would the scalp and soft tissues of the face and head." The Biophysics Division's scientists switched on their motion-picture camera and the gunners began their work, firing from ranges of fifty and one hundred meters. In every case at both distances, the impact of a military rifle bullet with a human head created what Dziemian and Olivier called "explosive hydrodynamic effects." The heads ruptured and the fragments scattered, due in large part to the shock wave traveling through the pseudotissue within the cranium, which could not contain it. This should have been predictable. La Garde, in a summary of his own work and case studies of others, had published a voluminous work in 1916 that detailed what he called the "explosive effects" to the human head when solidly struck by modern rifle bullets. His case studies included victims of battlefield injuries, a barracks suicide, and a prisoner who attempted to flee from a guard, who shot him high on the back of the head. Ample data had accumulated in the decades since, including studies of cranial injuries to Allied soldiers in World War II. Put simply, by 1962 it was well-known in the ballistics and medical communities that human heads broke apart when struck by military rifle bullets at the ranges in question in these tests. Nevertheless, the heads were shot, twenty-three with pseudobrains and four without.

Then things got interesting, to the point of forensic absurdity. After the heads were broken, Dziemian and Olivier and their scientists attempted to differentiate the damage. A simple matrix was established. At a range of fifty meters, the M-14 and the AR-15 both caused more cranial damage than the AK-47. At a range of one hundred meters, the AR-15 caused more damage than either the AK-47 or the M-14, which were roughly equal to each other. Presented this way in the narrative portion of the Biophysics Division's secret report, the information appeared methodically observed. The pictures published in the appendixes exposed the rankings as near meaningless. Some of the images showed cranial fragments arranged for assessment and display. Others, time-sequenced photographs excerpted from the thousands taken by the motion-picture camera, documented in slow motion the effect of a bullet penetrating and passing through a human head. The results, in practical terms, were identical. Each and every head containing a pseudobrain flew apart. Government scientists might care to count pieces and decide which rifle was more lethal, as if such measurements were revelatory. Soldiers would have better sense. Heads were heads, not ammunition cans, watermelons, cubes of gelatin, or blocks of pine. When attached to living men they contained brains. The shooting tests had established, unsurprisingly, that bullets fired from some military rifles caused human heads to fragment into more pieces than bullets fired from other rifles. But what exactly did this mean for either a rifleman or his victim? There is, after all, but one degree of death.

If General Wheeler wanted to know about the relative effectiveness of the rifles under review, this was not a measure. The lethality tests, in the end, offered little of obvious value. Every human bone struck by a rifle bullet had broken, every gelatin-filled cranium had shattered. The relative differences in damages were academic. And yet the test results still might have had a use in restoring a more realistic conversation about the AR-15. Dziemian and Olivier's final report subtly but clearly revealed that the army's terminal-ballistics experts were suspicious of the Project AGILE findings. "More shots were made with the AR-15 on legs than with the other bullets," it noted, "because of the rather startling results from limb wounds in combat described in the A.R.P.A. report."[24] The Biophysics Division's gunners shot legs at various orientations, with standard bullets and with bullets that had their tips trimmed off. No matter what they did, they were unable to reproduce the effects that the participants in Project AGILE claimed to have seen. At Aberdeen Proving Ground, the traumatic amputations simply did not occur. This result, coupled with the observation that all heads shattered when struck by any of the bullets, might have been a basis for the Pentagon to question the objectivity and methods of Lieutenant Colonel Hallock's team. But instead of having such a practical value, the lethality tests underlined other things: the risks of secrecy and the deep dysfunctions in McNamara's supposedly highly functional systems-analysis approach. There was no peer review of this kind of hushed work, and events that followed ensured that almost no one would ever find out about it.[25]

The deadline for an initial report was November 30,[26] seven weeks after Secretary McNamara raised the issue of American rifle choices with Secretary Vance. An understandable curiosity rose through the Pentagon. The possibility that scientists might tell soldiers which new American rifle was more dangerous was intriguing. Lethality data for the AK-47, a Soviet weapon the United States was beginning to face, added spice. But rather than allow a wider set of minds to examine the study and glean what they might from it—in other words, rather than being systematic—the army restricted its circulation reflexively and fiercely. Sometimes supervisors have to be wary of what they ask for, especially in institutions that mix secrecy, cash, and guns. Away from the Biophysics Division, where shooting body parts had become part of the job, the realization that federal employees were performing gunfire tests on human heads was at once unsavory and politically risky. Someone, it seemed, felt that this was something the United States did not want to get caught doing. In spring 1963, the staff of Charles Hitch, the Pentagon's comptroller, asked the army chief of staff's office for two copies of the lethality report. Worry and embarrassment crept in. The cover-up began. In a memorandum stamped SECRET the army chief of staff ordered Lieutenant General R. W. Colglazier, Jr., the deputy chief of staff for logistics, not to share the report, even with Hitch's office, "in view of the sensitivity and potential sensationalism with the use of human cadavers from India."[27] General Colglazier sought help from Vance. "Although this is not the first use of elements of the human cadaver for this purpose, I consider such use to be extremely sensitive," he wrote, in another secret memorandum, adding that the army would like Vance to ask Hitch to withdraw the request in "recognition of the potential sensationalism which could arise from public disclosure of this information."[28] The results of the lethality study remained hidden for forty-six years. And at the most important time, during the early and mid-1960s, the Project AGILE report, with its suspicious observations and false conclusions, remained uncontested.[29] The AR-15 continued its rise, boosted by a reputation for lethality and reliability that it did not deserve.

General Wheeler's larger set of worldwide tests also failed to provide a fully useful or enduring evaluation. This was in part because of the undue rush, but there were darker subcurrents, too. The study collapsed under the weight of allegations of bias and a climate of mutual recriminations between various camps. Proponents of the AR-15 accused the army and its evaluators of efforts at sabotage. The acidic climate prompted Vance to order an investigation by the army's inspector general, which found that at least part of the testing, a tactical assessment at Fort Benning, had been rigged against the AR-15. The results tainted the entire effort and provided the AR-15's backers with another argument they would use well: that their weapon was never treated fairly. Absent anything definitive to say, General Wheeler chose the safest path available. On January 14, 1963, based on the results of the worldwide tests, he delivered his recommendations. The army was most clear on one point—the pitfalls of the Soviet assault rifle. In his summary, General Wheeler dismissed the value of the AK-47, calling it "optimized for the submachine gun role" and declaring its "overall inferiority" to both the M-14 and M-16. Thus ending discussion about that, the general assessed the American arms. Being politically astute, he found merits in each. Both weapons, according to the army's assessment, had superior accuracy as well as acceptable durability, ease of maintenance, and other desirable characteristics. But the AR-15 had a consequential fault. The evaluation unequivocally rated it unsatisfactory in the important category of reliability. This was because, General Wheeler wrote, stoppages during firing were "so troublesome that soldiers might well lose confidence in the weapon." The general added that the army was optimistic that the deficiencies "can be readily corrected," though he was silent on what these corrections might be.[30]

Given the ferocity building in the argument over which rifle was best, General Wheeler was careful not to offend any camp too greatly. He seemed eager to step aside and let the defense secretary choose the next steps. The defense secretary, after all, was the one pushing the question. General Wheeler offered three recommendations: continue with the M-14 program, terminate the M-14 program and adopt the AR-15 as the new standard arm, or defer a drastic step and mollify all camps via what he called Option C. In this option, the army would buy AR-15s for helicopter-borne, airborne, and Special Forces soldiers and reduce its M-14 purchases accordingly. It would decide later which weapon would be the American shoulder-fired arm of the future: the AR-15, the M-14, or the SPIW, if the SPIW ever became feasible. Predictably, McNamara leaned toward Option C.

Now came the matter of readying the AR-15 for service. In early March, the Army Materiel Command formally opened an AR-15 development program, with an office at Rock Island Arsenal in Illinois headed by Lieutenant Colonel Harold W. Yount. This was not to be a normal program, and Colonel Yount's managerial control was titular. A special committee with oversight duties was formed. The committee included representatives from all the services but also put the program under the defense secretary's control: Two of McNamara aides were given seats on it, along with veto power over all its decisions.[31] This gave the AR-15 a high priority. It also left the program vulnerable to political interference on technical matters and introduced fresh tensions between the defense secretary's office and the ordnance service. McNamara had already expressed his dissatisfaction with the army's weapons experts, and the inspector general's investigation of the handling of the worldwide tests only added to the feelings of distrust. The defense secretary wanted to put his stamp on the AR-15 program and place it under his protection. But the top-heavy assignment of political appointees to the committee risked alienating or even removing people with weapons expertise from participation in the AR-15's development. McNamara's whiz kids were smart. But they had almost no experience in either war or weaponry, and were not necessarily an able substitute for those whose careers had been a study of ordnance and guns. One of the government's ballistic experts was appalled at their role. "Their qualifications," he said, "consisted of, and apparently were limited to, advanced academic degrees, supreme confidence in their own intellectual superiority, virtually absolute authority as designated representatives of OSD [Office of the Secretary of Defense], and a degree of arrogance such as I have never seen before or since."[32]

Firearms and their ammunition form a system. While that system can seem exceedingly simple compared to a fighter jet or a tank, it often is not simple at all. Automatic firearms and cartridges work together in complex ways, and changes to either a weapon or a cartridge can create pervasive disharmonies that can be difficult to pinpoint; ghosts can readily inhabit these machines, and they do. The services and the committee, working through both the government's arsenal and Colt's, proceeded to make changes to the AR-15 and the .223 round—more than one hundred in all. Many changes were minor and arcane. Others, including a change to the rifling in the AR-15's barrel and the addition of a device that could push the bolt forward manually, were significant and consumed months of infighting and interservice positioning. Throughout it all, as the members maneuvered and quarreled, the committee missed a basic step—ensuring that the rifle was resistant to corrosion. Previous generations of American military rifles had been plated with chromium within their chambers and barrels, which protected these areas from pitting and rust. The AR-15 was not. Colt's, and by some accounts Stoner, insisted that the barrel was made of a superior alloy, moly-vanadium, and would stand up to the elements without further protective steps. This was not the case. But the program rolled on, its momentum assured. In December 1963, the Pentagon purchased 104,000 M-16s—85,000 for the army and 19,000 for the air force, calling the procurement "a one-time buy." The rifle was renamed the M-16. Option C had been exercised.

If the 1963 purchase was meant to settle questions about which troops would carry which weapon, it failed. Instead, the M-16's anointment as an official American infantry arm made it influential in an unexpected way. The Marine Corps, long skeptical of Colt's offering, took note of the new flexibility in American rifle selection and proposed yet another path. The Corps had never been enamored of the AR-15. It accepted the merits of the assault-rifle idea, but for logistical reasons the Marines wanted an assault rifle and a machine gun to have the same caliber. Another new weapon caught its eye. After ArmaLite had sold the rights for the AR-15, Eugene Stoner, the inventor, had moved to another firm, Cadillac Gage. There Stoner designed a modular system of barrels, sights, and trigger assemblies that could be mixed and matched around a single receiver to create either a light machine gun or an assault rifle. In 1964 General Wallace M. Greene, Jr., the Corps' commandant, began lobbying the army to consider this new weapon, the Stoner 63. General Harold K. Johnson, who had replaced General Wheeler as army chief of staff, ordered a fresh round of tests. McNamara had opened discussions he had not anticipated. The American rifle program, once staid and organized, had become fully disordered. The army had developed one weapon, the M-14, and lobbied for its approval and survival. The air force had snubbed its sister service and adopted the AR-15, which was now called the M-16. McNamara had begun to push the M-16 into select units' hands. And the Marine Corps was campaigning for the Stoner 63. Just about everything had happened except what should have happened: an objective and open competition for assault-rifle design, with multiple submissions and a careful evaluation, which is what the Soviet Union had organized two decades before.

It is worth a pause to consider the significance of the step not taken. After Charles Hitch endorsed the assault-rifle concept, the United States military could have decided what it wanted an assault rifle to be and to do. This would have been a matter of conceiving and publishing proposed specifications for caliber, muzzle velocity, weight, accuracy, and any number of other characteristics. These specifications could then have been provided to both the government's designers and private industry—to Ruger, to Colt's, to Remington, to Winchester, to Browning, to Cadillac Gage, and to any other interested participants—with a deadline for design submission. In doing so, several things would have been achieved. McNamara's suspicion of the ordnance corps would have been placated. The intellectual capital of the private sector would have been notified and invited to compete. And when the deadline for submissions rolled around, the Pentagon would have had a range of competing designs from which to select the basis for developing an assault rifle.

Instead, it had argument, which now took the shape of an evaluation of firearms from a tiny field: the M-14, which the Pentagon had already acknowledged was not quite right, and two weapons—the M-16 and Stoner 63—that had been designed by the same man. No matter how well this evaluation would be conducted, the United States' rifle selection process looked less like deliberation than lunging. The new round of tests, called Small Arms Weapons Systems, or SAWS, tried to be everything that General Wheeler's worldwide tests had failed to be: thorough, objective, methodical. It did manage to serve a useful purpose. As the evaluators bore down on the many aspects of performance for the small assortment of rifles under consideration, they found something that McNamara's committee had missed: The M-16 was given to malfunctions.

One decision can affect another in unforeseen ways, and as the evaluators worked they came to realize that a decision made arbitrarily several years before—to have the rifle be accurate and powerful out to five hundred yards—was producing troubling side effects. Achieving that kind of ballistic performance required the bullet to travel at a very high velocity. But how much velocity was enough? Stoner's early AR-15 had fired a round with a propellant powder known as IMR 4475. In late 1963, the army allowed a different powder, WC 846, to be used. This powder, known as ball powder because of the shape of its propellant's pellets, appeared to offer advantages. It lowered the pressure in the chamber and it increased the bullet's muzzle velocity. But it came with worrisome traits. It burned dirtier than the IMR powder, and it increased the rate at which the rifle fired. Both of these side effects were potentially harmful. Unlike

what happened in the AK-47, in the M-16 the gas of the burning propellant did not push a piston. It vented into the bolt carrier, part of the
operating system of the rifle. This exposed the important moving parts
of the rifle to more heat and fouling. And dirtier powder meant more
fouling still. Moreover, the increase in the cyclic rate increased the rate
of jamming and the wear on the weapons' parts—two consequences that
could make the rifle both less reliable and less durable than it otherwise
might be. This is exactly what the SAWS test uncovered. By 1965 some of
the classified results of the SAWS test were circulating through the army's
upper reaches, and the evaluators had concluded that with ammunition
packed with ball propellant, the rifle had become six times more likely to
misfeed, and was prone as well to more fouling.[33] Perhaps it was time to
tap the brakes. But the war would not allow that. The American involvement in Vietnam was accelerating. In February 1965, the Viet Cong had
attacked the Pleiku air base, killing eight American soldiers. President
Lyndon B. Johnson escalated, authorizing the bombing of North Vietnam. The war was gathering momentum. New weapons were wanted.
Slowing the M-16's manufacture and distribution—no matter the unsettling results percolating from the tests—was not considered. In the rush,
those who could have exercised prudence had become impervious to the
signs.

In 1965, while the SAWS test was still under way, the M-16 received
its decisive boost. One of the American helicopter-borne units that had
received M-16s, the First Battalion of the Seventh Cavalry, was placed by
helicopters into the path of three NVA regiments that were trying to drive
from the Cambodian border and split Vietnam in two. For six days, the
outnumbered American soldiers faced communist forces in what General
William C. Westmoreland, the commander of American forces in Vietnam, described as "fighting as fierce as any ever experienced by American troops." After the battle, General Westmoreland attended a briefing
by the battalion commander, Lieutenant Colonel Harold G. Moore, Jr.,
who, according to Westmoreland, lifted an M-16 rifle and said, "Brave
soldiers and the M-16 brought this victory." General Westmoreland had
worried through much of 1965 over the small-arms advantage enjoyed
by communist fighters with AK-47s. General Wheeler's insistence on the
Soviet assault rifle's "overall inferiority" was not quite true after all. The
view might have looked that way from Washington when the army's de-

sign corps was under criticism, but the American commander on the ground was feeling outgunned. The M-16, it seemed to him, promised to be the equalizer.

Moore and many of his soldiers told me that the M-16 was the best individual weapon ever made, clearly the American answer to the enemy's AK-47. Most American units at the time were equipped with the older M-14 rifle, which was semiautomatic and too heavy for the jungle. Convinced that Moore and his men knew what they were talking about, I asked Secretary McNamara as a matter of urgency to equip all American forces with the M-16 and then also to equip the ARVN* with it. . . .

. . . The ARVN thus long fought at a serious disadvantage against the enemy's automatic AK-47, armed as they were with World War II's semiautomatic M-1, whose kick when firing appeared to rock the small Vietnamese soldiers back on their heels. Armed with a light carbine, little more than a pea shooter when compared with the AK-47, the South Vietnamese militia were at an even worse disadvantage.[34]

General Westmoreland's passion for Colt's automatic rifle would remain publicly unshaken throughout his life. But his description of the battle obscured a fuller view of what Colonel Moore's soldiers had experienced. Moore's own book, published years later, described several instances of M-16s jamming and failing in the fight. General Westmoreland also skipped details of the means by which the M-16 unseated the M-14 and finally became the American military's primary arm. James B. Hall, a sales manager at Colt's, described a more cunning process. By late 1965, Colt's had almost filled the 1963 order for 104,000 rifles and had no other significant contracts on its books. General Westmoreland wanted more M-16s but was getting little support from the Pentagon. McNamara and General Johnson had already exercised Option C. Their keenness for the M-16 did not yet extend to making it the standard American arm, especially with the prospects for SPIW unresolved, and because introduc-

---

* Army of the Republic of Vietnam, which fought with American forces against the North Vietnamese troops and Viet Cong guerrillas (author's note).

ing the M-16 to general issue would disrupt the hard-won small-arms standardization within NATO. Officials from Colt's, meanwhile, were working their contacts on Capitol Hill, trying to enlist congressional help.

General Westmoreland's frustration and Colt's sales push worked in concert in October 1965, when Hall sent a letter to a brigadier general he knew who managed logistics in Vietnam. Hall informed the general that "effective the following January [Colt's] would stop producing rifles for the Army and he was fighting a war without any support." If this was meant to be incendiary, it had its desired effect. The brigadier passed the letter to General Westmoreland, who called Senator Richard B. Russell, Jr., Democrat of Georgia. Russell, an ally of President Johnson and one of the deans of the hill, was touring Vietnam at the time as chairman of the Senate Armed Services Committee. Russell called McNamara on December 7 and issued a naked political threat: "Buy 100,000 rifles today, or I'm releasing the story to the press." Hall was summoned that day to Rock Island Arsenal to sign a contract.[35] Colt's position and profits were preserved. General Westmoreland would get his guns. For those who think that the United States chose its primary infantry rifle through orderly deliberation, or that systems analysis led to organized decision-making, the episode showed how things actually worked. This was how troops in Vietnam would receive their weapons, including the unready M-16s soon to be put into the hands of Hotel Company, Second Battalion, Third Marines.

After all these years of dysfunction, scandal was not far off. But first came celebration. At Colt's Firearms Division in Hartford, General Westmoreland's end run meant salvation. In 1963, Colt's had posted a million-dollar loss. It had hired and trained new workers and lured managers from other firms, staking its future, even its survival, on a gun without a market.[36] Floated by the Pentagon's order, the company entered a boom. The return on the AR-15 investment was at hand. When Colt's bought the manufacturing rights from Fairchild in 1959, it had gambled on a concept more than a product. ArmaLite's rifle had been rejected by the Pentagon. It had no powerful backers in the army or the Marine Corps. No domestic orders were expected. The nation was at peace. Almost seven years later, with the signing of the contract in December 1965, Colt's effectively became the sole-source provider of a weapon demanded by the army for an expanding war. The M-16, once roundly rejected, stood the chance of becoming the United States military's primary firearm, which would mean the allies would be seeking a new class of assault rifles, too. The company grew. Between May 1966 and April 1967, as rifle production jumped at the Hartford plant, Colt's military division hired 510 new employees.

Excitement surrounds a winner, and Colt's was suddenly a winner. The accompanying promotional push was striking, both for Colt's good luck and for the degree to which the gun press helped the company along. As part of the public-relations effort, William J. Curran, Colt's advertising and public-relations manager, succeeded in publishing a story under his byline in *Shooting Times,* naturally touting the M-16.[37] Gun companies and gun magazines have long had relationships beyond cozy. And now, when gun journalism was needed, *Shooting Times* failed. The magazine promoted the rifle further with a follow-up the next month. The second article detailed how Colt's provided the editors an M-16 for test-firing. The editors avoided putting the gun through what they called a "torture test," and were principally interested in its accuracy, its ease of use, and its bullets' penetration of various items the authors judged common to the battlefield, including bunkers and steel plates. But a funny thing happened on the way to plinking the selected targets. Of the first 450 rounds fired, the brand-new M-16 malfunctioned eleven times. Might not this have been the story? Not in *Shooting Times.* The writer, Major George Nonte, passed off the poor performance as related to one bad gun and not indicative of M-16s as a class. It was, Nonte wrote, "only logical to assume that any deficiencies such as those noted would be corrected (or the gun would be rejected) in the course of final inspection." He continued: "Before any single gun is actually accepted by Army resident inspectors and delivered to the military establishment, it must pass extensive firing tests."[38] This was not quite so. In fact, each rifle at Colt's factory had to fire only thirty-three rounds to pass its acceptance test, and the army would later admit that in order to ensure a high acceptance rate, the acceptance test was skewed in Colt's favor. Colt's was allowed to conduct the tests with ammunition containing IMR powder—not the ball powder the rifles would fire in Vietnam, which was known to cause a higher rate of malfunctions.[39]

The stories went to print even as the army conducted a survey of the small-arms use of 121 soldiers on infantry, cavalry, or airborne duty in Vietnam. Almost 90 percent were carrying M-16s. The results both confirmed the nature of ground fighting in the war and suggested that the M-16 was not ready for the job at hand. Eighty percent of the participants said they normally fired at enemy combatants within two hundred yards, and 95 percent said the enemy was within three hundred yards. Seventy-nine percent said that most or some of the time they fired at night, when more than half never saw the opposing soldiers clearly. Moreover, 95 percent of the combat veterans said that when they did see Viet Cong and NVA soldiers, the enemy was either running, prone, or in some sort of hiding.[40] What all of this meant was that one touted feature of the M-16—an ability to strike and penetrate steel helmets at five hundred yards—was almost irrelevant in jungle war. This was a dispiriting finding, given that the desire for this long-range performance had led the army to accept a propellant that made the rifle less reliable. And the soldiers' narrative comments hinted at burgeoning problems. Some soldiers liked the M-16. But many others said that while it was a good rifle when it worked, it jammed. Ominously, several soldiers pleaded for cleaning equipment.[41]

The National Rifle Association also was ready to give the rifle a boost, and prepared an article for the *American Rifleman* that praised the M-16. The article, published several months later, asserted that the rifle "bears up well under harsh field conditions" and that "dust, dirt, and rain do not make the M-16A1 less functional provided minimal care is exercised." As with the stoppages mentioned casually in *Shooting Times,* the NRA's article carried a strong whiff of the malfunctions plaguing the rifle. It mentioned problems with dirty chambers, extraction, and jamming, but only briefly. The *American Rifleman* concluded, without offering evidence, that the rifle "is proving itself in Vietnam."[42] The gun press, with access to arms and arms companies that the traditional media could not match, was missing the biggest small-arms story of the war. The troops would have to find out the truth themselves. They would get that chance.

In summer 1966 as General Westmoreland's M-16s were arriving in Vietnam, soldiers receiving the new weapons were finding them hard to clean, fussy, and prone to untimely stoppages. The scale of the problems was se-

vere enough that in fall 1966 the army requested help, and teams of technicians from the Army Weapons Command and Colt's were dispatched
to investigate. In meetings with several combat units, the inspectors from
Colt's discovered that "weapons were in an unbelievable condition of rust,
filth, and lack of repair." They also noted that the troops had received insufficient marksmanship training, and "there was a shortage of technical
manuals, there was a shortage of cleaning equipment, there was a shortage
of repair parts, and there was a shortage of officers and NCOs who knew
anything about the maintenance of the rifle."

The fielding of the M-16 had stumbled badly. In a flash, a disturbing reputation had taken shape. When M-16s worked, they were excellent. But with unsettling frequency, after a bullet was fired, the empty
cartridge case would not extract. It remained stuck in the chamber. The
process of firing—not only on automatic, but at all—abruptly ceased.
Making matters worse, sometimes the bottom of a spent cartridge case
was torn away, which made it exceptionally difficult to remove the remainder manually. This was in some ways a familiar story. M-16s and
their ammunition created jams as surely as Gatling and Gardner guns
had early in their long period of manufacture. Moreover, as these problems were being reported, the weapons, billed as being assembled from
modern components that gave the rifle an unsurpassed durability, were
literally rotting in the troops' hands. Another group of Colt's specialists
traveled to Rock Island Arsenal to inspect rifles returned from Vietnam.
Robert D. Fremont, a former ArmaLite employee who had joined Colt's,
reported to Hartford that "the exteriors of most weapons were corroded
and the bores and chambers almost universally fouled and dirty, showing
evidence of real neglect." Fremont suspected maintenance was a problem,
because soldiers either had not been issued proper cleaning equipment or
had not been trained. But he sensed as well that perhaps the M-16s were
not yet suited for combat duty. There was too much rust and corrosion.
He recommended "an investigation as to the possible use of stainless
steel for barrels or chrome plating the chambers and bores of the AR-15
weapons in order to combat corrosion and neglect." Fremont reached a
conclusion that the army's leadership and the president of Colt's Firearms
Division, Paul A. Benke, would not utter in public. "Colt's weapons," he
wrote, "are sadly lacking in corrosion resistance."[43]

It was a damning statement, though the public—and the troops—

would not hear it. For the manufacturer of a weapon distributed by the United States for jungle war, it must have been surprising. The M-16 was nearly ten years old, and the manufacturing steps necessary to ensure corrosion resistance were no secret. But the army and Colt's had neglected to follow them. At the same time, an army review team was finding that the army had issued new weapons but not the necessary cleaning gear to go with them.* Lieutenant Colonel Herbert P. Underwood, visiting Vietnam from Rock Island, watched the troops make do. His letter back to Colonel Yount detailed a supply failure. It also revealed his own uncertainty about the army's state of knowledge of the weapons it was handing out.

> The 173rd uses some field expedience, primarily for cleaning the chamber and the bore of the weapons. They either use a piece of commo wire, a shoe lace or a nylon cord which they carry with them. They take a 30 caliber patch cut it in half, fold it once and loop the string or what ever it is to the center of this patch. Then using oil they pull it through the bore of the weapon starting from the chamber. As they do this, they clean both the chamber and the bore and then dry it off. They also put a little bit of oil on it. I have not been able to find anyone that does not put a little bit of oil in the chamber of the weapon to prevent it from corroding. I try to discourage it, however I am not completely convinced myself that if you leave the chamber completely dry you won't have a problem resulting from corrosion, even if you cleaned your weapon every day.[44]

No one, it seemed, was quite sure what to do with this new rifle, not even the officers issuing it. Lieutenant Colonel Underwood had other problems to report. "The 173rd Airborne Brigade tells me that they have had at least 10 weapons, if not more, to blow up in the same manner as the exhibits that we had sent to us," he wrote. In at least one of these cases, the American soldier firing it was killed.[45] The problems were multiplying. Of 2,000 M-16s tested at the Twenty-fifth Infantry Division, 384

---

* The old cleaning gear was of little use. The M-14 had a bore diameter of 7.62 millimeters; the M-16 had a diameter of 5.56 millimeters. The cleaning rod used to push a patch through an M-14 barrel was too thick to pass through the newer rifle's barrel.

malfunctioned.[46] One company, B Company of the Twenty-sixth Infantry, made a list of malfunctions that read like a roll call: 527042 Gorton, 54 rounds fired, 2 failed to extract; 701693 Mason, 2 rounds fired, round stuck in chamber, 60 rounds fired, 1 failed to extract; 531240 Coolet, 60 rounds fired, 1 failure to extract, 1 failure to feed, 40 rounds fired, 1 failure to chamber; and on it went, man by man.[47]

Three weeks later, David Behrendt, a Colt's engineer temporarily assigned to Vietnam, mailed two audiotapes back to Colt's officials in Hartford. Behrendt groused that while from the air Vietnam was beautiful, "when you get down on the ground and walk around, it's something else, kind of cruddy. I told Jim I'll be glad to see a blonde again. Everything around here is black hair and slanty eyes." Behrendt had better reasons to feel indisposed. Many M-16s were jamming, and almost all were corroded. Working alongside soldiers at American bases and outposts, Behrendt restored most rifles to working order after cleaning them and replacing parts. But it was not a good sign that a corporate engineer with a bag of parts was required to keep a new rifle in service. Combat equipment was supposed to be more hardy than that. Behrendt noted, too, that the ball powder was making the M-16 run fast. Engineers at Colt's had been working on a replacement part—a buffer inside the return spring—that would slow the weapons down. But none were yet in Vietnam. Speaking into a tape recorder halfway around the world, he urged action.

> All the rifles have an extremely high rate of fire which isn't helping us in the least bit. You better get that new buffer over here right pronto to stop some of this malfunction. It sure will help. Finishes have been wearing off many of the weapons and I've actually seen holes eaten right through into the charging handle area and along the lower receiver area, underneath the dust cover. You can see right into the magazine. Carrying handles are pretty well eaten up on many of the weapons. Rust is covering quite a few of them.[48]

Behrendt's second tape detailed similar problems: "oily chambers, dirty chambers, dirty ammo, corroded ammo, or bent magazines, lips in particular." One infantry company had a 30 percent failure rate, Behrendt said. The problems did not recur on the next operation, after the company commander emphasized rifle cleaning. This was typical of the mixed reports making their way back to the States. There were many problems, though it was also possible to find troops who liked the M-16. But Behrendt put the positive comments in perspective. "This was the only unit that has been completely satisfied with the rifles," he said. The experiences elsewhere were disquieting. "We took three rifles to the range," he said. "This was with another unit. The rifles were pulled from their storage area and the condition they were in was the way they would be taken to an operation with the magazines they were going to use. On the three rifles tryed [sic], two of them failed to extract on the first round fired. One rifle fired 63 rounds before it failed to extract." Behrendt cleaned the rifles, replaced the extractor springs on one of them, and repeated the test the next day. With new ammunition, they worked well. With older ammunition, the jamming began on the fourth round fired. Behrendt said the platoon sergeants who watched the test were convinced the rifles *could* work. He was not sure they would be able to convince their men. And once again it was not a good sign that a Colt's engineer had to work on rifles one day for the rifles to function the next. He also had more bad news.

> I collected as many carriers and bolts as I could. Most of them are pretty much destroyed or battered up. I don't know why this is occurring. The men say they just fire and it happens. I'm sending a couple of barrels back with Jim for further investigation, I cleaned these barrels, chamber area especially as best I could, took them to the range and we still had the same fail to extract problem.[49]

Colt's data was accumulating. Another of its representatives in Vietnam, J. B. Hall, summed up the situation. Hall had met officers who fought during Operation Attleboro, one of the largest battles to date. The operation had been a startling experience for American troops. They faced heavy Viet Cong automatic-rifle fire from the dense vegetation. And their M-16s jammed. "There is no question that soldiers in Vietnam are losing confidence in the M-16 rifle," Hall wrote. "It is imperative that we take all steps possible to correct the situation." Hall's report was the most urgent, and it included a list: plate the bore and chamber with chromium, install heavier buffers, correct the corrosion problems on receivers and barrels, and find a way to cover the magazines when not being fired. On an internal Colt's channel, Hall offered a candid recommendation: "a crash program to provide a better weapon." Like Fremont, he also framed the problem in a way that the army and Colt's would never publicly dare. "While it is very true that there is a lack of rifle discipline by commanders, the statement that the M-14 fires with dirty ammunition while the M-16 doesn't, is a hard argument to counter."[50] This was exactly the case: When the same GIs in the same climates and conditions carried M-14s they had no problems like they did with their M-16s. Did not this suggest that the source of the problem was not the troops, but the rifles?

A little more than two weeks later, in early November 1966, the latest news of the M-16's poor performance in Vietnam reached top channels in the army. Colonel Yount visited the Pentagon to brief now-Colonel Hallock. Colonel Hallock's interest in the M-16 was zealous and personal. He had been an early supporter of the rifle, and a supervisor of Project AGILE more than four years before. The meeting marked a potentially agonizing moment. The SAWS test had zeroed in on problems with misfeeds and fouling related to ball powder. The new weighted buffer had been identified as a fix for at least part of the problem. But the buffer was available only for newly manufactured weapons at Colt's factory—not for the scores of thousands of rifles already in Vietnam. The weapon Colonel Hallock had advocated was failing, and as near as he could tell, the failures were getting American soldiers killed. What to do? Colonel Hallock filed a classified memorandum for the record based on his meeting. It left no doubt that the army had long understood the scope and nature of the M-16's problems, had done little to resolve them, and still was moving slowly to help soldiers with malfunctioning weapons in Vietnam. Colonel Hallock described his conversation with Colonel Yount.

> I asked if he had a plan to retrofit the weapons in the field with this buffer and he said he did not. First production of the new buffer, he said, would be in January and they would go on new weapons. He said that if the buffers were sent to the field for the old weapons they would not be available to go on the new weapons that also are going to the field. I asked if he had plans to get a special priority to increase the production rate and speed up availability of the buffer

and he apparently did not. I also asked about clearing up the fouling caused by ball powder. He did not say that anything definitive had been done to correct the problem.

I asked him if there were any reports yet from Vietnam indicating the occurrence, in fact, of the excessive malfunctions that one would expect to be occurring in the field as a result of breakages and malfunctions induced by excessive cyclic rate and the malfunctions induced by fouling, complicated by difficult cleaning conditions in jungle war and normal poor distribution of cleaning equipment. He said there were some, but didn't elaborate at this time.

Far from the war, the two colonels discussed a list of factors compounding the rifle's poor performance—lackluster weapons-cleaning habits, shortages of cleaning equipment, insufficient training, and a host of jerry-rigged practices by soldiers, including soaking ammunition with oil. This was not how the M-16's introduction as the primary firearm in Vietnam was supposed to go. And Colonel Yount's inaction was not how military officers were expected to carry out their duties. Colonel Hallock wanted the problems remedied. But his bureaucratic instincts interfered. He was equally interested in restricting who knew of the problems. There was a scandal to contain, even if it meant limiting the number of technicians working to fix the malfunctions. Colonel Hallock all but grilled Colonel Yount, and impressed upon him the need to keep the problems quiet.

I said, as I have on several other occasions during the last year, that this situation was potentially explosive with the Congress, within Defense, in the Army, and with the public, and that the malfunctions alone could be expecting to be causing loss of soldiers [sic] lives, even though the data showed the XM16E1 to be more effective than other rifles even with the malfunctions. Also, that if there were excessive malfunction rates, the troops would lose confidence in their weapon, even though the causes were not due to weapon design, and that it was a serious thing for the troops to lose confidence in their weapon. I urged again that highest priority be given to correct this situation and also that he consider the security aspect of the information in technical and other channels.[51]

Colonel Hallock stamped his memorandum SECRET HOLD CLOSE repeatedly, and sent it to Dr. Jacob Stockfisch, codirector of the Force Planning and Analysis Office, urging that the gloomy information be provided to the army chief of staff. (Stockfisch's office reported both to the secretary of the army and the army chief of staff; it was a strong proponent of the M-16.) Read against what was happening in Vietnam, and as more rifles known to be unreliable were being manufactured and issued to men headed to combat, the correspondence was chilling. The military had the option of delaying the issue of the M-16 until its shortcomings were worked out, and to allow troops to carry weapons that worked. But this would have meant admitting to a mistake and sounding an alarm. It would have required an officer to display courage. Instead, corporate instincts and self-protection had trumped integrity and good sense. After returning to his office at the Rock Island Arsenal, Colonel Yount made a change. As of November 29, his weekly "significant action report" as head of the office managing the M-16 carried a new line: "The report must not be reproduced, filed or referenced in any official correspondence." Colonel Yount added that only he and two other people were allowed to keep file copies of his reports. "All other copies," he wrote, "will be destroyed within 10 days of receipt."[52] At a time when the M-16 program desperately needed candor, attention, and more resources, and when commanders and troops in the field should have been informed of the problems emerging in Vietnam, another cover-up had begun.

It is easy, based on the existing records, to see Colonel Yount and Colonel Hallock as bureaucratic villains; certainly they acted against the interests of the troops in Vietnam. Their careerist behavior was of a familiar species, and ugly, even unconscionable, when revealed. If some of the men who had been in fighting in which M-16s had failed could have read what Colonel Hallock wrote, they would have demanded investigations. Rage was high enough in Vietnam that no small number of grunts would have wanted to do worse. Combat is an intensely personal experience, and it was especially so in the close-quarters savagery of Vietnam. Troops needed to have faith not just in their rifles, as Colonel Hallock suggested, but in their officers. And it was difficult to imagine an officer who believed men were dying because their rifles were failing but wanted to restrict who knew about the causes, or even that this was the case.

But these two colonels were hardly alone. They were part of a procurement and advocacy phenomenon that had slipped from control. Since early 1963, McNamara's office had pushed the M-16 along without check. Colonel Yount managed the program, but he did not provide its direction or have control over many of its decisions. With General Westmoreland calling for more rifles, all involved in the rifle program faced internal pressure to keep M-16s flowing off the assembly lines and into Vietnam. And yet it was a fateful moment to choose to play along quietly. It was in many ways a last chance. Effective November 4, the army had decided to adopt the M-16 as its standard rifle. Step by step, decision by decision, without clear signs of institutional intent, the watermelon shoot on Boutelle's farm and the untrustworthy Project AGILE report had led to policy. The M-16, a rifle with a flawed development history, was to replace the M-14, even though the army knew the powder-rifle mismatch was causing high M-16 malfunction rates, and before a technical solution had been put into place. The decision was made as reports were streaming back from Vietnam that the rifles were jamming, apparently for many different reasons, and that the rifles bound for jungle duty were "sadly lacking in corrosion resistance." As for the M-16's documented reliability problems, in a secret memorandum on November 7, General Johnson noted that "correction of deficiencies should be accomplished in a manner that does not delay new or on-going production. Priority will be given to eliminating any weapons malfunction problems in the field."[53] In other words, M-16s were to be rushed to Vietnam. The army would fix them later, if and when fixes could be found.

So the policy was set, and the people who knew most intimately of the problems were keeping mum. The questions now were of consequences. How bad would the problems in the field be? How would the army and Marine Corps react if the problems turned out to be worse than what was known? And what would the troops, who wanted to believe in their officers and their war, think when their new rifles suddenly went quiet in a fight?

Answers quickly appeared. In early February 1967, the armorers for Second Battalion, Ninth Marines, stationed near the coast at Phu Bai, Vietnam, grew concerned about the new rifles in the battalion's custody. The

Marine Corps was beginning to receive its share of M-16s. Though this battalion's rifles had been used just four times, and only for training, they were already pitted. The armorers reported their concerns and offered other observations as well. The weapons rusted easily; a recessed area on the bolt was difficult to clean; during firing, the trigger pin and hammer pin "tended to work their way out of the receiver." The armorers also wrote that "we experienced more than a normal amount of ruptured cartridges."[54] The mix of rapid corrosion and cleaning difficulties were an ill-boding combination for a rifle issued for fighting in rain forests and rice paddies. The Marine supply officers seemed alarmed. "This rifle is currently being utilized by units engaged in active combat," they wrote to the Rock Island Arsenal. "Therefore, an expeditious evaluation is requested."[55] The complaint reached the office of Colonel Yount. Before an army technician was able to examine the weapons, supervisors at the arsenal ordered him to hand out new maintenance instructions that were to be "taken by the user to correct reported problem."

The technician visited the battalion a month later. He confirmed the corroded condition of the M-16s. And he did as he was told. In his report back to the United States, he noted that he had furnished the Marines with the new literature and "intensive training on proper cleaning of weapons is planned." His report struck the official tone. It blamed the Marines for not keeping their weapons ready. There was no mention of what was known in the Pentagon and at Colt's: the tendency of the rifles to corrode, the need for a new buffer, the problems with failure to extract. Headquarters had spoken. Though the army knew the M-16 had technical problems that needed technical solutions, combat units were blamed for their rifle's worrisome traits. The troops entered the monsoon season of 1967 with rifles prone to fail, and a bureaucracy ready to scold them when they did.

The decisions to blame the infantry, and to keep the problems out of public discourse while issuing more rifles, were untenable. By early 1967, the sense that something was awry had reached Washington. Angry troops were sending home letters. Journalists were hearing complaints. Reports of the AK-47's reliability were also providing an obvious contrast. The *Washington Daily News* posed the question. How did the world's wealthiest nation lag behind communist countries in its most basic fighting tool?

In the past two years, with amazing competence and thoroness [sic],
the communists have replaced their earlier inferior weapons with
the rapid firing AK-47 automatic assault rifle of Soviet design and
Red Chinese manufacture. . . . The AK-47 is the regular weapon
for North Vietnam's army and main force Viet Cong troops. It is as
good as the new M-16 rifle U.S. troops use. It is less liable to jam
and therefore, in the opinion of some experts, may even be better.
Man for man, the regular communist soldier is a firepower match
for his American adversary—and is far more powerful than his South
Vietnamese foe. . . . Why is it that North Vietnam, with aid from its
Chinese ally, could foresee the need and meet it, despite all sorts of
obstacles? Why is it that the U.S., with its $25 billion to $30 billion
yearly war budget, superlative defense plants, and reputed logistic
superiority could not keep pace?[56]

No one in the United States government could adequately answer
that question. The chosen line—with roots reaching through General
Wheeler's memorandum to the first 1956 technical intelligence tests—was
to denigrate the AK-47 as a primitive but functional submachine gun and
insist that American weapons were in another category altogether. That
answer could not stand, not as long as the M-16 kept failing in fight after
fight, and not while General Westmoreland was demanding more guns
to improve his soldiers' odds. So why was the AK-47 operating smoothly
in Vietnam while the M-16 failed? When pressed on this, the United
States military eventually floated another answer: Kalashnikov rifles had
been in factory production for more than fifteen years, and these years of
product improvement gave them a temporary advantage over the M-16,
which had entered mass production only in 1964. There was at least a
kernel of truth in this. Teams of Soviet engineers had in fact worked out
many of the AK-47's design kinks. Weak or unsatisfactory parts from the
original design—the return spring, the hammer—had been identified and
upgraded, sometimes multiple times. Several poor design ideas, including
the receiver, had been reworked entirely. The AK-47 had been a conceptu-
ally sound weapon from the beginning. In the mid-1960s it was mature.
   But the performance difference between the M-16 and AK-47 had
more complicated origins than the weapons' relative ages. The two weapons were designed in fundamentally different ways and their differences

in lineage left the M-16 lacking in reliability for reasons that no manufacturing tweaks or upgrades could entirely fix. The AK-47's main operating system had been conceived to have a loose fit and massive parts, and
the resulting excess energy available in each firing cycle made it resistant
to jamming. The stroke of its operating system also exceeded the distance necessary to eject a spent cartridge and feed a new one by a full 50
percent. This meant that if the system did grow sluggish and unable to
move back and forth along its entire course, the motion produced would
still likely be sufficient to keep the rifle clearing, feeding, and firing in a
fight. Herein was a deceptive quality of the rifle: While it was externally
a crude-looking weapon, at least to those who believed a rifle was supposed to have a walnut stock, no tool marks, and a high degree of polish,
it was thoroughly engineered—not for aesthetics, but for reliability. The
Soviet Union and China also devoted the kind of attention to the rifle's
manufacture that further contributed to smooth operation. Two steps in
this respect were essential. Its bore and chamber were chromed, and it
was coated with an excellent protective finish. The weapon's workhorse
operating system became more durable and reliable when manufactured
to such standards and with such care. Taken together, the engineering
and manufacturing choices in the Kalashnikov line—signs that the communist world's arms-manufacturing skills were higher than its critics in
the West could appreciate—enabled the Type 56 rifles handed out for
jungle duty in Vietnam to resist rust and corrosion, even in the monsoon
season, and even with limited cleaning. The weapons *looked* primitive.
Looks were deceiving. The rifle had been made to be a peasant's gun, and
it worked exceptionally well in many conditions in which peasants fight.

The M-16 was the manifestation of a different set of design ideas. Its
parts were made to be a snug fit, almost in the manner of a manually operated bolt-action rifle. The tight fit helped make the M-16 more accurate
than the Kalashnikov, all the way out to the theoretically impressive five
hundred yards. It also seemed to make it undependable. Dust, dirt, sand,
rust, carbon buildup—all these things could slow or obstruct the movement of an M-16's bolt. Further, in the quest to keep down the weapon's
weight, the main moving parts of its operating system had been made
light. This added to the problems with reliability. The M-16 was easy to
carry, aim, and shoot. But the small mass of its bolt gave its operation
little excess potential energy; coupled with the tight fit, this was a design

recipe for stoppages in harsh environments, especially if the weapons were pitted or corroding. If this were not enough, certain manufacturing standards at Colt's through 1967 were also behind those in the Soviet Union and China. Colt's, the sole-source provider of the M-16, neither chromed the rifles' chambers or bores nor applied an adequate protective finish to the weapons—a pair of oversights that made the rifle prone to corrosion in Vietnam.

By spring 1967, the problems had become so widely known that Congress took an interest. On May 3, 1967, Representative L. Mendel Rivers, Democrat of South Carolina and chairman of the House Armed Services Committee, appointed Representative Richard H. Ichord, Democrat of Missouri, as head of a special subcommittee to examine "the development, production, distribution and sale of M-16 rifles."[57] Ichord steered wide of the question of which weapon was better—the M-14 or the M-16—for Vietnam or elsewhere. He left such questions to soldiers.[58] If the military wanted the M-16, so be it. He wanted to know why the M-16 was malfunctioning at an unacceptably high rate.

The appointment of the subcommittee coincided with a fresh round of malfunctions of M-16s issued to the Marines, including those issued to Hotel Company, Second Battalion, Third Marines. Its experience was instructive. In February, the battalion had been given its share of M-16s during a refit period on Okinawa. The rifles had initially been popular. The troops grasped the advantages of a lightweight automatic rifle with little recoil. They knew they could now carry more rounds into each firefight. They were satisfied with how the rifles, fresh from crates, handled on firing ranges. There was concern about a shortage of cleaning gear, but otherwise everything seemed in order. The Marines were pleased. A few weeks later, Hotel Company returned to Vietnam. On a sweep of the countryside on April 26, a few M-16s jammed. But the fighting was not intensive and the operation was not stalled. The problem was attributed to unfamiliarity with the rifle, perhaps combined with inadequate cleaning, though the Marines who were cleaning the weapons thought this was not the case.[59]

Then came the shock. On April 27, the battalion was preparing for combat against dug-in NVA units on Hills 861 and 881 near Khe Sanh. It spent much of the day watching artillery and air strikes pounding suspected NVA positions on the high ground. On April 29, the company moved toward Hill 881 North, and that night, after recovering the remains of a missing Marine, it spent the night in the bush on the approach to the southeast of Hill 881 North. On April 30, the company moved out on foot again, jumping into an attack at first light with Second and Third platoons abreast of each other and moving forward in a battle formation known as "on line." In Third Platoon, as Second Lieutenant Thomas R. Givvin, the platoon commander, walked uphill he found at least five M-16s with cleaning rods forced down their barrels resting on the ground.[60] These were the discards of Marines who had fought on the hill several days before. Hotel Company moved through tall elephant grass and was ambushed at a distance of about fifty meters by the North Vietnamese Army.

The ambush turned swiftly into a brutal close-quarters fight. Rifle by rifle, several of the Marines' new M-16s jammed.[61] The malfunctions had consistency, and most common was a failure to extract. To resume firing the troops needed to thread together several sections of narrow metal pipe, the military's standard-issue rifle-cleaning rods, and plunge the rod down the barrel from the muzzle to try to knock the spent shell case free. It was a movement akin to what Revolutionary War soldiers had had to do to reload muskets nearly two hundred years before. Only then could a grunt with a stopped rifle force out the empty cartridge case and load for another try. "Punching a bore," as this clearing action was called, was a tedious exercise on a rifle range. It was especially difficult to do when the spent cartridge case was torn. In battle it left riflemen unable to defend themselves and the men on their left and right, and was cause for fury and frustration. After conferring by radio with the battalion commander, Captain Raymond C. Madonna, Hotel Company's commander in spring 1967, ordered Hotel Company to fall back so they could call in air strikes and artillery fire. The two sides had been too close for the Marines to mass supporting fire without endangering themselves. The company relied on its own 60-millimeter mortars and 3.5-inch rockets for fire support. Hotel Company suffered eight dead Marines and one dead corpsman that day. Forty-three others were wounded.

On May 3, the remnants of Hotel Company and part of Foxtrot Company were ordered to help Echo Company, which had been pinned down in front of a network of NVA bunkers on Hill 881 North. Foxtrot Company would approach from the southeast. Hotel Company would envelop around Echo Company and attack from the north; the plan was to get behind the NVA bunker line and strike the enemy's rear. Captain Madonna and his Marines stepped off at dawn and began a long flanking movement on foot down a ravine and then through the triple-canopy jungle; they moved for as long as nine hours to get behind the NVA.

Hotel Company had only one platoon—First Platoon—that was still at fighting strength. As the sweat-soaked Marines at last moved near the enemy bunkers, and were preparing to rush, the captain gave an order over the radio to his platoon commander, Second Lieutenant Ord El- liott: *Fix bayonets.* He was effectively telling men to prepare to fight to the death, hand to hand. The order was superfluous. Lieutenant Elliott had come to the same decision himself. He had already told the men to ready their knives. With bayonets affixed, the officers thought, the Marines whose M-16s failed might slash or stab their way through the bunkers.[62] It was 1967, the age of the nuclear-powered aircraft carrier, the B-52 Stratofortress, and the submarine-launched Polaris ballistic mis- sile. A Marine Corps platoon and company commander were preparing their men for an attack in which they would wield their rifles like lances, swords, and spears. And that was Captain Madonna's assessment of Colt's assault rifle, circa 1967. "It was a pretty good bayonet holder," he said. "I knew those weapons were failing. I didn't know what the rate was, but I knew I couldn't rely on them anymore."

First Platoon had entered a gully where the elephant grass was tall and the air was silent; not even a bird could be heard. The fighting erupted as the platoon moved through the low ground, with North Vietnamese soldiers firing through dense vegetation, concealed in bunkers and spi- der holes. Under fire, the platoon's First Squad moved against one of the bunkers, with the leader of First Fire Team, Corporal Cornelio Ybarra Jr., crawling forward with a hand grenade. He tossed the grenade inside. There was a tremendous blast. Corporal Ybarra, known to his friends as Y, stood and headed for the next bunker. A close-quarters battle raged along the line, but each man was limited in what he could see by the heavy bush, and by the thick bursts of bullets cracking by. Luckily, the fire team was not spread too widely. One of its members, Private First Class Roy W. DeMille, was struggling with a jammed M-16. The team's grenadier gave him a .45-caliber pistol, so he would have a weapon that might work. DeMille was still trying to revive his rifle when he saw a bloody NVA soldier stagger out of the shattered bunker with a Kalashnikov. DeMille was helpless, holding a jammed M-16. He was about, it seemed, to die.

"Y!" DeMille yelled to his team leader. "A gook!"

Corporal Ybarra turned and reacted instinctively. His magazine had seventeen rounds. His M-16 was set on automatic. He fired at close-range until the clip was empty, killing the dazed Vietnamese man.

Fortunately for Private First Class DeMille, whose M-16 had failed, Corporal Ybarra's had not.[63]

The Hill Fights claimed more lives than any Marine action yet in the war. More than 150 Marines were killed. Several hundred more were wounded. Many elements of Marine firepower had worked together as two battalions had claimed the high ground. Attack aircraft, artillery, and mortars had pounded the North Vietnamese positions. The most basic piece of equipment had failed. By May 5, the jamming had been widespread enough that sadly surreal scenes unfolded at one helicopter landing zone on Hill 881 North, where wounded Marines, who had been hit in a mortar bombardment, were waiting to be evacuated. Marines who had not been wounded wandered among the casualties, asking their bloodied colleagues if their rifles had worked. When they found a wounded Marine whose rifle had performed well, they asked to trade and exchanged a faulty M-16 for the M-16 that had reliably fired. Other Marines had also found that three pins near the trigger assembly had a tendency to work loose and slip out, rendering the rifles useless.[64] Over several days, the Marines' initial satisfaction with their M-16s had turned to astonishment, then disgust. Emotions were further inflamed by a sense among troops that the Pentagon had failed to provide them with enough cleaning rods, as the army technical team had found when they visited Vietnam six months before.[65] One survivor vented to the *Asbury Park Evening Press:*

> Believe it or not, you know what killed most of us? Our own rifle. Before we left Okinawa, we were all issued the new rifle, the M-16. Practically everyone of our dead was found with his rifle tore down next to him where he had been trying to fix it.[66]

Back in Washington, the Marine Corps pushed back. It denied that the problems were extensive and insisted that the M-16 was reliable and that statements from Marines who said otherwise were exaggerated. There were, as is often the case, grains of truth in the official statements, just as there were errors and exaggerations in some of the troops' accounts. In the Hill Fights rifles failed; by most accounts, many rifles. But the claim that "practically everyone of our dead was found with his rifle tore down next to him" was overstatement, at least battalionwide. By seizing on such statements and becoming argumentative, the officers in Washington missed the substantial truth: M-16s were failing at an alarming rate, the failures put lives at risk, and the grunts had lost faith in their rifles and in some cases in their chain of command. The officers had entered an argument they could not win. This was in part because by this time, the congressional subcommittee was gathering its own information, which pointed to widespread malfunctions and a pattern of false official statements by generals who were trying to convince inquirers that all was well. In May, Ralph Marshall, a lawyer working for the subcommittee, visited the Great Lakes Naval Hospital in Illinois to interview wounded GIs. Marshall found twenty-two Marines who had fought with M-16s in Vietnam. Eleven had experienced jamming. Some of their accounts were jarring. "In a squad of 14 all rifles jammed—in another patrol 9 jammed," he wrote. "Several of the marines had requested the return of their M-14 rifles in place of the newly issued M-16 because they had lost confidence in the M-16."[67]

Marshall's findings were a drop in a cascade. In letters home and interviews with reporters in the war zone, soldiers and Marines told of weapons failing while troops were under enemy fire. One Marine lance corporal noted that "every private through sergeant that uses the rifle will tell you that it will jam about once every 2 magazines if it is on full-automatic and about once every 3 or 4 magazines on semi-automatic." How this translated into combat was captured in the last minutes in the life of Lance Corporal David C. Borey, a Marine from Massachusetts assigned to Bravo Company, First Battalion, First Marine Regiment. A fellow Marine mailed a letter home describing the skirmish, which erupted after his unit had been airlifted outside Da Nang and was caught in the open crossing a rice paddy the next day. "This is how it happened," he wrote:

> Like you said, Dad, we are all complaining about the M-16. When it works you can't beat it but it jams so goddamn easy. The only cover we had was a 5" dike to hide behind. There was a steady flow

of lead going back and forth and we were jaming [sic] left and right. And when they jam the only thing you can do is poke a cleaning rod down the bore and punch out the empty shell. Borey had the only cleaning rod in our group and he was running up and down the line punching out the bores. I knew he was going to get it and I think he did too. A man needed the cleaning rod and Dave jumped up and started running towards him. As soon as he got up he was hit in the foot. He was about 10 feet in front of me and he called to me and said—Hey Bert I'm hit. He couldn't stay where he was—bullets were hitting the dirt all around him. He had to get back to the dike. I told him to get up and run and I'd shoot grazing fire into the tree line where the VC were. I got three magazines and fired 60 rounds to cover him but as he was running a goddamn VC bullet hit in the back.[68]

The wall of silence had broken. One incident after another eroded public confidence. Senator Peter H. Dominick, a Republican from Colorado, visited Vietnam in May 1967 at roughly the same time that Lance Corporal Borey was shot. Dominick inquired about the M-16. He was told it was a good weapon and was invited to test fire a sample rifle himself. Someone produced an M-16 and handed it to the senator, who tried to fire it. It jammed.[69] In June, members of Ichord's panel held their own test fire with an M-16 provided by Colt's. If any one M-16 might have been expected to perform flawlessly, this should have been it: the test rifle a manufacturer facing congressional investigation presented as a sample to Congress. The subcommittee's rifle jammed several times. No one needed to be told what this might mean in combat. But another GI crystallized for the congressmen a particular species of nightmare:

The other night we got a radio message from one of our night ambushes. . . . The last words they said were, "out of hand grenades, all weapons jammed." The next morning when they got to them, their hands were all skinned up and cut and their stocks on their rifles were all broken from using them as clubs.

As the battlefield accounts piled up, the M-16's reputation sank so low that even troops waiting to ship to Vietnam worried about carrying it.

"I was horrified at the stories of whole units being pushed back because of the inability of the M-16 to sustain a heavy rate of automatic fire without a malfunction," wrote a navy lieutenant undergoing training in California. "It is terrifying and the stories and the opinions of the Marines regarding it have been ruthlessly suppressed. . . . I witnessed on the firing range malfunction after malfunction." A sergeant on predeployment leave wrote Ichord to ask whether he should seek alternative arrangements to fight. "Are we, the troops en route to SE Asia, supposed to arm ourselves with a backup weapon, which is widely done, or can we bet our lives on our M-16?" he wrote. "If you, in your capacity can answer the questions as expeditiously as possible I would certainly appreciate it very much—so would my wife."[70]

Colt's and the army agreed to change after change. The plastic stock would be thickened so it would be less likely to crack. The chamber would be chrome-plated, and then the barrel would be, too. The heavier buffer would be added, to reduce the rate of fire caused by ball powder. The gas tube would be made of stainless steel to resist corrosion. The anodizing on aluminum parts would be upgraded. A better phosphate coating would be applied to the weapon to resist rust.[71] Some of the steps were part of the normal debugging of a rifle. What made them remarkable was that they were being recommended for a rifle that had already been distributed for combat as the primary weapon for tens of thousands of American servicemen. The army and Colt's had effectively put a prototype into mass production, and were fine-tuning it as it failed in the troops' hands. Rifles shipped to Vietnam by late 1967 included some of these features, as one by one the changes were worked into the assembly lines in Hartford. But many changes identified as necessary in 1966 would wait until late 1968 to be incorporated on rifles being sent to the war. The improvements did no good for the thousands of troops carrying rifles issued until that time. Among the men on the line, their fates linked to rifles issued prematurely, anger boiled.[72]

Out in the field beside Ap Sieu Quan, Private First Class Nickelson worked on his jammed rifle. He had given away his position by firing. Bullets raked the grass nearby. He was terrified and enraged. He reached for a grenade, pulled the pin, and threw it as far as he could toward the trees; he hoped its blast would divert the attention of the enemy soldiers. After the explosion, he removed his rifle's magazine and pulled back on the charging handle to look inside the chamber. The empty cartridge was stuck there. He cursed again and reached for his cleaning rod, which he kept taped to the rifle. Around him was chaos. First Platoon was pinned down. Nickelson pushed the rod down the muzzle and knocked the empty cartridge case clear. He returned the magazine to its place and chambered a second round. Again he looked up to fire, and spotted the North Vietnamese soldier in the tree line. The man was on his stomach, prone and firing out at the platoon. Nickelson aimed his M-16 and eased back on the trigger again; firing on automatic, he hoped to hit the man multiple times. The first bullet hit the soldier in the left leg. He watched him roll out of sight into the bushes.

But Nickelson could not finish him. His rifle had jammed again. He reached for another grenade.

Up and down the scattered platoon the Marines' rifles were not working. A few Marines had defied the Marine Corps' orders and managed to acquire M-14s. These men were able to provide a degree of protection for the rest, but could not produce the volume of fire needed to push off the NVA. Staff Sergeant Elrod radioed the company commander and told him that his platoon had casualties and was stopped. He asked for an air strike on the village. The Marines of First Platoon backed away, putting distance between them and Ap Sieu Quan. Perhaps twenty NVA soldiers with automatic Kalashnikovs had turned back a Marine Corps rifle company. Two helicopters tried to land, one to carry off wounded Marines and another to drop off more ammunition. Both faced fire from the village and from among the vegetation. As they alighted, rocket-propelled grenades flashed out of the tree line and exploded in the landing zone. One helicopter was damaged. The pilots lurched their airframes back into the air and veered off, rotors thumping. The platoon pulled back farther. Two more helicopters arrived and hovered above the grass, noses high, while their crews dumped supplies off the back ramps. This was war in the assault-rifle era; the NVA volume of rifle fire was intensive enough that the company needed heavy fire support. After the helicopters were gone, Hotel Company escalated, with mortars, artillery, and the air strike that Elrod had asked for. Explosions flashed in the village and heaved rubble into the air. Ap Sieu Quan fell silent. The NVA soldiers slipped away.

Hotel Company stood. It had suffered miserably. Five Marines were dead, thirty were wounded.[73] Private First Class Nickelson had survived. He rose to his feet but left his jammed rifle in the dirt. He had arrived in Vietnam a month before. Until that day, he had never handled this kind of rifle. In the United States, the Marine Corps had trained him on an M-14. In his one previous firefight, his M-16 had jammed, too—after firing a single round. He had been in two firefights against NVA soldiers with automatic rifles, and he had managed to fire only three rounds back. What good was a rifle that did not work? Nickelson was new to war. He was no fool. He understood this was not right. A rifle that failed in battle was worse than useless. It was detestable. As far as he was concerned it was a discard. Upon arriving in Vietnam and before being assigned to the battalion, Nickelson had bought a .38 revolver from a soldier who was rotating home. He would carry that until the Marine Corps could give him a rifle he could trust.

An officer ordered him to pick up his M-16. Nickelson was incredulous.

"*Fuck* you," he said.

An argument broke out at the edge of the smoking village. Nickelson refused to carry a rifle that did not work. Other Marines intervened. Hotel Company had enough problems. A compromise was reached—he would carry an M79 grenade launcher. Someone produced his new weapon. The Marine who had carried it had been shot; it was available for anyone else's use. Nickelson slung it and walked into Ap Sieu Quan. The village had been partially rubbled. Shattered ceramic roofing tiles littered the ground. Blood-splattered trails showed where the North Vietnamese soldiers had dragged their dead away. A few chickens wandered the scene, the only remaining inhabitants. The Marines caught them, lit a fire from bits of rubble, and began to cook their birds. Nickelson settled into his new weapon. He would never carry an M-16 again.

By the time helicopters flew back to the USS *Tripoli* on July 26, the mood in Hotel Company was dark. The company's executive officer, Lieutenant Chervenak, had queried each platoon in Ap Sieu Quan and learned that forty rifles had jammed during the battle. *Forty rifles.* Roughly a quarter of the company had been under fire and unable to fight back. The officers in other companies in Second Battalion, Third Marines told him of similar problems in their own firefights during Operation Bear Chain.

Lieutenant Chervenak, lean and athletic, had taken a roundabout route to the infantry. Raised in west central Pennsylvania, he had been the quarterback of his high school football team, and then attended Pennsylvania State University on a military scholarship. After he completed the basic infantry course required of all Marine officers, the Corps assigned him to naval flight school in Pensacola, Florida. He hoped to fly jets. It was not to be. The Marine Corps needed more pilots for helicopters than for jets. He was assigned to the helicopter course. An assignment to flight school was coveted, one of the professional plums for a young military officer in the United States. When Lieutenant Chervenak learned he would not fly jets, he immediately did something officers in good standing at flight school rarely do. He quit. He asked for orders to the infantry. Soon he was en route to Vietnam.[74]

In May 1967, he arrived in Okinawa as one of the replacements assigned to restore the battalion to fighting strength after the fights for Hills 861 and 881. For the first time he saw an M-16. He started hearing the harrowing accounts. He also discovered that troops were buying M-14s from rear-echelon and aviation units that still carried them. Lieutenant Chervenak was new to the unit; he reserved judgment until he could see M-16s in action himself. But he sensed something was deeply wrong. The Marine Corps was organized around its rifles. The rifleman was at the center of its identity, training, and lore. And Marines were trying to get their rifles on a black market?

The Corps' reaction similarly stumped him. The Marine Corps had not been interested in the M-16 throughout the early 1960s.[75] But once the Pentagon took its decision, the Corps' generals adopted the Beltway stance. A din of complaints about M-16 jamming had risen from the ranks. The generals' replies mixed paternalistic denials that the M-16 was failing with strong defenses of the weapon's merits. The senior officers followed the army's pattern: They blamed the troops for the weapons' problems. At a press conference in Da Nang just after the battles for Hills 861 and 881, one highly decorated commander, Lieutenant General Lewis W. Walt of the Third Marine Amphibious Force, delivered a classic performance of an officer who has lost touch with his men. First he declared that the Marines in his command were "100 percent sold" on the M-16. Most of those who had relied on the weapon in battle, he added, "have nothing but praise for it." This can be read only as a lie. General Walt pressed on. He put blame for malfunctions squarely upon individual Marines and their officers and noncommissioned officers, saying they either had not adequately maintained their rifles or had tried to force too many rounds into their magazines. This was a slap at the men at war. In a booming slip of the tongue, General Walt added that "rumors" of unsatisfactory M-16 performance were started "by a very, very small majority."[76] Not long after the press conference, General Walt was reassigned to Washington and elevated to the post of the Corps' assistant commandant. In July, the commandant of the Marine Corps, General Greene, repeated General Walt's position, calling the M-16 "ideally suited" for the jungle warfare of Vietnam. The brass had set a tone. With the generals standing behind the M-16, complaints had little chance of finding a supporting audience. The young Marines in Vietnam were on their own.

The brass's position was reflected down the chain of command and in the army, too. One officer responsible for the Twenty-fifth Infantry Division's public statements described an official prohibition against mentioning M-16 malfunctions. This was a subject not to be broached in any army comments or in conversations with journalists, along with other topics officially deemed too unsettling for the public's ears: "the defeat of U.S. units," "B-52 and other bombing errors," "female VC," "very young VC," and the "use of flamethrowers, hand-held or track-mounted."

> MACV* told all information officers prior to my arrival that the M16 was not a topic for discussion. Newsmen were not to question soldiers about the weapon. No stories about the rifle jamming or malfunctioning were to be written.
>
> This was done despite the fact that many GIs hated the M16, felt they couldn't trust it. And until an order stopped the procedure, carried their own weapons instead: carbines, 45 caliber grease guns, rifles sent from home, captured AK47s, et cetera.
>
> At the same time the Army launched an all out propaganda campaign to make GIs in Vietnam more confident in the weapon they

---

*Military Assistance Command, Vietnam.

basically mistrusted. Special classes on the weapon were held in the units, new cleaning procedures were instigated, new lubricating materials were introduced. . . . A whole new campaign was initiated to instill in the American soldier the utmost confidence in a weapon that he didn't like.[77]

The Marines in General Walt's small majority, meanwhile, suffered on. They knew the truth was being suppressed. After being brought back to fighting strength in May, Second Battalion, Third Marines embarked on ships and sailed again toward Vietnam. While en route, the officers organized their own tests. The enlisted Marines cleaned their weapons repeatedly over several days. The fire team leaders and squad leaders looked over each rifle. On the ship's flight deck, platoon sergeants and platoon commanders inspected the rifles again. Each was parade-ground clean. Then the company commander and either the battalion commander or battalion executive officer repeated the step. At last the Marines were allowed to fire their M-16s off their ship's fantail. As many as 40 percent of the rifles jammed.[78]

Back on board the USS *Tripoli* after Hotel Company had suffered thirty-five casualties at Ap Sieu Quan, Lieutenant Chervenak seethed. He cleaned up and visited the stateroom where Captain Culver was bunking. The two officers talked about the M-16s' malfunctions. Lieutenant Chervenak asked for advice. What would Captain Culver think if he wrote a letter to newspapers and to Congress detailing the company's experiences? The Marine Corps was not helping its Marines. The truth about the M-16 needed to be told, somehow, if the problem was ever to be fixed. Captain Culver, a former enlisted man, was the son of a Marine. His father had enlisted in 1918 at the age of fifteen. Raised on Marine Corps bases and now commanding a company at war, he was more than reluctant to speak outside the chain of command. It was an agonizing thought. But Captain Culver knew Lieutenant Chervenak was right. Writing a letter, he told his executive officer, was a good idea.

Lieutenant Chervenak found a typewriter in the chaplain's stateroom. The captain and he composed a draft. When they finished, he climbed belowdecks to the enlisted quarters, and asked Staff Sergeant Elrod to read it.

I am a Marine First Lieutenant and have been serving in a rifle company in Vietnam since the 15th of May. Ever since my arrival, immediately following the battle of hill 881, one controversy has loomed above all others—that of the M-16 rifle.

I feel that is my duty and responsibility to report the truth about this rifle as I have seen it. My conscience will not let me rest any longer.

The idea of a lightweight automatic weapon is a fine idea and I do not categorically reject the M-16 rifle as being useless. I do believe, however, that there is a basic mechanical deficiency within the weapon which causes a failure to extract. This failure to extract a spent casing from the chamber allows another round to be fed in behind the unextracted casing causing the rifle to jam. When this occurs, a cleaning and rod and precious seconds are needed to clear the weapon. A marine in a firefight does not have those precious seconds.

We are constantly told that improper cleaning and unfamiliarity with the weapon cause any malfunction which may occur. Any rifle that requires cleaning to the degree they speak of has no place as a combat weapon. I believe that the cold, hard facts about the M-16 are clouded over by a fabrication of the truth for political and financial considerations. I have seen too many marines hiding behind a paddy dike trying to clear their rifle to accept those explanations any longer.

Our battalion has test fired these rifles on numerous occasions, aboard the ship and in the field, to try to find a solution to this problem. All rifles were cleaned and inspected prior to these tests. Having supervised several of these tests, I will swear to the fact that at least 25 to 40% of the rifles malfunctioned at least once under these optimum conditions.

During a recent fight on the 21st of July, no fewer than 40 men in my company reported to me that their rifles had malfunctioned because of failure to extract. Because of these inoperative rifles we were severely hampered in our efforts to extract a platoon which had been pinned down. Lack of sufficient firepower also caused us great difficulty in getting our casualties out. Having 40 rifles malfunction in any rifle company is a serious matter, and in an understrengthened company such as ours, the gravity of the situation is greatly increased. This problem is increasing in its seriousness and I know that is a major morale problem in the company. Unfortunately, all our complaints and the results of our tests never seem to reach willing ears.

I do not mean for this letter to slap at my battalion, the Marine Corps, the Colt Manufacturing Company, the Defense Department or anyone else concerned.

It is written out of concern for the safety of the men in my company and of the great morale problem that the M-16 causes. I will stand and stake my reputation on the fact that we have had men wounded and perhaps killed because of inoperative rifles. The men in my company have absolutely no confidence in the weapon they carry, and yet, they will be asked to go on another operation in the very near future carrying this very same weapon. Word will come down from higher up, however, stating that no one will take a negative attitude about the M-16, nor will they speak of the weapon in a derogatory manner to any newsman.

I can only hope that men such as yourself, who are in a position to do something, WILL do something. The search for the truth is paramount in all of us and I ask you to look into this problem and search for the truth there. I will stand behind every word that I have written. I think that this problem has been overlooked too long and too many attempts have been made to gloss over a situation that endangers the lives of men.[79]

Staff Sergeant Elrod finished the letter. He had served ten years in the Marine Corps. He had seen lieutenants come and go, and had a strong sense of how the officer ranks worked. Loyalty, by his reading of the inside game, meant working hard and shutting up. He handed the letter back to his executive officer. He liked it very much. "Hey, sir?" he said. "You're not planning to make the Marine Corps a career, are you?"

On July 27, Lieutenant Chervenak mailed four copies of the letter. He sent one to the *Barnesboro Star,* his hometown newspaper in Pennsylvania. He mailed another to the *Washington Post.* The last two went to Senator Robert F. Kennedy and Representative Ichord. On all four he signed his name officially: First Lieutenant Michael P. Chervenak, executive officer, H Company, Second Battalion, Third Marines.[80]

In all of the available records surrounding the bloody introduction of the M-16 to American military service, this stands as one of the few brave and candidly honest acts. The officers behind Project AGILE had produced a report no follow-up studies could support. General Johnson had quietly ordered the rifle into service knowing that it was unreliable. Colonel Hallock and Colonel Yount had enforced a hush about the M-16's many performance problems, even while agreeing that the weapons' failures were getting American soldiers killed. Officials at Colt's were insisting in public that the weapon worked well while they reviewed internal reports that said it did not. It fell to a twenty-three-year-old Marine lieutenant, his unit thinned by casualties while their rifles jammed, to stake his name on the truth.

That summer, when the Marines of Second Battalion, Third Marines returned to the bush, fewer of them carried the M-16. They defied policy and tried all manner of schemes to acquire M-14s, or anything else. Private First Class Nickelson continued to carry his grenade launcher and his .38. Few wanted an M-16; a rumor even circulated that the rifles were not made by Colt's but by Mattel, the manufacturer of plastic toys. For those who could not find an alternative weapon, the problems persisted. Private First Class Thomas C. Tomakowski, a radio operator in Hotel Company, was in a firefight and his M-16 froze, leaving him with only his wits with which to fight. A wounded North Vietnamese soldier surrendered to him.[81] Tomakowski pointed his jammed rifle at the prisoner and pretended all was fine, hoping the man would not change his mind. In Foxtrot Company, Second Lieutenant Charles Woodard, a platoon commander, carried an AK-47 on a mission, having made his own judgment about the relative effectiveness of the rifles available in Vietnam, no matter what the generals said.[82]

And during the heat of 1967, another officer, Second Lieutenant Charles P. Chritton, also of Foxtrot Company, began to have a recurring dream, which flowed from one of his own worst episodes. On June 28, one of his Marines had been killed while on a flanking move against a group of Viet Cong guerrillas on a ridge. A pair of Marines had swung far to the left during the firefight. They dashed through vegetation and surprised the guerrillas at close range. But as the Marine opened fire his M-16 seized up. One round did not extract and the rifle tried to feed a round in behind it, leaving the Marine with a jam that would take many seconds, even minutes, to clear. He was helpless. The Viet Cong turned and killed him. After recovering the Marine's body and the jammed rifle, Lieutenant Chritton allowed his fury to guide him. He and other Marines carried the dead Marine and his rifle to the battalion command post and entered the tent to confront the battalion commander with the facts. The commander and the executive officer pulled the lieutenant aside, away from the Marine's corpse. The executive officer produced a camera, placed the jammed rifle on a table, and made a series of photographs. "We'll take care of this," the commander told him. But nothing had come of it, and soon Lieutenant Chritton's dream started to follow him through his nights. In it, he was home in the United States, and he had kidnapped the president of Colt's and forced him to admit that Colt's was knowingly selling bad rifles to the government. Lieutenant Chritton was hardly the irrational sort. He certainly was no criminal. He left the Marine Corps and went on to a long civilian career as a lawyer. The dream stayed with him for his remaining months in Vietnam, and it visited him intermittently after he returned home to the United States.

Back in Washington, Representative Ichord's subcommittee ground toward its conclusion. The army had stonewalled the congressmen in many ways as they held hearings and lobbed correspondence back and forth with the Pentagon. Important witnesses were never produced. (Colonel Hallock, the supervisor of Project AGILE who later proposed and enforced a cover-up, avoided scrutiny. On May 31, as complaints from Vietnam reached high pitch, he retired.)[83] Many witnesses who did appear seemed to have been selected because they were not inclined to help understand the problems. The army produced a small stream of officers who insisted that the M-16 was excellent and dependable; those who had had the bad experiences under fire were kept away. Colonel Yount, who had been relieved of his duties by the army, did testify, but largely downplayed the scale of the problems and tried to assure the panel that solutions were well in place. The subcommittee emanated disgust. The congressmen understood viscerally that the M-16's performance in Vietnam was much worse than the army acknowledged, and that the army had not remedied the weapon's many early problems. On October 19 they published a scalding report. The report declared that the M-16's malfunctions were "serious and excessive" and labeled the army and Marine Corps negligent for failing to provide adequate cleaning gear and weapons-cleaning instruction. It scolded the army for not properly notifying the Marine Corps of the documented problems with the M-16 while encouraging the Marines to carry it, too. On one matter, the report accused the army of criminal negligence: the agreement between Rock Island Arsenal and Colt's to use cartridges packed with IMR powder for acceptance testing at the factory, knowing that the weapons would fire cartridges containing ball powder in Vietnam.[84] Representative William G. Bray, a Republican from Indiana and a subcommittee member, called the collusion "one of the most incredible and inexcusable exercises in duplicity I have ever seen."[85]

Ichord's subcommittee did not get everything right. Its emphasis on the IMR–ball powder controversy implicitly missed other causes of jamming, including problems related to corrosion. It attached little importance to chroming the bore and chamber. It did not examine the question of whether the ammunition cases were manufactured to a satisfactory standard, and whether their alloy was soft and prone to expansion and lodging snugly in the chamber when fired. But teasing out precise causes was difficult, especially in a short period of time and with the army unhelpful.* The report did succeed in capturing the broader institutional failure: The M-16 had been developed and distributed through a weak and troubled system, a system in which officers and officials alike neglected basic duties.

---

*What really caused the jamming? Ichord emphasized ball powder, a factor that a subsequent writer, James Fallows, endorsed. Thomas L. McNaugher, in his rigorous 1984 study, *The M16 Controversies: Military Organizations and Weapons Acquisition,* emphasized maintenance and noted that by 1970 the rifle was widely considered reliable. The most likely cause for most of the reported problems, based on the records now available, and the accounts of veterans, would seem to be corrosion in the rifles' chambers. This was caused in some cases by cleaning habits in the wet climate of Vietnam, but from a manufacturing perspective was related more strongly to the failure of the army and Colt's to chrome-plate the chambers of all M-16s leaving Hartford until late in 1968. Another likely factor contributing to the failures to extract, though as far as is publicly known the army never conducted extensive tests of the cartridge cases from 1966 to 1968, was that the ammunition cases were too soft and expanded under the pressures of firing, lodging into pitting and tool marks in the chamber. This intriguing and thoughtful theory was set forth by R. Blake Stevens and Edward C. Ezell in *The Black Rifle.* The rifle's inherently poor resistance to corrosion and insufficient ammunition standards likely combined to create the most intractable jams. Rifle cleaning habits were in all likelihood much less of a factor, considering that the same troops, when using M-14s in the same environments, reported few reliability problems. By 1970, when McNaugher noted that the M-16s in Vietnam were performing reliably, the many manufacturing changes meant that in many ways the troops were carrying a different rifle than what had been issued in 1966 and 1967.

The existing command structure was either inadequate or inoperative. The division of responsibility makes it almost impossible to
pinpoint responsibility when mistakes are made. There is substantial
evidence of lack of activity on the part of responsible officials of
highest authority even when the problems of the M-16 and its ammunition came to their attention. It appears that under the present
system problems are too slowly recognized and reactions to problems
are even slower.

Twelve days after the release of Ichord's report, on October 29, the
Washington Post, the newspaper of the nation's political class, published
Lieutenant Chervenak's letter.[86] His words had an instant effect. The Marine Corps opened an investigation—not into the causes of the rifle's failures or the slow reaction by the chain of command to troops' complaints,
but into the officer who dared to write to the *Washington Post.* General
Greene personally called the battalion, looking for Lieutenant Chervenak. By chance the lieutenant was on a rest period in Japan. The brass
could not find him. An investigating officer was assigned and canvassed
Marines in the battalion, taking sworn statements. He could establish no
real wrongdoing. Telling the truth was not legally forbidden, it was just
discouraged to tell the truth this way. The offense was a matter of protocol, not of law. When Lieutenant Chervenak returned, the battalion
executive officer presented him a letter of reprimand for failure to follow
proper channels.[87] Lieutenant Chervenak was unmoved. He listened politely. When the major handed the letter to him he did not bother to read
it. He was not by nature a troublemaker. But he knew that given the same
circumstances, he would do the same thing again.

The letter's effects did not stop there. In the unwritten rules of the
Beltway, the publication of Lieutenant Chervenak's claims in the *Washington Post* gave them a heft that dozens of other claims did not have.[88]
The Marine Corps began facing facts it had ignored. On December 3,
a pair of representatives from Colt's and the Marine Corps caught up
with the battalion at a base outside Da Nang. They had been ordered to
follow up on the lieutenant's allegations. Marines gathered in the theater for a presentation, at which the Marine Corps representative, a warrant officer, opened with the familiar lines. He told his audience that
the M-16 was a good rifle and if it was failing it was because they were

not cleaning it adequately. The Marines shouted and jeered. A near riot
ensued. The battalion commander demanded order and quiet. The representative from Colt's, Kanemitsu Ito, was so shaken he dared not take
notes.

The warrant officer and Ito held their own technical inspection, and
Marines filed by to show them their rifles. Ito was a war veteran himself,
and a former test officer in the army's ordnance service. He was small,
lean, and muscular, a fastidious forty-seven-year-old man with a record of
bravery who had roamed Vietnam for his employer, trying to understand
why Colt's rifles had performed so badly since at least 1966. He was conscientious to an almost excruciating degree. As the Marines filed past to
show him rifles that had failed them, he worried that the troops might label
him a profiteer as he and the warrant officer condemned pitted rifles. After
all, he thought, every rifle to be replaced might be seen as another sale for
Colt's. He decided to let the warrant officer do most of the talking. Quietly,
out of the center of attention, he watched. That night, emotionally and
physically exhausted, Ito typed a letter and sent it back to Colt's. He had
important news to share. What Lieutenant Chervenak had written to the
Washington Post was not quite right. Matters were actually much worse.

> I walked into a den of angry, feroucious [sic] lions when I visited the
> 2nd Battalion of the 3rd Marines. It was really a touchy situation. I
> would never ask anyone else to be in the situation I was in. The of-
> ficers and a great majority of the men hated the M-16A1 rifles. They
> had a right to hate it. The chambers of the rifles were so badly pitted
> that the only thing they could use the rifles were for a club.[89]

The examination of 445 rifles found that many had "chambers that
looked like the surface of the moon"; 286 rifles were immediately condemned as unfit for combat use. Ito understood how serious this was. He
sought as much information as he could get. He looked for Lieutenant
Chervenak, but by then the lieutenant had been reassigned out of Hotel
Company, and Ito could not find him. Ito read a copy of the battalion's investigation and discovered it contained ninety-six sworn statements from
Marines who agreed with the lieutenant's letter. If this were not enough, in
Hotel Company, where Lieutenant Chervenak had written of 40 jammed
rifles, his letter was more than vindicated: 67 of the company's 85 rifles

were so pitted that the warrant officer and Ito replaced them on the spot. And the charge that Marines had not been cleaning their rifles could find no traction here. The company commander during Operation Bear Chain, Captain Culver, had been a member of the Marine Corps' Rifle Team— a bunch of crack shots. Captain Culver was almost religious about forcing his Marines to clean their weapons. To him, any suggestion otherwise was a personal insult. ("To say that I had high standards of weapons cleanliness was an extreme understatement," he said.)[90] He warned the warrant officer not to blame the Marines again. They were the victims, the captain thought, not the culprits.

With unfiltered information about the M-16 now reaching General Greene, the commandant reversed himself. Ito could feel the tension. "Phone calls and secret messages were flying all over the Marine Corps area," he wrote. The Corps had decided to replace all of its M-16s. Rifles in the Corps' possession in Okinawa were "to be air lifted ASAP" to replace the rifles in Marines' hands in Vietnam, Ito reported. The Corps also put in a request to Colt's for twenty thousand rifles with chromed chambers. Ito saw the problems for what they were. His correspondence to Colt's did nothing to sugarcoat them. But he was in a difficult position. Colt's had wanted him to distribute surveys about the rifle. A lockdown was in place.

The questionnaires are out of the question. The M-16 rifle is a very hot topic over here. They don't want any names or units put on paper. I have been asked not to put anything down on paper. Unit COs [commanding officers] and staff officers forbid the use of the questionnaires. I go into the field armed (would you believe) with an M-16 rifle, when I can get one. Everything that I inspect and see, I must keep in my head until I can get to a place to write it down.[91]

Ito's letters suggest that he was a man of conscience. He had been telling his bosses at Colt's in clear terms for more than a year that the M-16 had real problems, and now he knew that these problems were worse than what the military or Colt's had ever publicly said. He had fought in Korea and been awarded a Silver Star. He was a professional engineer who had worked closely on the M-16, including working on ways to prevent malfunctioning. (At Colt's, between trips to Vietnam, he had designed a gauge to measure the dimension of a magazine to ensure it would feed the

M-16 optimally and reduce the incidence of jamming.)[92] He understood the anger of men who could not trust their rifles. A few days after meeting the Marines, he forced himself to confront the failures more personally. He visited the hospitals, to see men who thought that Colt's and the Pentagon had let them down at the most important moments of their lives. He wrote back to the States, hinting at his pain.

> Every time I think that I am tired, I do these things. As I said I have a lot of guts. I wished that others had the guts to look at things I see or ask questions. Some had reasons to hate me yet they like me because I am helping—a few don't really know. I don't know what to say to them—there are people with no arms, legs, faces and the rest. These are some of the places I go to find the information I need. I go every place, but I sure wouldn't ask anyone else to do it. . . .
>   . . . It is difficult working 18–20 hours a day—7 days a week. Any time I am tired I go back to the 24th, 93rd Evac or the 3rd Field Hospitals.[93]

Ito returned to the United States for Christmas and re-entered the delicate game of pretending things were better than they were. This remained Colt's posture. Even as late as summer 1967, while complaints of jamming rose to a roar, Colt's executives had been briefing journalists as if nothing were wrong. They told the executive editor of *Popular Mechanics* that they had received "no official complaints from their customer—the Department of Defense."[94] On December 28, Ito and Paul Benke, Colt's president, met at the Pentagon with officers from around the services involved in the M-16 program. Ito's presentation was direct: The new buffers were reaching many units, but severe problems persisted. About 70 percent of the rifles in the Marines' possession, he said, "should be condemned due to pitted chambers." More than one-fourth of the M-16 magazines in Vietnam should be condemned. He said he had seen several units that were still short of cleaning gear. He further noted that the army had no formal system for reporting M-16 malfunctions. This point raised a searing question. Now, two years after the problems had been identified, did the army's data, and its statements about the rates of failure, reflect anything like the truth?*

---

* The United States Army in the Republic of Vietnam would not require soldiers to report M-16

In the end, Kanemitsu Ito was a midlevel engineer. He could describe what he had seen. He could share what he knew. But Benke, the man who ran Colt's Firearms Division, would get the last word. Benke interjected. He told the military officers present that "the observations were based on very brief contact, hearsay, and single pieces of evidence, and that final conclusions would require added review and investigation."[95] By this time, Benke had been receiving frank, descriptive accounts of M-16 failures from his teams in Vietnam for more than a year. The accounts had come from multiple engineers—from Fremont, Hall, Behrendt, and others—and from multiple trips. Each of his company sources had relayed the remarks and experiences of many soldiers. Ito was neither treading new ground nor trafficking in rumor. He was sharing carefully observed details consistent with what others had seen and said. In November 1966, Benke had received a memo from another Colt's engineer, which summarized "discussions with one brigade commander, four battalion commanders and many other field and company grade officers." The memo specified "changes and things which should be expedited," including chrome-plating the bore and chamber, installing new buffers, and applying a better protective finish. More than a year had passed. Thousands of troops in Vietnam still had rifles without these improvements. They continued to suffer malfunctions. Colt's position, at the late date of December 1967, was now a matter of record: The reports of problems, even when supported by his own engineer fresh from Vietnam, were "hearsay."

More than forty years later, Paul Benke disagreed with any reading of the record that suggests that Colt's was not forthright and conscientious, or sold the Pentagon rifles unfit for combat duty in Vietnam. The M-16 rifle program suffered from problems, he said, but these problems were related to interservice rivalries, inadequate troop training, and bureaucratic opposition to the rifle within military circles. The problems with the rifle's reputation were exacerbated, he said, by the fact that he was opposed to the American involvement in Vietnam.

As for design or manufacturing shortcomings, he said: "We did have

---

malfunctions officially until spring 1968, making the military's data throughout the worst period of M-16 malfunctions, in 1966 and 1967, of dubious value.

some problems, including the corrosion of the aluminum receiver. The measure of them was not so much to cause a Congressional investigation." He also said the path the rifle took from the ArmaLite prototypes to the rifles issued in Vietnam was such that it was not exhaustively tested by the Army's ordnance corps, in part because the ordnance community resisted the rifle in both concept and particulars. "The M-16 never went through the testing process that other rifles had undergone," he said. "Had it gone through the normal cycle of introduction, it probably would have been a different rifle." As for the complaints by troops in Vietnam, like those of Hotel Company, Second Battalion, Third Marines, he said, "I think many of the tales have been exaggerated. We took them all seriously, but—" and he spoke about the political quarrels the company faced in Washington. When provided a copy of Ito's correspondence and of the memorandum of record from the meeting he attended with Ito in the Pentagon in December 1967, he said, "We never ever ever tried to hide anything." Their only concern, he said, was that soldiers had the best possible rifle.[96]

Several weeks after Benke and Ito appeared at the Pentagon, the Viet Cong and the North Vietnamese Army launched the Tet Offensive, striking scores of American and South Vietnamese positions across the country simultaneously. Tens of thousands of communist fighters had coordinated an action. In the matter of a rifle, the defending American troops, after several years in Vietnam, still did not have a fully reliable firepower match. Matters were more dire for the Americans' Vietnamese allies, who often were armed with surplus weapons from World War II. One of the senior South Vietnamese officers, Lieutenant General Dong Van Khuyen, lamented his soldiers' predicament against the better-armed foe. "During the enemy Tet offensive of 1968 the crisp, rattling sounds of the AK-47s echoing in Saigon and some other cities," he said, "seemed to make a mockery of the weaker, single shots of Garands and carbines fired by stupefied friendly troops."[97] With Tet, the war had changed. The American and South Vietnamese forces were not defeated in the field, and the South Vietnamese government did not fall, as the architects of the communist offensive had hoped. But the communists' ability to mass and fight shocked Washington, which had never expected the war to be this hard, or its foes this capable.

By late in 1968, the M-16 was performing better than it had, but it was far from good enough, and it was late. Survey teams were finding a higher level of satisfaction with the M-16. New troops arriving in Vietnam had been trained on the rifle, cleaning gear was available, and the rifles now had chromium-plated bores and the new buffer. The worst problems were past. But throughout the year, more problems were still reported—not at the rate of 1966 and 1967, but alarming nonetheless. A battalion in the 199th Infantry Brigade had seventeen rifles blow up on an operation conducted in muddy terrain and wet weather, and apparently water or mud had clogged the barrels.[98] The rifle, for all of its modifications, struggled to function when exposed to the worst sorts of field conditions. In Hotel Company of Second Battalion, Third Marines, Corporal Jack Beavers was in a battle in Quang Tri province on July 7, 1968. The NVA were firing artillery at the Marines, and as the corporal crouched and crawled to stay alive, his M-16 became coated with sand. Later, as his platoon assaulted across a rice paddy toward a village, the rifle jammed. So did the M-16s of other Marines around him. As Marines dropped, felled by NVA fire, he picked up their M-16s, only to have those rifles jam, too. Corporal Beavers went through three or four M-16s before the fighting stopped.[99] Seven Marines in Hotel Company died that day, including his best friend, Lance Corporal Gerald L. Baldwin, who was shot several times.

In autumn 1968, Ito was back in Vietnam, where he and another Colt's field representative toured military units around Saigon. They found that many magazines did not seat well on the weapons, which caused M-16s to fail to feed when fired on automatic. They found problems with the selector switch, which was often difficult to turn. And, even after all of the changes, they found that "quite a few rifles are rusting or corroding," especially around the selector switch. In a tape sent back to Colt's offices, Ito said that "damaged or poor functioning parts were noted in rifles which were only in use for two months maximum."[100]

The Pentagon eventually accepted that M-16s would jam at higher rates than it or its soldiers would have liked. One investigation early in the year found that during a seven-hour firefight near Chu Lai, Company D of the Fifth Battalion, Seventh Cavalry suffered many jammed weapons, and some were so severe that by the end of the firefight, of the sixty-five or seventy M-16s fired, "twelve were out of action." The Pentagon noted that "this was directly related to the inordinate amount of sand which was built up in the weapons during the rapid movement through the dikes and rice fields." "From past observations and tests," the official assessment continued, "it is known that small arms have difficulty in functioning satisfactorily in a severe sand environment."[101]

Such was the state of resignation. The M-16, which at the start of the war had been a symbol of innovation and technical promise, had become instead a symbol of the mix-ups of war, and of a dishonest Pentagon and a manufacturer with which it worked. As public opinion on the war shifted, America's undependable rifle became another element of disaffection, a symbol of failure for a military that had won World War II and for a nation that believed its industry was among the best in the world. It was a demoralizing comedown, as one embittered officer wrote:

> The M-16 sure is a marvelous gun,
> and in a god-awful war
> it provides some keen fun.
>
> The bullet it fires appears too small to harm
> but it makes a big hole
> and can tear off an arm.
>
> Single shot, semi, or full automatic,
> a real awesome weapon,
> 'tho in performance sporadic.
>
> But listen to Ichord and forget that stuck bolt,
> for you aren't as important
> as a kickback from Colt.
>
> So carry your rifle (they don't give a damn),
> just pray you won't need it
> while you're in Vietnam.
>
> The M-16 is issue, though we all feel trapped.
> More GIs would protest,
> but somehow they got zapped.[102]

* * *

Several months after the fight for Ap Sieu Quan, Staff Sergeant Elrod was reassigned from Hotel Company's First Platoon to become the battalion's intelligence chief, and was meritoriously promoted, to the rank of gunnery sergeant. The battalion continued to operate against the NVA in the provinces just south of North Vietnam. Throughout this time, he refused to carry an M-16. He had seen too many M-16s jam in too many fights, and lost too many Marines. After the battalion's rifles were replaced in December 1967, the newer rifles performed better, but many Marines still had problems, and the rifles with chromed chambers would not be available for months. The M-16 remained a bitter subject.

One day in spring 1968, after a skirmish in a gully near Khe Sanh, Gunnery Sergeant Elrod found an AK-47 beside a dead North Vietnamese soldier. The rifle was in excellent condition. He claimed it as his own, along with several magazines. This was not a trophy. It was a tool. Now he had an assault rifle he could depend on. The AK-47 did not solve all his problems. It solved one problem but replaced it with another. There was a special danger related to carrying the enemy's weapon: The M-16 and the AK-47 have distinctly different sounds, and whenever Gunnery Sergeant Elrod fired his new weapon, he risked drawing fire from other Marines. He considered this less of a risk than carrying a rifle that might not fire at all.

A few weeks later, Gunnery Sergeant Elrod was walking across a forward operating base near Khe Sanh with his AK-47 slung across his back. A lieutenant colonel stopped him.

"Gunny, why the hell are you carrying that?" he asked.

"Because it works," Gunnery Sergeant Elrod replied.

"It's going to get you killed," the colonel said.

Gunnery Sergeant Elrod knew something about how Marines were getting killed. In his experience, this was not one of the ways.

"Sir," he said. "My Marines know what my weapon sounds like. *And it works.*"

And that was the basic position from which any discussion about automatic rifles began and ended. It was well and good to design a rifle that fired bullets at tremendous velocity, or could achieve exceptional accuracy over substantial range. Soldiers would welcome a rifle that was especially lethal, just as they would praise a rifle that managed to be lightweight, or sturdy, or had recoil so slight that it almost could not be perceived. But none of these traits meant much if the rifle could not be relied upon to fire when a Marine pulled its trigger. If a rifle could not be trusted, its other characteristics were moot. Being a bayonet holder was not enough.

Gunnery Sergeant Elrod kept his AK-47 that day, and he carried it for several more months. He set it aside only when he rotated back to the United States.

CHAPTER 8

Everyman's Gun

Q: You said you killed an army officer?

A: *He was on a treetop on a small mountain near Kilak, Okidi Hill. The commander was in a tree. He was on a patrol or an observation post.*

Q: What happened?

A: *We were three. We came from behind. We saw him and he didn't see us. The commander was using his radio. The officer was not alone— the others were down below, cooking. They opened fire on us.*

Q: And then?

A: *The officer fell from the tree. It was my accurate fire that shot the officer.*

Q: After you knew he was dead, and the fighting was over that day, what did you think of the operation?

A: *I was so happy because I knew I would be promoted.*

Q: What was your new rank?

A: *I didn't get promoted.*

Q: There were other operations?

A: *My own group killed my mother. It was announced on the radio. I was involved in a raid, and later I learned my mother had died in the raid.*

—Notes from author's interview with Walter Ocira, a child soldier in the Lord's Resistance Army, in northeastern Uganda in 2007

THE EIGHT YOUNG PALESTINIAN MEN, DRESSED IN TRACK SUITS, reached the barrier outside Munich's Olympic Village in the darkness just after 4:00 A.M. on September 5. The fence was neither tall nor topped with razor wire, and an easy climb for a young man, even a young man with a duffel bag. The athletes and officials participating in the 1972 Summer Olympics slept on the other side. Though the compound was guarded, the security was relaxed, even casual. The West German government, eager to exorcise the memories of Hitler's Olympics in Berlin in 1936, had chosen a low-key police posture: an unarmed security staff, unimposing barriers, a climate of trust and accommodation rather than suspicion and control. The organizers had dubbed the competition "The Carefree Games." Like this motto, the public-relations ambition was unsubtle. The XX Olympiad was to be a global affirmation of Bavaria reborn, and a declaration of decency for a nation that had returned from fascism to the civilized world.

The men in the track suits were members of the Black September terrorist organization, a recently assembled cell directed to exploit the Games' officially friendly atmosphere. A police reconstruction would later claim that two of the cell's members had infiltrated the village weeks before and taken temporary jobs on the Olympic staff. The commander, Luttif Afif, a thirty-five-year-old émigré who had lived in West Germany for several years, had worked as an engineer; his deputy was a cook.[1] Afif had patiently watched this same section of fence the night before and observed athletes returning from parties outside. The athletes had scaled the barrier, dropped into the compound, and continued toward their apartments. No guard had stopped them. They passed unchallenged into the secure zone. Afif decided that his cell would imitate this behavior. The killers would masquerade as athletes coming home.

That night, before leaving their hotel, the Arabs slipped into athletic suits and packed their weapons into gym bags printed with the Olympic logo. Into each duffel they stuffed hand grenades, first-aid gear, amphetamines to ward off sleep, ropes cut to lengths ready for binding hostages, sections of pantyhose for masks, and a Kalashnikov assault rifle. Six of these rifles had been flown into Germany from Algiers, via Paris.[2] The world had not yet adapted to the idea that calculated menace, in the form of attacks upon civilians, might lurk anywhere. This was before air passengers and luggage were as a matter of routine thoroughly screened. The Kalashnikovs, tools designed for infantry, were in Munich to be used to corral and kill civilians. As they lifted each firearm and slipped it into the kit, Afif and his deputy gave it a kiss. "Oh, my love," they said.[3] Then the team set out, into the night.

One operating tenet of Black September was its almost airtight se-crecy. Even now, as they moved toward their crimes, six of the terrorists—Palestinians from refugee camps who had been trained in Libya—did not know what they had been ordered to Munich to do. Afif briefed them in a restaurant. They were to seize members of the Israeli delega-tion from their beds and then leverage their lives in a hostage siege. The world would be forced to hear the group's demands, including the release of more than two hundred prisoners, most of them Palestinians in Israeli jails. Afif had the list ready. For Black September, hostage-taking was not unfamiliar. Another cell had hijacked a passenger jet, Sabena Flight 572, several months before, and demanded a similarly extensive prisoner re-lease. Israeli commandos stormed the aircraft as the terrorists waited on the ground. The prisoners remained behind bars. This time Black Septem-ber had bolder plans and a grander stage. With an international press corps assembled for the Games, a hostage seizure in Munich would bullhorn the Palestinians' grievances as never before. Israel rarely bent to threats, the more so when demands were issued in public. Live television coverage was a more realistic aspiration than freeing prisoners in a swap. Afif told his cell what to expect. "From now on," he said, "consider yourself dead." Their status was predetermined, their fates known: "Killed in action for the Palestinian cause."

At about 3:30 A.M. the men stepped into taxis and were driven toward the section of fence Afif had selected. They arrived unmolested and met a group of Americans headed inside at the same time. The two teams—the athletes and the terrorists—helped each other over the top, gym bags and all.[4] Afif hurried his group toward 31 Connollystrasse, a residence where more than twenty Israelis slept. A new age of terrorism, long in the mak-ing, was about to introduce itself. By sunrise, eight men with assault rifles would command the attention of the world and change public security as it had been understood.[5]

The hostage siege in Munich, televised live worldwide, marked the next leap in the spread of automatic rifles, and the last tactical breakout, when assault rifles were applied to uses that the men and the governments that had given them their shape and numbers had not foreseen. Their steps in this direction, and use as a preferred tool for terror, predated Munich;

there are earlier examples.* But September 1972 in Munich brought the day that it became clear that whatever the Kalashnikov once was, whatever it had been meant to be, it had assumed a fuller and more universally dangerous character. After Munich, the Kalashnikov's utility in crimes against civilians and public order would be demonstrated repeatedly, in hijackings, hostage seizures, assassinations, suicide rifle attacks, and summary executions, sometimes before video cameras, designed to sow hatred and fear. The rifles' toll would become larger and their uses more ghastly with the passing years. They became requisite weapons for the massacres in Baathist Iraq, in Rwanda, and in the former Yugoslavia, for lawless formations of child soldiers, and for political crimes intended to jolt the world, from the Chechen and Ingush siege at a public school in Beslan to the Lashkar-e-Taiba raid into Mumbai. By the time the Kalashnikov line was a half-century old, its appearance as a central killing instrument in many of the most disturbing acts of political violence was no longer a shock. It was a norm. The people's gun, defender of Russian soil and socialist ideal, had evolved into a familiar hand tool for genocide and terror.

The processes that completed the Kalashnikov assault rifle's march out of communist garrisons were not random. They resulted from deliberate socialist arms-manufacturing, stockpiling, and transfer practices, followed by many means of distribution—some legal, some not—that followed.

After the establishment of Kalashnikov factories in the 1950s and 1960s, the early circulation of rifles followed predictable paths. The Soviet Union and other communist nations armed the Viet Cong and the North Vietnamese Army, equipping ideological partners for a war carried by ideological currents. Similarly, the gifts of AK-47s and an ammunition plant to Fidel Castro's Cuba during the 1960s fit with the mandates that armed the Warsaw Pact. These recipients were Kremlin allies. But as weaponry of Soviet provenance shaped socialist military forces around the globe, the Kremlin was also providing assault rifles and other armament to Arab states, seeking to blunt Western influence in the Middle East. By 1967, all of this was visible—as obvious as the Kalashnikovs in the hands of the NVA regulars in Vietnam, and as tangible as the piles of Ka-

---

* In May 1972, three members of the Japanese Red Army, a left-wing terrorist group, opened fire with Czech assault rifles on the crowd inside the terminal of Israel's international airport. They shot more than one hundred people, and killed twenty-four. They had smuggled their rifles in violin cases on a flight from France.

lashnikovs collected by the Israel Defense Forces after their defeat of Egypt's battalions in the Six Day War.* The state-to-state transfers were also unsurprising. They were for wars fought in an orthodox way, by forces whose organization and tactics were doctrinal and familiar. In the early years of its proliferation, the AK-47 was a calling card, an explicit mark of the socialist hand in wars in which its weapons appeared, even in wars, like the Six Day War, that were watched uneasily within the Kremlin and by the Eastern bloc's ruling elite.

The transfers of assault rifles to Arab governments were scarcely remarked upon as they occurred. Diplomats and commentators concentrated on Soviet military hardware thought to be more menacing—the artillery, tanks, armored personnel carriers, radar systems, missiles, and aircraft that might change the regional security equation. Rifles were just rifles. Who worried over a weapon with a range of a few hundred meters, which injured its victims bullet by bullet, when a neighboring state was updating its jet fighters and main battle tanks? What was lost to the security experts of the era was a process more dangerous than the introduction to the region of larger-ticket conventional arms: the prodigious migration of the rifle from state garrisons to those bent on unconventional war and crime. By the late 1960s, the ingredients enabling this migration were in place. Assault-rifle production had reached such levels that socialist military forces were well supplied, the proxy fights were established, and new armed political movements had taken shape. The movements represented a mix of nationalist, religious, and ethnic ambitions, and were organized by leaders willing to exploit arming opportunities made available by the Cold War. Within a very few years the Kalashnikov's attributes—its mechanical characteristics combined with its unprecedented availability—transformed Stalin's rifle, conceived as a tool of the state, into an engine for violence in the service of almost any cause.

Two phenomena paired to ensure this outcome. One was a socialist behavior: stockpiling, a behavior linked to the excessive rifle production in planned economies. The second was a capitalist axiom: the unrelenting energy of markets. Once excess socialist assault rifles existed, market forces ensured that they moved. Political motivations, not the laws of

---

*In one famous image, the cover of *Life* magazine displayed a young Israeli soldier, soaked and grinning, as he frolicked in the Suez Canal with a captured Kalashnikov.

demand and supply, were often behind early distributions. Moscow, Beijing, and Pyongyang provided rifles to curry favor among potential allies or to disrupt the activities of the West. Hard currency in return was welcome, but other motivations shaped deals. With time, rifles transferred in this way were redistributed by brokers and gun-running networks unencumbered by political concerns. Assault rifles became commodities. They recirculated by truck, train, containership, airplane, animal train, and brokerage. They often moved for profit alone. This migration accelerated throughout the later Cold War years and then beyond, when the stockpiles, less secure than in Soviet times, provided boundless new supply.

Decades of arms-manufacturing policies in the planned economies of the Eastern bloc had led, by the 1970s, to a material consequence: surpluses of arms without apparent use. The full extent of the Eastern bloc stockpiling is unknown. No thorough historical record has ever been assembled. Nor is it possible for a complete and accurate record to be made. All of the factors related to the socialist arms industry and the associated forms of trade—the conventions of state secrecy, the volume of production over time, administrative incompetence, personnel turnover, pervasive corruption, and other forms of criminal activity—worked to prevent accountability. Further, weapons and ordnance were stockpiled by a range of organizations, adding complexity to the problem. The Soviet army served as the primary storekeeper in many regions, but in each of the Warsaw Pact countries the national army, the federal police, and the intelligence services also had armories. Many nations also cached weapons for emergency issue to workers and ad hoc militias, and stored others in schools, where they were used for preparing teenagers for conscription and civil defense. Years later it is not possible to assemble the accountability puzzle fully. And yet in a few nations, enough arms eventually turned up, or enough researchers tried to document what was occurring as the weapons left government possession, to allow insights into the nature of stockpiling and the risks that accompanied amassing arms at such scale.

A pair of examples sketch the history. The urge to lay away weapons was powerful, and not readily deterred, even in the People's Republic of Albania, a founding member of the Warsaw Pact that broke from the Kremlin's orbit. From late in World War II through most of the Cold

War, Albania was ruled by Enver Hoxha, an avowed Stalinist. After Stalin died, Hoxha quarreled with the Kremlin. The tension grew severe
enough to cut off the Albanian police and military from the principal
source of socialist arms supply. The rupture in relations did not set Albania's state institutions back in their quest for arms. By the early 1960s,
Albania was receiving military aid from China, which was learning to use
its weapons programs to build relations with other governments. At first
China shipped in enormous quantities of arms and ordnance. Shipments
alone were not enough to satisfy Hoxha, who wanted the further security of domestic sources. By 1964 the aid reached the next step: China
was helping to build arms plants. Just as Soviet specialists had worked in
mainland China in the 1950s to modernize small-arms production and
train workers, Chinese technicians provided the same service in Hoxha's
Albania. Some of the visiting Chinese specialists remained in Albania at
least three years.[6] One project involved launching Kalashnikov production in the central mountain district of Gramsh, where output eventually
reached more than 275,000 assault rifles a year.[7] In these ways, the Hoxha
regime did more than stay apace in the arms race with other governments.
Albania under his hand became a bunker state. Vast storehouses of arms,
tinder for future wars in the Balkans and elsewhere, were stashed in buildings and tunnels across the land.

A different set of circumstances filled the Ukrainian Soviet Socialist
Republic with arms. Throughout the Cold War, the German drive across
Slavic soil in the Great Patriotic War was both a fresh memory and a core
narrative in Soviet national identity. The Kremlin considered Ukraine a
buffer in the event of another conventional war with the West. As Soviet
and Warsaw Pact forces arrayed along the borders of the capitalist world,
Ukraine was prepared as a second defensive line. Huge stockpiles were
cached on its territory, ready to be issued in any number of desperate
scenarios. The most spectacular of the storage sites was in Artemovsk, in
eastern Ukraine, near the border with Russia. Artemovsk lies in a region
atop geological deposits of salt, and when the Soviet army sought a place
to hide a reserve of conventional arms, the mines—out of sight of American spy planes—seemed ideal.

More than 150 meters belowground, in man-made caverns from
which miners had carted away salt, the army sequestered surpluses. The
mines became a repository of small-arms firepower on a scale unknown

in the West. The tunnels were filled with caches within caches, a layering of small arms reflecting generations of European war. Within them were weapons reaching to World War I, along with arms captured from the Third Reich or donated to the Red Army by the United States during the Lend-Lease program of World War II. Added to these were Soviet arms that the Red Army had used to fight the Wehrmacht, but subsequently replaced. There were newer additions: stockpiles of standard Soviet small arms from the Cold War, up to and including the most recent designs. The Artemovsk arsenal was an armory and a warren, a storage network mapped out by logisticians in which crates of weapons were separated by type and stacked toward ceilings, in places ten meters or more high. Electric cables and lights ran along the walls, keeping the place in a dim artificial glow. Beneath this maze and monument to Cold War thinking, farther below the earth, miners continued to extract salt. The depot was sealed off, separated by heavy doors and airlocks, the entrances watched by guards.[8] In all, the caves held some 3 million guns.

While Kalashnikov rifles were piled into storage, the assembly lines across the Warsaw Pact and Asia were producing more. Izhmash, the factory that began arms production in 1807, was now the busiest manufacturer of the Soviet Union's principal firearm and served as a routine stop for communist dignitaries visiting the Urals. The factory provided a source of national pride. The Kalashnikov assault rifle, like the caviar, like the vodka, like the furs, was seen as quintessential—a mark of the nation that produced it. Mikhail Kalashnikov had a new role. He was a tour guide. Early in the 1960s, before deposing his mentor, Nikita Khrushchev, Leonid I. Brezhnev visited Izhevsk as part of his duties as chairman of the Supreme Soviet, the union's legislature. Brezhnev was in his midfifties, dark-haired and emanating the insider confidence of a politician on the rise. Kalashnikov, ever capable of befriending and performing for power, was eager to escort the chairman on his rounds. In the Soviet Union, important decisions rested within few hands. Brezhnev was a potential patron, a man to be solicited, to be known to, no matter what.

I was entrusted with giving the necessary explanations. Of course, I was very enthusiastic about that assignment: as a rule, the future of the enterprise as a whole and the small arms business specifically depended on such visits. I wanted to bring up not only general prob-

lems but also my own, designer's problem—the construction of an
engineering building for small arms producers. Ideally it had to be
exactly like the testing range near Moscow that had been destroyed
so thoughtlessly years ago.

As always we began the tour in the experimental section, then
went on from there. We were passing a conveyor with suspension
brackets which held brand-new AKMs. Whenever Brezhnev picked
up an assault rifle, the first thing he looked at was the bayonet . . . I
did not really worry, but thought with curiosity: "Haven't the advisers of the esteemed guest notified him beforehand that the cardinal
merit of my creation was not the bayonet but other more essential
components and units?"

But everything soon became clear. Brezhnev bent down to me
and asked me in a subdued voice: "Can it be stolen?"

I had to make one of those vague gestures which could be interpreted in many different ways. One or two minutes later Brezhnev
said again in a conspiratorial tone: "What if I steal it?"

For that not to happen, I had to give Brezhnev the bayonet which
he liked so much. He was delighted as a boy. I reassured him sympa-
thetically: "You can always tell a hunter."[9]

Having played to the chairman's feelings, Kalashnikov asked for what
he wanted: an engineering building. The polygon at Schurovo, where
the design contest that led to the AK-47 had been held, had been closed
by Khrushchev. Kalashnikov seethed about this. He hoped Brezhnev
would replace what the small-arms designers had lost. The chairman did
not commit. (Some years later, Kalashnikov and officials from Izhevsk
landed an hour-long meeting with Brezhnev, who by then was the general
secretary—the Soviet Union's most powerful man. Brezhnev promised
them that they would have the building. It was never built.) The ex-
changes pointed to the perils of the Kremlin's governing style. A small-
arms research-and-development center was a cog in the national security
apparatus. Arguably it was an important cog. It was not of sufficient importance for its status to require a decision of the head of state. But the
concentration of power in few hands meant an endless scrum for access
and favor, and involved the most senior officials in matters better handled
by ministries and staff. It also colored the way midlevel bureaucrats acted

and thought. Kalashnikov blamed Khrushchev for Schurovo's closure. He could conceive of relief only through Brezhnev.

The Soviet Union's behavior, and that of its Warsaw Pact underlings, manifested itself in uglier ways.

As Brezhnev's power and stature were rising, the assault rifles being assembled in secret in East Germany had found their way to border guard detachments at the boundary with West Germany. The new knockoff was starting to replace the PPSh submachine guns that had been carried by the government's border guards since the units had formed. The guards stood grim duty. In 1961, the East German government had begun construction of what it called the Anti-Fascist Protection Wall, another milestone in doublespeak, considering that the purpose of the wall was not to keep Germans from the west from entering the east, but to stop the flow of émigrés fleeing the oppression and stagnation of the socialist side. The Kalashnikov's participation in state-directed violence against civilians here would be of a smaller scale than what had been seen in Hungary, but its introduction would be dark, and would resonate for decades.

Early on the afternoon of August 17, 1962, two young construction workers in East Berlin, Peter Fechter and Helmut Kulbeik, agreed not to return from their lunch break on a road-reconstruction project, opting instead to examine a building near the wall that separated them from West Berlin. They wanted to escape, and planned a reconnaissance. Any attempt would mean dashing across the open space, known as the "death strip," scaling the short wall on the far side, and passing under the barbed wire. The building, near Checkpoint Charlie, was beside the new wall. Perhaps it would offer a suitable leaping-off point, out of view of the armed East German guards. Inside the building, the pair found a storage room with a rear window that was not bricked over. The wall was in front of them. It was not much taller than a grown man. They had not intended to make their escape on this day. But the temptation was powerful. After observing the narrow space they would have to run across, Fechter and Kulbeik slipped through the window and landed on the death strip. Their sprint began.

The young men were quick, and they likely surprised the border guards watching the stillness below their posts. Both men reached the far wall. As they neared the concrete, the border guards opened fire with Kalashnikovs. Dozens of bullets flew toward the men. The range was short—perhaps sixty meters. The bullets missed Kulbeik. He scaled the wall and squeezed through the strands of barbed wire. Fechter was lean and fresh-faced; he looked fit. As he leaped to gain a hold with which to pull himself up, one of the rounds found its mark. He was hit. He fell, back to the eastern side.

Kulbeik sensed his companion's peril. But Fechter was so close. If only he could get up and try again. "Now go, go now, now move ahead!" Kulbeik shouted.

Fechter could not raise himself. He had been struck in the pelvis.

The hips, upper thighs, and pelvic girdle are among the worst places for a rifle bullet to smack into a human being. Wounds to these areas are often instantly immobilizing. Load-bearing bones rupture. Victims buckle and collapse. Complicating matters and raising the risk of swift death, large blood vessels follow the contours of bones. If cut, these blood vessels tend to bleed heavily and in ways that can be hard to stop. In the mad race to stop the flow, pressure and tourniquets are hard to apply.

Just a few feet from Kulbeik, at the edge of the communist world, Peter Fechter could not stand, much less scale a vertical concrete wall. Unarmed, eighteen years old, and at the mercy of two governments whose boundary he straddled, he slumped to his side, his blood draining from a wound almost impossible to treat. He was in need of immediate aid. His hasty attempt to escape had come to a full stop. He was not inches from freedom. He was a spectacle, watched by residents and officials from both sides, a helpless young man, minutes from death.

He shouted for aid. Surely he was not a threat, or capable of escape. Weapons were no longer required. But the wall was new, and the procedures for this kind of moment uncertain. From their posts on the east and from the west alike, the guards watched, joined by a growing crowd. No one dared to step into the strip and help. Fechter was thrown a bandage from the Western side. His wound was too severe, and too tricky, for him to hope to treat himself. Fechter bled. After several minutes he passed into unconsciousness, and fell silent. He slumped on his side, in the fetal position, wearing a dark sport coat. Later, the East German border guards, helmets on, their assault rifles slung across their dark coats, ventured to the wall and picked up Fechter and carried him away. An East German doctor soon pronounced him dead.

No one outside his own circle had heard of Peter Fechter before. He verged on anonymity in life. His death was of the most public sort, and

East Germany was unapologetic about how in his ending he realized instant and gruesome fame. Karl-Edvard von Schnitzler, the caustic East German television host, swept aside complaints, and defended the guards' decisions both to shoot and to leave the young man to die. "The life of each of our brave boys in uniform is worth more to us than the life of a law-breaker," he said. "One should stay away from our border—then you can save the blood, tears, and cries." The killing of Fechter also fit the use of the assault rifle for which Mikhail Kalashnikov had been rewarded: "reinforcing the power of the state." Here was the real Kalashnikov, 1962, propaganda peeled away.[10]

The Kremlin's posture toward its satellites and their yearnings for self-determination remained true to this form.

In early 1968, the Soviet Union faced another challenge from its western vassals, this time in the Czechoslovak Socialist Republic, where a reform-minded politician, Alexander Dubček, assumed control of the nation's Communist Party. Dubček sought change, including loosening restrictions on speech and on the press, liberalizing the economy, and offering citizens more consumer goods. The challenge to Kremlin hegemony was less confrontational than the uprising in Hungary twelve years before. But it was a threat. Its nickname, Prague Spring, suggested it was only a start. By July, with the Kremlin worried that tolerating one upstart might encourage others, the Soviet army was planning exercises—the word used to mask an invasion—on Czech and Slovak soil.[11] Soviet divisions struck in August, advancing alongside troops from Bulgaria, Hungary, and Poland. The airport outside Prague was seized, allowing transport planes to offload troops. Resistance was sporadic and mostly light. But more than seventy people were killed, and Moscow had sent a fresh signal to its satellites and to the West: The communists' hold on power would be preserved by force. When it felt threatened, the Soviet Union and its local partners would move past talk of fraternal relations and partnership and turn its guns on its own, just as they would fire on their unarmed citizens when they tried to flee.

The Eastern bloc had changed from Stalin's time. The Great Terror had given way to a less bloody form of centralized rule. But there would be no organic evolution from the totalitarian remains of what Lenin and Stalin had built. If the system were to give way, it would have to crack. The political consequences of this posture, and its effects on civil liberties and human rights, were obvious. The security implications were worrisome. One day, when the communist systems came under strain, or when they shattered, their huge storehouses of weapons might slip from state control to markets, where appetites for the arms were growing.

Eastern bloc infantry rifles had come to the Middle East in large numbers in the mid-1950s. The first large shipment to be widely recorded—the Kremlin-negotiated deal via Czechoslovakia to Nasser's Egypt in 1955—apparently did not involve AK-47s. Czech rifles were shipped. But not long after these transfers, Soviet AK-47s began to flow to the Egyptian army, as did M1943 ammunition and the technology to produce both the weapons and the cartridges. By the late 1950s, American technical intelligence officials were secretly testing Egyptian-manufactured 7.62x39-millimeter cartridges—a sign that a Middle Eastern version of the ammunition was already in significant circulation.[12] By the early 1960s, Egyptian soldiers were carrying an Egyptian-made AK-47 knock-off—the Misr, the first of many Kalashnikovs to be cloned in the Middle East. Soon the Kremlin's engagement with Egypt, Syria, Algeria, Tunisia, and Libya resulted in their militaries' adopting the Kalashnikov line. The timing was portentous. Unlike many military items the Soviet Union provided its customers in the region, small arms could be easily transferred to third parties, who could easily master their use. And the rush of Soviet infantry weapons into the region aligned with the rise of Palestinian nationalist groups, many of which engaged in campaigns of terrorism against Israel and its citizens.

Middle Eastern terrorism had been nurtured with state sponsorship. Soon after Israel declared independence in May 1948, Egypt's King Farouk I had organized unconventional fighters against the Jewish state. The fighters called themselves *fedayeen,* guerrillas prepared to sacrifice their lives. From bases in Jordan, Lebanon, and elsewhere, and with backing from Egypt's intelligence service, the Mukhabarat, they conducted attacks against Israelis in the early 1950s. After Farouk was deposed in 1952, in part because of Egypt's military failures, the Egyptians lent the fedayeen more support. Unconventional war and sabotage proliferated as other Middle Eastern governments and the Palestinian diaspora followed the Egyptian example. Unable to defeat Israel by conventional means, they maintained pressure in other lethal ways, while seeking a measure of deniability.

In the evolution of war, processes that develop in parallel—political, technological, or tactical—can suddenly cross, and at these points of intersection wars change. In the crucible of the Middle East in the 1960s, this was the case. The Palestinian groups that chose militancy soon procured the newly available rifles that the Eastern bloc had shipped to its Middle Eastern clients. The AK-47 and the AKM became standard arms for unconventional war. They were studied in militant training camps and carried on guerrilla and terrorist missions that entered the groups' tactical routine. Assault rifles, those lightweight instruments for concentrating firepower, multiplied the menace of individual insurgents and terrorists, elevating the danger they posed and the ambitions they voiced. The weapons' utility was not lost on the groups' leaders. Khalil al-Wazir, a commander who eventually led Fatah's armed war under the nom de guerre of Abu Jihad, embraced the AK-47 as a vehicle to victory. "The Kalashnikov is our only language until we free all of Palestine," he said.[13] From the fedayeen camps in the Middle East, the weapon, and the mentality for turning its barrel toward civilians, spread outward. Eventually a flight from Libya in 1972 carried six of the rifles to Munich.

By 4:30 A.M., the Black September cell members, assault rifles in hand, were trying to open the door to Apartment 1 at 33 Connollystrasse, where Israeli coaches and athletic officials were resting. One of the Israelis, Yossef Gutfreund, a wrestling referee, heard the noise. He opened the door and came face-to-face with the attackers. Gutfreund slammed the door, leaning into it and shouting to the other Israelis, calling them from their sleep. But the Palestinians had been quick. In the instant the door had been ajar, two of them inserted their assault-rifle barrels past the jamb, preventing Gutfreund from closing the door fully. They began to pry. Gutfreund was a huge man. He pushed back as long as he was able. For several long seconds he kept them out. His efforts saved a man. Tuvia Sokolovsky, a strength-and-conditioning trainer, scrambled from his bed and forced open a window. He dropped outside as the Palestinians rushed in. At least one of them opened fire as Sokolovsky dashed, but the bullets missed the man.

Inside the apartment, the attackers rounded up their captives: Gutfreund, Amitzur Shapira, Kehat Shorr, Andre Spitzer, Jacov Springer, and Moshe Weinberg. By this point, the Black September mission had already realized a measure of success. The cell had penetrated the Olympic Village and taken hostages, and its members were unharmed. But there was still a chance for the hostages to resist. Some of these Israelis were veterans of their country's many wars and possessed the light feet and powerful frames of lifelong athletes. These men had had an understanding of how and why to fight. Weinberg, a wrestling coach, acted first. He lunged at Afif with a kitchen knife. Another Palestinian fired. The bullet slammed into the side of the coach's mouth. Weinberg fell. It was a grotesque injury, but not fatal—a pass-through that missed his skull. He sputtered blood; his senses and much of his strength were intact. The Palestinians herded their unwounded captives through the apartment and bound them with their precut ropes.

Afif was not satisfied. With other members of his cell to help him, he forced Weinberg to his feet, ordered him outside onto Connollystrasse, and set out to seize more hostages. Weinberg was the quick-thinking sort, more than a match for the men who had captured him. He led Afif past Apartment 2, where smaller-statured Israeli athletes were quartered, toward Apartment 3, where Israeli wrestlers and weightlifters lived; these men brought muscle to a fight. Inside, Afif and his cell gathered six more hostages—David Berger, Zeev Friedman, Eliezer Halfin, Yossef Romano, Gad Tsabari, and Mark Slavin—and marched them at gunpoint outside, toward apartment 1.

Tsabari ran. One of the captors opened fire. Again the bullets flew wide. (As is the case with many who carry Kalashnikovs, the Black September terrorists were well armed but not crack shots.) Near the apartment's entrance, Weinberg lunged again. Even after being shot, he was formidable—a thick-necked career wrestler who had served as an Israeli commando. He punched one of the Palestinians in the face, fracturing his jaw. The man dropped his rifle as he fell. Weinberg scrambled to pick it up. There was not enough time. Another guard fired, shooting the coach several times. He collapsed. The remaining Israelis were forced inside, where Romano, a weightlifter on crutches from a recent training injury, sprang at their captors. After a struggle, one of the Palestinians opened fire. Romano's torso was shredded by automatic fire.

The Black September operation was a secret no more. The sounds of gunfire had awakened the Olympic Village, and an anemic counter-terrorism response began. A short while later, an unarmed German guard made his way on foot to the building, carrying a handheld two-way radio. There he spotted a man in a mask at the doorway, clutching a rifle. The security guard reported what he saw to his dispatch center, beginning a chain of notifications: to other apartments, to the Munich police, to the interior ministry of Bavaria, to the federal police, and to the German chancellor and diplomatic corps, which called Israel's ambassador at his residence in Bonn.

At 5:08 A.M., the terrorists dropped three pieces of paper from the apartment to a security officer below. The papers contained their de-mands. German police ringed the building and the world watched on live television as the first deadline for executions, and then others, passed. Israel reacted as expected. It refused to negotiate. A deal was struck on the ground: The Germans would provide passage by helicopter to a nearby NATO airfield, from where the hostages and their captors would be flown by passenger aircraft to an Arab nation. Much of the world had not yet organized for domestic counterterrorism action, and did not have highly trained units designated for these moments. The West Germans were un-prepared. The end came quickly. That night, after the Black September cell surveyed the Boeing passenger jet that was to carry the captors and captives from Europe, the Germans initiated an ambush at the airfield. It failed. The hostage seizure descended into a gunfight, in which the ter-rorists turned their Kalashnikovs on their hostages, who were bound and helpless before them.

On the morning of September 6, not quite twenty-four hours after Afif and his subordinates had scaled the fence, Jim McKay, an ABC televi-sion sportscaster, introduced the world to the age when military assault rifles had become elemental ingredients in forms of terrorism that would only grow. "Our worst fears have been realized tonight," he said, and then gave a summary of the number of athletes seized. Eleven men in all, he said, and added: "They're all gone."

Inside the Soviet Union, arms production continued. Throughout the mid-1960s, Soviet arms designers had watched the American rollout of the M-16 and had examined captured specimens from Vietnam. They had not been favorably impressed with Colt's rifle. (Kalashnikov himself called it "freakish," "prankish," and "capricious," and something that American soldiers "threw away.")[14] The M-16's ammunition was another matter. It demanded attention. By the early 1970s, within five years of the M-16's designation as the United States' standard military rifle, the Soviet army was at work on its own small-caliber, high-velocity round: the 5.45-millimeter cartridge. Once the round was available to armorers, Kalashnikov, whose weapons were now entrenched in the Soviet military to the point of enshrinement, led a design team that created the weapon the army chose to fire it: the *Avtomat Kalashnikova-74*, the automatic rifle by Kalashnikov, selected in 1974. The AK-74* was to the AK-47 what the AR-15 had been to the AR-10—a pre-existing design reworked for a smaller, faster round.[15] It entered mass production in 1976, and the Soviet army displayed it to the world in the 1977 October Revolution Parade in Red Square. It soon became the Soviet standard arm for many units, displacing the AKM.[16] Old patterns in West-East arms design had recurred. The Soviet army had eagerly grasped and imitated the technical thinking of an opponent. Small-arms design had further converged.[17] And again Mikhail Kalashnikov was toasted: He was named a Hero of Socialist Labor for a second time.

The award provided another curious glimpse into life in the center of Soviet arms-design circles. One of the honors that accompanied designation of a two-time Hero of Socialist Labor was the assignment of an artist to make a bust of the hero, to be installed at the recipient's place of birth. As Kalashnikov's bust was being shaped, he visited the studio of Anatoly Beldushkin, the artist commissioned to render him in bronze. He was surprised by what he saw. Beldushkin had fashioned the bust closely to Kalashnikov's likeness, but added a facial feature the designer did not possess: dense eyebrows. Kalashnikov understood.

I saw him make my brows very thick and protested half in jest: "What do I need brows like Brezhnev's for?" "Brezhnev has nothing

---

* This rifle was slightly longer than the AKM, but almost exactly the same weight, and the bullets it fired traveled at a higher velocity (more than twenty-nine hundred feet per second, as opposed to less than twenty-four hundred with the AKM).

to do with it," the sculptor tried to explain amicably to me. "Such brows are indicative of constant strain of thought."

Such was Kalashnikov's world, the Soviet Union of the 1970s, a system in which the habit of kowtowing was ingrained even in the sculptor's hands, and those enjoying its perks had casually, even cheerfully, accepted the strange rules. "I laughed merrily," Kalashnikov wrote. "'Couldn't you relieve me of this strain?'"[18] His bust was completed, bearing brows like those of the general secretary. It was placed on a pedestal in Kurya, the village from which the Kalashnikov family had been cast out during collectivization and sent into exile.[19]

By the 1970s, the Eastern bloc arms stores were proving to be of limited Cold War use, and the risks of the stockpiles and of greater assault-rifle distribution were becoming discernible. The war the rifles were to help the Kremlin win was not fought by the means the stockpilers had planned, and the armories stood as powerful attractants for all manner of opportunists. Illicit diversion was a natural risk. The pulls and pushes of demand and supply, along with ample precedents of diversions and their consequences, were in view. Three examples were instructive: the movement of firearm stocks left from World War II; the introduction of assault rifles to Uganda, where the government fell; and the assassination in 1981 of the president of Egypt, Anwar Sadat.

The bountiful trade in infantry rifles and machine guns assembled for World War II provided a useful precedent for understanding what was ahead. The war had pushed large quantities of military firearms around the globe, and when the fighting ended many governments were left with surpluses, sometimes staggering surpluses. For conventional forces, these excess weapons quickly became obsolete. In the arms-race climate of the Cold War, Western and Eastern armies adopted new standard cartridges and updated their standard arms. Where did the earlier generations of weapons go? Not into foundries. Some went into storage sites like the salt mines below Artemosvk. Others went to markets, wherever markets were. And once they entered markets, they turned up in conflicts everywhere. The gun-running business was often quiet and opaque, but one private dealer of the era, Samuel Cummings, an American who decamped for

Europe and made his fortune brokering deals, granted moments of transparency. In the mid-1970s, Cummings, by then a minor tycoon, offered a tour to a British journalist of part of his arsenal, and explained how small arms move liquidly from fight to fight.

> Here, he points out, is a stack of American Garand rifles which were first exported to Germany in the 'fifties for the first German re-armament. When Germany got more advanced weapons they were transported to Jordan in the late 'sixties, and when Jordan got more advanced weapons they were bought by Cummings and shipped to Manchester. From there many of them were shipped to the Philippines, to help fight Moslem rebels financed by Libya, while a few remain in Manchester waiting for customers. Here, just next door to the Garands, are some British Enfield rifles which were captured by the Japanese in Indo-China, then taken over by the Americans and used in Vietnam, before they were bought by Cummings. Here are some Springfield rifles which were first supplied to the French in Indo-China in the 'fifties. Here are Mausers which were brought over to Taiwan by General Chiang Kai-shek when he left the mainland in 1949. Over there are German ME42 guns which were left by Hitler's troops in Greece, Swedish guns made under license in Egypt and captured by the Israelis, British Sten guns dropped by parachute during the Second World War for the French Maquis, American Brownings for the Dominican Republic, Belgian Mausers from Venezuela, American M16s from the Chilean Army. . . . Cummings knows that his arsenals depend for their stocks on the aftermath of wars.

Cummings, in one of his signature one-liners, declared the flow of arms "an index of the world's folly."[20] Folly interested Cummings, and he made sure to read it well, because the business opportunities it presented interested him even more. What Cummings understood, and what his guided tour showed, was the durable nature of demand in a world in which the next local struggle was always about to start somewhere, and in which whenever one combatant adopted a new rifle its opponents wanted upgrades, too. There were almost always customers—if the price was right, the supply could be found, and weapons unneeded in one place could be married with a purchaser someplace else. If, as Cummings implied, today's arsenals depend on their stocks from the aftermath of yesterday's wars, then the Cold War had provided the biggest boon of all. Socialist stockpiling served as an immeasurably large, if latent, source of future supply—the greatest supplies yet. Cummings grasped this last point, too. He marveled at the appeal and practical merits of the Kalashnikov line, compared to what else was available. "If I was a Marine in Vietnam and was given one of those new ArmaLites," he said, during the height of the M-16 scandal in Congress, "I'd throw it away and say I'd lost it and try to get one of the Russian rifles off a dead V.C. They're the best."[21]

In his breezy and informed way, Cummings offered insights into private networks eager to move Kalashnikovs when the rifles became available. Idi Amin, in Uganda, offered a peek at a cruder form of transfer, which would be a factor in small-arms proliferation, too. Amin, a hulking career army officer, seized power by coup in Kampala in 1971. He was an outrageous character, a boxing champion and rugby player whose flamboyance and ease with spilling blood contributed to what became his international persona: brutish dictator and murderous buffoon. Some of those who knew him as a younger man, before his sadistic streak had manifested itself in wholesale executions, saw him as stupid, "a splendid type and a good player, but virtually bone from the neck up, and needs things explained in words of one letter."[22] But he possessed a viciousness, like Stalin's, that was chilling when connected to power. During more than eight years as head of state, Amin squirreled away weapons with the help of the Kremlin, East Germany, and Libya, and applied his soldiers' firepower advantage to the tasks of thwarting rivals and repressing Uganda's population. Amin relied on the tools of the purge: large-scale arrests of civil servants and suspected guerrillas and their supporters, followed by imprisonment without trial, torture, and extrajudicial killings, often by firing squads, sometimes by hammer blows. Like many despots, he overreached. As resentment and fear exhausted Uganda, he annexed a portion of neighboring Tanzania, triggering events that chased him from the presidential suite. Tanzania's army and a coalition of anti-Amin guerrilla groups invaded. Amin bolted. The disappearance of a commander in chief is never a good sign in a military government, and the Ugandan army took its cue from the boss. Officers and troops disappeared from many barracks. What happened next pointed to the risks ahead in Europe when communist nations crumbled from within.

In the northeastern region of Moroto, Ugandan troops vacated their garrison, leaving behind an armory. Moroto was inhabited by the Karamojong tribe, traditional herders who roamed the countryside in search of water and forage for their livestock. Their region was formally Ugandan but never fully under Ugandan control, and as a seminomadic people, many Karamojong saw themselves as unincorporated. They had paid for this perceived backwardness and disloyalty at the hands of Amin and his government. After the evaporation of the army at Moroto, local men looted the base and relieved it of weapons. This marked a consequential rearrangement. The Karamojong were already accomplished cattle rustlers, and with their newly acquired Kalashnikovs they could raid their neighbors' herds with heretofore unimaginable ease. The qualities that made a Soviet conscript with an AK-47 much more formidable than a Soviet conscript with a Mosin rifle or PPSh translated seamlessly to the business of rustling. But there was a difference. The introduction of Kalashnikovs to the Karomojong multiplied their firepower by a much larger factor than had the introduction of AK-47s to Soviet infantry squads, because the rustlers were not graduating from rifles and submachine guns. They were moving up from spears. In the ensuing years, traditional Karamojong power arrangements eroded, and the elderly leaders were supplanted by younger men leading bands of rustlers equipped with assault rifles. Warlords became a force. Karamojong raiding parties set upon their neighbors and claimed herds owned by the Iteso and Acholi people. Before the raids, the Acholi had three hundred thousand cattle. By 1997 many Acholi switched to raising donkeys. Their cattle holdings shrank to five thousand. Government efforts to control the Karamajong proved insufficient. Upheavals in Rwanda and Congo, and the eruption of an unrelated Acholi insurgency, brought more Kalashnikovs into the country. A local arms race matured. Attempts to restrict the flow of assault rifles were futile. The Ugandan government chose a new strategy. Hoping to co-opt some of the warlords and to create an informal buffer against the expanding Acholi insurgency, it urged Karamojong men to register their rifles in return for monthly stipends of about ten dollars.[23] What had been illegal in Uganda had become so entrenched that policy now sanctioned it with cash.

As the Karamojong were changed by their acquisition of Kalashnikovs, the Egyptian experience with the rifles also took an ugly turn.

Egypt's wars with Israel had yielded it little, whether under King Farouk or under Nasser, and its support for the fedayeen had fanned activities and sentiments it could not control. In 1979, President Sadat signed a peace treaty with Israel and agreed to recognize the Jewish state. The treaty enraged the fedayeen and their closest supporters, who turned on Sadat with a loathing reserved for traitors. On October 6, 1981, at a military parade in Cairo, assassins within the Egyptian army struck. While a ceremonial convoy passed the reviewing stand, a lieutenant ran toward the dignitaries standing for the pass and review. The officer with the Kalashnikov seemed part of the performance; perhaps he was to salute. He started firing. At the same time, more soldiers on a troop transport opened fire on the bleachers. Sadat and eleven other people were killed. Egypt passed under martial law.

These three examples—the savvy of Cummings, the vulnerability of Amin's armories, and the fate of Sadat, cut down by his own guns—were markers. And they were valuable for the smallness of their canvases. Cummings's business centered on himself, but he could explain the forces that drove a larger system. In Uganda, processes difficult to see in international arms transfers could be traced. In Egypt, the risks of sponsoring terror on a neighbor's soil had played out in full view, as had the ferocity of automatic-rifle power when miniaturized. The events in Uganda and Egypt also reflected an unstated but disturbing fact. The calamities that visited these governments had roots in steps intended to increase the governments' strength: acquiring assault rifles to be ready for any foe.

The Soviet Union, seemingly impregnable under Stalin after the Great Patriotic War, was not to last. While it did, its idiosyncratic rules held. By the 1980s, Mikhail Kalashnikov wanted to travel within the Warsaw Pact to observe the production of his rifles elsewhere. He mentioned this desire on a visit to Moscow to the office of Dmitri F. Ustinov, the Soviet minister of defense. Kalashnikov regarded Ustinov as a mentor and friend. The reaction was cold. He sensed his mistake.

> Hardly had I started to say that I wanted to see a weapons factory in Bulgaria, when Ustinov became gloomy and frowned. He said in a low voice: "Comrade Major."

I was in civvies as usual, but the minister's tone made me want to rise from the armchair and stand at attention.

It should be mentioned that this happened at precisely the time when the Americans had published an insulting story about "the Russian sergeant having armed the whole of the Warsaw Pact," and they started rapidly raising my military rank. In the morning, I found out that I had been given the rank of senior lieutenant, and in the evening I was already a captain.

Obviously, Ustinov personally monitored my "military career," and that was the case when I found out that I had been made a Major.

But that didn't change anything.

I felt a chill go down my spine when the minister said distinctly: "You have not said that. I have not heard you say that. Anything else?"[24]

Kalashnikov, for all his official achievements, lived within Soviet constraints, no matter that the series of arms carrying his name had entered the official national culture.* The Soviet Union maintained its military ranks through obligatory mass conscription, and before teenagers were drafted, they were required to master the assembly and disassembly of the AKM. The training was a part of the Program of Pre-Conscription Preparation of Youths, a Ministry of Defense curriculum managed by each school's military and physical-education instructors. In Soviet schools, rifles were the fourth R. The curriculum also included competitions in donning gas masks, thousand-meter cross-country runs, hundred-meter swims, pull-ups, and throwing simulated hand grenades. All male Soviet students were expected to perform these tasks, along with learning the rudiments of marching, civil defense, and first aid.[25] Even students from the most privileged families participated.

The program could be seen in Pripyat, founded in 1970 to support the Nuclear Power Station in the Name of Vladimir I. Lenin, which had been

---

*Its place was so complete that at times it was absurdly overstated. By one rumor, macaroni in Soviet pasta plants was required to be manufactured to a thickness of 7.62 millimeters; this, the story went, was because the machinery that produced pasta was ready, under secret decree, to be convertible to manufacturing cartridges. Nonsense, but a sign. Soviet priorities were such that a joke like this had currency.

constructed at Chernobyl. Its citizens were selected from accomplished families. Theirs was to be a model city, brick-and-mortar testimony to Soviet progress and the atom's peaceful use. In Pripyat as elsewhere, the AKM was as surely a part of the curriculum as Lenin, Pushkin, and the periodic table. In one set of evaluations, held at School No. 1 on April 10 and 11, 1986, the tenth-grade boys, most of them sixteen years old, were timed assembling and disassembling their school's assault rifles. The AKM's few parts and simple design made it ideal for the exam. Most students needed only thirty-four to fifty seconds to complete the test, held under the watchful gaze and stopwatch of I. D. Peshko, chief referee. Some students were remarkably fast. Andrei Avramenko, born in 1969, took apart his Kalashnikov and put it together again in twenty-eight seconds. Sergei Svirnov performed the chore in twenty-four seconds. Sergey Saliy was the best of all, completing the task in twenty-two seconds. His hands must have been a blur. Even the laggard, Oleg Bryukhanon, was capable. He needed seventy-five seconds—and that was the slowest of all.[26]

Two weeks later, the dream of Pripyat came to ruin. Reactor No. 4 exploded, bombarding Pripyat with radiation. Families were evacuated in an apocalyptic panic while the Kremlin pretended all was well. The evacuees left behind a world in freeze-frame—contaminated, sealed from intrusion, stopped in time. The abandoned city and its records, including I. D. Peshko's military preparation files, became an exhibit of the Soviet experience everywhere. The preconscription records showed the extent of assault-rifle infiltration into Soviet life. On purely ergonomic grounds they were consistent with records from tests organized by the United States Army in 1966, which underscored the simplicity of the Kalashnikov compared to American-designed arms. In those tests, conducted with American soldiers, the average assembly-disassembly times for the M-14, the M-16, and the AK-47 were seventy-one seconds, eighty seconds, and thirty-four seconds, respectively.[27] At sixteen years of age, the schoolboys of Pripyat were quicker than American soldiers with their own service rifles.[28] Assembly-disassembly times are not the most important measure of a rifle's design. But if a rifle is otherwise sound, they can be a measure of some significance. And the preconscription training, the tests held for teenaged boys handling assault rifles as part of their school day, established this: Children, it turned out, could figure out the basics of the Kalashnikov at least as quickly as soldiers could.

* * *

From school gymnasiums to jungle patrols to terrorist attacks, the AK-47 and its descendant arms seemed to be almost everywhere in the 1980s— in the Soviet Union and Warsaw Pact nations, in Central America, Africa, and Southeast Asia, in the Middle East. They were represented in the hands of state armies, police and intelligence services, and guerrilla formations and shadowy terrorist groups. The Iraqi and Iranian armies each carried Kalashnikov variants in the trench warfare along their contested border, as did the insurgents they underwrote on each other's soil. The weapons remained the tools of the strongman and the crackdown, and were used by the People's Republic of China to clear demonstrators from Tiananmen Square. In the Soviet war in Afghanistan, Kalashnikovs became the primary rifles of all parties—the occupying Soviet army and its Afghan government forces, as well as the mujahideen they fought.

The arrival of the Kalashnikov in Afghanistan predated the Soviet invasion in late 1979. As part of its military aid programs, the Kremlin had provided arms and training to Afghanistan's government since 1956. In the early 1970s, Pakistan was training insurgents as assets to undermine the presidency of Mohammad Daoud Khan. After the Marxist coup of 1978, and the Soviet invasion the following year, the insurgents acquired arms from several sources, ranging from battlefield collection to defecting Afghan government soldiers. Ultimately they received arms through a mechanism that brought the Soviet assault rifle nearly full circle: an international arms pipeline, fed by several nations, flowing through Pakistan.

The pipeline was an open secret. To feed it, arms were purchased by the Central Intelligence Agency, Saudi Arabia, and wealthy Arabs, among other sources, and moved by containership to the port of Karachi, where they were received by officers of the Directorate of Inter-Services Intelligence, or ISI, Pakistan's most powerful intelligence service. From Karachi, most of the arms moved by rail to the Ojhri Camp in Rawalpindi, which became an ISI arms depot—a reservoir of arms and ammunition to be sent over the border. The items were sorted there and carried by truck to Peshawar and redirected again, often to warehouses of Afghan commanders and groups fighting inside Afghanistan. The commanders' logisticians moved the arms to the border on their own fleets of trucks and passed them off to smaller camps, from where they sometimes moved by animal train. The system was slow. At any point after Karachi it could look mismanaged and vulnerable. Ammunition was piled high in Rawalpindi without adequate attention to safety (and in 1988 the Ojhri Camp depot exploded). The routes to the border were watched by Pakistani border guards and police officers who often extracted bribes. Afghan commanders diverted and resold weapons, redistributing them for cash. And inside Afghanistan, the Soviet army, while mostly road-bound, was actively searching for the pack trains. But the pipe was force-fed enough equipment in Karachi that arms and ammunition flowed out the other side, and the mujahideen were outfitted for war in remote terrain.[29] It also proved nearly impervious to interdiction at large scale. In time it was publicly acknowledged to have grown from ten thousand tons of weapons and ordnance in 1983 to sixty-five thousand tons in 1987.

> I would liken our system to a tree. The roots represented the ships and aircraft bringing supplies from various countries to Pakistan. The trunk lay from Karachi almost to the border, at which point the many branches lay across the frontier. These branches divided into hundreds of smaller ones inside Afghanistan, taking the sap (arms and ammunition) to the leaves (the Mujahideen). Lop off a small branch, even a large one, and the tree survives, and in time others grow. Only severing the roots or trunk kills the tree. In our case only the branches were subject to attack.[30]

The path of the Kalashnikov into Afghanistan and through generations of mujahideen has been well established and reasonably well traced. The value of its reconstruction lies in this fact: Processes hidden from view elsewhere in this case eventually came to be known. The sheer scale of shipments ensured that some portion of this movement came to light. In many other wars, determining the origins of arms with precision is more difficult, and few people attempt the task. Often, absent public accounts by people directly involved, inquiries into assault-rifle transfers become a frustrating exercise in working backward. Weapons identified in combatants' hands are traced, to the extent possible, to their sources. Such efforts have been intermittent, and even the most talented and industrious researcher rarely succeeds in connecting every dot. Most glimpses have been fragmentary. But fragmentary views have value. One of the finer examples, little known and scarcely studied, was the record assembled of weapons used in the 1980s by the Farabundo Martí Liberation Front, or FMLN, which at the time was a socialist insurgent group in El Salvador.

At the close of the Cold War, the Institute for Research in Small Arms in International Security, an assemblage of scholars and arms enthusiasts, underwrote a researcher who created a database of captured FMLN arms. The database grew to include 5,429 weapons, of which 4,713, or almost 87 percent, were assault rifles.* The database confirmed what anyone could see. Assault rifles, rejected by the United States until the 1960s, had come to be regarded as requisite equipment for modern war. But the data did more than document the obvious. They revealed the complexity and richness of a guerrilla movement's sources of supply. They also pointed to the ease with which assault rifles travel from place to place, overcoming logistical difficulties, geographical obstacles, or efforts at interdiction.

For the war in El Salvador, the majority of the assault rifles captured by the government, and the preponderance of the assault rifles captured early in the war, were American-made M-16s. Since the White House did not purposely supply the FMLN and backed the government the movement sought to overthrow, the natural deduction was that these weapons had traveled roundabout routes to insurgent hands. When the researcher traced serial numbers, the discovery was startling. Of almost 3,000 captured M-16s, nearly 1,900 could be traced back to a previous owner. Of these, 1,239 had once been in the inventory of the United States military, including 973 rifles documented as having been in Vietnam. The American military had left them in Asia, where they had been collected—perhaps by a private broker like Cummings but more likely by the intelligence service of a communist government—and shipped back across the sea. Another nearly 600 of the guerrillas' M-16s had been provided to the Salvadoran government as part of the American foreign military sales program and had leaked from government possession to the

---

* The remainder included 6 heavy machine guns, 54 general-purpose machine guns or squad automatic weapons, 182 carbines, 123 submachine guns, and a mix of grenade launchers and surface-to-air missiles.

insurgency.[31] In sum, the United States had armed its foes, indirectly but surely. The war echoed edicts of Mao: "Guerrillas must not depend too much on an armory. The enemy is the principal source of their supply."[32]

The channels of supply became more varied and sophisticated with time. Early in the insurgency, the Salvadoran government captured several primitively scrubbed FAL assault rifles; on each, a drill had been used to cut a hole through the magazine well where a crest identifying the nation of manufacture* had been located. Whoever attempted to hide the rifles' national origin had missed a step. The serial numbers remained intact. A review of these markings found that the rifles had entered the region in 1959 in Cuba, in the last moments of the rule of Fulgencio Batista, when Fabrique-Nationale, the Belgian arms manufacturer, had a contract to provide its NATO-standard assault rifle to Cuba.[33] The arms became property of Fidel Castro's government after revolution chased Batista from power, and from there they had been provided to like-minded revolutionaries a hop away. These rifles were old, worn, and heavy. As the FMLN picked up momentum and recruits, it sought newer arms, leading to the acquisition of M-16s—a much more impressive logistical feat. By the mid-1980s, the movement's sources of supply further diversified, and Kalashnikovs began to reach the insurgents, including large numbers of Kalashnikovs from North Korea and a smaller quantity from the East German plant in Wiesa. A few insurgents also carried Yugoslav RPKs. By 1989 Dragunov sniper rifles had been captured, too.[34] (These weapons also had been scrubbed. The serial numbers had been filed off, though their Cyrillic markings showed them to be of Soviet origin.) While the socialist suite of infantry arms edged in on the war, the markings on captured 7.62x39 cartridges used in FMLN Kalashnikovs revealed that their ammunition had been manufactured in Cuba. What did it all mean? The insurgents' arms-procurement arrangements had progressed, from rifles abandoned by capitalist enemies in Cuba and Vietnam, to interlocking and complementary socialist sources. The socialist system of export had matured. Kalashnikov assembly lines—created under the auspices of defending the Soviet Union and ensuring arms standardization for conventional communist forces—had developed into a supply

---

* The FAL originated in Belgium, but over the years was manufactured in several nations, including the United Kingdom, Australia, Argentina, and India.

network for insurgency in the Americas. This was armed revolution practically applied. It was also what it looked like, in logistical and ideological terms, when the Kremlin's brand of socialism worked. Each of these Kalashnikovs, and they were now appearing in every war, represented an incongruous achievement. As it groaned and buckled in its last years, the Soviet Union was struggling to deliver food to the citizens of Moscow. Its weapons reached the far corners of the world.

Then the system fell. Mikhail S. Gorbachev became general secretary of the Communist Party in 1985, and by 1986 the party was loosening its hold and allowing reforms. For those in Eastern Europe under communist rule and Soviet occupation, the desire for independence—suppressed by violence several times since World War II—was rekindled. In early 1989, the formerly banned trade union, Solidarność, exacted a commitment from Poland's communist government to hold elections, which it won overwhelmingly in June, creating an irreparable crack. Events accelerated. Czechoslovakia held its Velvet Revolution in November 1989; the Berlin Wall fell the same month. Romanians revolted in December. Hungary held free elections in spring 1990, and Bulgaria in June. Ukraine declared its independence that July, followed by Azerbaijan and Armenia. Georgia and the Central Asian republics announced their independence the next year. Albania voted its communists from office in 1992.

Violence marred communism's last hours. Deposed President Nicolae Ceaușescu of Romania was executed with his wife after a hasty victor's trial; they were shot, husband and wife standing side by side with hands tied behind their backs, by soldiers firing Kalashnikovs on Christmas Day. Elsewhere in the Soviet Union, much more blood was spilled, sometimes by officials trying to maintain power, other times because of ethnic tensions that had been both stoked and contained under Soviet rule. Riots were put down with Soviet force in 1986 in Almaty, in 1989 in Tbilisi, in 1990 in Baku, and in 1991 in Riga and Vilnius. Fighting broke out between Azeris and Armenians in early 1988, igniting a six-year war. In 1991, Georgia attacked separatist South Ossetia, and Chechnya declared its independence from Russia, setting a course for a larger and more costly war that would see human-rights abuses by Russia and its proxy forces on a grand scale, and the separatists' adoption of the tactics of terror.

Yugoslavia was fracturing, heading into a series of ethnic wars. Civil war erupted in Tajikistan in 1992, the year fighting broke out in Transnistria, and between Georgia and the Abkhaz.

During these years, an arms-pilferage drama unfolded across the Warsaw Pact. The events in the German Democratic Republic provided one example. The Berlin Wall fell in November 1989, pitching the country on a new course. During more than forty years of communist rule, East Germany had become an armed police state and well-stocked military front. The arsenals were large and varied, augmented by the secret production in the Wiesa rifle plant. The Nationale Volksarmee, or National People's Army, was the most heavily armed organization. But the police, the secret police, and the border guards had arms stores as well, and as many as four hundred thousand military weapons had been cached in factories, positioned to arm workers' militias ahead of national uprising or war. Party officials had another one hundred thousand small arms. The dismantling of the wall marked the beginning of German reunification. But the procedures of uniting the nation and its property were neither immediate nor clear. Nearly a year passed before the West German Bundeswehr, the federal defense forces, assumed responsibility for East German arms stores. By then, the depots were no longer full—large numbers of weapons had drifted from state custody into the possession of collectors, criminals, and faraway rebel bands. Adding to the arms-bazaar atmosphere was the presence of the garrisoned Soviet troops, some of whom remained on German soil into 1994. These soldiers and their officers were implicated in sales and diversions, too.

> Increasingly, Soviet soldiers are caught peddling small arms, hand grenades, and larger hardware to German citizens in exchange for alcohol, pornographic movies, and *Deutschmarks*. Pistols can be had for less than US$100, AK assault rifles along with ammunition is [*sic*] being sold on the black market for US$200 to US$300. Two journalists scored a scoop last autumn when they succeeded in buying from a Soviet major for a total of 3,000 Deutschmarks (approximately US$2,000) a number of hand grenades, an AK74, ammunition including an anti-tank mine along with one perfectly operational SAM-7, the Red Army's equivalent to the US Stinger shoulder-fired anti-aircraft missile.

Within the last year black market sales of ex-NVA or Soviet weap-onry has grown to unprecedented proportions in Germany. In Berlin everything including 120mm mortars had found their way into the hands of collectors. Much more of a problem than misguided gun-nuts are smuggling rings that recently have come to the attention of the police. One of these rings was uncovered when Stuttgart authori-ties got hold of two independently operating groups in the vicinity of that southwestern industrial city. Receiving AKs, pistols and am-munition from a Turkish connection in East Berlin, the two groups dispatched the guns to Yugoslavia's rebel groups in Kosovo province. One at a time, the weapons were carried past border checkpoints by returning Croatian and Serbian migrant workers using the weekly shuttle buses that travels [sic] from the Stuttgart area where many of the migrant workers have found work in the heart of Germany's automobile industry.

Various incidents prove that the above examples are not excep-tional occurrences but rather are the tip of a small arms iceberg.[35]

The iceberg extended beyond Germany. Other nations had larger stockpiles and less capable successor governments. In the early 1990s, Albania maintained a veneer of control over its postcommunist affairs. Appearances did not hold. Its leaders knew little of business, and beneath their assurances that an orderly transition from totalitarian bunker state to market economy was under way, the country's economy was carried along by Ponzi schemes fronting as legitimate investments. A large frac-tion of the population poured savings into these traps. In 1996 the end came. The schemes ran dry. The funds defaulted. The population's savings vanished. Panic came quickly as the pyramids collapsed. In 1997, public anger turned to rage. Rioting broke out early in the year, driven by popu-lar fury at the government for not protecting the people from nationwide fraud. Citizens ransacked government buildings and turned on the army and the police. Just as had happened in Moroto in Uganda, crowds seized the state's guns. The Kalashnikov factory at Gramsh was picked clean. Armed gangs formed, and in many regions anarchy prevailed. The high-est pitch of disorder lasted several weeks, during which hundreds of peo-ple were killed. By the fall, when the government offered an assessment of what it had lost, the numbers were staggering: nearly seven hundred

thousand firearms, 1.5 billion rounds of ammunition, more than 3 million hand grenades, and a million land mines. As much as 80 percent of
the army's small arms were missing. Researchers later claimed the official
estimates were low.[36] Some of these weapons were recovered through government offers of amnesty. Most were not. Many went north to the
Kosovo Liberation Army, or KLA, which at the time was listed by the
State Department as a terrorist group. The next year, the KLA was fighting a war against Serbian troops.

Ukraine provided another example, both of the incredible size of the
stockpiles and of a means of leakage. In the early 1990s, after the Warsaw
Pact had dissolved, Soviet military units gradually left the lands they had
occupied. They turned toward home—long, deflated columns rolling east-
ward by train and by truck. The remnants of the Soviet army lacked the
organization, will, and resources to carry all its equipment. It did try
to carry much of its weapons and ammunition. Many columns reached
Russia. Others made it only to Ukraine, where their journey stopped.
Ukraine, already a prestaged conventional arsenal, became an arms dump
along the army's road home, a nation where rail cars crammed with munitions were abandoned in the open air. (In the area around Odessa, 1,500
standard freight cars full of ammunition were idled and exposed; near
Chudniv another 330 cars were unattended; near Slabuta roughly 1,000
freight cars came to a stop.) The burden taxed Ukraine in extraordinary
ways. After trying to count its inheritance, the Ukrainian Ministry of
Defense claimed to own between 2.44 million and 3 million tons of ammunition in as many as 220 depots, and an estimated 7 million military
small arms*—roughly one hundred firearms for every soldier.

Once this sort of material was available, factors that ensured its travel
went to work: international demand, inadequate inventory procedures,
an overwhelmed and inexperienced government populated by corrupt
officials, weak international controls, and networks of brokers ready to
match buyers to goods. Little in the gun-runner's world is shared in public; transparency is typically accidental. The exact amounts of arms and
ordnance that leaked from Ukraine, and their destinations, will never

---

*This for an army that by 2007 would report having fewer than seventy-five thousand soldiers
and rarely had any soldiers abroad, aside from small contingents working under the auspices of
other organizations—such as the multinational force in Iraq or peacekeeping force in Kosovo—
that provided much of their logistics.

be publicly known. But two deals arranged by one particular broker, a debaucher of cartoonish proportion, did tumble into view.

In August 2000 the police in Italy raided a suite in a hotel outside Milan and arrested a large, naked man well into a night of prostitutes, drink, and cocaine. The man was Leonid Minin, a Ukrainian-born arms smuggler who had become a naturalized citizen of Israel. Arms dealing, to a large degree, had once been conducted between European courtiers and salesmen who wanted to be perceived as gentlemen. The Gatlings and Maxims and the former military officers in their company, with their fine dress, presented themselves as refined in experience and learning. Gatling insisted on being called Doctor. Maxim cultivated England's elite. Samuel Cummings, to the end, had panache. Theirs could be a dark business, but many practitioners put on airs. The upscale touch had its reasons. Some salesmen demonstrated weapons before princes and presidents, or generals who hailed from military academies where cadets learned to use their spoons. Minin was another sort. He was corpulent, hard-partying, and coarse—a dealer who moved casually through the post-Soviet underworld and all of its crudities, assessing weapons stocks and making useful friends. He fit a niche. He could hobnob with the warlord in need of weapons in one country and in another country speak the language of the shabby colonel whose nation had lost the Cold War and had excess weapons under lock and key. He was fifty-two years old, had many aliases, and was a streetwise businessman and able slob. In his possession at the time of his arrest, aside from the drugs, were five hundred thousand dollars' worth of unrefined diamonds and hundreds of pages of documents related to his business dealings, including the business of running guns. The documents showed that in a productive run of years seeking profits in the husk of the Soviet Union, Leonid Minin had assembled the social connections and basket of shell companies to obscure the movements of illicit cargo with paper shuffles that no one had managed to unwind. Some of these papers, once translated from multiple languages, offered a view of two weapons shipments to Africa from Ukraine.

For the first transfer, in March 1999, Minin organized the air shipment to Burkina Faso of three thousand AKM rifles, a million rounds of M1943 ammunition, twenty-five rocket-propelled grenades, and one type each of antiaircraft and antitank missiles, with eighty missiles in all. The shipment, sixty-eight tons of freight on an Antonov-124 cargo jet, was enough to arm a midsized rebel force. Though these weapons were officially listed as bound for Burkina Faso, they were not for that country's use. Once the plane landed in Ouagadougou, Burkina Faso's capital, the weapons were offloaded and transferred to another aircraft. This second aircraft, owned by Minin, shuttled the weapons by back-and-forth flights to Monrovia, the capital of Liberia, which was under United Nations arms embargo at the time. The second transfer, organized the following year, was larger. It included 10,500 Kalashnikovs, 120 sniper rifles, and 8 million rounds of ammunition. The cargo was flown out of the same Ukrainian airfield, at Gostomel, northwest of Kiev, and carried on the first leg by the same Antonov-124. The flight landed on July 15, 2000, in Abidjan, the capital of Côte d'Ivoire, and the arms aboard were reshipped to Liberia via a smaller cargo plane, which operated with a faked registration. Once in Liberia, the weapons and munitions were transferred overland to the Revolutionary United Front, or RUF, a rebel group in Sierra Leone backed by Charles Taylor, the former guerrilla who at the time was the warlord president of Liberia.

Under international rules, legal arms shipments are required to be accompanied by documents known as end-user certificates. These certifications, provided by the nation receiving the shipments, officially declare who the final recipient of the weapons will be. They serve as a government's seal of consent on arms deals on its territory. Minin's operation revealed how easily the rules could be sidestepped. He had provided the Ukrainian state arms export agency with end-user certificates signed by officials from Burkina Faso and Côte d'Ivoire; the documents claimed that these countries were the end users. They weren't. (Such records, arms dealers say, are easy to obtain, as simple as paying a bribe to a defense attaché on duty in Asian and African embassies in Europe. The paperwork can be arranged over dinner, even lunch. Brussels has been a favorite stop for procuring them, the dealers say, because many impoverished nations that have no representation in Eastern European capitals where arms deals are made have diplomatic representation there.)[37] The fraudulent certificates gave the Ukrainian arms export agency, which was riddled with corruption, plausible deniability, though many Ukrainian state officials were said to profit from the deals. By the time Minin was arrested in Italy, the weapons were already in the field, in the hands of the RUF. Minin's operation had other elements that easily skirted international controls, including shell companies registered in Gibraltar and the British Virgin Islands and banks that accepted wired deposits in Hungary, Cyprus, and the United States.[38] With air traffic control over Africa spotty, he had entered a business that was surprisingly secure.

If all of this looked complicated, it was complicated only in its unraveling. In practice, it was rather simple: Minin was a broker, a man who had access to both ends of an illegal arms deal—the people who wanted weapons in one country, and the people who controlled weapons stockpiles in another. With a bevy of bank accounts and shell companies created for the cost of registering them offshore, he assembled the mechanics of black-market transfers. The deals, to a casual observer, were masked by the patina of legitimacy. And once customers were assured of this, Minin passed along the prices for purchases and shipment, arranged transit, and ensured that each party at each leg had the necessary paperwork to present to the authorities, such as they were, to stamp, sign, or seal. All that was required was money, and contacts, and a willingness to break the law.

Once the payments from Africa were posted in his offshore bank accounts, Minin dispatched planeloads of Ukraine's weapons—made for the Cold War, cached in European bunkers, marooned by the Soviet collapse, and tended by government officials both incompetent and criminal—on their journey to Africa, thereby moving guns from a northern Cold War front to the postcolonial power struggles to the south. In this way, the Kalashnikovs and their ammunition, paired fuels for modern-day African war, were handed out to the thugs. These were not ordinary thugs. The RUF, among its many crimes, specialized in mutilation. In raids on villages along the Liberian border, it captured civilians and amputated limbs by hacking them off. It then released survivors and burned down villages as warnings to others. Its leaders with time were indicted on war-crime charges, as was Charles Taylor, who helped ferry them their guns. Sierra Leone and Liberia were not the only African countries to suffer from war criminals emboldened by excess Soviet guns, nor were they the only African countries that suffered atrocities and mutilations at such men's hands. The list is long: Angola, Rwanda, Sudan, the Democratic Republic of Congo, Uganda, and others. And thus the *Avotomat Kalashnikova* earned another name. To Europe's south, a busy destination for assault rifles made elsewhere, the acronym AK meant not just the Automatic by Kalashnikov. The letters stood for something more: the Africa Killer, the gun that helped sink country after country into fresh cycles of blood.

Almost no one was moving on the red dirt track leading to the village of Ajulu. The dozen or so young soldiers from the Sinia Brigade, hiding in the vegetation a few yards off the road, had little to do as minutes stretched into hours. They lounged and paced with their assault rifles, chatting, passing time between crimes. All the while they listened, waiting for a car or truck.

The group had been in place since 5:00 A.M., on orders from their commander, Joseph Kony. Their mission was not a hard one, at least not physically. They had been instructed to waylay travelers and lead them into the bush. Another team, responsible for administering warnings and collective punishment, waited in a gully a short walk away, ready with their razor blades. Only occasionally would a victim appear. It was 1998. The people of Acholiland, the area of northwestern Uganda where these fighters roamed the forests, had been living in fear for more than a decade. The survivors had adapted their habits to avoid the horrors of the roads. Yet even the most cautious could not stay off the roads entirely. People needed to go to market or for medical treatment in Gulu or Kitgum, or to visit relatives in the displaced-person camps near the Nile. From the rebels' perspective, the day had not been lost. They had captured several people, cut them, and released them to stagger home. One of the hidden fighters, Patrick Okwera, saw the next victim: a man about thirty years of age. He was pedaling toward them on a bicycle. The fighters prepared themselves. When the man came close, they would rush from hiding and seize him, too.

Patrick was fourteen years old and in his fifth year as a soldier of the Lord's Resistance Army, or LRA, the Sinia Brigade's parent command. His life, and that of his family, ran through Joseph Kony's nihilistic and inexplicable war. Patrick's parents had been abducted by the LRA when he was a small boy. The rebels released his mother. They chopped his father to pieces. Patrick's own encounter with the LRA came in 1993, when rebels kidnapped him from a stream in which he was bathing. Later, his younger brother, Jimmy, was abducted, too. The boys were reunited in LRA camps in southern Sudan, where they were taught to kill. They became child soldiers, molded for violence by commanders who led them back into the bush. Several years on, by the grisly standards by which the LRA judged him, Patrick Okwera was a success. He had been pressed into service as a nine-year-old and quickly sensed that survival required compliance. He had complied, becoming a killer within days of his capture. Now just past puberty, he was a veteran. He knew the tactics of the ambush, was experienced with the details of the kidnapping raid. He had fought in several battles and shown himself to be an effective supervisor of other children under arms. He had stormed enemy barracks, and helped cache weapons and ammunition throughout the countryside, so that if the Lord's Resistance Army lost Sudanese support its war might go on. By Patrick's own estimate he had shot at least thirty people with his automatic rifle. He had not hesitated yet.

Outside his depleted family, Patrick's kidnapping and conversion were barely noticeable. The Lord's Resistance Army relied on child abduction to maintain its ranks. Tens of thousands of children had been stolen from their lives, often under circumstances more spectacular than his, including raids in which children were roped together and led into the bush with wrists lashed behind their backs. Sometimes the miserable columns became death marches. Those who straggled risked execution at the hands of the other captives, who were forced to beat fellow villagers to death. The first ordeal ended only upon arrival at the rebel bases, where the survivors were reshaped. The boys became fighters. The girls were forced into lives as servants, cooks, and sex slaves. Awarded as wives to LRA commanders, they were repeatedly raped. Many bore children in forest encampments. Abducted children were the clay of the Lord's Resistance Army, a guerrilla force summoned into being by Kony, who claimed to channel holy spirits and follow the will of God.

Patrick stopped the man on the bicycle. He and several other children led their captive at gunpoint into the forest. The man trembled as they walked. He was silent. Patrick understood: The man knew what to expect. Up ahead was the cutting team, and there, with a razor, boy soldiers would slice away the man's lips and nose.[39]

The Lord's Resistance Army, sinister and bizarre, descended from a mystical guerrilla movement founded by Alice Auma, a childless Acholi woman who by various accounts was either Kony's aunt or his cousin. In 1985, Auma returned from a period of isolation on the banks of the Nile claiming to have been possessed by the spirit of an Italian army officer, whom she called Lakwena. Lakwena, she said, spoke dozens of languages. His name meant Word of God. In the early months after her supposed possession, Alice passed time aimlessly, working as a healer and oracle in Gulu; an enchanted freak. The spirit Lakwena grew into a taskmaster. He upped the duo's ambitions. Late in 1986 Alice announced that Lakwena had ordered her to organize a movement to overthrow the Ugandan government, which was led by Yoweri Museveni, a former guerrilla commander who had displaced a post-Amin Acholi president. At that, Alice Lakwena, a composite of personalities in the form of a young woman with no military experience, became as strange and underqualified a guerrilla leader as the world had known. Yet she found a following. Uganda was suffering, and the Acholi felt abused by Museveni. Her message of rejuvenation appealed.

Lakwena organized her recruits into a cultish military wing known as the Holy Spirit Mobile Forces, and channeled other spirits to assume each unit's command. Wrong Element led Company A; he claimed to hail from the United States. Ching Poh, from China, commanded Company B. A spirit variously called Franko or Mzee commanded Company C. He was responsible for food. Alice was fresh-faced and often dressed in long white robes. As the spirits seemed to alternate within her, she whispered, then raged. With her followers ringed round, she sat on a lawn chair and promulgated the Holy Spirit Safety Precautions, rules that required her soldiers to fight standing and never to hide behind cover. Service in her war demanded faith. But the precautions were more than instructions for battle. They formed a code of social behavior, which Lakwena insisted would protect her adherents from harm. Among the prohibitions were bans on stealing, smoking, drinking alcohol, carrying charms, killing snakes, or shaking hands with anyone while traveling to a fight. Sex was forbidden, as was killing enemy prisoners. Some precautions would seem easy to satisfy, like not carrying a walking stick into battle. For the movement's men Precaution Number Twenty was easier still: "Thou shalt have two testicles, neither more nor less."[40]

Rituals arose around Alice's invocations. Before battle, the soldiers attended purification ceremonies and were rubbed with shea butter oil, which Alice said would render their skin bulletproof. Many Holy Spirit fighters did not carry rifles. Those who did, at least in the beginning, were ordered not to aim at their enemies, but to fire in the general direction and allow spirits to guide bullets toward flesh. Others believed that if they chose the right rocks, those rocks, when thrown, would explode like grenades. The Holy Spirit Mobile Forces were not a rational military organization. But their cultishness gave them an early power against their foes, some of whom believed Auma's magic was real. Had she adopted classic guerrilla tactics, she might have led an effective insurgency. Instead, the mobile forces' tactics were theatric, a show resembling a parade. Their order of battle ensured the movement's short life.

> The Holy Spirit soldiers took up positions and, as ordered by the spirit, began to sing pious songs for 10, 15 or 20 minutes. Then the time-keeper blew a whistle. On this sign, the troops began marching forward in a long line, shouting at the tops of their voices: "James Bond! James Bond! James Bond!" Lakwena's chief technician was named James and called himself James Bond. The stone commanders led them and the line commanders ensured that the front line was maintained. Each stone commander carried a stone wrapped in cloth, which he threw at the enemy, at the same time calling to each company and leading spirit, "Ching Poh, Franko, or Wrong Element, take up your position, command your people!" This stone marked the limit past which the enemy bullets could not penetrate, thus creating a protective zone.[41]

After a few spectacular successes, the movement suffered its defeats. The ending arrived on the march on Kampala, Uganda's capital, when the Holy Spirit soldiers, many without weapons and calling for James Bond, were subjected to assault rifle and artillery fire. They were cut down. The survivors were put to flight. Alice promptly announced that the spirits had abandoned her. She slinked off for Kenya, where she was granted asylum and faded from view, aside from occasional interviews with journalists, who documented her end as an exiled lush, hooked on gin, spiritless, vowing a return.

Her homecoming was unnecessary. Joseph Kony replaced her as the possessed guerrilla leader of Acholiland. The new commander had learned what Auma had not. Kony did not ask his child soldiers to rest their faith on shea butter and stone grenades alone. He made sure to give them guns.

Joseph Kony raised Alice Auma's millennial weirdness several notches, blending her mystical persona with more practical ways to kill. He claimed to inherit her otherworldly contacts in 1987, when spirits took possession of him. His spirits formed a troupe. Juma Oris was their chairman, and mandated that Uganda be ruled by the Ten Commandants. Silly Salindi, a female Sudanese spirit also known as Malia Mackay, set down a fuller set of rules: no smoking or drinking, and sex only when allowed. She required prayer three times a day from the LRA's impressed conscripts, and ordered that whenever they crossed rivers or passed anthills they must make the sign of the cross. Who Are You, an American spirit, also had an alias: Zinck Brickey. He was in charge of intelligence. King Bruce controlled heavy weapons and kept alive the idea of the stone grenade as part of the army's supporting arms. Dr. Salan organized medical care, and insisted he could bring fertility to the barren. Willing Hing Sue, a Chinese spirit, was said to make the enemy hallucinate, even to imagine that the LRA had armored troop carriers that floated in the air. There were many more. A former LRA captain described how the spirits appeared.

> In the beginning he was possessed sometimes two or three times a day. . . . Kony would always be alerted by "Who Are You" that a spirit would come at a certain time to speak for a certain time (for example at 1400 hours for three or four minutes). Kony's secretary (Chief to Lakwena) would make the preparations, and Kony would dress in a white robe. A glass of water, a bible, and a rosary were placed on the table. To start the possession Kony would dip his fingers into a clear glass of water. Multiple spirits would pass through Kony in a single session. On average at least three spirits would talk in a session. Junior spirits always talked first. After the session the LRA commander would address the crowd. No one corrected what the spirits said, nor did people dare question the spirits.
>
> When Kony dipped his finger in glass [sic] of water he slumped forward for a few seconds, then sat up. Each spirit had a separate personality. His voice changed to a woman's tone of voice when pos-

sessed by Malia. Some spirits spoke faster than others. Who Are You was rude—quarreling—and he complained a lot. Chairman Juma Oris talked slow and calm with a flat tone like an "important person." Malia gave morale and hope after operations, and would say that those injured would recover with help from Dr. Salan.[42]

Kony's spirits set rules: Pigeons were sacred and not to be consumed; fish could be eaten as long as they had scales; eating pigs was forbidden, but warthogs were meat. Shea butter oil was believed to make LRA soldiers bulletproof; in time, this belief subsided, apparently overcome by facts.[43] Setting aside Kony's mimicry, there was an important difference between the movements. If Alice Lakwena had intended to purify Acholiland and then Uganda, Kony and his spirits had another plan—to subjugate it by force.

In almost any other setting or any other time, Kony would have been marked down as a barking madman, a person to be walked wide around when encountered on the street. But Acholiland was rife with cross-border intrigues, and across Uganda's northern line, in Sudan, Kony found support. Sudan was willing to arm him and the abducted children with whom he crossed out of Uganda, and to use the LRA to undermine a neighboring state. With support from Khartoum, Kony encamped in southern Sudan and built an army of children with Kalashnikovs. The guns were issued from Sudanese government trucks.[44] His soldiers carried thousands of rifles on raids back into Uganda, and to fight the Dinka, a Sudanese minority tribe that the government in Khartoum also wanted Kony to harass. They hid thousands more in the hills and forests along the border. In this way, Kony made his name. Acholiland burned. "The Sudanese government gave it a lot of firewood to make it cook well," said Lieutenant Colonel Francis Alero, another of Kony's former commanders.[45]

Assault rifles did more than amplify the war. They gave it stamina, a duration it otherwise could not have had. The children sensed this. "The Arabs gave Kony many weapons, and up to now that is how he has been able to resist," said one former soldier. "Without the guns it would have just been sticks."[46] The Lord's Resistance Army—its crimes and their consequences, along with its longevity—condensed the perils of assault-rifle proliferation. The simplicity of the Kalashnikov allowed Kony and his commanders to convert columns of abducted children, roped together like slaves, into a terrifying irregular force. Young and illiterate fighters, some as young as eight or nine, could be instructed on how to load and shoot their rifles, and how to keep them clean. "It takes only one week," said Colonel Alero. The boy soldiers were not good shots.* But in short-range ambushes and surprise raids, running and spinning and firing, often targeting civilians, they turned their own homeland into a hell.

The Kalashnikov's traits also allowed the LRA to keep its campaigns alive for years. Kony's brigades cached guns crudely. The Ugandan climate was harsh. And yet if the weapons were buried with a modest amount of care—first coated with oil and sometimes also with charcoal and ash to

---

* These two lines—*it takes only a week* and *the boy soldiers were not good shots*—serve as a departure point for further discussion about one element of Kalashnikov proliferation. The Kalashnikov is a very effective firearm at short and medium ranges. But its ease of use should not be confused with a user's ability to master marksmanship. Most anyone can load, carry, and fire a Kalashnikov, and so most anyone does. And often the poorly disciplined or the poorly trained use them ineffectively in fights. Any extensive reconstruction of the ways that warfighting has changed since handheld automatic firearms became prevalent in conflict zones will invariably turn up accounts of gunmen who fire wild bursts and hit nothing at all, even at close range. Such observations align with a school of thought that says that since assault rifles displaced bolt-action rifles, marksmanship skills in many fighting forces have declined. Why? Because of a reliance on automatic shooting, often without aiming. This behavior, combined with the trajectory of the medium-powered M1943 cartridge, limits the effective range of the weapon as commonly used. In the hands of unskilled gunmen, Kalashnikovs are effective for crime and for action against the unarmed, and for destabilizing regions not under tight government control. (The villagers in Acholiland are almost defenseless against them, and have suffered terribly.) But in the years since most well-off conventional armies developed or procured their own assault rifles, and often mounted optical sights to their updated arms, Kalashnikovs in such hands have proven at times to be less effective in fighting conventional forces with sophisticated training and modern equipment.

Sometimes the differences between a lightly trained Kalashnikov-wielding gunman and a modern Western soldier can be stark. In one example, from November 2005, a small convoy of American soldiers stopped outside the police station of the Afghan National Police, or ANP, in Zormat in Paktia province. The American patrol leader, from Charlie Company, First Battalion of the 504th Parachute Infantry Regiment, had planned to talk with the Afghan police chief. The soldiers, with the air force noncommissioned officers who coordinated the company's air support, waited outside, standing beside their vehicles and among the milling police officers. One of the Afghan officers leveled his Kalashnikov at the Americans and started shooting. The officer, according to one of the men who was attacked, "came toward our vehicles from the opposite side, maybe forty or fifty feet away before we noticed him and, without warning, raised his AK-47 to his hip and opened fire, yelling. He had wrapped the hand guard in red plastic and wasn't disciplined with his firing, shooting on full auto. We immediately took cover and none of his rounds hit anyone, but they did chew through the hood of the HMMWV [a military vehicle] I was standing beside, spraying fiberglass into the face of the sergeant standing beside me. Before anyone else had a chance really to react beyond taking cover, the gunner in the turret simply turned his M249 SAW [Squad Automatic Weapon, a light machine gun] and pretty much cut the ANP in half. After searching through his pockets, they found something along the lines of six months of pay which indicated he was likely paid off." (Personal communication from Staff Sergeant Bertrand Fitzpatrick, United States Air Force, who was present at the attack.)

repel insects—they could be retrieved as long as four years later and still be made to fire.[47] Ammunition was also stored underground, stuffed into jerry cans. One former child soldier, Dennis Okwonga, abducted at age thirteen, was ordered to restore rifles pulled from hiding. The Kalashnikovs had been buried in caves, towering ant colonies, or holes dug into the earth. Before being hidden, they had been oiled, bundled within tent tarps, and placed on a sheet of plastic in pits. A second plastic sheet had covered them, then a layer of rocks and dirt. Dennis helped dig apart an anthill that contained 240 Kalashnikovs and four 82-millimeter mortar tubes. The work began.

> Some were rusted and the ants had eaten the handgrips. We had to shape new hand grips with wood. It didn't take long to make them all work. There were three of us, sometimes more. We worked for one month to recondition them and we reburied them. We test-fired them—they all worked. We at first used water to wash them, to get rust off. Then we used oil, gun oil. One pit had 240 guns but they brought us guns from other places—898 in all. A storekeeper had to keep track of the numbers. AK-47s and mortars. All 898 worked after we cleaned them.[48]

In this way, the Acholi insurgency progressed from Alice Auma's hapless spirit show to Joseph Kony's organized brigades. The LRA was not alone in its use of child soldiers. But its development from sideshow movement into a near-permanent presence along Uganda's northwest border and the frontiers of Congo served to illustrate how such a force can be mobilized, set loose, and then survive. Armed with Kalashnikovs, Kony's brigades displaced more than a million and a half Ugandans. They punished suspected informants mercilessly and cut away the lips and noses of residents as a warning not to pass information to Museveni's soldiers. Their actions provoked reactions. The population suffered from both sides. The Ugandan government forced rural Acholi residents into displaced-person camps, both to protect and to control them. The Acholi economy withered. Eventually, the government invested in heavy weapons to chase the child soldiers down. The use of Mi-24 helicopter gunships was decisive in pushing the brigades across Uganda's borders. But Kony and his army's remnants lingered on, moving between Uganda,

Sudan, and the Democratic Republic of Congo, a force drawing strength from the resilience of its guns.

During the years of Kony's rise, the Kalashnikov was more than a requisite tool for regional African war. On the Pashtun frontier, where Kalashnikov saturation was as dense as anywhere, it became a gateway to international jihad. After the Soviet army's withdrawal from Afghanistan, the Taliban formed and claimed control of much of the country. Afghanistan and the tribal areas of Pakistan provided sanctuary for militant Islamic groups and parties. The international recruits who entered this world were ushered from guesthouses in Peshawar and Kabul to camps in the Afghan provinces, where they were trained for terror and guerrilla war.

Camps operated near Mazar-e-Sharif, Jalalabad, Khost, Kandahar, Kabul, and elsewhere. Different parties—some local, others from Central Asia, Kashmir, Africa, or Arabia—operated their own schools and taught their charges in a variety of languages, including Urdu, Uzbek, Tajik, Russian, Arabic, and Pashto.[49] The schools shared more than ideology and common purpose. They began instruction with an inaugural lesson—how to use the *Avtomat Kalashnikova*. Notebooks of students who attended these courses, recovered across Afghanistan in 2001, underlined the pre-eminent place that Kalashnikov rifles had realized in introducing new jihadists to their holy war. The handwritten notebooks the students left behind showed that the recruits attended classes covering the history and characteristics of the AKM and other Kalashnikov variants and received basic instruction in their use. Later lessons covered tactics, including the fundamentals of patrolling and ambushes, and immediate-action drills—the steps to be taken by small patrols upon making contact with a foe. The instruction was of mediocre quality. Some of it contained errors or unrealistic descriptions of the weapons' qualities. (A class given to Asadullah, a recruit in the Islamic Movement of Uzbekistan, which became an al Qaeda affiliate in the late 1990s, included charts claiming that an AKM had a one-thousand-meter range.) But the instruction was earnest, consistent, and meticulous, suggesting that whoever had organized it had given it considerable thought. The Kalashnikov was viewed by the jihad's trainers as a fighter's first tool.

Its prominence was demonstrated by a simple fact: The extent of Kalashnikov proliferation by the late 1990s was such that the only question for a fighter seeking to obtain one was price. The price of a Kalashnikov is often misunderstood, and in many conversations subject to distortion. One common view has long held, and falsely, that in many regions of the world an AK-47 can be purchased for the cost of a chicken or a sack of grain. Kofi A. Annan, the secretary general of the United Nations from 1997 through 2006, repeated these lines, and added that an AK-47 "can be bought for as little as $15."[50] Such prices may have existed in one place or another for a very brief time. But loudness and repetition are not truth, and these statements, echoed by journalists and arms-control advocates over the years, are best viewed with skepticism. The more realistic retail price range for a single automatic Kalashnikov in much of the developing world, depending on many factors (the rifle's exact type, nation of manufacture, and condition, the local laws and security conditions at the time and point of sale, the experience of the purchaser) is on the order of several hundred dollars. In some conflicts, a thousand dollars is not rare.

Prices climb when and where Kalashnikovs are difficult to obtain. In nations capable of enforcing the laws they pass, strict gun control can send prices soaring. In the United States, a well-used fully automatic Chinese Type 56 Kalashnikov, in 2005, could cost $10,000;[51] the price is higher as of this writing. But the United States is its own case, and prices there are not indicative of prices in regions where the Kalashnikov line is readily available or widely used. Other examples are more germane. In eastern Uganda in the late 1980s, after more than fifteen years of local Kalashnikov proliferation, an AK-47 could be bought for about $200, or traded for three or four cattle[52]—a good bit more than a chicken. In the arms bazaars along Pakistan's border with Afghanistan, prices for a Kalashnikov ranged from $1,500 to $3,500 during the early years of the 1980s, when demand for weapons for the war against the Soviet army outstripped supply. By the late 1980s, as other governments shipped hundreds of thousands of rifles to the war, Kalashnikov prices had dropped. They reached roughly $700 by the time the Soviet army withdrew. Prices then sank further, dipping nearly to $300 by 2000, before climbing again with the onset of new war.[53] In Iraq, Kalashnikovs could be purchased in early to mid-2003 for $150 or less, the soft retail prices reflecting an abundance of weapons available as the Baathist state security structures disbanded and weapons flooded markets, as well as the brief sense of optimism

immediately after Saddam Hussein was toppled.[54] As the insurgency grew
and sectarian violence spread, and as new forms of demand pressured
supply—including an influx of contractors seeking assault rifles for security duties—Kalashnikov prices moved up. By 2005, an AKM clone with
a fixed stock cost roughly $450. By 2006, these same rifles cost $650 to
$800, with higher prices being paid for Kalashnikovs with folding stocks,
which can be more readily concealed and are easier to fire from within a
car. In the end, a Kalashnikov on the retail market, which often means on
the gray or black market, is like a handmade carpet in a shop. It is worth
what a seller can convince a buyer to pay for it. Many factors determine
price, and an astute buyer and informed seller can haggle over the details
of a gun—not just condition, but Romanian versus Hungarian, Chinese
versus Russian, under-folding versus a side-folding collapsible stock—the
way collectors might debate the relative merits of a Turkmen, Azeri, or
Persian tribal rug.

Not just cash and barter have been used to acquire rifles; extortion has
proven an effective means. In Chechnya, insurgents often gain rifles and
ammunition through novel agreements. A local fighting cell will use middlemen to negotiate with Russian or pro-Russian Chechen units for truces.
In exchange for not attacking a certain Russian position for a prescribed
length of time, the insurgents exact a tax paid in armament—a rifle, a
can of ammunition, perhaps a sack of grenades. Sometimes to close deals,
they sweeten agreements by delivering vodka regularly to a government
checkpoint or position. In this way, Russian units have arranged quiet
tours.[55] Such arrangements are mercurial, and similar pressures can be
applied in the other direction and serve as a mechanism for disarmament.
Russian units, when seeking to capture weapons, have set up roadblocks
and impounded Chechen civilians' cars and trucks. For each vehicle to be
released, the soldiers tell the evicted drivers, the price is one Kalashnikov
rifle, to be obtained as the vehicle's owners see fit.[56] In such situations, a
rifle becomes very expensive—worth as much as a family's automobile.

Prices can be set in yet other ways, including special cases that have
little to do with needing a weapon for war, as when a weapon's novelty
or symbolism creates prestige. Prestige within Kalashnikov culture, like
prestige surrounding other product lines with large followings, almost
invariably drives up price. Brigadier Mohammad Yousaf, who headed the
Afghan bureau of the ISI, the Pakistani intelligence service, claimed that

the CIA paid $5,000 for the first AK-74—the new Soviet assault rifle that fired the smaller cartridge—captured in Afghanistan in the 1980s.[57] At other times a weapon can assume an aura, and aura similarly affects price. Weapons even resembling the smallest Kalashnikovs of all, the AKSU-74, a short-barreled, collapsible-stock design that American gun enthusiasts call the *Krinkov* and that Osama bin Laden has been photographed with, could cost more than $2,000 during the most violent period of the most recent war in Iraq.[58] This weapon had by then picked up a regional nickname that gave it jihadist cachet: "the Osama." Bin Laden's selection of this design (it is less than twenty inches long and weighs not quite six pounds) was on technical merits a strange endorsement. An AKSU-74 is inaccurate and fires rounds with less muzzle velocity than an AK-74, making it potentially less useful and lethal than many available choices. But people who regard themselves as warriors inhabit worlds in which symbols matter. And in the particular history of bin Laden's martial surroundings—western Pakistan and Afghanistan of the last three decades—a short-barreled Kalashnikov emanated a trophy's distinction. Relatively new, the AKSU-74 had been carried in the Soviet-Afghan War by specialized soldiers, including helicopter and armor crews, for whom a smaller weapon was useful in the tight confines of their transit. For an Afghan fighter, possession of one of these rifles signified bravery and action. It implied that the holder had participated in destroying an armored vehicle or aircraft; the rifle was akin to a scalp. By choosing it, bin Laden silently signaled to his followers: *I am authentic,* even if his actual combat experience was not what his prop suggested.

Symbolic power has been harnessed by owners of assault rifles since assault rifles became available. After Salvador Allende rose to the presidency of Chile in 1970, becoming the Western Hemisphere's first elected socialist head of state, Fidel Castro presented him with a folding-stock Kalashnikov bearing an inscription on a golden plate: "To my good friend Salvador from Fidel, who by different means tries to achieve the same goals."[59] The rifle served as 1970s leftist bling, though a golden plate was more Saddam Hussein than Karl Marx. Like so many other men with a Kalashnikov, like József Tibor Fejes with his captured AK-47 in Budapest, Allende could not resist a pose. He was photographed at least once playing with his keepsake rifle, looking down the barrel while pointing it into the air. If the most widely circulated accounts are to be believed, Castro's gift had a role in the final palace act, in which Allende, besieged in September 1973 during a CIA-backed coup, sat on a couch, placed his Kalashnikov between his knees, aligned the muzzle beneath his chin, and fired.[60] (Allende would not be the last head of state to die by Kalashnikov fire; the list would grow.)

The darker symbolism eluded those who maintained the celebration. Mozambique chose in 1983 to allow a Kalashnikov to adorn its national flag. At roughly the same time, Hezbollah formed in Lebanon, and its yellow flag bore the image of an assault rifle with features resembling those of a Kalashnikov.* Other groups have made the selection explicit. The Kalashnikov decorates the crest of Lashkar-e-Taiba, the South Asian Islamic terrorist group, and appears on flags and murals used by the New People's Army in the Philippines and the Revolutionary Armed Forces of Colombia, or FARC. In Iraq after the American invasion, the rifle became part of the murals and flags of Jaish al-Islami, the 1920 Revolutionary Brigades, the Mujahideen Shura Council, Jaish al-Taifa al-Mansoura, and the Salafist Group for Call and Combat.

The Kalashnikov, while by far the most common choice for recent martial art, was not alone in conveying political ideas. Fighters often choose weapons that broadcast messages. Palestinian insurgents often preferred to carry an M-16 or their carbine descendant, the M-4—the weapons of the Israel Defense Forces. Possession of an American rifle signified either Israeli corruption or Palestinian battlefield success; in either case, grounds to boost a Palestinian fighter's morale.[61] For these reasons, M-16s appear in the logo of Al Aqsa Martyr's Brigades and are sometimes superimposed on the emblem of Hamas, though the bulk of these organizations' fighters carry Kalashnikovs, which long ago entered the movements' symbols, lyrics, and slogans, too. One fedayeen song revered the "Klashin," local shorthand for the Kalashnikov line.

---

* The oft-repeated conventional wisdom is that the rifle on the Hezbollah flag is a Kalashnikov. The rifle's magazine resembles that of a Kalashnikov, as does its stock. The front sight post does not, and a case could be made that the image more closely resembles the G3 rifle, a widely circulated product of Heckler & Koch and another descendant of the *sturmgewehr*, which was designed in a Spanish–West German collaboration in the 1950s. Or it might simply be sloppy political art. Similar uncertainty surrounds the emblem of the Túpac Amaru Revolutionary Movement, or MRTA, which included the image of an assault rifle that is often called a Kalashnikov. The common assertion about Hezbollah's choice is not the most glaring error in the legends of Kalashnikov symbols. That distinction perhaps falls to the frequent claim that the logo of the Red Army Faction, the now-defunct left-wing German terrorist organization, bore the image of a Kalashnikov. The weapon on the group's red-star logo is an MP-5 submachine gun, also a product of Heckler & Koch.

Klashin makes the blood run out in torrents
Haifa and Jaffa are calling us
Commando, go ahead and do not worry
Open fire and break the silence of the night.[62]

But other weapons manage to have their moment, even as a pointed counterpoint. In the Caucasus, Ruslan Kuchbarov, leader of the Chechen and Ingush terrorist gang that seized more than eleven hundred hostages at School No. 1 in Beslan in 2004, strutted through the school's corridors and surveyed his captives while swinging a VSS—a silenced sniper rifle almost exclusively used by Russian *spetsnaz*.* His message was an underground staple. *Those men you sent to kill me? I've got their guns.* President Mikheil Saakashvili of Georgia, who cast himself as a post-Soviet Westernizer, initiated a program to replace his nation's stocks of Kalashnikovs with M-4s, choosing the rifle as if thumbing his nose at the Kremlin. The Kalashnikov, he said, was a symbol of communism, of centralization, of the Soviet Union, of the KGB-run government that rose on its remains, of an old and inhumane world he wanted Georgia to forget.[63] "Goodbye old weapon!" he shouted to formations of his country's soldiers as he personally handed out an early shipment of M-4s. "Long live the new one!"[64] Saakashvili was excitable, a president who knew more about symbols and speeches than about how wars were fought. On a Thursday night several months later, he ordered an attack on Russian-backed South Ossetia. His army was scattered by the weekend. It fled. The Russian soldiers who defeated them showed almost no interest in the M-4s the retreating Georgians abandoned, other than as trophies to be carried home. "Ours are better," one Russian soldier said, frowning over a captured American rifle in the briefly occupied city of Gori.†[65]

For most of those who seek assault rifles, these seesawing meanings are unnecessary. A pedestrian AKM or knock-off will do. For these buyers one

---

* Special Forces soldiers.

† Saakashvili and his military leadership also seemed not to know much about choosing its rifles—it bought thousands of Bushmaster M-4s, knockoffs that resemble the American military's standard Colt carbines but are not made to the same certified manufacturing standards. This was a strange choice, given that for roughly the same price, the Georgian military could have purchased the more combat-tested design. Military rifle choices have long confounded political and military leaders. This was another such case.

fact is irrefutable. The Kalashnikov, while more expensive than a chicken, has been an inexpensive choice. A record on the hard drive of a computer used by Mullah Mohammed Omar, the leader of the Taliban, showed that in fall 2001, as the Taliban priced out the costs of arming two thousand fighters, it anticipated spending about \$202* per Kalashnikov.[66] The comparisons on the ledger were useful—the rifle would cost twenty times as much as a uniform, and more than thirteen times as much as a pair of the shoes to be issued to each *talib* for the mullah's jihad. Another comparison was useful as well. Georgia, when it sought to replace M-4s lost in the war, accepted a price of \$870 per weapon for thirteen thousand rifles[67]—more than four times the price the Taliban was to pay for its primary arms. The United States military, by 2009, was paying roughly \$1,100 for each M-4 issued to its soldiers, more than five times the cost per rifle borne by its enemies in Afghanistan, if the Taliban's sources remained the same.[†68]

The United States government recognized this difference early in its engagement with the nascent Afghan and Iraqi armed forces, to which it provided hundreds of thousands of small arms. Mullah Omar's prospective cost—\$202 per Kalashnikov—was only slightly more than what the United States often paid on the way to becoming the world's largest publicly known purchaser of AKM knock-offs.

In those deals, brokers in Eastern Europe arranged purchases from stockpiles at bulk prices, often less than \$100 per assault rifle. By one example, Romanian surplus was initially sold at \$93 to \$98 each for a fixed-stock rifle, or \$115 for a rifle with a folding stock.[69] These prices were roughly comparable to the price of an M-16 rifle—in 1966.[70] The brokers then flipped the rifles at higher prices to the American companies awarded the Pentagon contracts, which in turn charged the Pentagon more—in the range of \$150 to \$165 a rifle, including air-freight delivery costs to Baghdad or Kabul. The rifles had typically been manufactured during the Warsaw Pact years and had sat unused in the decades since; they were considered new. Some vendors passed off used rifles to the Pentagon by reconditioning them with new finishes and lacquers. Newly manufac-

---

* The precise figure given was twelve thousand Pakistani rupees.

† Government purchasers can buy military-standard M-4s for about \$800 a rifle. The American military pays more because its M-4s include an after-market rail system to which accessories can be mounted. This pushes up the price.

tured rifles would cost significantly more, because of the increased costs of labor, energy, and commodities required to make them. The point, well-known among purchasers, is this: Because of the glut of rifles from Cold War–era stockpiles, it costs very little to outfit fighters with Kalashnikovs. The expense is small enough that many governments hand them out to those who might serve their bidding, as Egypt and Libya and other Arab states did with the Palestinians, as the United States did in Afghanistan and Iraq, and as Sudan did to the Lord's Resistance Army, whose commanders fought for years without worrying about running short of guns, or seeking funds to buy more. At the bottom of the hierarchy, where the fighting and killing and many of the crimes take place, those involved were armed almost effortlessly, and free of the burden of attending to the details. "The thing you get for free," one amnestied LRA commander said, "you don't bother to ask the price."[71]

Almost a century and a half after Dr. Richard J. Gatling developed a workable design for a rapid-fire arm, the armaments world had reached that stage. After decades of assault-rifle production in planned economies, eight-pound automatic rifles could be issued to child soldiers at no cost to their commanders, jihadist movements pitted against the world's most powerful and modern military force could arm fighters for about two hundred dollars a man, and the opening class in terrorist training camps was an introduction to the AKM. Outside the West, the rifle was at the very center of war and preparations for it. By 2001, when Mullah Omar received his price list, the United Nations had attempted a rough tally of the human costs to those in places where the rifles are used most. It found that small arms had been the principal weapons in forty-six of the forty-nine major conflicts in the 1990s, in which 4 million people died, roughly 90 percent of them civilians.[72] For most of these wars and most of these young conscripts, Kalashnikovs were the primary rifle. If the United Nations' numbers were accurate and hundreds of thousands of people were being killed by small arms each year—in wars, crimes, acts of state repression, or acts of terror—then it would never be possible to document, person by person, the Kalashnikov's role in what it all meant. Case studies would have to do, offering insights into the experiences of a victim here, or a victim there, serving as representatives of an enormous

class. Each war provides new casualties. Each day the tally climbs. But it
is possible to slow down and to examine what the weapons can do to an
individual victim, a man like Karzan Mahmoud.

Mahmoud was shot in spring 2002 in northern Iraq, a region that
had been an all-but-forgotten seam in the wars in the Middle East. No
one much noticed that day, though a new war was gathering. The American military had chased the Taliban from Kabul several months before,
and President George W. Bush's administration had switched focus. The
northern portion of Iraq, loosely protected by a no-fly zone, was a semi-
autonomous Kurdish enclave, a statelet within a state, where Washington
was quietly renewing engagement with the Kurds, seeking allies for the
war ahead. Ryan Crocker, an American diplomat, had come to Sulaimaniya, capital of the eastern portion of the Kurdish zone, to meet with the
officials of the Patriotic Union of Kurdistan, or PUK, one of two principal Kurdish parties. The PUK ruled Iraq's northeast, mixing promises of
democracy with old-time cronyism and centralized party power. It had
descended from a guerrilla force—the *peshmerga,* those who face death—
that waged mountain war against Saddam Hussein's Baathist Iraq. But
the party's surviving military leaders were now older and mostly softer,
interested in politics and business more than in fighting a lonely war. Its
military formations were small, inadequately equipped, and unevenly led.
And they had outright enemies—Hussein to the south and an Islamic
fundamental movement in their midst. This was the territory in which
Karzan Mahmoud operated, as a bodyguard, in a land of hidden danger
and treachery.

The three assassins arrived near the home of Prime Minister Barham
Salih at 3:45 P.M. on April 2, wearing a mix of traditional *peshmerga* dress
and modern camouflage uniforms. It was a chilly spring afternoon. A
light rain shower was falling. The assassins had shaved their beards and
looked neat, resembling officers from the local Ministry of the Interior.
For their approach, they had bought a local white-and-orange Volks-
wagen taxi so that they might blend in. The prime minister's residence, a
two-story house, was located several lots from the corner, set back several
yards from the road. As the taxi neared, Salih was finishing a meeting with
the city's director of intelligence and preparing to drive to meet Crocker.
The security teams of both men waited outside. The taxi stopped at the
corner. The assassins stepped out. They wore Kalashnikovs on slings. They

moved casually toward the officials' bodyguards, who suffered the confidence of numbers. The guards, after all, were twelve.

Mahmoud was Salih's driver that day. Moments before, he had left his white Nissan Patrol, and was walking through the drizzle toward the taxi when it pulled up. He was wearing a blue suit and red tie. He had intended to visit a market at the corner, but the taxi diverted his attention. Mahmoud was twenty-four, a *peshmerga* for six years. A polite man, he emanated decency, respect, and kindness of an order that could seem a fault. He approached the three men to tell them that they should move their car down the street. No one was allowed to park here. He was drilled in manners and protocol. It showed.

"How can I help you?" he asked.

The lead man had a question. "Is Dr. Barham home?"

"Yes," Mahmoud answered. "What do you need?"

About fifteen feet separated the two men. The man stepped forward, swung his Kalashnikov up to level, and fired a burst at Mahmoud's face.

Mahmoud was small statured, the sort of athlete whom larger and more powerful men misjudge. He had spent five years in intensive tae kwon do training, which had left him limber and loose and equipped him with dodges that could look instinctive. He sensed the shift—from routine traffic encounter to terrible danger—in the instant the assassin's face changed. The Kalashnikov muzzle rose. Mahmoud fell. He bent his knees, forcing his shins forward toward the ground. As his lower body dipped in that direction, he pushed off the balls of his feet and threw his shoulders in the other, backward, while raising his chin and arching his spine. His hands rose and extended, to protect his face. It was a blind rearward snap-dive, a desperate juke that risked slamming the back of his head onto asphalt. It saved him from the first blast. As Mahmoud arched while falling, his combined movements changed the angle his face presented as a target. Two bullets hit him in the head. They did not strike squarely. Both grazed him, each slicing a groove from his lower forehead, by his eyebrows, to his hairline. Then came more. He had pushed his hands up into the space between the muzzle and his face, directly into the path of a long automatic burst. Several bullets tore through Mahmoud's right elbow and forearm. At least two hit his left hand, shattering fine bones. An instant had passed. Mahmoud slammed onto the street, his right arm useless, his left hand ruined, his brow about to pour blood. He was alive.

He heard gunshots. The three attackers were striding forward and firing. He was at their feet. Mahmoud had a thought: *pistol.* The bodyguards kept a pistol in the map pocket of the door of his vehicle, which was running, doors closed, about twenty feet away. He needed this gun. He could visualize the weapon—a 9-millimeter semiautomatic with its magazine and fourteen rounds inserted. If he could reach it he could fight. The assassins must have thought they had killed him, because they were firing toward other bodyguards. Adrenaline had put Mahmoud in an extreme state of alertness. Now it propelled his will. He rolled onto his side, spun from his young legs to his feet, and bounded in his suit toward his SUV. His shattered right arm dangled in its sleeve. His face was wet with blood. His revival must have startled the assassins: The dead man rose. He reached the car in several wild, zigzagging lunges, each turn meant to frustrate attempts to shoot him in the back.

One of the gunmen zeroed in on Mahmoud a second time. He fired a burst. As with Mahmoud's first dodge, the zigs and zags kept him alive. They were not enough to spare him. A round hit his lower left back. Mahmoud reached the Patrol nonetheless. He was a lean young man, a martial-arts expert rippling with adrenaline and purpose, fired by the cornered animal's will to live, but without working fingers or hands. He swung his right hand at the door. The pistol was right there. *There.* His hand had no grip. He could not make it lift the handle. Karzan Mahmoud had performed his last act in the service of Prime Minister Salih's security detail. The assassin fired again. The burst rode up Mahmoud's left leg, shattering the femur and the hip, reducing to fragments the main load-bearing bones and joint on his left side.

The long arc of the history of automatic small arms was almost complete. From the days of Fieschi and Puckle, to the work of Gatling, Gardner, and Nobel, through the marvels of Maxim, who conceived the most important steps, rapid-fire infantry arms, at first a dream and then expensive, had become ordinary and available to almost anyone. At first, when few combatants had them, they were instruments of imperialism, state power, and army-meets-army international war. Now they empowered disorder and crime. In Iraqi Kurdistan, as in large tracts of the developing world, every party had assault rifles, and the assault rifles were almost all patterned on the original Kalashnikov. They had come here from many sources: from Iran, Romania, Russia, Egypt, Poland, the former Yugoslavia, and China. They had arrived to markets by many means: shipped across borders from outside, looted from state arsenals, handed out by neighboring governments hoping those who used them would frustrate Baathist rule. Some had been made in a factory that the Baathists had built for themselves. And now they were so locally abundant that buying one was only a matter of a young man's asking where to shop. Created in the race among nations to develop weapons that might ensure national security and improve soldiers' chances in war, they had been imitated, replicated, miniaturized, and fine-tuned, cycle after cycle, design by design, shipment by shipment, until something like parity among riflemen had been reached. Parity, it turned out, meant not just that any modern fighter could be well equipped. It meant that almost anyone could be shot. Parity looked like this: Karzan Mahmoud toppled and fell, landing in a puddle of cold standing water. There he lay, on his back, blinking up into raindrops peppering his face. He had no idea how many times he had been hit. His body was broken; his mind, for the moment, was strangely detached. His blood stained the puddle red. He thought he heard thunder.

Only a few seconds had passed. He did not have much time. Over the decades the men and women who studied the effects of modern military rifle bullets on the so-called human frame had documented the physical processes now playing out within Mahmoud. They knew the ways that different bullets fired at different ranges cut through human skin, human muscle, and all forms of human flesh. They understood how these bullets snap and shatter human bone, and how the knifelike shards of bullet jackets and ruptured bone intermingle and radiate outward, cutting more tissue as they scatter. Those scientists, and pseudoscientists, with their thawed human limbs and severed human heads filled with pseudo-brains, had documented and described how the parts that make up a man can be made to break. Many of their tests had been on cadavers. Karzan Mahmoud was not a cadaver. Not yet. He panted, moaned, struggled for comprehension, blinked through blood and gritted teeth. What was he to do? His wounds outmatched him. If the puddle were a bathtub, he would drown. He had reached incapacitation, that hard-to-measure but you-know-it-when-you-see-it performance state that ballistics scientists had tried to ascertain and guarantee. Theory was theory. Laboratory work was laboratory work. Forensic autopsies were forensic autopsies. From these pursuits, the physical processes happening within Mahmoud—who was suffering from a form of violence common in our time—were almost precisely sketched in the books and the minds of those who knew what firearms do to men. Technical studies did not sketch this: what it looked and felt like when military rifle bullets smacked human life, when incapacitation meant not just preventing action but summoning death, when rifles and gunfights were stripped of engineering, politics, romance, or any whiff of fable.

Gatling spoke of sparing men the horrors of battle, so that their lives might be saved for their country. Was Mahmoud lucky that those two early shots had grazed his forehead and not blasted his cranium into chunks, as the experts knew they could? He remained alive, spared not because the machinery of war had made his services obsolete, but because an angle of impact, twice, had been oblique. He was a leaking mess of holes, many of them limned with bullet fragments and the broken bits of bones that had given him his shape. His blood was flowing out and time had become excruciating, if short. Was this better? Not youth, not will, not fitness, neither training nor hard-won knowledge could bring a man broken in this way back to what he had been, seconds before. Slogans and money meant nothing here and now. Even ideas were few. Karzan Mahmoud was not a cadaver. Not yet. He was a man who wanted to stand and feel the handle of a pistol wrapped within his shooting hand. He could not. Instead, he was fighting sleep.

And the gunfight raged. The three attackers were all firing. The battle flowed around him. Mahmoud wanted to participate. But nothing worked. He felt cold.

"Yunis," he called to another driver. "I'm hurting."

"Yunis," he said. "Yunis?"

Time slowed for Mahmoud. For others, it raced. The street where Salih lived was an alley with the contours of a vertical-sided irrigation canal. In such a place, the members of a group could not readily disperse to fight, or even get out of one another's way. The guards returned fire. Mahmoud looked over and saw one of the attackers slumped on the ground nearby. A bodyguard had shot him. The man looked dead.

The two remaining attackers were charging, firing their Kalashnikovs on automatic as they came, sweeping the street with lead. Ramazan Hama-Raheem, one of the intelligence chief's guards, had been between the taxi and the gate. As Mahmoud was hit, he spun to face the fight. He had an instant to react. He fired his Kalashnikov, and thought he hit one of them in the leg. As he fired he was struck. A bullet blew apart his right shin, another broke his right hip. He twisted, falling, and was raked by more. A burst hit him in the back. Another shredded his left thigh. One round hit his upper left arm. Another grazed the top of his skull. He landed on the ground with one working limb: his right arm. His assault rifle was useless to him now. He could not lift it. But with a right arm, he had a chance. He drew his Makarov semiautomatic pistol. He fired and fired, but he struggled for aim and after seven shots was out of ammunition. With only one working arm, he had no way to reload.

Another guard, Balan Faraj Karim, who had been inside a guard hut when the attack commenced, joined the fight. He had not seen the taxi arrive, or the three assassins advance. He stepped into a shootout midway through its course. There had been two groups of bodyguards on the street. The attackers had charged into their midst, splitting and confusing them. Karim scanned the bedlam. He had only seconds to figure it out. It was not clear who was who. He saw a man trotting in his direction— a stranger in *peshmerga* dress. Karim decided: foe. He raised his weapon. The other man fired first, a long rippling burst. Karim felt the bullets splatter through him. They seemed to hit him everywhere. He collapsed. The man rushed by.

Gasping, Karim looked himself over. He had been shot in the stomach, the left shoulder, the right thigh, and multiple times in the left leg, including through the ankle and the calf. Another bullet had hit the back of his neck, probably as he spun and fell. It had passed through meat without hitting spine. He was helpless; a heap. He could do little more than watch, at least until his own time ran out. He looked around. He saw the collapsed forms of other guards, and that of the prime minister's secretary, Amanj Khadir, who had also rushed outside and been shot. He watched another friend from the prime minister's security detail, Shwan Khzar, firing his assault rifle. But Khzar's Kalashnikov ran out of bullets. As he tried switching to a pistol, the man who had shot Karim opened fire with another burst. Khzar fell. The attacker limped down the street, away from the gate, stepped around a corner of a cinder-block wall, and was out of sight.

This surviving gunman, Qais Ibrahim Khadir, had decided to forgo entering the prime minister's compound. His two accomplices were dead. He was alone now; there seemed little chance to press further. He hobbled across a vacant lot. He had a few seconds to think. A bullet had passed through his lower left leg, but missed bone. He could walk, and his uniform could help him. Passersby might not suspect him of his crimes. He reached the road and hailed a taxi. When it pulled over, he stepped in and gave an address. Soon he was moving away from the mess of bodies he had left behind, enveloped by city traffic.

The survivors in front of Salih's house stirred. The prime minister had by luck been kept from harm. He had been seconds from stepping outside, but a telephone had rung. An aide called him back, and he had not entered the kill zone. At the sound of gunfire his aides rushed him deeper inside. On the asphalt, Balan Faraj Karim, immobilized by his wounds but one of the few men outside still conscious, scanned the street. He did not see the prime minister. This was the only good sign. His eyes settled on Mahmoud. Karim called to him.

"Karzan?" he said. "Karzan?"

There was no answer. He knew that Mahmoud was dead.

Karzan Mahmoud was not dead. He was sliding back and forth between sleep and consciousness. Soon he was aware of being jostled. A white Land Cruiser was beside him. Hands lifted him and put him in the back. A shopkeeper's face was above Mahmoud, consoling.

"What happened?" Mahmoud asked. "Who shot us?"

The shopkeeper shushed him. "Don't talk," he said. "Don't talk. You're okay."

At the hospital, Mahmoud overheard that the prime minister's secretary had died. The staff cut away his blood-soaked suit and dress shirt. The doctors worked. Mahmoud was naked and sedated: the wrecked remains of a young man. He saw gloved hands pull fragments of bullet and bone from his arms. A policeman questioned him.

"What is your name?" he asked.

Mahmoud answered.

"What is your phone number?"

Mahmoud answered again, but now he had a headache. He was wheeled off for X-rays. Before surgery, he saw the prime minister at his side.

"You helped me," Salih said.

"You are okay?" Mahmoud asked.

"Yes."

"Be careful, Dr. Barham," he said. "Be careful."

The surgeons worked on Mahmoud, the first time, until 2:00 A.M. They tallied wounds from twenty-three bullets. None had hit his spine or vital organs. The bullet that entered his back had cut only muscle and flesh. The head grazes had not fractured his skull. Twenty-three bullets, the doctors said. While Mahmoud was asleep, and the anesthesia was wearing off, he heard his mother's voice.

"Karzan," she said.

He woke. The doctors, he learned through a haze, had quarreled over whether they should amputate his right arm and left leg. For now he retained them. He asked questions about the attack. No one wanted to answer. On the third day, he read a newspaper and learned that five of his friends had been killed. Three others, besides himself, had been crippled. Elsewhere in the hospital, Balan Faraj Karim woke to doctors who explained why they had amputated his left leg. He misunderstood. "No," he cried. "You do not need to cut my leg." He argued. "Send me somewhere," he said. "To Europe," he suggested. "A different doctor can keep my leg." But his leg was already gone.

The surviving attacker, Qais Ibrahim Khadir, did not make it far. He was captured while hiding in a house in the city. In the months that followed, Khadir occupied a solitary-confinement cell on the second floor of the city's jail, in conditions that might drive a sane man mad. His room was a concrete closet, chilly and unlit, accessible through a small steel door. There, before Kurdish security officials led him away and executed him, he sat in the darkness, his skin growing paler and his flesh growing softer, passing hours praying to his understanding of his god. He expressed no regret. When the opportunity presented itself, he voiced satisfaction, even pleasure, at what he had done. Conversations with Khadir did not follow linear thought, and his ruminations were prone to militant tautology. Doe-eyed and eager for company, he talked openly, but kept his history neat and free of gray. He had been born in Erbil in the mid-1970s and claimed to have left Iraq for study in a religious school in Yemen. He was cagey on the question of whether he met jihadists while abroad. He denied that he had. He also punctuated the denials with laughter and self-satisfied smirks. "I am very clever," he was given to saying. This confirmed something self-evident: *I lie*.

Khadir's militancy had wide-reaching roots. He had lived for a while with the Workers' Party of Kurdistan, or PKK, on Mount Qandil, the high-elevation base in Iraq near the border with Iran. But he felt little affinity for the PKK's fighters, whom he considered apostates. By 2001 he had come down off the mountain and taken up with Taweed, an armed Islamic movement. In a series of mergers with other local Islamic groups, Taweed became part of Ansar al-Islam, the Supporters of Islam, a confederation of armed Islamic parties that was emerging as a regional threat and demanded that the region be ruled by its interpretation of shariah law. It declared jihad against the PUK.

By 2002, Ansar al-Islam was large enough to field a visible guerrilla force of at least several hundred fighters, to run at least two jihadist training camps, and to control territory and several villages along the Iranian border. Its turf was a mountainous region, not the date-palm Iraq of the lower Tigris and Euphrates, but a zone of rolling foothills set against snowcapped peaks. There its fighters occupied trenches remaining from the Iran-Iraq War, augmenting them with bunkers and road checkpoints to create a statelet within a statelet that it governed its own way. The group closed a girls' school, forbade shaving, and desecrated a Sufi cemetery and mosque. It was northern Iraq's neo-Taliban.

Qais Ibrahim Khadir had taken an oath only to Taweed. But as Taweed evolved he changed with it. He rejoiced at the attacks on the World Trade Center and admired Osama bin Laden. "What does al Qaeda mean?" he asked, rhetorically. He had his own answer. "Al Qaeda," he said, "is a state of mind." Sitting in handcuffs in a room near his cell, Khadir gave himself high grades. Action, in his view, equaled accomplishment. Though he had failed to kill Barham Salih, he considered the operation an achievement. "We succeeded," he said. "According to our beliefs, any operation we do is a success when you do it."

Outside the prison, his victims suffered. The mother of one victim had died upon hearing of her son's death; she collapsed with a heart attack. Ramazan Hama-Raheem was handicapped, barely able to walk. "Only I know my pain," he said. "If you look at me now—look—my face, it is beautiful and calm. But inside, pain." He entertained a dark fantasy, which became a regular vision: He was alone and holding a pistol to his head. His depression was almost total. He was too strong to kill himself, not strong enough not to consider it every day. "My life," he said, is "jail, and I can't get out." Balan Faraj Karim had no fantasy whatsoever, not even the despairing fantasy of relief through suicide. He found sanctuary in sleep, which provided him with a dream. In this dream, he said, "I am sleeping in a bed in an American hospital and they have just finished the surgery to my shoulder and two legs." But always he would wake and find himself as Khadir had made him—a one-legged, disfigured man, unemployed, stuck in Iraq. He had two young children. His wife would later tell him that she did not know, hour by hour, what to do: to take care of their children, or to take care of him. Karim passed long days crying.

Karzan Mahmoud at first fared little better. He had lived to be reassembled, put back into the shape of a man with metal rods and screws. The shape of a man was not enough. Mahmoud had form, not function. His left leg and hip could barely support his weight, and his wounds, which had been soaked in a dirty puddle after he was shot, were contaminated. By late in 2002 his upper thigh was swollen, purple, and oozing; a deep and festering infection had settled in. His right arm did not bend. His left hand could not open and close. He was stooped and slowly weakening. His youth and the remains of his vigor kept him alive, though the infection and its fevers had such a hold on him that it seemed likely to finish his pain soon. Fortune and friendship intervened. Several months before he had been shot, Mahmoud had hired out as a driver for Kevin McKiernan, a reporter for ABC News. The two men became friends. McKiernan returned to Iraq in fall 2002. In the rush of work during the run-up to the American invasion, the two men met many times. Mahmoud brought McKiernan his medical records, and McKiernan taped the X-rays to a window, photographed them, and emailed them to a friend from high school, Dr. Michael Brabeck, who worked at Brigham and Women's Hospital in Brookline, Massachusetts. McKiernan and Brabeck, half a world apart, made Mahmoud their project.

By spring 2003, as the American war in Iraq began, Mahmoud was living in Dr. Brabeck's house in Massachusetts and receiving pro bono care that few victims of Kalashnikov bullets receive. By the summer, three surgeries later, his right arm had been reset with a ninety-degree bend at the elbow. His left hand was functional. His infection was defeated and his femur partially repaired, enough so that he was on a trajectory to walk without a cane.[73] His grimace subsided. His eyes brightened. By early in 2006, with Saddam Hussein ousted and the PUK's leader serving as Iraq's president, Mahmoud was working in Canada, at the Iraqi embassy in Ottawa. He was not, by any of the typical measures of mobility for a twenty-seven-year-old man, healthy and fit. He limped visibly, his right arm was almost useless, his right hand had little grip. And the former wiry bodyguard, adept at tae kwon do, was gaining weight, a consequence of his inability to exercise as he had before. But he was free from infection, able to dress and feed himself, and bathe, and shuffle up and down steps, and drive on the highway, and work at office tasks. He was blessed to be alive. He knew it. "My God helped me," he said one night in Ottawa. "I like my God." He had been helped, but not healed. He knew he never would be. And he found, when considering the rifle that had altered his body and diminished his life, that he wondered about Mikhail Kalashnikov, who lent his name to the weapon. He had a question for the man who proudly insisted he was the inventor of this device. "Why did you make this machine?" Mahmoud asked. "You don't like living people? You are smart. Why not make something to help people, not make them dead?"

Mahmoud was sipping tea, pinching the small warm glass with a mangled hand, furrowing his bullet-scarred brow. "Are you not afraid to see the judge?"*[74]

Mikhail Kalashnikov, in winter, adapted yet again.

The collapse of the Soviet Union both harmed and benefited him, and his world changed repeatedly. Financially, the end of the Soviet Union upended Izhevsk and the firearms industry. Defense budgets dried up.

---

* In an email later, Mahmoud expanded upon his question that night. The email read, in part: "I would like to ask Mr. Kalashnikov, what made you think about making such a horrible machine? What were you thinking about? Helping people or destroying their lives? I'm sure that you are a smart guy. Why didn't you go for finding a way to bring peace to life again? What we had—all those kind of guns through history—wasn't enough to make a man think about something more useful for people's lives rather than finding another killing machine? Why? I know that sometimes that piece of metal was helping nations to survive. But how about if there were no guns at all, not for attack and not for protection. What would happen? . . . It is not just me, and it is not only thousands who got injured or killed by your ideal machine. I'm wondering—how about if you tried it on yourself, one bullet into your feet before sending it out to the market. That might change your mind?"

Assembly lines fell quiet, and many workers, their salaries unpaid, left in search of work. Much of the labor force that remained was furloughed, called to work when orders needed to be filled but often told to stay home. Conditions on production days were gritty; sections of the factories were lit only by skylights, many workers had no protective clothing, and the ventilation was so poor that the air on days when weapons were assembled had a yellowish, particle-laden cast.[75]

Russia sought customers for its weapons. But its introduction to free markets was jarring. With so many assault rifles stockpiled, and other manufacturers competing—Arsenal in Bulgaria, Radom in Poland, Romtechnica in Romania, Norinco in China, F.E.G. in Hungary (now closed), Zastava in Serbia, and others—Izhmash and Izhmech, the paired companies in Izhevsk responsible for Kalashnikov production, struggled to make sales. Part of the problem was in management. The former communists who ran the companies knew much about their factories and almost nothing about marketing or service. They conducted business opaquely, and with patterns of patronage and nepotism not far beneath the varnish. But even sound managers might not have stopped the gun lines from stalling. Further Kalashnikov production fed a glut. The Russian arms-manufacturing sector was suffering from another of the varied ailments of the post-Soviet hangover. Several decades of mass production of the Kalashnikov line, which had once fit foreign-policy objectives and notions of national security, had destroyed business opportunities. Customers could always find other sellers. Those sellers undercut Russian prices.[76]

To keep workers employed and prevent the full erosion of the skill base, Izhmash produced a line of sporting rifles and shotguns, many of them using the underlying Kalashnikov design and some of them nodding to older gunsmithing traditions, with handsome wooden stocks and engraving. These were bourgeois guns. "We had to live on something," Kalashnikov said. "So we began to think about how to try, using our knowledge base and military-fighting designs, to create weapons for hunting."[77] The line was a limited success. Markets for sporting arms were similarly crowded, and Izhmash competed against established brands. In 2009 the company, its finances and behavior largely impenetrable to outsiders, entered Russian bankruptcy proceedings. Its operations were limited and its prospects for large orders grim. It seemed unlikely to shut down entirely, though its security rested not in its performance as a private enterprise but in a political fact: For the Russian military, the plants that produced the rifles remained a strategic enterprise. Similar problems manifested themselves throughout the firearms sector. Another Russian Kalashnikov manufacturer, the Molot joint stock company in Kirov, which complemented the production at Izhevsk, was so cash-strapped that in late 2008 it stopped paying wages to many employees. By 2009 it compensated workers not with rubles, but with food. This was, literally, subsistence labor.[78]

As the workers struggled, Mikhail Kalashnikov's stature spared him from both material suffering and idleness. He fared, if not well, at least better than many of his generation. Though there was little work, he retained the title of chief designer of the Izhmash gun works and consultant to the general director of Rosoboronexport, the state arms-export agency.[79] He also served as the informal ambassador of the sprawling Russian arms industry. Both the government and the factory had reason to ensure that he did not slide into the penury that enveloped Izhevsk's workforce. His ceremonial ascension from former noncommissioned officer to lieutenant general served him especially well. Because of it he received two payments a month from the government: a salary of about $575 from Izhmash and a general's pension from the military, too.*[80] His payments as consultant to the export agency were never disclosed. There was no doubt he was provided for—not lavishly, but far better than most.

The opening of borders and the loosening of restrictions also allowed Kalashnikov to travel, and beginning in the 1990s he was flying from place to place and seeing a world that for decades had been forbidden. Many trips followed invitations to military museums or gun clubs, whose members crowded around him at the chance to meet the face of the AK-47. He visited, among other nations, China, the United Kingdom, the Netherlands, Germany, Switzerland, and the United States, where he was a minor celebrity for many firearm owners: the aging Soviet general, hard of hearing, who had given the world its best-known gun. He seemed to enjoy these trips most of all. Kalashnikov, after a career as a state hero, was a man who liked being toasted as a genius. Other trips were part of his duties as Russia's ceremonial arms ambassador. The state arms-export

---

* His factory salary was roughly three times that of a typical worker at the plant, when the workers were paid at all.

agency shuttled him to arms shows to greet potential customers at the Russian booth. He claimed to have made more than fifty trips abroad, a pace of several expositions a year. In this way, he lived like Chekhov's wedding general—an elderly and avuncular officer whose presence lent weight to gatherings otherwise routine. Sometimes he arrived in a sport coat or suit, which he adorned with a diamond-studded tie clip in the shape of an AK-47—a touch as paradoxical as post-Soviet Russia itself.

In performing his public duties, Kalashnikov was often earnest. He could seem sincere. Yet his official appearances were sometimes accompanied by an undercurrent of shabbiness, of a geriatric man being used. His assignment was to be the embodiment and caretaker of an idea—the notion, welcomed after the Soviet Union's collapse, of Russian excellence. Post-Soviet Russia developed around him into an extraction state, an exporter of hydrocarbons, lumber, minerals, and people. It manufactured few commercial products widely recognized or sought beyond the borders of the former Soviet Union. In its lists of companies and exports, Russia had no Sony, Panasonic, or Samsung; no Mercedes-Benz, Toyota, or Nissan; no Vanguard, Lloyd's of London, or Sotheby's; no Gucci, Tag Heuer, or Cartier; no Coca-Cola, McDonald's, Nestlé, or Kraft; no Nokia, Black-Berry, Apple, or Microsoft. Russian fashions were not coveted, Russian popular music was scarcely listened to outside the former Soviet Union. But Russia had invented one commercial product that had overtaken much of the world: the AK-47 line. The paired Kalashnikovs, man and weapon, became secular icons and subjects of enforced celebration. Sometimes the celebratory nods took on an air that conflicted with Kalashnikov's talk of peace. For several years, the Museum of the Armed Forces in Moscow displayed a Kalashnikov that the museum claimed was used to kill seventy-eight American servicemen in Vietnam on a single spring day in the Tet Offensive of 1968.[81] The tale felt apocryphal. And the museum's presentation (the director of the museum pointed the rifle out proudly to an American newspaper reporter in 1997) seemed both gleeful and odd.

Part of Mikhail Kalashnikov's performances for the republic required more shading of the truth, including recirculating exaggerations about the degree of secrecy that had surrounded him during Soviet times. Kalashnikov and his handlers made it seem as if he had been locked off from the world and isolated even from his fellow citizens, a closely guarded national security asset who was prohibited from mentioning his work.

In the mid-1980s I went to my birth place in the Kuryinsky district of the Altai region for the unveiling of my own bust at the central square near the district library. My countrymen wanted to know how I became twice a Hero of the Soviet Union, they wanted details. But speaking about my work was not allowed.[82]

This was not exactly true. While some secrecy attended all Soviet arms enterprises, Kalashnikov's existence and work were openly acknowledged, and he was interviewed for a foreign publication as early as 1967.[83] Such remarks were a type, a feeding of a legend. Some of his statements were more boldly out of line with the record.

It was a complete secret. I wasn't allowed to speak to my family or have any contact with foreigners. Even after seven years of production, the gun was still secret: it had to be carried in a special case; there could be no specifications published; even the cartridge cases had to be picked up after shooting.[84]

These statements were laden with falsehoods. His assertion that no specifications had been published after seven years of production was demonstrably untrue. By 1955, the United States Ordnance Technical Intelligence Service had obtained and translated the 121-page Soviet Ministry of War's AK-47 manual, which, according to the date stamp on the original Soviet document, had been published in 1952—three years after mass production of the early AK-47s began in Izhevsk. The United States military began circulating the manual in its commands.[85]

The act had its purposes. To some, the general's appearances in his official capacities—as design virtuoso, lubricator of arms sales, a state secret emerging into the postcommunist light to dispense wisdom by the pearl—spoke to his commitment to the state. Others detected his discomfort, his fatigue, and a sense that he was performing services scripted by others.

He goes, frankly, as a bauble, a banquet boy in the rolling Russian hospitality suite, to lend the peddling of planes and tanks some historical gravitas. He helps get the checks written . . . it is a special torture custom-made for him in a special capitalist hell.[86]

And yet he appeared, again and again. For his participation, he was commended. The state piled prizes upon him with inventiveness and marked his birthday as an official holiday. Wearing his medals and carrying bouquets, which he often waved triumphantly above his head, the loyal veteran was a one-man advertisement for Russian arms and Soviet greatness. On his holidays he fulfilled roles that in latter-day Russia passed for news: state hero, grateful servant, living example of the talented Russian mind. In 2007, at the sixtieth anniversary of the creation of the AK-47, President Vladimir V. Putin issued a decree noting that Kalashnikov's "name is associated with the legendary pages of the history of Russian gun-making."[87] In November 2009, Putin's protégé, Dmitri A. Medvedev, followed the pattern. For Kalashnikov's ninetieth birthday, Medvedev awarded him the Hero of Russia medal—the highest honorary designation in the Russian Federation. Like Kalashnikov's accumulation of military ranks, each new award served to boost both the designer's stature and the stature of the state. This was a mutually supporting public-relations loop.

Publicly, Kalashnikov's standing remained large. Privately, his luck was fair. The end of the Soviet Union allowed challenges to the official Soviet story of his arms-design genius. Abroad, and in Rosoboronexport's sales kiosks and on state-controlled Russian television, Kalashnikov was lionized. But with prohibitions on free speech loosened, he faced criticism as strong and personal as when he had been accused in Khrushchev's time of being the center of a personality cult. Skeptics raised the possibility that Kalashnikov, like Aleksei Stakhanov, the celebrity miner who had supposedly mined fourteen times his quota of coal in a single shift, was a Soviet put-on, a heroic creation of a cynical state. Much of this line of inquiry was muted by the government's muzzling of journalists, but it was robust enough that credible counterclaims to the AK-47's parentage, and fuller explanations of the design process, emerged in Russian-language sources.

Kalashnikov, the man, pushed on. He slowed in his eighties and yet remained active, even spry—a case of will and Cossack hardiness besting advanced age. In the weeks and months between trips, he split time between his apartment in Izhevsk's center and a rustic but modern two-story dacha outside the city on a lake. He passed time with guests, often writing or listening to classical music; Tchaikovsky, he said, was a favorite.

His luck never quite turned. Many people tried to make money off him, and he became involved in private ventures, none of which proved lucrative. Local businessmen, backed by the government, borrowed his last name for a brand of vodka. But the Russian vodka market was as crowded as the international assault-rifle trade. The brand never captured market share. It filled store shelves in Izhevsk, but was almost unseen outside Udmurtia or the occasional duty-free shop, where it was packaged as overpriced kitsch. (One vodka offering at Sheremetevo Airport in Moscow, in a bottle shaped like an AK-47, carried a price tag of 150 euros. The vodka inside was worth a few dollars, at most.)[88] Kalashnikov's family groused about business arrangements that provided small returns for Kalashnikov and profits for the vodka producers; ill feelings lurked beneath the surface. The designer himself all but sighed when discussing his experiences in business—a concept foreign to an elderly worker from a state enterprise. "I do it very poorly," he said. "Private commercial interests were never realistic options for us."*[89] In interviews, he often downplayed the importance of money. "I am told sometimes, 'If you had lived in the West, you would have been a millionaire long ago.' Well, they value everything in that green stuff. But there are other values. Why don't they see these values?"[90] At other times, disappointment emerged. "Stoner has his own aircraft," he said of the inventor of the M-16. "I can't even afford my own plane ticket."[91]

If his own security was precarious, that of the rifles was not. The Kalashnikov line retained its place in Russian military life and in larger society. Preconscription training in public schools did not fade away with the Soviet Union, though the Kremlin, first under Putin and again under Medvedev, insisted the nation was shifting to a volunteer military force. The old pattern became the new. Russian students continued to study the

---

*A second try at the vodka market, this time through a British businessman who took the Kalashnikov name up-market with a brand to compete with Grey Goose, flopped, too. The designer's surname brought no magic; it might as well have been Scud. For several years, one of the general's grandsons labored to capitalize on it too, marketing a line of Kalashnikov pocketknives, snowboards, thermoses, sunglasses, and umbrellas. Brochures with the products were abundant at trade shows. Sales appeared negligible. By 2004, Mikhail Kalashnikov expected no turnabout. "For now I haven't experienced any financial benefit," he said. "There aren't yet any results." The ventures all suffered in part from their organizers' misunderstanding of the meaning of the Kalashnikov line. They insisted that the word *Kalashnikov* rang with the many admirable traits they saw in the rifle or the man: quality, reliability, fidelity to nation, and the rest. They did not grasp that among many would-be customers, away from the catechisms of Soviet propaganda, it might mean something else.

Kalashnikov at school, including gaining hands-on experience with the assault rifles as tenth and eleventh graders.[92] By 2010, virtually every adult male in the nation less than seventy years old had handled Kalashnikov's rifle and knew the designer's storied name and official history.

What of his legacy? One element was beyond dispute. Whatever notoriety the AK-47 and its knock-offs realized, Kalashnikov the man would be sure to defend to the end his nostalgic ideas of Soviet days. He was fastidious, proud of labor, and attuned to the rituals of Slavic collegiality. In formal settings, he would drink small glasses of cognac and vodka, shot by shot, gamely making toasts and wishing his many well-wishers well. Russia might have suffered its many deteriorations. He would not let that be said of him. He insisted on neatness. In public he often produced a comb and fussed his white hair into place. In his home, he offered pickles and fresh *kvass*. He could be a bewitching host, a man with a smile alternately warm and mischievous, if at times he grew evasive or combative on the central subjects of his life.

And he could confound. In one interview, he suggested that it was a compliment for his family to have been selected by party commissars in Kurya for exile during collectivization. As Kalashnikov framed it, Stalin knew which families were hardy and resourceful enough to tame Siberia. He chose the Kalashnikovs to help build a greater Soviet Union.[93] It was a sign of the dictator's wisdom, in this view, that he had chosen so well.

In his Russian-language writing, Kalashnikov stood in many different places at once. He wrote of his desire for peace and communal friendship, and of the perspectives of common soldiers. He wrote of international bonds between people and of his respect for, and relationships with, foreign arms designers. He also expressed disdain for American craftsmanship and American consumer attitudes, and gave voice to his satisfaction that his weapons had stymied American military operations—a roundabout way of expressing satisfaction that his weapons had killed American troops.

> Americans like to think that everything that is best is "Made in USA" and they would like very much that the period after World War Two would pass under the sign of their achievements and that "according to the law of the markets their American products would fly like a swarm." Unfortunately, everything was the opposite. The second half of the twentieth century is marked by the fact that the Americans

could not feel themselves absolutely unpunished either in Cuba or in Korea or in Vietnam or in tens of other places, which they believed were their zone of vital interests. And everywhere it was the AK that had a sobering effect on them.[94]

His zigzagging statements were unsurprising. He had lived a complicated life. With a complicated life came a complicated file—that of a survivor in a dystopia that first tormented his family, then championed him as a national hero. He presented a mass of ideas that cannot be squared.

Ultimately, Kalashnikov was left, by both his circumstances and his decisions, atop his contradictions. He clung to his mixed accounts of the rifle's origins and insisted upon respect while speaking of his own humility. To one interviewer he said: "As for the star sickness, I do not have it."[95] Yet when a museum was built in his honor in Izhevsk,* it compared him, with seriousness, to Galileo, and in his dacha, on the stair landing leading to the second floor, he hung a large Central Asian carpet bearing an image of himself. These were not marks of modesty. Kalashnikov also claimed to have bitterly told President Boris N. Yeltsin in writing that a pistol Yeltsin had presented him was a "mediocre decoration" that "humiliated the President of Russia even more than it did me."[96] This in spite of the fact that Yeltsin had made an exception to army personnel policies that forbade the appointment of a general in peacetime and elevated Kalashnikov from the rank of colonel to general grade.[97]

The references to Galileo and the outbursts were significant. They underscored the most consistent qualities of Kalashnikov's innumerable comments after the Communist Party's fall: his pride of association with the AK-47 and his sense of extraordinary accomplishment. This was his real position. It sometimes flashed itself in starkly unconventional terms. "With arms you have to understand it is like the idea of a woman who bears children," he said. "For months she carries a baby and thinks about it. The design work is similar. I felt like a mother—always happy when

---

*The museum, which struggled for years to raise money for its construction, provides a series of stories within a story. Kalashnikov derided the men who dismantled the Soviet Union and profited from the looting of state assets afterward. The museum in Izhevsk that is dedicated to him was built with donations from Anatoly B. Chubais, one of the main architects of the privatization of state assets, who profited handsomely in the process. The ironies only get richer. Chubais was nearly assassinated in 2005 by at least two men who ambushed his armored BMW on a road outside Moscow, spraying it with Kalashnikov fire.

her baby achieves something."[98] He added: "I have always tried to knock down that annoying stereotype: if you are a weapons designer, you are a murderer. . . . For people in my profession, all that comes down to one notion: Motherland."[99] Ultimately, in the service of this position, he assembled carefully disconnected lines of thought. He sought credit for the rifle when it was put to uses he liked. He rejected the notion that he was in any way responsible for problems the rifles caused.

These positions made him much different from another renowned figure in Soviet arms design: Andrei D. Sakharov. Sakharov, one of the physicists who led the Soviet nuclear-arms program, had contributed to the successful detonation of RDS-1 outside Semipalatinsk in 1949 while Kalashnikov was involved in outfitting the gun works in Izhevsk. His later work was a cornerstone of the development of the hydrogen bomb. He was a giant in Soviet weapons programs, a three-time Hero of Socialist Labor—one of the rare Soviet men more decorated than Kalashnikov. By the mid-1960s, burdened by the moral responsibilities of his work, he urged an end to the arms race that had been the center of his professional and intellectual life. Sakharov dared to question the entire socialist world. In doing so he rejected its rewards and brought upon himself its wrath. He called for rapprochement with the West and the development of a pluralistic society rooted in human rights and free expression. The Soviet Union ordered him into internal exile and restricted his travels and his writing. In 1973, Yuri Andropov, the chairman of the KGB, who had been the Soviet ambassador to Hungary during the crackdowns in 1956, labeled him "a person involved in anti-social activity."[100] The world saw Sakharov differently. In 1975, he received the Nobel Peace Prize.

Mikhail Kalashnikov was no Sakharov. But expectations of a Sakharov-style reorientation, implicit in the many questions he fielded over the years about what the AK-47 had become, were diversionary. For just as Kalashnikov was not the sole creator of the original AK-47, he was not responsible for the manufacture, distribution, or illicit use of the long line of derivative rifles that followed it. He was a midlevel player in a large system, and never its engine. The larger processes, globally and within Stalin's military complex, were in motion long before he participated in them, and the Soviet Union was determined to produce, and would have produced, a simple and reliable assault rifle for mass production whether or not Kalashnikov had lent his energies to the pursuit. This was a far simpler task than creating an atomic bomb. And once this new rifle was made, it would have been standardized throughout the communist bloc, as were many other martial products of Soviet provenance.

For all of Kalashnikov's unyielding insistence that he was accountable for nothing beyond being a gifted inventor, and for all of his moments of nationalism, he occasionally expressed remorse—at least at the rifle's association with atrocity, crime, ethnic war, and terror. His regret at times sounded tactical. A prepared statement about the perils of illicit small-arms proliferation read in part like a capitalist's complaint that other man-ufacturers had cut into Russia's business. At other times his misgivings sounded genuine. "Do you think it's pleasant seeing all of these hoodlums using your gun?" he once said, and then pointed to the post-Soviet war for Nagorno-Karabakh, the disputed territory along the border between the two former Soviet republics of Armenia and Azerbaijan. "Armenians and Azeris killing each other. We all lived so peacefully before." His memoirs touched difficult themes. "Arms makers have strange destinies!" he wrote. "They are saluted with shots they never expected, and it is not orations or music that remind one of jubilees but moans and screams."[101] These were hints at private pain. But almost always, after allowing such a tantalizing glimpse, he turned back to his fuller answers, the jumbled medley of a man whose name was attached to the world's most common rifle, and a killing machine.

> The constructor is not the owner of the weapon—it is the state. It does of course feel good when I know that many states used the arm. That something very worthy had been created . . . they spread the weapon not because I wanted them to. Not at my choice. I made it to protect the Motherland. Then it was like a genie out of the bottle and began to walk on its own in directions that I did not want. The positives have outweighed [the negatives] because many use it to de-fend their countries. The negative side is that sometimes it is beyond your control—terrorists also want to use simple and reliable arms.[102]

To this, on a summer day late in life, he added an answer to the victims, to men like Karzan Mahmoud, crippled by a terrorist carrying everyman's gun. "I sleep soundly," Kalashnikov said.

The Twenty-first Century's Rifle

Camp Lejeune, North Carolina, early 2006

The fourteen Marines, ready to dash, waited for the signal. It was a cold February morning on a firing range just inland from North Carolina's coast. The Marines, members of Second Battalion, Eighth Marine Regiment, were preparing for a deployment in the Anbar province of Iraq, and on this day they had set aside their M-4s and M-16s. In front of them, a short jog away, were fourteen Kalashnikov assault rifles, disassembled, unloaded, resting on the ground. At the signal, the Marines were to sprint to the rifles, reassemble them, perform a function check, load a magazine, and fire into a man-shaped target, aiming for the face and chest. Their rifles were a mix of Kalashnikov variants. They came from Romania, Russia, China, and North Korea. One was an original AK-47 from Izhevsk, assembled from solid machined steel, date-stamped 1954.[1] It was fifty-two years old—almost three times the age of some of the men about to fire it.

The Corps had a nickname for this test: *Just In Case.* In the tour ahead for these Marines, their officers wanted to be sure that they could pick up a Kalashnikov, in any condition, whether from an allied Iraqi soldier or from an insurgent in a close-range fight, and use the weapon immediately and well. The signal was given. The Marines were sprinting. Thirty seconds or so later, the first of them were firing. Holes began to appear in their targets' heads.

After almost six decades, the long travels of the Kalashnikov assault rifle had achieved the inevitable state: full saturation. Decades earlier the first AK-47s had left Soviet hands, and in the years since they had become the hand weapon of choice for strongmen, criminals, terrorists, and messianic guerrilla leaders. In time the Kalashnikov had also become a preferred arm for those who fought against the Soviet Union or Russia, and those who organized genocide. And now it was institutionalized in the training of American infantrymen. It could not, with all prudence, be any other way. In the battles ahead, every one of these Marines would encounter Kalashnikovs in the hands of allies and enemies alike. To see Marines prepare themselves around these simple facts, training with the signature socialist arm on one of the most prominent American military bases, was to grasp the extent of Kalashnikov saturation in modern war.

What does saturation mean? It would be naïve to think that war would stop without these weapons. It wouldn't. It would be just as naïve to think that many of the consequences of war as it has been waged in recent decades might not be lessened if these rifles were in fewer hands, and not so available for future conflicts. For how long will battlefields be so? The answer is straightforward—as long as the rifles exist in the outsized numbers the Cold War left behind.

Much attention is paid to accountability, security, and destruction of potential materials for weapons of mass destruction. With lesser urgency and smaller budgets, efforts to secure and destroy antipersonnel land mines have become widely accepted. In the past decade or so, similar attention has been given to efforts to eliminate stocks of shoulder-fired antiaircraft weapons, whose existence threatens the security of air transportation. The notion of regulating military firearms and destroying excess stockpiles enjoys much less support and faces considerable opposition, no matter that illicit uses of assault rifles have killed and wounded far more people than have all of these other weapons combined.

There are many reasons for this. Part of it is that surplus small arms are regarded as foreign-policy tools to be kept in reserve. Part of it is that to many government officials, honest and corrupt alike, surplus small arms are commodities, items to be converted to cash. Part of it is the manner in which priorities are set. Infantry arms that are loose in the field are exceedingly difficult to account for or collect. Surplus arms, locked up in armories, do not seem to cry for attention. Domestic and international politics play a role, too. The governments most responsible for the widespread distribution of military assault rifles—Russia, China, and the United States—have, for different reasons, shown little to no interest in destroying their excess weapons or those of other governments, even when they are not needed by standing military forces, and even when they endanger their own troops.

The United States has underwritten destruction programs. These have been small in ambition and scale, low in priority and funding, and undermined by official incoherence. Moreover, domestic politics in the United States have hindered any American government from trying to undo assault-rifle proliferation, at least as more than a backwater project. The climate of mutual distrust—between those who would seek to regulate and destroy more military assault rifles and those who claim that any such steps risk infringing the right of American citizens to bear arms—is of such an order that those who direct American foreign policy often steer clear of the issue. There is also a psychological hurdle. The near ubiquity of military assault rifles in conflict zones can send the subliminal signal that nothing can be done, except perhaps to arm more people against those who already have the guns. This is a typical course. Where armed groups threaten a perceived American interest, a common solution is to send in more guns to counter them. In this way, the United States military, since 2001, became one of the largest known purchasers of Kalashnikov assault rifles, which it has handed out by the tens of thousands in Afghanistan and Iraq.

The processes of arms reduction are not completely idled. Some aspects of nonproliferation have broad international support, and certain procedural and legislative elements of trafficking control are here to stay. But the efforts are patchwork and are undermined by inattentive and uninterested governments, and by governments that actively flout the rules. Local successes have occurred. More successes remain possible. Diligent researchers and nongovernment groups, along with individual officers, can stop bad practices here and there. But there is little momentum and many loopholes, and there is little reason to think that on the grand scale much will be done to keep the flow of illegal infantry arms in check. The case of Leonid Minin, the Ukrainian-Israeli arms dealer arrested near Milan, illustrated the state of affairs. Caught with documents describing the illegal shipment of nearly fourteen thousand Kalashnikovs and 9 million rounds of ammunition, Minin was released from custody after Italian courts ruled that Italy had no jurisdiction over his black-market brokering activities elsewhere. He walked. Had he been convicted and remained in jail, the trade would have continued. Where assault rifles are wanted, recent history shows, they appear. They move across borders like any other contraband, like heroin or hashish, like illegal immigrants, almost like rain. They are liquid. Demand ensures supply.

The comparison to illicit drugs has its limits. Like narcotics, assault rifles are difficult to find, secure, and remove once they have been distributed within a population. Unlike narcotics, they are not consumable. They remain in their users' possession, sometimes for decades. From 2001 through 2009, it was possible to find Kalashnikov assault rifles in Afghanistan bearing manufacturing stamps from as far back as 1953.[2] These were some of the very first AK-47s made. They had been forged, machined, and assembled nearly six decades before in Izhevsk. If they had been accompanied by log books revealing the names of those who had carried them, each would likely tell of years in the hands of Soviet conscripts, then of a period of reissue to the Soviet Union's Afghan forces. They survived from there, in militias and caches, until they resurfaced in the hands of the current generation of Afghan police officers and soldiers, the proxies of the United States, alongside Kalashnikovs that originated in arms plants throughout the former communist bloc—Bulgaria, Hungary, Romania, Yugoslavia, Russia, China, and elsewhere. The wooden stocks of these most aged AK-47s showed dents and dings. Otherwise most of these rifles appeared to be in excellent order, ready to fire for decades more.

Of all the methods to limit illegal trafficking in military arms, only one way is sure: destruction. Destruction can happen any number of ways. The most straightforward and effective method is to destroy excess rifles in government stockpiles, or those that are collected in conflict zones. Programs along these lines have faced obstacles of all sorts, ranging from practical to ideological. The urge to redistribute the arms often outweighs suggestions to destroy them. In this way, efforts to disarm Iraq and Afghanistan failed. Few arms were collected, and commanders who did obtain working rifles often reissued them to people considered, at least at the moment, supportive of the American military's mission. In stockpiles, other pressures prevented destruction, and many of the nations that have the largest stocks of weapons—Ukraine, for example—have participated in destruction programs only on a small scale. No sustained will has emerged to cut up the guns, in part because guns and ammunition can still be converted to money. The United States sent mixed messages and created uncomfortable situations in the Eastern bloc. During the past decade, one arm of the United States government, the State Department, was encouraging ministries to destroy excess weapons. Another, the Department of Defense, was shopping for the same items in the same countries and often purchasing through some of the same black-market middlemen who have been accused of smuggling.*

Is there an end? Yes. But the end of the Kalashnikov's role as a primary tool for killing will not result, in all likelihood, from any disarmament program or policies. The final factor will be time. Kalashnikovs are sturdy, but not indestructible. They can and do break—sometimes when backed over by an armored vehicle or car, sometimes when struck by bullets or shrapnel, occasionally when warped by fire. If left exposed and unattended long enough, they can succumb to pitting, corrosion, and rust. With the passing of many years, the combined tally of these forces will bring an end to these weapons. This will not be a short time. It will not even be decades. But in another half-century, or century, the rifles will have broken, one by one, and the chance exists that they will no longer be a significant factor in war, terror, atrocity, and crime, and they will stop being a barometer of the insecurity gripping many regions of the world. Until that time, they will remain in view and in use. Mikhail Kalashnikov was right. The AK-47 is one of the great legacies of the Soviet period. Its descendants will outlast the Soviet Union for decades more, products intended to strengthen nations that have made many nations weaker and put more people at risk.

---

* The Pentagon's distribution of automatic weapons in Iraq and Afghanistan was performed for years with scant controls. The situation improved after several years of war, but only after outcry, investigation, and scandal. Many of the weapons by then were lost from custody, and in the hands of insurgents, criminals, and sellers in bazaars.

A NOTE ABOUT THE
M-16 SERIES OF RIFLES IN 2010

A chapter in this book describes problems surrounding the introduction in Vietnam of the M-16 as a standard rifle for the United States armed forces. It is not an ambition here to trace the full evolution of the M-16 series in the decades since. Nonetheless, a few words are in order to distinguish the M-16 of the 1960s from its descendants.

The M-16 series, which was hurried into production as the Pentagon's response to the Kalashnikov, is more than fifty years old. Since the public controversy of 1967, this rifle and its offspring, including the M-4 carbine, have undergone many modifications, as has the ammunition they fire. The changes in design and in manufacturing standards have resulted in performance different from what troops experienced in Southeast Asia. The current generation of M-16s and M-4s are generally regarded by Marines and soldiers who carry them as reliable—not as reliable as the Kalashnikov, but arms that work.

The series' reputation does remain checkered. Part of this is a lingering hangover. The stories of failures in Vietnam have never been fully shaken. Misgivings are also related to accounts of rifles overheating in intensive combat or malfunctioning in sandy environments, and to complaints about the lethality of the rifles and their ammunition against lightly clad men. (This last complaint would seem related more to bullet composition than to the rifles.) Investigating each of these complaints is essential for public trust. But discussions about the current rifles should not confuse accounts of the M-16's failures in Vietnam with questions about performance of M-16 variants in current wars. Recent complaints are of an entirely different order.

Further to understanding the events depicted in this book, the current manufacturers of the American military's M-4 and M-16 rifles are Colt Defense LLC and FN Herstal USA. The Colt firm, located in West Hartford, Connecticut, is a successor company of Colt's Firearms Division of Colt Industries, which manufactured the original M-16 line for the Pentagon. Colt Industries, and its firearms division, no longer exist.

NOTES

This book's epigraph—"Inventors seldom benefit themselves. They benefit the people."—is from "Made the Gatling Gun: Inventor Sought to Decrease the Horrors of War. An Interview with Dr. Gatling," published in the *Washington Post* on October 29, 1899.

Prologue: Stalin's Tools of War

1. Drawn from the author's visit in 2004 to the test site and crater where RDS-1 was detonated, and interviews with the director of the National Nuclear Center of Kazakhstan, which is located on the grounds of the former Soviet institute, and the center's museum director and staff. Also from David Holloway, *Stalin and the Bomb: The Soviet Union and Atomic Energy, 1939–1956* (New Haven: Yale University Press, 1996), pp. 213–20.
2. Holloway, *Stalin and the Bomb*, pp. 213–20.
3. Interview with author, 2004.
4. Gene Roberts, "Enemy's Soviet-Designed Rifle Slows Marines' Drive in Hue. AK-47 Makes Sniper a 'Machine Gunner' Who 'Can Tie Up an Entire Company'—Cannons Used to Root Out Foe," *New York Times*, February 9, 1968.
5. Interview in 2002 of Ashrat Khan by author.
6. Interview in 2010 of retired general William M. Keys, president and chief executive officer of Colt Defense LLC, the principal manufacturer of the M-16 line. Colt had manufactured roughly 7 million M-16s and seven hundred thousand M-4 carbines. The weapon and its knock-offs have also been made in smaller quantities in several other factories in Singapore, Canada, and South Korea, by a division of General Motors and elsewhere in the United States.
7. Marius Broekmeyer, *Stalin, the Russians, and Their War* (Madison, Wis.: University of Wisconsin Press, 2000), pp. xiv–xv.
8. A useful and accurate English-language guide is Joseph Poyer, *Kalashnikov Rifles and Their Variations* (Tustin, Cal.: North Cape Publications, 2004), which expands upon the aggregation done by Edward Ezell's *Kalashnikov: The Arms and the Man* (Cobourg, Ontario: Collector Grade Publications, 2001).

1. The Birth of Machine Guns

1. E. Frank Stephenson, Jr., *Gatling: A Photographic Remembrance* (Murfreesboro, North Carolina: Meherrin River Press, 1993), p. 4.
2. "Death of Dr. Gatling, Former Indianapolitan Who Achieved World-Wide Fame, Inventor of the Gatling Gun, Grain Drill and Other Devices Which Have Benefited Many," in Gatling's obituary on February 27, 1903, in the *Indianapolis Journal*, his

impression from the caskets was quoted from an earlier interview. "The losses of life by disease rather than wounds caused me as a physician the idea that to shorten war would be to ameliorate it. This idea I got from looking at the boxes of dead bodies in the Indianapolis depot. I conceived a gun which should do the greatest execution in a brief space, by a revolving series of barrels loaded with a particular ammunition and shooting a double range."

3. This letter from Gatling to Miss Lizzie Jarvis on June 15, 1877, is cited in many books, including on page 27 of Julia Keller's *Mr. Gatling's Terrible Marvel: The Gun that Changed Everything and the Misunderstood Genius Who Invented It* (New York: Penguin, 2008).

4. Stephenson, *Gatling*, p. 10.

5. From a letter by Hugh O. Pentecost, Gatling's son-in-law, to the editors of the *Hartford Courant*, March 2, 1903. In Stephenson, *Gatling*, p. 81.

6. "Made The Gatling Gun. Inventor Sought to Decrease the Horrors of War. An Interview with Dr. Gatling," *Washington Post*, October 29, 1899.

7. Frink's role has not been widely documented. He is mentioned by Dr. Charles A. Bonsett in "Medical Museum Notes," a column in the December 1988 issue of *Indiana Medicine*. Dr. Bonsett cited a 1914 article about Gatling that described Frink as a "mechanical genius of this city [Indianapolis]." Personal communication to author from Charles Bonsett. Charles A. Bonsett, "Medical Museum Notes," from *Indiana Medicine*, December 1988, Vol. 81, No. 12. See also Fred D. Cavinder, *Amazing Tales from Indiana* (Bloomington, Ind.: Indiana University Press, 1990), p. 36.

8. From United States Patent No. 36,836, "Improvement in Revolving Battery Guns," awarded to Richard J. Gatling, November 4, 1862, by the United States Patent Office, p. 1.

9. A. Bouvieron, *An Historical and Biographical Sketch of Fieschi, with Anecdotes Relating to His Life* (London, 1835), p. 68. The dimensions were taken from the report of M. LePage, gunsmith to the king, who examined the device.

10. A copy of the patent submission is reproduced in George M. Chinn, *The Machine Gun: History, Evolution, and Development of Manual, Automatic, and Airborne Repeating Weapons*, Volume I (Washington: Bureau of Ordnance, 1951), p. 18.

11. "A New System of Artillery for Projecting a Group or Cluster of Shot," lecture presented to the Royal United Services Institute on May 9, 1862, and published in the institute's journal the following year, p. 377.

12. Chinn, *The Machine Gun*, p. 36.

13. The term was used in 1914 by Dr. Charles Dennis, a medical beat writer for the *Indianapolis Star*, writing under the pen name Dr. Oldfish.

14. *Indianapolis Daily Journal*, May 30, 1862.

15. From "On Mitrailleurs, And Their Place In The Wars Of The Future," by Major G. V. Fosbery, Her Majesty's Bengal Staff Corps, *Journal of the Royal United Service Institution*, 1870, p. 543.

16. Charles B. Norton, *American Breech-Loading Small Arms: A Description of Late Inventions Including the Gatling Gun and a Chapter on Cartridges* (New York: F. W. Christern, 1872), p. 240.

17. Lieutenant Skerrett's letter to Rear Admiral John A. Dahlgren, chief of the Navy's ordnance bureau, is printed in full in Norton, *American Breech-Loading Small Arms*, p. 241.

18. From Joseph Allen Minturn, *The Inventor's Friend; or, Success With Patents: A Practical Book Telling How to Discriminate Between Valuable and Worthless Inventions; How to Avoid Mistakes and Disappointment; How to Patent and Protect Inventions, and How to Dispose of the Monopoly* (Indianapolis: Meridian Co., 1893), p. 83.

19. Butler, who was nicknamed the Beast by the Confederacy, would become even more hated during Reconstruction. But long before that he was loathed. His military skills

were virtually nonexistent. Volume II of *History of North Carolina from the Earliest Discoveries to the Present Time,* by John W. Moore, 1880, summarized his reputation on p. 261: "Such had been his conduct that the Confederate government had, by proclamation, set a price upon his head and instructed its armies to show him no quarter, but slay him like a wild beast wherever captured."

20. Lieutenant W. W. Kimball, "Machine Guns," published in *Proceedings of the United States Naval Institute,* November 16, 1881, p. 407. Lt. Kimball did not cite his source for this information, and historians of the Civil War have largely concluded that the Gatling gun was not widely used in the war.

21. Paul Wahl and Don Toppel, *The Gatling Gun* (New York: Arco Publishing Co., 1965).

22. Louis M. Starr, *Bohemian Brigade: Civil War Newsmen in Action* (New York: Knopf, 1954), pp. 222–24.

23. General Ripley presents historians with a curious case. The nemesis of would-be arms dealers to the Union, he has been derided by many of Gatling's chroniclers as a small-minded officer who missed an opportunity to field a decisive weapon against the Confederacy. Interestingly, he also resisted the introduction of repeating rifles, missing another chance to equip his army with more lethal arms. He is, in this portrait, petty, unimaginative, inclined toward bureaucracy, and unresponsive. Ripley had a singularly difficult job. He needed to sort through the issues of arming a force that swelled severalfold within months, all the while puzzling through ways to keep the weapons flowing into service compatible with one another, and managing the weapons' disparate ammunition needs and soldiers' training. John Ellis, in his acidic treatise, *The Social History of the Machine Gun* (Baltimore: Johns Hopkins University Press, 1975), called him "an inveterate standardiser." Given the circumstances, this seems a reasonable approach, although standardization also thwarted the fielding of valuable weapons at a time when arms development was proceeding at a rapid clip. Ripley was hardly the first armorer who fought for standardization of infantry arms; the philosophy he embraced has become a foundation of modern military training and logistics. Standardization is part of the core of the Kalashnikov system, and one of the reasons for its martial success and its emergence, in the eyes of those who would more fully regulate the international small-arms trade, as a global scourge.

24. David Lloyd George, *War Memoirs of David Lloyd George, 1915–1916* (Boston: Little, Brown, and Company, 1933), p. 81.

25. David A. Armstrong, *Bullets and Bureaucrats: The Machine Gun and the United States Army, 1861–1916* (Westport, Conn.: Greenwood Press, 1982), p. 10.

26. W. Reid McKee and M. E. Mason, Jr., *Civil War Projectiles II: Small Arms & Field Artllery, With Supplement* (Orange, Va.: Moss Publications, 1980), p. 8.

27. The rumor was not substantiated and is offset by evidence otherwise. The Confederacy was no more disposed toward rapid-fire arms than the North. Whether the rumor was a product of war hysteria or a malicious plant by a competitor is unknown. But history would show that Gatling lived in the North, worked from the North, and saw himself as a man of Northern industry. No scholar of the Civil War has yet turned up evidence that he worked surreptitiously for the South, or offered his weapons for sale to the Confederacy.

28. This letter has been reproduced in several books about machine guns, gunnery, and Gatling. Chinn's work, *The Machine Gun,* is most useful, as it reproduced the original handwritten note, which shows Gatling's own underlining for emphasis.

29. William H. McNeill, *The Pursuit of Power* (Chicago: University of Chicago Press, 1982), p. 232.

30. McKee and Mason, *Civil War Projectiles,* p. 10. The data on the velocities and penetrating powers of the era's musket balls all come from this source, including the charts and text on p. 10.

31. Frank R. Freemon, *Gangrene and Glory: Medical Care During the American Civil War* (Cranbury, N.J.: Associated University Press, 1998), p. 48.
32. Ibid.
33. From Hannah Ropes, *Civil War Nurse. The Diary and Letters of Hannah Ropes,* John R. Brumgardt, ed., (Knoxville, Tenn.: University of Tennessee Press, 1980), p. 68.
34. Ibid., p. 88.
35. Nugent and Palmer litigated over the American patent from 1861. Ager received British patents for the gun in 1866. If the possibility of riches from future sales motivated the disputes, it was a battle over not much. There were no riches to be had. By the end of the war, in 1865, the Repeating Gun had been discredited due to its frequent jamming.
36. For many of the weapons described in these pages, a more thorough description of their design and operation can be found in Chinn, *The Machine Gun,* in this case, Vol. 1, pp. 37–40.
37. Robert V. Bruce, *Lincoln and the Tools of War* (Champaign, Ill.: University of Illinois Press, 1989), p. 119.
38. The prices were published by Lt. Col. Calvin Goddard, chief of the Historical Section of the U.S. Army's Chief of Ordnance, in *Army Ordnance: The Journal of the Army Ordnance Association,* and were reprinted in *The Machine Gun: The Period of Recognition,* Ordnance Department, Washington, 1943.
39. In fact, neither the Ager nor the Gatling were true machine guns, but Mills was the first to succeed in closing a sale of a rapid-fire weapon, and his sale presaged the widespread distribution of weapons of this sort in Europe and beyond.
40. Kimball, "Machine Guns," p. 406.
41. Armstrong, *Bullets and Bureaucrats,* pp. 18–19.
42. Test report of January 20, 1865, on file at Connecticut State Library, Record Group 103, Subgroup 12. Hereinafter referred to as "on file at Connecticut State Library."

2. Machine Guns in Action

1. From a letter to the Royal United Service Institute in 1875 by Captain Ebenezer Rogers.
2. Copy of contract on file at Indiana Historical Society Collection.
3. Quoted from a letter of July 14, 1866, from T. G. Baylor, captain of ordnance, to Major-General A. B. Dyer, the army's chief of ordnance. In Norton, *American Breech-Loading Small Arms,* p. 243.
4. Quoted from the report of three officers to Gideon Welles, Secretary of the Navy, May 30, 1868, in Norton, *Breech-Loading Small Arms,* p. 244.
5. Minturn, *The Inventor's Friend,* p. 83.
6. On file at Connecticut State Library.
7. Tatiana Nikolayevna Ilyina, *Voyenniye Agenty i Russkie Oruzhiye (Military Agents and Russian Weapons),* (Saint Petersburg: Atlant, 2008), pp. 75–83.
8. Peter Cozzens, *Eyewitness to the Indian Wars, 1865–1890: Conquering the Southern Plains* (Mechanicsburgh, Pa: Stackpole Books, 2003), p. 69.
9. *Gatling's System of Fire-Arms with Official Reports of Recent Trials and Great Success.* This undated brochure, printed by C. W. Ames in New York, is on file at Indiana State Library.
10. The test results are published in Norton, *American Breech-Loading Small Arms,* pp. 268–74.
11. Copies of correspondence are on file at Connecticut State Library.
12. Fosbery, "On Mitrailleurs," p. 547.
13. Letter from R. J. Gatling to General John Love, February 3, 1868. Gatling told

Love that he expected the French to buy his guns. "The best of the officers are of the opinion that the 1-inch Gatling gun will supercede the ordinary field guns now in use," he wrote. "If such should be the case, then making guns must soon grow [into] a large business."

14. Cited in Norton, *American Breech-Loading Small Arms,* p. 238.

15. Brevet-Colonel Edward B. Williston, "Machine Guns in War," *Army and Navy Journal,* May 20, 1886.

16. Major General Beauchamp, from the transcript of remarks at the Royal United Service Institution after a presentation, "Machine-Guns and How To Use Them," by W. Gardner. In Ordnance Notes No. 198, 1882, p. 7. That mitrailleuses were carted off no one disputes. It seems unlikely, however, that the quantity was 600; another officer noted that the year before the war, the French had 190 mitrailleuses.

17. Kimball, "Machine Guns," p. 413.

18. A series of letters in late 1869 between the secretary of state for war in Great Britain and officers of the Gatling Gun Company provide details. On file at Connecticut State Library.

19. *Abridged Treatise on The Construction and Manufacture of Ordnance in the British Service,* July 1877, p. 262.

20. *Gatling's System of Fire-Arms with Official Report of Recent Trial and Great Successes* (C. W. Ames, printer, circa 1874), pp. 6–7. On file at Indiana State Library.

21. Letter from W. H. Talbott, August 31, 1871. On file at Connecticut State Library.

22. G. A. Henty, *By Sheer Pluck: A Tale of the Ashanti War* (Glasgow: Blackie & Son, 1884), p. 197.

23. H. A. Brackenbury, captain, Royal Artillery, *The Ashanti War: A Narrative Prepared From The Official Documents By Permission of Major-General Sir Garnet Wolseley,* Vol. II (Edinburgh and London: William Blackwood and Sons, 1874), p. 44–45.

24. John H. Parker, *Tactical Organization and Uses of Machine Guns in the Field* (Kansas City, Mo: Hudson-Kimberly Publishing Co. 1899), p. 35–36.

25. A full copy of the handwritten test report is on file at Connecticut State Library.

26. Letter from R. J. Gatling to General John Love, October 26, 1873. On file at Indiana Historical Society Collection.

27. Letter from R. J. Gatling to General John Love. August 1, 1873. On file at Indiana Historical Society Collection.

28. Letter from Edgar T. Welles to General John Love, August 2, 1873. On file at Indiana Historical Society Collection.

29. Letter from R. J. Gatling to General John Love, November 30, 1873. On file at Indiana Historical Society Collection.

30. Letter from R. J. Gatling to General Love, November 8, 1873. On file at Indiana Historical Society.

31. Ibid.

32. "Letter from the Secretary of War Recommending Appropriation for Gatling Guns," Government Printing Office, 1874. On file at Connecticut State Library.

33. Letter from R. J. Gatling to General John Love, May 10, 1874. On file at Indiana Historical Society Collection.

34. Letter from R. J. Gatling to General John Love, March 26, 1874. On file at Indiana Historical Society Collection.

35. Letter from R. J. Gatling to General John Love, May 30, 1874. On file at Indiana Historical Society Collection.

36. "List of Guns Sold and Paid For," on file at Connecticut State Library.

37. "The Place of the Mitrailleurs in War," reprinted from *Saturday Review* in *Eclectic Magazine of Foreign Literature, Science and Art,* Vol. XII, July to December 1870 (New York: E. R. Pelton, 1870), pp. 725–28.

38. *Nature*, September 1, 1870, p. 361.

39. Letter from R. J. Gatling to General John Love, August 28, 1873. On file at Indiana Historical Society Collection.

40. Letter from R. J. Gatling to General John Love, November 9, 1873. On file at Indiana Historical Society Collection.

41. Letter from William Folger to General John Love, July 11, 1874. On file at Indiana Historical Society Collection.

42. Fosbery, "On Mitrailleurs," p. 557.

43. Ibid., p. 572.

44. Captain Rogers made a presentation, "The Gatling Gun: Its Place in Tactics," at the evening meeting of the Royal United Services Institution on April 19, 1875. The full text of his speech was published in the institution's journal, No. 19, 1876, London. The excerpt here is from p. 423.

45. Ibid., p. 427.

46. Letter from R. J. Gatling to General John Love, April 27, 1874. Letter on file at Indiana Historical Society.

47. Letter from R. J. Gatling to Love, May 30, 1874. The letter has a telling cross-out. After writing "five pounds" Gatling had originally added "or 10 pounds." The second amount was crossed out with four lines, suggesting that while Gatling sought Rogers's assistance, he wanted to secure it at minimal expense.

48. Rogers, "The Gatling Gun," p. 438.

49. Ibid., p. 440.

50. Red Horse was interviewed in 1881 by an army surgeon. His account was published by the Government Printing Office in 1893 and reproduced in *Lakota and Cheyenne, Indian Views of the Great Sioux War, 1876–1877*, ed. Jerome A. Greene, p. 37.

51. "On Little Big Horn with General Custer," *Army Magazine*, June and July 1894; republished in Peter Cozzens, ed., *Eyewitness to the Indian Wars, 1865–1890: The Long War for the Northern Plains*, p. 318.

52. Williston, "Machine Guns in War."

53. Peter Cozzens, ed., *Eyewitness to the Indian Wars, 1865–1890, Volume Two: The Wars for the Pacific Northwest* (Mechanicsburg, Pa.: Stackpole Press, 2002), p. 377.

54. Donald R. Morris, *The Washing of the Spears: The Rise and Fall of the Zulu Nation* (Cambridge, Mass.: De Capo Press, 1998), p. 567.

55. Ibid., p. 569.

56. "The Zulus Badly Whipped," *New York Times,* July 24, 1879.

57. Morris, *Washing of the Spears*, p 572.

58. Kimball, "Machine Guns," p. 410.

59. W. Gardner, "Machine Guns and How to Use Them," in Ordnance Notes. No. 198, Washington, D.C., June 1, 1882, p. 2.

60. Ibid., p. 6.

61. Ibid., p. 8.

62. *Lakeside Press,* Cleveland, N.Y., April 2, 1881.

63. Paul Wahl and Donald R. Toppel, *The Gatling Gun* (New York: Arco Publishing, 1965), p. 100. The authors cited the August 27 issue of the *Army & Navy Journal.*

64. Chinn, *The Machine Gun*, p. 58.

3. Hiram Maxim Changes War

1. "Evening News" of Baltimore, date illegible. From the Sir Hiram S. Maxim Collection, 1890–1916. Archives Division, National Air and Space Museum, Smithsonian Institution, Washington, D.C.

2. This number is from Maxim's memoirs, *My Life* (London: Methuen and Co., 1915).

In another account, to the Royal United Services Institution, Maxim said he had fired seven rounds.

3. "Sir Hiram Maxim, Inventor, Dies," *Rochester Herald*, November 25, 1916.

4. Hiram Maxim, *My Life*, p. 38.

5. Personal communication from Dr. Joseph Slade, of the University of Ohio, who has researched Maxim's life and holds copies of some of Maxim's personal papers.

6. Maxim, *My Life*, p. 40.

7. Ibid., p. 48.

8. Ibid., p. 86.

9. *Brooklyn Eagle*, November 24, 1916.

10. Maxim, *My Life*, p. 132.

11. Hiram Percy Maxim, *A Genius in the Family: Sir Hiram Stevens Maxim Through a Small Son's Eyes* (New York & London: Harper & Brothers 1936), pp. 21–25.

12. Maxim, *A Genius in the Family*, pp. 17–20.

13. Census data from personal communication from Dick Eastman, genealogist. Dr. Slade, who had researched Maxim's life, said, of Maxim's move to Canada during the war, "His wanderings are certainly suspicious" (personal communication with author).

14. "How I Invented Maxim Gun—Hiram Maxim. Outbreak of World-War Moves Veteran American to Describe for The Times His Epoch-Making Invention," *New York Times*, November 1, 1914. This was how Maxim himself quoted the advice in 1914. A briefer version is commonly cited: "Hang your chemistry and electricity! If you want to make a pile of money, invent something that will enable these Europeans to cut each other's throats with great facility." The second quotation has been used by many sources, including by Chinn in *The Machine Gun* (p. 128), and the many gun writers who borrowed from him. The reference to a "Jew" appears in Dolf Goldsmith, *The Devil's Paintbrush, Sir Hiram Maxim's Gun*, 2nd ed. (Toronto: Collector Grade Publication, 1993) p. 7, citing the *London Times*.

15. Chinn, *The Machine Gun*, p. 128. It was 1883. The idea was ahead of its time— machine guns were still struggling for military acceptance, and Maxim had conceived of an assault rifle, which would not be carried into combat for decades.

16. Maxim, *My Life*, p. 157.

17. P. Fleury Mottelay, *The Life and Work of Sir Hiram Maxim* (London: John Lane, 1920), p. 10.

18. A transcript of Maxim's presentation to the Royal United Services Institution on December 11, 1896, entitled "The Automatic System of Fire-Arms: Its History and Development," is on file at the Smithsonian. The account is taken from the opening page. Archives Division, National Air and Space Museum.

19. Ian V. Hogg, *Machine Guns: A Detailed History of the Rapid-Fire Gun, 14th Century to Present* (Iola, Wisc.: Krause Publications, 2002), pp. 34–35.

20. Goldsmith, *The Devil's Paintbrush*.

21. Maxim, *My Life*, p. 163.

22. Ibid., p. 170.

23. Chinn, *The Machine Gun*, pp. 134–35.

24. Julian Symons, *England's Pride: The Story of the Gordon Relief Expedition* (London: Hamish Hamilton, 1965), p. 196.

25. Lord Charles Beresford, *The Memoirs of Admiral Lord Charles Beresford*, Volume I. (Boston: Little, Brown & Co., 1914), p. 263.

26. Symons, p. 198.

27. Ibid., p. 203.

28. Alex MacDonald, *Too Late for Gordon and Khartoum: The Testimony of an Independent Eye-Witness of the Heroic Efforts for Their Relief and Rescue* (John Murray, publisher, 1887), p. 241.

29. Beresford, *Memoirs,* p. 267.
30. *The Nineteenth Century and After,* vol. 13, James Knowles, ed. (London: Sampson, Low Marston & Co., 1903), p. 91.
31. Chinn, *The Machine Gun,* p. 131.
32. Maxim, *My Life,* p. 203.
33. Ibid., p. 238.
34. Armstrong, *Bullets and Bureaucrats,* p. 175
35. Williston. "Machine Guns in War."
36. "Robari (The Story of A Very Little War.)" *MacMillan's* Volume LXXXI, Nov 1899–April 1900, pp. 99–105.
37. Details of Rattray's travels and life were provided to the author by his grandson, Alan Swindale.
38. Rattray's letter is posted on www.fivenine.co.uk, a British genealogy website.
39. "I am glad to learn the Fletcher note has been paid," Gatling wrote in a letter to General John Love, January 30, 1874. On file at Indiana Historical Society. The "Fletcher note" refers to the debt.
40. "Statement of the Condition of the Company," handwritten by Gatling for the shareholders, October 4, 1876. On file at Connecticut State Library.
41. "Cash Receipts and Disbursements during the year ending Sept. 30, 1889." On file at Connecticut State Library.
42. Armstrong, *Bullets and Bureaucrats,* p. 77.
43. Wahl and Toppel, *Gatling Gun,* p. 135.
44. Letter from Frederick W. Prince, secretary of the Gatling Gun Company, to the U.S. Navy Bureau of Ordnance, September 22, 1894. On file at Connecticut State Library.
45. Norton, *American Breech-Loading Small Arms,* p. 242.
46. *Army and Navy Gazette of London,* May 7, 1892.
47. G. S. Hutchison, *Machine Guns: Their History and Tactical Employment* (London: Macmillan and Co., 1938), p. 67.
48. The notes on Maxim's workplace personality are from a section of *Maxim Nordentfelt Days and Ways,* quoted at length in Goldsmith, *The Devil's Paintbrush,* p. 58. The details on overcapitalization are from a directors' report, quoted at length in the same book, p. 59.
49. "An Abridgement of Mr. Hiram S. Maxim's Lecture delivered at Dartford, March 16th, 1897," p. 5. On file at the Smithsonian.
50. John H. Parker, *History of the Gatling Gun Detachment, Fifth Army Corps, At Santiago, With a Few Unvarnished Truths Concerning that Expedition* (Kansas City, Mo.: Hudson-Kimberly Publishing Co., 1898), p. 11.
51. *Biographical Register of the Officers and Graduates of the U.S. Military Academy at West Point, N.Y., Since Its Establishment in 1802,* supplement vol. VI-A, 1910–20 (Saginaw, Mich.: Seemann & Peters Printers, 1920), pp. 642–44.
52. Parker, *History of the Gatling Gun Detachment,* p. 20. Parker's book, like his actions outside Santiago, was prescient. His suggestions for machine-gun employment presaged World War I. The book also serves as social criticism of the American army circa 1900. Parker championed the enlisted man, and his writing was spiced with his observations—and derision—of the machinations of army generals for status and power, and, chillingly, of what he saw as the abandonment by the army of soldiers in Cuba who had contracted tropical diseases. These men, he said, were not provided for as the army sailed home for victory parades. He was a tactical visionary. He was not popular.
53. Armstrong, *Bullets and Bureaucrats.* p. 83.
54. Goddard, *Army Ordnance,* pp. 8–9.
55. "The Yuma Penitentiary. One of the Most Remarkable Prisons in the United States.

Filled With Desperate Characters. In Many Years but One Has Escaped," *New York Times,* March 1, 1896.

56. *Times of London,* February 22, 1879. On file at Connecticut State Library.

57. All three newspaper clippings are on file, undated, at Connecticut State Library.

58. Peter Cozzens, *Eyewitness to the Indian Wars, Volume Five: The Army and the Indian* (Mechanicsburg, Pa: Stackpole Books, 2001). A soldier's diary on p. 319 describes the encounter. "With one Gatling on board, we started up the river Yellowstone. Had a lively target practice this P.M. at a large brown bear which was seen ahead on a sandbar. He made a lively retreat for the shore and into the thicket as we drew near. The men forward gave him a volley, but he still kept on." The entry thus is not fully clear, and can be read in two ways. The Gatling was certainly present, and the order of the writing strongly suggests it was fired. The phrase "gave a volley" indicates that the soldiers might have fired their rifles simultaneously. Armstrong, in *Bullets and Bureaucrats,* documented six uses of a Gatling gun against Native Americans from 1874 to 1878; p. 80.

59. Parker, *History of the Gatling Gun Detachment,* p. 14.

60. Ibid., p. 10.

61. "The Story of San Juan. How Parker and His Gatlings Turned The Tide Of Battle," undated newspaper clip, circa 1898, on file at Connecticut State Library. The report was written by Parker, who was given a tag line.

62. John H. Parker, *History of the Gatling Gun Detachment.* From the preface, written by Theodore Roosevelt.

63. Ibid.

64. Hutchison, *Machine Guns,* p. 67.

65. Ismat Hassan Zulfo, *Karari: The Sudanese Account of the Battle of Omdurman,* translated by Peter Clark (Bath, U.K.: Pittman Press, 1980), pp. 96–100.

66. Ibid., pp. 172–73.

67. Winston S. Churchill, *The River War* (originally published in 1900; reprinted by Kessinger Publishing, 2004), p. 150.

68. Hutchinson, *Machine Guns,* p. 69.

69. Rudyard Kipling, "Pharaoh and the Sergeant," 1897. First published in the *New York Tribune.*

70. Maxim, *My Life,* p. 182

71. Hiram S. Maxim, *Li Hung Chang's Scrap-Book* (London: Watts & Co., 1913). The first two quotations are excerpted from p. 19; the last quotation from p. 368.

72. Not long before his death, Maxim wrote of the inferiority of the freed slaves, describing his frustration at trying to keep the Kimball House lit and heated through a night with the help of only a black man. The company engineer had the same problem, he said, and finally told him he had concluded that "no amount of beating would keep a nigger awake at night."

73. *New Zealand Free Lance,* September 15, 1900.

4. Slaughter Made Industrial: The Great War

1. Sergeant A. J. Rixon papers, letter of March 17, 1915. On file at Imperial War Museum, London. Rixon added: "Not the St. Patrick's Day I'm used to."

2. Chinn, *The Machine Gun,* describes Browning's discovery and the series of experiments on pp. 160–63.

3. Ibid., pp. 150–70; also Major B. R. Lewis, *Machine Guns of the U.S., 1895–1944,* a series in *Army Ordnance.*

4. Chinn, *The Machine Gun,* pp. 209–10.

5. Julia Keller, *Mr. Gatling's Terrible Marvel* (New York: Viking, 2008), p. 203. The

text of Dr. Gatling's letter thanking his son for the five hundred dollars appears on p. 203.

6. Historians have excoriated Western officer corps for what would later seem monumental ignorance; it has become a bromide. Ellis's *Social History of the Machine Gun* portrayed the British generals thoughtlessly sending a generation to its doom.

7. Richard Meinertzhagen, *Army Diary: 1899–1926* (Edingburgh and London: Oliver and Boyd, 1960), p. 8.

8. Ellis, *Social History of the Machine Gun*, pp. 54–55.

9. "The United Service," *New York Times*, July 15, 1903.

10. Kimball, "Machine Guns," p. 417.

11. Armstrong, *Bullets and Bureaucrats*, p. 133.

12. Ibid., pp. 126–29.

13. Ibid., pp. 136–37.

14. Ellis, *Social History of the Machine Gun*, p. 55.

15. Hutchison, *Machine Guns*, pp. 82–83.

16. Charles à Court Repington, *The War in the Far East: 1904–1905* (New York: Dutton, 1908), p. 315.

17. Tadayoshi Sakurai, *Human Bullets: A Soldier's Story of Port Arthur* (Boston: Houghton, Mifflin, 1907), pp. 152–53.

18. Hutichison, *Machine Guns*, p. 89.

19. B. W. Norregaard, *The Great Siege: The Investment and Fall of Port Arthur* (London: Methuen & Co., 1906), p. 71.

20. Louis A. La Garde, *Gunshot Injuries: How They are Inflicted, Their Complications and Treatment*, 2nd Revised Ed. (New York: William Wood and Company, 1916). The precise losses remain a matter of dispute. La Garde, who apparently was working off medical data, put the number of Japanese killed in action at more than forty-seven thousand. With disease factored in, the number likely rises significantly.

21. Sakurai, *Human Bullets*.

22. Ibid., pp. 232–38.

23. Hutchison, *Machine Guns*, p. 84

24. Armstrong, *Bullet and Bureaucrats*, p. 139.

25. La Garde, *Gunshot Injuries*, p. 411.

26. Repington, *War in the Far East*, p. 490.

27. Armstrong, *Bullets and Bureaucrats*, p. 140.

28. From the handwritten letters of Alfred Dougan "Mickey" Chater, a captain in a Territorial unit who served on the Western Front from fall 1914 through March 1915, when he was struck in the face by a piece of shell. Captain Chater survived, but the injury and disfigurement were horrible. Letters on file at the Imperial War Museum, London.

29. David Lloyd George, *War Memoirs of David Lloyd George, 1915–16* (Boston: Little, Brown, and Company, 1933), pp. 61–74.

30. Goldsmith, *The Devil's Paintbrush*, pp. 131–60. The question of how many machine guns the Germans had at the war's outset has been clouded by unattributed guesses and estimates. Goldsmith provides the text of a report by "The German Government Agent at the Anglo-German Mixed Arbitral Tribunal," dated October 5, 1928. The report provided depot-by-depot totals from the former chief of the German Machine Gun Department.

31. Meinertzhagen, *Army Diary*. pp. 90–94. Meinertzhagen, a British intelligence officer, globe-roaming ornithologist, and self-aggrandizing figure, kept exhaustive diaries. His journals are both interesting and suspect, and his writings have been found to contain frauds. In this case, his account of the battle of Tanga is consistent with other sources, and one of his conclusions, that troops felt disgraced by being defeated by

black soldiers, was consistent with many of the misapprehensions of the ways that machine guns were changing warfare.

32. Chater, letter of December 13, 1914. On file at Imperial War Museum.
33. Martin Middlebrook, *The First Day on the Somme* (New York: Norton, 1972). Soldiers were surrounded by signs that, though the age of industrial warfare had arrived, many officers leading the army did not understand what this meant.
34. Ibid., p. 11.
35. Arthur Anderson, from a ninety-five-page hand-written manuscript. On file at Imperial War Museum.
36. Paddy Griffith, *Battle Tactics of the Western Front* (New Haven: Yale University Press, 1994), p. 49.
37. La Garde, *Gunshot Injuries,* p. 422.
38. Tim Ripley, *Bayonet Battle* (London: Pan Books, 2000), pp. 34–35.
39. A. J. Rixon, diary entry of April 1. On file at Imperial War Museum.
40. Rixon, diary entry of May 26, 1915.
41. Rixon, diary entry of September 25, 1915.
42. C. E. Crutchley, *Machine Gunner 1914–1918: Personal Experiences of the Machine Gun Corps* (South Yorkshire: Pen & Sword Military Classics, 2005), p. 15.
43. Middlebrook, *The First Day on the Somme,* p. 21.
44. André Laffargue, *The Attack in Trench Warfare: Impressions and Reflections of a Company Commander* (Washington, D.C.: United States Infantry Association, 1916), p. 27.
45. Ibid., p. 12.
46. Anderson, from his diary.
47. Middlebrook, *The First Day on the Somme,* p. 81.
48. Ibid., p. 106. The quoted section at the end of the excerpt is from Middlebrook's interview with Private W. J. Senescall of The Cambridge Battalion.
49. Ibid., pp. 137–38.
50. Ibid., p. 185.
51. Ibid., p. 123.
52. Anderson, from his diary.
53. Maxim, *My Life,* p. 313.
54. Ibid., p. 315.
55. Wilfred Owen, "The Spring Offensive," 1918. Owen, a lieutenant, was killed by a bullet a week before Armistice, roughly a month after writing these lines.
56. Crutchley, *Machine Gunner,* p. 15.
57. W. H. B. Smith, and Joseph E. Smith, *The Book of Rifles* (Harrisburg, Pa.: Stackpole, 1965), pp. 62–73.
58. Hans-Dieter Götz, *German Military Rifles and Machine Pistols, 1871–1945,* trans. Dr. Edward Force (West Chester, Pa.: Schiffer Publishing, 1990), p. 222.
59. Ian V. Hogg and John S. Weeks, *Military Small Arms of the 20th Century,* 7th Edition (Iola, Wis.: Krause Publications, 2000), p. 93.
60. Louis A. La Garde, and John T. Thompson, "Preliminary Report of Board to Determine Upon Bullet for Military Service Pistol." Written in Chicago, Illinois, March, 18, 1904.

5. Stalin's Contest: The Invention of the AK-47

1. *Kalashnikov: Oruzhiye, Boyepripacy, Snaryazheniye, Okhota, Sport.* Special Issue, 2004, p. 18. The polygon is also described several times in Kalashnikov's memoirs.
2. M. T. Kalashnikov, *From a Stranger's Doorstep to the Kremlin Gates,* (Moscow: Military Parade, 1997), p. 203.

3. Ibid., p. 164.
4. Dmitri Shirayev, "Legendarn Kalashnikov—Ne Oruzheinik, a *Podstavnoye* Litso," *Moskovsky Komsomolets,* January 3, 2002. *Moskovsky Komsomolets* is a Russian-language newspaper published in Moscow. Various sources say the artillery commission received from ten to fifteen submissions. Fifteen, the number provided by S. B. Monetchikov's *Istoriya Russkogo Avtomato* is used here, in part because Monetchikov lists the contestants' names. His book was published by Atlant in Saint Petersburg, 2005.
5. According to the State Statistics Committee in June 1946, out of 24 million workers and office employees who received their full wages or salaries 5.6 percent were paid about 100 rubles; 9.2 percent from 101 to 150 rubles; 10.7 percent from 151 to 200 rubles; 8.8 percent from 201 to 250 rubles; 8.7 percent from 251 to 300 rubles. Less than one-third of laborers and white-white collar workers were paid from 300 to 600 rubles. Research by Nikolay Khalip.
6. M. T. Kalashnikov, *From a Stranger's Doorstep.* The quotations from this section are taken from p. 152 and p. 166. This section was written by weaving together multiple sources, including Kalashnikov's memoirs, the displays and materials at the Museum in Izhevsk and St. Petersburg, Kalashnikov's speeches from 2004 to 2008, and multiple interviews with the author.
7. Kalashnikovs' stepdaughter's published remarks describe his relative material wealth in the postwar Soviet Union. Also, in Mikhail Kalashnikov and Yelena Kalashnikov, *Trayektoriya Sudbi* (Moscow: Vsya Rossiya Publishing House, 2004), Katya is shown in a knee-length fur coat in the photograph section between pp. 96 and 97.
8. Letter from M. T. Kalashnikov to Edward Ezell, dated June 1973. In the unsorted collection of Ezell's papers at Defence College of Management and Technology, Shrivenham, UK.
9. Letter from Edward C. Ezell to "Hal," dated September 18, 1973. Hal was Harold E. Johnson, an expert on Eastern bloc arms who worked at the Foreign Science and Technology Center of the U.S. Army Material Development and Readiness Command. He was also the author of the once-classified volume *Small Arms Identification and Operation Guide—Eurasian Communist Countries,* published by the U.S. Defense Intelligence Agency. In the Ezell Collection, College of Management and Technology, UK Defence Academy.
10. Personal communication to author from Dmitri Shirayev, a former Soviet arms design official.
11. The early versions of Kalashnikov's memoirs draw heavily from D. N. Bolotin's *Soviet Small Arms and Ammunition* (Hyvinkää, Finland: Finnish Arms Museum Foundation, 1995); later versions draw from A. A. Malimon, *Otechestvenniye Avtomaty* (Moscow: Minister of Defense of the Russian Federation, 2000). Translation by Michael Schwirtz.
12. Personnel communication to author by Maksim R. Popenker, editor of the www .guns.ru website and author of several books on Russian small arms.
13. Kalashnikov, *From A Stranger's Doorstep,* p. 128.
14. Mikhail Kalashnikov, at Rosoboronexport, summer 2007. In presence of the author.
15. Harold E. Johnson, "Assessing Soviet Progress in Small Arms Research and Development," *Army Research and Development News,* November–December 1974, pp. 31–32.
16. Y. A. Natsvaladze, *Oruzhiye Pobedy: Kollektsiya Strelkovogo Oruzhiya Sistemy A.I. Sudayera v Sobranii Muzeya* (Leningrad, 1988), pp. 4–17.
17. Marius Broekmeyer, *Stalin, the Russians and Their War, 1941–1945* (Madison: University of Wisconsin Press, 1999), p. 4.
18. Ibid., p. 45.
19. Georgy K. Zhukov provides an officially approved summary in his 1969 memoirs, *The Memoirs of Marshal Zhukov.* In the English-language edition, published in 1971 by Jonathan Cape, Ltd., of London, the summary appears on pp. 138–39.

20. N. Yelshin, "Soviet Small Arms," *Soviet Military Review,* 2, 1977, p. 15.
21. C. J. Chivers, "Izhevsk Journal: Russia Salutes Father of the Rifle Fired Round the World," *New York Times,* November 11, 2004. At the ceremony for Kalashnikov's eighty-fifth birthday, in Izhevsk, where he worked from 1948 until the present day, officials at the arms plant gave these figures.
22. Arthur J. Alexander, *Weapons Acquisition in the Soviet Union, United States and France.* The paper was prepared for a conference on Comparative Defense Policy at the U.S. Air Force Academy in 1973. In the unsorted Ezell Collection.
23. Adam Ulam, *Stalin: The Man and His Era* (Boston: Beacon Press, 1989), p. 464.
24. Bolotin, *Soviet Small Arms and Ammunition,* p. 107.
25. M. T. Kalashnikov, speaking at the sixtieth anniversary jubilee of the birth of the AK-47, in Moscow, 2007, in presence of the author.
26. Götz, *German Military Rifles,* pp. 198–204.
27. Ibid., p. 208, citing Lieutenant Colonel Dr. Rudolf Forenbacher, from the journal *Werhkunde,* 1, 1953.
28. Aberdeen Proving Ground Series, *German Submachine Guns and Assault Rifles of World War II* (Old Greenwich: W.E., Inc., 1968), pp. 1–10. The description of the development of the Kurz cartridge and the *sturmgewehr* was largely derived from Götz and from this document; the production numbers are listed on pp. 5 and 7.
29. P. Labbett and F. A. Brown. *Technical Ammunition Guide Series 3, Pamphlet 2: The 7.62mm x 39 Model 1943 Cartridge Communist* (London: September 1987), p. 1. The authors were skeptical of the official Soviet account and Soviet sources that relied on them. "Reliance has, perforce, to be placed almost entirely on Russian narratives, without original documents or other evidence being available. The total accuracy of Russian sources is hard to assess and the motivation and inspiration for the design and development of this cartridge may not have been exactly as the Russians portray it." This summarizes one of the central problems of assessing the Kalashnikov legend.
30. Bolotin, *Soviet Small Arms and Ammunition,* p. 97.
31. Ibid., p. 113.
32. Monetchikov, *Istoriya Russkogo Avtomata,* p. 24.
33. Broekmeyer, *The Russians and Their War,* pp. 12–13.
34. Bolotin, *Soviet Small Arms and Ammunition,* p. 113.
35. Monetchikov, *Istoriya Russkogo Avtomata,* p. 25.
36. Bolotin, *Soviet Small Arms and Ammunition,* p. 126. Hogg claims that nine thousand of Fedorov's *avtomats* were made, though he did not provide a source. Bolotin cited Soviet archives. His estimate is used here.
37. Bolotin, *Soviet Small Arms and Ammunition,* pp. 126–27.
38. Ibid., p. 54.
39. Ibid., p. 252. Bolotin provided a list: Tukhachevsky, Uborevich, Dybenko, Kuybyshev, Alksnis, and Unshlicht.
40. Yuri Sergeyev, *Tekhnika i Vooruzheniye,* No. 12, 1970.
41. Perry Githens, "How Good Are Russian Guns?" *Popular Science,* March 1951, p. 109.
42. Mikhail Kalashnikov with Elena Joly, *The Gun that Changed the World* (Cambridge, UK: Polity Press, 2006), p. 3.
43. Kalashnikov, *From a Stranger's Doorstep,* p. 25.
44. Ibid., p. 24.
45. Kalashnikov with Joly, *The Gun that Changed the World,* p. 4.
46. Kalashnikov, *From a Stranger's Doorstep,* p. 31.
47. Ibid., p. 404.
48. Ibid.
49. The first version is from *From a Stranger's Doorstep,* pp. 408–9. The second version is from *The Gun That Changed the World,* pp. 10–11.
50. Kalashnikov, *From a Stranger's Doorstep,* pp. 412–413.

51. Kalashnikov with Joly, *The Gun that Changed the World*, p. 26.
52. Ibid., p. 33.
53. Interview of Mikhail Kalashnikov by Nick Paton Walsh, who shared the notes of his interview with the author.
54. Catherine Merridale, *Ivan's War: Life and Death in the Red Army, 1939–45* (New York: Metropolitan Books, 2006), p. 84.
55. Kalashnikov, *From a Stranger's Doorstep*, p. 73.
56. Broekmeyer, *The Russians and Their War*, xiv–xv.
57. Vladimir N. Zhukov, *Second Birth*, translation by Army Foreign Science and Technology Center (Charlottesville, Virginia, 1974). Originally published by Voyenizdat, Moscow, 1963, p. 58. An official Soviet biography of Kalashnikov. Kalashnikov embraced this biography, and presented it as fact to his first Western biographer. Many passages are demonstrably false or at odds with Kalashnikov's later accounts.
58. Kalashnikov and Joly, *The Gun that Changed the World*, p. 19.
59. Ibid., p. 35.
60. Kalashnikov, *From a Stranger's Doorstep*, p. 75.
61. Zhukov, *Second Birth*, pp. 59–63.
62. Kalashnikov, *From a Stranger's Doorstep*, p. 76.
63. Some sources, particularly in the English language, say Kalashnikov was treated at Kazan. These stories appear apocryphal; the principal sources, including Kalashnikov himself, describe his treatment in Yelets.
64. Kalashnikov, *From a Stranger's Doorstep*, pp. 92–93.
65. Ibid., p. 87.
66. Zhukov, *Second Birth*, p. 85.
67. *Kalashnikov: Oruzhiye, Boyepripasy, Snaryazheniye, Okhota, Sport.* Special Issue, 2002, p. 17.
68. From interview of Kalashnikov by Edward Ezell in July 1989. A partial transcript of the interview was published in "Conversations with Kalashnikov," in the *Small Arms World Report*, December 1992, p. 5.
69. Zhukov, *Second Birth*, pp. 108–9.
70. Mikhail Degtyarov, in "Istoki 'Kalashnikov'" *Kalashnikov: Oruzhiye, Boyepripasy, Snaryazheniye, Okhota, Sport.* Issue 5, 2003, pp. 6–9. The year of birth of Kalashnikov's son, Viktor Mikhailovich, is from the museum in Izhevsk.
71. Kalashnikov has refused over the years to discuss the mother of his son, Viktor, saying only that she died when Viktor was young and he then received custody of the boy. The reasons Kalashnikov is otherwise silent on the subject are not clear.
72. Ezell, "Conversations with Kalashnikov," *Small Arms World Report*, December 1992, p. 5.
73. M. Novikov, "This is Kalashnikov," *Volksarmee*, No. 1, January 1968, p. 9. *Volksarmee* was the magazine of the National People's Army, the military of the German Democratic Republic.
74. Kalashnikov, *From a Stranger's Doorstep*, p. 122.
75. Ibid., p. 121.
76. Ibid., p. 132.
77. Ibid., pp. 133–34.
78. Viktor Vlasyuk, "Weapons Designer Vasily Lyuty," *Zerkalo Nedeli*, No. 12, March 23–29, 1996. Vlasyuk quotes Lyuty in the section cited. Translated by Viktor Klimenko.
79. Ezell, *Small Arms World Report*, December 1992, p. 6.
80. Kalashnikov, *From a Stranger's Doorstep*, pp. 237–38.
81. Ibid., p. 216.
82. Kalashnikov with Joly, *The Gun that Changed the World*, p. 61. Here Kalashnikov said that a year had passed before he returned to the Schurovo polygon for the competitive field tests.

83. Ezell, *Kalashnikov: The Arms and the Man*, p. 71. A photograph of the disassembled rifle appears on this page; the external shape of the AK-47 is evident, but the guts of the weapon have not yet been worked out.

84. Bolotin, *Soviet Small Arms and Ammunition*, p. 69, quoting remarks by Kalashnikov published on September 20, 1957, in *Krasnaya Zvezda* (*Red Star*), the official newspaper of the Red Army.

85. Kalashnikov with Joly, *The Gun that Changed the World*, p. 64.

86. Malimon, *Otechestvenniye Avtomaty*, chapter 9.

87. Ibid.

88. Kalashnikov, *From a Stranger's Doorstep*, p. 220.

89. Ezell, *Kalashnikov: The Arms and the Man*, p. 72.

90. Kalashnikov, *From a Stranger's Doorstep*, p. 209.

91. Ibid., p. 210.

92. The available sources differ on this point, and Kalashnikov has published inconsistent accounts. Bolotin listed three finalists: Kalashnikov, Bulkin, and Dementyev. The museum in Izhevsk listes four: Kalashnikov, Dementyev, Bulkin, and Sudayev. (The addition of Sudayev appears to be an error; he died in summer 1946, long before the rifles' field trials. His weapon was used as a control.) To these lists, Kalashnikov has at times added Sphagin and Degtyarev, two of the best-known figures in Soviet arms design.

93. Kalashnikov, *From a Stranger's Doorstep*, p. 213.

94. Bolotin, *Soviet Small Arms and Ammunition*, p. 69, citing *Red Star* newspaper, September 20, 1957.

95. Kalashnikov with Joly, *The Gun that Changed the World*, p. 63.

96. Malimon, *Otechestvenniye Avtomaty*, chapter 9.

97. Kalashnikov with Joly, *The Gun that Changed the World*, p. 62.

98. Ibid., p. 63.

99. Ezell, *Small Arms World Report*, December 1992, p. 7.

100. Bolotin, *Soviet Small Arms and Ammunition*, p. 70.

101. Bolotin's book was both accurate and authoritative enough, in Kalashnikov's view, that he cited it in his own memoirs, although not on the subject of Zaitsev's design contributions to the final AK-47 prototype.

102. Malimon, *Otechestvenniye Avtomaty*. Chapter 9 includes excerpts from a letter by Zaitsev. The book was published by the Russian Ministry of Defense and serves as both an official chronicle of the tests and a fuller account than Kalashnikov provided. Only five hundred copies were printed, and its circulation was tightly limited.

103. Pravda.Ru, a Russian news site, published its version on August 2, 2003, thirteen years after Lyuty died.

104. Vlasyuk, *Zerkalo Nedeli*.

105. Personal communication to author from Maksim R. Popenker.

106. Kalashnikov with Joly, *The Gun that Changed the World*, p. 65.

107. *Small Arms World Report*, December 1992, pp. 7–8.

108. Kalashnikov, *From a Stranger's Doorstep*, pp. 225–26.

109. In 1989, according to the transcript of their interview, Kalashnikov told Ezell he met Degtyarev during his early work at NIPSMVO, when Kalashnikov was still "a single country bumpkin." *Small Arms World Report*, December 1992, p. 6.

110. Zhukov, *Second Birth*, pp. 146–47.

111. Ronald F. Bellamy and Russ Zajtchuk, "Chapter 3: The Evolution of Wound Ballistics: A Brief History," *Textbook of Military Medicine, Part 1: Warfare, Weaponry and the Casualty Conventional Warfare: Ballistic, Blast and Burn Injuries* (Washington, D.C.: Office of the Surgeon General, United States Army, Walter Reed Army Medical Center, 1989), pp. 83–106.

112. Sergeyev, *Tekhnika i Vooruzheniye*, p. 27.

113. Robert H. Clagett, Jr, "How the Infantry Tests a Rifle," *American Rifleman,* October 1953, pp. 27–30. Clagett, a major, was a test officer for Army Field Forces No. 3 at Fort Benning, Georgia.

114. G. E. Hendricks, "Test Results Report on AK-47," November 7, 1962, Report No. DPS-800, to U.S. Army Test and Evaluation Command, and "Trial Report Soviet Machine Carbine 7.62mm Kalashnikov (AK)," August 1958, from the G-2 to the Netherlands General Staff. The Dutch report is on file at the Leger museum in Delft.

115. *Small Arms World Report,* December 1992, p. 7.

116. Kalashnikov, *From a Stranger's Doorstep,* p. 231.

117. Kalashnikov with Joly, *The Gun that Changed the World,* p. 66.

118. Malimon, *Otechestvenniye Avtomaty,* chapter 9. Kalashnikov has written that tests ended on January 10.

119. Novikov, from *Volksarmee.*

6. The Breakout: The Mass Production, Distribution, and Early Use of the AK-47

1. A. A. Grechko, *The Armed Forces of the Soviet State: A Soviet View* (Moscow: Ministry of Defense of the U.S.S.R., 1975). Translated and published by the U.S. Air Force, pp. 6–7.

2. Such reasoning has anchored popular assessments of the Kalashnikov line. The conventional wisdom runs like this: The AK-47 is an excellent and almost failsafe assault rifle, therefore it is ubiquitous. This is insufficient.

3. This sentiment informs Russian pride in Russian firearms to this day. Russia cannot point to a wide range of industrial successes. Against this background, the AK-47 and its related arms are Russian products that actually work.

4. Kalashnikov, *From a Stranger's Doorstep,* p. 234.

5. Kalashnikov with Joly, *The Gun that Changed the World,* p. 70.

6. Val Shilin and Charlie Cutshaw, *Legends and Reality of the AK: A Behind-the-Scenes Look at the History, Design, and Impact of the Kalashnikov Family of Weapons* (Boulder, Co.: Paladin Press, 2000), p. 28. There is no question that Kalashnikov, by mid-1948, began work here. But sources other than Kalashnikov point to a roundabout route, and say he first worked in Tula and Kovrov, but was unsatisfied with his professional life at both places, perhaps because of competition with other designers. (Bulkin, Simonov, and Tokarev worked at Tula, Degtyarev in Kovrov.)

7. Malimon, *Otechestvenniye Avtomaty,* Chapter 10.

8. Ibid.

9. Shilin and Cutshaw, *Legends and Reality of the AK,* p. 28.

10. Kalashnikov, *From a Stranger's Doorstep,* pp. 247–51. The dates here shift in Kalashnikov's multiple tellings; he said the meeting was in 1944, when Kalashnikov was working at Kovrov. But in 1944 Kalashnikov was not yet working on the AK-47, and was not yet assigned to Kovrov.

11. Kalashnikov with Joly, *The Gun that Changed the World,* p. 74.

12. This work fell to Valery Kharkov. Malimon, *Otechestvenniye Avtomaty,* Chapter 12.

13. Malimon, *Otechestvenniye Avtomaty,* Chapter 11, translation by Michael Schwirtz. Other changes were driven by economic concerns, including substituting expensive materials used on the prototypes with less expensive materials better suited for cost-conscious mass production. A few changes were minor: The screw fixtures in the stock and near the barrel were replaced with stronger fittings. The accessory panel at the butt plate, which provided access inside the stock for storing small items, such as rifle-cleaning materials, was changed to be similar to that of a carbine designed by Evgeny

Dragunov, another Soviet armorer. One change was to an accessory: Because it could fire automatically, the AK-47 built up more heat than most of the rifles and carbines that preceded it. A steel clip was added to the shoulder strap to prevent it from burning where it came into contact with the barrel.

14. For data on its imprecision, see the ballistic studies performed at the Aberdeen Proving Ground, including G. E. Hendricks, "Test Results on AK-47 Rifle," published on November 7, 1962, and filed as Report #DPS-800.

15. Dmitri Shirayev, "Who Invented the Automatic Kalashnikov?" *Soldat Udachi (Soldier of Fortune)*, Moscow, September 2000, pp. 30–34.

16. Personal communication to author in July 2009 from Norbert Moczarski, a German biographer of Schmeisser. Almost twenty years after the end of the Soviet Union, Schmeisser's activities at the time of the AK-47's development remain shrouded. There is no question of his presence in Izhevsk during the 1950s. But the Soviet archives have not been opened to allow an examination of how Schmeisser passed his time there and the reasons he had been sent to such a place. His biographers in Germany remain unsure what role, if any, he played in the development of the Kalashnikov prototypes, the fine-tuning and mass production of the AK-47 design, and the tooling of the Izhmash assembly line.

17. The first view was put forth by Russian *Life* magazine. Shirayev's quotation is from a personal communication to the author.

18. Shilin and Cutshaw, *Legends and Reality of the AK*, p. 29.

19. The heavier AK-47 that resulted from it probably reduced recoil, too.

20. Shilin and Cutshaw, *Legends and Reality of the AK*. Shilin does not provide his source.

21. Malimon, *Otechestvenniye Avtomaty*, Chapter 12.

22. After the monetary reform in 1947, the typical urban worker in the Soviet Union received a salary of five hundred to one thousand rubles a month (data of the Soviet State Statistics Committee; research conducted by Nikolay Khalip).

23. Irina Kedrova, in the Russian-language newspaper *Tribuna*, quoted Nelly Kalashnikov, Mikhail Kalashnikov's stepdaughter, in November 2004.

24. Mikhail Kalashnikov, in public remarks at sixtieth anniversary celebrations of the AK-47, in offices of Rosoboronexport, Moscow, in 2007, in presence of the author.

25. Kalashnikov, *From a Stranger's Doorstep*, pp. 429–30.

26. Kalashnikov with Joly, *The Gun that Changed the World*, p. 98.

27. Ibid., p. 104.

28. Ibid., p. 105.

29. William Taubman, *Khrushchev* (New York: W.W. Norton, 2003). Taubman provides a vivid description of Beria's last minutes on p. 256. The excerpt from Beria's letter, written on July 1, 1953, is from the translation of the document posted on the Virtual Archive of the Cold War International History Project at the Woodrow Wilson International Center for Scholars, at www.wilsoncenter.org.

30. Vojtech Mastny and Malcolm Byrne, *A Cardboard Castle: An Inside History of the Warsaw Pact 1955–1991* (Budapest: Central European University Press, 2005). The documents quoted were retrieved from archives and translated by the Parallel History Project on NATO and the Warsaw Pact. The document cited here, "General Provisions of the Warsaw Treaty Armed Forces Unified Command," is from pp. 80–81.

31. Mastny and Byrne, *A Cardboard Castle*. The language is from the Statute of the Warsaw Treaty Unified Command, Part II, Section B, p. 81.

32. Grechko, *The Armed Forces of the Soviet State: A Soviet View*, p. 342.

33. The Czechs resisted developing an AK variant and produced their own assault rifle, the vz-58, which fired the M1943 cartridge and superficially resembled the AK-47 but was otherwise a different rifle.

34. Guy Laron, "Cutting the Gordian Knot: The Post WW-II Egyptian Quest for Arms

and the 1955 Czechoslovak Arms Deal," Cold War International History Project, Working Paper No. 55. See also Jon D. Glassman, *Arms for the Arabs. The Soviet Union and War in the Middle East* (Baltimore: Johns Hopkins University Press, 1955).

35. Much of the information about the Chinese delegation and the details and dates of technical transfers are from the memoir of Liu Zhengdong, titled *Zhu Jian*. The book, a limited-edition memoir (press run, two thousand copies), was published in China in 2007. Its contents have never been distributed in English, and begin to fill in blank spots in the history of communist Chinese small-arms production. The translated title is *Casting of the Sword: Memoir of an Old Armorer.* Liu Zhengdong held positions within the Chinese defense industries for several decades. The account of Liu Shaoqi's visit to Stalin is from *Together with Historical Giants—Shi Zhe's Memoirs.* Shi Zhe was Mao's Russian-language interpreter. His memoirs were published in Beijing in 1992. The description of Mao's telegram to Stalin in the Korean War is from *Witness to Sino-Soviet Military Relations of the 1950s—Memoir of Military Staff of Marshal Peng Dehuai.* The marshal was the Chinese minister of defense in the 1950s. Translations by Lin Xu, an independent arms researcher.

36. Jenó Györkei and Miklós Horváth, *Soviet Military Intervention in Hungary* (Central European University Press, 1956), pp. 54–61. The order of battle is published on p. 59.

37. László Eörsi, *The Hungarian Revolution of 1956: Myths and Realities* (New York: East European Monographs, 2006), p. 14, with further notes on p. 28.

38. Ibid., p. 11.

39. Testimony of József Tibor Fejes, at closed-court hearing on January 20, 1959. From the Fejes file at Budapest Municipal Archives. Translated by Kati Tordas.

40. Paul Lendvai, *One Day That Shook the Communist World: The 1956 Hungarian Uprising and its Legacy* trans. Ann Major (Princeton University Press, 2008), pp. 58–62.

41. Eörsi, *The Hungarian Revolution of 1956.*

42. Transcript of conversations between the Soviet Leadership and a Hungarian Workers' Party delegation in Moscow, June 13 and 16, 1953, appearing in *Uprising in East Germany, 1953,* Christian F. Ostermann, ed. (Central European University Press; republished in 2001 by the National Security Archive), pp. 145–46.

43. Ibid., p. 147.

44. Ibid., p. 149.

45. Erwin A. Schmidl and László Ritter, *The Hungarian Revolution, 1956* (Oxford: Osprey Publishing Ltd., 2006), p. 7.

46. Ibid.

47. From the "Working Notes from the Session of the CPSU CC Presidium, October 23, 1956," an electronic briefing book prepared by the National Security Archive, Washington, 2002, and in *The 1956 Hungarian Revolution: A History in Documents,* eds. Csaba Békés, Malcolm Byrne, and János Rainer (New York: Central European University Press, 2002), pp. 217–18.

48. Eörsi, *The Hungarian Revolution,* p. 8.

49. The first translation is from Eörsi, *The Hungarian Revolution,* p. 191. The second is from *The 1956 Hungarian Revolution: A History in Documents.* The sources excerpt from the same document.

50. Györkei and Horváth, *Soviet Military Intervention,* pp. 54–61.

51. Schmidl and Ritter, *The Hungarian Revolution, 1956,* p. 57.

52. Court record Nb. XI. 8083/1958. szam. In the Budapest Municipal Archive, hereinafter referred to as the Fejes Court File. Fejes admitted to shouting "Russkies Go Home" but said he shouted no other demands.

53. Fejes Court File.

54. Fejes Court File, in this case, testimony by Fejes in response to a question from the presiding judge on January 20, 1959.

55. Fejes Court File. Prosecutors accused Fejes of stealing the watch from a Russian officer; he denied this in court and said he had taken it from a civilian.

56. The background on Fejes was from the court file. Further details were provided by László Eörsi, the Hungarian historian, who has spent years studying the Hungarian fighting groups and their members. The material from Eörsi was translated from Hungarian by András B. Vágvölgyi, director of the film *Kolorado Kid,* which chronicles part of the revolution.

57. Götz, *German Military Rifles,* p. 223. The MP-18 was too well regarded to disappear outright; a license was issued by the German firm that made them to the Swiss Industrial Company, SIG, which manufactured them for export in the 1920s.

58. Appointment letter of Captain John T. Thompson to the board of officers tasked with conducting the test. U.S. War Department. October 6, 1903.

59. La Garde, *Gunshot Injuries,* p. 135.

60. Report of the Surgeon General of the Army to the Secretary of War for the Fiscal Year ending June 30, 1893, pp. 73–96.

61. The quotations and descriptions of the Thompson–La Garde tests are from the officers' account of the tests, in the forty-three-page "Preliminary Report of a Board of Officers Convened in Pursuance of the Following Order, War Department, Office of the Adjutant General, Washington, Oct. 6, 1903," which was submitted to the War Department on March 18, 1904.

62. Ibid.

63. The cadaver-livestock tests did confirm that bullets encased in metal—so-called full-metal jackets—tended to cause less serious injuries than bullets that had lead exposed. The latter expanded on impact, often causing larger wounds.

64. William J. Helmer, *The Gun That Made the Twenties Roar* (Highland Park, N.J.: Gun Room Press, 1969), p. 77.

65. Ibid., p. 53.

66. Ibid., pp. 78–79.

67. From Memorandum of Discussion at the 302nd Meeting of the National Security Council, Washington, November 1, 1956, 9–10:55 A.M., in *The 1956 Hungarian Revolution: A History in Documents,* p. 324.

68. Györkei and Horváth, *Soviet Military Intervention,* p. 257.

69. The chronology here is drawn from the fuller timeline published in *The 1956 Hungarian Revolution: A History in Documents.*

70. Report of Georgy Zhukov to the CPSU, November 4, 1956, in *The 1956 Hungarian Revolution: A History in Documents,* p. 384.

71. Y. I. Malashenko, "The Special Corps Under Fire in Budapest. Memoirs of an Eyewitness," in Györkei and Horváth, *Soviet Military Intervention.* Malashenko led the operations section of the Special Corps.

72. The casualty estimates come from various sources, which all acknowledge the uncertainty of their numbers due to complicating factors: closed Russian archives, secret burials, wounded people who sought treatment in homes and not in hospitals, where they might be discovered, and so on.

73. Fejes court file.

74. Fejes court file, from the minutes of his police hearing on March 31, 1958.

75. Production of the solid-steel-receiver AK-47 was ceased in the Soviet Union, though its replicas would be made in other places—including China, North Korea, and Europe—for many years, and a few of these early style AK-47s are still made in the United States by Arsenal Inc. of Las Vegas, primarily for collectors. Mikhail Miller's work on the Soviet AKM is briefly discussed in Shilin and Cutshaw, *Legends and Reality of the AK.* Different sources give different weights for AK-47 and AKM. The weights used here are from Maksim Popenker.

76. Kalashnikov with Joly, *The Gun that Changed the World,* p. 87.

77. Kalashnikov, *From a Stranger's Doorstep*, p. 278.
78. Ibid., p. 275.
79. Bolotin, *Soviet Small Arms and Ammunition*, pp. 175–77.
80. The myriad knockoffs of the Kalashnikov would come with changes in barrel lengths, stocks, sights, muzzle brakes, flash suppressors, and other components, giving each weapon its distinctive differences. In later years some variants would change the caliber, often to the NATO-standard .223 round. None fundamentally altered the main Soviet design. All are often referred to as Kalashnikovs, some even (erroneously but almost universally) as AK-47s.
81. Design of the SVD began in earnest in 1958, when Evgeny F. Dragunov, a former army gunsmith who had become a designer in Izhevsk, competed against another *konstruktor*, Aleksandr Konstantinov, to make a prototype. As with the PK, longer range was necessary, and the prototypes were chambered to fire the Russian 7.62x54R cartridge. The competition lasted five years, and gradually, as Soviet officials demanded modifications, the two weapons—like Bulkin's and Kalashnikov's prototypes—began to grow similar. Dragunov's version remained more accurate, and in July 1963 it was selected as the new Soviet sniper rifle. A special solid-steel bullet was designed concurrently, which gave the rifle the ability to penetrate body armor and helmets, and to be a greater threat to vehicles, helicopters, and other heavy equipment.
82. This Soviet-era manifestation of rancor would resurface later, when Kalashnikov's colleagues would claim he had not given adequate credit to the people whose work had made the AK-47 possible.
83. Kalashnikov, *From a Stranger's Doorstep*, pp. 285–88.
84. Götz, *German Military Rifles*, pp. 154–58. Götz offers a plant-by-plant description of end runs on the treaty by German industrialists and military officers. Many German people considered the treaty an insult and did not betray work that should not have been hard to detect.
85. From Christa and Erika Schreiber, descendants of Kurt Schreiber. Interview with author in Wiesa, February 2005.
86. From Heinz Muhler, former employee, in interview with author, February 2005.
87. Interview with Dietrich Thieme, local historian, January 2005.
88. Details of the hiring procedures, the work conditions, and the oath were provided to the author by former employees of the gun works, and other residents of Wiesa, during the author's visits to the plant and the town in January and February 2005.
89. Personal communication to author from Dr. Thomas Mueller, former curator of Waffenmuseum in Suhl.
90. Interview with Peter, a former worker who asked that his surname be withheld. February 2005.
91. Schreiber interview, February 2005.
92. Personnel communication to author from Markku Palokangas, of the Finnish War Museum in Helsinki.
93. Personal communication from Markku Palokangas and Robie Kulokivi, a Finnish arms researcher.
94. Trial Report, Soviet Machine Carbine 7.62mm Kalashnikov (AK). Submitted to the Netherlands General Staff, August 1958. Copy provided to author by the Legermuseum, Delft, The Netherlands.
95. Yugoslavia had fought off the Axis without the Red Army's direct support, and it emerged from World War II without Soviet troops on its soil and with pride in the success of its partisans. Relations were further strained by the Soviet crackdown in Hungary in 1956 and the Soviet Union's deception during the arrest of Imre Nagy.
96. Personal communication from Branko Bogdanovic, a historian at the Zastava plant.
97. Ibid. The Yugoslavs had no Soviet license and were on tricky diplomatic trade grounds as they manufactured weapons based on Soviet patterns. After Yugoslavia

was dissolved and the archives were assumed by Serbia, the identity of the nation that leaked its AK-47s did not become publicly known.

98. The Zastava team hoped to make an entire family of arms based on the Kalashnikov system and experimented with means to modify the line, changing barrel lengths and adding features.

99. Personal communication to author from Branko Bogdanovic.

100. In time, Zastava would become a major Kalashnikov supplier and exporter, including export to the Pentagon's proxies in Afghanistan and Iraq, where Yugoslav Kalashnikovs are abundant.

101. Armstrong, *Bullets and Bureaucrats*, p. 152.

102. La Garde, *Gunshot Injuries*, p. 33.

103. At least two studies challenged the old guard: "Rifle Accuracies and Hit Probabilities in Combat" by Leon Feldman, William C. Pettijohn, and J. D. Reed, November 1960; "An Estimate of the Military Value and Desirable Characteristics of Armor Helmets for Ground Forces," a report published in 1950.

104. Those tests are covered in detail in the next chapter.

105. ORDI 7-101, *Soviet Rifles and Carbines, Identification and Operation* (published by the U.S. Army Ordnance Corps, May 1954), p. 1.

106. Report No. OTIO-471. The available documents accompanying the translation suggested that the United States military did not yet have possession of the new Soviet automatics and that technical intelligence officials had not yet tested and evaluated them. One line on the cover letter when the translation was submitted to the Army's chief of ordnance noted that "the technical accuracy of the source data has not been verified," indicating the military had not yet handled a specimen arm.

107. The Defense Intelligence Agency and the National Ground Intelligence Center (NGIC), the successor organization of the Army Foreign Science and Technology Center, said that record searches had not found most of the relevant documents from the era. The author assembled the records discussed here independently, from a range of sources, including the National Archives and several museums. Among the reports the U.S. military did find under a Freedom of Information Act request was a 1961 technical report on what the American army called a "Chinese AK-47." This report references two previous classified technical exploitations of the Soviet original—one published in mid-1956, the other in early 1957. The brief discussions of these reports in the 1961 document point to the first American military acquisition and tests of the AK-47.

108. Edwards's scoop carried whiffs of an insurgency within the army's ordnance department; reading between the lines suggests that his sources included American technicians who were testing the AK-47, and that they might have let him participate in a sample shoot.

109. William B. Edwards, "Russia's Secret All-Purpose Cartridge," *GUNS* magazine, September 1956.

110. Ibid. An editor's note said that Edwards's article had been ready for publication six months before, but the U.S. Army's chief of ordnance had asked the magazine not to print it. The magazine's staff complied. "*GUNS* was happy to cooperate with the Army in the interests of national security," the editors wrote, though it is hardly clear, looking back, what this national security interest was. By 1956, the AK-47 was no secret at all; Soviet newspapers and magazines had written about the rifle at length.

111. Personal communication to author from Casper van Bruggen, of the Legermuseum, in Delft. The Dutch unit had no further firefights with the Indonesian forces before the two sides reached a United Nations–brokered agreement in October, so the Dutch soldiers did not use their AK-47s in combat.

7. The Accidental Rifle

1. Personal communication to author from Alfred J. Nickelson.
2. The battalion's designation as a "landing force" allowed the Pentagon to exceed troop-level authorizations Congress had approved for Vietnam. Because it was formally assigned to ships, the Special Landing Force's Marines did not count against the number of troops on the ground though they spent most of its tour off the ships and in Vietnam.
3. Research & Analysis Study ST67-013, "Update: The NVA Soldier in South Vietnam." Combined Intelligence Center Vietnam, October 3, 1966, pp. 56–57.
4. Study ST67-064, "VC/NVA Techniques of Small Arms Fire," Combined Intelligence Center Vietnam, August 4, 1967, p. 8.
5. Technical Intelligence Study 66-12, "Viet Cong Munitions," March 26, 1966, p. 11.
6. One of the claims the AR-15's proponents would make was that the rifle had been proven to be highly reliable. In truth, the data was mixed. In some tests the weapon performed well. In others it did not. And from the beginning its manufacturer, ArmaLite, was in a poor position to know the behavior of its own products thoroughly: The company had a handful of employees and limited ability to subject its rifles to the examination that rifles in larger companies or in government development are subjected to.
7. "Rifle Squad Armed With A Lightweight High Velocity Rifle." Final Report, U.S. Army Combat Development Experimentation Command, May 30, 1959, p. 3.
8. Secret Memorandum from Robert S. McNamara to the Secretary of the Army, October 12, 1962. Declassified and on file at the National Archives.
9. *A Historical Review of ArmaLite,* published by ArmaLite, Inc., April 23, 1999.
10. William G. Key, "The ArmaLite Weapons System: Background Memorandum," Fairchild Engine & Airplane Corporation, December 7, 1956.
11. "Flight of the Friendship," *Time,* April 21, 1958.
12. R. Blake Stevens and Edward C. Ezell, *The Black Rifle* (Cobourg, Ontario: Collector Grade Publications, 1994), p. 56.
13. Dimensions and weights for the .222 Remington round are from W. H. B. Smith and Joseph E. Smith, *The Book of Rifles* (Harrisburg, Pa.: The Stackpole Company, 1965), p. 533.
14. The Army's Infantry Board at Fort Benning organized a series of evaluations of ArmaLite and Winchester test rifles in mid-1958 to assess their potential as replacements for the M-14. A review of the results by General Wyman's Continental Army Command endorsed the concept's merit: "Both test weapons were superior to the control weapon in lightness of weight and ease of handling. The significance of the weight-saving in the rifle-ammunition combination is such that a soldier with a battle load of 22.39 pounds, including his weapon and magazines, carries three times as much ammunition with either (SCHV) weapon as with the M-14 (actually about 650 rounds versus 220 rounds.)" The AR-15 had problems: the barrel of a test rifle had ruptured when fired after being subjected to simulated rainfall and water had collected in its bore. But the weapon was brand-new, and weapons early in their development cycle often showed mechanical and design problems. The supporters of the SCHV theory said it had "sufficient potential to justify continued development."
15. Letter from Paul A. Benke, president of Colt's Firearms Division to Earl J. Morgan, counsel to the Special Subcommittee on M-16 Program, August 24, 1967, p. 5.
16. Personal communication to author from Paul A. Benke. Benke described MacDonald as "a knowledgeable man but not a gracious man. Outspoken. He understood how to use a knife and fork, and how to use a soup spoon. He came from a good family. But gruff."

17. "Practical Penetrating Characteristics of the Colt AR-15 Automatic Rifle Chambered for the Caliber .223 Cartridge," August 15, 1960. On file at the Ezell Collection at Shrivenham.

18. Later tests would show that jacket rupturing seemed to be especially common when the bullets hit bone, which typically shattered into fragments that radiated through tissue and caused more damage. But the jacket fragmentation often occurred, ballistic tests would show, when the bullets did not hit bone.

19. Secret Fact Sheet "AR-15 Bullet Lethality" from Major General G. W. Power, Acting Chief of Research and Development, to the Vice Chief of Staff of the Army, April 24, 1963. Also, Secret Memorandum for Record on "Wound Ballistics" from the Office of the Chief of Staff of the Army, April 23, 1963. Records declassified and on file at the National Archives.

20. Confidential memorandum from Colonel Cao Van Vien to Commanding Officer of R&D Center, May 24, 1962. Declassified and on file at the National Archives.

21. "Report of Task No. 13A: Test of ArmaLite Rifle AR-15," submitted on August 20, 1962, by the Advanced Research Projects Agency. Declassified and on file at the Army War College Library.

22. Stevens and Ezell, *The Black Rifle*, p. 112.

23. In the six decades since the Thompson–La Garde pistol tests, questions had been raised in research circles about the utility and merits of firing into cadavers and live animals to determine how bullets wound human beings. Was there really a demonstrable correlation between injuries to cattle, pigs, and goats and injuries to men? These questions were unsettled, and at times the opposition to animal and cadaver tests was driven by concerns ideological as much as scientific. By the 1960s, newer means were available for assessing terminal ballistics, including firing into blocks of gelatin designed to simulate human tissue. The army's ballistics community had accepted these methods, but had continued with the old manner of testing, too.

24. Arthur J. Dziemian and Alfred G. Olivier, *Wound-Ballistics Assessment of M-14, AR-15, and Soviet AK Rifles* (U.S. Army Edgewood Arsenal, Biophysics Division, March 1964).

25. The preexisting state of knowledge about rifle injuries should have been adequate to put into context the damage to the heads and limbs of guerrillas shot in Vietnam. But the lethality tests at Aberdeen might have put the Project AGILE report into proper perspective once and for all, had the test results not been smothered.

26. The Biophysics Division would massage its data until March 1964, when it finally published its full report, which was not released to the public for almost five decades. After repeated inquiries, the author obtained a copy of the report in summer 2009.

27. Office Memorandum, from the Office of the Chief of Staff of the Army to Lieutenant General R. W. Colglazier, April 6, 1963. Declassified and on file at the National Archives.

28. Memorandum for the Secretary of the Army, signed by R. W. Colglazier, Lieutenant General, April 8, 1963. Declassified and on file at the National Archives.

29. Forty-nine years after the Project AGILE report, Paul A. Benke, the president of Colt's Firearms Division in the mid-1960s, referred the author to the report as a reference describing the M-16's merits.

30. Secret Memorandum for Secretary of the Army, "Comparative Evaluation of the M-14, AR-15 and Soviet AK-47 Rifles," January 14, 1963. Declassified and on file at the National Archives.

31. Stevens and Ezell, *The Black Rifle*, pp. 118–23.

32. Ibid., p. 99.

33. Office Memorandum from Director, FPAO, to General Johnson, November 30, 1966. Declassified and on file at National Archives.

34. William C. Westmoreland, *A Soldier Reports* (Garden City, N.Y.: Doubleday & Co., 1976), p. 158. Westmoreland's recollections did not square with accounts of the M-16's performance in the same battle as described by Harold G. Moore and Joseph Galloway in their book *We Were Soldiers Once . . . And Young* (New York: Random House, 1992). Moore commanded the battalion whose experience was cited.

35. Stevens and Ezell, *The Black Rifle*, pp. 196–97. The authors have excerpted from James B. Hall's background paper, "Acquisition of the M16 Rifle," 1975.

36. Ellsworth S. Grant, *The Colt Armory: A History of Colt's Manufacturing Company, Inc.* (Lincoln, R.I.: Mowbray Publishing, 1995) p. 179.

37. "In Defense of the M-16," *Shooting Times,* October 1966.

38. "M-16: Beauty or Beast?" *Shooting Times,* November 1966.

39. Letter from Paul A. Benke, president of Colt's Firearms Division, to Earl J. Morgan, counsel to the Special Subcommittee on the M-16 Program, August 24, 1967, p. 13.

40. The percentages come from U.S. Army Technical Note 5-66, "Small Arms Use in Vietnam: Preliminary Results, by the Human Engineering Laboratories, Aberdeen Proving Ground," August 1966.

41. Ibid.

42. Presley W. Kendall, "The M-16 in Vietnam," *American Rifleman,* May 1967, pp. 24–25.

43. "Trip Report, Headquarters AWC, Rock Island, Illionois," October 26, 1966, to Colt Inc., by Robert D. Fremont, Manager, Military Engineering, Colt's Firearms, October 28, 1966.

44. Letter from Lieutenant Colonel Herbert P. Underwood, who led an Army Weapons Command survey team in Vietnam, to Colonel Yount, October 30, 1966.

45. Letter of Koni Ito, a Colt engineer, to Robert Fremont, Colt's manager of military sales, October 30, 1966. On file at the National Archives.

46. Memorandum for the Record of Corrosion Control Meeting at Colt's Firearms Division, December 1, 1966.

47. List of Rifles of Lot # FC 1821 that malfunctioned, October 21, 1966.

48. Colt's Transcript of IBM tape received from David Behrendt, November 11, 1966, Tape #1.

49. Ibid., Tape #2.

50. Trip report to Colt's officials from J. B. Hall, Vietnam, November 5–9, 1966.

51. Colonel Richard R. Hallock, "Memorandum For Record: Vietnam Malfunction Information," November 15, 1966.

52. Stevens and Ezell, *The Black Rifle*, p. 210.

53. "Secret Memorandum For Deputy Chiefs of Staff, et al., from Department of the Army, Office of the Chief of Staff, November 7, 1966." Declassified and on file at the National Archives.

54. Unsatisfactory Equipment Report MCSA # 6069, February 8, 1967.

55. Letter from Marine Corps Supply Activity, Philadelphia, to Commanding General, U.S. Army Weapons Command, March 16, 1967.

56. "Vietnam Arms Race," *Washington Daily News,* unsigned editorial, March 26, 1967.

57. Appointment letter, on file at Western Historical Manuscript Collection–Columbia, at Ellis Library, University of Missouri. The collection is hereinafter referred to as WHMC-C, U. Mo.

58. Letter from Representative Ichord to Representative Charles Raper Jones, February 8, 1968. On file at WHMC-C, U. Mo.

59. Personal communication to author from Ray Madonna, who commanded Hotel Company, Second Battalion, Third Marines during spring 1967 in Vietnam.

60. Personal communication to author from Thomas R. Givvin, who commanded Third

Platoon, Hotel Company, Second Battalion, Third Marines in 1967 and participated in the actions related here.

61. Letter of Lance Corporal Larry R. Sarvis to Representative Ichord, June 17, 1967. On file at WHMC-C, U. Mo.

62. Personal communication from Raymond C. Madonna.

63. From unpublished manuscript of Raymond C. Madonna, who has written his own memoir of the Hill Fights, incorporating his recollections and his interviews of many of the Marines formerly under his command. Ord Elliott, who commanded First Platoon during the attack in which the Marines fixed bayonets, also discussed the events of that day with the author.

64. Personal communication from Charles P. Chritton, a lieutenant in Foxtrot Company, who witnessed the scene at the landing zone. The description of pins near the trigger assembly working loose is from Ord Elliott, David Hiley and Cornelio Ybarra Jr.

65. The shortages pointed to supply failures and to pilferage. Logistics units had not pushed an adequate amount of cleaning equipment to the troops in the field. But the light hands of war were a factor, too. Colt's included brass cleaning rods inside the cases of rifles shipped to Vietnam. One rod was shipped for every rifle. Colt's field teams later found the rods were disappearing even before the rifles were handed out, apparently as local Vietnamese employees on American bases stole them to sell on the scrap-metal market. It was frustrating for Colt's. This was a problem it could not fix. "They used them to make rice bowls or something," said Paul Benke, Colt's president at the time (personal communication to author).

66. "'Causing Deaths'—Marine Hits Faulty Rifles," *Asbury Park Evening Press,* May 20, 1967. After the letter was published, it was sent to Secretary McNamara by James J. Howard, a congressman from New Jersey, on May 22. Howard's letter is on file at WHMC-C, U. Mo.

67. Memorandum to Honorable Richard H. Ichord, from Ralph Marshall, May 31, 1967. On file at WHMC-C, U. Mo.

68. Letter from a Marine to his family, May 17, 1967. On file at WHMC-C, U. Mo.

69. "Memo to Mr. Findley re M-16 Events on Friday While You Were Gone," October 7, 1967. Mr. Findley is Paul Findley, then a Republic congressman from Illinois. The memo noted a call from Senator Dominick's office describing the incident in Vietnam and noting the senator's irritation. On file at WHMC-C, U. Mo.

70. The account of the night ambush was cited in a letter from Representative Dante B. Fascell to Representative Richard Ichord, August 2, 1967. The concerns of the navy lieutenant and army sergeant preparing to ship to Vietnam were sent directly to Representative Ichord. All three letters are on file at WHMC-C, U. Mo.

71. "M-16 or AK-47? The Right Rifle For the Right Job," a six-page fact sheet, dated November 25, 1968, intended to show the M-16's superiority to the AK-47. Circulated by Colt's, and on file at the Ezell Collection in Shrivenham.

72. Interviews with veterans still provoke disgust. Many believe they were guinea pigs. Charles Woodard, a young officer in the battalion at the time, called Colt and the military leadership's decisions "unconscionable." Givvin (see note 60, above) said the military leadership of the time "had blood on their hands." David Hiley, a platoon radio operator at the hill fights, said "They ought to give a million dollars to every Marine who had to carry one of those things."

73. Combat After-Action Report of Battalion Landing Team 2/3, July 30, 1967. Declassified and on file at the Library of the Marine Corps, Marine Corps Base, Quantico.

74. Interviews of Michael Chervenak by the author; the physical description of Chervenak came from Marines he served with in Vietnam.

75. The Marine Corps had not shown interest in the AR-15 as Colt's and its salesmen made the rounds with it in the 1950s and early 1960s. It wanted its rifle and machine

gun to be of the same caliber, thereby simplifying logistics. Though the Soviet Union had taken this step in the 1950s—fielding both the AK-47 and the RPK, which used the same cartridge—the United States was only beginning to go down the road toward a lightweight assault rifle and had no companion machine gun, even in the research-and-design phase, to fire the same cartridge. This would come later, as the M-249, the Squad Automatic Weapon, known as the SAW.

76. "Marines Hail M-16 Rifle, Army Accepts it Fully," UPI, published in the *Hartford Times,* May 11, 1967.

77. "House Ad Hoc Hearing for Vietnam Veterans Against the War," April 23, 1971. From the transcript, *Congressional Record* vol. 117, part 10, which was introduced into the public record on May 3, 1971.

78. Accounts of these inspections and function tests held at sea were shared with the author by former Marines who participated in them, including officers and staff noncommissioned officers who supervised them. These include Mike Chervenak, Chuck Chritton, Ed Elrod, Tom Givvin, Ray Madonna, Chuck Woodard, and Dick Culver.

79. Text of letter from First Lieutenant Michael P. Chervenak, USMC, to the *Barnesboro Star,* the *Washington Post,* Senator Robert Kennedy (D-N.Y.), and Congressman Richard Ichord (D-Mo.), as published in the *Barnesboro Star,* August 10, 1967.

80. A copy of the letter to Representative Ichord is on file at WHMC-C, U. Mo.

81. Personal communication to author from Thomas Tomakowski.

82. Personal communication to author from Charles Woodard.

83. From Hallock's brief biography in "The Hallock Soldier's Fund and Metro Works Columbus Home Ownership Center." Hallock entered the real estate business and died wealthy. He is a member of the OCS Hall of Fame at Fort Benning.

84. "Report of the Special Subcommittee on the M-16 Rifle Program of the Committee on Armed Services," October 19, 1967 (Washington, D.C.: U.S. Government Printing Office).

85. William G. Bray, "The M-16: A Report," *Data,* April 1968, p. 6.

86. Lieutenant Chervenak's letter took a winding course to public light. The *Barnesboro Star* published it in August. Senator Kennedy never replied. Representative Ichord's staff lost the letter (for which the congressman later apologized). The *Washington Post* held it, inexplicably, for three months. Throughout summer and fall 1967, as the M-16's problems were a national story, no one helped Hotel Company as its new rifles continued to jam.

87. The letter was a black mark on Lieutenant Chervenak's otherwise promising career. Although promotion from first lieutenant to captain is almost automatic, the more so in times of war, Lieutenant Chervenak was denied promotion when his time came. He served an extra year in the lieutenant rank. This effectively docked his pay.

88. Lieutenant Givvin wrote a letter detailing his platoon's experience in the same fight, and it was forwarded to the Marine Corps, which did not investigate. Lieutenant Charles Chritton, who was briefly the commander of Foxtrot Company, wrote to Congress describing his company's experiences with the rifle. One of the senators from his home state read the letter at a press conference on Capitol Hill, but there was no official reaction. The letter to the *Washington Post* changed the conversation.

89. Letter from Kanemitsu Ito to William H. Goldbach, vice president and general manager of Colt's Military Division, December 3, 1967.

90. Dick Culver, "The Saga of the M-16 in Vietnam (Part 1)." Culver served a career in the Marine Corps. Some of his experiences with the M-16 when he commanded Hotel Company, Second Battalion, Third Marines are posted on www.bobroher .com, p. 5.

91. Letter from Ito to Goldbach, December 3, 1967.

92. Patent No. 3482322, "Method of Preventing Malfunction of a Magazine Type Fire-

arm and Gauge for Conducting Same." Filed with U.S. Patent Office on November 6, 1967.

93. Letter from Kanemitsu Ito, Colt's field representative, to Misters Benke, McMahon, Hall, Fremont, December 9, 1967, re: "Return from Bear Cat to Saigon."

94. Daniel C. Fales, "M16: The Gun They Swear by . . . and At!" *Popular Mechanics,* October 1967.

95. "Memorandum for Record, Debrief of Colt's Vietnam Field Representative—Mr. Kanemitsu Ito," December 28, 1967. Prepared by Lieutenant Colonel Robert C. Engle, Project Manager Staff Officer, Rifles.

96. Personal communication to author by Paul A. Benke.

97. Lewis Sorley, *A Better War: The Unexamined Victories and Final Tragedy of America's Last Years in Vietnam* (Harcourt Books, 1999), p. 164.

98. "Memorandum for Army Chief of Staff, G4, Fact Finding Visit to 199th Infantry Brigade," March 28, 1968, by Lieutenant Colonel Robert L. Semmler, Chief, PM Rifles, Vietnam Field Office.

99. Personal communication to author from Jack Beavers.

100. Contents of tape recording received from K. Ito and J. Fitzgerald, September 27, 1968.

101. Letter from John S. Foster, Director of Defense Research and Engineering, to Representative L. Mendel Rivers, chairman of the House Armed Services Committee, February 2, 1968. On file at WHMC-C, U. Mo.

102. The poem, "Rifle, 5.56MM,XM16E1," is by Larry Rottmann, who served as an Army public-affairs officer in Vietnam in 1967 and 1968. Excerpted with permission of the poet from *Winning Hearts and Minds: War Poems by Vietnam Veterans* (1st Casualty Press, 1972).

8. Everyman's Gun

1. This is the official German version; Abu Daoud, who claimed to have organized the attack, later said it was false. As with many accounts of terrorism, many sources contradict one another. Given the speed with which the terrorists located the Israelis' apartment, their prior infiltration would seem probable.

2. "Munich 1972: When the Terror Began," *Time,* posted August 25, 2002 on www .time.com.

3. Ibid.

4. Simon Reeve, *One Day in September* (New York: Arcade Publishing, 2000), p. 2.

5. This section was assembled using information from several sources, including Serge Groussard's *The Blood of Israel: The Massacre of the Israeli Athletes* (New York: William Morrow, 1975), the most thorough and painstaking account of the act, by a journalist who covered the siege live and then investigated it. Reeve's *One Day in September,* and reconstructions by *Time* magazine were also helpful, as was a visit to the site as part of a lecture series on the attack for students of the Program on Terrorism and Security Studies at the George C. Marshall European Center for Security Studies, attended by the author in 2005.

6. Personal communication to author from Lin Xu.

7. Mike O'Connor, "Albanian Village Finds Boom in Gun-Running," *New York Times,* April 24, 1997. The factory manager is quoted as saying production reached twenty-four thousand AK-47s a month.

8. Descriptions, and a limited selection of photographs from within the Artemovsk cache, were provided by several people who have been inside the caves. The author was denied entry.

9. Kalashnikov, *From a Stranger's Doorstep,* pp. 302–3.

10 The account of Fechter's killing at the Berlin Wall was assembled from German

newspaper and academic accounts, as well as from records in the archive of the Stasi, the West Berlin police, and the Ministry of State Security. Von Schnitzler's quotation is from the transcript of the program he hosted, *Schwarze Kanal* (Black Channel), on GDR-TV, August 27, 1962. Research conducted by Stefan Pauly.

11. From "Meeting Notes taken by Chief of the Hungarian People's Army General Staff Károly Csémi On Talks with Soviet Generals to Discuss Preparations for 'Operation Danube,'" July 24, 1968, in *The Prague Spring '68: A National Security Archive Documents Reader*" (Central European University Press, 1998), p. 277.

12. OTIA 6129 Technical Report, bullet, ball. Report a.k.a. "Preliminary Technical Report, Egyptian 7.62mm, ball."

13. Neil C. Livingston and David Halevy, *Inside the P.L.O.* (New York: Quill/William Morrow, 1990), p. 38.

14. On visits in the United States, Kalashnikov has been gracious about the M-16, and complimented Eugene Stoner in person. Later, he placed flowers on Stoner's grave. But Kalashnikov is both competitive and attuned to his audiences. In Russia, away from Americans, he routinely criticized the American rifle. A sample, from public remarks at Rosoboronexport's offices in Moscow in April 2006, in the presence of the author: "They said that an American soldier would never take a Soviet AK-47 assault rifle in his hands. Oh how they lied! In Vietnam, the American soldiers threw away their capricious M-16s and took a Soviet AK-47 assault rifle from a killed Vietnamese, counting on captured ammunition. It all did happen, because the conditions in Vietnam were not as clean as conditions in the States where the M-16 works normally. Why am I talking about the past? You see it every day on TV. In Iraq, they openly show Americans with my machine guns, my assault rifles."

15. The theoretical range gains were offset to a degree by the short distance between the front and rear sights of the AK-74. This reduced accuracy with iron sights is a simple matter of geometry, and one of the trade-offs associated with having a shorter barrel.

16. Hogg and Weeks, *Military Small Arms,* p. 271.

17. Similar processes were at work elsewhere. In the 1960s, the Israeli military carried the Fabrique Nationale FAL automatic rifle. The FAL was a European competitor against the M-14 during tests in the United States in the 1950s. Like the M-14, it fired the standard NATO cartridge. The Israeli soldiers found it unsatisfactory, due to its heavy weight, its powerful recoil, and its performance shortcomings in the dusty conditions of war in the Middle East. After the Six Day War, the Israelis set out to find a better weapon. They were intrigued by the Kalashnikov's performance in the hands of their Arab enemies, and in the ensuing contest between arms two designers for Israeli Military Industries, Yisrael Galili and Yaacov Lior, submitted an assault rifle that knocked off elements of the AK-47 but chambered for the same American round fired by the M-16—the .223. The result—the Galil—was a fine example of convergence: the Soviet rifle design made to the American cartridge. It was fielded in the early 1970s. The rifle did not enjoy especially high popularity with Israeli soldiers, who at about the same time as the Galil became available were also issued American M-16s, which by then were largely debugged and were considerably lighter than the Galil.

18. Kalashnikov, *From a Stranger's Doorstep,* p. 431.

19. Author's visit to Kurya, 2004.

20. Anthony Sampson, *The Arms Bazaar: From Lebanon to Lockheed,* (New York: Viking Press, 1977), pp. 28–29.

21. *New York Times Magazine,* September 24, 1967.

22. Ian Johnston, "Death of a Despot, Buffoon and Killer," *Scotsman,* August 17, 2003.

23. Mustafa Mirzeler and Crawford Young, "Pastoral Politics in the Northeast Periphery

in Uganda: AK-47 as Change Agent," *Journal of Modern African Studies* 38, 2000, pp. 416–19.

24. Kalashnikov, *From a Stranger's Doorstep*, p. 17.

25. From "Programma Doprizyvnoi Podgotovki Yunoshei," published by the Ministry of Defense of the Soviet Union.

26. "Protocol of Pre-Draft Youth Competitions of Pripyat School No. 1." The hand-written ledger of student performance was found by the author in June 2005 in the gymnasium of the school. Translated by Nikolay Khalip.

27. *Small Arms Weapons Systems, Part One: Main Text,* published in May 1966 by the U.S. Army Combat Developments Command, Experimentation Command, Fort Ord, Table 4-1.

28. Similarly, a contest between two Russian soldiers at Mikhail Kalashnikov's eighty-fifth birthday celebrations in Izhevsk in 2004 was won by a soldier who disassembled and reassembled his Kalashnikov in twenty-six seconds. Author's observation.

29. Many sources describe the system that armed Afghan insurgents against the Soviet Union. This was condensed from Mohammad Yousaf and Mark Adkin, *Afghanistan—The Bear Trap: The Defeat of a Superpower* (Havertown, Pa.: Casemate, 1992).

30. Ibid., p. 109.

31. Lawrence J. Whelan, "Weapons of the FMLN—Part Three: Database Overview," *Small Arms World Report,* Vol. 3, Nos. 1 and 2, February 1992. Published by the Institute for Research on Small Arms in International Security, pp. 1–9.

32. Mao Tse-Tung, *On Guerrilla Warfare,* transl. Samuel B. Griffith II (Urbana and Chicago: University of Illinois Press, 2000), p. 83.

33. Lawrence J. Whelan, "Weapons of the FMLN—Part Two: The Logistics of an Insurgency," *Small Arms World Report,* Vol. 2, No. 3, May 1991. Published by the Institute for Research on Small Arms in International Security, p. 3. Also "Weapons of the FMLN," *Small Arms World Report,* Vol. 1, No. 4, August 1990, p. 3.

34. "Weapons of the FMLN," *Small Arms World Report,* Vol. 1, No. 4, August 1990, p. 3.

35. David Schiller, "Security Problems After Germany's Reunification," in *News from the Institute for Research on Small Arms in International Security,* Vol. 2, No. 2, February 1991, pp. 3–4.

36. Center for Peace and Disarmament Education/Saferworld, "Turning the Page: Small Arms and Light Weapons in Albania," December 2005, p. 6.

37. Personal communication to author from an international arms dealer in Ukraine.

38. There are many accounts of Minin's deals with Liberia. The facts here are condensed from the work of two international arms-transfer researchers, Brian Wood and Sergio Finardi, in Chapter 1 of *Developing a Mechanism to Prevent Illicit Brokering in Small Arms and Light Weapons—Scope and Implications,* published by the United Nations Institute for Disarmament Research, 2007, pp. 4–6.

39. Interview with Patrick Okwera.

40. Heike Behrend, *Alice Lakwena & the Holy Sprits: War in Northern Uganda 1986–97* (Oxford: James Currey Ltd., 1999), p. 47.

41. Ibid., pp. 59–60.

42. From "L.R.A. Religious Beliefs," an unpublished twelve-page manuscript prepared primarily by Captain Ray Apire, a former LRA commander and spiritual leader who defected from the LRA, and Major Jackson Achama, a former LRA administrator and "technician." Edited by Lieutenant Colonel R. W. Skow, a former defense and army attaché at the U.S. embassy in Kampala.

43. Ibid. Interview with Captain Apire.

44. Author's interviews with more than a dozen former LRA members and officers.

45. Interview with Lieutenant Colonel F. A. Alero.

46. Interview with Richard Opiyo, a child soldier in the LRA for six years.

47. Interview with Ray Apire, former LRA officer.
48. Interview with Dennis Okwonga, a child soldier in the LRA for slightly less than two and a half years.
49. Nearly two dozen students' or instructors' notebooks from several camps were collected in Afghanistan by the author and by David Rhode, a foreign correspondent for the *New York Times,* in late 2001. See further, C. J. Chivers and David Rhode, "The Jihad Files: Al Qaeda's Grocery Lists and Manuals of Killing" and "The Jihad Files: Afghan Camps Turn Out Holy War Guerrillas and Terrorists," *New York Times,* March 17–18, 2002. For a detailed description of one of the notebooks, a 190-page handwritten record made by a student in a camp run by the Islamic Movement of Uzbekistan, see "A Dutiful Recruit's Notebook: Lesson by Lesson Toward Jihad," by the same authors, *New York Times,* March 18, 2002.
50. Kofi Annan, A. "Small Arms, Big Problems," *International Herald Tribune,* July 10, 2001.
51. Author's observation at gun show.
52. Mirzeler and Young, "Pastoral Politics," p. 419.
53. Michael Bhatia and Mark Sedra, *Afghanistan, Arms and Conflict. Armed Groups, Disarmament and Security in Post-war Society* (New York: Routledge, 2008), p. 42. The historical trends in Kalashnikov prices are from this work, published in Chapter 2.
54. Author's observations and interviews in Iraq in 2003.
55. Author's interviews with Chechen insurgents in the Caucasus, 2005.
56. Author's interview in Norway in 2008 with Sharpuddi Israilov, a Chechen who had a vehicle impounded in this way before fleeing Chechnya.
57. Yousaf and Adkin, *Afghanistan–The Bear Trap,* p. 92.
58. Author's observations and interviews with arms dealers, customers, and intelligence officials in Iraq in 2006. For a further discussion, see "Black Market Weapons Prices Surge in Iraq Chaos," by C. J. Chivers, *New York Times,* December 10, 2006.
59. This is a commonly cited version, attributed to James R. Whelan, in his 1989 book *Out of the Ashes: The Life, Death and Transfiguration of Democracy in Chile* (Washington, D.C.: Regnery Gateway, 1989.) Other accounts differ, including one that claims the inscription read: "For Salvador, From his comrade-in-arms Fidel."
60. Like many of the legends of the automatic Kalashnikov, this account has been the subject of considerable dispute.
61. Author's interviews with Palestinian fighters in the West Bank and Gaza Strip in 2002.
62. Livingston and Halevy, *Inside the P.L.O.,* p. 278.
63. Interview with author in 2008.
64. Margarita Antidze, "Georgian Army Replaces Kalashnikov with U.S. rifle," Reuters, January 18, 2008.
65. Author's observation and interviews with Russian soldiers during Russian-Georgian War, August 2008.
66. From a memorandum in Mullah Omar's laptop, obtained in Afghanistan in 2001 by Alan Cullison, a reporter for the *Wall Street Journal,* who allowed the documents to be reviewed by the author. The contents of one particular memo—"In the name of God, most Merciful, most Benificent, Thank God and prayers and peace upon the prophet, Following is the cost of preparing one mujahid with weapons and costume"—are reproduced here.
67. "SUBJECT: Blue Lantern Level 3: Pre-License End-Use Check on License 50129249, United States State Department." Correspondence, unclassified, between the U.S. Embassy in Tblisi and Washington.
68. Author's interviews with officials at Colt Defense LLC, 2010.
69. Personal communication to author from Timothy Sheridan, who brokered the

American purchase of more than one hundred thousand Kalashnikovs for Iraqi and Afghan forces.

70. Ellsworth S. Grant, *The Colt Armory: A History of Colt's Manufacturing Company, Inc.* (Lincoln, R.I.: Mowbray Publishing, 1995), p. 180.

71. Personal communication to author by Francis Olero Okwonga, former lieutenant colonel in the LRA and a commander of Kony's security detachment.

72. United Nations Conference on the Illicit Trade in Small Arms and Light Weapons in All Its Aspects, July 2001.

73. Personal communication to author from Dr. Michael Brabeck. The section covering Mahmoud's and his friend's wounds was assembled from multiple interviews with participants, including Karzan Mahmoud, Balan Faraj Karim, Ramazan Hama-Raheem, and Qais Ibrahim Khadir.

74. Author's interviews with Karzan Mahmoud in Ottawa in 2007.

75. Edward Ezell, "Draft Trip Report, Izhevsk," November 6–14, 1994.

76. Author's interviews with officials at Rosoboronexport, the Russian state arms-export agency, in 2004 and 2007.

77. Interview with Mikhail Kalashnikov by Bryon MacWilliams, correspondent in Russia for *Newsweek* magazine, in Izhevsk in 2004. Mr. MacWilliams shared notes of his interview with the author.

78. Nadia Popova, "Russia's Obama Offers Change Kirov Can Believe In," *St. Petersburg Times,* May 5, 2009. See also "Kalashnikov Producer to Pay Wages in Sugar," *Russia Today,* April 10, 2009.

79. Remarks by Mikhail Kalashnikov in presence of author at the exhibition center in Izhevsk in August 2007.

80. Kalashnikov with Joly, *The Gun that Changed the World,* p. 143. Interviews by author with workers at plant in 2004.

81. Michael Gordon, "Moscow Journal: Burst of Pride for a Staccato Executioner," *New York Times,* March 13, 1997.

82. Igor Gradov, *Moskovsky Komsomolets,* November 9, 2004. Gradov published an interview with Kalashnikov in this Moscow newspaper on the day before the designer's eighty-fifth birthday.

83. An interview with Kalashnikov by M. Novikov appeared in the January 1968 issue of *Volksarmee,* published in Berlin.

84. "Brand Name: Mikhail Kalashnikov," *New York Times Magazine,* May 29, 1994.

85. "Report No. OTIO-471: Translation of a Soviet Manual Concerning a 7.62mm Rifle," September 13, 1955. Submitted to the Chief of Ordnance by H. H. Himmer, technical assistant, Ordnance Technical Intelligence Service. The report and a copy of the original Soviet manual are on file in the unsorted Ezell collection at Shrivenham.

86. Guy Martin, "(the killing machine)," *Esquire,* June 1997, p. 76.

87. DP No. 1195, issued from the Kremlin on July 5, 2007. Translated by Nikolay Khalip.

88. Author's observation.

89. MacWilliams interview with Kalashnikov.

90. Interview with author.

91. Holcomb B. Noble, "Eugene Stoner, 74, Designer of M-16 Rifle and Other Arms," *New York Times,* April 27, 1997.

92. Interviews in Russia by author. See also Nabi Abdullaev, "Russian High School Students Learn ABCs of War," *Moscow Times,* November 16, 2006.

93. Interview with author, 2004.

94. Mikhail Kalashnikov, *Ya S Vami Shol Odnoi Dorogoi* (Moscow: Vsya Rossiya Publishing House, 1999), p. 179.

95. Grador, *Moskovsky Komsomolets*.
96. Kalashnikov with Joly, *The Gun that Changed the World*, p. 112.
97. Ibid., p. 82.
98. Interview with Kalashnikov conducted by Nick Paton Walsh, July 3, 2003, at Kalashnikov's dacha at Izhevski Prud. Paton Walsh provided the interview notes to the author.
99. Kalashnikov, *From a Stranger's Doorstep*, pp. 260–261.
100. Letter from Andropov to the Central Committee of the Communist Party of the Soviet Union, February 18, 1973. From the Andrei Sakharov KGB file maintained by Yale University.
101. The quotation about Azeris and Armenian is from John Kampfner, from "Living Legend: The Private World of Mikhail Kalashnikov," *Telegraph* magazine, p. 20. The quotation about moans and screams is from Kalashnikov, *From a Stranger's Doorstep*, p. 162.
102. Paton Walsh interview with Kalashnikov.

Epilogue: The Twenty-first Century's Rifle

1. From author's inventory of the weapons used in the training.
2. Author's observation. In scores of patrols with the Afghan National Army and Police, the author identified seven Russian AK-47s with date stamps of 1953 or 1954.

ACKNOWLEDGMENTS

Alice Mayhew and David Rosenthal supported the too-long period of research for this book and offered patient encouragement throughout. As they waited, all manner of people helped.

Librarians, curators, collectors, historians, and independent and government researchers merit first mention. They found and offered materials I would not have turned up alone. Monique Howell at Indiana State Library and the staff at the Indiana Historical Society provided copies of Richard J. Gatling's letters and other records related to his life and work; more records of the Gatling Gun Company were retrieved by archivists at the Connecticut State Library. Dr. Charles Bonsett of Indianapolis rendered further assistance. The staff of the Naval Historical Center at the Washington Navy Yard provided references on machine-gun design and development. Kay Livingston of the Stimson Library at the U.S. Army Medical Department Center and School located early published ballistic studies of Dr. Louis La Garde. Joseph Slade, who holds a portion of Hiram Maxim's family papers, shared details of Maxim's life. The Maine Historical Society and Dick Eastman helped untangle an apparent falsehood Maxim circulated about the reasons he did not risk military service with his countrymen in the American Civil War. Alan Swindale discussed a letter his grandfather had sent from the campaign in Matabeleland. The staff at the reading room of the Imperial War Museum in London assisted by copying soldiers' diaries and reams of letters written at the Western Front in World War I. David Keough of the U.S. Army Military History Institute at the Army War College in Carlisle Barracks, Pennsylvania, pointed me to documents related to American rifle and machine-gun training (as well as declassified intelligence reports from Vietnam).

Mary Ellen Haug, at the Marshall Center Research Library in

Garmisch-Partenkirchen, Germany, located the United States government's translation of Vladimir Zhukov's hagiographic Cold War biography of Mikhail Kalashnikov. The librarians at the Museum of Artillery, Engineers and Signal Corps in Saint Petersburg and the Museum Complex of Small Arms of M. T. Kalashnikov in Izhevsk provided archival newspaper and magazine clippings that offered further insights into the official accounts of Kalashnikov's life and the weapons bearing his name. The museum in Izhevsk also allowed a viewing of their video collection of many of Kalashnikov's public appearances and statements. Max Popenker, founder of the website www.guns.ru, shared Soviet-era accounts of weapons designers and their work, including limited-edition and out-of-print references, that helped unpeel legends. Kristina Khokhlova assisted with translations. Lynne Seddon and the library staff at the College of Management and Technology College in Shrivenham, part of the Defence Academy of the United Kingdom, came in on weekends so that on visits from Moscow I could review the unsorted collection from the archives of Edward Ezell, a researcher of small arms and former curator at the Smithsonian Institution. When time ran short, they assisted with photocopying and shipped boxes of copies to my home.

Richard Jones, a curator of the Ministry of Defence's Pattern Room at the Royal Armouries, Leeds, helped with weapons identification and referrals to written sources related to the evolution of firearms and ammunition design. A meeting with him shaped years of further reporting and reading. Lin Xu, after a chance conversation in the Pattern Room, found and translated references in Chinese that yielded fresh accounts of the assault rifle's travels to China. He also explained technical aspects of small-arms operation and subtle shifts in Kalashnikov design in different countries over time.

Christian Ostermann, director of the Cold War International History Project at the Woodrow Wilson International Center for Scholars, repeatedly referred me to historians and regional specialists in the former Eastern bloc. The center's trove of translated records from government archives in the former Soviet Union and from Warsaw Pact nations were essential to understanding many events described in these pages. János Rainer at the Institute for the History of the 1956 Hungarian Revolution in Budapest searched the institute's archive of photographs and found several that showed revolutionaries carrying captured Soviet Kalashnikovs.

He then identified József Tibor Fejes and helped with gaining access to records in Budapest's city archives related to Fejes's trial and execution. Kati Tordas, a journalist and researcher, volunteered her time to sleuth out and translate details of Fejes's case. László Eörsi, the indomitable researcher of the Corvinists, shared his material.

Guy Laron provided data and context on Soviet arms deals in the 1950s. Mathieu Willemsen of the Legermuseum in Delft, the Netherlands, provided copies of declassified studies of an early AK-47 that was smuggled out of the Soviet Union. His colleague at the museum, Casper van Bruggen, provided information related to one of the first known battlefield collections of an AK-47 by Western combat forces, and secured permission to reprint a photograph of one of the Dutch soldiers with one of the guns. Alexandra Hildebrandt, chairwoman of the board of the Mauermuseum in Berlin, looked into the question of weapons carried by the East German border guards. Dr. Thomas Mueller, formerly of the Waffenmuseum in Suhl and currently of the Bayerisches Armeemuseum in Ingolstadt, assisted with the research in Wiesa, including providing the names of workers and firms involved in Kalashnikov production. Daniel Oswald assisted with research and translation in the former East Germany, and interpreted interviews in Wiesa. Norbert Moczarski helped explore the question of Hugo Schmeisser's involvement in AK-47 development in Izhevsk. Victor Homola and Stefan Pauly, in Berlin, assisted with details of East Germany's secret production, and Stefan spent weeks of his time examining the deaths by Kalashnikov fire of German civilians trying to flee to the West.

Brady Dolim at the National Ground Intelligence Center in Charlottesville, Virginia, helped release records offering details of the first American exploitations of Soviet small arms and M1943 ammunition. Branko Bogdanovic, of Serbia, assisted with information related to the copying in Tito's Yugoslavia of the Kalashnikov design. Markku Palokangas of the Military Museum of Finland met me in Helsinki and discussed his research into the Finnish acquisition of an early Polish AK-47 in the 1950s; Robie Kulokivi of WERETCO and Tapio Saarelainen, of the Finnish army, helped me further understand Finnish arming decisions and the origins of the Finnish Kalashnikov. Andreas Heineman-Gruder at the Bonn International Center for Conversion helped with information and contacts in Ukraine, which led to an understanding of small-arms stockpiles there; I was further assisted in Ukraine, with reports and pictures of the cache within Artemovsk salt mines, by people who asked not to be named. Hwaida Saad, in Lebanon, helped with research into Kalashnikov production in the Arab world.

William Stolz of the University of Missouri culled and copied reams of material from the records of Representative Richard H. Ichord. Among those records were copies of letters written to Congress and newspapers by First Lieutenant Michael Chervenak, and related correspondence and clippings. James Ginther, an archivist at the Special Collections Branch at the Library of the Marine Corps, provided digital copies of the 1967 and 1968 command records from Second Battalion, Third Marines, Chervenak's unit in Vietnam. Richard Verrone, formerly of the Vietnam Archive at Texas Tech University, helped with early clippings and with oral histories. The Marine Corps records, when set against the Vietnam-era military maps assembled by the university, made it possible to trace the location of the firefight in which forty American rifles jammed, prompting Chervenak to write. The current chief executive at Colt Defense, retired General William Keys, discussed in an interview the core aspects of the infantry's complaints about early M-16 performance in Vietnam. Keys was a Marine company commander in Vietnam; his Marines suffered from the problems documented in this book. Jeffrey Gould, with whom I served in a platoon in the First Marine Regiment in the 1980s and 1990s, and who is now an engineer at Picatinny Arsenal, in New Jersey, retrieved a reliability study of infantry arms conducted by the army in 1968, and arranged its public release. Gus Funcasta, also of Picatinny, offered smart insights and suggested smart questions. The staff at the National Archives assisted by providing access to records of the early M-16 program, which included the brief mention of the comparative study, using human body parts from India, of the lethality of the M-14, the AR-15, and the Kalashnikov. Thomas Blanton, of the National Security Archive, provided advice on how to obtain a copy of the report of those tests, which had been withheld from public view for more than forty years.

Veterans of Second Battalion, Third Marines in 1967 and 1968 spent long hours recalling their tours, and often providing records, photographs, and phone numbers or email addresses to other veterans of the same operations: Al Nickelson, Ed Elrod, Mike Chervenak, Chuck Chritton, Tom Givvin, Ray Madonna, Chuck Woodard, Dick Culver, Tom Tomakowski,

Jack Beavers, Rod Radich, Dave Smith, Ord Elliott, Cornelio Ybarra Jr., Roy DeMille, David Hiley, Bill Snodgrass, Don Aaker, and Stan Maszstak. Larry Rottmann, once forbidden by the army of speaking publicly about the M-16's failures, granted permission to reprint one of his poems.

Dr. Martin Fackler, the former army trauma surgeon and terminal-ballistics researcher, provided copies of many of his studies of wound ballistics, and patiently answered questions. Michael Rhode, an archivist at the National Museum of Health and Medicine in Washington, D.C., shared many referrals, opening a world of researchers and records explaining the changing ways that people have been wounded in war. Sanders Marble, senior historian at the Surgeon-General's Office of Medical History, dug up references and introduced me to several doctors familiar with wounds and wounding. These include Dr. Dave Edmond Lounsberry, a coauthor of "War Surgery in Afghanistan and Iraq," an invaluable public document for understanding the two most recent American wars, and Dr. Ron Bellamy, whose statistical studies of wounding agents in battle are a resource on this subject in which rigor rises above anecdote. Dr. Paul Doughtery provided copies of terminal-ballistic studies, old and new. Kevin McKiernan and Dr. Mike Brabeck shared email correspondence, documents, photographs, and memories of the treatment of Karzan Mahmoud, who met with me several times in Iraq, Canada, and the United States. Karzan also introduced me to other survivors, who walked me across the ground in Sulaimaniya and meticulously recounted the gunfight in which they were maimed. Security officials in northern Iraq allowed Kevin and me to conduct multiple lengthy interviews with Qais Ibrahim Khadir, the terrorist involved in the attack, who was later executed. I was further aided by many victims of assault-rifle proliferation in many other places, including the survivors in Beslan.

Several arms dealers helped me, too. The preponderance of them, due to the nature of their business, asked to remain anonymous here. Two don't mind a public thank-you: Reuben Johnson and Tim Sheridan. I was aided by many people engaged in many ways in researching ongoing conflicts: Tania Inowlocki, James Bevan, Aaron Karp, Robert Muggah, Tanya Lokshina, Phillip Killicoat, Brian Wood, Sergio Finardi, Peter Danssaert, Peter Bouckaert, Anna Neistat, Ole Solvang, Hugh Griffiths, Nicholas Marsh. Gary Kokalari, a one-man Albanian smear factory, provided a seemingly small tip that exposed a Pentagon-funded international scandal in the Kalashnikov ammunition trade, and deepened my understanding of arms and munitions movements. John Wallace and Ed Costello helped with recollections of time shared with General Kalashnikov, and with referrals. Ruslan Pukhov and Dmitri Bender helped with insights and materials in Russian. Virginia Ezell provided referrals and references, including useful copies of *Small Arms World Report.* Several government employees and military officers helped locate records or shared material and information that, because of a stubborn culture of government secrecy in the United States, are not accessible to the public. Their assistance enriched this book. Officials at Rosoboronexport in Moscow invited me to several ceremonies related to the Kalashnikov and its place in Russian arms history, discussed many aspects of the international arms trade, and through their colleagues at Izhevsk, arranged a rare tour of the Izhmash plant to observe the manufacture and final assembly of assault and sniper rifles.

They also arranged interviews with General Kalashnikov, as did Igor Krasnovksi, one of the general's grandsons. General Kalashnikov deserves a special thank-you for meeting several times in Izhevsk and Moscow, and for entertaining questions he has heard before.

The nudge toward this book, which ultimately led to those interviews, came from Samuel G. Freedman, who, in 2002, not long after David Rhode and I had returned from Afghanistan and completed a series of newspaper articles about guerrilla and terrorist training methods, suggested a more thorough examination of the Kalashnikov's origins and ubiquity. Stuart Krichevsky seconded the idea and shepherded it throughout.

Karen Thompson guided the book through its production, and worked around (and tolerated) my repeated long trips overseas. Jonathan Karp arrived with enthusiasm to publish the book she made possible. Outside of Simon & Schuster, several editors supported reporting into aspects of the military small-arms trade and its effects. At the *New York Times:* Susan Chira and Roger Cohen, who edited the foreign report, Matt Purdy and Paul Fishleder on the Investigations desk, Katie Roberts and Marc Charney at the Week in Review, Rogene Fisher and Jeff Delviscio at the At War blog, along with Ian Fisher, Kyle Crichton, Beth Flynn, and Bill Keller. Also, Mark Warren and David Granger at *Esquire.* Sid Evans and Anthony Licata at *Field & Stream,* with David DiBeneddetto and Colin Kearns. David Petzal, an army veteran and editor who has dedicated decades to understanding small arms, read the draft manuscript and applied an eye true to his reputation: thoroughly informed, unsparing, and welcome. Ethan Harper, Frank Kalesnik, Kenneth W. Noelsch Jr. and John C. Watson volunteered revisions from the hardcover edition.

Friends at the *Times* pitched in with information, referrals, translations, clippings, and other support: David Rohde, Nick Kulish, Paul Zielbauer, Eric Schmitt, Nick Wood, John Burns, Dex Filkins, Jim Dao, Thom Shanker, Michael Gordon, Jim Glanz, Carlotta Gall, Michael Slackman, Ellen Barry, Cliff Levy, Steve Myers, Andrew Kramer, Sophia Kishkovsky, Willy Rashbaum, Jeffrey Gettleman, Bobby Worth, Joe Kahn, Andrei and Oleg Shevchenko, Natasha Bubenova, Phyllis Collazzo, Cynthia Latimer, Flora Lee, Charlie Williams, Alain Delaqueriere, Ethan Wilensky-Lanford, Michael Schwirtz, Josh Yaffa, and Sasha Nurnberg. Photographers (and a videographer) joined me on many trips and indulged requests for detailed pictures of arms, ammunition, log books, serial numbers, shipping labels, munitions packaging, and markings: Adam Ellick, Luke Tchalenko, Joao Silva, Chang Lee, Christoph Bangert, Yuri Tutov, Justyna Mielnikiewicz, Joseph Sywenkyj, Sergei Kivrin, Dima Beliakov. Journalists from other news organizations helped, too: Nick Paton Walsh, Jeffrey Fleishman, Beth Noble, Arkady Ostrovsky, Alan Cullison, Aram Roston, Bryon McWilliams, and Bing West.

Several people listed here read portions of the draft manuscript, or drafts in their entirety, and offered suggestions and corrections. Other readers included Mark Greene and Kory Romanat.

I was assisted throughout by local journalists, guides, interpreters, and drivers in many different countries. Yuriy Tartarchuk escorted a small group of us through Chernobyl's ruins and the exclusion zone, and allowed Joseph Sywenkyj to photograph pages in the military instructor's log book detailing Kalashnikov drills performed by Soviet students. Yuri Strilchuk led us through the test site at Semipalatinsk, where the Soviet Union's first atomic bomb, Joe 1, was detonated, and explained the bomb's design, placement, and blast effects, allowing for this book's opening scene. Many people who helped in conflict zones or police states will not be listed, to protect them from retaliation from insurgents or from authorities who punish dissent or restrict access and honest reporting, including in Iraq, Afghanistan, Chechnya, Uzbekistan, Turkmenistan, and the Palestinian territories. Several can be named: Peshwaz Faizulla, Alan

Abdulla, Sangar Rahimi, Abdul Waheed Wafa, Pir Zubair Shah, Taimoor Shah, Nasir Ahmed, Arian Jaff, Abdul Samad Jamshid, Olesya Vartanyan, Dima Bit-Suleiman, George Kumagong, Jimmy Otim.

Much of my understanding of infantry tactics and how they have changed was gained in the Marine Corps, both in the field and via the Corps' emphasis on reading military history. This foundation was enhanced and enriched by countless military officals, officers, and troops who shared their experiences or who allowed me and a photographer to accompany them on the ground in Afghanistan and Iraq. A list of everyone would fill pages. Among those who helped with recollections, tips, suggestions, document review or arms or munitions identification were Nick Pratt, Mike Richards, Mike Bruce, Tom Wilhelm, Greg Sailer, Sulev Suvari, Rory Quinn, Ed Ota, Mike Mendoza, and Brett Bourne. Several public affairs officials assisted with documents or referrals: Bruce Zielsdorf, Frank Misurelli, Peter Rowland, Sheldon Smith, Dave Johnson, Daniel King, Christian Kubik, and more public affairs noncommissioned officers and officers in Afghanistan and Iraq than could be listed here. In the field, on patrols, raids, sweeps, medical evacuations, and other missions, and in long talks in the lulls, I was aided by and learned from Jimmy Howell, Josh Biggers, Paul Stubbs, Matt Baker, Ken Detreux, Sean Riordan, Dustin Kirby, Mark Grdovic, James McCarver, Bertrand Fitzpatrick, Richard Dewater, Colin Smith, Ramon Gavan, Daniel McKernan, Norberto Rodriguez, Douglas Terrell, Zackary Filip, Chuck Major, Walter De La Vega, Mark Trouerbach, Patrick Maguire, James Mingus, Stephan Karabin II, Tom Grace, Brian Rogers, Steven Green, Robert Smail, Gregory Veteto, Sean Conroy, Osvaldo Hernandez, Jarrod Neff, Cory Colistra, Adam Franco, Gordon Emmanuel, Jason Petrakos, Edward Mitchell III, Jeremy Owen, Joseph Wright, Matthew Dalrymple, Thomas Drake, Junior Joseph, Daniel Fuqua, Daniel Downes, Christopher Fine, Joshua Dolan, Brian Kitching, Moti Sorkin, Brian Christmas, Sly Silvestri, Jason Davis, Matt Stewart, Joseph Callaway, Deric Sempsrott, Ian Bugh, Grayson Colby, David Harrell, Chad Orozco, Zachary Kruger, Joshua Smith, Bill Yale, Eric Brown, Travis Vuocolo, Thomas Wright, Justin Smith, Robert Soto, Chris Demure, John Rodrigiuez, Tim McAteer, Chris Jones, Frank Hooker, Nick Rolling, and Brett Jenkinson. The last two on this list were fellow members of Class 1-90 of the Ranger Course whose paths crossed with mine in Kirkuk, Iraq, in Ghazni province or the Pech and Korangal valleys in Afghanistan. Our shared time informed my understanding of wars as they are fought, and of the experiences of combatants. They provided clarity and forcefulness to my thoughts.

The staff of the Maury Loontjens Memorial Library in Narragansett, Rhode Island, ensured that time at home was used productively, by searching for book after book, many of them out of print, and securing them for my reading via interlibrary loan.

My wife, Suzanne Keating, and our children supported everything and endured much, always offering understanding and love. Honey Keating made moonlighting possible, year after year.

Three colleagues deserve special mention: Nikolay Khalip and Viktor Klimenko of the *Times* bureau in Moscow traveled with me across the former Soviet Union, constantly providing advice and good judgment and sharing the work with good cheer. Tyler Hicks, a model of courage, talent, and professionalism, shared the patrols and many of the worst days, month after month for years. His photographs—disturbing, unflinchingly honest, and made at tremendous personal risk—show war for what it is.

My understanding of the consequences of assault-rifle proliferation, and the continued use of Kalashnikov rifles as instruments of state repression, was helped by Natasha Estemirova and Anna Politkovskaya in Russia, and Alisher Saipov in Kyrgyzstan and Uzbekistan. All three labored for justice and accountability in lands ruled by violence. All three were murdered for their efforts to uncover the truth, as was Umar Israilov, a source on the insurgency and counterinsurgency in Chechnya, who was shot dead in a contract killing in Vienna after sharing details of crimes by government officials in Russia. To these victims, and to the American, Afghan, Russian, and Iraqi service members wounded or killed on operations I was allowed to be part of or that I witnessed up close, words cannot convey the depth of my thanks, or of our loss.

None of the people mentioned above, or anyone else, deserves any blame for errors in this book or conclusions I have drawn that do not align with theirs. All responsibility lies with me.

INDEX

ABOUT THE AUTHOR

C. J. CHIVERS is a senior writer for *The New York Times* and its former Moscow bureau chief, and a frequent contributor to *Esquire*. From 1988 to 1994, he was an infantry officer in the U.S. Marine Corps, and served in the Gulf War and in the Los Angeles riots before being honorably discharged as a captain. His work has received several prizes, including a National Magazine Award for Reporting for the reconstruction in *Esquire* of the terrorist siege in Beslan and a shared Pulitzer Prize for International Reporting for coverage in the *Times* of combat in Afghanistan. His war reportage from 2003 through 2009 in Iraq and Afghanistan was selected by New York University as being among the Top Ten Works of Journalism of the Decade in the United States. He lives with his family in Rhode Island.